# Information Sciences Series

*Joseph Becker and Robert M. Hayes:*
INFORMATION STORAGE AND RETRIEVAL

*Charles P. Bourne:*
METHODS OF INFORMATION HANDLING

*Harold Borko:*
AUTOMATED LANGUAGE PROCESSING

*Russell D. Archibald and Richard L. Villoria:*
NETWORK-BASED MANAGEMENT SYSTEMS (PERT/CPM)

*Charles T. Meadow:*
THE ANALYSIS OF INFORMATION SYSTEMS, A PROGRAMMER'S
INTRODUCTION TO INFORMATION RETRIEVAL

*Launor F. Carter:*
NATIONAL DOCUMENT-HANDLING SYSTEMS FOR SCIENCE AND
TECHNOLOGY

*Perry E. Rosove:*
DEVELOPING COMPUTER-BASED INFORMATION SYSTEMS

*F. W. Lancaster:*
INFORMATION RETRIEVAL SYSTEMS

*Ralph L. Bisco:*
DATA BASES, COMPUTERS, AND THE SOCIAL SCIENCES

*Charles T. Meadow:*
MAN-MACHINE COMMUNICATION

# The Foundations of Education for Librarianship

**Jesse H. Shera**

Case Western Reserve University

A WILEY-BECKER AND HAYES PUBLICATION

BECKER AND HAYES, INC.
a subsidiary of John Wiley & Sons, Inc.
New York · London · Sydney · Toronto · Los Angeles

to

**John Schoff Millis**
**the best of listeners**
**the wisest of counselors**
**the warmest of friends**

*Library of Congress Cataloging in Publication Data:*

Shera, Jesse Hauk, 1903-
  The foundations of education for librarianship.

  (Information sciences series)
  Includes bibliographical references.
  1. Library education. I. Title.

Z668.S5      020′.7′1173      72-3851
ISBN 0-471-78520-2

Printed in the United States of America

10 9 8 7 6 5 4 3 2 1

# Information Sciences Series

Information is the essential ingredient in decision making. The need for improved information systems in recent years has been made critical by the steady growth in size and complexity of organizations and data.

This series is designed to include books that are concerned with various aspects of communicating, utilizing, and storing digital and graphic information. It will embrace a broad spectrum of topics, such as information system theory and design, man-machine relationships, language data processing, artificial intelligence, mechanization of library processes, nonnumerical applications of digital computers, storage and retrieval, automatic publishing, command and control, information display, and so on.

Information science may someday be a profession in its own right. The aim of this series is to bring together the interdisciplinary core of knowledge that is apt to form its foundation. Through this consolidation, it is expected that the series will grow to become the focal point for professional education in this field.

No one successfully investigates the
nature of a thing in the thing itself; the
inquiry must be enlarged, so as to become
more general.

*Francis Bacon*


I am only a restless searcher. Though I
have always sought the truth, I fear that
its hidden retreats, or a certain dullness
of mind may have obscured my vision
and in my quest after the thing itself
I have often become entangled in mere
opinion. Therefore, I have dealt with
these matters, not as one who lays down
definitions, but as one who tries to study
and observe with care. For to define is
the prerogative of the wise, and I am
neither wise nor close to wisdom; but in
the words of Cicero, only a great
conjecturer.

*Petrarch*

# Preface

In January 1956, the Carnegie Corporation of New York provided a generous grant to the School of Library Science of Western Reserve University for the author to undertake a study of library education. In the letter of transmittal, Frederick H. Jackson, writing for the corporation, expressed the desire that the study "would really be a distillation of" my "own thinking on this important subject." Such a "distillation" is exactly what the following pages are; this is a highly personal treatment of the subject, and its weaknesses and strengths are uniquely my own. However, many people have contributed in many ways to the formulation of these thoughts. It would be impossible to acknowledge my debt to all of them.

The study is a result of a theory of librarianship which has been in the process of maturation for more than a quarter century of teaching and administration, first at the University of Chicago, and subsequently at Western Reserve University, now Case Western Reserve University, and which has been elaborated in essays and addresses as the inquiry progressed.

My purpose has been to explore the role of the library as it contributes to the total communication system in society and the meaning of that role for the library profession, and having determined the requirements of that role to identify those which are appropriately met by graduate professional education. Therefore, the inquiry begins with a consideration of the communication system within the individual as related to his physiological, neurological, and psychological structure, and its meaning for learning and reading patterns and characteristics. The study then progresses to an exposition of the cultural environment and its communication system in society, together with the place of the library in it.

I have devoted considerable attention to the origins of libraries and to the history of library education. I believe that a knowledge of the historical development of any human activity is prerequisite to an understanding of it. It is essential that the librarian and the library educator have an awareness of the historical origins of the profession if library education is to be improved. From this background it becomes possible to determine with a reasonable degree of precision, the librarian's intellectual and educational requirements.

The concluding chapters of the study deal with curricular structure of the graduate professional program, and the place of research in it, the faculty, and general administration of the library school.

In the preparation of this work I have tried throughout to look critically at education for librarianship as it now exists, and to propose remedial measures, keeping in mind always that they must harmonize with the instructional and research aims of the university. In short, I have attempted to give education for librarianship a more meaningful theoretical and interdisciplinary perspective than has characterized it in the past. I have emphasized the Graduate Library School of the University of Chicago because of a sincere conviction that what took place there during the 1930s and the 1940s, exerted the most important single influence upon subsequent innovation in library education in transition.

Throughout the protracted period of inquiry I discussed the problems of library education with many people both within and without the library world, read as widely and omnivorously as possible, reflected on these discussions and on what had been read, and, combining these reflections with my own experience, conceptualized a general outline of a theory of librarianship and explored the meaning of that theory for library education. It was in a spirit of protest against provincialism in library education that the inquiry was undertaken, and it may be significant that, as the study progressed, I found the writings in fields other than those of librarianship and library education far more helpful and stimulating than the professional literature itself. Therefore, I have cited extensively from these readings in the hope that librarians and library educators may be led to explore this material in depth for themselves.

We cannot pursue our own limited calling with scarcely a thought for our place in the total drama of human endeavor. Admittedly, the librarian and the teacher in a library school may have a general awareness of the larger context to which they contribute; in the past they have seldom engaged in any protracted study of, or reflection on, their relations to the entire pattern of the social fabric. Francis Bacon was right in insisting that a subject should not be studied only within itself, the inquiry must be generalized.

Because the search is directed toward generalizable principles, I have not attempted to set forth in detail any precise description of an "ideal" curriculum. Such details must be worked out by each school in terms of its own objectives and its own academic setting. Merely to tinker with individual course offerings of the curriculum will not suffice to solve the problems of library education, for behind the library school there lies the *Weltanschaung* of the profession itself.

One cannot escape the fact that never in the history of the world have its people been so desperately in need of knowledge as they are at the present time; knowledge which the library should be uniquely prepared to provide.

Throughout, a constant aim has been to make this study reflective, provocative, enlightening, and constructive. I hope that this long journey has been worth the effort—for me it unquestionably was—I hope it will prove to be of value for the profession of librarianship.

Cleveland, Ohio                                        JESSE H. SHERA

# Contents

# The Foundations of
# Education for
# Librarianship

# One

# Communication and the Individual

The library is one element in the total communication system by which a society is held together and a culture is created and maintained. But understanding the communication system, and the role of the library in it, means first of all knowing what a communication system is and the ways in which it operates, because a society is an organized agglomeration of individuals. Thus to comprehend the social foundations of the library one must begin with some basic considerations and characteristics of the communication process and the ways in which that process relates to the individual. But one cannot pursue an inquiry into the nature of communication very far without being forced to consider in some degree the neuro-physiological functions by means of which man achieves a state of knowing, the characteristics of learning the nature of language and other forms of symbolism, as the vehicles of communication. In short, how man knows what he knows, and the ways in which that knowledge is communicated through the social fabric until it becomes the common possession of society and the fabric of the culture are all essential to an understanding of what librarianship is.

## THE ELEMENTS OF THE COMMUNICATION SYSTEM

The basic elements of the communication system, whether the act is personal, interpersonal, or mass communication, are four: (1) a transmit-

**1**

ter, (2) a message, (3) a means of transmission, which in indirect communication includes an intermediary agent, and (4) a recipient or receptor. Because the concern here is with human communication, two of these four elements, i.e., the transmitter and the recipient, are necessarily human, though this does not deny the reality of communication among other forms of life, nor does it reject the fact that human beings can receive meaningful messages from nonhuman sources. The remaining two elements, the message and the means of transmission, are either environmental or are products of human invention, ingenuity, and fabrication.

No communication system is perfect, though it is predicated on the assumption of perfection. The mathematical factor of entropy, which is a measure of the unavailable energy in a thermodynamic system, renders impossible the perfect transmission of a message from sender to recipient. The fact that in a closed system the message cannot transmit more information than that with which it was endowed by the transmitter does not deny the possibility that a recipient can "read" meanings into a message that the sender did not realize were there. Furthermore, every communication is subject to some "noise," where "noise" is defined as any extraneous matter—hum in a telephone system, static in radio, snow on the television screen—that is interjected into the message. Therefore redundancy, or repetition, is employed in an effort to ensure the accuracy of the transmission. Redundancy in language is so prevalent as to require no explanation, and one may observe that redundancy for its own sake often appears to meet a basic human need, like the fabled housewife who emphasized her dislike of gravy by proclaiming, "I don't want none never of no kind." Only in the English language, among those of the Western World at least, is the double negative interpreted to mean a positive.

Because the concern here is restricted to human communication, its characteristics, its nature, and the forces which act upon it, the present chapter will focus attention upon the capabilities and propensities of the human being in the role of either transmitter or receptor.

## CHARACTERISTICS OF THE BRAIN AFFECTING THE PATTERN OF COMMUNICATION

Communication is, of course, both physiologically and psychologically based; it is dependent upon the perceptive capacities of the senses and the interpretation of the resulting sensations, or stimuli, by the brain. Therefore, to understand the human characteristics which determine the pattern of communication one must necessarily turn to the findings of biology, physiology, psychology, and even the new and very specialized field of electro-encephalography.

To the normal human being in the twentieth century, the world presents a seemingly infinite variety of stimuli which continuously bombard the senses and, through them, the brain. Psychologists have now identified some twenty senses, ranging from the basic five to such as kinesthesis, the consciousness of muscular tension or motion. Except when there is some impairment or other inhibiting factor, all of them function constantly while their possessor is awake and, in variously altered ways, even during sleep.

All mental processes are, ultimately, derived from sensory perception. This perception, the continuous reaction to stimuli which are of sufficient magnitude or the proper quality to produce a sensation within the range of human sense organs, is conditioned by four factors: (a) the sensitivity of the "receiving" organism; (b) the character or quality of the stimulus; (c) the extent or degree of impact of past experience; and (d) the "set," or goals, of the recipient. These differ, of course, from person to person and from situation to situation, and though they have a physiological base, they are also conditioned by psychological, sociological, cultural, and other environmental factors. The amount of stimulus necessary to elicit a response is, in the language of the psychologist, the "threshold," which is said to be low when a response is easily induced and high when it is brought forth only with difficulty. These thresholds are both physiologically and psychologically determined, and vary even within the individual according to transient influences from both within and without.

Sensory perception stimulates—or, in reality, brings into being—mind consciousness, awareness, which has been considered the very essence of being; "cogito, ergo sum," wrote Descartes more than three centuries ago. As Neumann has pointed out, "ego consciousness is a sense organ which perceives the world and the unconscious by means of images, but this image-forming capacity is itself a psychic product . . . [this] psychic world of images is a synthesis of experiences of the inner and outer world."[1]

---

[1] Erich Neumann. *The Origins and History of Consciousness.* New York. Pantheon. 1954. p. 294. James J. Gibson rejects the belief that perception is based upon conscious sensation. Rather he holds that sensations, if they exist, are no more than byproducts of perception and are not basic to its occurrence. The senses, he maintains, are employed to detect objects, not to permit an observer to have sensations. The study of sensation would therefore be, according to him, irrelevant to the study of perception, and thus he rules out the study of receptor sensitivity, i.e., psychophysics and sensory physiology, as having no bearing on the problem of perception. *The Senses Considered as Perceptual Systems.* Boston. Houghton Mifflin. 1966.

Consciousness is that constructive psychological activity which continuously strives to bring the phenomena of the outer world into context in such a way as to deepen insight into the structure of psychological experience. Consciousness leads to action. Not only is the unconscious person excluded from the outer world, but also his social relationships are immediately changed. The loss of consciousness leads one immediately from a social into a private world, whereas clearness of consciousness makes man a social being. The complete awareness of an object is possible only on the basis of full cooperation with other people, and in this sense consciousness is in essence a social phenomenon.[2]

In supporting his provocative thesis—the ultimate reducibility of biology to physical science—Dean E. Wooldridge sets forth the hypothesis that consciousness is a passive phenomenon, that, as he says, "it doesn't *do* anything." He does not imply the existence of consciousness, but he does limit its role "to that of a sort of window through which we can observe a part of the workings of the brain without interfering with the orderly operation of the machinery we are watching."[3] Our mental experience, he argues, does not "*necessarily* preclude a physical explanation of thought" and "thought seems free and spontaneous only because most of the activity of thinking is unconscious and . . . only occasionally does a part of the action flash across our screen of awareness."[4]

Vinacke has identified four attributes of consciousness: (a) it can be understood strictly in terms of the electrochemical processes of the human body, especially the central nervous system; (b) it displays a structure which may be described in terms of "levels" or "areas" of awareness, i.e., selective mechanisms operate to determine what is to be included, at any given moment, within the conscious organization, and this organization and content are subject to continuous change; (c) it is conditioned by the individual's relation to the external world and to his internal environment; and (d) it is a continuum—present mental events are linked with past events and, by anticipation, with future events.[5]

---

[2] Paul Schilder. *Mind: Perception and Thought in their Constructive Aspects.* New York. Columbia University Press. 1942. pp. 341–42.

[3] Dean E. Wooldridge. *Mechanical Man: The Physical Basis of Intelligent Life.* New York. McGraw-Hill. 1968. p. 85.

[4] *Ibid.* p. 84.

[5] W. Edgar Vinacke. *The Psychology of Thinking.* New York. McGraw-Hill. 1952. pp. 33–34. For a mechanistic view of consciousness see: Dean E. Wooldridge. *The Machinery of the Brain.* New York. McGraw-Hill. 1963. pp. 219–20. Ralph W. Gerard. "Brains and Behavior," *The Evolution of Man's Capacity for Culture,* ed. J. N. Spuhler. Detroit. Wayne State University Press. 1959. pp. 14–20.

The relationship between the physiological and psychological factors in consciousness is still far from being understood, and science is not even certain whether the brain and the mind are two separate entities related to each other in ways that are not yet understood, or whether they are aspects of the same entity. Advances in electronics during the last 25 years have greatly increased understanding (both actual and potential) of the physiology of the nervous system, and have even made possible the construction of mechanical models which seem to embody some of the fundamentals which underlie the physiological bases of the brain. But even here, where the ground seems relatively firm, science is very willing to grant that the mind requires a great deal more to explain its workings than an understanding of physico-chemical characteristics of the brain.

The system by which the contents of the communication medium is transferred to the brain and stored there has been a mystery ever since the fifteenth century when that area of the brain was first discovered. The human brain is the most complex organization of matter and energy that man has encountered in all his explorations of the universe. The electrical properties of nerves which were discovered as early as the eighteenth century, and subsequent assumptions about the behavior of neurons have led many scientists, including such a distinguished figure as John von Neumann, to draw analogies between the brain and the computer.[6] Such conclusions are certainly not entirely to be rejected as invalid, and one cannot reasonably doubt that, as the science of computer engineering progresses and neurology and neurosurgery advance, the two areas will increasingly interrelate and each in its own specialized way contribute to the knowledge of the other. As Dean Wooldridge and others have shown, the operations of the brain are not to be understood exclusively in terms of binary logic. To be sure, the ten billion nerve cells of the brain, which receive and transmit countless messages every microsecond, can classify and store experience, solve problems, recreate the past, and anticipate the future. But, whereas the computer's operation is linear with relation to the stimuli it receives, the brain is nonlinear. The course which the stimulus traverses from the sensory organs to the brain may be described as linear, and the linearity of this pattern of signals may still be recognizable after the signals have fanned out through several connecting nerve cells. Up to this point the process can be accurately simulated on a computer. But when the signal reaches the brain, the bit of information that was communicated by the sensory organs is tremendously "spread-out" and "divided" into many

---

[6] John von Neumann. *The Computer and the Brain.* New Haven. Yale University Press. 1958.

bits so that linearity no longer exists, and the computer as it is known today and as it has been developed for business operations is entirely inappropriate as a model.

There is another and more realistic way of conceiving the brain than as merely a supercomputer, and that is as an organ of the body, with metabolic requirements and susceptibility to disease. Indeed, work in progress at the University of Chicago and the Brain Research Institute of the University of California at Los Angeles indicates that the operation of the brain in information storage and retrieval is as much chemical as electronic, that "memory" occurs by chemical change on the outside of the neurons instead of inside them, that electrical impulses flickering through spaces between the neurons are as important to brain function as the sending of electrical pulses along the nerves, and that the chemical bonding of calcium to the neuron's surrounding membrane may be the real key to the brain's capacity for information storage and retrieval.

Man is something more than a creature of habit, a biological organism, an animate being, just as his cognitive judgments, as the pragmatist would have them, are inspired by more than purposive interests. Man is likely unaware of his own cognitive behavior; "pure" thought is probably a figment of the metaphysicist's theorizing. Fish don't know they're wet, or, to adopt the imagery of Konrad Lorenz, wild geese don't intend to cast their reflection; they don't even see it in the waters; they don't even look for it. One might raise the query of the solipsist and question whether a reflection exists at all—unless there is a man there to see it.[7] "The last thing that man will understand in nature," wrote Sir John Eccles, "is the performance of his own brain."[8] Dr. Sidney Schulman of the University of Chicago implies only slightly less pessimism:

> Man's cranial computer doesn't come simple, fool-proof, and cheap from the shop of nature. Always pervading the intellectual activities of the brain are feelings, and the special sorts of awareness —like the knowledge of our own mortality—that go to make up the human condition. These come and go for most of us in combinations that are usually harmonious and sometimes even glorious. . . . In some way that seems naturally to make sense to us, but which we cannot begin to specify rigorously, good and evil are both inherent in

[7] Edward R. F. Sheehan. "Conversations with Konrad Lorenz." *Harper's Magazine.* vol. 236 (May 1968), pp. 69–77. Also, Konrad Lorenz. *Evolution and the Modification of Behavior.* Chicago. University of Chicago Press. 1965.

[8] Quoted by Sidney Schulman. "Brain Research." *Chicago Today* vol. 5 (Winter 1968) p. 8.

the complexity of the brain. It is this side of the frontier that has attracted poets, and philosophers for ages, and now, psychologists and psychiatrists.[9]

E. Roy John, who has written a particularly comprehensive treatise on the mechanisms of memory, does not reject the long-accepted belief that memory storage consists in the formation of specific pathways connecting receptors and effectors, and that information storage and retrieval involves alterations in specific cells in specific neural circuits. Rather, he seeks to harmonize accepted theory with the results of his own investigations. He holds that memory is based on the patterned activity of aggregates of cells, that experience caused by stimulation in a given environment alters the baseline activity of networks of cells. This alteration produces protein synthesis which modifies the responsiveness of the cell's membrane to particular sequences of stimulation. Thus, chemical changes occurring during memory consolidation increase the probability of modes of oscillation originally caused by the stimulus. According to John, memory retrieval requires a mechanism that assesses the congruence between the oscillations of cells which display invariant responses to afferent stimulation and that of cells the coherence of which has been influenced by prior experience. Initiation of oscillation in the plastic cells constitutes retrieval, and coincidence between the two modes indicates that the event is familiar.[10]

Finally, there are those like Sir Charles Sherrington, who hold that "mind" can never be explained in terms of "matter," because the two are incommensurable.[11] One may hope that eventually advances in the scientific investigations of the labyrinthian interrelationships of the brain will resolve some of the problems that now befog our understanding of the nature of human thought and consciousness. Sir Russell Brain suggests that such understanding may come through a new concept of the space-time relationship: it is possible that consciousness is essentially four-dimensional, but is experienced only in terms of man's "naive symbolism of three-dimensional physical space," and in the mind, events occur (as they do in the atom) which cannot be expressed in terms of the space man

---

[9] *Ibid.* See also: Jesse H. Shera. "The Cerebral Foundations of Library Science." *Library School Review.* (Department of Library Science, Kansas State Teachers College) Emporia, Kansas. (October 1968), pp. 3–6. Stanley Burnshaw. "The Body Makes the Mind." *American Scholar.* vol. 38 (Winter 1968–69).

[10] E. Roy John. *Mechanisms of Memory.* New York. Academic Press. 1967. pp. 25–39.

[11] Sir Charles Sherrington. *Man on His Nature.* Cambridge. Cambridge University Press. 1951. Chapters 7 and 8.

perceives.[12] But whatever the ultimate explanation of consciousness may prove to be, certainly science at the moment is dealing with those areas of mind which Grey Walter calls *silent* "because their oracles are dumb when threatened by the experimental intruder."[13]

The need of the brain constantly to receive and process new information is an inherent characteristic of, at least, the higher animals. Only a small portion of the central nervous system is developed at birth; the major part grows continuously through stimulation and experience— through the absorption, organizing, and processing of all information reaching the brain through sense perception. The total capacity of the human brain for handling information is, of course, sharply distinguished from that of even the higher animals—despite our colossal ignorance of the operations of the human brain, we know that the capacity of the mind to learn is far greater than is utilized. Though it varies from person to person, it is roughly constant for each individual—like the capacity of a waterpipe through which only a given amount of flow can be forced. But for the human brain, unlike the waterpipe, there seems to be an irreducible minimum below which the input of information cannot fall without damage. Attention can wander, and often does as every teacher knows; but it dare not cease.

To man's traditionally recognized need of air, water, food and shelter, Professor Platt has added "the need for what can be called—in a mathematical sense—'information,' for a continuous, novel, unpredictable, nonredundant, and surprising flow of stimuli."[14] The brain must have something upon which to exercise itself, and lacking external stimuli to process, it will, for better or worse, generate its own stimuli. In tests at McGill University, most subjects suffered hallucinations and other manifestations of mental disorientation after relatively short periods of sensory deprivation, though experiments at Princeton showed that confinement in the "black room" appeared in a number of instances actually to have im-

---

[12] Russell Brain. *The Contribution of Medicine to Our Idea of the Mind.* Cambridge. Cambridge University Press. 1952. pp. 23–24; J. Z. Young speaks of the "occult quality" of consciousness. *Doubt and Certainty in Science.* New York. Oxford University Press. 1960. pp. 155–56.

[13] W. Grey Walter. *The Living Brain.* New York. Norton. 1953. p. 72. See also: Walter R. Hess. "Causality, Consciousness, and Cerebral Organization." *Science.* vol. 158, no. 3806 (December 8, 1967), pp. 1279–83. A good review of the present state of research in neurophysiology is to be found in Ragnar Granit's *Charles Scott Sherrington.* Garden City, N.Y. Doubleday. 1967.

[14] John Rader Platt. "The Fifth Need of Man." *Horizon.* vol. 1, no. 6. (July 1959), p. 106.

proved learning ability and in other ways to have sharpened mental processes.[15]

But the interaction between the senses and the brain is not to be understood as a simple stimulus-response relationship in which the nervous system is likened to a telephone switchboard which connects the stimulus with the response. Rather, the brain may be characterized as a library or information center where stimuli, or messages, are received, interpreted, sorted, classified, arranged, and otherwise stored or acted upon before response, if any, occurs. Were man to utilize fully the exquisite capacity for making distinctions which enables him to perceive differences in like-seeming stimuli, he would of necessity respond to each as though it were unique. But this capacity is balanced by the ability to conceptualize, to categorize—to consider as equivalent things which are discriminably different—to group or relate like messages into classes, and to respond to them in terms of their class likenesses rather than of their uniqueness. Physiologically as well as psychologically man abhors chaos as nature is said to abhor a vacuum. It was not whimsy that led Sherrington to call man's brain the "magic loom," for it is necessarily a fabricator of patterns.

"Order is Heaven's first law," wrote Pope, and he might have added that pattern is the stuff of which it is made. Pattern, or conceptualization, may be viewed as any sequence or arrangement of events, or groupings of phenomena, so ordered as to be differentiated from or analogous to any other sequence, arrangement, or set. Deprived of the information provided by the senses, the mind would be a void, the barrenness of which it is difficult to imagine; deprived of the ability to categorize, to classify, to form concepts, the mind would be a hopeless confusion. From the overwhelming mélange of sensory perceptions, man formulates patterns of familiarity, patterns of experience, with which and to which new sensations or messages can be compared and related. A face, a series of sounds (a symphony, for example), a taste, are familiar or unfamiliar to the degree to which they conform or fail to conform to patterns created by past experience. Each new experience, each new sensation, is assimilated and interpreted by the brain, fragmented into patterns of relationships, and through integration with the patterns of past experience, is eventually brought into an organized whole. Thus experience, which in reality is symbolic representations of past perception organized in memory, may be said to be the conceptualized patterning of past sensory perceptions. Just as one may say that there is no history of, or for, that which has not sur-

---

[15] Michel Siffre. *Beyond Time*. New York. McGraw-Hill. 1964; Jack A. Vernon. *Inside the Black Room*. New York. Clarkson N. Potter. Publisher. 1964.

vived, so one can say that without memory there is no experience, only reflex.

Bruner has defined a concept as "a network of sign-significant inferences by which one goes beyond a set of *observed* critical properties exhibited by an object or event to the class identity of the object or event in question, and thence to additional inferences about other *unobserved* properties of the object or event."[16] Vinacke has expressed his definition somewhat less technically as "a kind of selective system in the mental organization of a person which links previous experience and current status with stimulus objects. Concepts are organized systems which have important structural relations with each other and which have dynamic functions in determining the outgoing course of thought."[17] Since concepts result from the interpretation and combination of sensory perceptions, they depend upon the individual's experience. Concepts then become systems and subsystems in the mental organization which are tied together, linked, or otherwise combined by sensory experience. Conceptualization represents selection as well as organization, and it is necessary in that through it the individual can make efficient use of past experience. As Rapaport has pointed out, the fundamental question which conceptualization answers is, With what does an idea belong? The answer is that everything belongs with everything that shares an attribute of, or relation to it, where attribute is regarded by Rapaport as "participation."[18] Memory provides a frame of reference, or context, in which the pattern of relationships created through the act of conceptualization is crystallized. Experience is assimilated in the memory as a multiplicity of concept-systems comprised of sense perception and previous abstract quality, expressed especially in terms of time, space, matter, energy, weight, color relationship, property, and essence.

George A. Miller maintains that the amount of information that the human being can receive, process, and remember is severely limited by the span of absolute judgment and the span of immediate memory of the individual. However, by organizing the imput simultaneously into related clusters, or chunks, and recoding, especially through the mechanism of

---

[16] Jerome S. Bruner, Jacqueline J. Goodnow, and George A. Austin. *A Study of Thinking.* New York. Wiley. 1956. p. 344.

[17] Vinacke. *Psychology of Thinking.* p. 100.

[18] David Rapaport. *The Organization and Pathology of Thought.* New York. Columbia University Press. 1951. pp. 708–9.

Ulric Neisser believes that those who hold the view that machines will replace man as a thinker reveal a misunderstanding of thought. Ulric Neisser. "The Imitation of Man by Machine." *Science.* vol. 139 (January 18, 1963), pp. 193–97.

linguistic recoding, the capacity to process information and the span of remembering can be materially extended. Miller sees in this recoding activity the very essence of the thought process itself.[19]

Science, says Holmstrom, "pursues its aim by observing the objects and phenomena and arranging the observations to form patterns such that regularities and recurrent rhythms of relationships, called scientific laws, can be discerned between their parts. Science, we may say, is 'true' to the extent that the self-consistent pattern which scientists build up in this way is 'similar' . . . to the basic pattern (hidden by the mists of our ignorance), of the universe itself." Holmstrom holds that science may be regarded as "being a human endeavor to understand and explain," and knowledge is described by him as being "a pattern of ideas existing in an individual human mind." One may be said to "know" or comprehend a science to the extent that this pattern in his mind is similar to the pattern which the general body of scientists have formulated.[20] In the beginnings of each of these sciences there were only fragments of information—fractional pieces separated, often, by large areas of the unknown. The Arabs' invention of algebra made possible patterns in which the visible and invisible pieces, the known and the unknown, could be manipulated, assembled, equated, evaluated, and otherwise dealt with in accordance with certain rules of logic. Thus does man's increased understanding of his environment owe as much to new patterning as it does to the discovery of new concepts. The distinction between science and art has been made that whereas science is the discovery of new patterns and relationships, art is the rearrangement of known patterns and relationships into new configurations or forms.

There are two major types of categorization or, more precisely, categorizing responses to stimuli—the identity response and the equivalence response. Identity categorization may be defined as the act of classifying a variety of stimuli as *forms of the same thing*. What gives rise to identity response is not clear, though it would seem that it is affected by learning. But there is still considerable uncertainty as to what constitutes an identity class and how one learns to categorize in terms of identity categories. "A rose, is a rose, is a rose" gives little help in the understanding of identity.

---

[19] George A. Miller. "The Magical Number Seven, Plus or Minus Two; Some Limits on our Capacity for Processing Information." *Psychological Review.* vol. 63 (March 1956), pp. 81–97.

See also: Stanley Burnshaw. "The Body Makes the Mind." *The American Scholar.* vol. 38 (Winter 1968–1969), pp. 25–39.

[20] J. E. Holmstrom. "The Relation Between Referencing Symbols and Language." *Review of Documentation.* vol. 17, fasc. 1 (1950), p. 20.

An equivalence class is composed of those things which, though discriminably different, are said to *be of the same kind* or *amount to the same thing*. Three broad types of equivalence categories can be identified: the affective, the functional, and the formal. The first of these consists of things which are united in the brain by a common affective response and are exemplified by the phrase "such-and-such reminds me of thus-and-so," though in many features they may be very far from being identical or, in the opinion of another person, related in any way. Functional categorization is based upon utilitarian necessity, and it fulfills concrete and specific task requirements. Formal categories are constructed by the act of specifying, or attempting to specify, the intrinsic attribute properties required by the members of a class. This is categorization in the taxonomic sense. It relates the content of any given message in terms of its essential or basic subject meaning in an attempt to substitute for its relativity of function, or relation, an absolute or essence.

Yet the brain can do more than process or manipulate information telegraphed to it by the senses, more than conceptualize, distinguish, and group—it can generate "new" information from stimuli received through clues and analogies; it can solve problems, apparently by fragmenting them into manageable parts having familiar connotations and then bringing all of its resources (such as memory) to bear on each fragment in turn; it can remember sights, sounds, tastes, smells, and physical contacts, and it can be trained to remember them better than it might be naturally inclined to do; it can "imagine," and direct the creation of things which have never before existed, by applying or relating some of its stored knowledge in new ways; it can retain, on a subconscious level, information which it is not aware of remembering; it can fill in information gaps created by the absence of sensory evidence, reaching conclusions or formulating concepts by intuition or postulation (as Northrop has shown)[21] through its capacity for closure; it can take the inductive leap "out of the reach of method" described by William Whewell.[22] The phenomena of hallucinations and dreams, psychosomatic illnesses, the hearing of nonexistent sounds, the feeling of nonexistent touches, all would seem to suggest that in certain circumstances, under certain conditions, the nervous system is also capable of feigning sensations in the absence of actual stimuli.

Understanding of the electronic circuitry of the brain and the ways

---

[21] F. S. C. Northrop. "Mathematical Physics and Korzybski's Semantics." *General Semantics Bulletin*. nos. 16–17 (1955), p. 2.

[22] William Whewell. *Novum Organon Renovatus, Being the Second Part of the Philosophy of the Inductive Sciences,* 3rd ed. London. John W. Parker. 1858. bk. 2, p. 88.

in which its messages are processed and manipulated is further complicated by the influence upon such mental behavior of the individual's drives, or in an older terminology, his instincts, the basic pattern of motivation.

## THE BASIC DRIVES

The pattern of motivation not only varies widely from culture to culture, society to society, and individual to individual, but it is constantly changing from hour to hour. The moments are few, however, when one is without motive or in a state of complete and conscious indifference. At any given moment one needs this, or wants that, is delighted by the achievement of a desired objective, or rendered miserable or unhappy by failure. Furthermore, motives, or drives, seldom operate singly, but usually occur in combination with other, perhaps conflicting, motives, and the extent to which a given drive is dominant is largely determined by its intensity. Intense drives, such as hunger, thirst, curiosity, greatly lower the threshold of perception with respect to any form of communication that relates to these motivations. All communication is in fact an attempt to lower the threshold of perception, and the ease with which it is achieved largely depends upon the degree to which it is coincident with the drive, or drives, of the recipient. But it is not only the ends which communication seeks which are conditioned by drives, the act of communication itself is an expression of motives, for man communicates not only for the satisfaction of others, but, and perhaps most of all, to relieve his own tensions and satisfy his own needs. As Keats has admirably expressed this urge in the famous lines of his so-called last sonnet:

> When I have fears that I may cease to be
> Before my pen has glean'd my teeming brain,
> Before high-piled books, in charactery,
> Hold like rich garners the full-ripen'd grain;

This same relentless drive toward composition is echoed in the frustrations of the blind Milton and the deaf Beethoven. Communication, then, is motivated not only by the universal urge for survival, but, for the artist at least, the act of communication is itself a drive that is not to be denied.

There is no general agreement on the basic drives and the role each plays, or may play, in communication. Nevertheless, it is not unreasonable to assume that communication among men contributed greatly to the satisfaction of such drives as: self-preservation (the gratification of hunger, the quenching of thirst, and the avoidance of danger or pain); self-reproduction (the sexual urge, parental protectiveness or solicitude); and security (physical, social, emotional, and intellectual). All of these may combine in a variety of ways to produce a general feeling of uneasiness in an unfamiliar or hostile environment or situation. To assuage such apprehensions and provide an escape from their materialization is the function of knowledge and its dissemination through communication. The role which these drives play in the communication process is further complicated by the relative emphasis, or intensity, which they exhibit among individuals and peoples, for the drives themselves are conditioned both by the physical and psychological complexion of the human being, and by his environmental and social orientation.

In a land flowing with milk and honey, motives which spring from the needs of the body may be subordinated to the urge to "be accepted" or to achieve prestige. Sex, which, of all the basic drives, has perhaps been most subject to social conditioning has, in many cultures, been intentionally sublimated by the creation of "substitute" drives or the social generation of psychological barriers such as secrecy, fear, embarrassment, disgust, and moral disapproval. Often society will create "artificial" goals, such as rewards for athletic prowess or mechanical achievement, to encourage the young to "forget about sex." Thus are the drives of the individual constantly subject to manipulation by the culture in which he finds himself.

A drive is a basic tendency to activity initiated by those shifts in, or deviations from, homeostatic balance (restlessness) which result in an increased sensitivity, or lowering of the threshold, to particular types of stimuli to the end that a compensatory response eventually occurs.[23] The basic drives are satisfied by means of activities, of varying degrees of complexity, which are conditioned by both individual and social factors. Collectively the group, in the process of exercising social control, is able to suppress certain drives and to create, emphasize, or stimulate others. Drives then, though they are physiological and psychological in origin, are also related to social action and social goals.

The activities through which these drives find satisfaction, involve, except for the simplest of reflexes, both the body and the mind, and as the complexity of the activity increases, the mental tends to overshadow the physical. This may lead to the disparagement of the physical—the rejection by the "intelligentsia" of all forms of athletics. In such a society the "egghead" and the "muscle-man" are mutually distrustful. So complex may the intellectual activity become, and so extreme its domination over

---

[23] Gardner Murphy. *An Introduction to Psychology*. New York. Harper. 1951. p. 569.

the physical that a Buddha, beneath the Bo tree, may achieve a state in which the body is completely subordinated to mind.

But whatever the social pattern, certainly man's drive toward a better understanding of his environment is one of the first to emerge, and one of the strongest. In its earliest stages it may be manifest only as curiosity, which in its most advanced form is dignified as "scientific research." The difference is only one of method, of systematization. Communication is fundamental to the satisfaction of this drive, for man's horizons will indeed be sharply limited if he cannot share his knowledge with other men. Communication is the sharing of knowledge, and one's understanding of the nature of communication will be incomplete so long as there is uncertainty concerning the nature of knowledge, the ways in which knowledge grows and is assimilated by the individual, the manner in which it is manipulated by the brain, and the true relationship between knowledge and the brain, or consciousness, itself.

Our understanding of the operation of the human brain, the processes of cognition, and the influence of communication upon man's basic drives, fragmentary though this understanding is at the present time, should be of concern to the librarian. No one expects the librarian to be a neurophysiologist or a psychologist, but he should be aware of the results of research in these fields, for much of what is being discovered is relevant to the ways in which he organizes his materials, the manner in which he indexes and in other ways processes his bibliographic store, and the search strategies he uses in reference work.

## LEARNING

As the individual progresses from infancy to maturity, and even to old age, he steadily assimilates into his own mental system elements originally external to him; these include symbolic representations of environmental objects, the norms of his culture, and the traits, both real and ideal, of those with whom he has emotional ties. This progressive incorporation or absorption is called by the psychologist the "internalization of experience."[24] This process results in a "mental context" in terms of which the thinking of the individual is carried out. The mental context thus becomes a complex of controlling and regulating systems established during the continuing course of learning. The process of thinking, then, can be fully understood only by relating it to the background of learning and the

---

[24] Vinacke. p. 266.

mechanisms by which that background influences behavior. Learning may, therefore, be defined, as Murphy has stated it, as "the process by which the organism becomes able to respond more adequately to a given situation in consequence of experience in responding to it."[25]

Again, Dethier has defined learning as "a process by which some event happening to the organism changes the nervous system so that a response to a future event is affected by the change. Nobody understands the nature of these changes nor in which part or parts of the nervous system they occur."[26]

Though the psychologist's comprehension of the learning process is still inadequate, it seems increasingly clear that learning always involves an interplay between the individual and the environment, and because both are extremely complex the possibilities for interaction are almost unlimited, and are difficult to isolate and study through laboratory experimentation. Learning may derive from direct experience and vicarious experience, and to the latter the communication system is fundamental. The former is the more vivid, more powerful, and in the popular view its effectiveness is epitomized in the phrase "experience is the best teacher." The latter may involve either direct, person to person communication, or indirect, i.e., graphic, communication. Formalized education then, is a social invention created to expedite the learning process through highly compressed and accelerated vicarious experience. All formalized education is predicated on the assumption that the efficiency of the learning process can be improved through controlled exposure to vicarious experience, though individuals differ in their responses. Of course, not all formalized education is vicarious experience, some of it may be direct, such as the classroom techniques of Dewey's progressive education, many industrial arts courses, laboratory exercises, and work-study programs. Some of it is synthetic, e.g., role playing, the lawyer's moot court, and debating; all of which are, in reality, sophisticated forms of the child's "play-pretend" games.[27]

---

25 Murphy. *Introduction to Psychology.* p. 574.

26 Vincent G. Dethier. *To Know a Fly.* San Francisco. Holden-Day. 1962. p. 97. He continues: "One of the simplest types of learning is termed habituation. It is defined as ignoring a continued stimulus that is not harmful. It is seen in the purest form in churches and college lecture halls. The stimulus in these cases is the human voice."

27 Herbert Simon examines the psychology of thinking as evidence of his contention that man is basically a simple system that becomes more complex as he adapts to the complexities of the environment. Herbert A. Simon. *The Sciences of the Artificial.* Cambridge, Mass. M.I.T. Press. 1969. chapter 2.

Despite the fact that psychological investigations into the nature of learning have been largely confined to the very simplest forms of learning behavior, some generalizations about learning can be set forth with a reasonable degree of certainty. *First*, there is an apparently strong relation between the complexity of the nervous system of an organism and the complexity of the things it can learn. *Second*, the importance of motivation in learning is very great, but one must not assume that motivation provides all the clues to the learning process for certain types of learning appear not to be goal directed. *Third*, there appears to be no one simple formula for learning applicable to all situations regardless of the individual who is doing the learning. *Fourth*, learning involves an interplay between the individual and the environment, and the environment may vary from idiosyncratic experience to those experiences shared by all men. The complex nature of this interplay is presented in Table 1-1. The infant is in a relatively unformed and helpless state, and he requires food, affection, protection, sleep, and a fairly constant temperature. But the conditions which will satisfy those needs, and the circumstances attendant upon their satisfaction are not fixed but vary according to the outline in the table. So, throughout life, the pattern of the individual's learning will be shaped by his biological character, his role, the groups of which he is, or will become, a member, his culture, and the idiosyncratic events which relate to him alone. Learning, then, involves an elaboration of this motive system. The original needs and impulses of the infant initiate learning acts which eventually become a complex pattern of striving and impulse satisfaction that persists, with varying degrees of intensity and emphasis, until death. Thus, as summarized by Vinacke, learning "is a function of dynamic interaction between the organism and the physical-social-cultural environment,"[28] with the resultant reshaping of the biological starting-points. *Fifth*, and finally, learning manifests itself in four ways: (1) there is a basic conditioned-response foundation of learning; (2) it progresses by trial-and-error; (3) learning is self-organizing and tends to promote permanence of result; and (4) it is symbolic in that it employs symbols and analogies. The first two of the above are so obvious as to need little explanation. Man knows from his experience in the training of animals and young children that much learning is gained through the development of conditioned responses, and certainly, he knows very well from his own experience that much of his learning is acquired through trial-and-error. It may not be an efficient way to promote learning, but there are times when it is the only available avenue.

---

[28] Vinacke. *Psychology of Thinking.* p. 266.

TABLE 1-1. Conditions entering into the learning process which shape the mental context*

| Conditions Which Influence Development | Degree, or Extent, of Generality | | | |
|---|---|---|---|---|
| | Universal | Group or Communal | Role | Idiosyncratic |
| Biological | Birth, death, appetites, physical needs | "Racial" traits, endemic disease | Age, sex, group affiliation as determined by birth | Physical "makeup," glandular balance, deformities |
| Physical-environmental | Time, temperature, gravity | Climate, topography, natural resources | Access to, or dependence upon, natural resources | Accidents, other unique events |
| Social-environmental | Infant care, contacts with other human beings | Size, density, and distribution of population, social organization, associations | Occupation, cliques, demands made by society | Social "accident," "lucky, or unlucky break" |
| Cultural-environmental | Tabus, certain forms or expressions of symbolism | Tradition, rules of conduct, manners, skills, knowledge | Culturally differentiated roles | Superstition, folklore individually communicated |

* Modified from Kluckholn and Mowrer. "Culture and Personality," *American Anthropology.* vol. 46 (1944), pp. 1–29; and Vinacke, *Psychology of Thinking.* p. 264.

Conditioning and trial-and-error lay the foundation for learning, the permanent effects of which may be found in the reinforcement of later experience, thus previous experience influences subsequent behavior. Learning, then, has certain permanent results, and these have a self-organizing effect on response. The activities of the individual depend, in varying degree, upon the results or effects of previous experience—stimuli impinge upon the organized results of previous stimuli—and responses emerge from these systems. The systems thus created by this self-organizing character of learning are not independent of each other, but have active interrelationships, and subsystems, which are close or remote as the case may be. These are "fields of force" in which a change in one area may result in a minor alteration or a complete realignment, depending upon the character of the stimulus. Within the individual, then, these systems and subsystems are interrelated in complex patterns and, in a sense, communicate with each other. Thus concepts, motives, behavior patterns, traits, attitudes, are not discrete entities, distinct and separate from each other, but are intricately interrelated, organized, and interdependent as a result of the self-organizing character of learning.

Of particular relevance, however, to the work of the librarian is the symbolic character of learning. As the infant or child matures in his experience, objects and acts acquire symbolic counterparts or analogies which can be employed or manipulated in lieu of the external object or act. Thus, through symbolization, the possibilities for learning become almost unlimited because symbols make possible: (a) the effective communication of experience from person to person or group to group; (b) the compression, or short-circuiting, of experience through the efficiency of symbolic manipulation; and (c) the utilization of past experience through storage and manipulation in the memory of symbolic representations.

In its earliest, or elementary, stages of learning the mastery of symbolic response is limited to simple conditioning by the repeated linking of words, or other symbols, and objects. This conditioning probably persists, in greater or less degree, throughout life, but as the individual achieves greater intellectual sophistication the word substitutes for the object until a point is reached at which words can themselves be reinforcements in the learning process and further learning can be expected upon them. Language, which is probably the most important manifestation of symbolism, can abbreviate, and often entirely eliminate, the long laborious process of learning through stimulus and physical response by itself becoming vicarious experience. Through symbolic representation it is also possible to bring large segments of past experience to bear on an existing situation, so that memory, working through language, can enrich, in many ways, the experience of the moment.

Robert Gagné has identified eight types of learning, most of which are self-explanatory and relatively obvious, though their categorization is useful in discussing the learning situation:

1. Signal Learning
2. Stimulus-Response Learning
3. Chaining, i.e., linking together two or more previously learned stimulus-responses
4. Verbal Association
5. Multiple Discrimination, e.g., the ability to overcome the "interference" that conflicting chains may generate and to sort out that which is useful, important, or needed to be retained
6. Concept Learning, i.e., the power to conceptualize
7. Principle Learning, where a principle is regarded as a relationship between, or among, concepts
8. Problem Solving[29]

Jerzy Konorski has turned to neurophysiology and the study of brain function as the key to our understanding of learning, and though his physiology is often oversimplified and his principles of learning at times conflict with more recent findings, his integrative approach is stimulating reading, and opens the door to an area of interdisciplinary study that needs further exploration.[30]

Despite the fact that Tilton insists that "a working psychology of learning is of central importance to the worker in the field of education," and that the "psychology of learning must bear upon *every* educational problem, upon *every* phase of the teacher's work,"[31] Delong complains

[29] Robert M. Gagné. *The Conditions of Learning.* New York. Holt, Rinehart, and Winston. 1965. pp. 33–57.

Comparison should also be made with Bloom's "Taxonomy." Benjamin S. Bloom, editor. *Taxonomy of Educational Objectives.* New York. McKay. 1956.

Arnheim presents the argument that visual perception and visual images play a very important role in the storing of information and the appraisal of experience. The author would have educators be systematically trained in "visual sensitivity." Rudolf Arnheim. *Visual Thinking.* Berkeley. University of California Press. 1969.

[30] Jerzy Konorski. *Integrative Activity of the Brain; An Interdisciplinary Approach.* Chicago. University of Chicago Press. 1968.

[31] J. W. Tilton. *An Educational Psychology of Learning.* New York. Macmillan. 1951. p. 7.

that the major weakness of current theories concerning learning "is its lack of usefulness to the teacher in the classroom."[32] He finds, however, certain encouraging trends in the literature of learning—that a new frame of reference for the investigation of learning is being accepted, that there is a change in focus from the experimenter to the learner, from emphasis upon results in learning to an emphasis on process, from independent findings to a synthesis of related results.

Thorpe and Schmuller, after an unusually exhaustive study of contemporary theories of learning, urge the need for their integration into a unified body of knowledge that will be adaptable and eclectic. The heterogeneity of contemporary society and its impact upon the learning of the individual demands a flexible theory of learning. The effect of the communication system upon the individual and its shaping of his learning is far too complex to be simply explained, though it has given relevance to McLuhan's belief in the importance of the medium. Learning should be considered, then, from an eclectic point of view, not in the sense of choosing or developing theories to fit passing fads, "but a *patterned eclecticism* which endeavors to construct an orderly framework which is both strong in itself and sufficiently flexible to meet the demands put upon it by vital and growing learners."[33]

Just how complex the problems of learning theory are in relation to such other factors as intelligence and cognition, is well illustrated by J. P. Guilford's study of the nature of human intelligence.[34] His work, which is a synthesis of some sixty years of effort in the attempt to understand intelligence, is particularly relevant to learning theorists, especially the behaviorists, for its denial of the widespread belief that the association principle can be applied to all learning, whereas it is but one of several kinds of intellectual products, or, as he says, "implications." He charges that the theorists in all areas relating to the intellectual processes have been guilty of oversimplification in failing to deal with the multiplicity of pro-

---

[32] Arthur R. DeLong. "Learning." *Review of Educational Research.* vol. 25, no. 5 (December 1955), pp. 439 and 445.

[33] Louis P. Thorpe and Allen M. Schmuller. *Contemporary Theories of Learning.* New York. Ronald. 1954. p. 437.

Konrad Lorenz's *Evolution and the Modification of Behavior* (Chicago. University of Chicago Press. 1965) is a study of "innate" and "learned" elements neither of which is applicable to fully developed behavior patterns. Information enters the organic system either through the species or through interaction with the environment, but there may be behavior patterns that originate from the evolution of the species.

[34] J. P. Guilford. *The Nature of Human Intelligence.* New York. McGraw-Hill. 1967.

cesses involved in perception, learning, creativity, and cognition. To bring order out of the chaos, Guilford has sought to provide a statement of the structure of intelligence, a classification of how man processes that which is discriminable. Thus, he has brought together the available empirical evidence regarding the biological and cultural factors involved in his model of the "structure-of-intellect," but thorough as his investigation is, it is still incomplete.

Because of the complexity of the intellectual process, Ulric Neisser sees little hope for any important developments in "artificial intelligence" in the near future. There are, he has written, three fundamental and inter-related characteristics of human thought that are conspicuously absent from existing or contemplated computer programs: (1) human thinking always takes place in, and contributes to, a cumulative process of growth and development; (2) human thinking begins in an intimate association with emotions and feelings which is never entirely lost; and (3) almost all human activity, including thinking, serves not one but a multiplicity of motives at the same time.[35]

Man is the product of an evolutionary process, says Linton, which ever tends toward increasing individualism. There is ample laboratory evidence to show that mammals are highly specialized in their abilities to learn, and by the time that man had reached a level where the establishment of cultures became possible he had lost most of his "instincts" and had to invent, or learn, practically everything he did. Thus, every individual is forced to develop his own patterns of behavior and, though these patterns are partially fixed through habit, they never become entirely stabilized in the sense usually thought of in reference to "instincts." The possibilities for variation in individual learning and, through learning, behavior are almost infinite. Intrinsically, then, members of the human species, because of greater capacity for, and variation in, the ability to learn have greater potentialities for differentiation than those of any other species. The whole trend of human evolution has, thus, been away from the production of standardized social units which, as Linton expresses it, "are the ideal building blocks for complex social structures."[36]

Teaching, as one form of communication, is an instrument for bringing organization and direction to what otherwise would be accidental or

---

[35] Ulric Neisser. "The Imitation of Man by Machine." *Science*. vol. 139 (January 18, 1963), p. 195. See also: Phyllis A. Richmond. "What Are We Looking For?" *Science*. vol. 139 (February 22, 1963), pp. 737–39.

[36] Ralph Linton. *The Cultural Background of Personality*. New York. Appleton. 1945. pp. 13–15.

fortuitous experience, and the incentive of the individual to learn lies in the satisfaction which it affords to his personal needs. So, as Linton says, "he takes the bait of immediate personal satisfaction and is caught upon the hook of socialization."[37] Thus, the individual eats to satisfy a strong hunger drive, but it is through learning that he is taught to "eat like a gentleman." This need to adapt one's self to the patterns of social behavior varies from individual to individual, and not everyone feels the desire to "eat like a gentleman," or, at least, to eat with the same degree of "elegance." Success in learning, therefore, is directly related to motivation, and the stimulation of that motivation is one of the teacher's most important obligations.

## VARIATION

No theory of learning can, however, be maintained unless it takes into account variations among human beings,[38] and there can be no understanding of the influence of communication upon the individual without an awareness of the great range in individual responses. The process of evolution results in increasing complexity and increasing variability; it does not promote uniformity. The nervous system in particular must be increasingly adaptable to variations in, and more effective integration with, the alterations in the environment. It may be more advantageous for survival to have better eyes, or better ears, but to have a better nervous system means being able to learn more quickly, to learn more different things, so that in modern society, and, indeed, perhaps in all societies, a premium is put upon the ability to learn, the capacity to assimilate communication. The rewards of adaptability, or variability, upon capacity to learn are all important in the background of mankind.[39]

The neglect of variation is, at least in part, the result of the need of science for generalizations and laws, and the eagerness to discover generalizations in all phenomena has blinded science to those distinctions which make of each man a true individual. The result has been that there is comparatively little literature dealing with the ways in which so-called normal individuals differ from each other.[40] Economists predicate an "economic

---

[37] *Ibid.* p. 25.
[38] Thorpe and Schmuller. *Theories of Learning.* p. 436.
[39] Murphy. *Introduction to Psychology.* p. 10.
[40] See: Roger J. Williams. "Chemistry Makes the Man." *Saturday Review.* (April 6, 1957), p. 42.

man," librarians talk glibly of the "average reader," and the mass media of communication are beamed at an assumed common audience with standardized tastes, interests, and emotional needs. Because nature produces an infinity of patterns, and man must make some order out of this diversity there has been neglect of those who have varied from accepted norms. This does not necessarily mean that science has been unaware of the problems posed by individual differences, but it has been impelled to seek out principles with the widest possible coverage. Because each variation is a potential threat to generalization, there is always the natural impulse to sweep the former under the rug. Yet Santayana has admonished the sciences to bestow, "infinite pains upon that experience which," in the vastness of science, "would drift by unchallenged or misunderstood."[41] Since education is considered to be the communication of knowledge, so directed that the individual's behavior is influenced favorably in relation to the social goals and values of his culture, the importance of Santayana's admonition to the student of the psychology of learning seems particularly apropos.

The democratic ethic recognizes the uniqueness of each individual, and holds that all are entitled to the opportunity to learn. There is, then, in the communication system, of which education as an institution is a part, the necessity to observe sufficient uniformity of procedure to create mutual understanding. The problem lies in the proper drawing of the line between uniformity and diversity, or more accurately, of allowing for diversity within uniformity; for in a democratic society both individuality and uniformity, within the context of equality, are recognized and encouraged.

In part, variation is inherent in the characteristics of the organism, and in part it is the result of the totality of the environment. The effect of physical factors is relatively obvious though the exact nature of that effect is not well understood. There is, however, evidence to show that the structure of the brain, the physical characteristics of the body and its chemistry, nutrition for example, influence the capacity to learn. There is evidence too, to show that the range of variation is probably greater among individuals than it is among "races." Alleged "racial" differences are more apt to be the result of environmental, especially cultural, factors. The emphasis which a culture places upon the education of the young, particularly the young of certain groups, the cultural differences in the attitude of a society toward the education of women, the social status that a society accords the professional person, the roles which are assigned to the constituent

---

41 George Santayana. *The Life of Reason.* New York. Scribner. 1905. pp. 37–38.

groups within the culture, the mores which may place a premium on manual skills or discredit "book learning," the distribution of wealth, especially the willingness of a society to pay for, or be willing to pay for particular services and the nature of those services with respect to educational requirements—all of these factors influence the *development* of the mental abilities inherent in the physiological and psychological capacities of the individuals who comprise the society.

One should not assume, however, that wealth or even prosperity is necessarily conducive to the development of mental abilities. Adversity may result in a selective process in which those with limited mental capacities fail to survive and only those who are richly endowed with a native capacity to learn, live to reproduce their kind. In this complex pattern of physical and social factors which influence, in a variety of ways, the capacity to learn and the opportunity to develop that capacity, cause and effect are so intricately interwoven as to make any kind of generalization extremely hazardous and all assumptions fraught with danger. Until there is far more complete understanding of the learning process than is now available, no one should have the temerity to assert that his educational theory is the only right one. Society is not yet ready to have any one educational system forced upon it, or any one institution or agency dictate what is "best."

That students learn more in "good" schools than in "poor" schools has long been accepted as axiomatic by the educational community, yet the monumental study of some six hundred thousand grade school children enrolled in approximately four thousand schools, which was sponsored by the U.S. Office of Education, seems to show, despite its methodological shortcomings, that "variations in school quality are not highly related to variations in achievement of pupils. . . . The school appears unable to exert independent influences to make achievement levels less dependent on the child's background."[42] This revolutionary suggestion that schools with widely varying characteristics differ very little in their educational effects needs more scientific examination than it has yet received, and one study is not sufficient evidence upon which to reject a traditional faith in educational excellence, but until such evidence is forthcoming, one way or another, educators cannot speak too confidently of their belief that equality of educational opportunity will increase the equality of intellectual achievement.

If it is the child's background rather than what takes place in the

---

[42] U.S. Office of Education. *Equality of Educational Opportunity*. James S. Coleman, Director. Washington. Government Printing Office. 1966. p. 297.

classroom that seems to be the major factor in his intellectual growth, then interest must center on the quality of the child's very early environment. Motivation plays an important role in education and environment has much to do with that motivation. Thus, it is logical to assume that the more important the library can be in stimulating voluntary education the greater will be the library's educational role.[43] It may be that both the school and the library have waited too long in becoming a part of the child's background, and that his intellectual growth could be substantially enhanced if he were exposed to learning opportunities at a very early age. For the librarian, this could mean in operational terms working with the parents as well as the children. Thus, an environment could be created in which the encouragement of learning would be given a high priority in the child's family life.

The present writer believes that the public library should experiment with library service to young children in highly localized situations no larger than the neighborhood, and perhaps with only the city block as the unit. These local centers could have some characteristics of the nursery school (though the child would be free to come and go as in any public library) with additional provision of library service to both child and parent. This blending of activities with the availability of books, under the direction of personnel competent to work with children and parents, could stimulate learning. The immediate costs would be high but the resultant social savings might very well return rich rewards.

## LANGUAGE

Of all man's mental powers which still remain inadequately explained despite advances in scientific inquiry certainly one of the most remarkable is the ability to recognize and attach meaning or value to any number of symbol-systems—visual, aural, even tactile. Without this capacity, which constitutes the very heart of language, communication, not only between individuals, but also within the individual himself, would be all but impossible and there could have developed no culture, no civilization, no social organization. Whether there could ever have been human thought without language is still debatable, but certainly most people find it difficult to "think" without the use of words.

Language is, indeed, as Susanne Langer has said, "the most momen-

---

[43] See: Kathleen Molz. "Education for Sensibility in the House of Facts." *American Libraries.* vol. 1 (January 1970), pp. 29–38.

tous, and at the same time the most mysterious, product of the human mind. Between the clearest animal call of love or warning or anger, and a man's least trivial word, there lies a whole day of Creation."[44] In language, man has achieved the free use of symbolism; his speech is the articulation of conceptual thinking, and his conceptual thinking is immeasurably facilitated, if not entirely dependent upon, verbalization. Yet there exists no evidence to show that there is any innate language-making instinct in the human being. Though every normal person is born with a remarkably flexible speech mechanism and a brain with the capacity for symbol recognition and manipulation as well as conceptualization and retention, it seems clear that language itself must be learned, transmitted as a message-carrying symbol-system from those who have mastered it to those who have not. "Language," wrote Edward Sapir, "is a purely human and non-instinctive method of communicating . . . by means of a system of voluntarily produced symbols."[45]

The very young child is first taught the names of things around him and (in most cases) the simple concept of "No," and thus the retentive, recognitional, and associative functions of his brain come into play when he is just beginning to relate himself to his environment. When he is of an age to speak, he is given reiterated examples of the words he is to say in order to identify an object he knows or a pleasurable experience he wishes to repeat. Only when the child enters upon his formal education is he initiated into the rules governing the proper usage of the vocabulary he has already achieved largely through imitation.[46] In due course he may

---

[44] Susanne K. Langer. *Philosophy in a New Key*. Cambridge. Harvard University Press. 1941. p. 83.

[45] Edward Sapir. *Language*. New York. Harcourt, Brace. 192?. p. 8. Also: Charles F. Hockett. "Animal 'Languages' and Human Language." *Capacity for Culture*, ed. Spuhler. pp. 32–39.

[46] Eric H. Lenneberg holds that while language obviously cannot be acquired in the absence of a speaking person, social contacts serve only as the releaser or resonator of innately developing mechanisms. In support of his view he cites the regularly successive stages that young children go through in learning to talk regardless of outside circumstances. Crying in infants is followed by cooing and then by babbling, the last being regarded as the first true language because phoneme units can be distinguished in its intonational pattern. Single words are uttered between the ages of twelve and eighteen months, followed by two-word combinations which are not random compositions but constitute a primitive subject-predicate organization. Such constructs, Lenneberg holds, are not imitations of adult speech but indicate that certain rules of grammar have been acquired. In brain-injured, deaf, or otherwise handicapped children the rate of language learning is slowed and the process extended, but the sequence is not altered. He further believes that a poor language environment does not handicap a child permanently, but if the social environment

wish to learn languages other than his own, and his familiarity with the structure of his native tongue will serve him well in such study. It is, however, useless if he embarks on other types of symbol-systems such as mathematics or music.

Because it is almost impossible to imagine the existence of natural language in the absence of speech, it may be said that man was not man until he spoke. No one knows how the originators of any language went about choosing sounds to designate what they wished to designate. The early theories of the origins of language set forth by the philologists have long since been discredited. Both the "ma-ma" (interjectional) and the "bow-wow" (onomatopoeic) theories of the origin of speech have, despite their picturesqueness, been found wanting because they represent relatively unimportant elements in speech. There now exists no language which is truly primitive in the psychological sense, and there seem to be no simple, amorphous, or imperfect languages remaining upon the earth; so the linguists have been forced to conclude that they cannot carry their investigations much beyond the perspective revealed by the study of known languages. The Australian bushman may live in the most primitive of dwellings and make use of only the crudest of implements, yet his language is more complex than English: "People who have not invented textiles, who live under roofs of pleated branches, need no privacy and mind no filth and roast their enemies for dinner, will yet converse over their bestial feasts in a tongue as grammatical as Greek and as fluent as French."[47] John Dewey has set forth the theory that "language, signs, and significance come into existence, not by intent and mind, but by over-flow."[48] The central problem faced by investigations into the origins of speech, however, derives from our inability to explain satisfactorily the ways in which vocal articulations of any sort become dissociated from their original expressive values and are stereotyped into conventional symbolic patterns which have a consistent and universal meaning.[49]

---

is enriched at an early chronological age, the learning process can be accelerated. Eric H. Lenneberg. *Biological Foundations of Language.* New York. Wiley. 1967.

Lenneberg's study brings up to date the earlier work by Leonard Bloomfield. *Language.* New York. Holt, Rinehart, and Winston. 1933.

Reference should also be made to Walter J. Ong's discussion of the word and the sensorium in his book: *The Presence of the Word.* New Haven. Yale University Press. 1967. Chapter I. Also: Arthur Koestler. *The Act of Creation.* New York. Macmillan. 1964. Chapters XIV and XV.

[47] Langer. *Philosophy in a New Key.* pp. 83–84.

[48] John Dewey. *Experience and Nature.* Chicago. Open Court. 1925. p. 185.

[49] "There is still no plausible explanation for the emergence of the cultural transmis-

Sydney Lamb holds that language is not to be understood in terms of words, but rather in terms of mental systems. Speech and writing, he believes, are not language, but rather the manifestations of the system which is language. Thus, he has carried forward Noam Chomsky's work on transformational grammar, which was a first attempt in recent times to link language with the mind, by what Lamb has called "stratificational grammar," a theory which presents language as consisting of several independent, but interconnected, codelike systems which appear at different levels or strata. Through the use of stratificational grammar to reveal structural correspondences between the formation of concepts and the neuron networks of the brain, Lamb hypothesizes that the whole system of a culture, the proper and expected behavior of all its members in all kinds of situations can be displayed.[50]

Though there is general agreement that language as an organized system of symbolic forms is distinctly a human achievement, it has been shown that some of the higher animals are capable of abstracting general forms from the detail of specific situations. This seeming ability of the higher vertebrates to interpret certain selected elements in a situation as signs, or indicators, of a desired or undesired total result may have led early man toward a dim feeling for the symbolism that, through ritual and metaphor, became formalized into language.[51]

At the moment it would appear that the anthropologists probably have more to contribute to the study of language than do the linguists and philologists. However, significant steps toward a synthesis of disciplines in attacking the study of language are to be found in the work of Ernst Cassirer, Otto Jesperson, W. M. Urban, and Charles Morris.[52] Such

---

sion of patterns of sound produced in man, the change must somehow have been related to the advantage of an increased repertoire and flexibility of sound patterns." Peter Marler. "Animal Communication Signals." *Science.* vol. 157 (August 18, 1967), p. 774.

Reference should also be made to: Thomas A. Sebeok, ed. *Animal Communication: Techniques of Study and Results of Research.* Bloomington, Indiana. Indiana University Press. 1968; and Eric H. Lenneberg. *The Biological Foundations of Language.* New York. Wiley. 1967. Also, Lenneberg deals with the biological context of the development of language in children in his article: "On Explaining Language." *Science.* vol. 164 (May 9, 1969), pp. 635–43.

[50] Sydney M. Lamb. *Outline of Stratificational Grammar.* Washington, D.C. Georgetown University Press. 1966.

[51] Edgar H. Sturdevant. *An Introduction to Linguistic Science.* New Haven. Yale University Press. 1947. Chapter 5. "The Origins of Language."

[52] Ernst Cassirer. *Language and Myth.* New York. Harper. 1946; Otto Jesperson. *Language: Its Nature, Development, and Origin.* New York. Holt. 1922; W. M. Ur-

scholars as these have recognized, on the one hand, the enormous importance of signs, symbols, and myth in human life, even in contemporary human life, and, on the other hand, despite the central position of language in all sociological and anthropological inquiry, the absence of precise scientific knowledge concerning its true nature. Such authors as these have set out to identify, describe, and differentiate the many elements in society to which language appears to be related, and in so doing have drawn upon the work, not only of linguists, but also of psychologists, semanticists, estheticians, psychopathologists, philosophers, and even engineers in particular fields. Significant use has been made of the work of such important scholars as Rudolph Carnap, I. A. Richards, Harold Lasswell, Hans Reichenbach, and Otto Neurath.

Not only was the spoken word the first winged thought, without language, explicit thought itself—thought recognized as thought—seems to be impossible.[53] Most of the mental classifications that man makes are part of his social heritage, for he is *taught* the names of categories. Once these names become fixed in language, they become a controlling factor in normal modes of perception and thinking. To borrow the terminology of William James, all things, including civilization, are held together by names; without names and the name-givers we would have chaos.[54] Once a native language is mastered, the brain operates with and on its symbols and, through them, the entities or ideas they represent. Only rarely does a conscious thought occur in a form other than words, and as every college student knows, it is impossible deliberately to think about nothing, even though the teacher may at times believe otherwise. (When the mind is said to be a blank, it is actually searching frantically for a piece of information which it has not yet found.) Thus, it is safe to say that the scope of an individual's thinking is determined by his vocabulary. Emotion, however, as distinct from thought is quite another matter.[55]

---

ban. *Language and Reality*. New York. Macmillan. 1939; Charles Morris. *Signs, Language, and Behavior*. New York. Prentice-Hall. 1946; Antoine A. Cournot. *An Essay on the Foundations of Our Knowledge*. New York. Liberal Arts Press. 1956. "On Language," pp. 306–23; Edward Sapir. "Language." *Encyclopedia of the Social Sciences*. vol. 9.

[53] Susan M. Ervin. "Language and Thought" *Horizons of Anthropology*, ed. Sol Tax. Chicago. Aldine. 1964. pp. 81–91; Dell H. Hymes. "A Perspective for Linguistic Anthropology." *Ibid*. pp. 92–107.

[54] Harold Hoijer, ed. *Language in Culture*. Chicago. University of Chicago Press. 1954.

[55] See Susanne K. Langer's discussion of language and feeling in *Mind: An Essay on*

One does not have to pursue very far the scientific literature on the operation of the human brain before it becomes apparent that man is still very ignorant of the mechanism of thought and the physiological and psychological conditions in which thinking occurs. However, the "motor" or "central-peripheral" theory of the operations of the brain, which is the most convincing in the impressive body of experimental evidence that can be marshalled in its support, clearly delineates the close relationship between language and thought. In its broadest outline, this theory postulates:

1. Thinking originates in sensory perception, i.e., through activation of the nerves through sensory perception.

2. Meaning is ascribed to these perceptions through the use of language habits which have resulted from conditioning during the socialization process of the individual. Thus, words come to be substitute stimuli for objects and situations in the environment.

3. These language or verbal habits are retained in the memory; in fact, memory is largely the storing or retention of these verbal habits. More precisely, memory is stored consciousness, and though animals can remember without the aid of language, such retention must be sharply circumscribed. One cannot remember that which he cannot conceive.

4. In time these verbal habits become perfected and automatic, with the result that less motor activity is required for their occurrence.

5. Words may become substitutes for objects, so that an individual may act as though the object were present when it is physically absent. Further, words may be invented to represent objects or concepts which exist only in the imagination. These concepts or objects can be endowed with attributes that are so generally understood that they may be communicated with relatively complete comprehension; e.g., honesty, patriotism, the philosopher's stone, the unicorn, the side-hill dodger. It is to be noted, however, that such concepts are at times, though not always, constructs or combinations of objects or parts of objects that do possess some physical reality, and hence, even abstractions can have a physical basis of some sort.

6. The word need not be spoken aloud. The implicit movement of the muscles activating the speech mechanism may take the place of overt language, but even movement is not necessary.

---

*Human Feeling.* Baltimore. John Hopkins University Press. 1967. vol. 1, pp. 102–103.

7.  A chain of such implicit responses may occur, as William James has pointed out, and one response may act as a stimulus to the next until the process reaches exhaustion.[56] This chain response corresponds to thinking. In short, thinking is "talking to oneself."

8.  With continued practice, which is an almost constant process often carried on without deliberate effort on the part of the individual, "silent talking" reaches the degree of complexity, speed, and efficiency that characterizes the mature person.

9.  In the use of "silent talking" in a problem situation, thinking appears to be essentially a trial-and-error process—witness the behavior of a person who talks aloud while seeking the answer to a problem.

10.  Much of this trial-and-error derives from association; i.e., the linkages of the chain. In fact, one may wonder whether it is possible to "think" apart from association.

11.  As suggested in point 7 above, a course of thinking is completed or, more accurately, terminated, when the original stimulating conditions are satisfied, or when an adjustment is achieved which renders the initiating situation inoperative. Fatigue may, of course, promote such a disturbance.[57]

Admittedly, the theory may overemphasize the vocal element in explaining the activity of thinking. Thinking probably involves the whole of the bodily organization including a substantial number of nonverbalized responses. But certainly language plays a very important role in man's ability to think.

Herskovitz has defined language as a system of arbitrary and vocal symbols by which members of a social group cooperate and interact.[58] A more elaborate definition has been developed by Charles Morris, who has identified five attributes of language: (1) a language is composed of a plurality of signs; (2) each of these component signs has a signification that is common to a number of interpreters, i.e., understandable to the members of the "interpreter-family"; (3) the signs constituting the language must be "comsigns," i.e., they must be producible by the members of the "interpreter-family," and they must have the same signification to the producer as they have to the interpreters; (4) the signs which constitute the language must be "pluri-situational" in that they must have a

---

[56] William James. *Psychology*. New York. Holt. 1890. Chapter 9. "The Stream of Thought."

[57] Adapted from Vinacke. *Psychology of Thinking*. pp. 63–64.

[58] Melville J. Herskovitz. *Man and His Works*. New York. Knopf. 1948.

relative consistency of meaning, or signification, in every situation in which a sign of the sign-family in question appears; and (5) the signs of the language must constitute a system of interconnected signs combinable in some ways, but not in others, in order to form a variety of complex "sign-processes." Thus Morris arrives at his definition of language as "a set of plurisituational signs with interpersonal significata common to members of an interpreter-family, the signs being producable by members of the interpreter-family, and combinable in some ways but not in others to form compound signs." Or, more simply, "a language is a set of plurisituational comsigns, restricted in the ways in which they may be combined."[59]

But language is much more than a set of intelligible signals verbally expressed; its *leitmotif* may be symbolism, but it is no mere agglomeration of symbolic units. Rather, it is an organic functioning system, an integrated whole, in which structure (if not logic) is always present.[60] Sapir and Whorf[61] have postulated that language is not only a vehicle, but also a molder of thought and that, far from being a simple technique of communication, language is itself a way or directing the perception of its speakers. It provides habitual modes for analyzing experience into significant categories.

Noam Chomsky holds that if man is to bring order out of the world about him his mind needs certain principles of inference which cannot be logically deduced from facts derived from experience alone but which must in some way "precede" experience. This axiom, Chomsky seeks to exemplify through his studies of the forms of language and the ways in which children and adults are able to grasp and articulate sentences that they have not heard before. Thus he argues that there are innate properties of the mind that make possible the acquisition of knowledge and belief, while determining its limits and scope. There are, he believes, deep-seated and rather abstract principles of a quite general nature that determine the form and interpretation of sentences, and there are the rules of grammar that seem

---

[59] Morris. pp. 35–36.

[60] John B. Carroll. The *Study of Language*. Cambridge. Harvard University Press. 1955. Chapters 4 and 6; Andre Martinet. *A Functional View of Language*. Oxford. The Clarendon Press. 1962. pp. 134-60; Macdonald Crichley. "The Evolution of Man's Capacity for Language" *The Evolution of Man*, ed. Sol Tax. Chicago. University of Chicago Press. 1960. (*Evolution After Darwin*), vol. 2, pp. 289–308; Max Black. *Morals and Metaphors*. Ithaca, New York. Cornell University Press. 1962. pp. 1–16.

[61] Sapir. *Language*; Benjamin L. Whorf. *Language, Thought, and Reality*. New York. Wiley. 1956.

to make visible the properties of a basic component of the human mind, which cannot be directly observed, but can be investigated as an idealized model. No observation, he argues, of stimulus-response connections, habit structures, or learning through imitation, will explain the central capacity of the human intellect to deal with the world freely, innovatively, yet under constraint of certain formal, logical rules of procedure.[62]

Western thought, including scientific knowledge, largely derives from Aristotelian origins which, in turn, was rooted in the subject-predicate structure of the Greek language. In Chinese logic, however, the subject-predicate dichotomy is avoided so that the subject of a discourse does not have to be stated nor does the level of abstraction need to be defined. Indeed Western science could develop only after it had evolved a language (mathematics) that was not bound by the subject-predicate structure of Western languages.

Marshall McLuhan has set forth the theory that it is the medium that shapes the content of the message, and hence the medium *is* the message. Thus he has written of language: "Speech acts to separate man from man, and mankind from the cosmic unconscious. . . . The power of the voice to shape air and space into verbal patterns may well have been preceded by a less specialized expression of cries, grunts, gestures, and commands, of song and dance. The patterns of the senses that are extended by the various languages of men are as varied as styles of dress and art. Each mother tongue teaches its users a way of seeing and feeling the world, and of acting in the world, that is quite unique."[63] Linguists do not agree on the limits to which the Sapir-Whorf hypothesis, much less the McLuhan thesis, should be pushed, but even if, in their extreme form, they are invalid, language certainly is one of the channels through which the cultural environment exerts its formative influence upon the personality of the individual. This was exactly the inference drawn by D. D. Lee, who argues that people of different cultures not only act differently, but also have different bases for their actions; they act upon different premises because they perceive and codify reality differently. In this codification Lee holds language to be fundamentally involved.[64]

---

[62] Noam Chomsky. *Problems of Knowledge and Freedom*. New York. Pantheon Books. 1972. Also, "The Formal Nature of Language." *The Biological Foundations of Language*. by Eric H. Lenneberg. New York. Wiley. 1967. pp. 397–442.

[63] Marshall McLuhan. *Understanding Media; The Extensions of Man*. New York. McGraw-Hill. 1964. p. 80.

[64] D. D. Lee. "Being and Value in a Primitive Culture." *Journal of Philosophy*. vol. 46 (1949), pp. 401–14. Also: Theodosius Dobzhansky. *Mankind Evolving*. New Haven. Yale University Press. 1962. pp. 71–73.

Yet, despite Langer's praise of language it is, at best, a very imperfect means of communication. It must often rely upon other forms of representation of thought, such as nonverbal communication. It is, also, loaded with redundancy to make certain that the meaning of the message is not misunderstood. Professor Sze-Hou Chang of Northwestern University has asserted that the analysis of spoken English by the use of the oscillogram chart shows the language to be so filled with redundancy that the ordinary telephone system could carry up to six hundred times its present message-carrying capacity if all but the significant portions of man-made speech could be eliminated.[65] Through the work already done, using this so-called extractive method of speech analysis, it appears that there may be considerable promise for the improvement of speech communication by developing mechanical dictionaries based on key sound impulses, and through the fabrication of machines that will successfully transmute speech into writing.

## NONVERBAL LANGUAGE

Language, of course, is not limited to verbalized forms. As indicated above, Charles Morris defined language as a plurality of signs that can be produced by human beings, the significances of which are sufficiently standardized to be known to a number of individuals. These significances must remain constant within differing situations, and they must be set in patterns that are sanctioned by the community in which they are used. There will, of course, be some degree of individual variation in interpretation; no communication is perfect, but such variation will be due largely to the fact that human beings are rarely able to do more than suggest what they desire to express, thus it may often be left to the receptor to fill in detail. Thus Michael Polanyi speaks of "tacit knowing" or the "tacit dimension" by which he means that we "can know more than we can tell." Again he speaks of "a gap to be bridged by an intelligent effort on the part of the person to whom we want to tell what the word means. Our message had left something behind that we could not tell, and its reception must rely on it that the person addressed will discover that which we have not been able to communicate."[66]

Dr. Jurgen Ruesch, professor of psychiatry at the University of Cali-

---

[65] Sze-Hou Chang. "The Research Frontier." *Saturday Review*. (July 6, 1957), p. 46.
[66] Michael Polanyi. *The Tacit Dimension*. Garden City, N.Y. Doubleday. 1966. pp. 4 and 6.

fornia, and Weldon Kees, artist, poet, and film producer, have joined forces to lay the foundations for a theory of nonverbal communication. They hold that there are three such forms of codification:

1.  Sign language which includes all those forms of codification in which words, numbers, and punctuation signs have been supplanted by gestures. (kinesics)

2.  Action language which embraces all those bodily movements that are not used exclusively as signals, but which may, in particular situations, have considerable communicative power.

3.  Object language which includes all intentional and nonintentional displays of material things, i.e., implements, machines, art objects, architectural structures, signs, and all other symbolic representations on material substances.[67]

To these Edward T. Hall would doubtless add the element of time itself, for "time" talks. It speaks more plainly than words. The message it conveys comes through loud and clear. . . . The structure and meaning of time systems, as well as the time intervals" possess important communicating capabilities.[68]

Ruesch and Kees have set down certain other basic considerations with respect to the role of nonverbal communication: (1) the selection of a particular type of codification depends upon the versatility of an individual and his ability to vary statements in keeping with the character of a particular situation; (2) nonverbal languages become of prime importance in situations where words fail completely; (3) the characteristic functions of each of the types of nonverbal languages are not necessarily interchangeable; (4) objects may be specifically and intentionally shaped as symbols or they may come to have symbolic meaning quite apart from the original purpose for which they were fabricated; (5) object language may also be used when the communicator wishes to conceal unethical, immoral, slanderous, or profane statements, i.e., as a form of euphemism; (6) in contrast to object language, action language is transitory, though it represents the most universal kind of language; (7) action language is the principal way in which emotion is expressed; (8) action

---

[67] Jurgen Ruesch and Weldon Kees. *Nonverbal Communication.* Berkeley. University of California Press. 1966. p. 189.

[68] Edward T. Hall. *The Silent Language.* Garden City, N.Y. Doubleday. 1959. pp. 15–16.

Also his *The Hidden Dimension* (Garden City. N.Y. Doubleday. 1966) deals with the role of space in communication.

languages are closely related to sign language and kinesics; and (9) verbal languages are based upon principles that are entirely different from those upon which nonverbal communication is predicated.[69] Nonverbal languages are, perhaps, less subject to Polanyi's "tacit dimension" than are the verbal languages, because man can show more than he can tell and hence people tend to resort to analogic forms of expression. Admittedly, the librarian is not primarily concerned with these nonverbal means of communication, but certainly he should be aware of the extent to which they are important in the entire communication system, for only by an emphasis upon the total individual, with all of his personal and unique characteristics, including to a great extent the nonverbal, can the librarian serve the patron most fully. In Loren Eisley's words, "It is the human gesture by which we know a man, though he looks upon us under a brow reminiscent of the ape."[70]

## READING AND ITS SOCIAL EFFECTS

Writing probably ranks second only to language as man's greatest invention in communication, and like language, its origins are obscured in the mists of an antiquity that stretches back some twenty thousand years to the Upper Paleolithic Age. It is easy to see embryo-writing in the geometric patterns and crude representations of objects and animals that are to be found on the cave walls of northeastern Spain, southwestern France, the eastern Mediterranean, northern Europe, and North Africa. But whether such survivals are to be regarded as art, expressions of magic, or the earliest attempts at communication probably depends upon the point of view or interest of the archaeologist who studies them. Certainly they belong to a yet undivided, or undifferentiated, form of human activity from which, at a later time, more specialized forms have gradually separated themselves. They do not meet the criteria of communication in the modern sense in that they are static, that is they are disconnected and arbitrary images which cannot convey to us even the simplest ideas or the simplest sequence of narrative.

A somewhat closer approach to the modern concept of communica-

---

[69] Ruesch and Kees. pp. 189–93. See also: R. A. Gardner and B. T. Gardner. "Teaching Sign Language to a Chimpanzee." *Science*. vol. 165 (August 15, 1969), pp. 664–72.

[70] Quoted by René Dubos. *The Dreams of Reason*. New York. Columbia University Press. 1961. p. 99.

tion than that represented by these cave markings, may be seen in the use of knotted ropes and notched sticks; the latter especially may have been used by one individual in communicating with another, but that they were mainly ritualistic or mnemonic devices can also be assumed.[71] True writing begins, so far as modern scholarship has been able to discover, with the cuneiform script of the Sumerians, and dates from approximately the fourth millenium B.C. For fifteen hundred years they were the dominant cultural group of the Near East, produced a mature and highly developed literature, and left behind, recorded on clay tablets, a large and impressive body of complex law, documents relating to administration and trade, and religious writings.[72] From the days of the Pharaohs to the present, the history of graphic communication has been amply documented. The interest, in the present survey, is less with the evolution of writing and its deviant forms than with the impact of graphic communication upon the individual reader. The concern of the librarian is with the consumer of the record; the form of the record itself, though it may have implications for the administration and management of libraries, is incidental to the librarian's intellectual task. The important consideration here is the impact of the graphic message upon the individual and the variations in his reaction to it.

Fundamentally the motives which impel the individual to read are no different from those which prompt other forms of human action. Such motives might be cataloged interminably: to improve the capacity to earn, to achieve power, to increase security, to escape anxiety, to solve personal problems, to experience vicarious adventure, to indulge aesthetic enjoyment or emotional excitement, to gratify a desire for prestige, to identify one's self with a group, and many others. Motivation in reading, then, is based on the assumption, usually vaguely expressed, that there are certain values capable of realization through reading.

Literary figures, and other scholars before and after the time of Lord Verulam, have imputed certain values to reading because their fortunes and their reputations have been made by writing and by reading and criticizing the writings of others. It is not surprising then that those such as publishers and librarians for whom writing and the dissemination of the written word is a vested interest should declare that reading is an

---

[71] David Diringer. *Writing.* New York. Praeger. 1962. Chapters 1 and 2.

[72] Samuel Noah Kramer. *The Sumerians.* Chicago. University of Chicago Press. 1963. pp. 302–326; Edward Chiera. *They Wrote on Clay.* Chicago. University of Chicago Press. 1934; John A. Wilson. *Signs and Wonders upon Pharaoh.* Chicago. University of Chicago Press. 1964. Chapters 2–3.

unmitigated good, and that the reader is wiser, possesses superior taste, and is more perspicacious than the nonreader. This incessant reiteration of the virtues of reading has carried great conviction, a conviction that has been intensified by an educational system that is itself book-centered, and which is under the direction of faculties which are recruited from the ranks of the book-users.

But what must not be forgotten in all this admirable enthusiasm for the highest values of reading is that today the disproportion between writing that is excellent in its aesthetic and intellectual standards and the total output of contemporary graphic materials is rapidly decreasing. During the past half century the total spectrum of print has been greatly extended in scope, especially in those areas of operational materials. Reading today is much more directed toward utility than toward recreation. In this dichotomy, however, one may recognize the two main values of reading, as one may identify the two main uses of language itself— the symbolic use, to convey meaning, and the rhetorical use, to stimulate emotions.

Douglas Waples has attempted to classify the motives for, or alleged values in, reading (on the basis of such relevant evidence as is obtainable) in terms of three related and progressively general categories, visualized as three concentric circles. The innermost represents the reader's ability to understand and recall what he reads:

> Hence, the schools traditionally conceive reading values in terms of the students' abilities to remember and criticize. The more the reader remembers the more valuable the reading.[73]

The very simplicity of this notion has brought it widespread acceptance, and in its wake has come distortion of the layman's understanding of reading values. Yet, as Waples pointed out, this quality of absorption offers the only basis upon which the values of the same publication to different readers can be easily and objectively compared, and certainly the individual does read in order to assimilate and retain the content of graphic records.

The second circle represents the instrumental, or "transfer" values of reading as they may be inferred from the reader's behavior. Thus,

> . . . by reading some books in Russian the reader has learned to read *any* book in Russian, or by reading about a strange city the

---

[73] Douglas Waples, Bernard Berelson, and Franklyn R. Bradshaw. *What Reading Does to People.* Chicago. University of Chicago Press. 1940. p. 26 ff.

visitor can find his way about, or by reading about children a teacher can manage them more successfully.[74]

These transfer values are more comprehensive than the mere ability to recall what has been read, but the experiences of the individual form complex patterns, and these transfer values of reading are often difficult to isolate from other experiences, so their contribution to the total personality of the individual is difficult to measure. Certainly there can be little doubt that much reading is motivated by "the need to know" for very specific and practical purposes.

The third circle represents motivation that originates in a highly generalized belief in the normative values of reading as they appear in traits of character associated with certain types of reading or certain kinds of publications.

Such values were widely assumed even before Francis Bacon's famous essay. Examples would include the belief that readers of philosophy or law or biology will acquire the intellectual traits of the philosopher, the lawyer, and the biologist.[75]

An examination of the effects of reading may begin with the preconditions of publication, i.e., the characteristics of the society and of the persons and groups who produce publications. Obviously the effects of reading are dependent upon what there is to read, and what is available to be read is determined by: language; religion; tabus and fetishes; the division of labor; nationalism; regional differences; available leisure time; social pressures for "education"; trends in the educational level; the age distribution of the population; the impact of current events, both national and international; the active agents of publication, i.e., the personal and group conditions affecting the author, the publisher, and the sponsor; the social psychology of authorship;[76] the influence of the publisher, which appears to diminish as one progresses from newspaper to magazine to book; economic controls; merchandizing; the influence of the market, either real or assumed; the power of pressure groups; the influence of government, either directly as publisher, or through legislative control— all are preconditions of publication that determine the character of graphic records to which readers are exposed. The character of publication reflects the character of the people "behind" it; in a sense society "demands"

---

[74] *Ibid.*

[75] *Ibid.*

[76] See particularly: Harold D. Lasswell's "Research on the Distribution of Symbol Specialists." *Journalism Quarterly.* vol. 12 (1935), pp. 146–56.

certain kinds of publications from the universe of all conceivable print and "rejects" others. The effects of reading, then, must be understood in terms of the effects of what there is to be read.[77]

Because the reading of most people is largely determined by the materials that are most easily available to them, the effects of reading must also be understood in terms of the distribution of the printed word. Given the necessary incentive, a reader will persist until he obtains the publication he needs, e.g., the scholar in pursuit of research, the mechanic wishing to learn more about the operation of a machine, the administrator in need of certain economic data, but in the total volume of reading such incentives are relatively limited, and most reading represents a complacent acceptance of what the agencies of distribution supply.

The distribution system, therefore, exhibits both a negative and a positive effect. It is negative when it fails to supply the reader's desire; it is positive when it brings readers and congenial publications together. The reader, even under the most favorable conditions, is seldom a free agent; his exposure to reading is limited by the state of the market. The reader is, therefore, blocked in some directions and pushed in others by the system of publication and distribution. The total world of graphic records, then, is filtered through a series of screens before it reaches the reader, and each screen represents some particular agency of publication or distribution. Obviously those agencies which exist for the sole purpose of making money will exert quite a different influence upon the flow of print from those agencies which serve an educational purpose. The action

---

[77] The several types of studies respecting the preconditions of publication may be represented by the following:

Ernst Kohn-Bramstedt. *Aristocracy and the Middle Classes in Germany; Social Types in German Literature, 1830–1900.* London. P. S. King. 1937.

E. Wyndham Hulme. *Statistical Bibliography in Relation to the Growth of Modern Civilization.* London. Grafton. 1923.

Helen Martin. "Nationalism in Children's Literature." *Library Quarterly.* vol. 6 (1936), pp. 405–18.

David Daiches. *Literature and Society.* London. V. Gollancz. 1938.

Walter E. Bruford. *Germany in the Eighteenth Century; the Social Background of the Literary Revival.* Cambridge. Cambridge University Press. 1935.

Leo C. Rosten. *The Washington Correspondents.* New York. Harcourt Brace. 1937.

Frederick G. Melcher. "The Publisher as a Factor in Popular Reading." *The Practice of Book Selection,* ed. Louis R. Wilson. Chicago. University of Chicago Press. 1940. pp. 272–87.

James L. McCamy. *Government Publications for the Citizen.* New York. Columbia University Press. 1949.

of these screens is also determined by economic factors—the ability of individual societies, or cultures, to support certain agencies but not others.[78] They are also influenced by a variety of social factors: the density of the population, the occupational pattern of the society, the educational level of the people, the existence of pressure groups in the community, and the sanctions with which a culture favors certain types of reading at the expense of others. Even the most favored individual will doubtless find that his reading is affected by the fact that newspapers and magazines, being delivered to his door, are always at hand; whereas books, particularly the exceptional publications, are often secured only with the greatest difficulty.

If there can be said to be a central factor in the total effect of reading upon the individual, it lies in the content of the publications read, for the two main parts of the reading situation are the reader and what is read. Content may, of course, be classified in a variety of ways—by level of difficulty, by subject treated, by standards of literary merit, by its relevance to human needs or wants, by the type of reader toward whom it is directed, or by its observed effects upon the reader. But whatever the classification may be, the content of any graphic record may be regarded as mediating between the reader's predispositions and the effect that his reading produces. The content of any given graphic record, then, is the resultant of many forces, a complex of a variety of determinants: the structure of the language and the technical difficulties it presents, its literary merit, the symbolism employed, the subject matter communicated, the graphic methods used in the presentation. Preceding generations have interpreted content largely in terms of aesthetic values or judgments. Recent research in content analysis has swung to the other extreme of attempting to quantify certain observable properties in the text, particularly certain forms of symbolism, e.g., by counting the frequency of certain connotative words. Though the latter pretends to greater "objectivity" it is no less subjective than those forms of literary criticism against which it is supposed to be a "reaction." One does not achieve objectivity through the quantification of that which is itself subjective. Failure to recognize this has invalidated much of the work in so-called content analysis carried out during the past four decades.[79] The investigator is probably on more solid ground when he is investigating the simplicity of the idiom employed, but there is little relation here with the maturity of the ideas expressed

---

[78] Louis Round Wilson. *The Geography of Reading.* Chicago. University of Chicago Press. 1938.

[79] See, for example; Bernard R. Berelson. *Content Analysis in Communication Research.* Glencoe, Ill. The Free Press. 1952.

in the text. The syntactic structure of the Gettysburg Address is a model of simplicity and clarity, yet the ideas which it has immortalized can be fully comprehended by only the mature mind.

Descriptions of the subject content of the book customarily employ the generally understood divisions of knowledge. Traditional book classification strives to associate like publications and to separate those which are unlike in an arrangement of progressively narrower, or more specialized, categories. Following the principles set down by Bacon and Comte, book content has been, long before the days of Melvil Dewey, classified taxonomically on the assumption that readers used books in such a patterned context. But it may be that subject classification of book content becomes more useful when it is based upon a better understanding of the uses which readers make of graphic records, i.e., the differences in reader use rather than differences in publications *per se*. The latter may reveal, with reasonable validity, what the book is *about*, but this may be less important than what it is likely to do *to* or *for* the reader.

The term "predispositions" includes all the personal conditions involved in the reading experience, or more broadly, the experience of the individual with any form of communication. Such conditions derive from the many aspects of the individual's total personality, and they affect both his selection and his interpretation of the form of communication to which he is exposed. They are the resultant of age, intellectual capacity, education, economic status, group affiliations, psychological complexion, his roles in society; all the factors which shape his attitudes toward life contribute to the effect which the reading of a particular document, the viewing of a certain picture, the hearing of a musical composition will have upon him. The problem arises when one attempts to differentiate from among these many influences, to isolate one from another, to ascertain the role of each in shaping the effect of communication upon the individual.

Historically, the development of print and the growth of literacy and of the reading public have been well documented but have not been put together with other relevant evidence to construct a representation of the changing patterns of reading through time, or the impact that such reading has had upon history itself. The historian of ideas has paid scant heed to problems of communication via the printed word.

There is some research literature which suggests that reading can change attitudes,[80] and that, in general, the less the individual knows

---

[80] Gordon W. Allport. "Attitudes" in Carl A. Murchison, ed. *A Handbook of Social Psychology*. Worcester. Clark University Press. 1935. pp. 798–844.

about the subject the greater a change in attitude is likely to be.[81] The change in attitude will be influenced by the intensity of feeling that the reader brings to the written word, and by the ability of the individual to retain what he has been reading. Studies of the effectiveness of advertising have indicated that such textual properties as vividness, novelty, and other attention-getting techniques greatly prolong the reader's retention of what he reads.

The application of the case study method to investigations into the effects of reading indicates that the instrumental value of reading is one of major importance, both with respect to motivation and result. These instrumental effects appear in the behavior of the individual toward the many problems of health, vocation, social relationships, the family, politics, science, and the manipulation of the mechanisms—"apparatus"— which are a formidable part of his everyday living. These instrumental effects differ widely in the areas of application, in scope, in the complexity of secondary effects, and in duration. Instructions printed on a can of paint may be read, utilized, and immediately forgotten, whereas Luther Burbank was said to have read *Darwin* with his whole soul, and with a fullness of motivation that explains its lasting influence upon his life.[82]

Typical case studies also reveal that reading may result in intense emotional experience, sorrow, pleasure, and pain, deriving in part, at least, from identification of self with the experience recorded in the book. Reading may also engender escape from reality, self-esteem, a sense of oneness with history, diversion and relaxation, an increased sense of security, or its opposite, fear. Many have been converted to a particular religious faith or social philosophy through the influence of a single book or a prolonged exposure to many writings. Finally, the reader may undergo what has been called "an enriched aesthetic experience," though this phenomenon is characteristic of a relatively high degree of literary maturity. Aesthetic experience is more a totality of the other elements than a unique phenomenon. It may involve in greater or less degree any or all of the other effects of reading, though basically it is a form of emotional exultation.

Case studies, based as they are on actual experience, would appear to be the most reliable form of evidence for the effects that reading pro-

[81] Franklin H. Knower. "Experimental Studies of Changes in Attitudes." I. "The Effect of Oral Argument." *Journal of Social Psychology.* vol. 6 (1935), pp. 315–47. and II. "The Effect of Printed Argument." *Journal of Abnormal and Social Psychology.* vol. 30 (1936), pp. 522–32.

[82] Emory S. Bogardus. *Leaders and Leadership.* New York. Appleton-Century. 1934.

duces in the individual. But, in a substantial part of the published testimony on the influence of reading upon the individual, one wonders whether it is not a reporting of undifferentiated experience founded on the impressions and appraisals of complex phenomena made by individuals whose predispositions favor *ex parte* conclusions. One wonders whether there has not been a strong tendency to dramatize, a desire, perhaps quite unconscious, to favor the fortuitous, the unusual, or the picturesque. The temptation to enhance prestige by mild boasting about the effects of reading "great books" may be too strong for many to resist. The present writer could make a good "case" on paper, for the impact of *King Lear* on his adolescent mind, but he knows now that most of those impressions were quite wrong, and probably his behavior was more influenced by Christy Mathewson's *Pitching in a Pinch!* Thus, all testimony based on undifferentiated experience needs careful scrutiny, particularly by those who are disposed to generalize about the process of communication.

Though there is almost no scientific evidence to demonstrate the influence of reading upon human conduct, sentimentalizing over the values of reading, the laws of censorship, the burning of books by totalitarian governments, and the very existence of the public library itself are all predicated upon the assumption that reading does affect human behavior. With so much uncertainty concerning the factors which contribute to the effects of reading, it is not surprising that the effects themselves are only vaguely comprehended.

For some people the physical act of reading is a barrier to the communication of thought. But for most people reading is a labor-saving device in that it frees communication from the restrictions of space and time ("time-binding" the semanticists call it), makes discourse wait upon the convenience of the reader, and brings the distant and the past to the ever-present here and now.

Lewis Mumford associates the clock and the printing press as the two greatest technic innovations, and in this merger of time-keeping and record-keeping he sees man released from the domination of the immediate and the local.[83] However, he finds dangers, too, in the reaction of the individual to the printed word: Gutenberg's invention contributed to the dissociation of medieval society, but

> print made a greater impression than actual events, and by centering attention on the printed word, people lost their balance between the sensuous and the intellectual, between image and sound, between

---

[83] Lewis Mumford. *Technics and Civilization.* New York. Harcourt. 1934. pp. 134–36.

the concrete and the abstract. . . . To exist was to exist in print; the rest of the world tended to become more shadowy. Learning became book-learning and the authority of books was more widely diffused by printing, so that if knowledge had an ampler province so, too, did error. The divorce between print and firsthand experience became so extreme that one of the first great modern educators, John Amos Komensky, advocated the picture book for children as a means of restoring the balance and providing the necessary visual associations.[84]

John Dewey's philosophy of education represented a degree of reaction against the domination of print in the education of the child and a revolt against the classical tradition in the curriculum.

Dependence, or rather excessive dependence, upon the written word, can, by substituting symbols for reality, stifle thought and limit progress. Reading may make a full man, but Sir Francis Bacon did not say with what man is thereby filled, or whether such stuffing is in itself an unmixed blessing. The book has earned all the tributes that have been heaped upon it over the centuries, but there can be a surfeit of books, even of "good" books, just as there can be embarrassment from the accumulation of any form of riches.

Lacking any scientific knowledge one is thrown back upon the obvious platitudes: that individuals read from a variety of motives; that their ability to learn, to absorb vicarious experience from the printed page, exhibits a wide range of variation; that an excess of reading may be as harmful to the individual as its neglect; and that for many people reading, because of individual differences, may be a complete waste of time. One cannot assume that because a "teen-ager" is struggling over the obscurities of *Hamlet*, or attempting an *explication* of Othello's

> Put out the light, and then put out the light.
> If I quench thee, thou flaming minister,
> I can again thy former light restore.

that his soul is therefore with the immortals. Though graphic records are so fundamental to our culture that the law quite properly demands that every individual has the right to literacy, legislation cannot force down upon the brow of man a laurel crown. Not all men can be guided by symbols, or symbolic representation. For some there is no substitute for reality.

Despite the fact that our contemporary mores have elevated the act

---

[84] *Ibid.* p. 136.

of reading to a position of esteem, that the reader is generally regarded as being superior intellectually to the nonreader, that our educational system is book-centered, and that vast sums have been spent during the past century in the creation of an elaborate and extensive public library system that is used by a relatively small proportion of the total population, very little is known concerning the effects of reading upon the individual and, through the individual, upon society. During the 1930s, Douglas Waples and his graduate students at the University of Chicago began to lay a solid foundation for scientific inquiry into the effects of reading, which culminated in the publication of *What Reading Does to People*.[85] This work was to have been a prologue to more sophisticated research. But the intervention of the Second World War and the diversion of Waples's interests into the study of mass communication and propaganda analysis arrested further inquiry into this important subject. Thus the questions which Waples had so appropriately raised have largely been left unanswered.

Waples's probings into the social effects of reading were more than an expression of the normal inquisitiveness of the research investigator; they were a reaction against the excessive sentimentality by which the act of reading had long been colored. Yet, one must admit that there are dangers, too, in what he was attempting to discover. Once we know what reading does to people we may have taken the first step toward the domination of men's minds. The Soviets had not long been in power before they became aware that the liquidation of illiteracy was requisite to the control of the collective mind and the opening of a door to effective propaganda. There exists always a conflict between the ends of research and the potential ability to use the results for antisocial purposes. The conflict resolves itself into the age-old unanswered question of how much knowledge can the human being be entrusted to have.

Paramount to the problem of the knowledge process is the problem of *control*. Mastery over communication in any form is an open invitation to the manipulation of thought. Who will be the manipulators and who the manipulated? Such power in the hands of the unscrupulous could mean that the library will experience pressures the intensity of which it has never before known. With the increasing misuse of scientific discovery are we approaching Orwell's world of 1984, and will the terrors of C. S.

---

[85] Waples, Berelson, and Bradshaw. *What Reading Does.* Earlier studies were: Douglas Waples and Ralph W. Tyler. *What People Want to Read About.* Chicago. University of Chicago Press. 1931; and Douglas Waples. *People and Print.* Chicago. University of Chicago Press. 1937.

Lewis's science fiction trilogy become a reality? Would that little band of scientists, who in the late 1930s were exploring the atom, have continued their search had they been able to envisage the consequences at Hiroshima and Nagasaki and to foresee that even the peacetime uses of atomic energy are not an unmitigated good? The pressure to push into the unknown is relentless. But science has seldom been able to control the social consequences of its search for truth.[86]

Equally, the librarian cannot escape the consequences of what he is doing. He cannot be certain that information networks, or the replacement of the human being with computers for information retrieval, or even the abrogation of his responsibilities for the building of the book collection by resorting to "blanket ordering" of books, are not two-edged swords.

Society must reconcile the legitimate search for truth with the social consequences of research. Science has brought changes, most of which we should welcome rather than reject, and it has illuminated our understanding of values. But science must be seen in its proper social perspective. The value system by which society lives evolves empirically and determines the conditions under which social decisions are made. Fully as urgent as the proper use of scientific capabilities by society is the development of appropriate social values. To inculcate these values, derived from a future-oriented scholarship, is the great responsibility of education. As Lewis M. Branscomb has written, "Mankind must react rationally to the opportunities as well as the problems created by technology. On one side lies a harmonious world of interdependent societies, enjoying decentralized power and shared wealth, leisure, and learning. On the other is a despoiled planet of charred earth, dead lakes, and an acid atmosphere."[87]

## THE LIBRARY AND THE INDIVIDUAL

Though the library is an instrumentality created to maximize the utility of graphic records for the benefit of society it achieves that goal by working with the individual, and through the individual it reaches society. Therefore, the proper study of the librarian is man—man's neurophysiological communication system, the ways in which he learns, his language,

---

[86] See account by Robert C. Cowen of the conference, sponsored by the British Society for Social Responsibility in Science, London, 1970. *The Christian Science Monitor.* December 9, 1970. p. 8.

[87] Lewis M. Branscomb. "Taming Technology; A Plea for National Regulation in a Social Context." *Science.* vol. 171 (March 12, 1971), p. 977.

his reaction to the recorded word, and the influence of record upon his behavior. The librarian as mediator between man and his graphic record stands at the point where man and book come together in a fruitful intellectual experience. Thus, the education of the librarian must encompass much more than a technical proficiency. No one can properly deny that the librarian must "know books," but he must know much more than that; in the broadest and richest sense he must be an educated person. It is the man-book interface that holds the key to a philosophy of librarianship and defines the intellectual content of the librarian's education. What is a book that a man may know it, and a man that he may know a book? That is the overriding philosophical question to which library education and research must ever be addressed.[88]

---

[88] Shera. "Cerebral Foundations." pp. 3–6.

# Two

# Society and Culture

For untold centuries man has dreamed of Elysian fields, of a Happy Hunting Ground, of distant lands flowing with milk and honey. Such faith, which appears essential to the psychological life of mankind, is a natural human response to the fact that man is confronted by an environment that is basically hostile, with which he is more or less constantly at war for survival; an environment which compels his never-ending attention to the overwhelming business of everyday living.

The ceaseless struggle to maintain life necessitates (even within primitive societies) a division of labor. As the cultural pattern becomes more complex, specialization follows: specific responsibilities are assumed by, or assigned to, particular individuals because they possess special aptitude, skill, physical prowess, or knowledge which sets them apart in some way from their fellows. The advancement of even the most primitive civilization, in the face of a continually threatening environment, is possible only through the cooperative and cumulative contributions of such individuals.

## THE DEVELOPMENT OF THE ROLE

Almost four centuries ago, Shakespeare declared all the world to be a stage upon which "one man in his time plays many parts." Yet only recently have sociologists become aware of the importance of the "role" to social organization and structure. A role is a complex of many elements, a dynamic system of interrelationships which are subject to constant change.

**50**

A role may be fortified by legal sanction, in which case the appropriate pattern of behavior is explicitly formulated as a legal or ethical norm. Again, a role may be determined and stabilized by a group or other association of individuals. In other situations the pattern of each role is not explicitly rationalized, but is husbanded by a closed community which carefully transmits it from generation to generation through initiation, education, and discipline.

There may be different ways of performing in a role, determined by the environment, the mores of its contemporary culture, the dominant active tendencies of the performer, and the sociopsychological demands of the moment. The role of father, for instance, connotes a very special set of relationships—biological, psychological, legal, social—between a male parent and his offspring; hence the role of father may be "played" in a variety of ways.

Historically, man's increasing attempts at mastery of his environment, the maturing of cultures, the growing complexity of the patterns of social organization, and the accumulating store of collective knowledge by evolving social groups, have been reflected in an increasing specialization of functions into definable social roles. As the desires and needs of men became continually more diverse, and as the very specialization of functions itself created the opportunity for new kinds of activity, these roles became more sharply differentiated and more exacting in the demands placed upon those who performed them. The setting-apart of certain competent individuals could no longer be based upon sex, manual dexterity, physical strength, or keenness of perception alone; assumption of particular roles came to depend upon the mastery of certain acquired skills, the acquisition of specialized knowledge, or the possession of rare talents or wisdom. The stern injunction of the Puritan community of Colonial Massachusetts that "he who will not work shall not eat" gave way, eventually, to social acceptance of roles which are not directly related to the wresting of subsistence from the productivity cycle of the earth.

With the specialization of social functions came stratification into social classes, followed by social recognition that "status" attached to these roles. The status of any one role assumes certain qualifications on the part of every person in the role-group and reflects obligations which are enforced and standards which can be invoked, through common consent, to protect the group from interlopers. In return, this status affords certain rights and benefits which must, of course, take some form highly prized by the community—physical, social, legal, economic, ethical. But as a condition of such rewards, the role demands of him who fills it that he perform the associated social function in a prescribed manner, and that he meet certain moral, ethical, or performance standards delineated by the group, or its supporting society. Thus, some form of *noblesse oblige* is both derivative from and contributory to the status associated with the role.[1]

A hierarchy of statuses has derived from the fact that some roles require, for their proper fulfillment, certain abilities, capacities, skills, or knowledge possessed by a relatively small proportion of the population and consequently are highly valued by all. Such roles are regarded as having special social significance because they are concerned with a function particularly important to society and meet a vital social need. Roles which demand long periods of training for their performance, or the mastery of highly specialized techniques, tend to acquire greater prestige, higher social status, and more generous economic rewards than those which can be played with little rehearsal.

In general, an individual's social status is dependent upon the role he plays to earn his living or to support a family. But "one man in his time plays many parts," and each of the several separate roles which every individual assumes brings him into association with a different subgroup of society—his family, his business associates, the congregation of his church, the teachers of his children, his fraternity brothers. Role-groups are, as Kenneth Boulding suggests, not made up of "men but, as it were, parts of men, men acting in a certain role."[2] Within each of these subgroups, the role he plays in it, and the status associated with it, has particular meaning or significance. Though society itself recognizes a given role and relates it to a particular status, the subgroup may attach additional importance to it and hence elevate its status. For example, those individuals who specialize in the cultivation of knowledge and are denominated "scholars" are accorded a particularly favorable status in those segments of society in which knowledge, especially systematized knowledge, is held in high

---

[1] John W. Bennett and Melvin M. Tamin. *Social Life: Structure and Function.* New York. Knopf. 1948; J. O. Hertzler. *Social Institutions.* Lincoln, Neb. University of Nebraska Press. 1946. pp. 162–66; Florian Znaniecki. *The Social Role of the Man of Knowledge.* New York. Columbia University Press. 1940. pp. 13–22.

Bennett and Tamin argue that the social role is the "dynamic aspect" of the status; an individual is socially assigned to a particular status and occupies that status with respect to other statuses. But when he exercises the rights and duties which comprise that status, he is performing a role. Thus, a role is defined as those activities or modes of behavior which a society expects of an individual occupying a given status, and any status is functionally defined by the role attached to it.

The same view is held by Ralph Linton. *The Study of Man.* New York. Appleton-Century-Crofts. 1936. p. 114.

[2] Kenneth Boulding. *The Image.* Ann Arbor. University of Michigan Press. 1956. p. 27.

esteem. The status of the scholar in certain circles is evidence that these subgroups consider his abilities, wisdom, and skills, to be necessary, even essential, to society's achievement of certain desirable goals. In other segments of society, however, the role of the scholar has a very low valuation or status, and he is regarded, if not with contempt, at least as being an "egghead," whose head is stuffed with "book larnin'," who never did an honest day's work, and never met a payroll. "Ambition," then, as it is popularly, and often disparagingly, understood, is in essence a striving to improve one's role in the role-group, and the status of the role group itself.

A community, whether the term be used in the political, economic, or sociological sense, may well be regarded as a structure of interrelated roles and role-groups coalesced into cellular units of organization and tied together into a cultural pattern by lines of communication. It is man's capacity for abstract communication and his peculiar ability to enter, by means of his imagination, into the lives of others that makes it possible for him to create social organizations of a magnitude and complexity far surpassing those of the lower animals, even of the social insects. It was these same capacities that made possible, also, the emergence and development of cultures, and the evolution of cultural patterns from the most primitive to the most complex. Thus, social organization, culture, and man's ability to communicate are inseparable; they cannot exist in isolation, and one cannot properly be studied without reference to all.

## THE NATURE OF CULTURE

Even though one must recognize that the interdependence and interrelationships of social organization, the culture, and the ability of man to communicate, all as seen against the background of the physical environment, are complex, subtle, and imperfectly understood, they are, and especially the concept and relationships of culture itself, extremely important to an understanding of the library as a social invention. Therefore, it is important that the librarian have some awareness of the meaning of *culture* in its sociological sense, for it underlies all the social forces and demands that brought the library into being.

For at least a century the popular meaning of *culture*, and the one most generally held by librarians even today, has been colored by Matthew Arnold's interpretation of it as the study and pursuit of perfection by the individual.[3] Culture, for Arnold, meant the complete and harmonious

---

[3] Harry Levin. "The Semantics of Culture." *Daedalus.* vol. 94 (Winter 1965), pp. 1–13.

development of all the faculties that make for the beauty and the strength of human life—an inward condition of mind and spirit, not an external social phenomenon. From Arnold, it was an easy step to the use of culture as a synonym for refinement, gentility, and even sophistication and elegance in matters of etiquette. Such interpretations were sharply attacked by the sociologists, and particularly by William Graham Sumner who regarded the term as "illustrating the degeneracy of language," a term "stolen by the dilettantes and made to stand for their own favorite forms and amounts of attainment. Mr. Arnold, the great apostle, if not the discoverer, of culture, tried to analyze it and he found it to consist of sweetness and light." Sumner charges that "the stuff of culture is all left out of it [so that it] comes to represent only an external smoothness and roundness of outline without regard to intrinsic outline."[4]

A society, says Robert Redfield, "is people doing things with and to and for each other to the interests of each and all in ways that those people have come to accept," but a culture "is an organization or integration of conventional understandings . . . the acts and the objects, in so far as they represent the type characteristic of that society, which expresses and maintains these understandings. In the folk society this integrated whole, this system, provides for all the recurrent needs of the individual from birth to death and of the society through the seasons and the years." Again he has spoken of culture as a specialized term that "is unique, complex, self-consistent. A culture, like a personality, is a way of life. It is the way of life of a particular society." But in its generic sense it is "the inventions, arts, and ideas of all mankind, those characteristics which set off man from the animals."[5]

Kroeber and Kluckhohn, in their exhaustive and critical review of the concepts and definitions of culture, have identified no less than thirteen attributes implicit in the concept, of which "Group or Social Reference" is almost universally accepted by contemporary social scientists. Many also agree that it relates to social behavior, is a nongeneric historical product transmitted from generation to generation through tradition, or "heritage," and is a "totality" of the social environment; that it is "pat-

---

[4] William Graham Sumner. *Essays.* New Haven. Yale University Press. 1934. pp. 22–23. See also: René Dubos. "The Shaping of Culture." *Graduate Journal.* (University of Texas), vol. 7 (Winter 1965–66), pp. 45–68.

[5] Robert Redfield. *Human Nature and the Study of Society.* Chicago. University of Chicago Press. 1962. pp. 418 and 236; idem. *The Social Uses of Social Science.* Chicago. University of Chicago Press. 1963. p. 112.

terned," systemized, or organized; that it is adjustive and adaptive; and that it must be learned.[6]

But even Kroeber and Kluckhohn, after their extensive investigations, have not formulated a universally acceptable definition, rather they attempt to limit the term to the patterning of behavior, and not to behavior itself. Thus, they leave the reader free to make his own choice or to fabricate a definition of his own that most nearly meets his needs. Sir Edward Tylor, who adopted the term from the German *Kultur*, has given what is generally regarded as the classic definition: "That complex whole which includes knowledge, belief, art, morals, law, custom, and any other capabilities *acquired* by man as a member of society."[7]

To Wilson and Kolb, culture "consists of the patterns and products of learned behavior—etiquette, language, food habits, religious beliefs, the use of artifacts, systems of knowledge and so on."[8] Finally, the biologist Paul Sears has defined culture as "the way in which the people in any group do things, make and use tools, get along with one another and with other groups, the words they use and the way they use them to express thoughts, and the thoughts they think—all of these we call the group's culture."[9] The common denominator in all of these definitions, and many others which might have been quoted, is that culture is transmitted through tradition and assimilated from the group, or as Kluckhohn has briefly summarized it, "culture consists of all transmitted social learning."[10]

During the past ten years, however, a group of younger anthropologists have been attempting to broaden the classical concept of culture by viewing it as a complex of strategies by which a society attempts to

---

[6] A. L. Kroeber and Clyde Kluckhohn. *Culture, a Critical Review of Concepts and Definitions*. Cambridge, Mass. Peabody Museum, Harvard University. 1952. (*Papers*, vol. 47, no. 1). Also: Edmund R. Leach. "Culture and Social Cohesion; An Anthropological View." *Daedalus*. (Winter 1965), pp. 24–38.

[7] E. B. Tylor. *Primitive Culture*. 7th ed. New York. Brentano. 1924. (Italics mine.) Also: Read Bain. "A Definition of Culture." *Sociology and Social Research*. vol. 27 (1942), pp. 87–94.

[8] L. Wilson and W. L. Kolb. *Sociological Analysis*. New York. 1949. p. 57. (Italics mine.) *cf.* Ralph Linton. *The Tree of Culture*. New York. Knopf. 1957; and H. R. Hays. *From Ape to Angel*. New York. Knopf. 1958. Chapter XXXII.

[9] Paul B. Sears. *Who Are These Americans?* New York. Macmillan. 1940. pp. 78–79.

[10] Clyde Kluckhohn. "Report to the Sub-Committee on Definitions of Culture of the Committee on Conceptual Integration." 1942. p. 2 (mimeographed). Also see: Kluckhohn. *Mirror for Man*. New York. Whittlesey House. 1949. Chapter VIII; Kaj Birket-Smith. *The Paths of Culture*. Madison, Wisc. University Press. 1965. Chapter I.

maximize its adaptation to the physical environment. Thus, culture is seen as a complex of highly organized feedback systems in which seemingly nonproductive activities, such as religious ritual or food tabus, serve adaptive functions. Thus, the "sacred cow" of India actually plays an important economic role by providing motive power for agriculture, dung for fuel, and protein for non-Hindu consumption, or again, the ritualistic pig festivals of New Guinea, are not barbaric gluttony, but a device for the maintenance of an ecological balance among men, pigs, and food supply.[11]

## THE TRI-PARTITE STRUCTURE OF CULTURE

Culture may also be viewed as a tri-partite unity, or a complex structure most easily analyzed in terms of three major aspects. These were first identified by Alfred Weber in Germany, and later by MacIver in the United States, with subsequent agreement of many of the anthropologists. The nomenclature of this classification has been variously expressed, as is evident from the table in Kroeber and Kluckholn,[12] but, in substance, the major domains of culture are essentially (1) the relation of man to nature —subsistence concerns, techniques, and physical equipment; (2) the more or less fixed interrelations of men resulting in social contacts—social organization; and (3) the subjective or "spiritual" culture—ideas, attitudes, and values, and actions due to them, insights (*Einsicht, Geistige Kultur*), the totality of verified or generally accepted knowledge and beliefs, the *scholarship* of the culture.

Thus, culture is diagrammed as a triangle in Figure 2-1. It is to be noted that Cornelius Osgood, in his monograph on the Ingalik Indians of Northern Canada, has called these three modes of culture, material culture, social culture, and mental culture.[13]

These three elements, or aspects, of culture are so interdependent

[11] Alexander Alland, Jr. *Evolution and Human Behavior*. Garden City, N.Y. Natural History Press. 1967. Chapter 8. "Culture and Human Behavior."

See also the treatment of Milton Singer in "The Concept of Culture" (*International Encyclopedia of the Social Sciences*. New York. Macmillan. 1968. vol. 3, pp. 527–43) and Herbert A. Simon's *The Sciences of the Artificial* (Cambridge, Mass. M.I.T. Press. 1969), which treats the complexities in society, how they arise, how they can be adapted to, and understood by human beings.

[12] Kroeber and Kluckholn. *Culture, a Critical Review*. p. 98; Edward T. Hall. *The Hidden Dimension*. Garden City, N.Y. Doubleday. 1966. Chapter 1.

[13] Cornelius Osgood. *Ingalik Mental Culture*. New Haven. Yale University Press. 1959. (*Yale University Publications in Anthropology*, no. 56.)

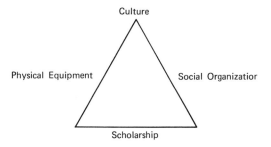

**Figure 2-1.**

that they tend to advance or retrogress in unison, and any disproportionate development of one at the expense or neglect of the others results in serious maladjustments throughout the entire culture. Thus, it is important for the welfare of a society that a reasonable balance among the three be maintained. But it is also important for the librarian to note that, close as this triadic relationship is, the three aspects differ markedly in the extent to which each is dependent upon communication, particularly graphic records. Even in primitive societies the scholarship soon transcends the capacities of oral communication and human memory so that some more permanent form of record becomes essential if the scholarship is to be preserved. The very essence of scholarship is that it deals with abstract concepts and with generalizations which cannot be directly observed and mastered as is possible with the techniques of a simple mechanical device or the social relations and procedures of a small homogeneous community. It is true, of course, that books dealing with the physical equipment and the social processes of cultures have existed from very early times, but they developed as technology and social organization increased in complexity. The intermingling of religious ritual with agriculture, the healing arts, and all public projects resulted in a literature that combined all three aspects of culture.

## PHYSICAL EQUIPMENT

The physical equipment of a culture is, perhaps, its most conspicuous element; certainly it is the most tangible and hence the most easily identified and understood. The archaeologist, digging among the physical remains of ancient civilizations, was the first to gain insight into the nature of prehistoric societies. The artifact has a physical permanence that enables it to survive long after all else has perished. Similarly, the child's first real feeling for the actuality of pioneer life on the American frontier comes from an examination of arrowheads, stone axes, and other physical remains left by the Indians as they retreated across the Western plains. The physical equipment, then, because it has form and can be readily perceived by the senses, is frequently accorded an exaggerated importance in the assessment of a culture's maturity. This tendency to attribute excessive weight to the artifact as an indicator of civilization is particularly strong in a society such as our own in which the physical equipment, the technology, has been developed to an extremely high degree of complexity.

The sophistication of the physical equipment of any culture is dependent upon two basic factors, the human and the environmental. A society cannot develop an elaborate physical equipment if its members lack the physical and mental aptitude for such development. This is in part a matter of intellectual capacity and in part the consequence of physical adaptation or dexterity. Such aptitudes and capabilities are popularly understood as ingenuity. But the importance of the environment must not be neglected, for the physical equipment can be developed no further than the natural resources which support the society will permit. The culture of the Iron Age could not have developed had there been no iron, and there are those who argue that our contemporary culture would be impossible without the materials from which paper is made. Thus there exist ecological determinants of cultural potentialities, natural resources which place limits beyond which the culture cannot develop unless its scholarship is capable of finding substitutes to circumvent these limitations. Ultimately some hypothetical point is reached beyond which no society can go.

Elting Morison holds that the rapid technological development of the past one hundred years took place in a "cultural surround" that had been evolved over previous centuries to deal with only minor or low-powered technical systems. At a time when man seems capable of performing almost any engineering, or technological, feat that occurs to him, it would seem that if society is to manage the powerful system it has created, it must reestablish a balance among the three elements of culture "that will give clear definition to what, in the new scheme of things, our interests really are."[14] Thus Morison sees the contemporary conflict between C. P. Snow's "two cultures"[15] as being not so much a cleavage in

---

[14] Elting Morison. *Men, Machines, and Modern Times.* Cambridge, Mass. M.I.T. Press. 1966. p. 214.

[15] C. P. Snow. *The Two Cultures and the Scientific Revolution.* New York. Cambridge University Press. 1959.

human understanding, as a division between those who are eager to change conditions by expanding man's technology and increasing the physical plant of society, and those who are seeking "to protect a set of definitions —a culture—that had been designed to permit man with limited knowledge and inadequate physical plant, to deal with conditions that often seemed unchanging."[16] It is as if man were trying to answer Huxley's classic question, "What are you going to do with all these new things?" without taking into account man's place in the new environment created by "all these new things."

## SOCIAL ORGANIZATION

Not until the rise of the modern science of anthropology, was the role of social organization in the determination of culture adequately recognized. Prior to the advent of the anthropologist, the archaeologist was the authority on culture, or "civilization," as was indicated above, and he characterized its sophistication in terms of its physical equipment; thus the early stages of man's history became known as the "Stone Age," the "Iron Age," the "Bronze Age," and the like.[17] With the rejection by anthropologists of an earlier antiquarian curiosity that was fascinated by the aberrant manifestations of human social behavior among the "barbarians," the new science began to direct its attention toward a better understanding of cultural patterns with the objective of interpreting the contemporary world. Anthropologists thus began to consider such problems as the relation between the total culture and its constituent elements; the extent to which unconscious patterns of thought, emotion, and action are conditioned by or revealed in the language of the culture; the relativity of cultural values and the importance of those elements which are common to all cultures.

Human societies require a certain minimum of reciprocal behavior, a standard system of communication, and a set of shared values, for these elements underlie all cultures and are evident in all cross-cultural comparisons. The human being can tolerate only a small degree of uncertainty; there is a basic need for order in human life—some semblance of predictability as to what can be expected from one's fellows if one's behavior follows a certain path. Cultures are integrated wholes in which the constituent elements are interdependent and interrelated, and these interrelationships

---

[16] Morison. p. 215. Also: Emmanuel G. Mesthene. *Technological Change; Its Impact on Man and Society*. Cambridge, Mass. Harvard University Press. 1970.

[17] Gordon Childe. *What Happened in History*. New York. Penguin. 1946.

must be understood as the implementation, or actualization, of the theme that is central to the whole culture.[18] The study of culture, then, becomes in part the study of regularities, for cultures have organization as well as content.

Basic to the regulatory function of culture is social organization, the second of the three elements of culture. Such organization begins with isolated, autonomous groups, such as tribes, states, nations, which may in themselves represent either the totality or only one segment of the social pattern. Within the basic unit of the social structure there exist subordinate groups which may be few in number and simple in relationship or many in number with a multitude of intricate and interwoven relationships with overlappings and interstices at many points. A culture, then, must be regarded as a web, or network, in which the pattern is not only determined by the strands of social organization, but also each strand gains its significance, in part, from being at a particular point at a particular time, or being, or failing to be, in conjunction with other strands. This intricate pattern is further complicated by the fact that social organization does not always parallel, or is not always coterminus with, the culture. The accidents of migration, colonization, common cultural heritage, or other provisions for the transfer of cultures, may result in the dispersion of a single culture over more than one nation, or other political or economic unit. Thus, Canada and the United States, or the United States and the United Kingdom, exhibit the same basic cultural pattern.

Subgroupings within the culture may be derived from or based upon, a variety of determinants: as clans or classes within a culture they may derive from the accident of birth, or blood relationship, the possession of material wealth and the transmission of that wealth by the regulations imposed by the culture, the ability to perform certain functions or roles (either intellectual or physical) which are of particular value to the group. When a subgroup represents capabilities essential to the culture it is endowed with prestige by the mores of the culture and so enjoys a prestigious role.

Castes and clans, as customarily understood, are usually defined in terms of blood relationship or the accident of birth. The individual is born into such groupings and remains in them throughout his life. In the caste system the element of human volition is reduced to the minimum. There are also territorially defined groups—states, cities, villages—which may represent a cultural unit, or these may cut across cultural lines. Large metropoli-

---

[18] See: Clyde Kluckholn. "New Uses for 'Barbarians.'" *Frontiers of Knowledge in the Study of Man*, ed. Lynn White, Jr. New York. Harper. 1956. pp. 33–47.

tan centers may be, and in the United States usually are, constellations of a variety of smaller cultural units, "little Italy," "Chinatown," etc., which struggle to preserve their cultural heritage against powerful forces pressing for amalgamation. Similarly, occupational groupings within a culture may be either geographically compact, a local association of the bar or an employees' association in a single company, or they may be dispersed geographically, as a national professional association or a national labor union. This spatial distribution may, or may not, be an important factor as a determinant in cultural configuration.

Further, society evinces many examples of agglomerations of individuals representing many cultures, or at least exhibiting a wide variety of cultural orientations or residues, united for the pursuit of a common purpose or objective. Thus the modern industrial corporation unites, for the purpose of production and distribution of its product, many occupational and professional groups, some of which may even be socially antagonistic. The sublimation of such antagonisms, the attainment of like-mindedness (cf. the German *Gemeinschaft* as distinct from the *Gesellschaft*) may itself be an important group-welding principle.

Though there are dangers in an excessively hasty assumption that there exists real social unity—because the precise definition of a social or cultural unit, even for purposes of a particular study, presents some serious theoretical difficulties—there is now widespread agreement among social and cultural anthropologists that social phenomena must be seen, not as a collection of discrete elements, but rather as integrated parts of a total social pattern or field.[19] Thus Radcliffe-Brown, following Durkheim, developed the thesis of functional interconnectedness, by which he means that the role of any social activity is the part it plays in the culture of the community as a whole, thus contributing to the maintenance of the social organization of the total culture. Russell Lynes pictures the social structure of contemporary American culture as a series of freestanding occupational pyramids with relatively little communication among those at the several apexes.[20] In the cultural pattern he postulates, money is less important than position and accomplishment. Income can no longer establish a man's social position; it can make him only rich or poor.

Lynes's analysis does point up the fact that, even among societies and

---

[19] Margaret Mead. *Continuities in Cultural Evolution.* New Haven. Yale University Press. 1964.

[20] Russell Lynes. *A Surfeit of Money.* New York. Harper. 1956; Birket-Smith. Chapter 6; Claude Lévi-Strauss. *Structural Anthropology.* New York. Basic. 1963. Part 2. "Social Organization"; Ruth Benedict. *Patterns of Culture.* Boston. Houghton Mifflin. 1941. Chapters 7–8.

cultures which are regarded as relatively stable, cultural patterns become modified, sometimes rather drastically during a period of rapid social change. Particular social groups may make no contribution, or even a negative one, to the structural continuity of the culture. Thus the concept of "role" or function of a social group within the culture implies as its correlative the idea of dysfunction or negative "role." But, regardless of the role of any particular group within the social organization of the culture, the important fact, here, is that social phenomena present patterned regularities, that they may form structures which can be compared from one society, or culture, to another, and that these societies, or cultures, may properly be regarded as totalities of which the parts are interrelated.

## THE INSTITUTION IN SOCIAL ORGANIZATION

Cooley defined the organization of a culture as a "vast tissue of reciprocal activity, differentiated into innumerable interwoven systems."[21] In social organization, the tasks involved in patterning social behavior are brought to a focus and epitomized, and the social organization of any culture is determined by its underlying social institutions. Thus the social institution, with its agencies and associations, is the very foundation of social organization and its most vitally influential element.

The word "institution" is a verbal symbol devised by the social scientist to designate that cluster of social phenomena, conventions, or formalized structures whereby a society fixes the limits of, exercises control over, or imposes form upon, the activities of human beings. Institutions are the instruments by which a society imposes its will upon its members and shapes their behavior in accordance with the goals which it seeks to achieve; they grant sanctions, impose *tabus*, and in general lord it over some human concern. An institution may be rigid or flexible, exacting or lenient, and it may discharge its functions through associations or other groups to such an extent that it is frequently difficult to distinguish the institution from the association. But always it is the institution that establishes the standards of conformity from which the individual may depart only at his peril.

Sumner holds that institutions are produced out of mores, and that each institution is comprised of a concept (idea, notion, doctrine, or interest) and a structure.[22] The structure consists of personnel, equipment,

---

[21] Charles H. Cooley. *Social Process*. New York. Scribner. 1922. pp. 19 and 29.
[22] William Graham Sumner. *Folkways*. Boston. Ginn. 1940. pp. 53–54. *Library Quarterly*. vol. 7, no. 4 (October 1937), pp. 546–63.

organization, and ritual. By personnel he means the qualified members of the group, those whom the group certifies as "belonging" in distinction to the "outsiders." The equipment is that apparatus through which the members function—all the possessions of the group, both material and non-material or intellectual. The organization is the manner in which the personnel and equipment are arranged to form a working system of interrelated responsibilities and functions. Finally, the ritual consists of its customs, the rules and ceremonies by which the institutional behavior of the individual members is regulated and through which those who do not belong are kept at a respectable distance. A physician who does not practice his profession in the proper manner not only loses his patients, but also is subject to penalties imposed by the medical authorities of his state and the medical associations to which he belongs.

The structure of the institution embodies the concept and furnishes the instrumentalities or agencies for bringing it into the world of social action in such a way as to serve the interests of the culture. According to Sumner

institutions are either crescive or enacted. They are crescive when they take shape in the mores, growing by the instinctive efforts by which the mores are produced. Then the efforts, through long use, become definite and specific. Property, marriage, and religion are the most primary institutions. They began in folkways. They became customs. They developed into mores by the addition of some philosophy of welfare, however crude. They were made more definite and specific as regards the rules, the prescribed acts, and the apparatus to be employed. This produced a structure and the institution was complete. Enacted institutions are products of rational invention and intention. They belong to high civilizations. . . . Pure enacted institutions which are strong and prosperous are hard to find. It is too difficult to invent and create an institution, for a purpose, out of nothing. . . . All institutions have come out of mores, although the rational element in them is sometimes so large that their origin in the mores is not to be ascertained except by an historical investigation. (legislatures, courts, juries, joint stock companies, the stock exchange). Property, marriage, and religion are still almost entirely in the mores.[23]

---

Another use of the term *social institution*, which shall not be used here, is to designate an entity or a practice which has been devised by society to perform a specific service, such as the library, the school, or the church; e.g., Lowell Martin's use of the term in "The American Public Library as a Social Institution."

[23] Sumner. *Folkways.* p. 54.

The social agencies including the professions and the associations, are derivatives of the social institution. In primitive cultures, and when a group or society is small, a single social institution may assume responsibility for an agglomeration of functions, as have the family and the church in times past. But the growth and increasing complexity of a culture brings a corresponding growth and complexity in social functions, which affect the responsibilities of existing social institutions and may lead to the evolution of new institutions. These new institutions, in their turn, under the impact of continued cultural maturation, must create mechanisms whereby their responsibilities may be discharged and the objectives of society may be achieved; thus they give rise to social agencies as instruments through which to operate and, incidentally, as means by which to exercise their social control. The distinction between institution and agency, though sometimes unclear, is more than a matter of degree, since it involves structure and the exercise of power and authority. Both institutions and agencies exert their measures of social control, but that of the institution is primary and basic, acting upon the individual in his chosen role, while that of the agency is secondary and derived.[24]

Once established, agencies (as well as institutions and individuals) have roles of their own to play, and the pattern of these roles creates the profile of a social organization. Thus, at any given time, an advanced society may be seen as a system in pyramidal form of interrelated and interlocking social agencies, the respective roles of which interact at many

---

Constantine Panunzio subscribes to the theory that the origin of social institutions is to be found in "experience deposits." He sees institutions as "mainly the products, the fructifications, or the embodiments of human experience in associated living. In their essentials they consist of the accumulation of the group-experience of the race." *Major Social Institutions; An Introduction*. New York. Macmillan. 1939. p. 145.

[24] MacIver makes a different distinction between institutions and associations. For him, the former are "the established forms or conditions of procedure characteristic of group activity," while the latter are "groups organized for the pursuit of an interest or group of interests in common." The term *institution* stresses the impersonal factor in social relationships; it is a system of controls which extend beyond personal relations. It is the bond between the past and the present, and between the present and the future. It links men, not to their families and their neighbors, but to their ancestors and to their gods. One may belong to an association, but not to an institution. MacIver considers the church to be an association and communion an institution; the trade union an association, the union label an institution; the family an association, primogeniture an institution. He points out that the terms have been confused because the same word may mean institution in one instance and association in another. See: R. M. MacIver. *Society*. New York. Farrar and Rinehart. 1937. pp. 4–19 and 193–323.

points and in many complex ways. In them exists the social organization of the given culture, and the basic orientation of the roles they enact is derived from the strategic position which they occupy with respect to the hierarchical pattern of that culture.

All manifestations of social organization are the products of social stress and strain. In a stable or slowly changing society there is little conflict with the cultural environment, but in periods of disorder, when change is rapid, any social agency may be compromised by an inflexible structure. No such cluster of usages that is unresponsive to alteration can ever quite escape its slavery to the past. The tendency toward tradition and inertia are inherent in the nature of formal organization. Yet persistence of an agency, after the need for it has disappeared, makes it an impediment to social adaptability; when the spirit becomes the letter, and allegiance is to vested interests, vested habits, and vested ideas, then formalism and ritualism remain only as fetishes to be served, and what may have been a way of intellectual integrity and social significance becomes mere guardianship of an anachronistic faith. Evidence of this phenomenon can already be seen in the thrust, or intrusion, of information science into librarianship.

Adaptation and adjustment, adventitiously or by design, may create for an existing agency an entirely new role or roles quite different from those with which it was originally charged. The roles it abandons may be filled by an entirely new agency; for that matter, a new agency may arise to preempt these roles on the grounds that it can perform them in a new, and presumably better, way. Or the first agency may fragment its responsibilities, giving rise to new kinds of agencies and associations each to perform a part of a coordinated whole which remains (at least nominally) under the control of the parental body. Upon occasion an agency may be introduced from an alien society. Freed from its own cultural matrix, it will be shaped by the usages and folkways of its new societal setting; and it may prompt the emergence of a new and quite indigenous agency. The action of these various processes—ossification, adaptation, replacement, absorption—can have very serious consequences, either for good or ill, for a culture, because of the dependence of social organization and social functioning upon the interaction of agencies. For example, an educational system which does not keep pace with the changing conditions of its society will produce citizens who will be a drag upon the intellectual advancement of that society.

Indeed, the public library is very far from being immune to the fate of social obsolescence, as Philip Ennis has warned. "The general level of affluence in American life," he has written, "the relative leveling in income differentials, coupled with the widespread accessibility of books from other channels all have robbed the public library movement of some of its most important imperatives."[25] As a consequence the public library "has become socially invisible. Trying to do everything means not only a dissipation of energies, but a loss of well-served and loyal clientele who will promote and defend the library."[26] He argues that, if public libraries are to survive, they must reexamine their objectives and establish for themselves new priorities in service which will be appropriate to the communities in which they exist. In one community the priority might be service to business and industry, in another service to those portions of the population which are deprived of educational and cultural resources; in a third the library might ally itself with other cultural agencies such as art museums, musical organizations, and other associations for high cultural attainment.

But what is the public library today? As Kathleen Molz has pointed out, "Society, with its shorter view that the public should get what it pays for, has so chipped away at the concept of a public library that, in all too many communities, it has become little more than an informational hodge-podge, furnishing its staff and resources as a solver of riddles for the community's contestants, a reference arm for the burden of community homework, and a supplier of cheap best sellers for the titillation of the middle class."[27] The future of the public library as a viable social instrument is very far from a certainty; it has a perilous knife-edge to travel, and it could fail.

## THE PROFESSIONS AS AN ASPECT OF SOCIAL ORGANIZATION

Present-day professions are one expression of the social process, one example of that adaptation and growth whereby men, and groups of men, adjust to the totality of their environment. They operate within the framework of social organization comprised of the interrelationships between institutions, and agencies. Certainly professions are associative in their structure and they serve as one bond through which the institution maintains its control. Myron Lieberman goes so far as to distinguish *institutional* professions from those which he calls *scientific*: "Some profes-

---

25 Philip H. Ennis. "The Library Consumer; Patterns and Trends." *Library Quarterly.* vol. 34, no. 2 (April 1964), p. 176.

26 *Ibid.* p. 178.

27 Kathleen Molz. "The Public Custody of the High Pornography." *American Scholar.* vol. 36, no. 1 (Winter 1966–67), p. 103.

sions, notably the ministry and law, are based primarily upon the practitioner's understanding of certain religious or social institutions. . . . In contrast to the basically nonscientific professions such as law and the ministry, there is a large and growing number of professions which are primarily dependent upon the empirical sciences for their subject matter [such as] medicine and engineering. No profession is completely scientific or completely institutional, but most professions are chiefly one or the other."[28]

In all of their manifestations, the professions, like other socially-created entities, are living things having a tangled identity. They cannot be displayed in perspective or revealed in detail by any strictly logical method of inclusion and exclusion. They show the vestiges of purposive design and fortuitous circumstance; they are the stuff of idea and custom inherited from many ages, societies, cultures, civilizations, and climates of opinion; they are the product of notions, procedures, sanctions, and values drawn from cultural foci often far distant in space as well as time. Like the other components of a patterned social organization, the profession emerges as an imperfect instrument of order and purpose in a constantly changing culture. In common with other agencies and the parent institution, it imposes its special form of regulation upon the activities of men, thus shaping the course of future events; it is an aspect of all that has gone before, a potential part of that which is to come; it is both directive and responsive, destroyer and preserver, a spur to and a check upon change, a creature of means and a master of ends; it can be only partially understood through its life history, even the genetic method cannot teach all that should be known of what such social phenomena are, how they come to be, and what they may become. Between the profession and its institution (and even the social order) is a complement and antithesis; each is forever remaking the other in the constant and unending ebb and flow of social evolution and change.

Use of the term *profession* to designate, and especially to dignify, almost any form of human occupation is not nearly so recent in origin as one might suppose. For four centuries the word has been loosely employed to cover a multitude of activities and, yes, even a multitude of sins. Thus, the *Oxford English Dictionary* lists among its usages of *profession*:

1541.   The parties of the art of Medycyne . . . can not be separated one

---

28 Myron Lieberman. *Education as a Profession.* Englewood Cliffs, N.J. Prentice-Hall. 1956. p. 2. Also: Everett C. Hughes. "Professions," and Bernard Barber. "Some Problems in the Sociology of the Professions." *Daedalus.* vol. 92 (Fall 1963), pp. 655–58, and 669–88 respectively.

from the other without the dommage and great detryment of all the medicynall professyon. R. Copland, **Galyen's Terap.** [A nice statement, incidentally, of professional unity.]

1577.   Princes...delighted with ye profession of husbandry. B. Googe, **Heresbach's Husb.**

1600.   Their profession is to robbe and steale from their neighbours, and to make them slaues. J. Pory, tr., **Leo's Africa.**

1601.   (Being Mechanicall) you ought not walke upon a labouring day, without the signe of your Profession. Speake, what Trade art Thou? Shakespeare, **Julius Caesar.**

1898.   He is doing a very nice trade in the muffin "profession." **Westm. Gaz.**[29]

Contemporary understanding and usage of the term seem to date from 1915, when Abraham Flexner considered the characteristics of a profession in order to discover whether or not social work could at that time qualify as professional. Though he modestly commented that his criteria would "need recasting from time to time," they have become generally accepted as valid, and hopeful professions have been measured against them instead of the reverse.

Let me now review briefly the six criteria which we have mentioned: professions involve essentially intellectual operations with large individual responsibility; they derive their raw material from science and learning; this material they work up to a practical and definite end; they possess an educationally communicable technique; they tend to self-organization; they are becoming increasingly altruistic in motivation. It will be interesting to submit various forms of activity to the test in order to determine whether these criteria work.

After applying his test, Flexner concluded that medicine, law, engineering, literature, painting, music are "unmistakable professions."[30]

Carr-Saunders and Wilson, describing the state and nature of profes-

---

[29] *Oxford English Dictionary.* Pierce Butler saw in some current practices vestiges of the religious signification of the term: "Originally, the word 'profession' meant an acknowledgment or declaration and referred to the vow taken by the cleric or monk. Thus the word is a linguistic fossil from the age when religion was the only profession. The same idea still prevailed as medicine and law slowly freed themselves from ecclesiastical connections: the neophyte physician took the Hippocratic oath, and the beginning lawyer a similar one as a barrister." See: "Librarianship as a Profession." *The Library Quarterly.* vol. 21, no. 4 (October 1951), p. 237.

[30] Abraham Flexner. "Is Social Work a Profession?" *School and Society.* vol. 1, no. 26 (June 26, 1915), pp. 902, 904, and 906.

sionalism in England in 1933, identified professions in the following manner:

> . . . the term profession, as emphasized in the introduction, clearly stands for something. That something is a complex of characteristics. The acknowledged professions exhibit all or most of these features; they stand at the centre, and all around them on all sides are grouped vocations exhibiting some but not all of these features.[31]

Though these authors state that law and medicine stand "near the centre," they cite no occupation as being *at* the center and thus, presumably, exhibiting *all* of the characteristics of a profession.

Some twenty years later, Morris L. Cogan undertook to summarize and analyze definitions of the concept *profession*; and there is no need to retrace his steps here. He concludes with his own tentative definition:

> A profession is a vocation whose practice is founded upon an understanding of the theoretical structure of some department of learning or science, and upon the abilities accompanying such understanding. This understanding and these abilities are applied to the vital practical affairs of man. The practices of the profession are modified by knowledge of a generalized nature and by the accumulated wisdom and experience of mankind, which serve to correct the errors of specialism. The profession, serving the vital needs of man, considers its first ethical imperative to be altruistic service to the client.[32]

In a later paper, Cogan attributes some of the confusion surrounding the problem of definition to the fact that "a single term (profession) is used to designate disparate referents." He identifies three levels of definition—historical-lexicological, persuasive, and operational—citing his own, which was based on analysis of standard etymological works and other writings, as an example of the first type. The second, "designed to redirect people's attitudes," he illustrates with Flexner's definition, which he says has been "translated into the program and behavior of contemporary medical societies." The third he describes as "the guide-lines for the practitioner as he faces the day-to-day decisions of his work," resulting from "a demand for the observable and the measurable [which] will not be satisfied by lexicological and persuasive statements."[33] He finds further

---

[31] A. M. Carr-Saunders and P. A. Wilson. *The Professions.* Oxford. Clarendon Press. 1933. p. 284.

[32] Morris L. Cogan. "Toward a Definition of Profession." *Harvard Educational Review.* vol. 23, no. 1 (Winter 1953), pp. 48–49.

[33] Morris L. Cogan. "The Problem of Defining a Profession." *The Annals of the*

confusion in the fact that the term itself has been applied "indiscriminately to three different concepts. The word is employed to indicate: (1) An occupation differentiated from other occupations; (2) a formal vocational association; (3) a licensed vocation."[34] The relevant *Webster's Third* definition, which represents current usage, reflects this diversity of meaning:

4a.　A calling requiring specialized knowledge and often long and intensive preparation including instruction in skills and methods as well as in the scientific, historical, or scholarly principles underlying such skills and methods, maintaining by force of organization or concerted opinion high standards of achievement and conduct, and committing its members to continued study and to a kind of work which has for its prime purpose the rendering of a public service.

4b.　A principal calling, vocation, or employment.

4c.　The whole body of persons engaged in a calling.

One would hardly expect to find precision of analysis in the definitions propounded by the U.S. Government for the purpose of categorizing occupations in statistical studies, but the *Dictionary of Occupational Titles* (1949) does describe in detail, if not in explicit terms, the criteria for inclusion in its Professional Occupations category:

> This group includes occupations that predominantly require a high degree of mental activity by the worker and are concerned with theoretical or practical aspects of complex fields of human endeavor. Such occupations require for the proper performance of the work either extensive and comprehensive academic study, or experience of such scope and character as to provide an equivalent background, or a combination of such education and experience.
>
> Typical professional occupations are those of doctor, lawyer, architect, mechanical engineer, chemist, physicist, astronomer, editor, actor, and musician. Of these, mechanical engineer, architect, astronomer, and doctor are primarily concerned with the development or the practical application of formal and well-organized fields of theoretical knowledge; whereas such occupations as editor, actor, and librarian are concerned with activities that demand acquired abilities

*American Academy of Political and Social Science; Ethical Standards and Professional Conduct.* ed. Benson Y. Landis. vol. 297 (January 1955), p. 108.

34 Cogan. "Definition of Profession." p. 47.

which may properly be considered of a professional character, but may not require the background of a formal field of knowledge.[35]

This same publication identifies another group as Semiprofessional Occupations, which are described as follows:

> Included in this group are occupations concerned with the theoretical or practical aspects of fields of endeavor that require rather extensive education or practical experience, or a combination of such education and experience for the proper performance of the work; such fields of endeavor, however, are less demanding with respect to background or the need for initiative or judgment in dealing with complicated work situations than those fields which are considered as "professional." These fields of activity, many of them being concerned with the technical or mechanical details of the broader and possibly more theoretical fields of endeavor.

> Chiropodists, tree surgeons, draftsmen, aviators, laboratory technicians, and fingerprint experts are typical semiprofessional occupations.[36]

Perhaps an explanation for the recurrent phenomenon of definitions of this term is the persistent conviction, on the part of practitioner and public alike, that there is some unique advantage—to both—in an occupation's being designated as a profession. Because of the position of respect and deference accorded to the physician, the lawyer, the minister, in most communities; because of the generally favorable financial situation achieved by at least the best known or "most successful" of these individuals; because everybody knows that they had to pass through long and difficult (and expensive) courses of study in order to become qualified in their specialties; because the people with whom they deal, recognizing the necessity for superior specialized knowledge in the area of their particular "complaint," put themselves entirely in the hands of these individuals, trusting completely to their judgment, performing whatever actions they recommend, and paying whatever price they ask; for all of these reasons, it is easy to conclude that if the trappings of these vocations are set to adorn any occupation, the form within will become the reality which it appears to be. Thus eventuated the proliferation of "professional schools" and "professional associations."

---

[35] *Dictionary of Occupational Titles.* 2nd ed. (U.S. Employment Service, Division of Occupational Analysis) Washington. Government Printing Office. 1949. vol. 2, p. 1.
[36] *Ibid.* p. 13.

One is compelled to conclude that there is no sound basis upon which to build a definition of a profession, since the only manner of approaching the problem seems to be by identifying those occupations which society is willing to accept as professions and then accepting whatever characteristics they display as essential to any occupation purporting to be a profession. Nor is consensus any more useful, at least until it becomes so widespread that it can be described as "current usage," for as in all scholarly fields, authorities consult and repeat each other in arriving at their opinions. Nor do historical studies yield any useful insights, for the tendency is to seek in history the antecedents of those characteristics which comprise each author's own understanding of the term. It is possible to find the antecedents of the rite of transmission of specialized knowledge to a carefully selected group in the ritual, or witchcraft, of primitive societies, and some may see the establishment of standards of conduct for a privileged few foreshadowed in the highly structured codes of chivalry. Whitehead, convinced that concern with theory is the primary attribute of the professions, traces their "faint anticipations" to the academies of Plato, Aristotle, and the Stoics.[37] But Carr-Saunders and Wilson emphasize the desire for association and the possession of intellectual technique as the salient attributes of the professions, and thus find their beginnings in the guilds, the early universities, and the scientific societies of the seventeenth century.[38]

The weight of history would appear to confirm the present-day acceptance of law, medicine, and the ministry as so-called true professions. However, it does not follow that the characteristics they display necessarily represent the essence which makes them professions. As Ennis has remarked, law and medicine, "after all, are crisis professions—the layman's health and legal emergencies are the professional's routines";[39] and while one might not make so strong a statement about the work of the minister (excluding, for this discussion, his possible function as an intermediary between God and man), it is clear that the layman who makes a personal demand upon his clergyman is generally impelled by something which he would likely classify as a crisis. Might it not be true that these three vocations have been generally accepted as professions simply because of the fundamental human needs with which they deal?[40]

---

37 Alfred North Whitehead. *Adventures of Ideas.* New York. Macmillan. 1933. p. 79.
38 Carr-Saunders and Wilson. *Professions.* p. 286.
39 Philip H. Ennis. "Seven Questions about the Profession of Librarianship: Introduction." *Library Quarterly.* vol. 31, no. 4 (October 1961), p. 301.
40 Cf. Cogan. "Definition of Profession." p. 36. See also Myron Lieberman: "The

The observable features, which they have built up over the years to ensure the honorable and capable fulfilling of these needs, then, are seen to be mere mechanisms, safeguards, structures, channels; and what does it profit one to study these features as though they would yield the magic formula for professionalism?

Over the years, librarians have argued among themselves about many things—whether their occupation should be described as an art, a craft, a science; whether or not there is a body of theoretical knowledge underlying what they do; what kind of background and educational preparation best qualifies the recruit for proficiency in librarianship. They too have succumbed to the almost universal conviction that more prestige, more respect, more income would accrue if only they, collectively, could achieve for their activities the status of a profession. They too have adorned themselves with some of the outward forms which they see as distinguishing the profession from the vocation. They too have studied the characteristics of "accepted" professions and measured their own practice against them —some concluding that librarianship is a profession, some that it is not and never will be, still others reaching no conclusion.

As Pierce Butler said in 1951, "We all do believe that librarianship is a profession."[41] In this tacit assumption there is certainly an element of desire to validate librarianship's credentials in a bid for improved social status. But it is not the label which is to be affixed to librarianship, nor yet the respectability of the credentials which librarianship can offer society —rather the proper focus of concern is on the place of the library in contemporary culture and in the translation of that understanding into appropriate educational programs.

It is unfortunate that the English language affords no adequate substitute for the word *professional* as opposed to *nonprofessional*. Furthermore, the American academic structure has created a distinction between graduate schools and professional schools according to the fields

---

notion that the service performed be an essential one goes back to the origin of the professions. The professions arose because people believed that certain services were so important that they should be made available to everyone who needed them, regardless of whether the recipient of the services was able to pay for them or not." Lieberman. *Education as a Profession.* p. 2.

[41] Butler. "Librarianship as a Profession." p. 238. But as early as 1936 Ernest Reece refused to have any part in the debate over whether librarianship was, or was not, a profession. ". . . some persons may interest themselves in debating whether it has become a profession. Such a discussion is of dubious profit, since to recognize an occupation for what it is signifies more than to label it." Ernest J. Reece. *The Curriculum in Library Schools.* New York. Columbia University Press. 1936. p. 26.

for which the students therein are to be prepared. Therefore, in this study the word *professional* and its derivatives will continue to be used for the sake of differentiating some aspects of librarianship from others. There is no intention to establish the professionalism of any given task, or to argue that an aggregation of tasks or a type of education designated professional constitutes a profession. But as a matter of convenience in communication, the term will be used to designate the holder of a Master's or Doctor's degree in library science, or the tasks appropriate to the holder of such a degree, or the educational preparation encompassed by the curriculum leading to such a degree.[42]

But whatever one may decide about the credentials that librarianship has to offer as a profession, a body of theoretical knowledge would seem to be an important characteristic of a profession in the classical sense, and a consideration of the concept "profession" logically brings one, then, to the third element of culture—its scholarship.

## THE SCHOLARSHIP OF CULTURE

The scholarship, or intellectual content, of any culture may be understood as its totality of verified or accepted body of knowledge and belief, which includes not only science but also attitudes, value systems, mores, ethical and moral codes, superstitions, folklore, "revealed" knowledge, religious dogma, and the human understanding of the life of the spirit, or the "Good Life." It may be regarded as Bacon regarded it, from the standpoint of the three faculties of the human mind—Memory, Reason, and Imagination. It may be dichotomized, as by Hobbes into natural and civil philosophy; or by Kant, who distinguished the Pure, or Rational,

---

[42] For those who would pursue the argument further and for samples of disparate conclusions, see: Melvil Dewey, "The Profession." *The Library Journal.* vol. 1 (September 1876), pp. 5–6; Bernard Berelson, ed., *Education for Librarianship*; *Papers Presented at the Library Conference, University of Chicago, August 16–21, 1948.* Chicago. American Library Association. 1949; Lester Asheim, ed., *The Core of Education for Librarianship*; *A Report of a Workshop Held Under the Auspices of the Graduate Library School of the University of Chicago, August 10–15, 1953.* Chicago. American Library Association. 1954; Henry Miller Madden. "Is Librarianship a Profession?" *California Librarian.* vol. 25, no. 3 (July 1964), pp. 163–65; John S. Diekhoff. "The Professional School in the University." *Journal of Education for Librarianship.* vol. 6 (Fall 1965), pp. 103–10.

from the Applied or Empirical; or by Comte, who disparaged all speculative knowledge as Metaphysics, and insisted that true knowledge, or science, was confined to the study of nature or of human nature; or by Spencer, who held that all knowledge could be bifurcated into the Abstract and the Concrete. But to prepare a construct of the scholarship of contemporary culture would, of course, plunge one into the task of designing a classification of all human knowledge, an undertaking which has fascinated man from the Greeks to Whitehead, but which every generation must "solve" for itself. Suffice it here to identify two major areas of scholarship: (a) that which is composed of all verified, or generally accepted, knowledge, and (b) the body of folklore, beliefs, attitudes, and value systems.

Further, one may partition the first category into such subgroupings as: (1) abstract, or "pure" scholarship, or knowledge; (2) scientific, that knowledge which has been "verified" by having successfully passed the "tests" of "scientific" or "objective proof," and hence is presumed to be or is generally accepted as "true"; (3) practical or pragmatic scholarship, including knowledge of the environment; (4) technological and operational scholarship; and (5) revealed, or religious, knowledge. Obviously, cultures vary with respect to the emphases which they place upon these several categories of the scholarship, and varying prestige values are awarded, in any given culture, to the roles assigned to their development, promotion, or execution. For example, in contemporary American culture, greater prestige is accorded by academicians to the "pure" scientists than to the engineers, while the mathematician regards the geographer with contempt because his "science" is "only descriptive."

But cultures can be threatened by such cleavages within the scholarship, for its several segments, like the components of the social organization, are not only interrelated, but interdependent. The engineer can go little further than the foundations laid by "pure" research will permit, yet "pure" research, in turn, can be seriously hampered by the absence of "machines," of mechanisms developed by the technology of the engineer. Thus all scholarship is dependent upon what Morison calls "the cultural surround."

The scholarship of a culture must, therefore, be thought of as a unity of materials, methods, and products, controlled by certain economic laws or principles, and subject to standards which are compatible with the standards of the culture of which it is a part. Because the concept of scholarship is fundamental to the present study it will be dealt with in some detail.

## THE UNITY OF SCHOLARSHIP AND THE UNITY OF CULTURE

The *materials* of a scholarship are necessarily limited to experiential possibilities actually explored by any individual or group within the cultural field.[43] These possibilities are, of course, highly complex but all may be reduced to four constituent categories:

1.   Natural elements. The physical and biological constituents and forces of nature and the laws, principles, and rules which govern them. These are universals.

2.   Cultural elements. The existing cultural boundaries (of equipment, organization, and scholarship) within which certain human experiences are included and from which others are excluded.

3.   Contingent elements. The fortuitous action of the environment (time, place, and participants involved) that condition the experiential possibilities of human life. The environment is further modified by the particular events or occurrences that take place in any given moment.

4.   Spiritual elements. The value system which establishes the norms of truth, virtue, beauty, and similar nonphysical forces, to which the individual reacts with varying degrees of sensitivity depending upon his environment, his innate or acquired behavior patterns, and his propensity for imitation or originality. His awareness of these intellectual, esthetic, and ethical compulsions comprises conscience.

The methods of scholarship may be dichotomized into form and process. If an individual's experience derives from an awareness of an activity occurring within his environment or within himself, it follows that there are three modes of scholarship: the intuitive, which implies the formation and use of direct cognition or state of understanding; the inductive which leads to the inference of laws, principles, and rules from rational observation; and the deductive which is the dialectic development of such generalizations. Scholarship that is stored, either in human memory or recorded in some graphic form, may be said to be potential; to become kinetic it must be brought to the consciousness of some individual, but if it is to affect society the individual must play some recognized social

---

[43] Much of the material on which this section is based is drawn, with the permission of Mrs. Ruth L. Butler, from Pierce Butler's *Scholarship and Civilization*. Chicago. University of Chicago. Graduate Library School. 1944.

role. It is in this consciousness that man recognizes the content of his experience and thus acquires knowledge. When he arranges this experience, or knowledge, in order and sequence he attains understanding through the process called reasoning. Reasoning, therefore, is a process or ordering, arranging, relating, and classifying, through which each idea is brought into congruity with all other thoughts or ideas to form a rational system.

Man seeks to master his environment through exploration and invention. The first involves simultaneous experiences of a thing and of its human utility. The second may derive either from a recognition of a human need and a quest for a means to satisfy it, or recognition of the properties of a thing or force and a quest for possible human exploitation.

Thus there are three major processes by which scholarship originates: (a) the immediate recognition of the content and order of fortuitous experiences; (b) the emergence or development of a specific curiosity and a resultant search for a specific answer; and (c) the exploration of an idea merely to find whatever may be discovered. The last two are characteristic of all formal research. Man's purposive investigation, as distinct from the accidental or incidental, may be pursued for a variety of motives. Some labor to produce ideas in a desire for private or public profit; others are driven by pure intellectual curiosity without a thought for the effect of their findings; some seek altruistic ends, the improvement of society and the amelioration of the hard lot of their fellows; some work as a matter of pure routine; and some from pure enjoyment of the activities themselves. Such motives may operate separately or in concert or combination, and different motives may activate one individual at different periods of time.

Scholarship, like the other aspects of culture, must be equitably distributed throughout society, and this process of distribution must be continuous, because the oncoming generation must be prepared for the time when it will take possession of the society. Recruits must be enlisted in sufficient numbers to fulfill the specialized social roles necessary to the operation of the society. Current additions and corrections to the scholarship must be made available to all who have need for them. Finally, whenever the occasion demands, the relevant scholarship of a culture must be brought to bear at the point where it will result in maximum benefit to its society.

From what has been said above, the essential unity of scholarship emerges as a spectrum, or continuum, in which there are no breaks either within or between the ranges. In nature the physical seems to merge imperceptibly into the animate and the animate into the mental. So, too, in the realm of scholarship there is a continuous transition from the universals of physical properties and chemical reaction to the uniques of aesthetic manifestation. However, the gradations in the spectrum of experience and scholarship represent real differences and not arbitrary blendings. The sciences are quantitative and inductive, for exactly the same reason that they are experimental and presentational. The humanities are qualitative and deductive for the same reasons that they are comparative and representational. But the characteristics of the range of any scholarship are determined by the characteristics of the range of experience to which it corresponds, for there are limits imposed upon any given scholarship at any given time. In an individual these determinants are his intellectual capabilities, education, sensitivity, direction of attention, and the capacity and vividness of his memory. For the scholarship of a society the determinants are the development of the preceding factors in the individuals of which it is composed, and the stock of recorded knowledge that has been accumulated through inheritance and collective effort including borrowings from other cultures. The scholarship of a society, or a culture, is more than the sum of the individuals of which it is composed. It achieves this increment not only through the group memory preserved in its graphic records, its transcript, but also through the division and specialization of intellectual labor. Thus, a society can expand the scholarship of its culture far beyond the capacities of any individual human mind.

Violation of the unity of scholarship is the result of an abnormal development in one of its constituent parts, just as a culture can suffer from excessive differentials in its trivium. Such aberrations may be the result of one or more of the following fallacies:

1.   The fallacy of *constants* attributes to a variable certain values and characteristics of a constant. Because of this fallacy men have held that the entire range of physical, social, and mental phenomena are all manifestations of a single "substance." The materialist identifies this "substance" with matter, the Berkleian idealists or the Christian Scientist with mind.

2.   The *operative* fallacy leads to the identification of a problem with its solution. Because of this fallacy men have been led to reject, or at least neglect, those data of experience from which generalization cannot easily be developed at the moment. Thus the "scientist" may reject humanistic experience as "subjective and intangible," and hence unworthy of serious consideration. The operative fallacy also results in the investigation of trivialities merely because the apparatus of investigation is easily available, witness the irrelevancy of much of the present-day "fact finding" in sociological research.

3. The fallacy of *process*, or mechanistic fallacy, results in confusion between an end result and the activities which lead to it. Thus are ideas often identified with the intellectual operations by which they are developed from experience. In this way the medieval logician mistook the syllogism for scientific proof.

4. The fallacy of *origins* leads to the identification of a totality with its components. A whole is something more than the sum of its parts, so, too, a society is more than the arithmetic sum of its physical and biological elements. This is the fallacy of many statistical analyses and the assumed identity of like units.

5. The fallacy of *specialization* arises from an excessive devotion to the division of labor and leads to fragmentation of the scholarship. Because specialists are committed to a compartmentalized pattern of thought they become isolated from each other and from the general field of inquiry. Specialization in its extreme form denies synthesis, and the professional recruit, in his haste to become a specialist, scurries through his preprofessional liberal studies with no thought of synthesizing and incorporating his experiences into permanent cultural insights. So, too, a culture that is overcommitted to the specialization of its scholarship may eventually destroy itself through pulverization.

The interdependence among the three aspects of culture has already been noted, but it should be emphasized that each to a substantial degree limits or facilitates the development of the others. Certain of these relationships are quite obvious. The *technology* of physical equipment cannot advance further than the *scholarship* will permit, for man cannot *do* what he does not *know*. Technology is a corollary of the *scholarship*, and it is upon this technology that the *physical equipment* of a culture rests. Similarly, the social organization of a culture reflects both the state of the *physical equipment* and the *scholarship*: note the changes in social organization brought about by the industrial revolution. One can only guess the impact of the invention of the wheel upon the culture that devised it. Admittedly, a technology can develop to a point without an understanding of its meaning; Squanto taught the early settlers of New England to place a fish in each hill of corn, though there was no understanding on his part of the chemistry of soil fertilization. But a technology that is based on simple observable facts (the corn grew greener where the refuse of the catch was dumped) cannot advance very far.

Further, the pronounced characteristics of any one of these three aspects of culture may determine the characteristics of the other two, though it may not always be easy to distinguish between cause and effect.

Certainly the value systems of India and China differ sharply from those of the United States, and this contrast is reflected in the social organization, and the physical equipment of their very different worlds. Even within a culture, contrasting value systems may reflect the influence of those groups which devote major attention to certain aspects of the scholarship or the social organization. Such conflicts may be not only intense, but also may twist or shape the entire cultural pattern: witness the conflict between the humanistic as opposed to the scientific, or technological, point of view in determining the value system of our contemporary society.[44] Again, the value system reflects a shift from man as an individual to man as an organized, or organizational, being. The growth of anti-intellectualism among certain groups in a population, especially if those groups are important either because of their numbers or the influence which they exert in other ways upon the cultural pattern, could lead to the destruction of an entire culture, or at least transform it to the point at which it becomes something quite different from what it had been.

Though there are forces within a culture which tend toward its alteration or even destruction, there are also stabilizing forces which exert powerful influences for cohesion and resistance to change. Cohesion within the culture is the result of: (1) similarity of interests, that is identity, or near-identity of values, beliefs, shared-knowledge, and economic interests; (2) the interdependence of interests which compels groups with differing cultural traits, knowledge, or skills to unite in striving for a common goal; and finally (3) there are such powerful forces tending toward regularization and stability as: habit, mores, physical or geographical propinquity, and an effective communication system—a common language. Thus, from a somewhat different point of view, communication, with the possession of a common language, is again revealed as an essential part of culture. Communication is the adhesive which binds the culture together; it is the very soil from which culture springs—lacking it there could be no culture.

---

[44] Note the argument that arose over C. P. Snow's now famous Rede Lecture on "The Two Cultures and the Scientific Revolution" and the rejoinder by F. R. Leavis in his Richmond Lecture at Cambridge on "The Significance of C. P. Snow."

Three

# Communication, Culture, and the Library

## COMMUNICATION AND CULTURE

The view of culture as a control mechanism of society begins with the assumption, as Clifford Geertz has said, that "human thought is basically both social and public—that its natural habitat is the house yard, the market place, and the town square. Thinking consists not of 'happenings in the head' (though happenings there and elsewhere are necessary for it to occur) but of a traffic in what have been called, by G. H. Mead and others, significant symbols."[1] And again, a little later, "Man is not to be defined by his innate capacities alone, as the Enlightenment sought to do, nor by his actual behavior alone, as much of contemporary social science seeks to do, but rather by the link between them, by the way in which the first is transformed into the second, his generic potentialities focussed into his specific performances. It is in man's *career*, in its characteristic course, that we can discern, however dimly, his nature, and though culture is but one element in determining that course, it is hardly the least important. As culture shapes us as a single species—and is no doubt still shaping us—so too it shapes us as separate individuals."[2]

---

[1] Clifford Geertz. "The Impact of the Concept of Culture on the Concept of Man." *New Views of the Nature of Man*, ed. John R. Platt. Chicago. University of Chicago Press. 1965. p. 107.

[2] *Ibid*. p. 116. It is important to note that the main meaning of modern electronic

**81**

Communication, then, is essentially a social phenomenon, and because of its importance to the structure, organization, and behavior of society, as well as to the character of the individual, it is central to the study of librarianship. Indeed, the very word *communication* itself means *share*, and when two people are communicating they are a unity. A culture, then, can be regarded as people in communication who are sharing language, customs, habits, and beliefs.[3] Communication in relation to culture must exclude, by definition, stimulus reception from the physical environment and the kind of behavior exchanges accepted by the biologists and biometricians as communication.[4] Communication may be regarded, as Marler does, as being essentially "the evolution of synergistic interplay between participants both of whom are committed to maximizing the efficiency of interchange."[5] No man, indeed, "is an island entire of itself."

From the grottoes of Combarelles and Altamira to the galleries of the Louvre, the walls bear eloquent testimony to man's basic need for pictorial representation. First, say the historians of art, there was sculpture; "the object represented through all its profiles," writes Faure, "having a kind of second real existence." Sculpture was followed by the bas-relief, "which sinks and effaces itself until it becomes engraving,"[6] and finally there was pictorial convention, the representation of the object painted on a cavern wall. The modern archaeologist, armed with the tools of science such as carbon 14 dating, might disagree with Faure's sequence, but the argument is irrelevant to our purpose. What is important is that man needed pictorial representation both for communication with his fellows and for self-expres-

---

communication, by its speed and ability to span great distances, is that it enlarges the potential scale of social organization and greatly enhances the possibilities for centralization and imperialism in culture. An excellent survey of the impact of electronics, or as the authors call it, "the electronic utopia" or "technological sublime," upon social history appears in James W. Carey and John J. Quirk. "The Mythos of the Electronic Revolution." *American Scholar.* vol. 39 (Spring 1970 and Summer 1970), pp. 219–41 and 395–424.

3 Colin Cherry. *On Human Communication,* 2nd ed. Cambridge, Mass. M.I.T. Press. 1966. Chapter 1.

4 Norbert Wiener takes the position that communication can occur between man and machines and even between machines. *The Human Use of Human Beings.* Boston. Houghton Mifflin. 1950. Chapters 4 and 5.

5 Peter Marler. "Animal Communication Signals." *Science.* vol. 157 (August 18, 1967), p. 789.

6 Elie Faure. *History of Art: Ancient Art.* Garden City, N.Y. Garden City Publishing Company. 1921. p. 13; also, J. Pijoan. *History of Art.* London. Batsford. 1933. Chapter 2. "Art in the Reindeer Epoch"; and R. Huyghe. *Ideas and Images in World Art.* New York. H. N. Abrams. 1959. pp. 104–24.

sion. Pictorial representation can be traced back to the Reindeer Epoch and the dawn of civilization; it shares with language, writing, kinesics, and all the variant forms of nonverbal communication a major role in that total process by means of which cultures came into being and evolved.[7] From the bison of Font-de-Gaume to the image from an overhead projector is quite a leap technologically, but the intervening millennia have not altered the human compulsion to outwit time, as it were, by re-creating and attempting to hold unchanged forever the fleeting image of a moment.

Communication is both personal and social, and it is difficult to discuss it in relation to one without also considering it in relation to the other. Man must communicate both with himself and with his fellows, and the same elements of the communication system—a transmitter, receptor, medium, and message—are present in both intra- and interpersonal communication contexts. Communication is essential to natural interaction and conjunction in specific conditions of social organization. It is a mode of interaction between or among two or more individuals. In its cultural relationships it presupposes the existence of an organized group to which the communicators belong, from which they have acquired their speech and other communication patterns or habits. Communication, in the social sense, then, implies a relationship. But communication is not only an essential part of culture, it defines and even limits culture.

Peter Drucker has drawn an important and basic distinction between *information* and *communication*, which he says are opposite yet interdependent. Information is purely formal and has no meaning in and of itself. Information is impersonal, whereas communication is interpersonal. Information can be freed of the human component. "All through history, the problem has been how to glean a little information out of communication, that is, out of relationships between people, based on perception. All through history, the problem has been to isolate the information content from an abundance of perception."[8] Yet, at the same time, information presupposes communication. *Knowledge*, by contrast, is information that

---

[7] I. J. Gelb. *A Study of Writing*, 2nd ed. Chicago. University of Chicago Press. 1963; Cherry. *Human Communication*. Chapter 7. "On Cognition and Recognition"; E. T. Hall. *The Silent Language*. Garden City, N.Y. Doubleday. 1959; J. Ruesch and W. Kees, *Nonverbal Communication*. Berkeley. University of California Press. 1957. Cf. E. H. Gombrich. *Art and Illusion*. New York. Pantheon. 1961. Chapter 2; and the same author's delightful *Meditations on a Hobby Horse*. London. Phaidon. 1963. See also: Gelb. *Study of Writing*. p. 35 ff.; L. Hogben. *From Cave Painting to Comic Strip*. New York. Chanticleer Press. 1949. pp. 179–83.

[8] Peter F. Drucker. *Technology, Management, and Society*. New York. Harper and Row. 1970. p. 12.

is applicable to work. "Only when a man applies information to doing something does it become knowledge. Knowledge, like electricity or money, is a form of energy that exists only when doing work."[9] Such a distinction is, of course, that of the economist, and would be somewhat at variance with that generalized concept held by the "intellectual" who prized knowledge for its intrinsic worth, its inherent beauty, and the wisdom it is supposed to bestow.

It is man's capacity for organizing information into large and complex configurations, and his ability to transmit that information to other men, that is the great glory of the human species. Though the propensity to communicate would appear to be inherent in the human organism, even as it is in the world of the lower animals, there are a variety of acquired characteristics which influence the ability to carry on communication. These are said to be "acquired" because they do not originate in the physical reality of the human organism, but are socially induced or culturally determined. Yet so powerful and so well concealed may be these social determinants, that their effects upon behavior may appear to make that behavior seem intuitive. Language is itself acquired, yet it lies at the basis of all communication, determines its patterns or modes, and so plays a determinant role in the ability to communicate. It logically follows that the efficiency of language establishes, in large measure, the efficiency of communication.

The structure of the communication system, especially the language, can shape a culture's representation of the universe. For centuries linguists shared the Greek belief that language was derived from a universal uncontaminated essence of reason shared by all men, and that words were merely the vehicle, or medium, by which this essence was expressed. Thus, a thought that was capable of expression in one language could be translated without loss of meaning into any other language. But Whorf's investigations into the Hopi Indian language presented a concept of linguistic relativity that somewhat altered traditional beliefs about communication and society.[10]

The principle that all observers are not led to the same representation of the universe by identical physical evidence unless their linguistic backgrounds are similar is not derived solely from Whorf's studies of Hopi. There are a multitude of other languages imposing widely differing views of nature and the environment upon those who speak them. The validity of

---

[9] Peter F. Drucker. *The Age of Discontinuity*. New York. Harper and Row. 1968. p. 269.
[10] Benjamin Lee Whorf. *Language, Thought, and Reality*. New York. Wiley. 1956.

the Aristotelian law of identity, "A is A," is denied by the Chinese because the logic of their language does not admit of such polar words as "redness," "hardness," "longness," or "shortness." Rather, the Chinese say that "the long and the short are mutually related"; for Chinese is a "multi-valued" language in contrast to the dichotomies of bi-valued English. Thus, the Chinese see most situations in terms of shades of gray, rather than in the absolutes of black and white. The Wintu Indians of North America go even further than the Chinese in avoiding the "is of identity," and say, for example, not "this is bread," but "we call this bread." The Coeur d'Alene Indians of Idaho do not speak in terms of simple cause and effect relationships, but rather in terms of *process*, and other languages employ nouns which represent identities capable of motion.

Thus, modern research in linguistics reveals language not only as an instrument by means of which human beings communicate with each other, but also as a tool that shapes the cultural pattern. Further, there is no reason to suppose that any of the languages of the Indo-European family, with their bi-valued logic, subject-predicate syntactical structure, and their law of identity, represent ultimate perfection of the communication system. Today science is feeling the restraint of assumptions imbedded in language, and is seeking to improve communication by the invention of new media.

Communication is that form of conscious interaction by means of which a stimulus, signal, or symbol, or a pattern of these elements in any combination, transmits meaning through space and time from one living organism to another. Without communication, society could not be. It is, as Cooley has expressed it, "the mechanism through which human relations exist and develop—all the symbols of mind, together with the means of conveying them through space and preserving them in time. . . . Communication makes up an organic whole corresponding to the organic whole of human thought, and everything in the way of mental growth has an external existence therein."[11] Or, as Pierce Butler has stated, "Communication is the process by which indirect experience is established. . . . By a manifold of cultural structures and agencies, communication of experience takes place not only among the living but also through successive generations."[12]

So uncertain is man's knowledge of the effectiveness of his com-

---

[11] Charles H. Cooley. *Social Organization.* New York. Scribners. 1910. p. 61. Also: Cherry. *Human Communication.* Chapter 3; and George A. Miller. *The Psychology of Communication.* New York. Basic Books. 1967. pp. 45–55.

[12] Pierce Butler. *Scholarship and Civilization.* Chicago. University of Chicago Press. Graduate Library School. 1944. p. 5.

munication system, that he utilizes every device that his ingenious mind can conjure up in the effort to deliver his message, and the more nearly complete his mastery over the techniques of communication—the more language he knows, the more symbols he can command—the greater his influence upon others. Lacunae in speech may find a degree of compensation in gestures, facial expressions, and other bodily movements—a shrug of the shoulders, a blush, the touch of hands (ranging from caresses to benedictions to blows), a hanging head, even a tone of voice. All of these can convey meaning; they can reinforce the spoken word; they can negate it; they can clarify, emphasize, and reinforce it; in certain circumstances they can transmit a message with far more clarity and accuracy than verbal language is capable of achieving. Some students of kinesics have estimated that nonverbal communication accounts for half of all messages between human beings and all messages from animal to animal and animal to man.[13]

Various kinds of representational and symbolic nonlinguistic devices can be used for the transmission of information from person to person. Works of art and instrumental music, for example, communicate without words, as do any number of symbolic forms which possess (or have been assigned) personal or general connotations. Signs used for traffic control, which may or may not include words, are frequently differentiated by shape so that the driver can recognize the message of a sign by its outline alone. A waving flag often means more to an observer than the most eloquent Fourth of July harangue. Like words, such symbols may carry a wealth of meaning or significance out of all proportion to their actual informational content. Every crucifix stands for a complex structure of faith, doctrine, dogma, and practice, and the simple words "one if by land and two if by sea" conjure up a moment which bore the weight of an empire and the future of a nation.

For the purposes of this study, the dimensions of communication will be limited to the interpersonal—transmission of messages between and among human beings by means of "natural" language,[14] and evincing the

---

13 See: Jurgen Ruesch and Weldon Kees. *Nonverbal Communication.* Berkeley. University of California Press. 1957; Ray L. Birdwhistell. *Introduction to Kinesics.* Washington. Foreign Service Institute. 1952; Edward T. Hall. *The Silent Language.* New York. Doubleday. 1959; Charles F. Hockett. "Animal 'Language' and Human Language" in J. H. Spohler, ed., *The Evolution of Man's Capacity for Culture.* Detroit. Wayne State University Press. 1959. pp. 32–39; and Miller. *Psychology of Communication.* pp. 83–86.

14 As opposed to "artificial" languages, such as codes, computer languages, and the like. The distinction is, of course, ridiculous since all languages are "artificial." There

essential elements of interpersonal communication: i.e., the transmitter, the message, the mutually intelligible means of communication, and the receptor or receptors. In most instances, it is important that both transmitter and receptor be consciously aware that communication is in process. In the majority of situations there is a single transmitter[15] at any given time, but there may be any number of receptors; the classroom situation provides the traditional example of single transmitter and multiple receptors.

Message content is potentially infinite, within the limitations imposed by the message-carrying capacity of the language, or medium, used. The content of any given message is conditioned by (a) the situation which motivates the origin of the message, that is, the environment which gives rise to it, and (b) the characteristics, purpose, and competence of the sender. The degree to which the sender is aware of the characteristics of the recipient (or expected recipient) and thus shapes the message as best he can to conform to or coincide with those characteristics, is to be understood as part of the sender's purpose and competence.

Interpretation of the message, on the other hand, is conditioned by (a) the abilities and characteristics of the recipient, including the past experience he can bring to bear, and (b) the environment or situation in which he finds himself at the moment of reception. The same message transmitted to the same individual under different circumstances may evoke varying responses. P. B. Medawar holds that the "capacity of a system of communication obviously depends on the range of different configurations of symbols at the command of the transmitting agent."[16] He is assuming, of course, that an act of communication, a specific message, owes its uniqueness, or as he says, "its property of being *this* message and not *that* message, to the particular configuration or sequence of the symbols" of which it is composed, for "a random or disorderly configuration of symbols does not make sense."[17]

In general, one may say that the goal or objective of communication is the achievement of "likeness of mind"—which is not to be equated with persuasion, but more nearly with understanding or comprehension. As Park has expressed it, "Communication creates, or makes possible, at least,

---

is no such thing as a natural language, but the term is used to designate the language of a people.

[15] Musical groups may be considered to be multiple transmitters, unless one wishes to quibble over the role of the conductor.

[16] P. B. Medawar. *The Art of the Soluble*. London. 1967. p. 50.

[17] *Ibid*. Also: Edward T. Hall. *The Hidden Dimension*. Garden City, N.Y. Doubleday. 1966. Chapter 1.

that consensus or understanding among the individual components of a social group which eventually gives it and them the character not merely of society but of a cultural unit. It spins a web of custom and mutual expectation which binds together social entities as diverse as the family group, a labor organization, or the haggling participants in a village market. Communication maintains the concert necessary to enable them to function, each in his several ways."[18]

In communication theory, which calls the achievement of like-mindedness a form of action, *all* action is considered to be controlled by information. Primary, direct, or person-to-person communication is almost always an interchange, a give-and-take process in which statement, question, comment, and rejoinder follow hard upon each other in mutual stimulation. Receiving communication, as Mortimer Adler points out, is not like "receiving a blow, or a legacy, or a judgment from the court." It is more nearly comparable, he asserts, to the relationship between pitcher and catcher in baseball. "Catching the ball is just as much an activity as pitching or hitting it. The pitcher or batter is the giver here in the sense that his activity initiates the motion of the ball. The catcher or fielder is the receiver in the sense that his activity terminates it. Both are equally active, though the activities are distinctly different."[19]

The vehicle for interpersonal communication is principally natural language, with all the capabilities, limitations, and complications which inhere in such an arbitrary and yet amorphous symbol-system. Natural language (as opposed to artificial) is a social phenomenon, and even the dictionary-makers (and, on some points, the grammarians) have been forced to yield to the harsh truth that usage ultimately determines the "correctness" of any linguistic practice. As Humpty Dumpty said, "When *I* use a word, it means just what I choose it to mean—neither more nor less." After such behavior patterns have become so widespread that they are accepted as "common usage," they become a part of the language-system and carry generally understood meanings. The forces for regularization have only this constantly evolving practice to work with, and such laws or rules as can be established for the governing structure and use of a language are of necessity based upon recognition of the manner in which that language is—and has been—used.

Speech—direct communication—is transitory, condemned forever to an eternal now. Furthermore, the capacity of the human brain to remem-

18 Robert E. Park. "Reflections on Communication and Culture." *American Journal of Sociology.* vol. 44 (1939), p. 191.
19 Mortimer J. Adler. *How to Read a Book.* New York. Simon and Schuster. 1940. pp. 23–24.

ber, though it is remarkable, is not infinite, and the processes of conceptualization and generalization involve selection, and thus mental rejection,
as well as recognition and retention. As the quantities of information
provided to the brain increase, fragments may be dropped from the
memory-store, perhaps beyond the ability of even the subconscious to
recall. Man, both individually and collectively, has invented certain
mnemonic aids to recollection in his efforts to transmit important knowledge accurately from generation to generation; for example, a large part of
the oral tradition of many cultures is in song or verse. Primitive and uncomplicated societies can depend upon oral communication for the transmission of knowledge and information essential to the efficient conduct of
their affairs; recent studies have shown that the elders of certain illiterate
tribes in Uganda, Kenya, and Tanganyika base their judicial decisions
upon a body of tribal precedent transmitted solely by word of mouth.[20]
But advanced civilizations demand written records, particularly in matters
of great moment.

There can be little doubt about the primacy of the word in all forms
of communication, despite the fact that man communicates with his whole
body and makes use of all the senses in conveying thought to others.
"Communication through sound is paramount," Walter J. Ong has written.
"No matter how familiar we are with an object or a process, we do not
feel that we have full mastery of it until we can verbalize it to others. And
we do not enter into full communication with another person without
speech. . . . Written words are substitutes for sound and are only marks
on a surface until they are converted to sound again, either in the imagination or by actual vocalization."[21]

The advance of the technology of communication has tended, however, to obscure the importance of the word, of the oral-aural character of
communication. The spoken word has become inextricably amalgamated
with other forms of graphic record: writing, print, pictorial representation,
and even computer languages. Ong has identified three stages of communication development: the unrecorded word—oral culture; the de-
natured word—alphabet and print, the sound-sight split; and, finally, the
electronic stage.[22] Yet for all of these alterations and advances in the
technology of the media of communication the word is still basic as it was
in the "beginning."

"The bondage of words was broken by writing them down," Professor

---

[20] Interview with W. C. Brown reported in the *New Yorker.* January 12, 1957. p. 18.
[21] Walter J. Ong. *In the Human Grain.* New York. Macmillan. 1967. p. 2.
[22] Walter J. Ong. *The Presence of the Word.* New Haven. Yale University Press. 1967.
   Chapter 2.

Denys Hay of the University of Edinburgh has written. "The availability of the written word conditioned the whole development of civilization. A new dimension was given to the mind of man; he could afford to forget since he could store his information outside himself."[23] "Vox audita perit, littera scripta manet" wrote Caxton almost five hundred years ago, in his *Mirror of the World*, and thus expressed an advantage the graphic record still enjoys over the fleeting shadows of the television screen.

## SECONDARY COMMUNICATION

Indirect or secondary communication may be defined as that in which a graphic record intervenes between transmitter and receptor.[24] When languages were reduced to writing, as ideas were reduced to pictures, it became possible for individuals to communicate across unimaginable distances in time and space. The invention of phonetic writing, which represents sound as well as ideas, expanded opportunity for human expression, and eventually led to the development of artificial languages for the communication of highly specialized types of information, and to the conversion of natural language to the capabilities of mechanical or electronic mechanisms.

Next to language itself, writing is probably man's greatest invention. It became an important element in the complex of factors that brought forth the city-state from barbaric tribal origins and raised that state to the magnitude of nations and empires. It confirmed the power of priesthoods and the might and prestige of kings. It fixed historical tradition and strengthened social cohesion. It has preserved the wisdom, the ignorance, the grandeur, the pride, the intellectual curiosity, the prejudice, the loves and hates, the arrogance and humility—in short, the thoughts, strivings, and interpreted actions—of generations. It is an instrument of both liberation and bondage. It has been a major means of intellectual growth and creative achievement (the founding fathers of these United States viewed universal literacy as the essential strength of their concept of a democracy) but it has also strengthened those conservative forces that stifle growth and adventure. It standardized the codes, the classics, and the scriptures.

---

[23] Denys Hay. "Fiat Lux." *Printing and the Mind of Man*, ed. John Carter and Percy H. Muir. London. Cassell. 1967. pp. xvi–xvii.

[24] Precise distinctions between primary and secondary communication are not easy to make. A teletype "conversation" may be regarded as primary, despite the intervention of an intermediary mechanism, because there is a direct exchange between transmitter and receptor.

There is no need to dwell at length on the characteristics of communication by means of written rather than spoken language. Both written and oral communication have their own unique assets and liabilities. The advantage to the receptor, which lies in the unambiguous understanding of what word is meant, is perhaps counterbalanced by the fact that if the receptor is not clear as to what that word itself means, or how in particular it is being used, the transmitter is not present to supply an explanation, a synonym, or an illustration. The advantages allied to the permanence of written records may be somewhat offset by the sheer volume of accumulation which the refinement of techniques for the generation and preservation of such records has made possible.

The peculiar quality of secondary communication that distinguishes it from the primary is not that it is usually permanent whereas primary communication is generally transitory, or that it requires the interposition of an intermediate agent between transmitter and receptor, but that it is unidirectional. One can only soliloquize to the printed page, the radio, or the television screen, or write letters to the editor or to the station. Thus in all forms of secondary communication there is a barrier between the source of the thought and its object.

Of the three aspects of culture the scholarship would seem to be the most dependent upon the development of graphic records, and it is conceivable that it was the scholarship that was responsible for the "invention" of writing. Indeed, Summerfelt goes so far as to say that "not improbably" the Sumerian priests were the originators of the written word,[25] and Sir Leonard Woolley has written that "it was in the temples and in the service of the god that writing began."[26] Gelb did not differ markedly from this point of view when he wrote, "Sumerian writing owes its origin to the needs arising from public economy and administration."[27] Church and state were essentially one in Mesopotamia during the fourth millennium B.C.[28]

In contrast to the other two aspects of culture, then, the scholarship could make little, if any substantial progress without the support of graphic records. Communication bridges the gap between the existence of things and their meaning, and in acquiring meaning they acquire representatives,

---

[25] A. Sommerfelt. "Speech and Language." *A History of Technology*, ed. Charles Singer et al. Oxford. Clarendon Press. 1954. vol. 1, p. 101.

[26] Jacquetta Hawkes and Sir Leonard Woolley. *Prehistory and the Beginnings of Civilization*. New York. Harper and Row. 1962. p. 633.

[27] Gelb. *Study of Writing*. p. 62.

[28] David Diringer. *Writing*. New York. Praeger. 1962. pp. 27–46; Herbert Landar. *Language and Culture*. New York. Oxford University Press. 1966. pp. 8–23.

surrogates, signs, symbols, and implicates which are far more amenable to manipulation, management, accommodation, and permanence than are the things or events in their original state. Past events are able to survive the ravages of time only because someone has written them down; orally transmitted history soon becomes little more than folklore. Thus man finds himself increasingly in a world of graphic symbols, a world in which, for real property, there are only symbols of real things. The value of those pieces of paper, stock certificates, which we treasure in our portfolios, has a much closer relation to similar pieces of paper at a place called Wall Street than to the buildings, equipment, and products or services of the corporation these certificates represent. One speaks glibly of the "information explosion," but the phenomenon to which he refers is really more of a "paper explosion," and if, in one way or another, man cannot find ways to deal with this paper flood, his inundation by it is not impossible. In the meantime, he who cannot read, who cannot make his way in this world of symbolic representation, is in a serious plight indeed. Thus, though the scholarship of the culture may be more dependent upon communication than the other two aspects, as a culture matures and grows increasingly sophisticated and complex, communication becomes increasingly important to all three aspects.

As a burgeoning technology depends more and more upon graphic communication, so technology itself contributes to the development of secondary communication. The modifications in the printing process that have been developed since the time of Gutenberg have brought important quantitative changes to the communication process without materially altering its basic structure. The high-speed rotary press, the typewriter, the mimeograph, the variety of photographic techniques have exponentially extended the boundaries of secondary communication, though the relationship between the communicator and that which is communicated has remained essentially unaltered. But in the communication process this very magnitude is in itself of fundamental importance. Graphic records tend to beget graphic records, and as this autogenesis progresses there comes a time when man himself may be enslaved by the phonetic symbols of his own thought.[29]

As mechanical duplication of the written or printed word extended the boundaries of the original document, so the interposition of certain mechanical and electronic devices extended the dimensions of human voice and sight. The semiphore and the heliograph were the first attempts to

---

[29] Derek J. de Solla Price. *Science Since Babylon*. New Haven. Yale University Press. 1961. Chapter 5. "Diseases of Science."

bridge the void over which the voice could not be made to carry. The telegraph and the early so-called wireless were further extensions of this same technique by the use of electrical and electronic transmission for the reproduction of mechanical signals. The invention of the gramaphone made possible the recording and reproduction of relatively crude facsimiles of sound patterns, a process to which modern electronic engineering brought considerable refinement through the high fidelity phonograph and its related sound systems. Further dimensions were added to the communication process by combining certain of these techniques, e.g., the recording of telegraphic symbols on tape, the association of the telegraph with the typewriter to make the teletype, and the use of electronic technology for the recording, not only of sounds but of pictures. Radio, television, and their use of communication satellites, extended the range of the human voice and human sight to almost limitless dimensions so that virtually instantaneous communication from transmitter to audience became possible and practicable.

Thus, the invention of printing with movable types was the real harbinger of a change in magnitude rather than in the basic elements of communication, which is not to say that the cultural revolution engendered by the printing press was not a true revolution.[30] A society in which written records are the exclusive possession of a limited elite is a very different society from one in which the written word is common property. During the first fifty years of printing, over eight million books were produced, probably far more than the total European output of manuscripts during the entire medieval period.[31] On this rising tide of print were borne the Renaissance and the Reformation, the precursors of science, the Age of Enlightenment, social and political power for the masses of the people, and the Industrial Revolution. Typography weakened the authority of the written word, weakened the prestige of the scholar, marked the demise of the polyhistor, the man of universal wisdom; and paradoxically, by swelling the bulk of scholarship to inhuman proportions, it made men slaves of print. So long as books were few in number, men were forced to rely heavily

---

[30] One could argue that the first real revolutionary step came with the invention of the codex, for in many ways it was, and still is, a highly economic and effective mechanism for the presentation and retention of the social transcript. It can be efficiently produced; it is compact and portable; its contents are readily accessible; and its storage capacity is great. Of all the forms of secondary communication the book is the most intimate and personal. It can, of course, be directed to a mass audience, but the act of reading is still a personal act.

[31] Pierce Butler. *The Origin of Printing in Europe.* Chicago. University of Chicago Press. 1940. p. 21. Also: Hay. "Fiat Lux." pp. xv–xxxiv.

upon their own immediate experiences, word of mouth, correspondence, broadsides, and their own imaginations for knowledge and entertainment. Originally the spread of book knowledge was regarded as a supplement to the more familiar means of acquiring and enlarging experience, but increasingly, as the centuries passed, the synthetic environment of the printed word became a substitute for experience until, under the impact of the mass agencies of communication, men are held in the grip of an instrument for the universal dissemination of synthetic experience to the point that contact with the realities of social existence are being seriously threatened. To quote Lewis Mumford: "The mass production of books which the invention of printing made possible was followed immediately by the demand for the mass production of suitable standardized minds; indeed, one was dependent upon the other, and they were tied together by a common belief in the reproductive process itself."[32] Therefore, whenever one celebrates the benefits that the printing press has brought—and they are indeed many—the cruel price which it, as well as the electronic innovations in mass communication, has exacted, must not be forgotten. When the leaves of the *Mainz Psalter* of 1457 slipped from the press of Fust and Schoeffer, a force for both good and evil was unleashed upon the world.

A Paul Revere and a Samuel Prescott, galloping into the April night, could arouse but a handful of "embattled farmers" to the defense of their homes; less than two centuries later millions of television viewers watched Neil Armstrong take his "giant step for mankind" from his lunar module. The importance of this contrast is so great and so far-reaching in its influence that there are now those who share the belief of Archibald McLeish, expressed in 1956, that "the printing press is manifestly doomed as the propagator of the obvious, and the time cannot be far off when the greater part of the books on the best-seller lists will go directly into the cameras of the picture machines without pausing to pass a pupal stage in print."[33] Similarly, in lamenting the demise of "Buch-und-Lesen Kultur," Spengler charged that "democracy has by its newspaper completely expelled the book from the mental life of the people. The book-world and its profusion of standpoints that compelled thought to select and criticize, is now a real possession only for a few. . . . The age of the 'book' is flanked on either hand by that of the sermon and that of the newspaper. Books are a personal expression, sermons and newspapers obey an impersonal purpose."[34]

---

[32] Lewis Mumford. *The Condition of Man.* New York. Harcourt, Brace. 1944. p. 256.
[33] Archibald MacLeish. "In Praise of Dissent." *New York Times Book Review.* December 16, 1956. p. 1.
[34] Oswald Spengler. *The Decline of the West.* New York. Knopf. 1932. vol. 2, p. 463.

But Hay has stoutly reaffirmed his confidence in the permanence of the book for any serious purpose, and especially as a 'vehicle for the transmission of the scholarship of the culture from generation to generation. "It is surely inconceivable," he has written, "that the impresarios of the future will succeed entirely in persuading the creators, the makers, to consign their inspiration to the ether, to be bounced about between the earth and the Heaviside Layer until the waves peter out in inaudible murmurs. Authors are not like children, content to see their beautiful pebbles flung into the pool of eternity. The student and the scholar, at any rate . . . will want a measure of continuity. They will want shoulders to stand on as they peer at the past and future. . . . Perhaps some day it may be possible to devise ways of recapturing the flying words and images of the past. Unless that happens there will be no substitute for print and the book will remain the only way by which one age can speak to another."[35]

In 1909, at the very beginning of the modern era in communication, Cooley identified four basic characteristics that contribute to the effectiveness of a communication system: (1) its *expressiveness*, the range of ideas, or information it is able to carry (in present-day terminology this would be its information carrying capacity); (2) the *permanence* of its record, or its effectiveness in overcoming time; (3) its swiftness, or its ability to span space (*range* would seem to have been a better term); and (4) its *diffusion*, or availability to all classes of the population, or society to which it is directed.[36] The implications and significance of the first three of these characteristics are so obvious as to need no explanation; nor does one need to belabor the point that it is in both the enlargement and the animation of the communication process that the most spectacular advances have been made during the present century. The diffusion of communication, however, is important in relation to its impact upon the social structure of a culture.

## CLASS DIFFERENTIALS IN THE PRODUCTION AND UTILIZATION OF COMMUNICATION

To say that communication is the cohesive force in a culture and the vehicle that makes possible the development of human social relationships, does not imply that it necessarily permeates uniformly throughout a society, or that it does not vary from one subculture to another. Communication sustains the social units of a culture in a kind of colloidal suspension, but,

---

[35] Hay. "Fiat Lux." p. xxxiv.
[36] Cooley. *Social Organization.* p. 63.

to carry the metaphor further, its concentration, or density, is neither uniform nor consistent. There are within the complex structure of modern society great differences in the degree of exposure to, utilization of, and dependence upon the communication system itself, and on the types of communication media of which the system is comprised.

Within any given social class, or culture, the utilization of the communication system is dependent upon, as Talcott Parsons has said, "the empirical knowledge necessary to cope with situational exigencies and sufficiently integrated patterns of expressive symbolism and of value orientation."[37] Individuals are combined in biological families and households, in gregarious circles of acquaintance, more or less geographically concentrated, and in social corporations and civic units. Social corporations may be economic, vocational, recreational, and creedal, of which the last has to do with belief (churches, fraternities, political parties). Civic units include the state and the entirety of its structural and operative components. Collectively they present a general pattern of class structure, within which there are subordinate patterns some of which may be peculiar to individual groupings. Each of these groups or classes is a communicating unit, though the communication medium, or media, may vary widely.

Class differences in the utilization of, or dependence upon, the communication system date from the earliest times, and "elite" communication as opposed to "mass" communication may be traced to the magic and secret ritual of the Stone Age. Even primitive social structures include those groups the members of which earned a livelihood through the utilization of some form of special, or elite, communication. The priests, the medicine men, the architects of ritual, both sacred and profane, all maintained their positions through some form of mastery over the communication process. Sometimes, perhaps often, this mastery was spurious, but always the outward semblance of superiority was maintained. By contrast, the slave, the peasant, the common man lived by myth, legend, folklore, and he recognized the superiority of the elite ritual even when it was nothing more than a meaningless mumbo-jumbo. But however humble its origins, certainly there emerged a form of elite communication that was the possession of a privileged class, or classes, and a body of legend and folklore that was the common property of all.

As primitive tribes coalesced into city-states, which in turn grew into nations and empires, the tribal chieftain was replaced by the king, emperor, or other political leader at the apex of the social pyramid, and the possession of property, or other forms of wealth, displaced a monopoly on

---

[37] Talcott Parsons. *The Social System.* Glencoe, Illinois. Free Press. 1951. p. 34.

"learning" as the prerequisite to promotion up the social ladder. But this did not diminish the prestige of elite communication. Rather it brought a new form of specialization, creative art, the practitioners of which were the recipients of special favor, patronage, from those in the topmost economic or political levels of the social hierarchy. The masses of the people, however, still retained their myths, their folklore, their legends, and from these the artists and other intellectual workers drew heavily. Thus the communication system was far from immune to the impact of changes in the social structure.

The graphic communication system was the monopoly of an elite class and was supported mainly by that social stratum. Literacy drew a sharp line between the scholar, or artist, and the remainder of society. This was true even though, for a time, the scholarship of Rome leaned heavily upon the services of Greek scholars who had been colonized by their conquerors. In both Greece and Rome it was generally true that scholarship was the possession of the more favored classes supported by a slave economy. But even in the age of Plato and Aristotle memory was still a most important repository of human scholarship, perhaps the most important vehicle of the communication chain. As Alfred North Whitehead has said, "Writing was an invention which took about two thousand years to make its effect felt . . . even in Plato's Dialogs, the discussions are seldom if ever about what the participants have 'read' but invariably about what they 'remember.' The amount of memorizing must have been tremendous . . . for a long time after writing had been invented it was little more than a keeping of accounts, a business of kings and bankers, promulgating orders and computing moneys. Only when men began putting down their thoughts did the effect of the written word begin to be felt on the intellectual progress of mankind."[38]

The folklore of the masses of the people was still predominantly unrecorded except as it was absorbed into the literary creations of the elite. Essentially the same situation persisted through the medieval world, with its monastic monopoly of learning, and on into the Renaissance and the Age of Enlightenment. The system of graphic communication was not only most accessible to the world of the elite, but also it was largely under the control of the intellectual class. Even under the system of patronage the scholar and the nobility were members of the same elite social stratum and the one mingled freely with the other.

At the present time, society, because of its increased mobility—

---

[38] Alfred North Whitehead. *Dialogues of Alfred North Whitehead*, ed. Lucien Price. Boston. Little Brown. 1954. p. 153.

geographic, economic, occupational, cultural—may be moving toward an essentially classless structure in which there may be relatively little domination by an elite. Folklore was probably the first form of communication to feel the impact of these changes; for folklore appears to flourish most abundantly during long periods of social stability and cultural isolation. Tradition, myth, and legend are born of the soil and man's attachment to the soil. For over a century the constant change and expansion of population have hampered the growth of an indigenous folklore. Despite the efforts of the literati and the sophisticates in art to espouse an enthusiasm for the primitive, an enthusiasm for folk culture, the "common people will not buy it."

As the folk culture of past ages drew from the culture of the elite, and peopled its fanciful world with kings, noblemen, and merchant princes, so, during the past century, the literature of the elite has turned to the "common man," the underprivileged, the downtrodden, for its themes. A tragedy which once was thought to be tragic only when it befell a royal personage or royal family, now is sought in the drab and hopeless lives of little people. This intermingling of class identification and symbolism in the thematic content of contemporary communication is paralleled by innovations in the mechanisms of the communication process which may be destroying, probably forever, the old monopoly of the elite. Illiteracy in the Western World has been all but obliterated. The new instruments of mass communication have brought to vast segments of the population identical stimuli and vicarious experiences. The scholarship of cultures has been made accessible with a uniformity and a magnitude of inclusiveness that is unequalled in the history of mankind, and may be expected to become even greater in the decades ahead. Such levelling may be expected to destroy still further the class patterns of society.

## COMMUNICATION AS THE MATRIX OF SOCIAL STRUCTURE

Since all human activities are expressions of man's thought, will, or emotion, an effective pattern of social organization should provide the opportunity for a balanced release of these manifestations in ways that will bring the maximum benefit to the society. As Graham Wallas has pointed out in *The Great Society*,[39] however, man's success in organizing

---

[39] Graham Wallas. *The Great Society*. New York. Macmillan. 1914. Chapters 11–13.

his activities to such an end have been distressingly inadequate. The earlier social structuring exemplified, as Giddings has shown, component groupings based upon geographical propinquity and genetic segregation. The tribal or kinship form of component societies were successfully bound together by the older methods of stimulating thought through oral communication. Indeed, oral communication compelled geographic aggregation, whereas the invention of indirect communication contributed to the mobility of peoples, loosened the bonds of geographical propinquity, and encouraged the development of a "constituent society" in which the members are united by special forms of activity or particular interests. These *constituent* societies are differentiated by Giddings, in his *Scientific Study of Human Society*, from the *component* form by specialization of function, voluntary and purposive association, coordination, mutual-aid, and division of labor. Constituent societies could not develop very far if they lacked the medium of graphic communication.[40]

In a civil society the most important purposive organization is the state itself. Through the state the social mind operates to achieve the coordination and domination of the whole community and its lesser purposive associations. Its functions are coextensive with the entire range of human interests, and its communication system is directed toward the achievement of "like-mindedness," because its primary purpose is to perfect socially integrated action. Basic as the state is to a civil society, one may doubt whether it could exist in a free and democratic form were it not supplemented and supported by private and voluntary associations. As Giddings has said, "Whatever belittles the state or destroys belief in its power to perform any kind of social service, whatever impairs the popular habit of achieving ends by private initiative and voluntary organization, endangers society and prevents the full realization of its ends."[41]

For centuries the dominant social pattern was a form of class ladder, with the state itself at the top, on which the position of the individual was largely determined by his economic or family status. Mobility, the opportunity to climb from rung to rung, varied, of course with the specific culture, but the factors which determined position were relatively universal.

In the wake of the industrial revolution, however, came the rise to power of two new aberrations in the structural pattern of Western civilization. Both were rooted in the human propensity for voluntary association,

---

[40] Franklin H. Giddings. *The Scientific Study of Human Society*. Chapel Hill. University of North Carolina Press. 1924. p. 10.

[41] Franklin H. Giddings. *Descriptive and Historical Society*. New York. Macmillan. 1906. p. 515.

both had their origin in man's innate gregariousness, but both altered rather drastically the social organization of the culture. One was the development of the corporation as an instrument of economic enterprise, the other was the rise of the professional or vocational association. So deeply rooted in human society is the need to form associations, that even the attempts of the extremists of the French Revolution to destroy corporate freedom served only to stimulate new associations and communities: financial companies, agricultural associations, life insurance organizations, and a host of other voluntary associations for the promotion of public works, amelioration of human misery, and improvement of the human intellect. Thus the growth of corporate organizations which cover every aspect of life attenuates the threat of the ever-present conflict between the individual and society or the state.

As component groupings of society gave way to the constituent form, communication became increasingly important as a cohesive agent. Both the corporation and the professional or trade association brought into close contact individuals from a great variety of disparate economic and social backgrounds, people who had played and were playing a multitude of roles some of which were mutually antagonistic or antithetical. Thus, if the organization is to prosper, like-mindedness, at least with respect to its aims, methods, and operations, is essential, and it is the achievement of this unanimity that is the burden of the communication system. Similarly, each individual, as he comes into contact with various corporations and associations finds that he himself must play many roles, roles which he can master only to the extent that the communication system makes such mastery or proficiency possible. Communication, when it operates effectively, subdues and holds in bondage that anarchy that inheres in the social roles and may even threaten the well-being of every individual.[42]

Both the corporation and the association have sought every opportunity to adapt the media of communication to their needs. The growing body of corporate administrative or managerial theory is increasingly dependent upon an understanding of the communication process. Much of such effort masquerades behind the form of public or employee "relations," but the achievement of like-mindedness is always the goal. Thus,

---

[42] John A. Clausen, Orville G. Brim, Jr., Alex Inkeles, Ronald Lippitt, and M. Brewster Smith. *Socialization and Society*, ed. John A. Clausen. Boston. Little, Brown. 1968.
   Also: Hugh Dalziel Duncan. *Communication and Social Order*. New York. Bedminster. 1962; and his study of symbols in the maintenance of social order and promotion of social relationships: *Symbols in Society*. New York. Oxford University Press. 1968.

in the effective operation of the modern corporation, the house organ may well be as vital to company management as the research report is to its technical staff.

The promotion and stimulation of communication was, of course, the very *raison d'être* for the creation and development of the professional society. During the centuries, even millennia, that preceded the invention of printing and the beginnings of scientific inquiry, learning was intensely individual, and often isolated. Until the rise of the scientific societies in the seventeenth century, the only means of professional communication among scholars was achieved through travel and private correspondence, and many of the most important figures of this early period made surprisingly frequent excursions about the continent of Europe and across the channel to England, and maintained a voluminous and steady exchange of letters. But the unreliability of such forms of communication are self-evident, success was too dependent upon the fortuitous: the establishment of a friendly relationship rather than a hostile rivalry, or even geographical propinquity and the vicissitudes of travel.

The dissemination of knowledge and the opportunities for cooperation were greatly facilitated when, in the seventeenth century, scholars began to form societies for the oral exchange of their accumulated knowledge and, very soon thereafter, sought the preservation of their group deliberations in published transactions and proceedings.

"Science developed its social character," Gillispie has written, "out of the necessity for cooperation, communication and patronage. . . . Ephemeral literary and cultural academies . . . [which] abounded in Renaissance Italy . . . [were] called into being as the ornament of some court, the pastime of some prince, and vanished as easily as formed."[43] It was the emerging interest in scientific inquiry, however, that gave the movement a reasonable degree of permanence. In 1603, the Accademia dei Lincei (lynx-eyed) was founded under the patronage of Prince Federigo Cesi, but it could not survive his death in 1630. A much more stable organization was the Accademia del Cimento, of Florence, founded in 1657. But historically, the two most eminent bodies were the Royal Society of London (1662), and the French Academy of Sciences (1666). The future of scientific publication was clearly foreshadowed when, in

---

[43] Charles C. Gillispie. *The Edge of Objectivity*. Princeton, N.J. Princeton University Press. 1960. pp. 109–10.

Also: Talcott Parsons. "The Institutionalization of Scientific Investigation." *The Sociology of Science*, ed. Bernard Barber and Walter Hirsch. Glencoe, Illinois. Free Press. 1962. pp. 7–15.

1665, Denis de Sallo published the first volume of the *Journal des sçavans*, which in its earlier years was dominantly concerned with the work of the scientific societies. During this same year the Royal Society, founded on a pattern set forth many decades before by Francis Bacon,[44] began its long and important series *Philosophical Transactions,* and, as Martha Ornstein observed, "all subsequent scientific periodicals developed in imitation of these two."[45]

It is important to note, however, that the learning of this early period in the history of professional association was retrospective and book-centered. These scholars, these savants, these wise men, who were devoting themselves to the discovery of new knowledge, sought it through reexamination of that which had been accumulated in the past. To be sure, there was a limited amount of crude apparatus from the use of which men were able to probe somewhat more deeply into the nature of their physical environment than was possible with the unaided senses, but their probing was largely book-, rather than laboratory-centered. Even Bacon, the great exponent of the inductive method and the wringing from Nature of her secrets, has left no record of any extensive experimentation. Though this early science drew from, and built upon, the past, it was historical only in the sense that it made use of a great heritage of accumulated record from which it drew its substance. In the fields of the pure and applied sciences this historical approach was dominant. Miss Ornstein has estimated that in the publications of the first years of the *Journal des sçavans*, "possibly one-third of the articles are on historical researches."[46] In those instances in which elementary laboratory investigations were employed, the techniques developed, and the results, were carefully checked against the published findings of previous investigators. Much of the scholarship, though, was a kind of intellectual rumination of the writings of others, but this too can be a sign of ferment. To quote Newton's epigram, "If I have seen farther, it is by standing on the shoulders of giants."

As learning advanced and became increasingly specialized, this was reflected in the professional association and in the journal publication. Though these specialized journals were designed to meet the needs of their immediate clientele, the wider dissemination of such publication

---

44 Jesse H. Shera. "The Dignity and Advancement of Bacon." *College and Research Libraries.* vol. 23 (January 1962), pp. 18–23.

45 Martha Ornstein. *The Role of Scientific Societies in the Seventeenth Century.* Chicago. University of Chicago Press. 1938. p. 202.

46 *Ibid.* p. 201.

brought the innovations and discoveries of one field to the scholars of another, and thus made possible the development of social cohesion among groups the members of which might otherwise have found communication difficult.

## THE LIBRARY AS A LINK IN THE COMMUNICATION CHAIN

The library is a product of cultural maturation.[47] It came into being when societies ceased to be nomadic and became urbanized, and when graphic records became important to the effective operation of organized human relationships. There is no record of when, or how, libraries began, but one can assume, from the scattered and fragmentary evidence that has survived, that early libraries were essentially archival—storage places for the preservation of records that were necessary for the transaction of business or commerce, the administration of the state, and the communication of belief to succeeding generations. In short, libraries were nothing more than a facility for extending the effective life of the written word. Thus, from the very beginning the library has been a product of social organization and a handmaiden of scholarship, and during those centuries when learning was so intensely individualistic it was almost the sole resource of the philosophers, the literati, the probers of the unknown. The library was created of, by, and for the elite; not until the nineteenth century did it begin to assume any responsibility for the masses. The contents of the library were closely guarded, partly because the materials were scarce and partly because they contained information that was held to be inappropriate for indiscriminate dissemination because it was vital to the state.

This close association of the library with the elite soon brought to the library a prestigious status, and it is not surprising that the patronage or possession of a library soon came to be a symbol of social position and opulence. Men in positions of power or influence in public life, such as the Ptolemies, a Charlemagne, or a Cardinal Mazarin, began to build libraries. Such men were patrons of literature and learning, and to their libraries they brought such scholars as Demetrius of Phalerum, Richard de Bury, or Gabriel Naudé to collect materials, keep them in order, and see that they were made available to those who had the right

---

[47] See: Jesse H. Shera. *The Sociological Foundations of Librarianship.* Bombay. Asia Publishing House. 1970.

to their use. The relationship between the library user and those in control of the library was also intensely personal. Because the doors of the library could be opened or closed at will, according to the personal whim of those in authority, the course, as well as the flow, of scholarship was always under the authority of the Establishment. There were no inherent rights, only special privilege.

With the rise of scholasticism, the founding of monasteries and cathedral schools, the establishment of the great universities, and the coming of the Renaissance and Reformation, accessibility to libraries was somewhat broadened, but the mission of the library was still restricted to service to the elite. The invention of printing and the great proliferation of recorded information that was stimulated by the Enlightenment brought to these earlier barriers to library resources a steady and continuing dissolution. Slowly there began to develop a formalized body of library practice, heralded in 1345 by the *Philobiblion* of Richard de Bury, and the even more important *Avis pour Dresser une Bibliothèque* of Gabriel Naudé, which first appeared in 1627 and was translated into English in 1661 by the famous diarist, John Evelyn.[48] The role of bibliography as an instrument in the communication process and as an aspect of scholarship had, of course, been recognized much earlier. In the latter half of the thirteenth century, the Franciscans compiled the *Registrum librorum Angliae* and, early in the fifteenth century, John Boston de Bury prepared a union list of manuscripts owned by the English monastic libraries, under the title *Catalogus scriptorum ecclesiae*. Perhaps of even greater significance was the appearance in 1494 of Johann Tritheim's *Liber de scriptoribus ecclesiasticis*, a chronological listing of the writings mainly, but not exclusively, ecclesiastical, of nearly one thousand authors. A year later he published at Mainz his *Catalogus illustrium virorum Germaniae*, in which were chronologically enumerated over two thousand works by more than three hundred authors.

During the manuscript age, copies of works were so rare that it was a matter of great importance to the scholar to know where a copy of a given title might be found. But as a rule, such information was passed from person to person and became part of the substance of scholarship. As a result, bibliographic compilations were relatively few until the invention of printing made impossible the retention of such information in

---

48 Richard de Bury. *Philobiblion*, intro. Archer Taylor. Berkeley. University of California Press. 1948.

   Gabriel Naudé. *Advice on Establishing a Library*, intro. Archer Taylor. Berkeley. University of California Press. 1950.

the human memory. Between 1450 and 1500, some thirteen thousand incunabula were issued. In 1545, Konrad Gesner published his *Bibliotheca universalis* and rightfully earned the title of "the father of universal bibliography." The magnitude of the task confronting Gesner, even at this early stage, may be seen in the fact that this work, a folio of thirteen hundred pages, listed approximately twelve thousand titles—all the Latin, Greek, and Hebrew books known to Gesner.[49]

Thus by the end of the sixteenth century the volume of recorded knowledge had become so great that scholars felt the need for some systematization of it. Problems of bibliographic organization are at least as old as the printed book itself, and the need for bibliography as a channel of the communication system becomes intensified with each change in the volume and methods of publication. Bibliography, like the library, is to be seen as an instrument for widening the scholarship of the culture to an ever increasing segment of the population.[50]

The accessibility of library resources was further increased when the university libraries began slowly to open their doors to scholars and other professional groups, notably the law and the clergy, who were beyond the strict confines of academic walls. But the most drastic transformation in the role of the library in the democratization of scholarship came toward the close of the seventeenth century and, in America, the beginning of the eighteenth, when groups of individuals from all walks of life began to associate for the purpose of creating a library that would make a modest supply of books available to those who otherwise would have been denied such benefits. These voluntary associations assumed a variety

---

[49] Three years later Gesner published his *Bandectarum sive partitionum universalium*, in which the titles in the preceding compilation were arranged according to subject classes. See: Theodore Bestermann. *The Beginnings of Systematic Bibliography*. Oxford. Oxford University Press. 1935.

Ernest A. Savage. "Cooperative Bibliography in the Thirteenth and Fifteenth Centuries." *Special Librarianship in General Libraries*. London. Grafton. 1939. pp. 285–310.

Jesse H. Shera. *Historians, Books, and Libraries*. Cleveland. Western Reserve University Press. 1953. pp. 35–37.

John L. Thornton. *Chronology of Librarianship*. London. Grafton. 1941. pp. 157–66.

P. Delaunay. "Humanism and Encyclopedism." *The Beginnings of Modern Science*, ed. René Taton. New York. Basic Books. 1958. pp. 3–10.

[50] Margaret E. Egan and Jesse H. Shera. "Foundations of a Theory of Bibliography." *Library Quarterly*. vol. 22 (April 1952), pp. 125–37. Reprinted in Jesse H. Shera *Libraries and the Organization of Knowledge*. London. Crosby Lockwood. 1965. pp. 18–33.

of forms: simple book clubs, more formally structured proprietary or corporate organizations, rental collections, Sunday school libraries, parish libraries, and, occasionally, small collections of books maintained by municipalities and towns.

Seeking the all too meager resources of these collections came, not only the professional men of the community, the doctors, the lawyers, the teachers, and the ministers, but also the artisans, the laborers, the young merchants' clerks, all in pursuit of information and knowledge that would improve their skills and advance their occupational status. There came too the girls from the textile mills of southern New England, the children, the housewives, and even the merchant princes of Rhode Island, the Middle-Atlantic colonies, and the Southern plantations. They came for a variety of reasons, and by no means all of them were impelled by a consummate dedication to the life of the scholar. But the eagerness with which these libraries were established and the books which were placed on their shelves are eloquent testimony to the passing of the old monopoly of learning by a privileged few.[51] In the middle of the nineteenth century, the citizenry of Boston established their public library, the first such major collection to be created as an aspect of municipal government, and thereby established the principle that free access to books was, in a democracy, a fundamental human right.[52] This idea was implicit in the proceedings of the librarians' conference of 1853, and it was certainly present in the first American Library Association conference of 1876.

To be sure, Edward Everett argued strongly that the newly formed Boston Public Library should provide books that would have little use beyond a select group of highly educated individuals, and George Ticknor, for all his insistence upon the need for a public library that would provide reading materials for the entire population, was actually not far behind his colleague on the Boston library board; but not many years were to pass before the public library began to desert the more definitely articulated demands of its original clientele and sought to direct its attention toward the reading interests of people in the mass. Then it began to assume its present structure and become a people-centered, or centrifugal, rather than a book-centered, or centripetal, agency. This shift in point of view, made in the declining years of the nineteenth century, drew the

[51] Jesse H. Shera. *Foundations of the Public Library.* Chicago. University of Chicago Press. 1949. Chapters 3 and 4; Gladys Spencer. *The Chicago Public Library; Origins and Backgrounds.* Chicago. University of Chicago Press. 1943. Chapter 15.

[52] *Report to the Trustees. July 1852.* Boston Public Library. (Boston City Document No. 37) Boston. 1852.

attention and professional concern of the great majority of public librarians away from the communication of specialized information to an elite clientele as the central focus of librarianship, and substituted for it an almost religious dedication to the cause of popular education; they called it "popular culture."[53]

The history of the library as an agency of communication, then, reveals a variety of forces and pressures that have shaped and reshaped its social role. In its earlier stages it was an archive, where the records essential to the preservation of the church or state, were preserved from destruction. As such it was a handmaiden of power and authority, and locked behind its doors was the very substance of monarchy in ecclesiastical as well as civil affairs. But it was also, in part, a museum of bookish treasures, a storehouse of artifacts, and thus it became a symbol of social position. It was also a manifestation of conspicuous consumption, one of the means by which the nobility and men of property displayed their achievements. For centuries the library was a laboratory, often the only laboratory, the sole resource of the scholars by whom it was used. So it served learning, as it served the nobility, in the interests of special privilege.

After the breakup of the old order, and in the wake of the revolutions, both political and industrial, that swept the continent of Europe in the nineteenth century, new social groups, or classes, came to power and the library was called upon to serve "the common man." It brought to-

---

[53] By contrast, many of the world's greatest libraries, particularly those in Europe, were centripetal, drawing toward their vortices the cream of their coeval scholarship. Often they began as clusters of private libraries, the personal collection of some savant with a strongly acquisitive instinct and the financial resources for its indulgence. Such collections were reshaped to meet the needs of successive owners as they passed, through inheritance or by sale, from generation to generation, until they found a final resting place in a monastery, a university, or a municipal library. But this merging of ownership did not alter their original character, nor did the change affect their objective. They still strove after excellence—the most complete collection of the most authoritative works, in whatever field, be it law, medicine, theology, or belles letters. They held fast to their precious books and manuscripts and paid scant heed, indeed, to the user. The custodians knew that their resources would appeal only to that class of readers who could make use of such volumes and that their collections were sufficiently great of their kind that those who needed them would seek them out. That these users were but few in number was no cause for concern.

See: Jesse H. Shera. "Emergence of a New Institutional Structure for the Dissemination of Specialized Information." *American Documentation.* vol. 4, no. 4 (October 1953), p. 164. Reprinted in his *Libraries and the Organization of Knowledge.* pp. 34–50.

gether, perhaps for the first time in its long history, not a tight homogeneous little world of philosophers, divines, or scientists, but men from many walks of life, men who were playing many roles, men who demanded of the library quite different benefits, but who might find in its resources a common bond of understanding.

Thus in an age of specialization, of social fragmentation, the library like the communication system of which it is a part, can become a great cohesive force at a time when social cohesion is most vital. But unlike the mass media of communication it need not be an instrument for the achievement of conformity. It is, and should remain, the stronghold of individualism. Whereas the mass media, the newspaper, radio, television, are declaratory, the library is interrogative. To the library men come seeking truth, each in his own way and for his own ends. In the library the patron is not told what to think or when to think it, but in his search each must discover for himself the thoughts and opinions of others and try to understand them, to appreciate them for what they are, even though he may not share them. The library, then, must be a force for understanding, for cohesion, in a world of antagonisms, conflict, and specialization, but it must be a unifying, not a homogenizing force. The social role of the library is a very complex role and the responsibilities which society, often quite unwittingly, has placed upon it are very heavy. Certainly there is no one library form that can achieve them all; there must be many types of libraries to assume so varied a burden. But there is a unity in the library process as an agent of communication. In the character of that unity lies the key to the dilemma which the library faces today.

Gone forever is the librarian as sorcerer-priest with his papyrus rolls, as monastic recluse pouring over vellum codices of Biblical texts and commentary, as bibliophile perched high on a ladder in a book-lined vaulted chamber, as maiden aunt presiding, with muted voice and padded footstep, over the whispered silence of the library reading room. Each in his own way was a response to the social need of his time, the creation of the cultural milieu in which he pursued his career; and by the same token, and for the same reasons, the modern librarian, in whatever branch of librarianship he elects to serve, must be well educated, professionally competent, and highly qualified to play an important part in the communication process of today's world.

Four

# An Epistemological Foundation for Library Science

"I have often thought," wrote George Beadle in *Phage and the Origins of Molecular Biology*, "how much more interesting science would be if those who created it told how it really happened, rather than report it logically and impersonally as they so often do in scientific papers. This is not easy, because of normal modesty and reticence, reluctance to tell the whole truth, and protective tendencies towards others."[1] Beadle's wish comes very close to being fulfilled by James Watson's account of the discovery of the structure of DNA.[2] In the pages of *The Double Helix*, are recorded the steps and circumstances involved in an act of creativity, a major scientific discovery. But Watson's book deals with the interaction of no more than the five characters of his drama and their search for scientific knowledge; it is, as it had to be, a record of the drive for new knowledge by only a few individuals.

As the need for information and knowledge drives the individual, so also it drives the society.[3] It is the basis of collective, as well as of individ-

[1] George W. Beadle. "Biochemical Genetics: Some Recollections." *Phage and the Origins of Molecular Biology*, ed. John Cairns, Gunther S. Stent, and James D. Watson. Cold Spring Harbor, Mass. Cold Spring Harbor Laboratory of Quantitative Biology. 1967. p. 23.

[2] James D. Watson. *The Double Helix*. New York. Athenaeum. 1968.

[3] The rest of this chapter is an extension and revision of the author's "An Epistemolog-

ual, behavior. As the brain deteriorates when deprived of information to be processed, so a society, if it is to avoid decay, must make constant provision for the acquisition and assimilation of new information and knowledge. But to be transmitted within, and absorbed by, any group, that which is known must be communicated and communicable. Society knows both more and less than the individual; collectively it knows the entire contents of all the encyclopedias it has produced and all the contributions to the proceedings of all the learned societies. But it does not know the warm and intimate experiences that make up the beauty and texture of an individual life. Each individual possesses, through his personal experiences, knowledge not possessed by those whose experiences have been different. Because perfect communication does not exist, much of this knowledge can never be shared, even by those with unusual talent in the creative arts. But knowledge and language, which is social in origin, are essentially inseparable, for language is the symbolic structuring of knowledge into communicable form, and because it is the agent by which knowledge is communicated, it can shape the knowledge both of the individual and of the group.[4] Modern society is a duality of action and thought bound together by the communication system. Without language—a system of communication—group action, if indeed it can be said to exist at all, becomes no more than the product of fortuitous circumstance or random behavior—the mere swarming of agglomerations of individual organisms, like Emerson's four snakes at Fresh Pond, gliding up and down a hollow "for no purpose that I could see—not to eat, not for love, but only gliding."[5]

## THE NEED FOR A NEW EPISTEMOLOGICAL DISCIPLINE

The communication process is a duality of system and message, of that which is transmitted as well as the manner of its transmission. Therefore, the librarian must see his role in the communication process as being more than a link in a chain; he must also concern himself with the knowledge he communicates, and the importance of that knowledge both to the individual and to society. Yet the study of the nature of knowledge, and

---

ical Foundation for Library Science" (*Foundations of Access to Knowledge*, ed. Edward B. Montgomery. Syracuse, N.Y., Syracuse University Press. 1968. pp. 7–25), and is used here with the permission of the editor.

[4] See: Bertrand Russell. *Human Knowledge, Its Scope and Limits.* New York. Simon and Schuster. 1948. Chapter 1.

[5] Entry in his Journal for April 11, 1834.

the relationship between the structure of knowledge as it has developed in contemporary civilization and the librarian's tools for intellectual access to that knowledge, have received almost no attention and certainly no intensive exploration.

We are, therefore, here concerned with the need for a new epistemological discipline, a body of new knowledge about knowledge itself. The manner in which knowledge has developed and has been augmented has long been a subject of study, but the ways in which knowledge is coordinated, integrated, and put to work is, as yet, an almost unrecognized field for investigation. There have been systems of logic and formulations of scientific method. Man knows with some exactness how scientific knowledge is accumulated and transmitted from one generation to another; historians of science, for example, have become increasingly interested in the growth of scientific knowledge.[6] Many philosophers have speculated about the nature of knowledge, its sources, methods, limits of validity, and relation to truth. Until relatively recent times, epistemology was a branch of speculative philosophy, concerned with *how* we know. The evolution of the science of psychology, however, left epistemology relatively poor in intellectual substance. Today, "scientific epistemology," to use Eddington's term, has transformed the earlier philosophic and speculative approach into a scientific, and largely theoretical study that is concerned primarily with what man cannot know, i.e., with the *limits* of human knowledge. In the terminology of cybernetics, these limits are referred to as "constraints" on knowing. Such constraints may be physical, biological (or physiological), psychological, or determined jointly by the environment and the organic and electronic structuring of the human body. But almost invariably the study of epistemology has been seen against the background of the intellectual processes of the individual.[7] The psychologists have carried the philosophers' speculations into the laboratory and have made some progress in understanding mental behavior—but,

---

[6] See: Karl R. Popper. *Conjectures and Refutations*. London. Routledge. 1963. Also: Karl R. Popper. *The Logic of Scientific Discovery*. New York. Basic Books. 1959; Philip P. Wiener and Aaron Noland, eds. *The Roots of Scientific Thought*. New York. Basic Books. 1957; Lewis S. Feuer. *The Scientific Intellectual*. New York. Basic Books. 1963; Bernard Barber and Walter Hirsch, eds., *The Sociology of Science*. Glencoe, Ill. Free Press. 1962; Susanne K. Langer. *Mind: An Essay on Human Feeling*. Baltimore. Johns Hopkins University Press. 1967; Arthur Koestler. *The Act of Creation*. New York. Macmillan. 1964.

[7] Hans Reichenbach. *Experience and Prediction*. Chicago. University of Chicago Press. 1938; Michael Polanyi. *Personal Knowledge*. Chicago. University of Chicago Press. 1958; Karl Mannheim. *Ideology and Utopia*. New York. Harcourt Brace. 1936.

again, of the individual. Neither epistemologists nor psychologists have developed an ordered and comprehensive body of knowledge about intellectual differentiation and the integration of knowledge within a complex social organization. The sociologists, though they have directed their attention toward the behavior of men in groups, have paid scant heed to the intellectual forces that shape social structures and institutions.

The new discipline that is envisaged here (and for which, for want of a better name, Margaret E. Egan originated the phrase, *social epistemology*)[8] should provide a framework for the investigation of the complex problem of the nature of the intellectual process in society—a study of the ways in which society as a whole achieves a perceptive relation to its total environment. It should lift the study of intellectual life from that of a scrutiny of the individual to an inquiry into the means by which a society, nation, or culture achieves understanding of stimuli which act upon it. The focus of this new discipline should be upon the production, flow, integration, and consumption of communicated thought throughout the social fabric. From such a discipline should emerge a new body of knowledge about, and a new synthesis of, the interaction between knowledge and social activity. In recent years there have appeared two important books that are aimed in the direction of providing a foundation for the kind of discipline here indicated.[9] Neither work could properly be called "social epistemology" as the term is here employed, but each is dealing in certain ways with the problems with which "social epistemology" is concerned.

In recent years William Goffman, Dean of the School of Library

---

[8] So far as the present writer knows, Miss Egan never used the phrase in any published writing, but she used it frequently in class lectures and in conversation.

L. B. Heilprin has criticized the term for being redundant, if not internally inconsistent or paradoxical. "Social epistemology," he has written, ". . . is described as a new kind of epistemology—a theory of knowledge about how society knows as a whole. This apparently contrasts it with traditional epistemology . . . based on the knowledge of the individual. However, we know only as individuals, never as a group or a society. The referent of the concept 'society' is not a single superbeing but a set of individuals. . . . Evidently [the intent is] to place a new emphasis on an old area. We need to study that part of access to knowledge which affects us all and on which we must act together." Laurence B. Heilprin. "Critique and Response to Paper by Jesse H. Shera 'An Epistemological Foundation for Library Science,' Symposium on the Foundations of Access to Knowledge, Syracuse University, July 28–30, 1965." *The Foundations of Access to Knowledge*, ed. Edward B. Montgomery. Syracuse, N.Y. Syracuse University Press. 1968. pp. 26–27.

[9] Fritz Machlup. *The Production and Distribution of Knowledge in the United States.* Princeton. Princeton University Press. 1962; and Frederick Harbison and Charles A. Myers. *Education, Manpower and Economic Growth.* New York. McGraw-Hill. 1963.

Science, Case Western Reserve University, has been working on a mathematical approach to the dissemination of scientific ideas[10] and, together with Dr. Vaun Newill, formerly of the Medical School faculty of the same university, has been developing an analogy between the dissemination of scientific knowledge and the spread of epidemics.[11]

Though "social epistemology" should have its own corpus of theoretical knowledge, it should be truly interdisciplinary in its heavy dependence upon many fields—sociology, anthropology, linguistics, economics, the physiology of the human nervous system, psychology, mathematics, and information theory, to name but a few of the most conspicuous areas. It may also be expected to have practical results, and one of the most practical applications will be in librarianship, for there exists a very important affinity between it and the role of the librarian in society. Librarianship, whether its practitioners recognize it or not, is based on epistemological foundations. The aim of librarianship at whatever intellectual level it may operate is, as has been shown in the earlier chapters of this study, to bring to the point of maximum efficiency the social utility of man's graphic records, whether the patron served is a child absorbed in his first picture book or the most advanced scholar engaged in some esoteric inquiry. Clearly, if the librarian is to become an effective mediator between man and his graphic records, librarianship must be much more than a bundle of tricks taught in a trade school for finding a particular book on a particular shelf for a particular patron with a particular need. Such techniques have a place in the skills of the librarian, but the librarian will do his job badly if he does not possess a true mastery over the means of access to recorded knowledge. This mastery implies not only a thorough understanding of the nature of that knowledge, but also an appreciation of the role of knowledge in that part of society in which he operates. If the librarian's bibliographic and information systems are to be structured to conform as closely as possible to man's uses of recorded knowledge,

---

[10] William Goffman. "A Mathematical Approach to the Spread of Scientific Ideas—The History of the Mast Cell Research." *Nature.* London. vol. 212, no. 5061 (October 29, 1966), pp. 449–52.

[11] William Goffman and Vaun A. Newill. "Generalization of Epidemic Theory; An Application to the Transmission of Ideas." *Nature.* London. vol. 204, no. 4955 (October 7, 1964), pp. 225–28.

William Goffman. "An Epidemic Process in an Open Population." *Nature.* London. vol. 205, no. 4973 (February 20, 1965), pp. 831–32.

William Goffman and Vaun A. Newill. "Communication and the Epidemic Process." *Proceedings of the Royal Society.* Series A. vol. 298, no. 1454 (May 2, 1967), pp. 316–34.

the theoretical foundations of his profession must eventually provide answers to such questions as:

The problem of cognition—how man knows.

The problem of social cognition—the ways in which society knows and the nature of the sociopsychological system by means of which personal knowledge becomes social knowledge.

The problem of the history and philosophy of knowledge as they have evolved through time and in variant cultures.

The problem of existing bibliographic mechanisms and systems and the extent to which they are in congruence with the realities of the communication process and the findings of epistemological inquiry.

Traditionally, the tools and methods of the librarian for the control of his collection—his classification schemes, subject headings, indexes, and other devices for the subject analysis of bibliographic units—have been based on the assumption of permanent, or relatively permanent, relationships among the several branches of knowledge. Thus they tend to become largely inflexible, closed, fragmented and nonholistic systems into which each unit of information is fitted. The structure and communication of knowledge, by contrast, form an open system which changes as the functions and needs of the individual and society shift to accommodate the increasing differentiation of knowledge as well as its consolidation resulting from the coalescence of two or more disciplines.

Marjorie Grene, taking as her point of departure her interpretation of the theory of knowledge developed by Michael Polanyi,[12] has set forth the thesis that modern philosophy is held captive by the alleged objectivity of science. Therefore, philosophy has been unable to develop an adequate theory of knowledge, for knowledge is a venture of living individuals endeavoring to make sense of their experience through the limited endowments of their time and space. She argues that philosophy in the tradition of Descartes and Newton has been powerless to interpret living nature,

---

[12] Michael Polanyi. *Personal Knowledge*. Chicago. University of Chicago Press. 1958. Polanyi holds that the term is not internally inconsistent despite the fact that knowledge is customarily regarded as being impersonal, universally established, objective, and true. He holds that there is personal participation of the knower in all acts of understanding, but our understanding is not, thereby, made subjective, it is objective in the sense of establishing contact with a hidden reality. Comprehension is neither an arbitrary act nor a passive experience, but a responsible act claiming universal validity.

that we have come to the end of the lifeless world of objectivism and are in the midst of a philosophical revolution that is drastically revising the concept of knowledge. Thus, from her study of the theories of knowledge held by Hume, Kant, neo-Darwinism, Whitehead, Merleau-Ponty, and Polanyi, she reaches the conclusion that knowledge is inescapably conjectural.[13]

## THE NATURE OF KNOWLEDGE

Thus one is brought squarely into confrontation with the basic problem of what knowledge *is*. Webster's Third Edition records no less than twelve definitions, all but two of which describe the term as denoting a "fact or condition." The compilation accepts seven terms (including *knowledge* itself!) as synonyms—science, learning, erudition, scholarship, information, and lore—saying that they "agree in signifying what is or can be known." It is interesting that the definition of knowledge as *that which is known* is considered by the pundits of Springfield to apply *only* to that which is known by society: "The sum total of what is known: the whole body of truth, fact, information, principles, or other objects of cognition acquired by mankind."

The compilers of the *Syntopicon of the Great Books of the Western World*, after having surveyed the use of the term by the authors of the Hutchins-Adler classics, conclude that "knowledge, like being, is a term of comprehensive scope," and that "its comprehensiveness is, in a way, correlative with that of being." For the only thing, they argue, that cannot be an object of knowledge, which cannot be thought about in any way except negatively, is that which has no being of any sort, in short— *nothing*. Admittedly, not all things may be known to man, but things beyond man's knowledge are knowable. Thus, the definition of knowledge extends to all things knowable, to all kinds of knowers, to all the modes of knowledge, and all the methods of knowing.[14]

Karl Deutsch holds that, though knowledge is a broader concept than "mere data suitable for tabulating," the term includes "data and quantitative formulae," along with "understanding, 'knowing' what to expect, how to act, and even how to compose or manage one's own mind." It in-

---

[13] Marjorie Grene. *The Knower and the Known*. London. Faber and Faber. 1966.
[14] Mortimer J. Adler and William Gorman, eds., *The Great Ideas; A Syntopicon of the Great Books of the Western World*. Chicago. Encyclopedia Britannica. 1952. vol. 1, p. 880.

cludes both the " 'tragic knowledge' of such philosophers as Karl Jaspers," and intuitive knowledge, "or what Pascal calls the 'esprit de finesse.' " The acquisition of knowledge, both analytic and synthetic, factual and abstract, repetitive and unique, forms "a part of the growing-up process of every child, as he remembers and orders his experience, and as he begins to project inferences from it into the future, and it becomes the main vocation of some adults." Similarly, on the social level, knowledge is used by every human group to abstract data "from its experiences and [use] them to guide its future behavior."[15]

Kenneth Boulding has used the term *Image* for that which we would call knowledge. Thus he writes in defense of his terminology: "What I have been talking about is knowledge. Knowledge, perhaps, is not a good word for this. Perhaps one would rather say *Image* of the world. Knowledge has an implication of validity, of truth. What I am talking about is what I believe to be true, my subjective knowledge. It is this Image that largely governs my behavior."[16] But he warns that a careful distinction must be made between this Image and the messages that reach it, for "the messages consist of *information* in the sense that they are structured experiences. . . . *The meaning of a message is the change which it produces in the image.*"[17] In the great majority of encounters between message and Image the latter remains unchanged; that is, much of the information received has little impact upon knowledge. But the message may alter the Image in some regular and well-defined way, in which case the information may be said to constitute an addition to, or clarification or substantiation of, existing knowledge. In other instances the message—the information—may cast doubt upon the Image and thus undermine confidence in some aspect of knowledge, which in turn may stimulate the desire for additional information; for instability in the Image engenders emotional distress and a certain loss in orientation. Again, the information may work a revolutionary change in the Image: "Sometimes a message hits some sort of nucleus or supporting structure in the image, and the whole thing changes in a quite radical way,"[18] as the work of Darwin revolutionized the scholarship of his own, and succeeding, gen-

[15] Karl W. Deutsch. "Scientific and Humanistic Knowledge in the Growth of Civilization." *Science and the Creative Spirit*, ed. Harcourt Brown. Toronto. University of Toronto Press. 1958.

[16] Kenneth Boulding. *The Image*. Ann Arbor. University of Michigan Press. 1956. pp. 5–6.

[17] *Ibid*. p. 7. (Italics throughout are his.)

[18] *Ibid*. p. 8.

erations and wrought a drastic revolution in man's knowledge of himself and his place in the universe.

This subjective knowledge structure—the Image—incorporates a system of values according to which certain types of information are rated on a series of scales of "betterness" or "worseness" as determined by the individual, organization, society, or culture. These value scales play such an important role in determining the effect of information upon knowledge, that one might go so far as to say that there are no "facts" in the absolute sense—only messages filtered through a changeable value system.

We follow Boulding in distinguishing between information and knowledge, despite Fritz Machlup's proposal "that we get rid of the duplication 'knowledge and information.' . . . We may occasionally refer to certain kinds of knowledge as 'information,' but we shall avoid the redundant phrase 'knowledge *and* information.' "[19] The present writer, however, sees a clear distinction between the two, probably derived from the terminology of information theorists: information is the input of knowledge, and is always received through the senses, no matter what or how many devices may intervene between transmitter and receptor. The word *information* is a collective noun for a part of the sum total of that which can be known, and in our opinion it is a misuse to employ it to represent the whole of knowledge.

Knowledge, on the other hand, is that which an individual, a group, or a culture, "knows," and there can be no knowledge without a knower. Stated another way, knowledge is everything an organism has learned or assimilated—values as well as facts or information—organized according to whatever concepts, images, or relations it has been able to master.[20] From the universe of experience, man individually and society collectively select what Margenau has called the *cognitive component*—that which is "known" and hence the substance of knowledge.[21] Knowledge exists as soon as one person has acquired "it" through discovery, invention, or some other means. But it does not grow simply by the intake of messages; there is within the individual and within society an active internal organizing mechanism which shapes and molds the intake, so that knowl-

[19] Fritz Machlup. *The Production and Distribution of Knowledge in the United States.* Princeton. Princeton University Press. 1962. p. 8.

[20] Cf. George A. Miller, Eugene Galanter, and Karl H. Pribram. *Plans and the Structure of Behavior.* New York. Holt. 1960. p. 18.

[21] Henry Margenau. *Open Vistas.* New Haven. Yale University Press. 1961. p. 29.

edge becomes more than the sum of the stimuli that each organism receives.

Knowledge is always *of* or *about* an actual or supposed object. This characteristic Ledger Wood has called "referential transcendence (that is, the intellectual *milieu*)," which itself is an indispensable characteristic of all knowledge, and is responsible, Wood contends, in large measure for the structure of what he calls the *knowledge-situation*. This cognitive transcendence may be either perceptual, relating to an outer reality or assumed reality either present or remembered, or conceptual, directed toward abstract systems or universes. Cognitive transcendence, mysterious as it is, gives man the power to conceptualize. It relates exclusively to conscious content and does not characterize extramental objects. Strictly speaking, one object can never refer to another object, even though the one may signify the other by virtue of the inclusion of the two in the same referential scheme. Reference is a property characteristic only of the mind, and only the mind can refer one object to another.[22] Thus the knowledge-situation, and especially the principle of cognitive transcendence, lies at the foundation of all facets of the library as an information system, its subject analyses, and its reference operations.

The extent to which the library as an information system is involved in the knowledge-situation is not accidental. The use of the library and the knowledge-situation are generically related inasmuch as the former is one manifestation of the latter. The knowledge-situation, or knowledge-process, is a unity of subject, vehicle, and object. Expressed in psychological terms, the subject is the *self*, the perceiver; it may even be understood as the simple act of awareness. The vehicle encompasses all that is given to the subject through which it knows the object. The object is the ultimate goal or referent of knowledge; it is that which the knowledge is "about." Transferred to the library situation, these terms may be illustrated thus:

| | | Intellectual Content of |
|---|---|---|
| The Library User | The Library's Bibliographic | the Library |
| ——————→ | Apparatus | Store ——————→ |
| (Subject) | (Vehicle) | (Object) |

Thus, the library is more than an important link in the communication chain; as an intellectual system it is part of the total knowledge-situation.

---

22 Ledger Wood. *The Analysis of Knowledge*. London. Allen and Unwin. 1940. Chapter 1. Cf. William James's treatment of *Erkenntnisstheorie* in *Psychology*. New York. Holt. 1890. vol. 1, pp. 216–23.

The librarian must be concerned not only with that which is known, but also with the intellectual condition or state of knowing. This condition is both personal and social, and the librarian must operate in two worlds at once, the microcosm of the individual and the macrocosm of the culture in which the individual resides and with which he must work out a harmonious relationship.

## THE CLASSIFICATION OF KNOWLEDGE

The classification of knowledge is not a form of mental exercise pursued merely for the entertainment of philosophers. Classification is a form of analysis, and often it can be more enlightening than definition in establishing the nature and function of knowledge in society. But classification can be of little value unless its purpose (or purposes) is stated. An exhaustive classification is closely akin to definition; a less refined classification involves less precise definitions; and an elementary classification indicates no more than the range and variety of that which is being classified. Even a simple enumeration of constituent elements can be of considerable value by laying bare much of the meaning of the term in question.

Knowledge can be classified in many ways for a variety of purposes according to the particular frame of reference in which it is viewed. To the librarian as well as to many philosophers, the classification of knowledge means its formal structuring in accordance with certain real or assumed relationships among the several disciplines as determined by their respective intellectual content. Man has evolved certain specialized orders for the branches of knowledge—a developmental order, a pedagogic order, a pragmatic order, and even an "order of nature" which is supposed to represent *the way things really are* as determined by an individual, or by what Bliss called the "scientific consensus."[23] Such approaches to classification are irrelevant to the present discussion, which is concerned with the nature and utilization of knowledge rather than its substantive content.

As with all attempts of man to classify phenomena, the classification of knowledge has been strongly influenced by the urge to dichotomize, to bifurcate knowledge into two parts of a whole. Thus some philosophers of science have distinguished between "scientific" and "historical" knowledge, the former being concerned with generalization and the latter with

---

[23] Henry E. Bliss. *The Organization of Knowledge and the System of the Sciences.* New York. Holt. 1929.

individual facts and unique events. Such a dichotomy confuses the valid distinction between knowledge and information, and forces upon both science and history a strange and limited meaning. Others have denominated their two divisions of knowledge "general-systematic" or "general-abstract," and "particular-concrete." To improve the discrimination of the two categories, some epistemologists have used a tri-partite distinction of "logically necessary universals," "empirically probable universals," and "particulars." Again, to divide knowledge into that which is of enduring worth and that which is of only transitory value would seem to introduce judgments which are themselves ephemeral and relative to the individual and to a given time and place. Nevertheless, if knowledge is to be classified according to the uses to which it is put, there should be some recognition of relative permanence of that utility even though it should not be a basis for classification in and of itself.

Friedrich Hayek has drawn a sharp line between "scientific knowledge"—the knowledge of general rules—and "the knowledge of particular circumstances of time and place." He regrets that "today it is almost heresy to suggest that scientific knowledge is not the sum of all knowledge," and that "it is fashionable today to minimize the importance of the knowledge of the particular circumstances of time and place."[24] "We need to remember," he adds, "only how much we have to learn in any occupation after we have completed our theoretical training, how big a part of our working life we spend learning particular jobs, and how valuable an asset in all walks of life is knowledge of people, or local conditions, and of special circumstances."[25]

The general distinction that is often made between "scientific" and all other forms of knowledge is of little value because the term "scientific" is subject to as wide a variety of interpretations and definitions as the term knowledge itself. The terms "basic" and "applied" knowledge do suggest certain functional relationships in which the latter may be said to derive from the former. But there are many instances in which an application has suggested clues to the discovery of basic concepts, and moreover the line of demarcation between the two is not always clear. "Basic" and "applied" are often only relative terms, and the two not infrequently exist in combinations in which the degree of emphasis of each can vary widely, like Polonius's classification of drama into

---

[24] Friedrich A. Hayek. *Individualism and Economic Order*. Chicago. University of Chicago Press. 1948. pp. 80–81. Originally published under the title, "The Use of Knowledge in Society." *American Economic Review*. vol. 35 (September 1945), pp. 519–30.

[25] *Ibid*. p. 80.

"... tragedy, comedy, history, pastoral, pastoral-comical, historical-pastoral, tragical-historical, tragical-comical-historical-pastoral, scene individable or poem unlimited."

Society has allocated vast resources for the production of practical knowledge in the form of technology for which a vast store of basic knowledge is a prerequisite, but, at the same time, there is much practical knowledge that is not based on anything that can be attributed to science or scholarship of any kind. Indeed, there are those who believe this statement to be true of all library technology, and who hold that the procedures and processes of the librarian have been derived from purely *ad hoc* experimentation based upon nothing more than trial and error viewed against a background of unsubstantiated assumptions about the ways people consult a library file or extract information from a book.

The Germans have long distinguished between *wissen* and *können*, or the "knowing what" and the "knowing how" of Gilbert Ryle, while Michael Polanyi has developed the concept of the "tacit dimension" and "tacit knowing," by which he means that a man knows more than he can say.[26] But a classification that is markedly superior to the simple dichotomies mentioned above has been devised by Max Scheler, who distinguished three classes of knowledge: *Herrschaftswissen*, knowledge for the sake of action or control; *Bildungswissen*, knowledge for the sake of nonmaterial culture; and *Erlosungswissen*, knowledge for the sage of salvation.[27] These three categories have been interpreted by Fritz Machlup as, respectively, instrumental knowledge, intellectual knowledge, and spiritual knowledge. Scheler denied the existence of knowledge for its own sake: "There is no such thing as knowledge just for the sake of knowing," he wrote, and he added that "the purpose of intellectual knowledge is the free self-fulfillment of all mental capacities of the individual and the continual growth of his mind."[28] Machlup has criticized Scheler's scheme because it makes no provision for transitory or ephemeral knowledge, though he concedes that such knowledge might be subsumed under instrumental knowledge.[29] He has seriously doubted whether "most of our film or television plays or our books and magazines" could be accommodated in Scheler, but again one encounters the problem of defining *knowledge*

---

[26] Michael Polanyi. *The Tacit Dimension.* Garden City, N.Y. Doubleday. 1966. Chapter 1. Also: Polanyi. *Personal Knowledge.*

[27] Max Scheler. *Die Wissensformen und die Gesellschaft.* Leipzig. Der Neue-Geist Verlag. 1926. pp. 250–51.

[28] *Ibid.* p. 251. After Machlup.

[29] Machlup. *Distribution of Knowledge.* p. 20.

and its differentiation from *information*, or mere sensory perception or stimulation.

Benjamin Bloom and his associates in their study of the taxonomy of educational objectives, have also evolved a tri-partite division of knowledge as:

1. Knowledge of specifics—the recall of specific and isolated bits of information.

2. Knowledge of ways and means of dealing with specifics—organizing, studying, judging and criticizing ideas and phenomena.

3. Knowledge of the universals and abstractions in a field—an understanding of the major ideas, schemes, and patterns by which phenomena and ideas are organized.[30]

Anthony Downs has divided all knowledge into "entertainment" knowledge, which he says is "procured solely for the edification it provides," and knowledge used in the decision-making process. The latter category he subdivided into "production" knowledge, "consumption" knowledge, and "political" knowledge.[31] His classification makes no advance over that of Scheler, and though he would seem to have satisfied Machlup's demand for the classification of ephemeral knowledge in his "entertainment" category, he does not recognize spiritual knowledge. One wonders whether he would regard it as entertainment or decision-making. Hertz and Rubenstein have classified knowledge according to the type needed by operations research teams: i.e., conceptual, empirical, procedural, stimulatory, policy, and directional.[32] But this categorization, because it is related to the needs

---

[30] Benjamin S. Bloom et al. *The Taxonomy of Educational Objectives: The Classification of Educational Goals. Handbook I. Cognitive Domain.* New York. Longmans Green. 1956. pp. 63–77.

They define knowledge as "those behavior and test situations which emphasize the remembering, either by recognition or recall, of ideas, material, or phenomena." *Ibid.* p. 62.

The authors speak of the three domains of the educational process: (1) the Cognitive—which deals with the recall or recognition of knowledge and the development of intellectual abilities and skills; (2) the Affective—which deals with changes in interests, attitudes, and values, and the development of appreciation and adequate adjustment; and (3) the Manipulative—which deals with the development of motor skills. *Ibid.* p. 7.

[31] Anthony Downs. *An Economic Theory of Democracy.* New York. Harper. 1957. p. 215.

[32] David B. Hertz and Albert H. Rubenstein. *Team Research.* New York. Eastern Technical Publication. 1953. pp. 4–11. Their classification as it relates to the information needs of research is discussed in Chapter VI.

implicit in the research process, does not provide for the role of knowledge in a number of important human activities and needs. Ledger Wood has turned to psychology for the frame of reference of his classification: Sensory Knowledge, Perception of "things"—knowledge from direct experience, Perceptual Memory—knowledge from recall, Introspective Knowledge, Knowledge of Other Selves, Conceptual Knowledge, Categorical Knowledge, Formal Knowledge, and Valuational Knowledge.[33] But, as his classification clearly shows, Wood is concerned primarily with knowledge possessed by the individual rather than knowledge as a social product.

The same observation can be made of the elaborate categorization, of the ways in which knowledge can be viewed, which the compilers of the *Syntopicon* developed from their analysis of the Great Books. Adler and Gorman have identified six ways in which knowledge can be classified:

1. According to diversity of objects.
   a. Being—becoming, intelligible—sensible, the necessary—the contingent, the eternal—the temporal, material—immaterial.
   b. Knowledge of natures or kinds as distinct from knowledge of individuals.
   c. Knowledge of fact—knowledge of ideas or relations.
   d. Phenomenal—nomenal, sensible—suprasensible.
2. According to the faculties involved in knowing.
   a. Sense perception.
   b. Memory.
   c. Rational or intellectual.
   d. Understanding, judgment, reason—intuition, imagination.
3. According to methods of means of knowing.
   a. Vision, contemplation, or intuitive as distinct from discursive.
   b. Immediate—mediated judgments, induction—reasoning, principles—conclusions.
   c. Innate—acquired.
   d. *A priori*—*a posteriori*, transcendental, or speculative—empirical.
   e. Natural—supernatural, sense or reason—faith or inspiration.
4. According to degrees of assent.
   a. Certain—probable.
   b. Types of certainty—degrees of probability.
   c. Adequate—inadequate, perfect—imperfect.

---

[33] Wood. *Analysis of Knowledge.* Chapters 2–10.

    5.  According to the end, or aim, of knowing.
        a.  Theoretical—practical, for the sake of knowing—for the sake of production.
        b.  Types of practical knowledge, the use of knowledge in production and in the direction of conduct, technical—moral.
    6.  According to the media of communicating knowledge.
        a.  Means and methods of communicating knowledge.
        b.  Value of the dissemination of knowledge, freedom of discussion.

The editors of the *Syntopicon* have also analyzed the Great books with respect to the nature of knowledge, the relation between the knower and the known, the international character of knowledge, man's natural desire and power to know, the principles of knowledge, knowledge in relation to other states of mind, the extent or limits of human knowledge, the comparison of human with other kinds of knowledge, the use and value of knowledge, the growth of human knowledge, the history of man's progress, and failure in the pursuit of knowledge.[34]

As the study of communication seeks an answer to the question "Who says what to whom, by what means, and with what effect?" so the study of the functions of knowledge in society asks the question, "Who knows, and why, and for what purpose?" Thus, there can be no absolutes in the classification of knowledge according to function. Instrumental knowledge, to use Scheler's grouping, for the professional man may be intellectual knowledge for laymen: a knowledge of thermodynamics is instrumental knowledge for the physicist and intellectual knowledge for the librarian, while the understanding of the principles of bibliographic organization is instrumental to the librarian and intellectual to the physicist. To the bibliophile, however, the lore of books is probably more spiritual than either instrumental or intellectual.

However favorably or unfavorably one may regard some of Machlup's distinctions, his classification of knowledge according to function, or as he would say, "the subjective meaning of the known to the knower," is the most useful for present purposes. He has distinguished five types of knowledge of which the first has six subordinate classes:

    1.  Practical knowledge—that which is useful in one's work, in the making of decisions, and in the determination of action. (Can be subdivided according to activity.)

---

[34] Adler and Gorman. *Syntopicon.* vol. 1, pp. 887–89. (Somewhat modified.) Note the use of dichotomy.

      a. Professional knowledge
      b. Business knowledge
      c. Workman's knowledge
      d. Political knowledge
      e. Household knowledge
      f. Other practical knowledge

2. Intellectual knowledge—that which satisfies intellectual curiosity. Usually associated with cultural values; an important ingredient in general, or liberal education.

3. Pastime knowledge. Satisfies nonintellectual curiosity and the desire for light entertainment and emotional stimulation. Usually acquired passively. (In this category Machlup's insistence upon the identification of information with knowledge becomes particularly troublesome.)

4. Spiritual knowledge—related to religious belief.

5. Unwanted, or useless, knowledge. (Here again, Machlup would appear to be speaking of information rather than of knowledge.)

Machlup raises a question about ethical knowledge which, he says, might represent a separate category, except that to the extent that it serves as a guide to action it is a part of practical knowledge, and to the degree that it represents a knowledge of values recognized by others it is a form of intellectual knowledge.

A distinction should also be made between knowledge that is subjectively new, that which has not heretofore been known to a particular individual, and that which is socially new, having not previously been known to anyone. Though the resources devoted to the generation of socially new knowledge are still relatively small compared to the vast sums spent on the dissemination of existing knowledge, it is increasing steadily as more and more of the nation's economic and intellectual capabilities are directed into research and development. Furthermore, much of the energy channeled into the production of new knowledge, in both the physical and social sciences at least, is designed to obtain generalizations about the predictable effects resulting from specified acts under certain conditions. Many of these generalizations are of enduring value, though some of the technological knowledge may be of value for only a relatively short period of time. Investigations into the rate of obsolescence of knowledge are still far from extensive and would be of tremendous value to the librarian, even though social utility is not necessarily to be measured only in terms of its rate of decay.

The above distinction between subjectively new and socially new knowledge points up a further distinction, that between knowledge dissemination and knowledge production. From modern communication theory comes a description of the process by which information is transferred from one unit to another within a system. The transmitter selects the message from the information store, or aggregate of stimuli, and communicates it to the receiver over the network or channel that is available, usually after encoding it into a "signal." The receiver, after decoding the message, incorporates it into his own information store. Upon processing by the receptor, the information received becomes knowledge.

Though there appears to be good reason for faith in the progress of human knowledge, understanding of the process of knowledge growth is still lamentably inadequate. S. R. Ranganathan has suggested that knowledge grows, or, more specifically, throws forth new subjects, in four major ways: denudation, dissection, lamination, and loose-assemblage. These he has illustrated as a series of circular diagrams shown in Figure 4-1. The concept of denudation Ranganathan has derived from geology, where it signifies the exposure of formations or structures through the removal of overlying material; by analogy, an innovation or breakthrough in knowledge may expose an entirely new area of investigation and reveal an unsuspected source of information. Dissection is the fragmentation of a field into two or more segments which may or may not retain their association with the parent discipline, depending upon the magnitude and depth of the cleavage and the sociological character of the dissociation. Lamination is the association or federation of two or more fields because of the emergence of common elements of concern, as illustrated by the rise in recent decades of interdisciplinary studies. Loose assemblage differs from lamination mainly in the degree of the intensity of association. It, too, works to weaken the conventional barriers between disciplines, though its results may be limited mainly to "borrowings" by one field from another in order to improve insights and understanding.

In a recent study of the kinds of bonds between two subject fields, Ranganathan has revised his terminology, though this does not alter materially his analysis of knowledge growth and intraknowledge relationships. He now employs the term "fission" to replace the earlier terms *dissection* and *denudation*. "Fission," he has written, "gives canonical division of a main subject."[35] But what is more important for the present discussion than his terminological revision, he has added to his list "fusion," though he has not as yet fully developed this concept. Thus he has written:

---

[35] S. R. Ranganathan. "Kinds of Bonds Between Two Subjects, Including Fusion Bond." *DRTC Seminar Paper. B*. 1967. p. 35. (Mimeographed.)

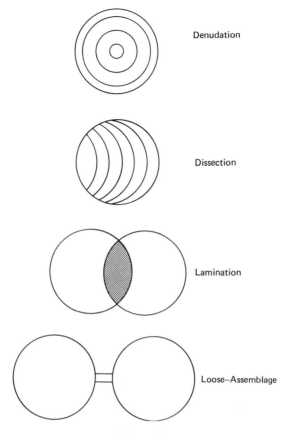

**Figure 4-1.**

"We have just now begun to see the possibility of a fifth way in which two Main Subjects may be bonded. We propose to call it 'Fusion.' In Fusion, the two Main Subjects bonded lose their individuality . . . the Subject which is the result of the Fusion can have its own set of compound subjects going with it."[36]

But Ranganathan has cautioned that "the field of knowledge is an infinite universe. So we do not know all its specific subjects. It is an infinite universe of unknown and unknowable entities. There is, therefore, an element of uncertainty. Any specific subject may crop up in any specific corner of the field of knowledge and at any time."[37] He has spoken of the

---

[36] *Ibid.* p. 36.
[37] S. R. Ranganathan. "The Colon Classification and its Approach to Documentation."

importance of an understanding of the patterns of knowledge growth to the "tactics, the corresponding counter-tactics, and the machine tools" of the library system, but he has applied his theories mainly to the problem of bibliographic classification.

## SOCIAL EPISTEMOLOGY AND THE SOCIOLOGY OF KNOWLEDGE

As Kenneth Boulding has so aptly pointed out, the entire social system of a culture is a process centrally concerned with information and knowledge, and even the most "responsible" political decisions are made in the light of the image of the world that the decision-maker possesses. His image is largely the product of the information he receives, and hence is controlled by the nature of the information systems by which he is surrounded. If political decisions are to be controlled, they must be seen by society as an integral part of a much larger structure in which information is collected and transformed into images of the world. Science, for example, derives much of its political importance from the fact that it has become an increasingly significant part of the total social process by which images of the world are created.[38]

Don K. Price holds that there are four estates—the scientific, the professional, the administrative, and the political—all of which are largely differentiated by the ways in which they utilize or apply information and knowledge. The scientist is concerned with pure truth. The professional applies truth to particular or specialized purposes, such as healing the sick or educating the young. Administrators design and implement the social structure necessary to carry out a particular purpose. Politicians, or, more accurately, statesmen, proclaim and promote the larger and ultimate goals of society. These estates are not always sharply defined, says Price, but tend to merge into a spectrum or continuum, so that one individual can assume roles in more than one estate. Also there must be checks and balances working among these estates, so that no one dominates the others, just as the three constituent elements of culture must be maintained in reasonable balance.[39]

---

*Bibliographic Organization.* University of Chicago, Graduate Library School. Chicago. University of Chicago Press. 1951. p. 96.

[38] Kenneth Boulding. Review of Don K. Price's *The Scientific Estate. Scientific American.* vol. 214 (April 1966), pp. 131-34.

[39] Don K. Price. *The Scientific Estate.* Cambridge, Mass. Harvard University Press. 1966.

Social epistemology is related to, but in a sense is the reverse of, the sociology of knowledge. The latter deals empirically with the social determination of knowledge to discover the extent of influence of social factors upon ideas, and seeks to isolate those influences in society by which knowledge is conditioned. The sociology of knowledge arose over a recognition that the older methods of intellectual history, which were oriented about an *a priori* assumption that changes in ideas were to be understood only on the level of the ideas themselves, were interfering with an understanding of the impact of the social process upon man's intellectual sphere. This sociologically oriented history of thought recognized that there are collective purposes of the group which underlie the thought of the individual, and that a large part of thinking and knowing cannot be correctly understood so long as the social implications of human life are not taken into account. As this social background becomes recognizable as the invisible force underlying knowledge, one comes to realize that thoughts and ideas are not the result of the isolated inspiration of great geniuses. Beneath even the profound insight of genius lies the collective historical experiences of a group. But this influence of the group is not to be confused with the popular notion of "the group mind." Underlying human knowledge there is not merely one complex of collective experience with one exclusive tendency; the world of knowledge for any individual evolves from many different orientations because there are many simultaneous and mutually contradictory trends of thought of unequal value competing with each other, each with its different interpretation of a "common" experience.[40]

The sociological history of art has shown fairly conclusively that art forms may be definitely dated according to their style, since each form has evolved from certain given historical conditions and hence reveals the characteristic of its epoch. What is true for art is also true for knowledge. Just as art forms can be dated on the basis of their association with particular periods in history, so also for knowledge one can detect with considerable exactness the perspective attributable to the historical setting. *Perspective* as used here signifies the manner in which one views a particular segment of knowledge, what is perceived in it, and how it is construed in thought. Perspective is something more than a merely formal determinant of thinking; it is qualitative in that it relates to the traits by which knowledge at any given stage may be characterized—the nature of the concepts used, the absence or presence of synonymous or counter concepts, the levels of abstraction, and the structuring of the concepts. Thus, the sociol-

---

[40] See: Karl Mannheim. *Ideology and Utopia.* New York. Harcourt Brace. 1936. Chapter 5.

ogy of knowledge reveals very clearly the distinction between *information* and *knowledge*, for the former does not admit of the sociohistorical perspective; the assertion, to cite the simplest example, that two plus two equals four gives no clue as to when, where, and by whom it was formulated. Perspective becomes important when the validity of the information is in doubt. We cannot here become involved with a consideration of the nature of truth, but it is important to record that it is at the point of validation that information passes the barrier into knowledge. "Knowledge is subjective information," says Heilprin, "which is not merely communicated, but compared and found identical by a group of scientists or scholars who share their concepts. It is above all a social product, dependent upon agreement among a group of technical persons who perform the operations characteristic of their field. And it is a function of time, since any member of the group can challenge its consensus."[41]

Every culture, as Boulding has shown, produces a "transcript," a record in more or less permanent form which can be handed down from generation to generation. In primitive, nonliterate societies this transcript takes the form of verbal ritual, legends, myth, poems, ceremonies, the transmission of which from generation to generation is one of the principal concerns of the group. The invention of writing marked the beginning of a degree of dissociation between the communicator and that which is communicated.

In primitive cultures where the transcript is oral tradition, and transmission is difficult, there is great resistance to, and even fear of, change once the transcript has been "approved" by society. Emphasis is upon the "right" thing to do at the "appropriate" time, once this rightness and appropriateness has been socially determined. The advent of a recorded transcript accelerated the growth of knowledge by freeing the mind from the necessity to retain tradition so that mental energy could be expended in innovation.

Society achieves its knowledge through two main channels, direct experience and the record or transcript, and areas of knowledge and different cultures vary in their proportion of dependence upon one or the other. History, for example, can be known only through the transcript, but the principles of physics have their origin largely in direct experience, though the transcript passes that experience on. It is important to remember, however, that the value system of a culture also has its effect on the transcript. A value system that assigns great weight to those messages which conform to tradition, i.e., to the transcript, will tend to suppress or

---

41 Heilprin. "Response to Shera." p. 11.

reject those messages which do not conform. The value system of science can be as ruthless as that of primitive man in censoring messages which threaten the system—witness the drag upon scientific innovation by the closed corporations that were the academies. The value system of a culture exerts a strong influence upon the communication of knowledge within a society and the ways in which the society utilizes knowledge. As in the biological world one is aware of only those mutants that survive; so in a society there is doubtless a substantial amount of knowledge that fails in the ruthless competition for acceptance. There is no guarantee, of course, that ability to survive is a reliable test of validity, yet there is no substitute for competition, and without it a culture would either become a chaos or subside into stagnation.

Very little is known about the appearance and ultimate fate of the mutant in knowledge. At times the intellectual climate seems right for innovation and there is no innovator; again, there is an innovator who speaks only to deaf ears. One dare not press historical determinism too far; without St. Paul the history of Christianity would have been vastly different; Luther had to find his princes and Newton his Royal Society. Yet in spite of the power of chance and the mutational character of alterations in the knowledge possessed by society, after considering the long course of recorded history one cannot avoid the impression that there is an orderly development in public knowledge as recorded in the transcript of successive civilizations and societies. From man's conception of himself as standing at the center of a small three-dimensional locality to his awareness of the four-dimensional relativistic universe in which space and time are not the continuum he once believed them to be—though the record has its extravagances, blind alleys, and periods of decadence—the overall development would seem to be neither random nor haphazard. Early knowledge can often be recognized as a special case of that which has come later. Algebra generalized the operations of arithmetic as calculus generalized some operations of algebra, and Keynesian economics is a generalization of the classical system of Adam Smith.

Since knowledge feeds upon social values, like any other organism it moves inevitably toward that part of a possible field of action where the values and rewards seem highest. Society, guided by its own sense of values, opens wide the sluices to irrigate certain fields and closes them to others. The growth of public knowledge is part and parcel of the growth and organization of society. "When we look at the whole range of human cultures," writes Margaret Mead, "and follow out the types of multilinear evolution . . . the evolutionary potentialities of human culture seem to be very high indeed. So also when we follow out the cultural development that has occurred in some one part of the world over a relatively long period of time . . . the rather monotonous potentiality for civilization to develop in one direction is striking." But she also adds that "the lower in the scale of cultural evolution we go . . . the greater is the possibility that a culture will be caught in a blind alley, as when a people become preoccupied by obsessive ritual, or find a stop-gap solution to the food problem, or build in a politically limiting institution like headhunting."[42]

## SOCIAL EPISTEMOLOGY AND THE LIBRARY

The philosophy of librarianship delineated here does not exclude the important contribution that the physical sciences can make to the intellectual arsenal of the librarian. Because a culture, and the subcultures of which it is composed, is a complex social structure created by men who are themselves composites of psychological, biological, and physical phenomena, the physical as well as the social sciences are relevant to the whole problem of social epistemology. If librarianship is to be concerned—as it must be—with the epistemological problem in society, it must also be interdisciplinary. Few will deny, we believe, that the human use of the graphic records of society (the social transcript, to borrow Kenneth Boulding's term) is a scientifically based study to which all branches of human knowledge can contribute. Because librarianship is primarily concerned with the utilization of the social transcript by human beings it is fundamentally a behavioristic science, but because the methods and findings of the physical and biological sciences are being increasingly applied to the study of human behavior, librarianship must be "scientific" even in the classical use of the term. A librarian, therefore, must be a scientist, not only because he may be doling out scientific literature to scientists and will perforce need to communicate intelligibly with his patrons, but also because science, in its broadest sense, is a part of the foundation of the librarian's scholarship.

The interdisciplinary focus of systems analysis and operations research has direct relevance to the librarian's procedures and technology, and a symbolic meaning for the growth of knowledge in society. Just as systems analysis directs scrutiny to the interrelations among the component parts

---

[42] Margaret Mead. *Continuities in Cultural Evolution.* New Haven. Yale University Press. 1964. pp. 285–86.

of an operating whole, so social epistemology places its emphasis upon the whole man and the whole society, and all of their ways of thinking, knowing, feeling, acting, and communicating. Science itself is a major social enterprise, carried on by individuals to be sure, but in the present day increasingly by individuals working in concert within the context or environment of educational, research, industrial, and governmental organizations and institutions.

But librarians do not live by the bread of mathematics alone, nor by the succotash of systems analysis; to say that system is the essence of the science of librarianship states a very narrow and restricted view. The librarian's responsibility is the efficient and effective management of the transcript, the graphic record of all that society knows about itself and its world.

Heilprin has admirably summarized the importance of the epistemological approach to the problems of the librarian and his professional education, in a review of the earlier version of this chapter:

> If the librarian (or more generally, the information scientist) is actually an important service link in optimizing the use of graphic recorded information, then success depends on how much of this process he understands. He must see it all in profile—how we manufacture knowledge, starting with direct sense impressions and including (in science, at least) careful comparison of communicated abstractions. Publication in symbols usually follows. Often all of this happens before the librarian sees the product. But with increasing frequency he must take part in the manufacturing process by supplying some of the communicated concepts in various pretested states, with evaluations of these states. This requires expertise on subjects, not merely references. He also will tend to *be* more of a scientist, and in particular will have to understand the way in which what once has been accepted as objective tends with the advance of knowledge to slip back into its prior state of subjectivity. If epistemology encompasses this entire field, including all of communication science, clearly a large expansion is needed in the background of the information scientist. He must at least be aware of the entire process of knowledge, and of the principal constraints on and weak points in its communication. Educators who have to construct courses to guide and instruct the information scientist cannot be less broad than those they are trying to educate. To be a competent teacher in this field will indeed be a challenge. We may conclude that perhaps the main reason why in-

formation science has progressed such a short distance as a science is that we do not understand the connections we are groping for here. Lack of knowledge of epistemology is possibly the greatest barrier to improving library and information science.[43]

---

[43] Heilprin. "Response to Shera." pp. 39–40.

# Five

# The Role of the Library
# in the Social Process

In the preceding chapters society has been presented as a complex system of interlocking and interdependent roles—institutional, associational, and individual—united by a communication network which operates through a variety of media, at varying degrees of sophistication, and which evinces greater or less complexity depending upon the demands of the culture of which it is a primary cohesive force. The library, by definition, is an agency of communication, principally of secondary, or graphic, communication. Therefore, to understand what librarianship is, one must begin with an assessment of the roles which the library has played in the communication process throughout its history. In part, these roles have evolved naturally as a consequence of social need, in part they have been imposed upon the library as a result of theorizing as to what the library might or should do. Social institutions or agencies are the creation of human beings engaged in group activity, therefore any institution or agency may assume whatever role man assigns to it. There are no "natural" or "logical" roles except insofar as man himself is a manifestation of nature and, therefore, what he does may be said to be "natural." Social consensus, then, is the ultimate authority in determining roles. Society has determined what the library of the past has been, and it is society that will determine what the library of the future shall be. This statement does not mean that the patterns of social acceptance cannot be shaped and molded in response to the activities or insistence of specialized groups, nor does it deny the values of such social "pressures"; indeed, man as a responsible

member of society has the obligation to contribute his share to the directing of social action toward those goals which seem to him to promise the
fullest and richest life. But one must remember that a society, consciously
or unconsciously, creates its own goals, and that these establish the outer
boundaries within which any agency must operate.

The functions of the library as a social agency, and the roles which
have been established for it, must, therefore, be sought in two ways: (1)
implicitly, through an analysis of the historical development of the library
and the roles the library has assumed during the centuries of its existence;
and (2) explicitly, in the form of stated theories of the functions of the
library in society. At times these will be congruent, but again they will
diverge sharply; in part they will represent almost universal acceptance,
or they may be little more than the theorizing of a limited few. But whether
the role of the library is large or small, important or insignificant, central
or peripheral, essential or ornamental, it is ultimately socially determined.[1]

## CONSERVATION

Though the library has traditionally been dedicated to the preservation of the graphic records of society, ironically, its own historic origins
are obscured by the very absence of those records it was created to preserve. One can, therefore, only assume that as prehistoric cultures achieved
a stage in their development at which graphic records became essential
to communication, some form of mechanism for the preservation of these
records was devised. Libraries, then, would seem to have been born of
the coincidence of social need and physical scarcity; graphic records were
few in number and relatively fragile, yet indispensable to the operation
of the society.

The important historic fact is not whether libraries began as archival
collections—certainly the conservational role was one of the earliest for
which record survives—but that they were essential to cultural survival.
As graphic records themselves transcended the limitations of human speech
and memory, so the library, by its guardianship of the written word, increased the life expectancy, and hence the utility of the document. In a
very real sense the library was the group memory, not only was it the
intellectual center of the culture it served, but also it was a form of in-

---

[1] John M. Christ argues for the use of functional analysis as the best approach to an
understanding of the role of the library in society. "Functional Analysis and Library
Science." *College and Research Libraries.* vol. 30 (May 1969), pp. 242–46.

surance against social disintegration and decay. The central position of the library in early cultures is implicit in the derivation of the term *archive* (which the early libraries seem to have been) which comes from the Greek *arkheion*, a magisterial residence, a public office, or the French *arché*, an ark, a place of first things.[2]

Discoveries of agglomerations of clay tablets from the Assyro-Babylonian civilization and papyrus scrolls from Egypt show clearly that libraries were accumulated not only for the preservation of official state records, but also for the effective transaction of private business enterprise.[3] The importance of libraries in the preservation of the scholarship of the culture is, again, implicit in the story that Shih Huang Ti, founder of the Ch'in Dynasty, ordered the destruction of all books except those treating of agriculture, divination, and medicine.[4] It was, therefore, not consideration for the future historian, but the practical and immediate needs of the hour that prompted early civilized man to accumulate his graphic records in centers where they would be readily available for consultation by himself and his descendants. Libraries did not begin as monuments to individual or national glory, nor as the adornments of a regime, though they in time became such because of the human drive for prestige and a propensity to embellish. Though they may have been incorporated in the tombs of royalty because the king would need these records in the proper conduct of his afterlife, they were not regarded as in themselves sepulchral, nor is there any surviving evidence to suggest that a Hittite king thought the royal library an ideal place for the disposition of a deserving maiden aunt. The library was a necessary adjunct to the court room, the council chamber, and the marketplace, and it long antedated the laboratory as the cradle of knowledge.

So important was conservation that the early writers on the management of libraries—De Bury, Naudé, Blades, and a host of others—devoted much attention to the custody of books as physical entities, as artifacts.[5]

---

[2] *Oxford English Dictionary; Webster's New International Dictionary; The American Heritage Dictionary.* See also: T. R. Schellenberg. *Modern Archives: Principles and Techniques.* Chicago. University of Chicago Press. 1956. pp. 11–12; Hilary Jenkinson. *A Manual of Archival Administration.* London. Percy Lund. 1937. pp. 2–3; S. Muller, J. A. Feith, and R. Fruin. *Manual for the Arrangement and Description of Archives.* New York. H. W. Wilson Company. 1940. pp. 13–14.

[3] Edward Chiera. *They Wrote on Clay.* Chicago. University of Chicago Press. 1938. pp. 67–79 and 201–4; Allan Nevins. *The Gateway to History.* Boston. Heath. 1938. pp. 83–85.

[4] John L. Thornton. *The Chronology of Librarianship.* London. Gratfon. 1941. p. 13.

[5] Richard De Bury's *Philobiblion* was written in 1345 and first published in Cologne

For many centuries the physical care of books was the central task of librarianship, and perhaps nowhere is the role more drastically expressed than in the annals of early American colleges. At one time the regulations of Harvard College required the librarian to have all books available on a stated day for inspection by the Visiting Committee,[6] and similar regulations maintained at other institutions. As Walton points out, this practice of the annual inspection of books has its origin deep in the history of library development, and it came to America with the books themselves.[7] So serious was the threat of loss that in 1667 the overseers of Harvard insisted that "upon the new choice or removall of the Librarian Keeper the fellows shall look over the Library & see that all the books be actually in their places; if any be wanted the Library keeper shall make them good."[8] A century later, in 1765, the laws required that "if any Damage come to the Library, by the neglect of the Librarian, or his Inobservance of the Laws of the Library, it shall be made good out of his Salary or otherwise."[9] Though the Harvard librarians of the nineteenth century were not actually required to make good the book losses, academic law continued to create for the librarian a role which emphasized, above all else, custodial responsibility for books as property, and for many librarians this role fitted, as Brough says, "like a glove."[10] In 1848, in a letter to President Everett of Harvard, Walter Mitchell complained of "the sleepless vigilance of three lynx-eyed librarians," and insisted that "the labor of getting *one* reference, given us in the recitation, was rendered too tedious and formidable by the restrictions of the library."[11]

Even today there are those who still regard custody of the book as a material object the supreme expression of the librarian's art, and this veneration of the rare book room or the bibliographic museum as the *sanctum sanctorum* of the library world has fostered the popular misconception of the librarian as being one who is more concerned with preservation than with use. Thus, the librarian has become an easy scapegoat for every disgruntled undergraduate and has perpetuated such shopworn tales

---

in 1473. Gabriel Naudé's *Avis pour Dresser une Bibliothèque* first appeared in 1627, and William Blades's *The Enemies of Books* was first published in 1887.

[6] Kenneth J. Brough. *Scholar's Workshop.* Urbana, Ill. University of Illinois Press. 1953. p. 17.

[7] C. E. Walton. *The Three-Hundredth Anniversary of the Harvard College Library.* Cambridge, Mass. Harvard College Library. 1939. p. 38.

[8] *Ibid.*

[9] Colonial Society of Massachusetts. *Publications.* vol. 15 (1925), pp. 195–96.

[10] Brough. *Scholar's Workshop.* p. 19.

[11] Keyes D. Metcalf. "The Undergraduate and the Harvard Library, 1765–1877." *Harvard Library Bulletin.* vol. 1 (1947), pp. 43 and 45.

as that told of the Harvard librarian John Langdon Sibley, who went forth happily to retrieve the only two volumes missing from the library shelves.

One may regret that a social function as important as the conservation of the cultural heritage should lead to the excesses of bibliomania, but it must be admitted that almost inevitably conservation for immediate and practical use merged into conservation for its own sake, an aberration that was fostered by a scarcity of writing materials and the premium on literacy. Because graphic records were both useful and scarce, they were highly prized. Of all forms of life, man is the most acquisitive, as well as the most destructive, probably because he has the greatest resources for the exercise of both propensities, and, as it became possible, he began to accumulate graphic records as he had accumulated other forms of wealth or property. Thus, the possession of a private library became a symbol of social distinction, and the endowment of a public institution the highest expression of social consciousness. At times the hard core of utility tended to be obscured by the trappings of social stratification. But even at its most flamboyant, the library as museum fulfilled a social need. Society, then, did not create a library as an outlet for its acquisitiveness; it accumulated and preserved the records of its scholarship against the ravages of time and the depredations of men because such records were essential to the culture and because they were scarce, but in the evolutionary process of library development, man discovered that not only could conservation for its own sake become intellectually and emotionally satisfying, but also it could be made to serve the urge toward personal achievement, distinction, and prestige. In time, then, the purpose of conservation became blurred and indistinct, when it was not actually discredited and even ridiculed, until today the most damning charge which one can bring against the library is to call it a "storehouse" and the librarian its "keeper." So intense is the contemporary drive for the "dynamic" program, that society has largely forgotten that books, like people, may "also serve who only stand and wait."

But in a sense, as will be indicated later, all functions of the library converge in conservation; for however much the role of custodian runs counter to the mores of contemporary society, and however much we may embellish it with ancillary objectives, conservation is basic and fundamental to the library.

## EDUCATION

The intellectual content of the culture, its scholarship, had to be actively transmitted from generation to generation as well as preserved.

Indeed, the two are halves of the same unity, and in the historical evolution of the library as a social agency, it is often difficult to separate the one from the other. Originally, this scholarship was dominantly concerned with the relations between man and his spiritual life. "We must look to the temples of ancient Egypt for the first libraries," writes James Westfall Thompson, "for the earliest books were religious, liturgical, and ritualistic. . . . The recording of secular thought, even the decrees of the pharaohs, must have begun to obtain long after religious teaching and ritual had been reduced to writing."[12] The temple was the focus of all community life. It was much more than a sanctuary for the worship of the gods, it was the seat of government from which the oligarchy ruled. Surrounding it were the dwelling-places of the priests and public officials, storehouses, granaries, workshops, law courts, the library, and the school. Even more than the medieval monastery, the pre-Christian temple was the focus of community life and the seat of government. Every sanctuary possessed its library and school, "the House of the Tablet" or the "House of the Seal," in which the temple archives and liturgical texts were preserved, and the young were instructed in the art of writing. Along the banks of the Nile, in the valley of the Tigris and Euphrates, scholars pored over ancient texts in theology, astrology, medicine, agriculture, and passed on to younger generations the recorded wisdom in the temple libraries.

For centuries, even for millennia, the library was, as Oliver Wendell Holmes said, "a nest in which to hatch scholars." Callimachus and his associates at the Alexandriana compiling that great catalogue known to us as the *Pinakes*; the distinguished Hellenic grammarian Euphorion who presided over the royal library at Antioch; Tyrannica and Andronicus of Rhodes, librarians to the emperor Sulla, laboring over the texts of Aristotle; Varro, commissioned by Julius Caesar to organize a public library for Rome, writing his treatise *De bibliothecis*, which has since been lost; all were typical of the scholar-librarians of the classical world and the esteem in which they were held. Many were tutors to the royal family and to the youth of the wealthy noblemen; many, like the distinguished sophist L. Julius Vestimus, were granted the title *procurator bibliothecarum* by the emperor in recognition of their scholarly achievements. Under the emperor Hadrian, Vestimus was the chief administrative officer for all the public libraries of Rome, and the *bibliothecarius* in each of the individual libraries was responsible to him. Roman organizational genius

---

[12] James Westfall Thompson. *Ancient Libraries*. Berkeley. University of California Press. 1940. p. 1.

developed a distinction between the administrative officers proper and the scholarly directors, each with his own staff of slaves or freedmen, and each operating within well-defined boundaries of responsibility.[13]

The Dark Ages were very dark indeed, and in the turmoil that followed the triumph of barbarianism, the monastic libraries and the schools attached to them were the sole resource for the preservation and dissemination of the intellectual heritage of central Europe. In its earliest expressions, Christianity was essentially a movement among the "lower" classes, and only gradually did it acquire better-educated leaders hospitable to the idea that citation of the secular classics gave strength to the arguments against paganism. The church had been born into a world of collapsing civilization, and in the beginning was itself carried down into the degradation of anti-intellectualism. But, fortunately, Christianity was essentially a bookish religion, and such leaders as Cassiodorus at Vivarium came to realize that classical learning was complementary rather than hostile to Christianity. By reorganizing the monasteries and monastic schools and their libraries, such leaders lifted these organizations from the neglect and degeneration that was threatening them with fanaticism and even moral disaster.[14] Cassiodorus was the first to bring order out of the monastic chaos, and he pioneered in the promotion of a sound scholarship, both in church and secular learning, as the only foundation for the educational discipline of those who had dedicated their lives to the promotion of the Christian life.[15] The history of the Graeco-Roman libraries covers a period of some six centuries, during which more was achieved in the dissemination of education and learning than the Christian era encompassed during a period three times as long. The founders of the medieval monasteries and their affiliated cathedral schools recognized this inferiority, and the traffic in books across the Continent and into England and Ireland is eloquent testimony to the importance of the written word in the promotion of the church.

While Western Europe was in darkness, Byzantium enjoyed a brilliant civilization with imposing libraries and schools where the classics were assembled, taught, and imitated. The Jews have always evinced a reverence for books, and in many ways their religion promoted a Christian

---

[13] Thompson. *Ancient Libraries.* p. 33; Alfred Hessel. *A History of Libraries.* Washington, D.C. Scarecrow Press. 1950. p. 6.

[14] James Westfall Thompson. *The Medieval Library.* Chicago. University of Chicago Press. 1939. pp. 30–35.

[15] Cassiodorus. *An Introduction to Divine and Human Readings*, trans. Leslie W. Jones. New York. Columbia University Press. 1946. pp. 131–39.

attitude toward letters long before the Reformation and the Renaissance, and their synagogues and their libraries were centers of teaching, edification, and intellectual discipline as well as of worship.[16] To the time of Mohammed, the Arabs had almost no written literature; Mohammed himself could neither read nor write, and the culture of the Arabs was transmitted almost entirely by word of mouth. But with the conquest of Persia, the libraries of which were well stocked with Persian literature and Greek philosophic writings, creative authorship and learning slowly came to be admired and revered in the Muslim world until the "house of wisdom" and the "house of learning" became characteristic of the Arabian community to an extent that even the depredations of the Mongols and the Tartars could not completely eradicate a devotion to learning.[17]

In the Western World, the rebirth of learning and the beginnings of science reaffirmed the library as the focus of education and the laboratory of incipient scientific inquiry, and with the Age of Enlightenment its contribution became even more significant. In colonial America the library was the greatest single physical asset of the new Harvard College, and according to tradition, Yale College began as a collection of books. At the beginning of the eighteenth century, Rev. Thomas Bray became so alarmed over the low educational state of the Anglican clergy in the colonies of North America that he organized a society for the establishment of parish libraries in Maryland, Virginia, and other colonies along the Atlantic coast.[18] Legislation for the promotion of libraries, introduced first into the colonial assemblies and later into the state legislatures, was almost inevitably referred to the committee on public education. Library encouragement throughout American history to the close of the Civil War was the special concern of those who, like Henry Barnard and Horace Mann, regarded public education as fundamental to the new democracy.[19]

This close affiliation between the library and the formal educational system was an inevitable result of the fact that the latter, in Western civilization, has always been book-centered. Even at a time when books were scarce and highly prized, both teacher and pupil leaned heavily upon the book, whether it was a papyrus roll, a vellum codex, or a *McGuffey Reader*. This dependence of the educational system upon graphic records

[16] Saul K. Padover. "Jewish Libraries." *Medieval Library*, Thompson. pp. 338–46.

[17] Saul K. Padover. "Muslim Libraries." *Medieval Library*, Thompson. pp. 347–68.

[18] Charles T. Laugher. *The Beginnings of the Library in Colonial America; Dr. Thomas Bray and the Religious Societies 1695–1795.* Unpublished doctoral dissertation. Western Reserve University. 1963.

[19] Jesse H. Shera. *Foundations of the Public Library.* Chicago. University of Chicago Press. 1949.

was inherited from Oxford, Cambridge, and the great universities of the Continent by the early American colleges. Carlyle's definition of a true university as a collection of books was repeatedly echoed on this side of the Atlantic. "Everything else may admit of a substitute, or may be dispensed with," wrote Christopher Columbus Langdell, dean of the Harvard Law School, to President Eliot in 1873, "but without the library the School would lose its most important characteristic, and indeed its identity."[20] Three years later, President Eliot himself wrote that "the Library is the centre of the University . . . it would be easier to carry on the University without productive funds than without books and reasonable facilities for their use."[21] So important were books to the educational process that, lacking an adequate college collection, students not infrequently made use of the voluntary association, particularly the campus literary society such as *Linonia* or *Brothers in Unity* at Yale, as an instrument for the collective purchase of books that would be available to all members of the group.

With the election of Andrew Jackson to the Presidency of the United States came a new awareness that this high office was attainable by every industrious American boy, however humble his origins, and with this new faith in the political and social importance of the "common man" came belief in the efficacy of universal education. The importance of an educated electorate to democracy in time became interpreted to mean that education could guarantee the success of popular government. Those who rode the crest of the wave of universal education were not bothered by the thought that they might be forcing upon a society that was consciously democratic an educational philosophy developed from the leadership of an intellectual aristocracy and a master and slave economy.[22] Blinded by achievements at Oxford, Cambridge, and Göttingen, America was determined to be cultivated, as William H. Prescott wrote in 1840, "up to the eyes."[23] "The first principles of popular government," wrote Edward Everett to Mayor Bigelow of Boston, "require that the means of education should, as far as possible, be equally within the reach of the whole population. . . . the sons of the wealthy alone have access to well-stored libraries; while those whose means do not allow them to purchase books are too often deprived of them at the moment when they would be most

---

[20] President of Harvard University. *Annual Report, 1872–1873*. Cambridge, Mass. 1873. p. 63.

[21] *Ibid. 1875–76*, pp. 26–27.

[22] Alfred North Whitehead. *Dialogues of Alfred North Whitehead*. Boston. Little, Brown. 1954. p. 110.

[23] Van Wyck Brooks. *The Flowering of New England*. New York. Dutton. 1937. p. 172n.

useful.''[24] By the middle of the nineteenth century those who believed that education could save the world and that the library was the handmaiden of universal education—"the crowning glory of our public schools"—were in full cry. "How much more ignorance would thus be removed," thundered Rev. John B. Wight before the Massachusetts General Court in defense of the public library act of 1851, "how much vice reformed, how much slumbering talent awakened, how much awakened talent aided and made efficient, how much done to make many in a high degree intelligent, well informed, useful and respectable citizens, and to correct, improve, and elevate the general character of the whole community in five, in ten, in twenty, in fifty, in a hundred years."[25] From across the Atlantic, Victor Hugo echoed, in *Les Miserables*, "Light, light in floods, no bat resists the dawn, illuminate the bottoms of society."

## SELF-EDUCATION

The frenzy of enthusiasm for universal education that engulfed the new nation during the first half of the nineteenth century had its origins deep in the Colonial period. For two centuries the town meeting house had been the intellectual center of community life. At the turn of the eighteenth century, Cotton Mather had organized discussion groups or "neighborhood benefit societies,"[26] which a few decades later were, consciously or unconsciously, revived in Benjamin Franklin's *Junto*, the Literary and Philosophical Society of Newport, Rhode Island, and similar voluntary associations for self-education.[27] It was not long before individuals from a variety of occupational and economic groups, but particularly from the professions of law, medicine, education, and the ministry, desiring more books to read than they could purchase individually, began to pool their funds to establish voluntary corporations. In most instances

---

24 Quoted by Major Benjamin Seaver in his *Message of the Mayor on the Subject of a Public Library.* Boston. (City Document No. 10.) 1852. pp. 4–5. See also: Shera. *Foundations of Public Library.* pp. 216–26; Sidney Ditzion. *Arsenals of a Democratic Culture.* Chicago. American Library Association. 1947. Chapter 5. pp. 77–96.

25 John B. Wight. "Public Libraries." *Common School Journal.* vol. 13 (1851), p. 261.

26 Samuel Mather. *Life of the Very Reverend and Learned Cotton Mather.* Boston. Samuel Gerrish. 1729. p. 56.

27 Austin K. Gray. *Benjamin Franklin's Library; A Short Account of the Library Company of Philadelphia, 1731–1931.* New York. Macmillan. 1937. pp. 3–4; George C. Mason. *Annals of the Redwood Library and Athenaeum.* Newport. The Redwood Library. 1891. pp. 2–53.

their memberships were composed of laymen more interested in general literature than in strictly vocational reading, but whatever the motive, much the same procedure was adopted spontaneously and independently in towns throughout America and Europe.[28]

From Millbury, Massachusetts, in 1826, Josiah Holbrook set forth his plan for a "Society for Mutual Education," and the modern adult education movement may be said to have begun.[29] The fortunes of the lyceums, the mechanics' institutes, the literary circles, the workers' education groups, the women's societies, the agricultural extension programs, ebbed and flowed, and when they died, their place was taken by the chautauquas. The chautauqua movement, which ended with the passing of William Jennings Bryan, was reborn in the adult education movement of the 1930s, and "Reading with a Purpose" gave way before the onslaught of the "Great Books."[30] At the present time the same spirit is revealed in the poverty programs, illiteracy classes, and "Books and Jobs." This expression of the librarian's role has been so persistent that it merits consideration in some detail.

Attempts to graft the library onto these self-education programs have not been conspicuously successful, but at the height of the first wave of enthusiasm for "self-improvement," librarianship was beginning to experience the first stirrings of professional awareness—public libraries were becoming altruistically self-conscious. The movement was gradual, but it was also seemingly irresistible, and slowly the librarians became "socially minded." At first the emphasis of the public librarian was upon the salvation of the individual and, through him, of society, but by the late 1920s, the focus had shifted to the community. Librarians began by looking to schools, clubs, and factories as possible sources of patrons; they now consider them as recipients of library "service." Thus "group dynamics" became the librarians' favorite phrase. In short, librarianship had "turned the corner and begun to proselyte."

In 1924, William S. Learned of the Carnegie Foundation wrote that

> the chief business of a community library is to produce a general diffusion of knowledge among small, ill-defined, and constantly shifting groups, where each need is peculiar to the individual himself, and must be dealt with separately. Such a function involves a multi-

---

[28] Shera. *Foundations of Public Library.* Chapters 2–4.

[29] Carl Bode. *The American Lyceum.* New York. Oxford University Press. 1956. pp. 3–40.

[30] Victoria Case and Robert O. Case. *We Called It Culture.* Garden City, N.Y. Doubleday. 1948.

tude of minute adjustments each of which is essential in certain cases, but no one of which is exceptional, and all of which together make up the main amount for which the library stands as a whole.[31]

Thus was Learned led to the view that the public library "is an indispensable basis for a community intelligence service,"[32] but a survey of the services offered by a variety of the larger municipal public libraries in the United States indicated to him that the potentialities for library service to community interests were only just beginning to be realized by the librarians.[33] Thus, he reached the conclusion that "a free community book exchange is destined to be transformed into an active intelligence center, . . . a genuine community university bringing intelligence systematically and persuasively to bear on all adult affairs, . . . [and] the elementary and secondary schools would be the subsidiary feeders for the greater institution, serving the special needs of the young citizen, and training him for progressive self-education in the larger environment."[34]

If Learned represented a transition from the individual-centered to the community-centered library, it was Alvin Johnson in *The Public Library—A People's University* who gave the new movement its most strident voice. Writing at the behest of the American Association for Adult Education and in the shadow of the Great Depression, Johnson found a ready audience among librarians. In the early 1930s, many of the jobless had turned to the public library in the hope of acquiring new skills or in other ways to improve occupational competence and hence employability. This resurgence of interest in "serious reading" proved to be only transitory, but it had been sufficient to rekindle the professional fervor of the librarians who, themselves, had suffered economic frustration, and Johnson's words were doubly welcome. "Even the best library with the finest collection of books, can not be a really successful adult educational institution if it confines its activities to pure librarianship," and "pure librarianship" to Johnson meant only conservation and custody.[35] Though Johnson admitted that "library intervention in the intellectual lives of the masses is still sporadic,"[36] nevertheless, "the adult educational undertakings

---

31 William S. Learned. *The American Public Library and the Diffusion of Knowledge.* New York. Harcourt Brace. 1924. pp. 27–28.

32 *Ibid.* p. 26.

33 *Ibid.* p. 52.

34 *Ibid.* p. 56.

35 Alvin Johnson. *The Public Library—A People's University.* New York. American Association for Adult Education. 1938. pp. 68–69.

36 *Ibid.* p. 57.

of the public libraries are in the aggregate impressive."[37] After demolishing the image of the librarian as custodian, Johnson argues strongly that the public library is the logical institution to conduct a national program of community education beyond the years of formal instruction. "It was never imagined by the early proponents of universal public education that the instruction given by the schools could in itself equip the child or young person with the political and cultural ideas that would be needed in later life."[38] For education for effective citizenship, as well as for improving the technical proficiency in those who have completed their years of formal vocational training, the "library is so obviously its proper center that not even the purest pure librarian can be against it."[39] Thus, Johnson concluded his study with the ringing challenge that brought courage and exultation to the heart of every librarian:

> It would be foolish and unjust to fail to acknowledge the fact that the American public library, as it stands today, is a remarkable achievement, indeed, one of the outstanding American contributions to civilization. I know of no department in our national life that exhibits a greater proportion of able and devoted leaders, men and women of outstanding personality whose work will live on beyond them, beneficently. They have laid a broad base for an institution that will have an even greater future when it shall boldly take to itself the leadership in adult education which it alone is capable of developing, and shall make itself over into a people's university, sound bulwark of a democratic state.[40]

From cover to cover Johnson's book is pure emotionalism, but it was a beacon to a profession that was losing its way in a "Slough of Despond."[41] Marion Humble surveyed the reading habits of the American farmer and concluded that rural America really does use the public library for adult education.[42] James Truslow Adams, in his study of adult education in American democracy, though he questioned Johnson's observation, that if libraries were to play their most effective role in adult education, they might have to publish books of their own which would avoid profes-

---

[37] *Ibid.* p. 61.
[38] *Ibid.* p. 65.
[39] *Ibid.* p. 64.
[40] *Ibid.* p. 79.
[41] Kathleen Molz. *"The Public Library: The People's University."* *The American Scholar.* vol. 34 (Winter 1964–65), pp. 95–102.
[42] Marion Humble. *Rural America Reads.* New York. American Association for Adult Education. 1939.

sional jargon and be "readable, sound, small, and inexpensive,"[43] concluded "most emphatically" that "in our opinion our American free library system, both potentially and actually, is one of the finest instruments for Adult Education possible by any people."[44] A more quiet but scarcely less emphatic voice was that of Robert D. Leigh who, in summarizing the findings of the Public Library Inquiry, wrote concerning adult education:

> In many places, especially as larger library systems are organized, the public library would appear to be well suited to provide the materials and sometimes the meeting centers which these formal educational enterprises require. Direct functioning in connection with such adult education enterprises would be an expansion of public library activity in line with the accepted library objectives.[45]

No one has yet adequately defined "adult education," nor stated with any degree of precision just what it is supposed to accomplish. In its broadest sense it may be regarded as any informal but directed learning for those who have passed the years of adolescence, and its objectives are, presumably, much the same as those of formalized education. In this broadest sense, then, the public library has long been an agency of adult, or self-, education. It was designed to serve the potential *individual* reading and information interests of the adult population of the community, or some specified segment thereof. It has striven to supply an omnibus service that may proceed in any direction that *individual* adult needs and *personal* circumstances may dictate. If the "educational" objective was not always clear, it was so because the ends of education itself have not been well defined.

Increasingly, however, "adult education" has been defined in terms of organized groups, and particularly within the last generation, library service to adult education has been thought of as attempts to identify and give service to more or less formal class situations. As indicated above, this organized learning for adults has had a long, though not always conspicuously successful, history. It was dependent upon the decentralization of initiative in organizing its programs of activity; it operated through a loose framework of committees; and it achieved such unity as it possessed

---

[43] James Truslow Adams. *Frontiers of American Culture; A Study of Adult Education in a Democracy.* New York. Scribner. 1944. p. 230.

[44] *Ibid.* p. 232.

[45] Robert D. Leigh. *The Public Library in the United States.* New York. Columbia University Press. 1950. p. 233.

in an omnibus federation that encompassed a wide, not to say indiscriminate, variety of educational projects. To the fluidity of this pattern, the services offered by the public library seemed almost ideally hospitable, despite the fact that all the historical evidence pointed to failure in attempts to graft the library movement upon such weak organizational stems. Certainly there is no evidence that American librarianship has ever given the adult education movement any professional leadership or any degree of continuous direction. Even the staff of the Public Library Inquiry was unable to discover any indication that the public library had "become either a major center of formally organized adult education under its own initiative, nor does it serve as the officially designated library for the existing major agencies of formal adult education."[46] One must recognize, of course, that a social instrument can alter its objectives, change its course and revise its role, but the change should be recognized as such, and there should be awareness that the new course runs counter to the course of history.[47]

No one can reasonably doubt that the movement for self-education was born of the most admirable of motives and the highest of ideals. Deeply rooted in the midnineteenth-century faith in the perfectability of man, the conviction of Horace Mann that "in a Republic ignorance is a crime," adult education has reflected the extravagant reliance of the American upon education to solve specific social problems, to improve income and hence social status, and generally to break down the barriers to social mobility. In the field of adult education, librarianship found a fertile soil into which it might thrust new roots. The very nature of their calling demands of librarians a professional optimism concerning the efficacy of the printed word in ameliorating all human social ills. The adult educators, and among them the librarians, followed unblushingly and unapologetically the Jacksonian goal of success, and an educational philosophy which would treat every mind as equal and make the educational resources of the nation accessible to all, regardless of capacity. It created for itself no demanding standards of excellence, insisted that education was an inalienable right, and held that reading or discussion was in itself good, however lacking in direction or inept in leadership. In short, the movement for self-education, both inside the library and out, was emotional rather than intellectual.

The contribution of the movement for self-education to the role of

---

[46] *Ibid.* pp. 107–8.

[47] Jesse H. Shera. "On the Value of Library History." *Library Quarterly.* vol. 22 (July 1952), pp. 240–51.

the library, evolving as it did from the voluntary library societies, the social libraries of the eighteenth century, represents an important historical development. Though it was a patchwork, often without form and all too frequently without much substance, there can be no doubt that it did meet certain individual needs. It did open doors which, for some, might forever have remained closed. By supporting the American belief in rugged individualism and the self-made man, it brought the library into closer harmony with the American culture, and made it more conspicuously a part of the total fabric of American life. Self-education gave the public library a conscious social orientation that it had previously lacked—if the goals were not always the best, at least they were goals—and as such they helped to make the library dynamic rather than passive. It contributed to the weakening of the traditional role of conservation which had, over the centuries, ossified the library, and it helped to alter the role of conservation itself by enlarging the concept of library material from the codex form to all forms of graphic communication, films, sound recordings, and microphotographic reproductions. Though it may have blurred the lines of demarcation between the library and the museum, the library and the archive, and even the library and the schoolroom, it emphasized the interrelationships of all three institutions. It moved, as Leigh points out, "the claim for support of library service away from rather meaningless totals of registration and circulation toward concrete services whose value can be measured and appreciated in terms of the group activities served."[48] It strove to provide appropriate books for each individual, according to his own intellectual capacities, to the end of enriching his life. It probably experienced its finest hour in the acculturation of the immigrant during the early years of the present century. Finally, and perhaps most important of all, it produced a response on the part of the library to an apparent social need. The very vitality of the movement for self-education is convincing evidence of the importance of its role in society, and the reaction of the librarians to this persistent demand for an expanding intellectual horizon demonstrated that librarianship was at least started on the road to maturity and social responsibility.

On the other hand, the formally organized adult education groups may be regarded as having performed something of a disservice to the public library by diverting the attention of the profession away from the individual reader, who had been the object of its historic role, and toward readers in the mass, even to the point that the Public Library Inquiry itself became confused, and its director could write:

---

[48] Leigh. *Public Library.* p. 106.

From their official statements of purpose, it is evident that public librarians conceive of themselves as performing an educational task. The library, however, may also be thought of as a constituent part of public (or mass) communication; the machinery by which words, sounds, and images flow from points of origin through an impersonal medium to hosts of unseen readers and audiences.[49]

The Inquiry held that the public library was "in direct though often unacknowledged competition"[50] with the other agencies of mass communication, particularly the commercial media, and concluded,

It would seem, then, that the public library's natural role as an agency of public communication is to serve the group of adults whose interest, will, and ability lead them to seek personal enrichment and enlightenment.[51]

Thus was left to the public library an almost residual role:

Our review of the characteristics of the commercial agencies indicates that they leave undone or slight the performance of communication services which are indispensable for the health of our society. The unperformed tasks would seem to constitute the uniquely appropriate functions for noncommercial agencies of communication of which the public library is one.[52]

The Inquiry then identified certain of these "unperformed tasks" which seemed to define the educational role of the public library. These may be summarized as the obligation to serve as "centers" for the "selection, organization, and promotion" of "materials," both contemporary and historical, that had social utility, both immediate and permanent. The Inquiry concluded that

if we turn back to compare this definition of appropriate function arrived at by our survey of the whole machinery of public communication with the public library's own statements of historic faith and current official objectives, it seems evident that the librarians have been on the right track in describing their purposes.[53]

---

[49] *Ibid*. p. 25.
[50] *Ibid*.
[51] *Ibid*. p. 48.
[52] *Ibid*. p. 50.
[53] *Ibid*. p. 51.

Much less restraint than that employed by Leigh was used by Campbell and Metzner who surveyed for the Public Library Inquiry the use made of the public library by the adult population of eighty selected communities, and concluded that "the library suffers from being a quiet voice in an increasingly clamorous world." They expressed the opinion that "there is reason to believe that through broader services and a more active information program this fraction of the population (which it now serves) could be considerably increased."[54] Thus they charged that the public library is "failing to a considerable extent as an agency of mass communication and enlightenment."[55] Yet, despite this clamor for a more "dynamic role" for the library, Leigh, surveying a decade later "The Changing Concepts in the Public Library's Role," found that very little change had taken place, and therefore, confined his observations to minor modifications in administrative and organizational patterns.[56] Speaking at the same conference to which Leigh addressed his remarks, Dan Lacy echoed once again the old refrain:

> Perhaps the greatest opportunity for expanding library usefulness lies in closer identification with all the manifold wealth of group discussion and informational activities which we loosely call adult education.[57]

But, despite the lesson of library history and the findings of the Public Library Inquiry, he added,

> The problem is not that of the library *creating* adult education activities; it is to find a role in providing effective library service for the enormous range of activities originating in other institutions and organizations—including those that have not realized their need for service.[58]

The assumed role of providing effective library service to adult educa-

---

54 Angus Campbell and Charles A. Metzner. *Public Use of the Library and Other Sources of Information.* Ann Arbor. University of Michigan. Institute for Social Research. 1950. p. 45.

55 *Ibid.* Also see: William S. Gray. "Summary of Reading Investigations, July 1, 1949, to June 30, 1950." *Journal of Educational Research.* vol. 44 (February 1951), p. 403.

56 Robert D. Leigh. "Changing Concepts of the Public Library's Role." *Library Quarterly.* vol. 27 (October 1957), pp. 223–34.

57 Dan Lacy. "The Adult in a Changing Society; Implications for the Public Library." *Library Quarterly.* vol. 27 (October 1957), p. 292.

58 *Ibid.*

tion agencies arises from a failure to recognize that the self-education movement, unlike formal education, has never been dominantly book-centered. The lyceum, the mechanic's institute, the chautauqua, the literary circle, were dependent primarily upon the lecture platform as their major means of communication, and books had little part in any of their programs. Even in the Agricultural Extension Service, it was the county agent, not the county library, who was the main source of information. Of the contemporary adult education movement, Cyril O. Houle, who perhaps more than most education specialists urged integration with library operations, asserted, in 1956, that the formalized programs of adult education were decreasing in their use of printed materials, and that such materials as were used were specially prepared pamphlets.[59] Even when programs were devoted to the "Great Books," the participants were often supplied with capsule collections of excerpts provided by the sponsoring organization and did not make use of the texts of the books themselves. Again, Dan Lacy reported,

> A national program of world politics, also often sponsored by libraries, set forth in its promotional literature: "You could do it alone and spend months collecting and reading a costly library of scores of volumes," and suggests instead that one do it the easy way by reading a few pamphlets and then discussing.[60]

Not only did organized adult education fail to make extensive use of books, but also adults did not represent a major segment of the users of the library. As Berelson's studies of the library's public showed, children and young people were the dominant groups in public library patronage, "the public library retains only a small part of its younger users after they have entered adulthood"; and again "the use of the library falls off sharply at the school-leaving age"; or again, "by and large the older the people the less they use the library"; and, finally, "in this country the public library is today a young people's institution."[61] But most important of all, Berelson pointed out, was the fact that adult use of the public library varied directly with educational achievement, and "the educational level emerges as the most important single factor affecting adult use of the American public library."[62]

---

[59] Cyril O. Houle. "The Use of Print in Adult Education Agencies." *Adult Reading*, ed. Nelson B. Henry. Chicago. University of Chicago Press. 1956. pp. 157–87.
[60] Lacy. "Adult in Changing Society." p. 289.
[61] Bernard R. Berelson. *The Library's Public.* New York. Columbia University Press. 1949. pp. 21–24.
[62] *Ibid.* p. 30.

In general, Berelson's 1949 data are still valid today, and the public library is not so much a place where adults get education as where educated adults get books. Robert Leigh once stated this point succinctly when he said, "The public library is not the people's university but the *library* of the people's university." Few libraries have either the personnel or the physical equipment—books and plant—adequate to the needs of an adult education program, and few librarians have the training that prepares them for such educational responsibilities.

There was an element of prophesy in Leigh's aphorism, for in recent years libraries have been working with groups in the community interested in particular aspects of civic life, such as the environment, drug addiction, unemployment, and related problems. Such activities, now generally referred to as adult services, rather than adult education, represent a broadening of the earlier concept and a more rational view of the role of the library in it. Adult education in the earlier sense still persists in some communities, but many of these activities, with the cooperation and assistance of the public library are being carried on outside the library walls.[63] More and more the library is assuming its proper role as "the library of the people's university."

Through the mastery of his bibliographic resources, aiding the adult in broadening his educational and social horizons is the business of the librarian. Three powerful tendencies in contemporary society will compel the librarian to define his role in ministering to the intellectual needs of the adult citizen. The first, and most obvious, is the success of modern medicine in conquering disease, and especially the diseases of childhood and youth. The expectation of life, at all ages, has been steadily lengthening. Regardless of the behavior of the birthrate, the proportion of the population in the higher age brackets seems certain to increase substantially in the foreseeable future. Thus there will be a growing number of adults to be served. The second influence derives from the rising enrollments in higher education and the growing numbers of the population who will be college graduates and the holders, even, of advanced academic degrees. It would seem logical to assume that those who are educationally advantaged will place more demands upon the library than their neighbors who, for whatever reason, have not been exposed to the academic life. One may also anticipate that the character of the demands placed upon the library will change as the educational level of the patron changes.

Finally, there is the ubiquitous impact of automation, and the promise

---

[63] See: Margaret E. Monroe. *Library Adult Education; The Biography of an Idea.* New York. Scarecrow Press, 1963.

which it brings of drastic reductions in the demand for labor. Substantial increases in leisure time will create new and serious problems for which society is completely unprepared. The ethic of work is so deeply imbedded in our culture that the prospect of nonwork as a virtue can throw our whole system of social values into chaos. Robert Maynard Hutchins has stated the problem of the machine in relation to leisure time clearly:

> The great question about the reduction of hours of labor always is: What are we going to do with ourselves? One thing we might do is learn; and we might do it all our lives. The new technology could make it possible to develop a learning society. Every home could be equipped with a television set that would give access to educational material of every kind at every level. The knowledge and the wisdom of the race would be available at last to every member of it.
>
> The problem of technology in education is the same as that of technology generally. What are we going to use it for? These devices may strengthen the worst tendencies in education, which are to confuse it with training and the accumulation of information. . . . They may diminish the attention given to reasoning and judgment; they may reduce discussion; they may promote centralization. . . . Everything depends upon the conception of education held by the people in charge. . . . Hence it is important to begin thinking now about how the enormous power of educational technology is to be guided and controlled. . . . One of the most important social changes in history is impending. We shall have to develop new social and political institutions to cope with it.[64]

A culture, as has been shown, is comprised of a cluster of subcultures, each composed of people living by different "time clocks," and each with its own bundle of habituations, each age group formed in a different period with different sets of conditionings and different attitudes toward the future. In ameliorating the strain which shifts in the value system place upon a culture, the library can play a vital role. Through gerontology and related sciences, and through fundamental research into the problems of the aging process (both physical and psychological), the librarian must seek to understand the adult, particularly the aging adult, as they have sought to understand the physical, emotional, and educational problems of the child.[65] To create an atmosphere of understanding

---

[64] Robert Maynard Hutchins. "New Computer Technology May Revolutionize Educational Process." *The Plain Dealer.* Cleveland, Ohio. (August 7, 1966), pp. 5–AA.
[65] See: Max Lerner. *America as a Civilization.* New York. Simon and Schuster. 1957.

and mutual respect among the disparate ethnic, social, and religious groups in our culture is one of the most serious problems facing society today. Librarians have had considerable experience in interpreting their role in the acculturation process with respect to youth, but the attitudes of the adult are equally important.

## THE PROMOTION OF READING

The role of the library as an agency for the promotion of reading is historically a later expression of its role as an agency of education. The extent to which the promotion of reading is accepted as the proper role of the library is evident from the fact that when Robert D. Leigh and his associated experts in the social science disciplines began their "appraisal in sociological, cultural, and human terms of the extent to which librarians are achieving their objectives,"[66] they unquestioningly accepted the time-honored assumption that "the major objectives of the American public library are . . . education, information, aesthetic appreciation, research, and recreation."[67] This was more a statement of book selection policy than a formulation of objectives, but it derived from the belief that though "the objectives of the public library are many and various . . . in essence they are two—to promote enlightened citizenship and to enrich personal life. They have to do with the twin pillars of the American way, the democratic process of group life, and the sanctity and dignity of the individual person."[68] Gerald W. Johnson expressed the same point of view when he wrote the introduction to the ALA public library standards:

> The key to this broader world is the possession of books, but if the door stands wide open there is no need of a key. It is the business of the public librarian to keep the door open and to see that no stumbling block lies in the way of those who would enter. Any-

pp. 611–20. See also: Robert J. Havighurst and Ruth Albrecht. *Older People.* New York. Longmans, Green. 1943; Warren S. Thompson. *Population Problems.* 4th ed. New York. McGraw-Hill. 1953. pp. 373–75.

[66] Leigh. *Public Library.* p. 3.

[67] American Library Association. Committee on Post-war Planning. *A National Plan for Public Library Service.* Chicago. American Library Association. 1948. p. 107. Summarized from the Committee's *Post-war Standards for Public Libraries.* Chicago. American Library Association. 1943. pp. 19–24.

[68] *Ibid.* p. 16.

thing that contributes to this end is good library practice; anything that blocks it is bad, no matter what the rules may say. . . . It is the responsibility of the operating personnel not only to see that the open door shall remain open, but also that it shall be inviting.[69]

We are here confronted by a positive value judgment on the act of reading itself, based upon a faith in the importance of the act as contributing to the moral and intellectual welfare of both the individual and the community. In our contemporary culture the motivation of this faith is largely socioeconomic, for economic amelioration and improved social status depend largely upon knowledge, and reading is one of the most important means for the acquisition of knowledge. Therefore the library, if it is to achieve its fullest role in society, is not passively to make books available when needed by a potential reader, but actively to stimulate the use of books.[70] S. R. Ranganathan enunciated the classic statement of this philosophy when, in two of his Five Laws of Library Science he wrote, *"Every Reader His Book*, and *Every Book Its Reader.*" Books, he insisted are not for preservation or for the chosen few, but for all.[71] But the supreme, not to say extreme, statements of the role of the library as an agency for the stimulation of reading occur annually with the conferring by the American Library Association of the Clarence Day Award "to a librarian for outstanding work in encouraging the love of books and reading,"[72] and the April celebration of National Library Week. Both are publisher sponsored and publisher-bookseller oriented, and the latter should probably be known as National Reading Week. But they both bear the blessing of the American Library Association which conceals the stigma of commercialism and may even yield some tax benefits to their sponsors.[73] Thus, it became customary to pronounce a value judgment upon the number of users to which a library is accessible and the numbers it serves, and circulation figures were assumed to be a valid measure of a library's success in meeting community needs. When these figures were numerically unimpressive in comparison with attendance at athletic events

---

[69] Gerald W. Johnson. "Role of the Public Library." *Minimum Standards for Public Library Systems, 1966.* American Library Association, Public Library Association, Standards Committee. Chicago. American Library Association. 1967. p. 3.

[70] See: B. Landheer. *Social Functions of Libraries.* New York. Scarecrow Press. 1957. p. 93.

[71] S. R. Ranganathan. *The Five Laws of Library Science.* Madras. The Madras Library Association. 1957. Chapters 1–5.

[72] *Literary and Library Prizes.* New York. R. R. Bowker Company. 1967. p. 241.

[73] Jesse H. Shera. "The Cult of Reading." *Wilson Library Bulletin.* vol. 40 (April 1966), p. 767.

or the sale of cigarettes, as they would almost inevitably be, the librarians sought comfort in the sociologists' principle of "widening circles of influence." "For the overwhelming majority," writes Gerald W. Johnson, "the quickest and easiest access to the world's best thought is through the public library. To maintain this source of information open to all and unpolluted by any self-seeking interest is a task important beyond all computation." For the library "is at once the most easily available and the most independent" of all the agencies of information. "It is not . . . committed to a particular point of view, . . . primarily concerned with events of the moment, nor . . . hampered by the physical restrictions of its medium."[74]

Johnson's point of view, which probably represents the attitude of most librarians toward the role of the public library in society, has been of great value in freeing the agency from the shackles of censorship, and making unpopular the notion that the reading of certain types of literature might engender in the reader certain "harmful" or "socially unacceptable" ideas. But on the other hand, and despite the fact that the censor has never been able to produce evidence to support his case, uncritical acceptance of the Baconian doctrine that reading makes "a full man," has encouraged librarians to foster reading as implicitly desirable and to hypothesize a "general reader" as the stereotype of the public library patron. To imply that reading should be a generalized habit, and that when a child has a book in his hand his soul is with the immortals leads to confused thinking about the role of the written word in society. When librarians are confused about the role of the book in their culture, they, quite obviously, can not think clearly about the purposes of the library. Lacking a clear understanding of what the public library is for, the public librarian will stand, as Kathleen Molz has so aptly said, "dead center in the midst of muddle."[75] One may assume that the habit of reading has a structure of its own and that enthusiasm for one kind of reading will not necessarily spread, contagion-like, to other, especially to more difficult, types. If one seeks to encourage reading *qua* reading it would seem logical to expose the reader to only that which is in itself excellent and hope that eventually the reader will develop standards of value of his own; to do otherwise would be an implicit denial of the educational role of the library and an argument for keeping reading guidance to a minimum.

There has always been a fine line between censorship and education, between giving the reader what is "good" and keeping from him that which

---

[74] Johnson. "Role of Public Library." p. 4.
[75] Molz. "The Public Custody of the High Pornography." *The American Scholar*. vol. 36 (Winter 1966–67) p. 102.

is "bad." Freedom of the *press* is not the same as "intellectual freedom" in the *library*. Again, to quote Miss Molz, "In this age of assets, people have every right to *buy* what they want to read, and the question of pornography, or smut literature, or whatever other designation it goes under, will eventually boil down to nothing more than what is encompassed in the old phrase, *chacun à son goût*."[76] The disciples of "intellectual freedom" are on extremely shaky ground when they try to argue that the reading of "good" books is beneficial while the reading of "bad" books will do one no harm. They cannot have it both ways. There may be no reliable evidence that the reading of "violent" literature will stimulate violent acts, or that reading is in any way related to social behavior; yet we cannot divest ourselves of the belief that the reading of "trash" injures the *taste* of the reader in very subtle ways.[77] "Over many American lunch counters," Douglas Waples told the University of Chicago's 1938 Institute on Current Issues in Library Administration, "hangs a sign, 'The bank has agreed to sell no sandwiches and we have agreed to cash no checks.' How about a sign in front of the loan desk, 'Mike Flanagan's drug store, for obvious reasons of self-interest, has agreed to stock no books of importance to the serious reader, and we, for the same reason, have agreed to stock nothing else.' "[78]

Such statistics as are available seem to suggest that there may possibly be a positive correlation between the complexity of socioeconomic structure, the production of print, and the number and size of libraries. There is also some evidence to suggest that book production per million of population is, at present, highest in the smaller countries with relatively high standards of living. A similar correlation appears to exist between standard of living and the size and use of libraries.[79] But such correlations cannot be taken as proof of cause and effect. Historical evidence, however, seems to prove that book production, reading, and library development are the products of a maturing society, and that when a culture achieves a certain level of sophistication, libraries begin to emerge. The urge to seek satisfaction from reading is one of the last of the human wants to be expressed, and, despite the efforts of the librarians, it will not manifest itself until certain prerequisite socioeconomic conditions have been met.[80]

Every historical period has its own "mentality," and the mentality of

---

[76] *Ibid.* p. 103.

[77] Jesse H. Shera. "Intellectual Freedom—Intellectual? Free?" *Wilson Library Bulletin.* vol. 42 (November 1967), pp. 323 and 344.

[78] Douglas Waples. "Peoples and Libraries." *Current Issues in Library Administration,* ed. Carleton B. Joeckel. Chicago. University of Chicago Press. 1939. p. 370.

[79] See statistics in Landheer. *Social Functions of Libraries.* pp. 103–8.

[80] Shera. *Foundations of Public Library.* Chapter 7.

each period tends to stress certain ideas more than others. Thus, historians have been able to characterize each cultural period in terms of its dominant orientation or ideology. But these dominant ideas do not necessarily reflect the entire culture of a period; within a given culture or cluster of subcultures a variety of divergent philosophies may compete, so that the influence of a particular idea may vary within a particular culture and its subcultural pattern at any one time. Thus the need of the individual is, to a large extent, determined by the culture in which he lives, and the choices which he may make for himself are sharply limited by his intellectual as well as his physical environment. One may say that an individual has a choice between reading and nonreading, and that the librarian can direct that choice toward the use of books, but in practice such choice operates only within very narrow limits. If the individual is a member of a highly developed culture, his "status" largely determines his needs. He needs certain information in order to participate as a member of his group, and the character of that need determines whether he will read more or less, or more of one kind of material than another. Even recreational reading is largely conditioned by the rhythm or social speed of the culture and the frustrations, pressures, and maladjustments created by it. Therefore, the rate and direction of change in a society will influence considerably the reading patterns of its members, and one dare not assume that reading habits are transferable from social segment to social segment or from time period to time period.

There have been many attempts to classify the spectrum of reading according to type. Librarians, as previously noted, have tended to accept the categories of "education, information, aesthetic appreciation, research, and recreation," and from these they derived a statement of the function of the public library. Oskar Thyregod, in his study of the cultural function of libraries, follows the distinctions made by Max Scheler of "salvation-, culture-, and achievement-knowledge."[81] Landheer has modified these to "devotional, cultural, achievement, and compensatory" reading,[82] and there are others. But these are fundamentally only variants in nomenclature, emphasis, or points of view; all have been used at one time or another to define the role of the library, but their very diffuseness demonstrates their unfitness for definition, and they may have done more harm than good in blunting the objectives which they were supposed to clarify. Such

---

[81] Oskar Thyregod. *Die Kulturfunktion der Bibliothek.* The Hague. Martinus Nijhoff. 1936.

[82] Landheer. *Social Functions of Libraries.* Chapters 3–5.

categories of reading behavior say, by implication, that the role of the library is to play every role associated with reading, that it must be all things to all men, that it must promote all kinds of reading for all kinds of purposes. When one is not certain of what "reading is for," it may be prudent to promote reading for everything; but this is scarcely an acceptable credo for a profession, and it does not demand much knowledge for its implementation.

Most thinking about reading has been along the narrowest of lines. One can be reasonably confident that reading, like all other forms of human activity, must involve some effort on the part of the reader if it is to achieve rewards. Where there is no challenge, there is little or no response, and therefore, if reading is too closely adjusted to the mentality of the reader, it will fall short of its goal. There is also considerable evidence to show that relatively few people within even the most mature of cultures are willing to make the effort required of the reader, regardless of the promotional efforts of the librarian. One may seriously doubt, then, whether the role of the library as an agency for the promotion of reading will ever be statistically very important.

A much more basic problem is the impact of reading upon the mind that will subject itself to the discipline that reading requires. The social and psychological factors involved in reading are still to be explored. Reading may "improve" the mind, but such "improvement" probably does not result from reading in its generic form; it results rather from specific types of reading, but the nature of these types and their psychological interrelationships with other forms of mental and emotional activity are still to be explored. Librarians, who themselves are compulsive and omnivorous readers (that is probably why they became librarians) cannot afford to comfort themselves by "spraying" the community with a wide variety of reading matter, predicated on the assumption that somehow the objective will be hit and that, effective or not, the very barrage is itself a bastion against "censorship." Philip C. Ritterbush, of the Smithsonian Institution, put his finger squarely on the central problem that has been discussed here when, in reviewing Mortimer Adler's *The Difference of Man and the Difference it Makes*, for *Science*, he wrote:

> We have no reliable index of public enlightenment, and the efforts of our principal institutions and organizations devoted to this objective are distorted by a host of conflicting presuppositions about what the layman "needs to know" and whether or not there exists an unsatisfied "demand" for knowledge . . . on the part of the public. I do not know

of a serious student of the sociology of knowledge who has devoted himself to this matter or even of an introductory historical survey of past efforts at popularization.[83]

---

[83] Philip C. Ritterbush. "Interpreting the Human Species." *Science.* vol. 160 (April 5, 1968), p. 57.

# Six

# The Role of the Library in the Dissemination of Information

Every culture has had to evolve for itself the plan of its own social systems. One age is concerned with the role of Divine power in guiding the behavior of man, another with that of reason, a third with the democratic ideal. Present-day culture seems to be largely concerned with the utilization of applied science in the design of society. Applied science is directed toward the practical solutions of technical problems and it utilizes the methods of observation, reason, test, and verification. To this experimental approach to technical problems, pragmatism brings a philosophical base.

The dissemination of information is, as has already been emphasized, one of the most basic of social activities, and one of the most essential. Perhaps no culture is more dependent upon the successful communication of information than one based on applied science. Therefore, it is not surprising that the role of all types of libraries as centers of information is more important today than it has ever been. Because this role of the library has grown to such proportions that it is arousing widespread interest beyond the ranks of the professional librarians, it seems advisable to devote an entire chapter to it.

## THE MEANING OF INFORMATION

"Information" is a term to which usage has given many meanings, but for which there are few definitions. In the generic sense, it is that which is transmitted by the act or process of communication, it may be a message, a signal, a stimulus. It assumes a response in the receiving organism and, therefore, possesses response-potential. In the present context, however, a more restricted interpretation must be understood. Its motivation is inherently utilitarian, and it is akin, if not completely synonymous, with Landheer's "achievement knowledge."[1] It is instrumental, and it usually is communicated in an organized or formalized pattern, mainly because such formalization increases potential utility. Since it is instrumental, utility is its major criterion of social value, and it promotes adaptive behavior.[2]

The librarian's preoccupation with the printed word has disposed him to regard information as being derived from graphic records and, indeed, librarians are still not infrequently taught to place greater value on the printed statement than on oral communication. The dissemination of information, then, may be regarded as a role in which the functions of conservation and education coalesce.

## THE ORIGINS OF INFORMATION SERVICE

From the surviving legal codes of the Babylonians, Assyrians, and Hittites, it is apparent that at least as early as 2,000 B.C. the law required that every business transaction, even the smallest, be preserved in written form and duly authorized, and the spades of the archaeologists have exposed large agglomerations of clay tablets on which were scribed vast quantities of such instrumental or "achievement" records.[3] Long before the days of Assurbanipal, the records of business and government were systematically collected and preserved.[4] One may properly assume, then,

---

[1] B. Landheer. *The Social Functions of Libraries*. New York. Scarecrow Press. 1957. pp. 72–90.

[2] Reference should be made to discussion of information and knowledge in Chapter 4.

[3] Edward Chiera. *They Wrote on Clay*. Chicago. University of Chicago Press. 1938. pp. 67–79.

[4] Allan Nevins. *The Gateway to History*. New York. Heath. 1938. pp. 79–85. Also: Leo Deuel. *The Testament of Time*. New York. Knopf. 1965. pp. 55–56.

that from their beginnings, libraries were essential centers for the preservation and utilization of information necessary to the operation of the economic life of the people, and that to the library went civil authorities seeking the knowledge that was required for the adequate performance of their respective roles. This function of the library as a center of information was continued in the Christian era, the Middle Ages, the Renaissance, and grew in importance with the expansion of trade and commerce that followed the age of reconnaissance. During the latter half of the sixteenth century, the House of Fugger brought together, through the effective operation of its "intelligence system," perhaps the greatest concentration of economic and social information that the world has yet known.[5]

With the increasing complexity of Western culture and the elaboration of its physical equipment came a parallel increase in dependence upon graphic records which further intensified the role of the library with respect to information. Similarly, the spread of literacy enhanced its availability to growing numbers of the population. But professional awareness on the part of the librarian of his responsibilities for the active dissemination of information developed with surprising slowness. Ticknor and Everett and their associates on the first board of trustees of the Boston Public Library devoted much attention, in their first report on a public library for Boston, to the library as an agency of education and an instrument for the promotion of reading, and they also recognized that a certain proportion of the library collection was sufficiently important for reference use that it should not be permitted to circulate—"Cyclopedias, Dictionaries, important public documents"—but they apparently failed to perceive, in any formal sense, the implicit importance of the library in the distribution of information.[6] Similarly, at the first librarians' conference held in 1853, though there was much attention given to problems of cataloging and other forms of bibliographic organization, the development of popular libraries, the acquisition of government documents, and the promotion of international exchanges, the role of the library in the dissemination of information was almost entirely ignored. Only Charles Folsom of the Boston Athenaeum, in discussing the *Duties and Qualifications of Librarians*, mentioned, as being more or less secondary to the custodial function, that "the dispenser of a great library" should "have some notion" of the

---

[5] *The Fugger News-Letters*, ed. Victor von Klarwill and trans. Pauline de Chary. London. John Lane. 1924. pp. vii–xxxiv. Also: George T. Matthews, ed. *News and Rumor in Renaissance Europe*. (*The Fugger Newsletters*.) New York. Putnam. 1959.
[6] Trustees of Boston Public Library. *Report; July 1852*. (City Document No. 37) Boston. J. H. Eastburn, City Printer. 1852. p. 16.

library's contents in order to understand its "scope and bearing, so as to be able readily to follow out subjects, and to put inquirers upon the right track."[7] Even the monumental 1876 *Report on Public Libraries in the United States*, which appeared a quarter of a century later, evinced no greater awareness of this aspect of the librarian's role than did the conference of 1853; the idea that the library should actively promote the dissemination of information, even through assistance to readers, was given only the most casual attention and was generally regarded as a distraction from the librarian's more important duties. The prevailing assumption seems to have been that reference works should be made easily available to the public so that the library staff might be free for more important tasks.[8]

This strange failure of the early professional librarians to recognize a library function that was indigenous to its social role may be attributed to a variety of causes: an excessive preoccupation with custodianship and preservation; the struggle to gain public recognition and more nearly adequate public support; early concern with the development of management and housekeeping methods to the exclusion of more professional responsibilities; the shackling of the college library by academic regulations which were directed more toward book preservation than toward book use, and hence hampered the librarian in performing any important service function to the academic community; and the relative poverty of most libraries, both in book stock and in staff.[9] Not entirely facetiously, one might add to this list a current and rather widespread belief that was cogently stated as early as 1790 by an anonymous contributor to the Boston *Independent Chronicle* for May 13th of that year. Condemning even a very modest expenditure of public funds for the formation of a library for the Congress of the United States, he wrote with some heat:

> It is supposed that the Members of Congress are acquainted with history; the laws of nations, and possess such political information as is necessary for the management of the affairs of the government. If they are not, we have been unfortunate in our

---

[7] Proceedings of the conference as reprinted in George B. Utley. *The Librarians' Conference of 1853*. Chicago. American Library Association. 1951. p. 96.

[8] U.S. Bureau of Education. *Public Libraries in the United States of America; Their History, Condition, and Management.* Special Report, Part 1. Washington. Government Printing Office. 1876. p. 688.

[9] See: Samuel Rothstein. "The Development of the Concept of Reference Service in American Libraries 1850–1900." *Library Quarterly.* vol. 23 (January 1953), pp. 1–15.

choice. . . . The design and end of the Constitution are for quite different purposes, than for the amusement, or even instruction of Congress. I would ask wherein is a public Library conducive to the purposes mentioned in the preamble of the Constitution?. . .it is supposed that the members are fully competent. . .without being at the expense of furnishing them with Books for their improvement. . . . The people look to *practical politics*, as they presume the Theory is obtained previous to the members taking their seats in Congress.[10]

Such reasoning, one must admit, is not entirely alien to contemporary thought, even among professional librarians who (collectively, if not individually) have failed to perceive the importance of the library as a source of information of immediate and practical utility in the business of living.

It is not surprising that the first professional recognition among librarians of the importance of the dissemination of information should come from the public librarians. The emerging public library presented to its supporters the problem of justifying the expenditure of municipal funds by demonstrating the values the community might derive from it. Even in those early days, volume of borrowings and services rendered were the customary criteria of library utility, and there was always present, therefore, a definite incentive to devise new ways in which the librarians could increase their usefulness. Nor is it surprising that leadership in this movement should come from such larger municipalities as Boston, Worcester, and (later) Newark, where book stock and staff were sufficiently adequate to enable their librarians to look beyond the daily routines.

The first serious proposal for library service that would promote its role as an information source was made at the Philadelphia Library Conference in 1876 by Samuel Swett Green, librarian of the public library at Worcester, Massachusetts. His paper, entitled "The Desirableness of Establishing Personal Intercourse and Relations Between Librarians and Readers in Popular Libraries,"[11] argued modestly that because the bibliographic tools devised by the librarians were unfamiliar to the public, the librarian should make his professional knowledge of graphic records "accessible" to the library patrons. But, as Rothstein pointed out, Green was promoting a new technique of library service rather than a new theory

---

[10] Quoted by David C. Mearns. *The Story Up to Now. The Library of Congress, 1800–1946*. Washington. The Library of Congress. 1947. p. 3.

[11] Samuel Swett Green's paper was published under the title: "Personal Relations Between Librarians and Readers." *Library Journal*. vol. 1 (October 1876), pp. 74–81.

of librarianship, for even he did not regard information service as a central professional responsibility of the librarian.[12] His proposal was mainly a public relations gesture.

The reception which greeted Green's proposal was mixed; it was generally approved by his colleagues at the 1876 Conference, newspapers in Boston and New York greeted it with favor, contrasting the hospitality of the Worcester public library with the "unaccommodating spirit" found in the libraries of their respective cities. On the other hand, the London conference of English and American librarians of 1877 was less enthusiastic about the idea. Charles Ammi Cutter believed that librarians should put more reliance on the bibliographic tools than on personal assistance, a point of view favored at the Boston Public Library; and even those who spoke out in favor of Green's point of view—W. F. Poole, Otis Robinson, and Reuben Guild—were agreeing with rather than emulating the Worcester librarian.[13] Actually, Green is probably more significant for what he represented—the changing pattern of library use in America—than for his professional influence. At Harvard, Justin Winsor envisaged the college library as having an important role in the research and educational program of the college, a role which, in a sense, was being forced upon the academic library by the importation from Germany of the seminar method and the Teutonic faith in the pursuit of new knowledge and the promotion of research as the most important functions of the university. The broadening of the curriculum to include scientific, technical, and professional education, the inauguration of the graduate school for the training of scholars, the elevation of research to a position coordinate with teaching, transformed the academic world of the last quarter of the nineteenth century, and in the wake of this transformation there came a slow but unmistakable shifting of the library's course; it became user- rather than book-centered. This new structuring of academic scholarship, as Robert C. Binkley says, raised research from "an honored sport" to "an exclusive profession,"[14] and brought scholars, who had hitherto been working largely in isolation with few resources other than their own, together into centers

---

12 Samuel Rothstein. *The Development of Reference Service Through Academic Tradition, Public Library Practice, and Special Librarianship.* (A.C.R.L. Monograph No. 14) Chicago. Association of College and Reference Libraries. 1955. p. 22.

13 *Ibid.* pp. 21–23.

14 Robert C. Binkley. "New Tools for Men of Letters." *Selected Papers of Robert C. Binkley,* ed. Max H. Fisch. Cambridge, Mass. Harvard University Press. 1948. p. 191.

of concentration where the tools of research, including libraries, could be made more readily available.

The new role which was being imposed upon the academic library spread, in a modified form, to public libraries, and during the 1880s many public librarians began to take more seriously their responsibilities in "aiding readers," though there was generally no clear-cut distinction between a true "information service" and assistance in "the improvement of reading taste." As the information role gained increasing professional acceptance, the term "reference work" slowly replaced the vague and ambiguous "aid to readers."

By 1885, Melvil Dewey had introduced an incipient form of subject specialization into the "reference department" of the Columbia University Library.[15] By 1890, William E. Foster at the Providence Public Library was exerting much influence for the promotion of a unified concept of reference work.[16] Soon the professional literature contained a substantial quantity of reporting on the nature and methods of reference work in a number of the larger public and academic libraries, and, in 1895, Adelaide Hasse reported an increasing attention to reference work in the training programs of many institutions.[17] Admittedly, in the eyes of the professional librarian this information role was still vague, and its outlines fragmented; yet there was unmistakably a growing awareness that it was somehow central to the librarian's task, and there were even those, like William I. Fletcher of Amherst College, who went so far as to challenge the supreme authority of the library catalog and insist on the need for "a quick-witted intelligence" to supplement and interpret the bibliographic mechanisms the librarians had created.[18]

---

[15] Columbia College Library. *First Annual Report of the Chief Librarian, 1884.* p. 6; *Second and Third Annual Reports, 1886*, p. 39. Also: Columbia University. School of Library Service. *School of Library Economy, Columbia College, 1887–1889; Documents for a History.* New York. School of Library Service. Columbia University. 1937. pp. 31–32.

[16] William E. Foster. "The Information Desk at the Providence Public Library." *Library Journal.* vol. 16 (September 1891), pp. 271–72.

[17] Adelaide R. Hasse. "The Training of Library Employes—IV." *Library Journal.* vol. 20 (September 1895), pp. 303–4.

[18] U.S. Congress. Joint Committee on the Library of Congress. *Report Under S.C.R. 26 Relative to the Condition and Management of the Library of Congress, With Hearings, March 3, 1897.* (54th Congress. Second Session. Senate Report 1573, 1897), pp. 232–33. In contrast to Fletcher, William H. Brett had argued that the catalog revealed the complete contents of the library. pp. 264–65.

## THE RISE OF TWENTIETH-CENTURY RESEARCH

At the turn of the twentieth century, this new awareness of an amplified role for the library in society was to receive a new and very different emphasis from forces quite unforeseen by American library pioneers. Admittedly, the development of research and the professionalization of scholarship prepared the way for the large research library—indeed, made such collections an absolute necessity. The sharp increase in interest in research that characterized the scholarship of the late nineteenth century did not long remain confined to academic walls. Research was becoming important in commercial and industrial enterprises. A seemingly unlimited supply of abundant raw material and natural power, coupled with the protective tariff, were no longer sufficient to ensure a permanent flow of profits. Confronted by sharpening competition and declining supplies of raw materials, industry began to look critically at its processes and to seek in applied scientific research the answers to its problems of production.[19]

This awakening of private enterprise to the potential value of research stimulated the sponsorship of scientific investigation by the federal government, though the foundations for government participation in scientific inquiry had been well laid by Joseph Henry and Samuel Langley at the Smithsonian Institution. The Department of Agriculture, after its establishment in 1864, quickly assumed leadership in the promotion of research that was to prove of great benefit to rural America. There followed such agencies as the Bureau of Mines, the Bureau of Standards, and others.[20] These were but foreshadowings of what was to come a half-century later; for though by the end of the nineteenth century, and even well into the twentieth, research was dominantly university oriented, the foreshadowings were unmistakable.

Collaboration between academic institutions and the federal government may be said to have begun with the passage of the Morrill Act, which created the land grant colleges. But any similar cooperation between industry and the universities was of much later origin—delayed, perhaps, by the fear that the world of scholarship might lose its soul in

---

[19] U.S. National Resources Committee. *Research: a National Resource*. Washington, D.C. Government Printing Office. 1939–41. vol. 2, pp. 24–28.

[20] A. Hunter Dupree. *Science in the Federal Government; a History of Policies and Activities to 1940*. Cambridge, Mass. Harvard University Press. 1957. Chapters 8, 10, and 13.

the marketplace.[21] Today government, industry, and education, encouraged by the philanthropic foundations, have joined in a concerted attack upon the barriers to human knowledge. This collaboration has been one of the distinguishing characteristics of twentieth-century American scholarship, and its results have deeply influenced the totality of the American cultural pattern. This process of reshaping the American culture through the growing force of research created an insatiable demand for information, a demand that traditional instruments of communication could not meet.[22] Never has a culture been so dependent upon communication and graphic records, yet human inventiveness has lagged behind the attempt to maintain a proper balance between the resources for utilizing graphic records and the demands which society is making of them, and nowhere is this lag more apparent than in the library. So deeply steeped have the librarians become in the genteel tradition of their profession—conservation, popular enlightenment, the improvement of taste—that they have tended to ignore the demand for information.

So drastic a break with tradition did this "new" role appear at the turn of the century, that the librarian as disseminator of information became known as a "special librarian," because John Cotton Dana and his associates could think of no other name, and there were many who questioned whether such a librarian was really a librarian at all. So rigidly was this line drawn that one librarian could write, in 1915, "The main function of the general library is to make books available. The function of the special library is to make information available."[23] It was indeed difficult for librarians to define their role apart from the type or kind of materials handled. The word itself came from the Latin *librus*, which meant *book*. There could be no getting around it.

Though the modern expression of the role of the library as an information center may be said to have begun with the legal profession, particularly in assistance to legislators and others charged with governmental responsibility,[24] it was John Cotton Dana who was the first professional

---

[21] Eric Hodgins. "The Strange State of American Research." *The Mighty Force of Research*, ed. Editors of *Fortune*. New York. McGraw-Hill. 1956. pp. 1–20.

[22] See Fritz Machlup. *The Production and Distribution of Knowledge in the United States*. Princeton. Princeton University Press. 1962. Chapters 9–10.

[23] Ethel M. Johnson. "The Special Library and Some of Its Problems." *Special Libraries*. vol. 6 (December 1915), pp. 158–59.

[24] The lawmakers have, of course, always depended heavily upon the library for the information they need for the prosecution of their work. This is probably due to the fact that the control of human conduct was one of the first responsibilities

librarian to campaign actively for assumption by the library of a role in serving the informational needs of its society. At the Breton Woods Conference of 1908, when Dana assumed the leadership in organizing the Special Libraries Association, he proclaimed his philosophy of librarianship:

> The Library idea has always been more or less academic, monastic, classic. . . . The rapid development of special libraries managed by experts. . . is simply an outward manifestation that the man of affairs has come to realize that printed things form the most useful and most important tools of his business, no matter what that business may be.[25]

But so drastic seemed his philosophy to the majority of his colleagues that, a year later, his attempts to bring the newly organized Special Libraries Association into the American Library Association met with only a rebuff from what he termed "the cumbersome A.L.A." He wrote in the *Library Journal*:

> My suggestions to the Executive Board in this line were as definitely ignored by the Board as have been many other suggestions from me. That there is a very active library organization, affiliated but not a definite part of the American Library Association, is a fact which is not due to me but to shortcomings elsewhere.[26]

How accurately Dana assessed the role of the library and the extent to which the rank and file of professional librarians eventually deserted one of their original mandates, has been adequately proved by subsequent events. The movement envisaged by Dana grew slowly but steadily, until in 1935 the *Special Libraries Directory* listed 1,154 such organizations, but this same directory for the year 1953 lists 2,489 libraries, an increase of 115.6 per cent in less than two decades.[27] The increase in membership

---

of a society and also one of the first to require considerable dependence upon graphic records. But even in modern times, the legislative reference library was probably the first form of the "special library." See: Louis J. Bailey. "Legislative Reference Service." *Special Libraries*. vol. 21 (January 1930), p. 7. Also: Rothstein. *Development of Reference Service*. pp. 54–61.

25 Quoted in Chalmers Hadley. *John Cotton Dana, A Sketch*. Chicago. American Library Association. 1943. p. 88.

26 *Ibid*. pp. 88–89. It is interesting to note that Dana's experience with the A.L.A. had a definite parallel in England where, at the Hoddesdon Conference of 1924, the Association of Special Libraries and Information Bureaux, now ASLIB, was formed and went its own way quite independent of the Library Association.

27 Special Libraries Association. *Special Libraries Directory, 1935*. New York. Special Libraries Association. 1936; *Ibid. 1953*.

of the Special Libraries Association itself rose from 1,100 in 1930 to 5,716 in 1970, a five-fold increase.[28] By contrast, the membership of the American Library Association grew during the same period from 12,000 to 28,641, slightly more than doubling membership in 40 years.[29] The contrast is made even more striking by the fact that the growth of the Special Libraries Association represents by no means all librarians engaged in information work. During the period covered by the above statistics, there was also established the American Documentation Institute (which changed its name in 1967 to the American Society for Information Science), the Division of Chemical Literature of the American Chemical Society, and lesser "splinter" groups or subgroups. Even the American Library Association formed, in 1965, its Information Science and Automation Division. Many of the members of these groups, though they are engaged in library work, do not consider themselves librarians and hence do not affiliate with either the A.L.A. or the S.L.A. In fact, so repugnant is the term "librarian" to many of these individuals that they take advantage of every opportunity to dissociate themselves from it, a phenomenon which, in itself, is a sad commentary on the failure of the library profession to perceive the growing importance of one of its most fundamental responsibilities.[30]

The increasing dependence of our contemporary culture upon information is conspicuous. Our economic structure, our standard of living, and what we are prone to call our age of "progress," are based upon research. Raymond H. Ewell of the National Science Foundation reports that expenditures for research and development in the United States have been growing at approximately an exponential rate. Annual expenditures for such purposes have passed the sixteeen billion dollar mark, more than three times as much as was spent for research during the entire period of our national history from 1776 through 1935, and equal to twelve percent of the annual *Federal Budget*. The magnitude of this investment is further emphasized by the fact that the annual expenditure for research and development is now over three percent of the gross national product, or approximately the same as the annual growth rate of the gross national

---

[28] Annual reports of the Membership Committee of the Special Libraries Association, as given annually in *Special Libraries*.

[29] American Library Association. Reports of membership in *A.L.A. Handbook* for the appropriate years.

[30] Jesse H. Shera. "Special Libraries—Why Special?" *Special Libraries; Problems and Cooperative Potential*, ed. Robert J. Havlik, Bill M. Woods, and Leona M. Vogt. Washington, D.C. American Documentation Institute. Mimeographed. Special Report for the National Commission on Libraries. 1967. pp. 5–16.

product since 1920. The relative portion of GNP devoted to research and development rose almost seven and one-half times between 1940 and 1960, and twenty times in the thirty years between 1930 and 1960.[31] Research lies at the foundation of the scholarship of our culture, and upon it the physical equipment and social organization are heavily dependent.[32] It is our collective obligation, as a people, to make certain that the uses of research are directed into socially responsible channels.

## THE INFORMATION NEEDS OF RESEARCH

The mission of research is, of course, the solution of problems, and it is certainly obvious that the solution of problems requires information. Research, then, as an asking of questions and a searching for valid answers, is as old as man himself, for problems have always been present in the environment, and man has been a constant seeker after their solution. Thus, out of random inquisitiveness emerged system, organization, and method, and the key to this trivium is communication. Even the lone research worker is not isolated from society. He must bring to his problem a certain reservoir of information that has been communicated to him through his past experience and stored in his memory. Though there may come a time when he can dissociate himself from the outside world and live upon his accumulated store of information, it is more probable that he will find it necessary to maintain a continuing communication—either directly through primary communication or indirectly through secondary communication—with the informational resources of the outside world. But in either situation there are certain types of information which he must have, and these, as was mentioned in Chapter 4, have been identified by Hertz and Rubenstein[33] as:

---

[31] R. H. Ewell. "The Role of Research in Economic Growth." *Chemical and Engineering News.* vol. 33 (July 18, 1955), pp. 2980–85. Also: "The Inventor." *Wall Street Journal.* (June 7, 1968), p. 1; and Machlup. *Distribution of Knowledge.* pp. 155–56. One should not forget, however, that the ancient libraries were centers of "research" though it was a very different type from that to which we today are conditioned. Also, the monasteries of the Middle Ages were centers of research, and it is entirely possible that even more of the GNP of the world of the Middle Ages went into research than is true today.

[32] Hodgins. "Strange State of Research." pp. 1–20.

[33] David B. Hertz and Albert H. Rubenstein. *Team Research.* Boston. Eastern Technical Publications. 1953. pp. 5–10.

1. Conceptual information: The ideas, theories, hypotheses about the relationships which exist among the variables in the area of his problem.

2. Empirical information: Experience, the data of research, may be drawn from one's self or, through communication, from others. It may be laboratory generated, or it may be the product of the "literature search."

3. Procedural information: The methodology which enables the investigator to operate more effectively. Procedural information relates to the means by which the data of the investigation are obtained, manipulated, and tested; it is essentially methodological and from it has been derived the "scientific attitude." The communication of procedural information from one discipline, or field of investigation, to another may illuminate vast shadows of human ignorance.

4. Stimulatory information: Man must be motivated, and there are but two sources for such motivation, himself and his environment. Stimulatory information that is environmentally derived is probably most effective when it is transmitted by direct communication—the contagious enthusiasm of another individual—but whether directly or indirectly communicated it is probably the most difficult of all forms of information to systematize. It is by nature fortuitous; it submits unwillingly to direction or compulsion.

The growing emphasis on "team" research derives from the natural gregariousness of man and his inherent propensity for group organization and has been stimulated by the growing magnitude of the research task itself. The body of accumulated knowledge has assumed such vast proportions, and its mastery has become so highly specialized, that an increasing number of research undertakings require the concerted attack of many minds, with varying skills, aptitudes, experience, and points of view. Team research magnifies and complicates the informational task, and greatly increases its importance. To the four types of information listed above, team research adds:

5. Policy information: This is the focus of the decision-making process. Collective activity necessitates the definition of objective and purpose, the fixing of responsibility, the codification of rights and privileges, and the delineation of function.

6. Directive information: Group activity cannot proceed effectively without coordination, and it is through directive information that this coordination is achieved.

The Hertz-Rubenstein study places primary emphasis upon the importance of the total communication process in team research, with the objective of identifying useful measures for improving the communication system in research laboratories, but its implications for the future role of the librarian as a disseminator of information throughout society are unmistakable. The informational needs of our culture must be met—indeed, they will be met—if not by the librarians, then by some other breed of cats who will groom themselves for the task.

There may be considerable relevance for librarianship, and particularly for library education, in the fact that much of the inquiry into the information needs of research workers has been done by those who are not librarians, or at most only "marginally" librarians, such as information scientists. The field has been especially attractive to specialists in communication and other aspects of the behavioral sciences. Also from the voluminous studies of user needs that have been made, it has become apparent that the library is only one channel within a communication system and that it is most difficult to study library use independently of the other sources of information. Certain questions inevitably arise to plague the investigator: What is the differential performance of library and extra-library information channels? Do the same people use both, in what sequence, and to what effect? A study by the Auerbach Corporation, which appeared in 1965, showed that the library ranked ninth among the communication channels used by scientists and engineers in the Department of Defense.[34]

It is also important to point out that in studies of the information needs of scientists and others, "needs" is generally interpreted as having to do with *kinds of messages*, in terms of subject, currency, language, or source, but the term has also been used to signify the *means* for supplying them. Confusion over these two possible uses of the term "need," has certainly not contributed to the clarification of the problems under study. Furthermore, these inquiries into the uses of information divide into two major types: the first might be called basic because its objective is to obtain an understanding of communication patterns and the influences that determine their configuration; the second is a form of applied research as it is directed toward the answering of questions or the formulating of decisions with reference to specific entities, such as library programs, retrieval sys-

---

[34] Auerbach Corporation. *DOD User Needs Study. Phase I.* Philadelphia. (May 1965) Final Technical Report 1151-TR-3. (AD 615-501; AD 615-502). Reference should also be made to William D. Garvey and Belver C. Griffith. "Studies of Innovation in Scientific Communication in Psychology." *American Psychological Review.* vol. 21 (November 1966), pp. 1019–36.

tems, or aspects of publishing.[35] Despite the substantial amount of material that has been published about information needs, the quality of the materials is disappointing. As Saul and Mary Herner have pointed out, a relatively few techniques have been employed in pursuing the inquiries; the techniques have been applied to a diversity of users that tend to make the studies incompatible; the language is often ambiguous; innovation is lacking; there has been a failure to profit from earlier mistakes; and rigorous experimental design is frequently absent.[36]

But research, whether it is practiced individually or collectively, is not confined to those who may be pursuing it as a form of enterprise; it is not something that only the professional research investigator does. Increasingly, research as a method of instruction and an environment for formalized learning is being introduced into undergraduate as well as graduate programs. This undergraduate research, or more properly, inquiry, has its own characteristic information needs, though academic librarians generally have given these requirements slight attention, while the faculty has tended to ignore them almost entirely. This neglect may doubtless be attributed to the fact that the instructors themselves were not properly encouraged in the use of the library in their own undergraduate years. The textbook and the reserve collection, which in the final analysis is only a kind of multiple text, have too long dominated undergraduate, and even graduate, instruction. The teacher's own mimeographed reading lists and bibliographies have been imposed between the student and the total library collection, largely because the typical faculty member does not trust either the bibliographic mechanisms of the library or the competence of the librarians, while the librarians, for their part, have never developed a theory of the role of the library in the student's intellectual experience. This neglect has been intensified by the absence of any real communication between teacher and librarian, both have paid lip service to the library as a "learning center," and having said that satisfied their sense of obligation with a short course or a few lectures on "How to Use the Library."

---

[35] See the chapter on user needs in the successive volumes of the *Annual Review of Information Science and Technology*. vol. 1. New York. Wiley. 1966.

[36] Saul and Mary Herner. "Information Needs and Uses in Science and Technology." *Annual Review of Information Science and Technology*. vol. 2. New York. Wiley. 1967. p. 2. William Paisley provides an excellent description of the strengths and weaknesses of the methodologies used in these user studies, and offers convincing reasons for the proliferation of such a large number of them. William J. Paisley. *The Flow of (Behavioral) Science Information—A Review of the Research Literature*. Palo Alto. Stanford University. Institute for Communication Research. 1966.

The pioneering work of Patricia Knapp at Monteith College of Wayne State University stands not only as the first important effort to bring the academic library actively into the educational process, but also it is the most important innovation in academic librarianship since libraries first gave the student free and unrestricted access to the book stacks.

The Monteith pilot experiment was designed to explore the relations, if any, between (a) faculty-library participation in course planning and student use of the library for courses so planned, (b) student use of the library and the building of student use of the library in design of the course, and (c) student understanding of the library and competence in its use and student use of the library for course work, and, finally, the experiment was to ascertain whether expert bibliographic assistance provided by the library to the faculty will positively affect the three preceding relationships.[37] The results of the study appeared to validate the methods of inquiry used by Mrs. Knapp and her associates. With respect to student use of the library they found that "there are so many variables involved in the use of the library tools and resources that it would seem wise for investigators to make the most of methods which provide an opportunity for studies in depth of a small number of cases."[38] This conclusion substantiates our own belief that the use of the library is a more complex phenomenon of human behavior than librarians and others have assumed it to be, and hence the need for a better understanding of the mental processes involved than science now possesses. With respect to faculty use of the library's bibliographical services, the Monteith study found that "faculty did, indeed, use the bibliographic service as a resource for teaching," and that "whether the tasks assigned were for teaching or for research, they were much more likely to be bibliographical than informational. And of the bibliographical tasks, most called for selective and scouting activities. We concluded, therefore, that training for bibliographic service to academicians should minimize retrieval of specific information and should stress, instead, bibliographies and indexes, particularly selective bibliographical tools, scouting techniques, and the apparatus of reporting and communication in the academic disciplines."[39] That funds were not provided for the continuation of the experiment, and that it has been almost completely ignored by the educational and library world raise serious questions about the sincerity of educators and librarians in their pious and now platitudinous pronounce-

---

[37] Patricia B. Knapp. *The Monteith College Library Experiment.* New York. Scarecrow Press. 1966. p. 131.

[38] *Ibid.* p. 139.

[39] *Ibid.* pp. 142–43.

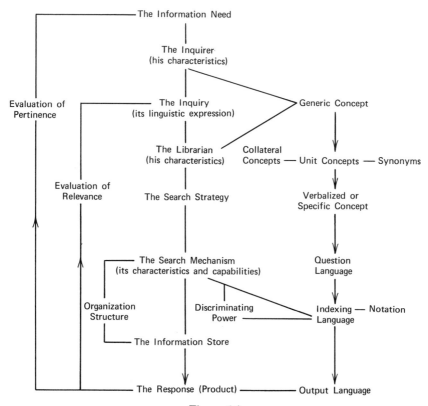

**Figure 6-1.**

ment that the library "is the heart of the university" even when they summon up the ghost of Thomas Carlyle as their witness.

Some awareness of the multitude of variables in the information search process of which Mrs. Knapp speaks may be obtained from the diagrams in Figures 6-1 and 6-2, prepared by Alan Rees:

In both of these diagrams it is important to note that *pertinency* is an expression of the relation of the answer to the user's need, whereas *relevancy* relates the answer to the user's question. If the question does not accurately reflect the need, or if the reference librarian fails to interpret the need accurately the answer may be relevant but not pertinent. Obviously there are many opportunities for a search to go wrong, and it often does, hence the importance of search strategy as every experienced reference librarian can testify.[40]

---

[40] Alan M. Rees. "Conceptual Analysis of Questions in Information Retrieval Sys-

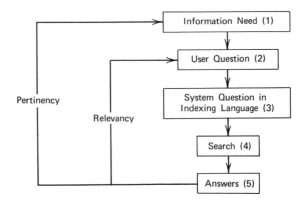

**Figure 6-2.**

## BIBLIOGRAPHIC ORGANIZATION

The fullest and most efficient use of a library's resources depends upon the organization of its materials; this is an axiom that was as well

tems." American Documentation Institute. *Proceedings; 26th Annual Meeting. Chicago, Illinois, October 1963.* Washington, D.C. American Documentation Institute. 1963. pp. 175–77.

Alan M. Rees. "Broadening the Spectrum." *The Present Status and Future Prospects of Reference/Information Service,* ed. Winifred B. Linderman. Chicago. American Library Association. 1967. pp. 57–65.

Alan M. Rees and Douglas G. Schultz. *A Field Experimental Approach to the Study of Relevance Assessments in Relation to Document Searching.* Cleveland. Case Western Reserve University. School of Library Science. 1967. pp. 277–84.

Tefko Saracevic. *The Effect of Question Analysis and Searching Strategy on Performance of Retrieval Systems; Selected Results from an Experimental Study.* (Center for Documentation and Communication Research. Comparative Systems Laboratory: Technical Report No. 15.) Cleveland. Case Western Reserve University. School of Library Science. 1968.

Jesse H. Shera. "On Keeping Up with Keeping Up." *Documentation and the Organization of Knowledge,* by Jesse H. Shera. London. Crosby Lockwood. 1966. pp. 72–83.

Jesse H. Shera. "Foundations of a Theory of Reference Service" and "The Challenging Role of the Reference Librarian." *Reference, Research, and Regionalism.* Austin. Texas Library Association. 1966. pp. 13–20 and 21–34.

Philip H. Ennis. "The Library Consumer; Patterns and Trends." *Library Quarterly.* vol. 34 (April 1964), pp. 163–78.

Philip H. Ennis. "A Study of the Use and Users of Recent Knowledge." *Ibid.* (October 1964), pp. 305–14.

known to the ancients as it is today. Man had not long begun the accumulation of his graphic records before the inadequacies of "simian search"[41] became apparent. This discovery is not surprising, for man is by nature an inveterate classifier, arranging objects, ideas, even his own kind in accordance with criteria which for him have meaning and value. Libraries offered a natural outlet for this propensity to organize, inventory, and arrange, a propensity which was encouraged by the futility of examining seriatim an agglomeration of papyrus rolls or clay tablets in search of desired information. Bibliographic organization, then, was rooted in man's intellectual nature.

The scholar-librarians of the great *Alexandriana*—such as Zenodotus of Ephesus, Eratosthenes, or Aristophanes of Byzantium—not only edited the manuscripts entrusted to their care, but also arranged and catalogued them; and Callimachus compiled his *Pinakes*, which was to form the basis of all later bibliographies of antiquity.[42] Bibliographic organization as a basic tool of scholarship existed long before the period of the manuscript came to an end. Indeed, there is evidence that an early form of library cataloging or inventory, existed in the age of the clay tablet. In the seventeenth century B.C., a library was built at Akkade, or Agade, by Sargon I, founder of the Semitic empire. This collection, if the results of excavations are to be trusted, had been arranged and classified by its librarian Ibnissaru. The library at Edfu in Upper Egypt was inventoried on the walls of the library building itself. Such early attempts at crude classification and inventorying of library holdings were extended by the scholar-librarians and others into the beginnings of a more broadly based bibliography. The transition required centuries for its completion, but there can be little doubt that historically, the library was the cradle in which all bibliography was nurtured.

As early as the second century A.D., Galen found it necessary to compile a classified bibliography of his writings, and in 731 the Venerable Bede appended to his *Ecclesiastical History of Britain* a list of some forty works arranged in a roughly classified manner. Late in the thirteenth century there was compiled a cooperative catalog, perhaps of Franciscan origin, the *Registrum librorum Angliae*, which is a form of union list of holdings of English monastic libraries—as Savage says, "a directory to the where-

---

[41] Verner W. Clapp. "Subject Controls; Nature and Levels of Controls." *American Documentation*. vol. 3 (January 1952), p. 11.

[42] Edward A. Parsons. *The Alexandrian Library*. New York. Elsevier Press, 1952. pp. 204–18; Dorothy M. Norris. *A History of Cataloging and Cataloging Methods*. London. Grafton. 1939. pp. 1–6.

abouts of books."[43] At the beginning of the fifteenth century, John Boston, monk of the Abbey of Bury St. Edmunds in Suffolk and almost certainly the custodian of the abbey library, used the *Registrum* in preparing his *Catalogus scriptorum ecclesiae*, in which is brought together a list of the books held by the libraries of the monasteries and other ecclesiastical houses of England.[44] This union list included materials drawn from no less than 195 such repositories and was arranged alphabetically by author, followed by a partial classification of the writers under the several books of the *Bible* about which they had written.[45]

At the end of the fifteenth century, Johann Tritheim compiled his *Liber de Scriptoribus Ecclesiasticis* and his *Catalogus Illustrium Virorum Germaniae*, and half a century later Konrad Gesner prepared his *Bibliotheca Universalis*, a first attempt at a true universal bibliography. In the last work, a folio of thirteen hundred pages, were listed (with annotations) approximately twelve thousand titles—all the Latin, Greek, and Hebrew works known to the compiler. The arrangement of this work was alphabetical, by the Christian names of the authors, but it was followed, three years later, by the *Pandectarum sive Partitionum universalum*, in which the titles were arranged in some twenty major subject classes, though those for medicine and theology were never published. The works of Tritheim and Gesner were followed by a considerable proliferation of subject bibliographies, catalogs, and inventories of particular library collections; but the significant fact for the present discussion is that by the time of Gesner, bibliographic organization had assumed three major forms: crude subject classification of the rolls or codices themselves, catalogs or inventories of the holdings of individual libraries or groups of libraries, and attempts to compile universal bibliographies.

Historically considered, then, if the first responsibility of the librarian was to preserve the records of his culture, his second obligation was to look to their effective organization. For centuries librarianship has been almost synonymous with bibliography, and the progenitors of the modern public library movement saw the problems of improving the techniques of bibliographic organization as central to the practice of librarianship itself. The growth of graphic records and the multiplication of libraries brought

---

[43] Ernest A. Savage. "Cooperative Bibliography in the Thirteenth and Fifteenth Centuries." *Special Librarianship in General Libraries,* by Ernest A. Savage. London. Grafton. 1939. p. 287.

[44] *Ibid.* pp. 298–306.

[45] Theodore Besterman. *The Beginnings of Systematic Bibliography.* Oxford. Oxford University Press. 1935. pp. 2–6.

refinement of the techniques of library and bibliographic organization. Librarians grew to depend increasingly upon bibliography as an essential aid to their book acquisition programs. In England, the formulation in 1841 of the famous "ninety-one rules" laid the foundation for library cataloging practice for generations to come, on both sides of the Atlantic Ocean. A decade later, Charles C. Jewett and his contemporaries urged the creation at the Smithsonian Institution of a great national bibliographic center and proposed at the first American library conference, in 1853, a union catalog of all the major American libraries.[46] So important was the work of Dewey and Cutter in the library philosophy of their contemporaries that there developed an almost naive faith in the self-sufficiency of the classification scheme and the dictionary catalog, and even so eminent a library pioneer as William H. Brett could assert that one "could find in a properly made catalog everything the library has on the subject, no matter what it is."[47] Parenthetically, it might be added, the middle decades of the present century brought a reaction against the conventional catalog on the part of the information scientists that in the extremities of its manifestations was equally irrational.

The growth in importance of the periodical as a medium of publication had, by 1850, become so great that librarians were convinced that its subject analysis was a proper library function. In 1848 William F. Poole issued, under the auspices of the Brothers in Unity Library of Yale University, his *Alphabetical Index to Subjects Treated in the Reviews and Other Periodicals,* and librarians undertook to index, cooperatively, this increasingly important segment of the library's resources.[48] Unfortunately, the librarians discovered that a local autonomous agency, such as the library, predicated on the assumption that both physical accessibility and content accessibility could be provided on a local and self-sufficient basis, was not adequate to the demands of an interorganizational cooperation envisaged by Poole and, earlier, by Jewett. Furthermore, the mechanisms of library organization, the classification scheme and the card catalog, were devised for the book or monograph as the standard bibliographic unit, whereas the journal was a composite of many, and often largely unrelated,

---

[46] Utley. *Librarians' Conference of 1853.* Also: Joseph A. Borome. *Charles Coffin Jewett.* Chicago. American Library Association. 1951. Chapters 4–5.

[47] U.S. Congress. Joint Committee on the Library of Congress. *Report under S.R.R. 26. Relative to the Condition, Organization, and Management of the Library of Congress. March 3, 1897.* Senate Report 1573. 53rd Congress. 2nd Session, 1897. pp. 264–65.

[48] William L. Williamson. *William Frederick Poole and the Modern Library Movement.* New York. Columbia University Press. 1965. Chapter 8.

bibliographic units assembled in a single physical volume, and for dealing with it the traditional tools of the librarian were dull indeed. Though the standardization of the journal, the presentation of identical content to all libraries, was an almost perfect subject for cooperative action, the professional immaturity of library organization prevented the establishment of centralized and cooperative indexing. Thus, an important part of the bibliographic mechanism for providing content access to a large and significant body of contemporary literature slipped from the hands of the librarians.

Here was a turning point in the profession, for this abandonment of "Poole's Index," which had previously been an important and well-recognized professional responsibility, not only weakened the prestige of the librarian among other professional groups, but also—more important— immeasurably circumscribed the growth of the intellectual discipline of librarianship.

At the time when the professional librarians in the United States were abandoning the concept of bibliographic organization as their central role, and were turning toward the path of universal education blazed a half-century before by Mann, Barnard, and their disciples, important developments were taking place on the continent of Europe. Paul Otlet and Henri La Fontaine laid the foundation for an international movement for world documentation at their historic meeting in Otlet's home in the Rue de Florence, Brussels, in 1892. From the meeting of these two men came a series of important events that shaped the progress of bibliographic organization for more than a generation. It was they who planned the Office International de Bibliographie which, after a series of changes in name, eventually became the Fédération International de Documentation. It was they who conceived a universal international bibliography to which was to be attached an international reference library of subject bibliographies. And it was they who, in 1895, called the first international conference on bibliography.[49]

At almost the same time, the Royal Society of London began to address itself to the need for the systematization of scientific literature, a problem which had been emphasized by Joseph Henry of the Smithsonian Institution when he addressed the British Association for the Advancement of Science at its meeting in Glasgow in 1883. Henry's proposal for a catalog of scientific papers was brought nearer realization when the Royal Society, at its meeting in July of 1896, laid the foundation for its *International Catalog of Scientific Literature*, which began publication in 1901.

---

[49] S. C. Bradford. *Documentation*, 2nd ed. London. Crosby Lockwood. 1953. "Fifty Years of Documentation." pp. 132–43.

The emerging pattern of bibliographic organization at both the national and international levels has been admirably treated by Miss Ditmas and Mrs. Murra,[50] and need not be described in detail here. However, it should be pointed out that this movement was deeply rooted in the older discipline of archival practices which had grown up over the centuries, but which had not begun to achieve professional maturity until the work of Muller, Feith, and Fruin in the Netherlands, Hilary Jenkinson in England, and Posner and Schellenberg in the United States gave it some semblance of systematization. In the beginning, then, one might say that librarianship, documentation, and archival custodianship were one, and the reasons for the development of the three separate and sometimes hostile groups, to administer observedly similar processes for providing access to recorded knowledge, are to be found in the dynamics of social structure and the fact that very early, subtle forces began to divide those who were concerned with this tri-partite unity into separate groups which eventually became intolerant of each other.

## THE LIBRARIANS' RETREAT FROM BIBLIOGRAPHY

From the increasingly difficult problems of analyzing and organizing recorded knowledge for effective use, the librarians turned to the new faith in the education of the masses that followed the Age of Enlightenment. The growth of mercantilism and the dawn of the industrial revolution demonstrated the need for a substantial body of workers who were both literate and trained in specific manual skills. This practical need was reinforced by the results of the political revolutions in England and on the Continent, and the creation in the United States of a rapidly growing democracy based on almost universal male suffrage.

Nurtured by a new awareness of the importance of the individual, a new credo of social progress, a reorientation of social values, and a new stratification of the structure of society, there emerged on both sides of the Atlantic a belief that in universal education was to be found the key to the advance and improvement of mankind. The librarians joyfully flocked to join the ranks of those zealous individuals who were crusading

---

[50] E. M. R. Ditmas. "Coordination of Information; A Survey of Schemes Put Forward in the Last Fifty Years." *Journal of Documentation.* vol. 3, no. 4 (March 1948), pp. 209–21; Katherine O. Murra. "History of Some Attempts to Organize Bibliography Internationally." *Bibliographic Organization.* (Chicago University. Graduate Library School.) Chicago. University of Chicago Press. 1951. pp. 24–33.

for a fusion of popular culture and the traditional classical education of the aristocracy. But, while the librarians were busily polishing the lamp of culture so that even the poorest man could be guided into a Utopia that would make him, through the medium of the public library, rich in the wisdom of the ages, others began to attack, albeit somewhat amateurishly, a few of the bibliographic problems in a search for answers that a new and science-oriented society needed. However, librarians in growing numbers became increasingly indifferent to the elements of the bibliographic process within their profession and grew more and more deeply involved in the democratization of education, while nonlibrarians, especially those interested in the organization of the literature of science, picked up the tasks of bibliographic organization.

This diversion from the bibliographic responsibilities of librarianship would not have occurred had there been a proper understanding of the role of the library, its functions and objectives, and an adequate recognition that there were many different kinds of libraries, with collections that were strikingly dissimilar, necessitating an adjustment in organizational machinery required to satisfy a wide variety of divergent demands.

Renunciation by the librarians of much of their historic role as mediators between man and the graphic record, and hence an indifference to the natural leaders in bibliographic organization, contributed to the dispersion of bibliographic activity in the United States and encouraged its uncoordinated and often fortuitous development. (See Figure 6-3.) Such a generalization does not deny the fact that there are libraries which have been conspicuously successful in establishing continuing bibliographic services of recognized excellence. The development of MEDLARS climaxes a long history of bibliographic achievement by the National Library of Medicine. The work at the National Agricultural Library emerged from a variety of specialized bibliographic services initiated by the library of the U.S. Department of Agriculture. The MARC project at the Library of Congress is only one example of its achievements in bibliographic innovation. To the Economics Division of the New York Public Library must go the credit for the great utility of the *Public Affairs Information Service*. The Business Branch of the Newark Public Library and the Business Information Bureau of the Cleveland Public Library established patterns of bibliographic service to business and industry that have been taken as models by others. The several libraries of the industrial relations centers on university campuses throughout the East and Midwest have promoted a cooperative system for the exchange and centralization of bibliographic information, and the *Engineering Index* is a product of the Engineering Societies' Library in New York.

The importance of all of these activities, and others that are less conspicuous, is not to be minimized, but the fact remains that a great volume of bibliographic development and research is being increasingly carried forward outside library walls. National and trade bibliography and the more general forms of periodical indexing have long been the responsibility of the H. W. Wilson Company and the R. R. Bowker Company, who seem to have proved that bibliography can return a profit to privately invested capital. Conspicuously successful continuing bibliographic and abstracting services in such fields as chemistry, biology, psychology, metallurgy, physics, mathematics, and many others have been maintained by professional associations. The Library of Congress, despite its many achievements, and unlike many other great national libraries, has never assumed leadership in organizing and coordinating our national bibliography, or even the bibliographic activity of the Federal Government. Certainly it has not fully realized the potentialities which came to it with the establishment under its administrative jurisdiction of the Copyright Office. The history of American librarianship during the past century is indeed a record of lost opportunities.

Dissociation from the ranks of professional librarians of such organizations as the American Documentation Institute, which in 1967 became the American Society for Information Science, and the Special Libraries Association, together with the assumption by nonlibrary personnel of bibliographic undertakings, as is shown in Figure 6-3, has weakened the hold of the library profession on its own discipline and in many instances has encouraged a widespread belief that librarians were not qualified to undertake the tasks they were supposed to perform. Such doubts as to the librarian's competence have often erupted into open and not always irrational hostility, which has been only partially attenuated by the formation of the A.L.A.'s Information Science and Automation Division. There can be no doubt that the librarians have been vulnerable to the charge of excessive conservatism, that they have been lacking in imagination and quite inhospitable, when not openly antagonistic, to attempts to improve the effectiveness of their tradition-bound bibliographic techniques, particularly when such innovation implied any suggestion of mechanization. The seriousness of this indictment is implicit in the fact that in a 1957 survey conducted by the Office of Scientific Information of the National Science Foundation of twenty-four nonconventional systems in current use, not one had emerged from a traditional library situation. Of the total, nineteen are industrial installations, most of which are in the field of chemistry, and the remaining five are in government agencies: The National Institutes of Health, the Naval Ordnance Test Station at China Lake, California, the

| The Popular Library | Chronology | The Scholarly Library |
|---|---|---|
| | Preclassical Era | Babylonia, Assyria, Egypt —temple libraries |
| | Classical Period | Ancient libraries—Greece, Rome |
| | Hellenistic Period | Alexandria, Pergamum |
| | Middle Ages | Monastic and cathedral libraries |
| | Islamic Civilization | Baghdad, Cairo, Cordoba |
| | Renaissance | University libraries in Western Europe |
| | Beginnings of Science | |
| | Enlightenment | |
| Private library clubs | Eighteenth Century | Great research libraries of |
| Social libraries | Library scholarship | Europe—British Museum, Bibliothèque Nationale |
| | Nineteenth Century | |
| Public library movement | Boston Public Library | Beginnings of research |
| Adult education | Librarian's Conference of 1853 | libraries in U.S.A. |
| Popular culture | | |
| Free public schools | | Documentation movement |
| | | Otlet and La Fontaine |
| Public Library Act, United Kingdom | | Bibliographic activity |
| American Library Association | | Poole's index |
| Carnegie grants— Carnegie libraries | | |
| | Twentieth Century | |
| Local and regional library associations | | Special Libraries Association —Chapters |
| State associations | Council of National Library Associations | Special library movement ASLIB |
| | | American Documentation Institute—Chapters |
| | International Federation of Library Associations | Chemical Literature Division American Chemical Society |
| | Education for librarianship | American Association for the Advancement of Science, Information Science Division |
| | Conventional — Documentation | National Microfilm Association |
| | | Association of Technical Writers and Editors |
| | Information science | National Federation of Science Abstracting and Information Services |
| | Associations of special types of libraries: Medical, music, law, Catholic, college and university | Special bibliographic services Chemical abstracts Biological abstracts, etc. Research in library automation and information science |

Figure 6-3.

Biological Warfare Laboratory of the U.S. Army, the U.S. Geological Survey, and the Patent Office.[51]

In 1966, when the fourth edition of this compilation appeared, it reported 175 such systems, but the situation with respect to libraries had changed only slightly. Library listings were confined to national institutions such as those in medicine, agriculture, and the Library of Congress. Industrial installations still dominated the scene, though it should be pointed out that in many of these the library may have played some part. In industry the nomenclature is so loosely used that it is difficult to distinguish between special libraries and information centers.[52] This lack of interest on the part of librarians in the improvement of retrieval systems is further confirmed by current surveys of library research as related to documentation, classification, and other aspects of the information problem. The National Science Foundation's 1966 survey of research and development, for example, shows that only in a limited number of university libraries is there any apparent interest in such inquiries,[53] while librarians occupy no conspicuous place in ASIS' *Annual Review*.[54]

Traditionally librarian philosophers have addressed themselves to a search for *universals* and *standards*. They have sought to serve a "universal" man by contributing to a standardized system of education, through the promotion of standardized techniques. Thus they have been led to stereotype their bibliographic processes into a "universal" classification system, a "universal" subject-heading list, a standard code for bibliographic description, but in so doing, they have made a fetish of generality. The librarian as generalist in a world of increasing specialization is, indeed, a noble ideal, but it must be based on a recognition that generalization is itself a form of specialization, that it must develop its own specialized processes, and not become just a composite of the specializations into which librarianship can be fragmented. Librarianship has many tributaries, each with its own particular needs and use-patterns of graphic records to which the instruments and methods of bibliographic organization must be ad-

---

[51] National Science Foundation. Office of Scientific Information. *Nonconventional Technical Information Systems in Current Use.* Washington, D.C. National Science Foundation. 1958.

[52] National Science Foundation. Office of Science Information Service. *Nonconventional Scientific and Technical Information Systems in Current Use.* (No. 4.) Washington, D.C. Government Printing Office. December 1966.

[53] National Science Foundation. Office of Science Information Service. *Current Research and Development in Scientific Documentation.* (No. 14.) Washington, D.C. Government Printing Office. 1966.

[54] *Annual Review of Information Science.*

justed and within which there are powerful elements of unity. But this unity is to be sought internally, within the nature of the bibliographic process itself, not forced from above by the imposition of "standard" or "universal" procedures or techniques. The librarian's attempts to be all things to all readers must not be mistaken for a search after fundamental and unifying principles.

## THE SEARCH FOR UNITY

The functions of all social agencies are shaped by two forces: (a) the demands made upon the agency by society and the alterations in those demands resulting from social change, and (b) the professed objectives of professional leaders of the agency. But demands and professed objectives are not always coincident and, indeed, may in extreme situations be actually contradictory. In such a conflict, society has the upper hand, for an agency that does not meet the social demands placed upon it will ossify or decay, and be replaced. This assertion does not negate the possibility that professional leadership may alter social demands, nor does it raise the question of moral or ethical values. It simply emphasizes the truth that when an agency and its society part company, something must yield, and the odds favor society. "Society is our trustees," Dr. Francis Peabody told the medical profession, "it is to it that we are responsible."

But failure by the professional group to accept the functions defined for it by society or, conversely, the inability or unwillingness of society to accede to the professional objectives established by the agency, creates a vacuum, and a vacuum is as abhorrent to society as it is to nature. Thus does social change beget readjustment of traditional agencies, or the creation of new ones structured in response to unfulfilled demand. Every agency, then, is threatened by social shifts which may leave it with only residual functions and waning support, or no functions at all—an anachronism, a ghost, a memory. The cyclical pattern of history may suggest the possibility of eventual rebirth—but it will probably be a long wait.

The library, throughout its history, has not been immune to such social change. For centuries it remained essentially stable, but, during the last hundred years particularly, it has often yielded to pressures, even fads, without recourse to a guiding philosophy or theory of its own. Though librarians have been dedicated to preserving the historical records of others, they have been singularly indifferent to the meaning of their own past and, as Pierce Butler has pointed out,

among the learned professions librarians and lawyers occupy a peculiar status. Both know very well how to do things, but both have only vague notions of why they do them. Both have developed highly efficient systems of practice, but neither has developed a corresponding system of theory to elucidate, justify, and control that practice. . . . In short, both are still empiricists.[55]

Yet the historical role of the library is very far from being complex, nor has it been difficult to define. One may even suggest that this very simplicity explains the absence of an underlying philosophy; for from its very beginnings, the central and unifying concept of the library has been its dedication to *assembling, preserving, and making available for use the records of human experience*—it's as simple as that. Why then, one may ask, is an elaborate delineation of its philosophy necessary? The answer lies in its assumption of functions, rationalized as a more dynamic program, which it was never designed to perform. Such deviation may signify that the library is attempting to respond to significant change in its function—change that may be the result of pressures from society or from a leadership within the profession which believes that the old functions must be replaced or supplemented by new if the library of the future is to be preserved from erosion or decay. But there is also the possibility that changes in the library may be the result of emerging functions which, though marginally related to librarianship, are not at any given moment being met by any social agency. Born and nourished in the parent organization, these may either become the new masters of the house or eventually take flight and establish their own identities. Such readjustments are not necessarily harmful—indeed they may be necessary—but they are not usually accomplished without considerable temporary maladjustment with attendant agonizing reappraisals. Such alterations are disastrous only when they so weaken the agency that it loses control of functions and responsibilities inherently its own.[56]

A maladjustment between a statement of goals and the means for their achievement creates a crisis not only for the operating units, but also

---

[55] Pierce Butler. "Survey of the Reference Field." *The Reference Function of the Library*. University of Chicago, Graduate Library School. Chicago. University of Chicago Press. 1947. p. 1.

One may question the author's comparison of librarianship with the law, since the philosophy of law is an old and highly respected discipline, but he is certainly correct in accusing the librarians of "intellectual barrenness of their vocational equipment."

[56] Elting E. Morison. *Men, Machines, and Modern Times*. Cambridge, Mass. M.I.T. Press. 1966. Chapter 1.

for the professional schools which are expected to provide personnel trained to understand these new goals while achieving mastery of the old techniques. Thus, an obligation is placed upon the professional school somehow to reconcile the newer functions with the old techniques in ways that will not violate the unity of underlying professional theory, but will preserve the internal consistency of the educational program. Failing such a reconciliation, the parturition process must be so expedited that no serious distortion of either the old or the new functions is possible, for unless a harmonious relationship between ends and means is preserved, the effectiveness of both will be destroyed.

Librarianship today stands in precarious balance between ends and means. As a social agency it is being pulled in a variety of directions, some of which are in direct conflict, and it must choose either reconciliation in a stable professional unity, or disastrous schism. The ultimate decision will profoundly affect the library schools of the future. The true role of the library, then, must be sought in a body of rational professional theory that will distinguish it from all other social agencies, a body of theory that will belong to it and it alone.

## TOWARD A UNIFIED THEORY OF LIBRARIANSHIP

It is important to examine (as has been attempted in the preceding chapters) the major social process—communication—of which librarianship is a part, and the changes in the library brought about by changes in the pattern of communication. One may logically assume that the library has influenced, and been influenced by, all forms of communication, but the particular concern here is graphic communication, especially those forms of graphic communication with which the library has traditionally concerned itself. Changes in society, even the value systems of good and evil, have placed new demands upon the library throughout its historical development, and most of these demands have resulted from differing theories of human behavior and intelligence, of goals, and norms of civilization in its march over the treadmill of time. In the ancient East and in the Graeco-Roman world, the library was the handmaiden of scholarship and, in its baser manifestations, a symbol of prestige. In the medieval world, it was the last bastion of civilization in an age of barbarism. The modern public library was rooted in the Age of Reason, when man's faith in continuing progress and ultimate perfectability was based upon a conviction of the indomitability of human reason. But the library as an instrument for the perfectability of man's mind has been questioned not only by historical events, but also by changing theories of human behavior and new knowledge of human variations and limitations. Yet all these changes have not been systematically incorporated in a library philosophy. One must read into the record of what the librarian does, the *credo* of why he does it.

The examination in the preceding pages of the processes of society in the ways it shapes, and the demands it makes upon, its libraries, and our knowledge of the development of library policies and services, makes possible the formulation of certain basic propositions fundamental to a systematic statement of the role of the modern library in contemporary society. Such statements, of course, define the role of the library as a generic form and are not to be assumed as describing the operations of any particular library. These propositions are, however, the standards against which the several manifestations of library specialization are to be measured and judged.

1.  The *book*, or *graphic record*, by which is meant any physical entity upon which is recorded a transcript of human experience, is, and must remain, the central concept of an acceptable theory of librarianship. The role of the library is defined in the origins of the word itself and is subject to modification only to the extent that time has added to the book other media of graphic communication. Thus a fundamental theory of librarianship must recognize the library as an agency of secondary or indirect communication, and the role of the librarian in society as that of a mediator between man and his graphic records.

2.  The processes of selecting, acquiring, and making available for use the contents of graphic records comprise the operational aspects of librarianship. Librarianship is a trinity of acquisition, organization, and dissemination, in which acquisition relates to the selection and accumulation of materials, organization to their preparation for efficient use, and dissemination the processes of making the contents of graphic records available to the user.

3.  The resources at the disposal of the library profession for the achievement of its goals are, then two: (a) collections of graphic records, selected for their potential utility to a defined clientele and organized for efficient use; and (b) the body of intellectual skills necessary for the selection, organization, and dissemination of materials in ways that will meet contemporary social needs. Librarianship, therefore, implies a body of material and a corpus of skills for its manipulation, to the end of serving the culture.

Thus one is led to the conclusion that *the only legitimate functions of the library are those which can be satisfactorily fulfilled by the means and resources available.* This would seem a truism, but it must be emphasized, for the assumption of functions or goals for which the librarian does not possess the necessary resources is a disservice to both the library and society. In their misguided zeal to make of librarianship a "cultural" force in the community, the librarians have assumed responsibilities which they could not properly perform, which have weakened their professional position and impeded the development of groups which might perform such functions or services with far more effectiveness. Librarianship began, and for centuries remained, as a highly respected profession. The scholar-librarians from the ancient world to the close of the nineteenth century were generally men of intellectual stature and attainment, but with the spread of literacy and the educational elevation of the masses came an anti-intellectualism in which the librarians suffered, as did many other segments of the scholarly world, a significant loss in prestige. This was, of course, unfortunate, just as any manifestation of anti-intellectualism is unfortunate; but the remedy lies in reshaping the value structure of society, not in attempts by the librarians to assume alien responsibilities which seem of a higher order in the social grade, but for which the profession is not equipped. Librarianship, then, if it is to survive as a profession in its own right, must surrender its attempts to assume the attributes of another profession—education, social work, group leadership —and return to itself for its true objectives.

The role of the library in the communication process and in the civilization that process serves is to *maximize the social utility of graphic records.* This is the standard against which all librarianship must be judged. The key words here are *utility* and *graphic records*—use and books. Thus librarianship is bibliographic, not bibliophilic. It seeks to unite in a fruitful relationship the book and the user. This does not exclude the possibility of sentiment or emotion in such a relationship, but it is the utility of the tool and the skill in its manipulation that justify an art, a profession, or a craft.

# Seven

# What the Librarian Needs to Know

"Your librarian should be, above all, a learned and profound theologian; but to this qualification, which I shall call fundamental, should be united vast literary acquisitions, an exact and precise knowledge of all the arts and sciences, great facility of expression, and lastly, that exquisite politeness that conciliates the affection of his visitors while his merit secures their esteem."[1] Such was the profile of the librarian that Jean-Baptiste Cotton des Houssayes drew for the general assembly of the Society of the Sorbonne on December 23, 1780, and, in general terms, it represented the image of the librarian from the priest-scholar-librarians of the ancient world to the American scholarly librarians of the second half of the nineteenth century. Not until the movement for popular education began to receive general acceptance and the emancipation of women brought young ladies seeking library careers did this venerable prototype change substantially. This transition offers a fertile field for exploration by the social historian.

Both scholarship and service were explicitly set forth in des Houssayes's exposition, but the former was dominant. By the turn of the present century, however, service had gained the upper hand, and librarian-

---

[1] Jean-Baptiste Cotton des Houssayes. *The Duties and Qualifications of a Librarian.* Chicago. McClurg. 1906. pp. 36–37.

ship was losing its status as a scholarly career; thus did des Houssayes's librarian as "learned and profound theologian" yield to the librarian as missionary. The role of the librarian as the arch-priest of reading for purposes of education, information, recreation, aesthetic appreciation, and civic responsibility even today possesses strong emotional connotations. The importance of reading is not to be rejected, but the emphasis is shifting, and it is being expressed in new bibliographic configurations, new needs, and new materials. The librarian, confronted by accelerated change, especially in the technology of his culture, soon discovers that many of his complacent assumptions of the past are being left behind. He discovers, to quote Elting Morison, that if life does not "proceed in good order along the whirring grooves of change," and "that if great care were not taken in the ordering of the new energies, things would jump the rails."[2] It is entirely possible, of course, especially if one disregards the long-term view, to assume that innovation is a hostile force, that it is a form of dislocation of existing values, a way of disturbing comfortable routines and calculations. Morison goes on to say that the present age of rapid change "must open as an era of destruction. It must from its very nature destroy many of the conditions which give most interest to the history of the past, and many of the traditions which people hold most dear. . . . There must be great destruction both in the physical and in the intellectual world, of old buildings and old boundaries and old monuments and, furthermore, of customs and ideas, systems of thought and methods of education."[3] Danger lies in the hiatus between destructive change and the innovations which take its place, when "people do not know enough to recognize their limitations but know too much to follow loyally the direction of better qualified leaders."[4] The major task of education is to close this gap between changes that destroy and the innovation that creates that which will supplant the old. The librarian, if he is to meet the needs of a new society must think of better solutions than that devised by the old teamster who mended the harness after the horses were gone.

Our task in the present chapter is to re-examine "the new librarianship" in the light of what has been said about the social role of the library, in the hope of evolving some insight into the knowledge and skills that the librarian of tomorrow should possess.

---

[2] Elting E. Morison. *Men, Machines, and Modern Times.* Cambridge, Mass. M.I.T. Press. 1966. p. 5.

[3] *Ibid.* pp. 13–14.

[4] *Ibid.* p. 14.

## THE LIBRARIAN'S UNIQUE RESPONSIBILITY

One must begin by asking what is the librarian *qua* librarian, what is his *unique* responsibility, what does he do that no one else does? To answer that librarianship is what librarians do is not very illuminating, though, consciously or not, a substantial portion of the profession has been guilty of just such circularity. In the preceding pages of this study we have attempted to lay a foundation for the proposition that the librarian is a mediator between man and the graphic records that his and previous generations have produced, and that the goal of the librarian is to maximize the social utility of graphic records for the benefit of humanity. The most important contribution which this definition makes to an understanding of librarianship as a discipline in its own right is that it represents a shift in emphasis from librarianship *qua* librarianship to society itself and makes possible a substitution for the librarian's own subjective judgment or opinion an objective study of what society expects to get from books or records at any stage of its cultural development or in any part of its social structure. Here is implicitly defined an activity that is peculiarly the responsibility of the librarian and is shared with other groups only at its margins; yet it is intimately intertwined with the needs of society. It minimizes the *a priori* value scale which the librarian usually cherishes, in common with other devotees of the library faith, and broadens the bases of its value judgments to a consideration of that which is good for society. Here is a recognition of the fact that the library is shaped by society, changing as society changes.

In the past the profession has maintained that what the librarian needs to know depends upon the kind of librarian he is, or expects to be —a children's, school, academic, or special librarian. Such a point of view is especially prevalent among the new advocates of librarianship as information science. The value of specialization and the utility of specialized knowledge is not to be minimized, but unless it is held together by the cohesive force of a generalized concept of librarianship that underlies all that the librarian does, the inevitable result is fragmentation of the profession to the point at which all standards of performance and all criteria of excellence will be lost. All library specializations, in one way or another, serve social ends, thus it is in the library as an instrument of society that the universals that underlie the profession are to be sought.

If it is the unique responsibility of the librarian to assemble, to organize, and to facilitate the use of graphic records, his genuinely professional activities must lie in these three areas. But the focal point of this activity is that moment when a book, a graphic record, passes into the hands of the reader. If this event takes place frequently and fruitfully the library may be said to be successful; if it never takes place, nothing the library could be or do would justify its existence. This is the *sine qua non* of librarianship in relation to which the relevance of all other possible activities must be judged.

Use, in the sense that something a reader has read has its impact on society and is therefore a matter of concern to society, occurs beyond the point at which the librarian puts the book, graphic record, or information, into the hands of the reader. If this particular event is to become a drop in the pool of accumulating knowledge there must be some impact, the book or the information must "do something" to the reader, though it need not take the form of, or be expressed in, overt action. A change within the individual, a deepening or an enrichment of the quality of experience in a single life, is a contribution, and often a very important contribution, to society. Indeed, our culture is so oriented that the quality of a civilization is measured by the degree to which it provides this enrichment, this opportunity for self-development, for its members. Yet, whether or not this relationship between book and reader is barren is largely beyond the control of the librarian once the book has reached the reader. The best that the librarian can do to facilitate a fruitful contact is to utilize fully all of his resources in making as nearly certain as possible that the best materials for the particular purpose find their way to the reader. Policies of selection, methods of organization, and media of interpretation must be chosen with this end in view; this is the standard by which the knowledge that the librarian must possess, if he is to perform his professional activities adequately, must be judged.

It has long been an axiom of the profession that the librarian cannot be responsible for evaluating the worth of the materials that he puts in the hands of the patron, that the librarian is not, and cannot be, a subject specialist. Therefore, it has been argued, the librarian must provide in breadth what he cannot achieve in depth; there is safety in numbers, and from that point on it is up to the reader to "make his own evaluation." Yet, almost a half-century ago, James I. Wyer argued for exactly the opposite point of view. In his treatise on reference work, Wyer is severely critical of those librarians who are content merely to guide the reader in the use of the bibliographic resources that the library provides. He rejects as conservative those librarians who hold that the prime duty of the librarian is to acquire and organize the materials of the library and "aid" the user to help himself. "To *interpret*," he wrote, "seems a much more exact and satisfying verb than to *aid*, to *help*, or to *assist*. . . . It connotes not merely less of mechanism and more of humanism; it suggests thoroughness (even in helping) as against superficiality; . . . a colleague rather than a clerk; informed leadership rather than a steering committee; in a word, understanding."[5] Wyer supports his point of view with the picturesque example, "The Gloversville milkman who, with one eye on his horse and wagon at the curb, shouted through the public library door for 'a book to cure my best cow' would never have left $70,000 to the library if he had been told to 'Consult the card catalog under *Cows*,' only to flounder among references to *Cattle, Diseases of, Bovine therapeutics*, etc."[6]

Similarly, Bundy and Wasserman are right when they charge that librarians have failed to evolve a practitioner-client relationship that is truly professional, and that the librarian's "willingness to play an inexpert role may well have been reinforced by the fact that the librarian has had some little knowledge about many things but not very much genuine understanding of anything."[7] They lament "the extinction of the reader's advisor, that breed of librarian who could, would, and did actively channel readers along rational and productive lines by making concrete recommendations and introducing taste and discrimination into such choices."[8]

## DISTINGUISHING CHARACTERISTICS OF THE SPECIALIST'S SUBSTANTIVE KNOWLEDGE

The focus of the librarian's professional knowledge, then, is this interaction between users and graphic records, and the influences which shape that relationship. It is this orientation that sets him apart from specialists in the more traditional, and well-defined, academic disciplines. The physicist, chemist, astronomer, economist, or historian have little interest in the relation between themselves or their colleagues and the literature of physics, chemistry, astronomy, economics, or history. The man of letters is more concerned with what takes place between book and

---

[5] James I. Wyer. *Reference Work*. Chicago. American Library Association. 1930. p. 5.
  Wyer is especially critical of the conservative point of view taken by William Warner Bishop in *The Backs of Books*. Baltimore. Williams and Wilkins. 1926. pp. 149–64; and by John Cotton Dana in "Misdirection of Effort in Reference Work." *Public Libraries*. vol. 16 (March 1911), p. 108.
[6] *Ibid.* pp. 9–10.
[7] Mary Lee Bundy and Paul Wasserman. "Professionalism Reconsidered." *College and Research Libraries*. vol. 29 (January 1968), p. 8.
[8] *Ibid.* p. 9.

reader, but even he probably works as much from an inner compulsion to purge his own brain as to induce a desired effect in his readers.

At this point it becomes necessary to consider certain important differences between the kinds of knowledge required of a subject specialist in the formal academic disciplines, and that of a practitioner in a profession such as law, medicine, dentistry, nursing, social work, and librarianship. The importance of this distinction can scarcely be overemphasized for it is, in part at least, in the kinds of knowledge required that is to be sought the key to any educational program. It has been the failure to create an harmonious relationship between the kinds of knowledge required and the program of formal instruction in librarianship that has often led the professional educator astray.

The specialist in the formal academic disciplines, and especially the student who is preparing himself for a career in such a branch of scholarship, must equip himself with three distinct types of knowledge, and his program of formal instruction must be so oriented.

a. *The Theoretical Framework of the Field*: He must be familiar with the structure of his field, and the interrelationships of its major parts. If he is a physicist he understands the basic relationships within that massive structure that has been erected upon those great traditional pillars of mechanics, heat, sound, light, electricity, and magnetism, and, more recently, the nature of matter and energy. Or, to use a metaphor, when he plunges in among the trees and the undergrowth, he must know the contours of the forest or he will surely lose his way. In short, he must know what the field is "about," what its contents, and what its goals are, and the ends it seeks.

b. *The Appropriate Methods of Research*: He must know the methods of research appropriate to his field of specialization, the ways in which new knowledge in the field is generated or discovered. This means knowing what methodology is appropriate and also what is inappropriate. He must know how the materials with which he works respond, or fail to respond, to specific methods. He must be able to evaluate the results of the research of others in terms of the efficacy of the methods used. Thus he develops what has been loosely known as a "scientific attitude."

c. *Major Contributions to Verified Knowledge*: He must understand, for his particular specialization, the major contributions to verified knowledge. This is particularly important for the sciences, which are *cumulative*; they are built up over relatively long periods of time until a formalized discipline is created. Some ideas are still held to be true, others have been added to the original stock, and many have been discarded as false. Thus there emerges a discipline, a science, with a solid and generally accepted vortex of accumulated knowledge surrounded by a constantly shifting and changing outer rim of new knowledge. Dispute generally centers on the outer edge; that which is within the vortex consensus has accepted as being true, though this does not deny the possibility that new knowledge is eventually drawn into the vortex, and may even alter drastically the basic form of the discipline. Such a transformation took place in physics with the impact of Einstein's work. It is, however, the vortex that the student must master before he can be trusted to venture into the turbulent waters at the periphery.[9]

To the above three forms of knowledge should be added some awareness of the integration of knowledge, the relations between the field of specialization and other fields, but in the past this has generally suffered neglect except as it is incorporated in an understanding of the theoretical framework of the field or provides the scholar with tools essential to the prosecution of his own work. The educational program of the specialist in the formal academic disciplines is designed to impart a mastery of one subject field and of the intellectual skills required for the extension of knowledge in that field, without regard to what the student will do after the completion of his formal training. That is, the educational program of the subject specialist, at both the graduate and undergraduate levels, is predicated on the assumption that the student will eventually become a research worker, an investigator, a productive scholar, in the area of his choice.

## THE INTELLECTUAL EQUIPMENT OF THE PROFESSIONAL

Every profession is a blending of theory and practice, a science and an art, *wissen und können*, to understand and to know how. Both of these elements are essential, both must be maintained in an harmonious and proper relationship. Like the rungs of a ladder, if they are allowed to become separated too far, the one cannot be reached without losing contact

---

[9] Crane Brinton has drawn a distinction between *cumulative* and *noncumulative* knowledge using the sciences and the humanities to exemplify the two forms. One may properly ask, however, is not all knowledge cumulative, and are not our advances over the Greeks in all fields more a matter of relativity, or degree, rather than of kind? See: Crane Brinton. *Ideas and Men.* New York. Prentice Hall. 1950. pp. 12–14.

with the other. If there is an excess of know-how the profession degenerates into a mere craft, while too much theory leads to the sterility of empty formalism.[10] By contrast to the subject specialist in the formal academic disciplines, the student in a graduate professional school must be prepared for the *practice* of his profession, for the professional is basically a *practitioner*. Most physicians practice medicine, most lawyers practice law, ministers preach, and teachers conduct classes. Admittedly there are medical men engaged in medical research, lawyers pursuing legal research, ministers who devote some of their time to Biblical criticism, and teachers who are engaged in research in their own right. But the pedagogy of all of these professions centers about practice rather than the assimilation of pure knowledge, for professional training, by definition, is a composite of theoretical knowledge and specialized intellectual and physical skills.

But this body of knowledge and these skills are not necessarily drawn from any one subject field, for the profession is, by its nature, interdisciplinary. Medicine draws from biology, chemistry, physics, and psychology; the practicing lawyer must be familiar with many departments of knowledge: economics, political science, medicine, chemistry, or any subject to which a particular case might relate. In a sense, nursing is a specialized form of medical practice, and social work represents the application of the social and certain of the biological sciences to the practical problems of family and community living. Because a profession is a composite of a variety of disciplines, it must fashion from them a consistent and integrated pattern unique and relevant to its own needs. Furthermore, it must maintain contact with the sources of its discipline, the fields of knowledge from which its principles and techniques have been derived, so that as each source field develops new insights and new knowledge, those relevant to the profession can be absorbed into its own theoretical structure or body of practical skills. It is not a disparagement of the professions to say that they are essentially parasitic, that they must be nourished by the formal academic disciplines. Their justification depends upon the success with which they convert this subsistence to socially useful ends. The great danger that threatens every professional school is that, through eagerness to achieve intellectual self-sufficiency, it suffers from intellectual isolation; for professions, like nations, cannot live unto themselves. The professional worker should be the first to recognize the unity of knowledge.

Of all the professions, that of the librarian is probably the most derivative and synthetic, is most dependent upon the more formal disciplines

---

[10] See: Michael Polanyi. *The Tacit Dimension.* Garden City, N.Y. Doubleday. 1966. Chapter 1. "Tacit Knowing."

for the derivation of its own theoretical structure and its corpus of practice. In the past, librarians have been disposed to view this characteristic as a fundamental weakness, and it has therefore generated a considerable feeling of professional inferiority. Yet this very quality has given librarianship a uniquely strategic position of leadership in the integration of human knowledge, and it could make of librarianship a great unifying force, not only in the world of scholarship, but also throughout all human life.

This type of knowledge, which is drawn from the formal academic disciplines, e.g., psychology, logic, mathematics, sociology, to name but a few, and which is basic and fundamental to the library profession, is identical with that imparted in the traditional graduate program of the university; thus it would seem reasonable that the librarian should acquire it academically. Certainly such knowledge constitutes that part of the librarian's intellectual equipment, which, though fundamental to librarianship, has been woefully neglected in the past despite many pronouncements respecting its importance, and without recognition of the fact that university administrators and other critics of librarianship have decried such neglect. It is particularly important, therefore, that these studies are properly seen as central to the librarian's body of professional knowledge, and not as tinseled embellishments that will transform a set of clerical tasks into a body of professional practice.

Neglect of fundamentals has brought the profession of education to a separation that is almost complete between the techniques of instruction and the subject that is to be taught. Librarianship can easily suffer the same fate if it continues to concern itself primarily with the refinement of its technical skills and neglects its professional responsibilities.

## THE ANCILLARY INTELLECTUAL EQUIPMENT OF THE LIBRARIAN

Despite the fundamental importance of the formalized disciplines to the librarian's intellectual equipment, not all of his professional knowledge is externally derived. There remains a very substantial body of knowledge and skills that are essential to the librarian, yet may or may not be appropriate to a formal academic program or encompassed within the traditional academic disciplines. These ancillary bodies of knowledge, which are no less important because of their auxiliary position, may be grouped into six main classes or types:

 a.   Organizational—The organization and management of libraries, including the historical development of librarianship, as well as present practice, and potential future trends.

b. Environmental—Those agencies and other social structures and instrumentalities with which the library must interact: governmental, academic, corporate, and associational. Here are included not only those social groups which the library serves, but also those which, in one way or another, serve the library, such as publishers, booksellers, and bookbinders.

c. Cultural—The immediate cultural context of the variant forms of library specialization. This includes the general culture in which the library as a social agency operates and the specialized interests or concerns, the local culture, by which each library is shaped and to which it must respond.

d. Physical—The materials and equipment with which the librarian must deal: the planning and maintenance of the physical plant, custody of the book stock, development and supervision of the library as a physical entity.

e. Clerical and Office Routines—The routines and procedures customarily identified as office routines, the clerical routines in library operations, accounting, management procedures and operations.

f. Personnel—The librarian and his staff as gainfully employed human beings, personnel and the management of personnel, supervision, administration of staff, and direction of work effort.

Each of these areas of knowledge, as they are related to the profession of librarianship will be more fully discussed, in subsequent pages, in terms of the librarian's total intellectual equipment.

## THE LIBRARIAN'S FUNDAMENTAL KNOWLEDGE

The fundamental knowledge of the librarian can be understood only in terms of the function, or role, of the library; for the doctrine of the architect that form follows function may be applied, as well, to social structures. The librarian, regardless of the kind of clientele he serves, may be said to be concerned with the interaction of human minds communicating across the barriers of space and time through the media of graphic records, the content of which may be conveyed through the senses of sound and touch, as well as sight. For it is understood that a graphic record may be audible and tactile, as well as visual.

Therefore, the professional knowledge of the librarian must be centered about:

a.   The content of the record of human knowledge and experience. If the function of the library is to promote the interaction of human minds through the medium of graphic records, it is axiomatic that the intellectual content of graphic records, rather than the graphic records (books) themselves as artifacts, must be known and understood by the librarian. A corollary of this axiom is that the book needs of, or the graphic records relevant to, a particular clientele must likewise be known and understood.

b.   The manifestations of a desire on the part of the individual to participate in, or share vicariously, the experiences of others. Thus, the librarian's sphere of intellectual competence is represented as the triangle in Figure 7-1, of which one side is the individual, the other side, graphic records, and the base the conjunction of the two in a socially fruitful relationship.

Such a triangular representation is characteristic of the use of graphic materials, through the medium of the library system, at any age, under any circumstances, and for any level of sophistication.

Thus, the unit of library service is the communication of some fragment of library content, or library resources, to a reader or inquirer, and the measure of library success may be expressed as the number/value of such units effectively and efficiently transmitted. The central act, or objective of librarianship may, therefore, be expressed as,

> Books
> or
> Information about  ————————————————→ Readers
> or Contained in Books

and the fundamental professional knowledge necessary for the successful consummation of this act may also be represented in triangular form as shown in Figure 7-2.

Because the role of the librarian is one of mediation in the world of recorded knowledge, his understanding of the communication process must be interdisciplinary in its roots; the librarian must comprehensively relate communication to a wide spectrum of human activities, involving a divergent variety of cultural groups, encompassing all ages and strata of intellectual competence, operating in many subject fields. Further, he must strive to maintain a balance among these demands, pressures, and interests, even when at times they are in conflict, for society cannot afford to sacri-

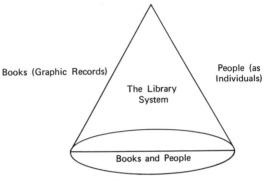

**Figure 7-1.**

fice one for the benefit of another. There will be times when the librarian must be a humanist among scientists, a champion of the young in a world of adults, a philosopher in the marketplace, an idealist surrounded by realities.

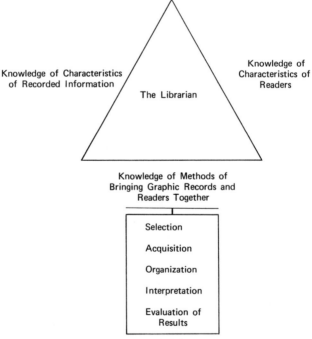

**Figure 7-2.**

But such knowledge, however thoroughly mastered, remains static until the skills of the practitioner give it life. A surgeon may know how to operate, but he is of little value to his patients if he cannot transform that knowledge into effective remedial action. A lawyer who knows the theory and philosophy of law will starve if he cannot win a case. A librarian, however scholarly, is of scant value to society if he cannot translate that scholarship into an effective program of action that will in some way be profitable to the community he is supposed to serve. Librarianship, therefore, like any other profession, is a composite of theory and practice, of knowledge and skills, and the one without the other is barren and sterile. Thus, if librarians have anything of importance to contribute to the culture of their society it must be transmitted by those special skills that they have developed through centuries of practice. Quite obviously, skills developed in one profession can successfully and profitably be transmitted to another, and the librarian must so prepare himself that he can benefit from skills and competencies borrowed from other fields.

The task of defining a skill is not easy; even its mere description is difficult. As Boulding has written:

> Ask the ball player how he manages to hit the ball and he will not waste time in words but will grab the bat and say, "Like this." A physiologist or psychologist might, of course, have a different (and more verbose) view of the matter. However lengthy their explanations they would be incapable of transmitting the skill verbally. . . . There is no substitute for the simple demonstration and really no way of learning but by trying, and failing, and trying again until the skill is built into the organism.[11]

Intellectual skills, like muscular skills, have something of this imitative quality, and they, too, are products of the whole organism. The skill must be fused into an organic whole. "The student plays all the time with pieces which never form a pattern, the place and purpose of which he never quite sees. One cannot, however, help him much by *describing* the skill which he is supposed to have even though once acquired he may say, 'Why didn't you tell me these things before?'—to which the only answer is, 'I did!' "[12]

The property of a skill that makes it difficult, if not impossible, to explain verbally, even granting the subtleties of language, is what Michael Polanyi calls "tacit knowing," or the "tacit dimension" in human thought. Thus he has written:

---

[11] Kenneth E. Boulding. *The Skills of the Economist.* Cleveland. Howard Allen. 1958. p. 7.
[12] *Ibid.* p. 8.

I shall reconsider human knowledge by starting from the fact that we can know more than we can tell. . . . Indeed my definition of a word denoting an external thing must ultimately rely on pointing at such a thing. This naming-cum-pointing is called "an ostensive definition"; and this philosophic expression conceals a gap to be bridged by an intelligent effort on the part of the person to whom we want to tell what the word means. Our message had left something behind that we could not tell, and its reception must rely on it that the person addressed will discover that which we had not been able to communicate.[13]

All skill relates to a "system" of some kind, that is, to a coherent set of quantities, properties, and relationships, which have been, or may be, abstracted from the totality of the environment. The successful exercise of any skill depends upon the ability to create an abstract system from the complexities that comprise the real world in which the practitioner is operating. Thus the skill of the librarian will depend upon his ability to abstract a system from the intellectual, emotional, social, and physical world around him—the world he "serves," whether it be that of the housewife, of the college student, of the business man, or of the scholar. The basis of the librarian's system is the communication of information, where *information* is to be understood as any graphic manifestation of intellectual activity; thus the librarian must view the world professionally as an intricate pattern of communications. It is in this abstraction of librarianship that the peculiar skill of the librarian is to be sought.

## THE LIBRARIAN'S ORGANIZATIONAL KNOWLEDGE

The professional worker, whether in medicine, law, education, or the ministry, stereotyped as an isolated practitioner, working almost, if not entirely, alone, with a minimum of equipment, and with no "home" except the four walls of his study or his office, has all but vanished. By contrast, today, as Henry E. Bliss has written, "the communities of minds in schools, associations, and nations, the cooperative tendencies of modern society, the interrelations of business, of art, of sciences, of societies, have produced a mental, social and economic tissue."[14] This intricately patterned tissue is

---

[13] Polanyi. *Tacit Dimension.* pp. 4–6.

[14] Henry E. Bliss. *The Organization of Knowledge and the System of the Sciences.* New York. Holt. 1929. p. 60.

the result of an organizational revolution in modern society which, Boulding says "has received little study, and is not something of which we are particularly conscious. It has crept upon us silently. It is something which we accept as 'natural' almost without thinking. And yet the whole movement raises problems with which we are ill-equipped to deal. . . . We are still often . . . thinking in terms of a society in which organizations are rather small and weak, and in which the family is the dominant institution."[15] This remarkable growth in the number, size, and power of organizations that has taken place during the past seventy-five years, and which has permeated all areas of human activity, came relatively late to the library. Though librarians have always been tied to a physical plant to a greater degree, perhaps, than other professions, for centuries their organic structure, like the buildings in which the library was housed, was small, relatively simple, and intimate. Moreover, the fact that librarianship has been for much of its history dominantly custodial, has increased the difficulty of perceiving the pertinence of an understanding of organizational structure and function to the specialized knowledge that the librarian is generally supposed to have. Not until the coming of the early 1930s could even a relatively few librarians be said to have become actively aware of the institutionalization of their profession and come to realize that the library was a part of a larger social structure. The revelation that librarians do not live quiet uncomplicated lives in their own tidy little worlds was something of a shock; the hunger to "get back to the book," is an understandable craving, but in the world of today it foreshadows the onset of professional starvation.

The library system is represented as the diagram in Figure 7-3.

In the economic turmoil of the early 1930s there was great appeal in the assumed security that group affiliation promised. When the Second World War brought a crisis that demanded united action, not only within but among nations, one may be scarcely surprised that organization in and for its own sake came to be regarded as a right and proper goal for individual effort, and that the greatest of all personal sins was that of social maladjustment, of failure to integrate oneself into the group. But the excesses of this movement brought many faults, not the least of which was a blind worship of administration and the administrator,[16] a conviction that

---

[15] Kenneth E. Boulding. *The Organizational Revolution.* New York. Harper. 1953. pp. 3–4.

[16] William H. Whyte, Jr. *The Organization Man.* New York. Simon and Schuster. 1956. pp. 14–22 and 32–59.

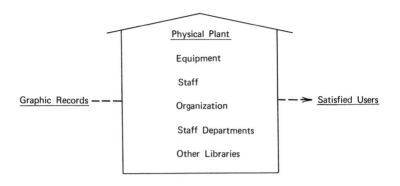

**Figure 7-3.**

managerial responsibility was the highest reward that society could bestow and its efficient prosecution the greatest proof of devotion to that trust.

All of the professions reflected this trend, medicine, teaching, even the ministry. The legal profession had long been highly structured through its affiliation with the courts and the bar associations. Likewise in education the pull toward group affiliation had been strong from the days of Henry Barnard and Horace Mann, but the twentieth century brought a substantial increase in the formation of educational associations, centralized schools, and universities which were great centers of organized teaching and research. In medicine, the country doctor was replaced by the clinic, and hospital management and administration became a specialized field. In religion, the divinity schools began the preparation and training of pastors' assistants, and considerable attention began to be directed toward the church as an administrative system as well as a house of worship. To these forces the library was not immune. The history of the American public library is a record of the delegation of responsibilities by the library board to the librarian and, subsequently, his professional staff. In the early years of the Boston Public Library, its distinguished board, under the domination of Ticknor and Everett, allowed the librarian few responsibilities other than the most elementary housekeeping routines, and virtually all duties now regarded by librarians as "professional," were firmly held in the determined hands of the trustees. Not until the appointment of Justin Winsor did this grip begin to loosen. But even well into the twentieth century, the typical director of the larger libraries was more of a scholar than an administrator.

It was with the establishment of the Graduate Library School at the

University of Chicago, however, that library administration came into its own. Following a preliminary period of uncertainty as to the areas of advanced graduate study appropriate to the practice of librarianship, the school, largely through the influence of Dean Louis Round Wilson and Carleton B. Joeckel focussed its program of teaching and research primarily upon library administration. This movement was stimulated in part by the work of Douglas Waples in measuring statistically the social effectiveness of the public library, but an even greater influence was exercised by the University itself which, during this period in its history, was especially strong in the social sciences, particularly in the areas of public administration and government. This tendency was intensified by the proximity to the University Quadrangles, of the Public Administration Clearing House. Students in the Library School were strongly urged to supplement their courses in librarianship with programs of study in these adjacent administrative areas. Lured by the financial rewards that were beginning to be offered to library administrators, the school experienced little difficulty in attracting ambitious young men and women to its doors.

The profession of librarianship was ripe for the Chicago "point of view," and a new enthusiasm for scientific administration and management spread rapidly to other library schools and throughout librarianship generally. Admittedly librarianship had been suffering from an excessive bibliophilism that, for all its richness and depth, had led to a serious neglect of the library as an organized system. This new desire to examine critically the operations of the library, and to evaluate its social contribution, as well as its efficiency was, indeed, badly needed, and there can be little doubt that it raised the professional prestige of the librarian. Many of the libraries, even some of the largest and most important, had fallen into a sorry state of administrative neglect; salaries were low, working conditions were far from ideal, and the physical plant was, in many instances, becoming obsolete. Encouraged by the growth in the size and complexity of libraries, their increasing interdependence, and the need for new administrative machinery for their effective operation, attention to administrative knowledge increased until at times it came to be regarded as the most important segment of the librarian's professional equipment. This enthusiasm for administrative competence was in no way diminished by the obvious fact that, largely because of it, the "outside world," especially the world of government, industry, and business, were paying generously for administrative competence. This interest in administration is not likely to diminish; as "larger units of library service" give way before the rise of "information networks," the role of management, systems analysis, and other forms of programming unit operations are likely to increase. All of these activities, however, will probably draw more heavily from such fields as management and applied mathematics than from librarianship.

To decry the excesses of the doctrine of "every librarian an administrator" does not detract from the importance of managerial knowledge in the professional equipment of the librarian. The fallacy in this belief arose from the failure to recognize the essential similarity in the problems encountered by the library administrator to those of other administrators operating in other fields. Both the doctor and the lawyer, for example, must be familiar with the structure within which they operate. The doctor assigns to others the administration of hospital and laboratory facilities, while the lawyer in general divorces himself from the administration of the penal system, and devotes little attention to the administration of the courts. By contrast, excessive preoccupation on the part of the librarian with administrative and managerial problems has, in turn, led to neglect of the essentially bibliographic character of his profession. One must, therefore, bear in mind that administrative knowledge is *necessary*, but not *central*, to librarianship, and its place in education for librarianship must reflect its ancillary character.

Though administration has been practiced from the time when man first began to organize himself into groups, only recently has there emerged a separate profession of administration with its own theoretical structure and body of generalizations presumably applicable to a wide spectrum of diverse situations of which the library is but one instance. Whether large organizations should be operated by professional administrators or by those skilled in the substantive knowledge from which the organization derives its objectives and functions is a problem that is not peculiar to librarianship, and it cannot be categorically answered here. Certain of the larger libraries have experimented with professional administration, particularly with respect to financial and budget operations and the management of personnel, and with considerable success. So far as librarianship is concerned, any valid answer to this question of the role of the professional administrator is obscured by the fact that the main avenue to advancement in librarianship has led up the ladder of the administrative hierarchy. Often the skills of administration have been overemphasized, and many ambitious and able librarians have been compelled for financial reasons to accept administrative positions for which they were both temperamentally and intellectually unfitted. Though no successful tests for the prediction of administrative success have as yet been devised, one may guess that administrative competence and scholarly ability, if they are not actually antithetical, are often very far from being compatible.

An excessive emphasis upon administrative skills at the expense of fundamental subject knowledge cannot be corrected by the library schools alone; it is a reflection of our national mores. But it is the schools' responsibility to assess the amount and kind of administrative knowledge that should be incorporated in the basic and advanced curricula, and to determine how and at what point in the professional program of study additional training in administration is desirable. There are valid historical reasons for the emphasis upon administration in the traditional program of education for librarianship, but the time has come for its rigorous reexamination in terms of the patterning of the library as it exists today and as it may be expected to develop tomorrow.

In the present study, four basic types of knowledge are considered to be organizational. The first is concerned with the internal organization and management of the library as an individual enterprise, with its own specific objectives and environment, e.g., public, school, college or university, government, business, or other form of specialization. It is fallacious to assume that each of these has its own peculiar body of administrative theory. Though each type may introduce variations and alterations unique to it, all relate to a common body of managerial knowledge. One may suggest that the size of the unit is the most important administrative consideration and that administratively the librarian of the small specialized research library has more in common with the high school librarian or the librarian of a small urban community than he has with the librarian of a large metropolitan system or a great university.

Second, the growth of libraries and the exponentially increasing volume of literature have dispelled, probably forever, the old myth that a library should strive for completeness in its book collections. Today no library, however large, or however limited its field, can aspire to completeness. Further, the rapid advances in the technology of communication, such as teletype, facsimile transmission, and electronic character recognition, have made completeness unnecessary and have placed in the hands of the librarian powerful new tools for the coordination of bibliographic services and systems that can be national and even international in their coverage. New techniques in photographic reproduction, particularly extremes in miniaturization, have laid the foundation for a new age of interlibrary cooperation, a cooperation that has transcended conventional technology, and are manifest in a slowly growing spirit of interdependence.[17] The Farmington Plan, the Center for Research Libraries, EDUCOM, and the

---

[17] See: John R. Platt. "Where Will the Books Go?" *The Step to Man*, by John R. Platt. New York. Wiley. 1966. pp. 3–18.

Ohio College Library Center, are doubtless harbingers of this new age, and are emphasizing the need of the librarian for that aspect of administrative knowledge which treats of cooperation at the local, regional, national, and international levels.

Third, librarians, in common with other Americans, are "joiners," and the professional association is playing an increasingly important role in their lives. Fostered by the need for increased cooperation and interdependence, this dedication to associational activity is not likely to decline. Though many have become disillusioned with the impotence of associational activity in promoting the efficiency and effectiveness of the profession, this disappointment may well be due to the failure of most librarians to understand the nature of professional associations, their proper objectives, the character of their activities, and the nature of their limitations. Much of the inadequacy of professional library associations has arisen from the simple fact that they were asked to perform functions that exceeded their abilities and powers. Therefore, the librarian of the future must be equipped with an understanding of the structure of the voluntary professional association, and not look to it for that which it cannot give, or direct it along paths which it cannot, by its nature, successfully traverse. In directing the destiny of the professional association, pride and yearning for prestige must give way to knowledge and understanding.[18]

Finally, the administrative knowledge of the librarian must reflect an historical awareness; he must understand how the library, as an agency, has developed through the centuries, how it has responded or failed to respond to the changes in its environment, and wherein it has succeeded or failed in its services to mankind. Not until the 1930s was library history freed from an interminable sequence of narratives depicting the growth of individual libraries, so that it might present the library as an emerging social invention conditioned by its social *milieu*. This unfettering of library history redirected all library philosophy, and made possible a new and far more useful understanding of the role of the librarian in society.[19]

---

[18] Most library associations are, by the nature of their membership, promotional. The only bond by which their diverse membership is united is the desire to "sell" libraries to the public generally or to some specialized groups. Only incidentally do they promote professional knowledge within their own ranks. Any attempts to remodel them into engines of scholarship and research are doomed to failure from the beginning. The frequent efforts of the American Library Association to reorganize, is striking proof that change that is not based solidly upon a definition of purpose and objective is only a nominal reorganization. Likewise the attempt to graft research onto the ALA, which is not a research organization, is not likely to be successful.

[19] See: Jesse H. Shera. *Historians, Books, and Libraries.* Cleveland. Western Reserve University. 1953.

Organizational knowledge, then, embraces far more than an understanding of the functions of management and administration. It encompasses in addition the fundamentals of interlibrary cooperation, professional association, and the history of the library as a creation of society.

## THE LIBRARIAN'S ENVIRONMENTAL KNOWLEDGE

The environment may be defined as that totality of elements which individually and collectively establish the requirements which must be met by the library. In part these relate to the system of which the library is one segment and within which it must operate. Only in a relatively few instances, such as the Boston Athenaeum, the Redwood Library of Newport, Rhode Island, and other surviving social libraries, or such libraries as the Newberry and, formerly, the John Crerar Library in Chicago, is the library organizationally independent. The public library is a part of municipal government, the academic library is an integral part of the college or university community, the "special" library is often a part of a business or industrial organization. In each of these situations, and in many others, the library is required to operate in an environment the general structure of which is established by a superior authority, and within which the freedom of the librarian is in greater or less degree circumscribed. The librarian, therefore, must be familiar with the characteristics of this environment; he must know in some substantial detail the way in which government operates, a business enterprise functions, a school system or academic community works. He must know something of the legal structure which will influence his policies and the laws and regulations which he must observe.

There is a second environment which is created by the clientele the librarian serves, the graphic records they will use, and the areas of knowledge to which these graphic records must be related. He must understand the social organization and structure of the environment and he must speak the language of his clientele. It is this environment that has brought his library into being and he cannot afford to be a stranger in the world it represents.

Finally, there is the environment of the library itself, the physical world of buildings, furniture, and equipment, the book stock, the staff, and the universe of ideas which is the intellectual content of the library. This universe may be the pedestrian world of trade discounts, binders' schedules, of jobbers' catalogs, of fines to be collected, and invoices to be processed; yet within the boundaries of this environment is to be found the excitement of developing a collection that precisely meets the needs of the users, and the thrill of a successful chase for a particularly treasured or elusive book. It is a kaleidoscopic world into the changing pattern of which each part must fit, and in which each segment has its own unique value.

Each library then exists in an environment peculiar to itself, an environment that influences its success or failure, and within the limits of which the librarian must operate.

Inasmuch as the library is a service agency, it is the second of these environments, the environment of the clientele, that is the librarian's *raison d'être*, and it is because of its importance that so much attention has been devoted, in recent years, to user-interest studies, profiles of user interest, and selective dissemination of information (SDI). The diversity of this environment for the public librarian makes his task especially difficult, and his burden has been made heavier by his failure to come to grips with the dimensions of his problem.

The boundaries of this world are limited, in a variety of ways, by the other two environments and hence they, too, are important to the librarian. The task, then, becomes one of bringing into an harmonious and effective balance and relationship these three environments. Furthermore, each of the three is unique to any specific situation, yet it is possible to generalize in ways that will make them applicable to classes of situations, or even define them as universals.

This tri-partite character of environmental knowledge presents a problem to those concerned with the professional education of the librarian. That environmental knowledge is important to the librarian can scarcely be denied, and that much of it can, and should, be reduced to principles and types appropriate to formal education is equally clear. But what portion is properly within the sphere of professional library education, and what is most effectively mastered outside the classroom through practical experience has not been adequately determined. Formal education is, of course, condensed experience, but not all environmental knowledge can be compressed into the Procrustean pattern of classroom presentation. Much of it is to be mastered only through the slow laborious process that is the characteristic of apprenticeship, practice, and experience; much of it is the kind of knowledge that each person must discover for himself.


## THE CULTURAL CONTEXT

Enough has been said in the earlier chapters of this study to indicate the importance of an understanding of the culture in the librarian's arsenal of professional knowledge. The librarian should understand the position of the library in its historical and contemporary setting. Much of this knowledge should be acquired in the librarian's undergraduate education; the graduate professional program should stress the role of the library in the cultural *milieu*. Here, it is sufficient to emphasize that the librarian operates in two cultures, first, in that generalized realm in which the library as a social agency exists, and second, in the specific culture which his own library serves. The first is appropriate to formal education; the second is largely the result of experience, supported by appropriate professional education, and requires knowing his clientele and the materials that should be provided for it.

For the cultural context with which the librarian finds himself associated he must become familiar with its specialized terminology, its social structure, its patterns of thought, the ways in which it operates, and its peculiar problems. There are certain library procedures and methods appropriate to specific cultural groups, special classification schemes, special systems for the analysis of varying types of graphic records for special purposes, and there are particular bibliographic or reference services for identified clienteles.

Thus, the librarian's knowledge of the cultural context of that segment of the profession in which he works, and the area he serves, may be, like the environment itself, diversified or highly specialized, flexible and responsive, or rigid and predetermined. Only through an understanding of the cultural setting can the librarian expect to render his most effective service.

## PHYSICAL EQUIPMENT—PLANNING AND MAINTENANCE

A knowledge of physical equipment, its planning and its maintenance, is requisite to the immediate environmental knowledge discussed above. A library, even a small one, is a physical entity, a plant, a structure, that originally required planning and, once built, demands constant surveillance. The librarian, therefore, must have some knowledge of architecture, especially library architecture, of space requirements and their relationships, of traffic and work flow, both with respect to the staff and the clientele, of lighting, of heating, of humidification, of flooring, and of furniture design, and even of computers and their capabilities—all the innumerable minutiae which make the library plant an efficient physical organism. Even more important than the foregoing is a knowledge of that equipment which, if not unique to librarianship, is at least so closely a part of it that the librarian may quite properly be expected to be competent in its evaluation and use.

In addition to the physical care of books and other library materials, the repair and preservation of bindings, the librarian must also be familiar with the needs of films and phonograph recordings for maximum life expectancy. He should also have some understanding of such equipment as bookmobiles, and book trucks, electronic charging devices, photocopying, audiovisual, and card-sorting equipment, protective mechanisms, and the various computer applications for control and information handling. He cannot be expected to be an authority in all of these, and indeed there are many library positions in which no knowledge of them will be required, but at least he should be prepared to know where trustworthy information about them is available, and have enough of an understanding of the mechanical and electronic world of which they are a part to be able to interpret the information available to him, and thus protect himself and his library from the glibness of the huckster.

## CLERICAL AND OFFICE ROUTINES

Clerical and commercial procedures and routines are likewise a segment of environmental knowledge, though few of these are unique to librarianship. Here are included such skills as typing, filing, bookkeeping and accounting: the procedures of budget management, ordering, the handling of invoices; the general law of taxation, contracts and leases; the basic principles of insurance; and an understanding of the regulations governing employment, civil service, social security, and other supplemental benefits. For many of these the basic knowledge and skills may well be acquired outside the field of librarianship, and subsequently adapted to library needs—just as they must be appropriately modified for an administrator in a hospital, an automobile factory, or a department store. But he must not forget that the library as it exists now is almost unique in that it maintains a constantly increasing inventory, and this fact alone necessitates certain adaptations in its economy; eventually, it would seem the inventory must stabilize.

In many ways the knowledge of physical equipment and of clerical and commercial procedures is a composite of detail, a heterogeneous body of precise information that may shift or be superseded almost from month to month. Collectively it can impress the layman and hence can be easily mistaken for profound managerial competence and knowledge. More than one librarian has gained a reputation as a great administrator because he could quote formulae for the spacing of book-stack ranges or the seating capacity of reading rooms. Admittedly such knowledge can be extremely important, even vital, when a new library is to be built or an old one remodelled. But the tricks of "scientific management," of time and motion studies, of performing efficiently that which probably would be better left undone, these are not to be mistaken for true administrative wisdom, and certainly they are not librarianship. There is no denying the fact that the librarian must be assumed to be as able as any other intelligent person to *obtain* and *use* the information from other fields that he may need, and to adapt it, or supervise its adaptation to librarianship. But because a library administrator possesses this technical knowledge from such areas as management and administration, one may not assume that he is an able library administrator.

## PERSONNEL

Any organization is people working together for the benefit of the whole, and most of the problems of administration begin and end in personnel. The task of personnel administration is more of an art than a science, and most of the literature on the subject trails off in an elaboration of the obvious, or retreats to vapid platitudes about *esprit de corps* or emotional appeals for "team work."

Yet, of all the responsibilities of administration, the management of personnel is perhaps the most neglected. People are not by nature cooperative, and each member of the staff must learn to understand the problems of the others. How much of this art can be taught in library school is open to question. Success largely depends on the personalities of the people involved, the creation of an atmosphere hospitable to group effort and incentive. Communication is certainly one of the most important elements in the process, but communication must be a "two-way street." Every staff member has the right to be heard, and as long as the lines of communication are open employee dissatisfaction can be held to a minimum.

It is probably true to say that good personnel relations filter down from the top, but the staff members, too, have a responsibility to appreciate the problems of the administrator. They cannot do this unless they are kept informed of what those problems are and how their solutions are being realized.

The problem of personnel raises the question of "loose" versus "tight" administration, and that in turn rests largely on the personality and work habits of those in administration. The choice of either alternative raises its own peculiar problems for there are advantages and disadvantages in both. Whatever one may say about personnel management, examples could probably be cited to prove the opposite. There are even people who work best under a "straw boss." If responsibility is to be delegated, as it must be in every complex organization, then it must be accompanied by the appropriate authority to act. Perhaps the best guide is to study the operations of other administrators, both successful and poor, or to read the autobiographical writings of those who have had long and successful careers in the management of personnel. The staff should never feel that they are being manipulated no matter how worthy the end. What then can one say about the management of personnel? Not very much. A genuine liking for people, the ability to understand another's point of view, the capacity to recognize that every individual is a distinct and separate human being, certainly these are important, but success in the promotion of group effort is something more than any of these, they do not guarantee success. Each administrator must find his own way in his work experience, and he must be ever critical of himself.

A generation ago one could say with considerable accuracy that the library was neglecting the important role of "middle management," but this is no longer true. Growth in the size and complexity of libraries has had much to do with the change. But whatever the reason, personnel management in libraries is improving, though one must not forget that some of the great librarians of the past elicited the strongest of loyalties from those fortunate enough to work under their direction.

## THE RELATION OF A THEORY OF LIBRARIANSHIP TO THE LIBRARIAN'S REQUISITE KNOWLEDGE

The role, or roles, that the librarian is called upon to play in any culture reflects implicitly a theory, or theories, of the social function of the library. Explicit statements of these theories have, in the past, been relatively few, but there is ample evidence to prove that different library groups, as well as groups of laymen, have represented very different ideas respecting the central purpose of the library and the clienteles it is supposed to serve. Though these groups may not have thought of themselves as exponents of a particular library philosophy, or even as library theorists, yet each holds tenaciously, and often vocally, to the belief that the educational program of the library recruit should be based upon, or at least should emphasize, those kinds of knowledge which seem most appropriate to its own concepts of library function. This attitude toward education is by no means unique to the library; it is characteristic of every professional and indeed every vocational point of view. Education is constantly being threatened by both curricular expansion and attrition. As new functions develop and old services expand, there follows a corresponding demand for the addition of new courses to the curriculum or, at a minimum, the inclusion of new information in existing courses. But this specialization does not always represent a net increment, for there is present a counter tendency to encroach upon and erode the basic program of study, particularly those parts of the undergraduate course of study which relate to "general" or "liberal" education. The classical curriculum is not necessarily sacrosanct, but all too frequently rejection has been permitted to proceed with little regard for the value of what is being lost.

Thus, in the library school, as elsewhere in the educational spectrum, this process of cumulation and erosion has taken place until the present curriculum represents a heterogeneous composite of attempts to meet new demands by grafting new specializations upon a stem that has been weakened by repeated amputation.[20] Library service today has grown to such proportions and encompasses such a wide range of materials and interests that any attempt to create a median upon which a universally applicable curriculum can be postulated has become impossible. Each phase or type of library operation has rapidly become a field of specialization in itself for which an increasing amount of specific education is required. In the late 1940s, when the present writer was a member of the faculty of the Graduate Library School of the University of Chicago, he shared with his colleagues the belief that there is a very substantial body of knowledge common to all aspects of librarianship, and this point of view was given its fullest expression in the conference, held in Chicago in 1953, on *The Core of Education for Librarianship*.[21] Today, however, it is becoming increasingly clear that that which provides unity for the profession, for librarianship as a whole, is not a particular set of courses in a library school, but an understanding of the *functions* of the *library system* in its entirety, the relationships among the various parts and aspects of librarianship, and a sense of the necessity for a wholesome respect on the part of

---

[20] Perhaps the most striking example of this development in librarianship is to be seen in the battery of specialized curricula prepared in the 1950's under the auspices of the Sub-Committee on Special Librarianship of the Joint Committee on Library Education, an instrumentality of the Council of National Library Associations. See: "Education for Special Librarianship." *Library Quarterly*. vol. 24, no. 1 (January 1954), pp. 1–20.

[21] Lester Asheim. *The Core of Education for Librarianship*. Chicago. American Library Association. 1954.

each group comprising the profession for the functions and responsibilities of all the other groups. In short, librarianship, like knowledge itself, is a unity which must be comprehended by all who are engaged in its practice, improvement, and promotion. Beyond this common basis of understanding, each area of specialization is entitled to an educational program which will be adequate, in both content and numbers of students, to its own peculiar needs. In terms of educational organization this implies a necessary agreement among library schools respecting the content of the basic courses needed by all students, and a willingness to formulate a program of cooperation in which each participant will accept responsibility for one or more areas of specialization. Not even the largest schools can provide instruction in every phase of librarianship. Further, certain schools are strategically better situated than are others in geographical propinquity to resources for offering instruction in certain areas. Therefore, the minimization of duplication, the elimination of the least efficient or marginal units, and the promotion of cooperation comprise the only rational approach to the solution of the problem of education for librarianship.

In childhood, in youth, during the years of formal education, in the pursuit of a vocation or an avocation, in playing the many roles that every individual is called upon to assume, in the prosecution of the most esoteric research, in the most casual concern with the trivial and transitory, through graphic records the services of the library touch life at every point. Thus, the relationship between the flow of life and the library may be represented pictorially as a chronological continuum, a stream into which flow many tributaries each representing a specialized individual role. Because the library touches the life of the individual at every point through every age, it must of necessity reflect in its own structure the growing complexity of life itself. Thus the task of education for librarianship is two-fold: (1) to prepare the student by equipping him with the necessary specialized knowledge that will enable him to contribute effectively to a profession that is constantly changing and becoming increasingly specialized, yet, at the same time (2) to exert a cohesive force that will promote communication and understanding among the constituent parts of the totality of librarianship so that the profession will not be fragmented into a variety of isolated and even discordant specialisms. In short, the librarian of the future must help to build a professional world in which the public librarian, the children's librarian, the school librarian, the academic librarian, the so-called special librarian, the documentalist, and information scientist can live in harmony with mutual understanding and respect and with maximum opportunity for the fulfillment of each particular role.

The relationship between the function of the library and the knowledge that the librarian may need to execute that function may, perhaps, best be presented in graphic form in Table 7-1, though, to achieve a degree of clarity in presentation, such a tabulation must be relatively superficial in the depth of its analysis. One should also point out that the theories of library function as generally set forth in the literature do not always correspond to the principles of operation within a particular library. Therefore, the following tabulation of knowledge needed by the librarian in a few of the areas of specialization is based upon a limited number of observable principles of operation rather than any formally expressed theories or objectives of librarianship.

Despite its length, the preceding tabulation is only a partial listing of the types of knowledge required by the various library specializations, but it is sufficient to suggest the magnitude of the demands that are made upon library schools and the impossibility of satisfying all of them with the limited resources in time and faculty that are characteristic of the typical library school program of study. The ideal curriculum would provide an introductory survey of the total library field followed by extensive and intensive discipline in the relevant specialization. Such a program should be based on the recognition that each specialization necessitates its own unique preliminary training, that the responsibility of the student is *to learn* rather than to be taught, that even the most nearly ideal curriculum can be only the beginning of the educational process, and that the student's years of formal education can accomplish little more than create an awareness of the knowledge he must master and the ways in which such mastery may be achieved over his entire professional life. "The lyf so short, the craft so long to lerne," wrote Chaucer in the opening lines of *The Parlement of Foules*, in recognition of learning as a life-long process.

Specialization in library education there inevitably must be, but before there can be an effective assumption of responsibility among the several library schools, consideration must be given to the number of workers required by each specialty, the possibility of a geographic pattern of such demand, and the resources available to each school with respect to the specializations which it is qualified to offer.

The preceding pages have dealt almost exclusively with functional specialization, with but scant attention to such operational specializations as cataloging, reference work, or administration. One hardly need labor the point that the specialized requirements of each of the functional fields will be reflected in adjustments and modifications in the operational specializations. The cataloging (to choose an extreme example) in a children's library will be quite different from that in a library serving the research

TABLE 7-1.

| Library Function | Specialized Knowledge |
|---|---|
| **I.  *Conservation*** | |
| Ranges from the pure museum collection and care of rare books and manuscripts for their own sake to the preservation of such material for present and future use in a specialized field, e.g., history of medicine.<br><br>To a limited degree permeates all librarianship, but achieves its fullest expression in such libraries as Folger, Morgan, Huntington, Newberry, and small special collections in university or public libraries. | Literary history (perhaps of a particular field)<br>Paleography<br>History of printing and publishing, including methods and styles of the scriptoria during the manuscript age<br>Classical languages<br>Markets, sources, and prices of rare books and manuscripts<br>Care and preservation of bindings, paper, etc.<br>Methods and techniques of photographic reproduction |
| **II.  *Education—Formal*** | |
| School (elementary and secondary) | Education theory and practice<br>Curriculum<br>Organization of school system<br>Characteristics of children or adolescents, child or adolescent psychology<br>Literature appropriate to the age group concerned |
| College | Much the same as the above, adjusted for higher age bracket<br>Organization and administration of higher education<br>The aims and methods of scholarship and research |
| Graduate Study (special departmental libraries) | Special subject knowledge<br>Research methods, especially literature, searching in research context in special field |
| **III.  *Education—Informal*** | |
| Public Libraries | |
| Children | Characteristics of children, child psychology<br>Children's literature<br>Parents groups<br>Community and home contact methods |

TABLE 7-1.—*Continued*

| Library Function | Specialized Knowledge |
|---|---|
| III. *Education—Informal*<br>    Public Libraries—*continued*<br>    Young People | Characteristics and psychology of adolescents<br>Literature for youth and appropriate literature for adults<br>Youth organizations<br>Methods of youth contacts |
| Adults—Individuals<br>Here two poles of opinion are represented though they are not always clearly defined or specified. One extreme holds that the efforts of the librarian should be directed toward serving the intellectual "elite" through the use of only those materials of the highest quality even though the appeal may be limited. At the other extreme are those who would emphasize service to the near illiterate, the foreign-born, and others for whom the most elementary of materials are appropriate. Between these extremes are those who emphasize service to all intellectual strata in the community and would acquire for their libraries materials that meet a reasonably acceptable standard, predicating their point of view on the assumption that the library as a public agency has an obligation to all—to meet any reasonable demand. Thus the library, to them, becomes in effect a "free retail" operation. | The first need here is for a clarification of theory and objectives—a point at which the library schools might well assume some leadership<br>Knowledge of the nature, history, and present complexities of "culture"<br>The sociology of knowledge<br>Psychology of the adult—individual differences in human abilities and interests<br>Wide range of reading materials, standards of excellence, and appropriateness for specific needs and interests |
| Adults—Groups<br>The area of formalized "Adult education," civic groups, social clubs, group work with older people, or people with limited abilities | Much of the material included in work with the individual adult<br>Community group organization<br>Methods and techniques of group contacts<br>The psychology of group activity<br>Materials appropriate to group use |

TABLE 7-1.—*Continued*

| Library Function | Specialized Knowledge |
|---|---|
| IV. *Service to Specialized Interests* | |
| Includes special librarianship, documentation, and all forms of library service in specialized subject fields. Emphasis upon service to research; e.g., library service in chemistry, medicine, law, business, government, legislative reference, public administration | Knowledge of the subject field or fields<br>Knowledge of the social and organizational pattern of the field<br>Knowledge of the organization served<br>Special sources (nontrade) of relevant materials<br>Special materials by form and substance<br>Evaluation of materials (to a limited extent)<br>Special methods of organization of materials—classification systems, mechanized techniques<br>Abstracting and bibliographic summaries |

staff of a chemical industry. A cataloger in a small municipal public library may need to be familiar with only the techniques of ordering Wilson or Library of Congress cards and the simpler means for achieving consistency in applying the standard classification schemes. By contrast, the cataloger in a large research library may need to know the intricacies of manuscript description, the rules of transliteration from Russian or Arabic into English, or the methods for developing a special classification or subject heading list for his own peculiar needs. Moreover, the present methods and approaches in the teaching of cataloging may be completely revolutionized by the advent of computer refinements, and the networks of cooperative effort such technology could make possible.

In the past, the traditional librarian's enthusiasm for standardization has forced operational specializations into a uniform pattern, and discouraged their emergence from functional specialization. This tendency toward standardization may be reinforced by the network development. Yet, operational specialization should follow, or develop from, functional specialization in *librarianship*. Specialization may decrease the professional mobility of the librarian, but it should engender intellectual and economic rewards, through the improvement of professional standards of performance, to a point at which the incentive for the individual to transfer from one functional specialization to another will be minimized. The great need is for reliable information that will relate the changing face of librarianship to manpower resources, both today and in the future.

# Eight

# The Search for a Format

Philosophers of higher education have always been ambivalent about the appropriateness of professional education to the university community. At one end of this spectrum of theory stands Robert Maynard Hutchins who has rejected all vocational education as being anti-intellectual. If his philosophy were adopted, "the professional schools of the university would disappear as such. Education for the learned professions would be conducted in the three faculties of metaphysics, social science, and natural science, with prospective clergymen graduating under the faculty of metaphysics, lawyers under that of social science, and doctors and engineers under that of natural science. . . . Those professional schools which have no intellectual content in their own right would disappear altogether, except as their activities might be thought worthy of preservation in research and technical institutes."[1] At the other extreme stands Andrew Dickson White's now famous iteration of the words of Ezra Cornell, immortalized in Cornell's Great Seal, "I would found an institution where any person can find instruction in any study."[2] Ironically, the University of Chicago has a library school and Cornell does not. The idea of vocational training as an integral part of higher education did not originate with either Cornell or White, but goes back at least as far as Benjamin Franklin and

---

[1] Robert Maynard Hutchins. *The Higher Learning in America.* New Haven. Yale University Press. 1936. pp. 111–12. Jacques Maritain is, of course, even more rigid than Hutchins. See: Jacques Maritain. *Education at the Crossroads.* London. Oxford University Press. 1942.

[2] Morris Bishop. *A History of Cornell.* Ithaca, N.Y. Cornell University Press. 1962. p. 74.

Thomas Jefferson, and, as Morris Bishop has pointed out, Dr. Samuel Johnson observed to Boswell, "I would have the world to be thus told, 'Here is a school where everything may be learnt.'" In anticipation of Eliot's elective system at Harvard, President Francis Weyland reported, in 1850, to the Corporation of Brown University, that "every student might study what he chose, all that he chose, and nothing but what he chose."[3]

During the decade that followed the Civil War almost every overt change in the pattern of American higher education was rooted in concessions to those who were demanding that it become more utilitarian, more vocational, than the classical tradition. Laurence Veysey has shown that the advocates of practical training came largely from two groups: many, "particularly on the East Coast, were men of established backgrounds who sought to effect a generous compromise with the external clamor for change. Others, more often from the Middle West, represented in true fashion the sometimes shrill invective and the humbler circumstances of the non-academic clamorers."[4] Today, Clark Kerr's "Multiversity" admits professional and vocational education without strain. The university, he said, "becomes the chief port of entry" for the professions, both the new and those that have been sanctified by tradition. "In fact a profession gains its identity by *making* the university the port of entry. This creates new roles for education; but it is also part of the process of freezing the structure of the occupational pyramid assuring that the well-behaved do advance, even if the geniuses do not."[5]

Despite the fact that, in 1855, Frederick A. P. Barnard denied that vocationalism would ever intrude itself upon institutions of formal learning —"While time lasts, the farmer will be made in the field, the manufacturer in the shop, the merchant in the counting room, the civil engineer in the midst of the actual operation of his science"[6]—higher education has always been broadly vocational. College prepared the student not merely for life, but also to earn a living as a prospective minister, lawyer, teacher, or one of the other professions. The needs of a growing industrial society and its attendant technology merely broadened the scope of formal education and obscured a vocationalism that had always been present in greater

---

[3] *Ibid.* p. 74n.

[4] Laurence R. Veysey. *The Emergence of the American University.* Chicago. University of Chicago Press. 1965. p. 60.

[5] Clark Kerr. *The Uses of the University.* Cambridge, Mass. Harvard University Press. 1963. p. 111.

[6] Frederick Rudolph. *The American College and University.* New York. Knopf. 1962. p. 338.

or less degree. Quite rightly, Frederick Rudolph has accused the universities of blurring the distinction that had long existed between the connotation of *profession* and that of *vocation*.[7] But the battle which Hutchins has waged at the University of Chicago has by no means been lost. The ideal of general, or liberal education, and the pursuit of the "well rounded man" has given new vitality to the undergraduate curriculum while deepening and enriching the professional school.[8] The professions have come to realize that skill, technology, even specialized knowledge, are not enough, even to the point at which one finds at M.I.T. and Cal. Tech. educational programs which, for their breadth and liberal outlook, rival the best academic institutions and are superior to many.

## HISTORICAL BACKGROUND

Thus, when Melvil Dewey opened in 1887, at Columbia University, the first library school, then known as the School of Library Economy, he was, consciously or unconsciously, squarely in the rising tradition of vocational and professional education of which Ezra Cornell and the Morrill Act were the harbingers. It is easy to see in these early ventures into professional training for librarians, which coincided roughly with the decline of the scholar-librarian of an earlier day, some positive relation between the two, and hence to conclude that professional education damaged the status and respectability of the librarian. Such an assumption, however, overlooks the historical fact that the scholar-librarian was basically a scholar rather than a librarian. His library duties were almost entirely routine; he was, indeed, a "keeper" of the books. Moreover, on many academic campuses at the turn of the century there was no great enthusiasm for libraries, to say nothing of facilities for the training of librarians. At the newly established University of Chicago, William Rainey Harper displayed a singular indifference to the growth of the University library, and permitted the faculty to take books from the collections, purchased in Berlin, to their private offices with no control over their return to the university collection. At Harvard, Eliot even expressed the opinion that it would be better to throw away many of the books in the College Library than to spend money on a new building to house them.[9]

The movement for vocational education for librarians also coincided

---

[7] *Ibid.* p. 339.
[8] Veysey. *Emergence of University.* pp. 197–203.
[9] *Ibid.* pp. 96 and 376.

with the rise of the economic emancipation of women, and many have argued that the influx of women into the profession lies at the roots of its loss of prestige. Certainly Melvil Dewey's school did attract young ladies in substantial numbers, and when John Simmons, the prosperous Boston clothing merchant, endowed Simmons College he declared,

> It is my will to found and endow an institution to be called Simmons Female College, for the purpose of teaching medicine, music, drawing, designing, telegraphy, and other branches of art, science, and industry best calculated to enable the scholar to acquire an independent livelihood.[10]

It was Henry Lefavour, dean at Williams College, and consultant to the Board of Simmons College, that recommended instruction in library science, as being among those subjects requiring "a certain intellectual maturity" and which would equip the College's graduates "with both a broad intellectual or artistic foundation and a specialized technical training that will open to them some avenue of remunerative labor."[11] But however one may explain the characteristics of the first attempts to establish formal library education, it must be admitted that the beginnings were not impressive; it was vocational and there was only slight intellectual content.

Doubtless a number of explanations could be advanced for the deterioration in the position of the librarian, and each might have a measure of validity. Such social phenomena are usually complex, but underlying them all was a fundamental failure to develop an intellectual content to librarianship that would give meaning to its burgeoning technology and to its contribution to social communication.

Historians of library education are generally agreed that its history divides into three distinct periods: the period of apprenticeship and inservice training that prevailed from ancient times until 1887, and to a lessening degree, for some time thereafter; the period of organized library school training from 1887 to 1923, when the Williamson report appeared; and the period of academically-centered library school development that may be said to have begun with the publication of the Williamson report and continued to the years immediately following the end of the Second World War.[12] At the present time the profession would appear to be in a

---

[10] Kenneth L. Mark. *Delayed by Fire, Being the Early History of Simmons College.* Concord, N.H. Rumford Press. 1945. p. 24.

[11] *Ibid.* p. 28.

[12] Robert D. Leigh. "The Education of Librarians." *The Public Librarian,* ed. Alice I. Bryan. New York. Columbia University Press. 1952. p. 300ff.

confusion of innovations, including revision of the Master's program, addition of the doctorate to the curricula of a number of schools, experimentation with a sixth-year degree, and, perhaps most important of all, as a result of the impact of the computer, the rise of "information science," especially in those universities not previously engaged in the teaching of library science. This period was also marked by substantial growth in the number of accredited library schools, a renaissance in undergraduate courses in librarianship, and the rise of the community college with its unblushingly technical training in library practice. Never in the history of library education has there been so much activity by those in charge of post-secondary school education in library training and education, but the old doubts and uncertainties about the best road, or roads, to follow still remain.

---

Sarah K. Vann. *Training for Librarianship Before 1923*. Chicago. American Library Association. 1961. Chapters 1–3.

Carl M. White. *The Origins of the American Library School*. New York. Scarecrow Press. 1961. Chapters 2–5.

Joseph L. Wheeler identified fourteen significant events in the progress of library education from Dewey to the close of his own survey in 1946: the work of Dewey and his associates in establishing the Columbia school; Poole's opposition to Dewey; the Williamson report; creation of the Board of Education for Librarianship; Ralph Munn's report of 1926; Ernest Reece's study of the library school curriculum; Louis Round Wilson's analysis of budgets, salaries, teacher qualifications, and students; the study by Metcalf, Russell, and Osborn for the fiftieth anniversary of the University of Illinois library school; the demand for fewer, but better, schools; the influence of the Chicago school; the report on the training of school librarians issued by the Board of Education for Librarianship and the American Association of Teachers Colleges; rejection of correspondence courses by the BEL; founding of the Association of American Library Schools; organization in the ALA of a Professional Training Round Table. Joseph L. Wheeler. *Progress and Problems in Education for Librarianship*. New York. Carnegie Corporation. 1946. pp. 36–84. It is to be noted that chronology did not seriously bother Wheeler.

The source materials for the history of library education, except for the Vann and White studies, both of which end with the Williamson report, are fragmentary and widely scattered. Columbia is the only school that has a full-dress history. Ray Trautman. *A History of the School of Library Service, Columbia University*. New York. Columbia University Press. 1954; and Ernest J. Reece, ed. *The School of Library Economy, Columbia College, 1887–1889, Documents for a History*. New York. School of Library Service. Columbia University. 1937.

Also important are the Leigh study mentioned above; Alfred Pradeek and Lawrence S. Thompson. "Bibliothekarische Fachausbildung." *Handbuch der Bibliothekswissenschaft*, ed. Fritz Milkau and Georg Leyh. Weisbaden. Otto Harrassowitz. 1957. vol. 3, pp. 817–19, Harriet E. Howe. "Two Decades of Education for Librarianship." *Library Quarterly*. vol. 12 (July 1942), pp. 557–70. Other material will be noted in this chapter.

In a day when library collections were small and recorded knowledge so limited that one man could encompass it all in a lifetime of scholarship, the librarian needed no esoteric skills, except possibly those of calligraphy, to be effective. This situation maintained through the Renaissance and long after the invention of printing. Even Gabriel Naudé needed only eighty pages to set forth his advice for organizing and administering a library. Not until the middle of the nineteenth century is there much to suggest that library work might require anything more than the qualifications that a well-educated man might possess.

The growth of library collections and the demand for their increased availability to the public which characterized the library after 1850, altered dramatically the duties of the librarian and necessitated the formulation of a body of techniques appropriate to the librarian's expanded tasks. Similarly, increased staffs added substantially to the librarian's burden of administration, while the proliferation of public libraries brought a need to understand governmental procedures. Thus, there arose a breed of librarian who was less of a scholar and more of a man skilled in the business of running a library. Since the librarianship of that day was rooted in *a priori* assumptions about what the librarian should do, the training of the librarian was basically empirical, and apprenticeship or on-the-job training met adequately the intensely practical need for a limited body of skills. Like the doctor and the lawyer, the librarian's training began by precept and example in imitation of the elders.

The development of the public library, especially in the English speaking world, established the character and was the strongest single influence in determining the pattern of library training. The public librarian, together with his staff, was responsible for a miscellany of duties and routines in which professional and clerical were seldom clearly differentiated. His was the responsibility to select books (when this duty was not, as it often was, retained by the library's sponsors) with consideration for the value of their content, their relative permanence, and their cost, but always with regard to an assumed clientele who would be using them. His was the obligation to buy the books advantageously and with due regard to the established routines of a purchasing office. He arranged the books in a meaningful order and cataloged them accordingly by author and subject. He maintained accurate records of the whereabouts of the volumes on loan. He occasionally arranged for display and promotion, and provided, at appropriate intervals, inventories of the book stock. He looked to binding, repair, cleaning and replacement. He gave adequate attention to the building or buildings in which the library was maintained. Finally, he familiarized himself with the laws and regulations under which the library operated and by which its management was governed, and he reported annually on his stewardship to his governing board.

The education of the librarian, therefore, prepared him to meet these very immediate and practical ends. Dewey stated the aim at Columbia in pragmatic terms "to give the best obtainable advice, with specific suggestions on each of the hundreds of questions that rise from the time a library is decided to be desirable till it is in perfect working order, including the administration"[13] and with a similar objective he set forth in 1889, the Civil Service examination for prospective library school teachers at the New York State Library.[14] Thus the pattern became fixed. The head of the Pratt Institute Free Library declared that its training class "takes up the library processes in systematic order, beginning with the order department and following a book through its course into the hands of the borrower and back again."[15] The same point of view was characteristic of Drexel, Armour Institute, and the other pioneer library schools.[16]

Early education for librarianship, then, was not only faithful in reflecting library work, but also almost exclusively concerned with acquainting the students thoroughly, and at first hand, with the actual tasks the practice of librarianship entailed. Columbia insisted that its purpose was "entirely practical" and that its aim was "object teaching."[17] The *Annual Report* of the school asserted that "however excellent may be the results from the lectures, instruction, seminars, problems and visits, the main reliance must be on experience."[18] Pratt and Armour institutes attached great importance to "apprenticeship,"[19] Drexel to its "work assignments,"[20] and Armour was reported as surpassing even Columbia in the stress "laid

---

[13] Columbia College. Library and School of Library Economy. *Circular of Information.* 1884; Melvil Dewey. "School of Library Economy at Columbia College." *Library Journal.* vol. 9 (July 1884), pp. 117–20.

[14] Melvil Dewey. "Civil Service Examination for New York State Library." *Library Journal.* vol. 14 (April 1889), pp. 118–21.

[15] Mary Wright Plummer. "Brooklyn Library Training Class." *Library Journal.* vol. 16 (December 1891), p. C87.

[16] "Drexel Library Class." *Library Journal.* vol. 17 (December 1892), p. 488; Armour Institute Library. *Preliminary Circular of Information.* 1893.

[17] Columbia College. *Circular of Information*; and Dewey. "School of Library Economy."

[18] Columbia College. Library and School of Library Economy. *Annual Report, 1886–87.*

[19] Plummer. "Brooklyn Library"; and Armour Institute. *Department of Library Science.* 1894–95.

[20] Drexel Institute. Library Class of 1892. "Drexel Institute. . .Record of Library Training Classes." *Library Journal.* vol. 19 (September 1894), pp. 307–8.

upon the practical things of Library life."[21] Thus, there is ample evidence to show that the pioneers in American library education conceived the need of the profession as being mainly for people skilled in the techniques of library operation and maintenance.

Substantively, then, the post-Dewey period differed little from that which had preceded the establishment of the Columbia school. Dewey was a promoter, not a scholar or educator. He gave the training class program a kind of academic respectability by establishing it at Columbia, but did not hesitate to move it to Albany where it was under the aegis of the University of the State of New York, when he became State Librarian. In Dewey's mind a library school meant little more than an efficient place where technical subjects could be taught, and a center from which people trained in standardized techniques, especially the Dewey classification, could go forth to positions in which they would spread the gospel of uniform practice. Perhaps Columbia's main contribution to the development of professional education was that it was a center for instruction that was not associated with a single library, but to which could come students from many places for training that would prepare them for work in many libraries. That the school began at a university was almost incidental, and it did not, as Leigh has shown, establish a pattern that was widely accepted. Of the fourteen schools established before 1920, no more than three began as schools of a university. Ten of the remainder were in libraries or vocational institutes, while the eleventh was in a vocational college for women.[22] During the entire period between Dewey and the Williamson report of 1923, only the Columbia-Albany school, and that of the University of Illinois required college degrees for admission. Some schools, recognizing that a librarian needed to know something more than the techniques of his craft, offered lectures or courses in literature, foreign languages, or "current events," but these were sporadic, uneven, and quite superficial. The period of study was also pragmatic, being based mainly on the time that candidates were willing to devote to it. Programs varied from three months to a year in duration though in time the academic year slowly became accepted as the ideal. The part-time student was a conspicuous feature of library education from the start. As many as fifteen or twenty "courses" or "units" were crammed into this year of study, but eventually there was general acceptance of a "core" comprising cataloging and classification, reference and bibliography, book selection, and

---

[21] American Library Association. Committee on Library Schools. "Report. 1896." *Library Journal*. vol. 21 (December 1896), pp. C93–97.
[22] Leigh. "Education of Librarians." p. 303.

administration, and beyond these there were a variety of electives. But even in the core courses there was great variation in content and a failure to differentiate between that which was clerical and the more clearly professional. Leigh has characterized them as "a hodgepodge of major problems and minor routines,"[23] supplemented by classes in filing, shelf-listing, indexing, inventorying, lending routines, binding, and book repair, to which were not infrequently added handwriting, accounting, business routines, and, eventually, typing. One need scarcely be surprised that university administrators looked askance at vocationalism as unfit for the university campus. In fact, these programs offered so slight an advantage that, as late as 1917, Azariah Root could say that the auxiliary training agencies were turning out two to three times as many librarians as the library schools.[24]

## FIRST STEPS TOWARD STANDARDS

The period from Dewey to Williamson was one of controversy, divisiveness, and a measure of experimentation. It was a time when conservatism was arrayed against progressivism, when many ideas expressed in 1923 and thereafter were first enunciated. That the period produced its share of inconsistencies and anomalies is symptomatic of the changes in library education that were beginning to take place. Since the studies by both Vann and White have described this transition period in considerable detail, it is only necessary here to summarize the more conspicuous trends.

During this period there was growing criticism of instructional methods both from the graduates of the programs, and certain leaders such as: Aksel Josephson, who proposed a two-year program of which the first would prepare librarians for minor positions while the second year would be devoted to advanced graduate study at a senior university;[25] Mary Wright Plummer, chairman of the ALA Committee on Library Training when the 1906 standards were formulated; Azariah Root, who vigorously opposed high school graduation as a minimum requirement for entrance into the schools, and proposed a second survey of library education that would revise the 1906 standards; Mary Eileen Ahern who, as editor of

---

23 *Ibid.* p. 305.

24 Azariah S. Root. "The Library School of the Future." *ALA Bulletin.* vol. 11 (March 1917), pp. 157–58.

25 Aksel G. S. Josephson. "Preparation for Librarianship." *Library Journal.* vol. 25 (May 1900), p. 226.

*Public Libraries*, was in a particularly strategic position to influence trends in professional education; and, of course, C. C. Williamson who was emerging as a leading critic of library education. "Within the schools themselves," as Miss Vann has written, "it was an era in which the tendency existed 'from the beginning for library schools to be more or less dominated by a single personality.' "[26]

The American Library Association, confronted by a variety of conflicting points of view, contained within its membership too diverse a group of interests and factions to permit it to exercise any real leadership in library education, a malady from which the Association also suffers today. It has expressed official interest in library training as early as 1883; when Dewey first began his plans for a library school, it appointed a committee to consider not only Dewey's proposal but also other matters pertaining to library education. Opposition arose almost immediately from William Frederick Poole and a number of his sympathizers. Contact with the schools, however, was not lost, but maintained first through the Association's Standing Committee, which, in 1903, had developed from the original committee, and subsequently the Committee on Library Training. The latter Committee sought to formulate standards and had even examined certain library schools, though its efforts had little impact upon educational programs. It also fostered a section of the ALA on Professional Training to encourage discussion of educational problems. Its most successful achievement, however, was to promote, in 1923, the formation of a Temporary Library Training Board, which was charged with the formulation of tentative standards and the making of plans for accrediting library training agencies under whatever auspices they might exist.

The library schools themselves showed remarkably little success in achieving unity or formulating standards. On December 9, 1910, a communication signed by Phineas L. Windsor of Illinois, Mary Emogene Hazeltine of Wisconsin, and Julia W. Whittlesey of Western Reserve was sent inviting the library schools to a meeting to discuss certain problems relating to their work. The response was gratifying, and from the meeting there evolved the Round Table of Library School Instructors, an antecedent of the Association of American Library Schools. But for reasons which no one has been able to explain, the Association has not evolved an effective program of action for itself, nor has it contributed materially to the raising of standards. Its main success, apart from sponsoring the

---

[26] Vann. *Librarianship Before 1923.* p. 192. But, during this period in the history of higher education in America such domination by individuals was doubtless true of most departments and schools of the university.

*Journal of Education for Librarianship*, has been to cling tenaciously to a tenuous life, just outside the official jurisdiction of the ALA, yet always with that organization's sympathetic support and encouragement. Louis Round Wilson has said of it that "its effectiveness, however, was severely limited and continues to be limited . . . the importance of the organization derives from its potentialities rather than its past accomplishments."[27]

It became increasingly clear, during the early years of the present century, that if anything was to be done about standards and accreditation of library education it would have to come from the ALA itself, especially its Temporary Library Training Board of 1923. Slowly and haltingly the groundwork was being laid for Williamson. As Sarah Vann has said, the period from 1887 to 1923 "may seem to have accomplished little within its own time, but, in reality, the post-1923 achievements may be viewed as the culmination of the forces at work in the 1876–1923 era."[28]

## THE WILLIAMSON REPORT

In 1917 the Carnegie Corporation employed Alvin Johnson to study the results of its philanthropy in behalf of libraries. His report emphasized the need for improving the proficiency of library personnel, and recommended financial support for library schools, scholarships for students, and the establishment in a limited number of strategic centers of model libraries.[29]

As a result of the Johnson survey, the Corporation, in 1919, commissioned Charles C. Williamson, a librarian who had previously been an economist, to make a field study of existing facilities for library training. The study, which was completed in 1921 and published in 1923, is reported to have "struck like a thunderbolt."[30] It was factual, forthright in

---

[27] Louis Round Wilson. "Historical Development of Education for Librarianship in the United States." *Education for Librarianship,* ed. Bernard Berelson. University of Chicago. Graduate Library School. Chicago. American Library Association. 1949. p. 46. A quarter of a century since Wilson wrote this, the AALS is still trying to realize its potentialities. (*Education for Librarianship* will hereinafter be cited as Chicago. *Librarianship.*)

[28] Vann. *Librarianship Before 1923.* p. 193.

[29] Alvin Johnson. *A Report to the Carnegie Corporation of New York on the Policy of Donations to Free Public Libraries.* New York. Carnegie Corporation. 1917. See also: Robert M. Lester. *Review of Grants for Library Interests. 1911–1935.* New York. Carnegie Corporation. 1935; and Florence Anderson. *Library Programs, 1911–1961.* New York. Carnegie Corporation. 1963.

[30] Leigh. "Education of Librarians." p. 307. This study was not as much of a thunder-

its criticisms, and specific with respect to its recommendations. Williamson lost no time in stating the central burden of his argument:

> Each of the two general types of library work, which may be called
> "professional" and "clerical," demands general education of differ-
> ent grades and vocational training quite distinct in character and
> method. . . . Professional training calls for a broad, general educa-
> tion, represented at its minimum by a thorough college course of
> four years, plus at least one year of graduate study in a properly
> organized library school. For the clerical work of libraries, training
> may consist of a general education of high school grade, followed by
> a comparatively short period of instruction in library methods com-
> bined with sufficient practice to ensure proficiency and skill in clerical
> and routine work. . . . Library schools should confine themselves
> to training of the professional type. Training of the clerical type
> will be provided through the so-called training classes conducted by
> libraries.[31]

Williamson found just about everything wrong with the schools. Salaries were inadequate, faculty lacked appropriate academic education and
professional experience. Admission standards, classroom teaching, and
"field work" were ineffectual. The curricula were crowded with inappropriate subjects. In addition to his eight specific recommendations listed
below, he proposed that not more schools, but better schools were needed;
schools with adequate faculties, financing, and equipment. Specifically he
urged that: (1) a four-year baccalaureate degree be prerequisite for admission; (2) schools be affiliated with universities, either as departments
or autonomous professional schools; (3) curricula be enriched by the
total educational resources of these parent universities; (4) curricula be
revised to provide for the first year a general program in basic library
subjects followed by a second year devoted to specialization, with an
intervening year of practical experience; (5) adequate texts and other instructional material be prepared; (6) provision be made for programs of

---

bolt as it would have been had Williamson not yielded to advice and suppressed
the first version of his report. This first report was not made public until 1971
when it was published in one volume together with the 1923 report. A supplementary volume containing a commentary on the two reports appeared at the
same time. See: Charles C. Williamson. *The Williamson Reports of 1921 and
1923*. Metuchen, N.J. Scarecrow Press. 1971.; and Sarah K. Vann. *The Williamson
Reports; a Study*. Metuchen, N.J. Scarecrow Press. 1971.

[31] Charles C. Williamson. *Training for Library Service*. New York. Carnegie Corporation. 1923. p. 136. But this quotation is foreshadowed on pp. 3–4.

continuing education through summer schools, institutes, and correspondence courses; (7) voluntary certification of professional librarians be
instituted; and (8) procedures and facilities for the accrediting of the
schools be created.[32]

The great weakness of the Williamson report was that it approached
the education of the librarian from the standpoint of what librarianship
*was* and what librarians *did*, rather than what librarianship *should be* and
what librarians *should do*. To state this weakness another way: Williamson
was trying to improve the breed of librarians rather than to evolve an
entirely new breed educated for the social role the library should perform.
This failure to consider the social role of the library as the intellectual
and educational matrix of librarianship is especially surprising, coming as
it did from one who had been trained in the social sciences. But the report was "strong medicine," perhaps as strong as librarianship of that day
could take, and even today the symptoms that Williamson isolated have
not been entirely corrected. As Leigh has said, it would certainly seem
that the profession has had ample time to recover from the shock and
it should be busy with a reconsideration of the Williamson recommendations.[33] Leigh's criticism remains valid today.

## EFFECT OF THE WILLIAMSON REPORT

Williamson's study may not rank in importance with Abraham Flexner's revolutionary inquiry into the professional education of the doctor,
but one must admit that it did propel education for librarianship out of
the infancy of apprentice training and into the early years of professional
adolescence. Despite its limitations, the report did focus the attention of
librarians in general, and the American Library Association in particular,
upon the need for educational reform.

During the year following the publication of the report, the Board
of Education for Librarianship, which replaced the earlier Temporary
Library Training Board, was created by the ALA, and the new body immediately began to formulate standards for the accreditation of the schools
according to three basic types of programs. It enlisted an interest in library
education not only on the part of the Carnegie Corporation but also of the
General Education Board of the Rockefeller Foundation, and the Rosen-

---

[32] *Ibid.* Chapter 19.

[33] Robert D. Leigh, ed. *Major Problems in the Education of Librarians.* New York.
Columbia University Press. 1954. p. 16.

wald Fund, all of which provided substantial grants for a wide variety of purposes relating directly to the improvement of education for librarianship. The two largest grants made by the Carnegie Corporation went to Columbia University for the establishment of its School of Library Service, of which Williamson became the dean in 1926, and to the University of Chicago to inaugurate the Graduate Library School. During the ten years that followed the publication of the Williamson report the Corporation poured $5,000,000 into library education activities which provided the ALA with an endowment to support a permanent staff, made possible the preparation of textbooks for use in the library schools, subsidized almost one hundred fellowship grants to library school students, and otherwise aided the schools in improving the quality of their programs.[34]

In 1936, Louis Round Wilson reviewed the changes that had taken place in library education during the ten years that followed the establishment of the Graduate Library School, and declared that the Williamson recommendations were well on their way to accomplishment. The bachelor's degree, he pointed out, had been accepted by two-thirds of the accredited schools as a prerequisite to admission; all of the schools had become affiliated with teaching institutions, and faculty salaries and academic recognition had improved appreciably. There was, he admitted, still much opportunity for improvement, but Williamson had been successful in establishing a distinctively different pattern for library education.[35] Wilson's acknowledgement of the profession's debt to Williamson is probably not excessive in its statement, nevertheless, one cannot but wonder what the state of library education might have been today had Wilson himself not appeared on the Chicago scene when he did; certainly his vision of what library education should be was far in advance of anything that Williamson was able to evolve at Columbia, and it was the flesh and blood of the Chicago graduates, rather than those one hundred and fifty printed pages that are the Williamson study, that have shaped and are continuing to reshape education for librarianship today.

One must not overlook the influence of the Board of Education for Librarianship in crystalizing curricula patterns during the years immediately following the appearance of Williamson's work. The Board brought the schools face to face with the problem of meeting standards imposed by an outside agency; it discussed administrative problems relating to the schools with the administrative officers of the universities with which the schools

---

[34] Anderson. *Library Programs.* pp. 10–12.

[35] Louis Round Wilson. "The American Library School Today." *Library Quarterly.* vol. 7 (April 1937), pp. 211–45.

Carmichael's study does not have the extensive statistical base of Berelson's, indeed he made considerable use of Berelson's work in developing his own recommendations, but the program he suggested has particular relevance to graduate education in librarianship, especially as it relates to the articulating of graduate study and undergraduate preparation for it. There is also pertinence for librarianship in his introductory statement: "Despite all the studies, reports, discussions, debates, and criticisms, little progress has been made toward the solution of the problems which, by unanimous agreement, are recognized as serious stumbling blocks affecting adversely all phases of education. No new issues have appeared, and no fresh approaches have been suggested for the resolution of the old ones."[90] Here are sentiments with which every library school dean or director can emphatically agree.

## COLLECTIVE SEARCH FOR A PROGRAM

Two heads may be better than one, but this venerable proverb cannot necessarily be extrapolated to mean that the degree of success of an undertaking is necessarily related to the number of people engaged in it. Too many cooks *can* spoil the broth. Perhaps it is the democratic ethic that gives us this faith in the safety implicit in numbers; perhaps it arises from a feeling of individual inadequacy; but whatever the explanation, librarians have long adhered to a confidence in the group approach to any problem, even though this collectivization of effort has not, as it has not in the case of library education, been particularly fruitful.

For more than a generation the Association of American Library Schools has annually convened to address itself to common problems of library education, but its deliberations have been uniformly sterile, repetitious, and demonstrative of the *malaise* by which the Association has long been beset. The University of Chicago conference of 1948[91] accomplished little more than the presentation of the state of library education as it then existed. Neal Van Deusen, in his summary declared that he had "a feeling that some schools would not have to change very much in their present thinking. The main areas of subject matter needed have been reviewed many times and I believe there is considerable agreement."[92] Thus, he saw only "shifts in emphasis," rather than any revolutionary or drastic innova-

---

[90] *Ibid.* p. 3.

[91] Chicago. *Librarianship.*

[92] Van Deusen. "Summary." Chicago. *Librarianship.* p. 200.

tions. Consequently, he was content to propose that the schools should increase their attention to the needs of the individual student, provide for field work experience with academic credit, organize "prelibrary school and postlibrary school educational functions," and "attract highly qualified teachers."[93] There is scant evidence anywhere in the proceedings that there was any real awareness that even then the winds of change were beginning to blow through library halls, changes that might drastically alter the professional education of the librarian.

By 1948, most of the accredited library schools were moving rapidly toward the elimination of the fifth-year bachelor's degree in librarianship and substituting for it the master's degree, a trend which greatly distressed those who had received the master's degree already, for they believed with considerable justice that their degree had been cheapened. Unfortunately, despite talk about curricular revision, in many instances the change was little more than an alteration in nomenclature, the new M.S. in L.S. being only a new name for the B.L.S. In December 1948, a conference, sponsored by the Council of National Library Associations and supported by the Carnegie Corporation, was held at Princeton University to consider the issues then confronting library education. The thirty-six invited participants, of whom about half were engaged in library education, recommended that: (1) a joint committee be established on education for librarianship; (2) the *Newsletter* of the Association of American Library Schools become the official organ for the dissemination of information about library education; (3) recruitment be recognized as a profession-wide responsibility, and funds be sought to support a long-range program for the Committee on Library Work as a Career; (4) the Board of Education for Librarianship serve as the official accrediting body for the profession, that adequate funds for its support be sought, and that it undertake a study of the several types of undergraduate library education then in existence; (5) and there be an agency established to serve as a placement service to aid both librarians seeking staff and those in search of professional positions.[94] The recommendation that aroused the most lasting interest, however, was that which urged the proposed Joint Committee on Library Education to undertake a study of the educational needs of those preparing themselves for service in special libraries. Little of lasting importance came of this conference except the establishment of the Joint Committee on Library Education and its subcommittee on Special Library Education.

---

[93] *Ibid.* pp. 199–203.
[94] Harold Lancour, ed. *Issues in Library Education. Report of the Conference on Library Education, Princeton University, December 11–12, 1948.* New York. Council of National Library Associations. 1949. pp. 5–6.

The 1953 Chicago conference, on the *Core of Education of Librarianship*, dealt with a problem that was not new; library schools had recognized the existence of a "core" for years, and attempts to define a core evaporated in the implicit decision that there were a multitude of "cores" one for each specialization, while the common core remained what it had always been, administration, book selection, cataloging and classification, and reference work.[95]

In April 1962, the Library Services Branch of the U.S. Office of Education, in cooperation with the School of Library Science at Western Reserve University sponsored a conference in Cleveland on library education which was under the leadership of Ruth Warncke of the Western Reserve faculty. The invited participants, who numbered almost one hundred, evolved some fifty suggestions and recommendations, not all of which received unanimous approval and some of which were mutually contradictory. The group, however, did agree in strongly urging that the ALA increase its involvement in library education by providing increased support for the Library Education Division and the Committee on Accreditation which had replaced the original Board of Education for Librarianship.[96]

As a more or less direct outgrowth of the Cleveland conference, the H. W. Wilson Foundation provided a grant to the ALA for the calling of a conference, and such other action as might be appropriate, to formulate a National Plan for Library Education. The Executive Secretary of the Library Education Division, Sarah Rebecca Reed, assumed the initiative in assembling a National Commission on Library Education which held its initial meeting in Chicago on January 24–25, 1963. The Commission, however, found itself completely impotent, dragged out a moribund existence, and in 1967, voted itself out of existence, the new Office of Library Education at ALA headquarters having then been established by a grant from the Wilson Foundation.[97] The Office of Library Education has concerned itself mostly with the accreditation of newly established library

---

[95] Asheim. *Core of Education.* The workshop reached the rather astonishing conclusion that librarianship is "encyclopedic—an amorphous mass with no pattern—and it would be better to have library school graduates represent mastery of different areas rather than an identical core of knowledge." (p. 4) Whatever one may think of this characterization of librarianship, "amorphous mass with no pattern" is certainly a strange way to describe "encyclopedic."

[96] Frank L. Schick, ed. "The Future of Library Education; Proceedings of an Institute. . .April 25–28, 1962." *Journal of Education for Librarianship.* vol. 3 (Summer 1962), pp. 53–60.

[97] See Jesse H. Shera. "In Defense of Diversity." *Journal of Education for Librarianship.* vol. 4 (Winter 1964), pp. 137–42.

schools and the preparation of Lester Asheim's "Policy Statement" on an educational "ladder."[98]

In recent years, such conferences as have been held have tended to focus on specific problems in library education and were designed for particular audiences. In the spring of 1965, the U.S. Office of Education sponsored a conference in Washington, again under the direction of Sarah Reed, designed for recently appointed library school deans.[99] The meetings were notable for the fact that the formal papers were presented by experienced library school directors, though much of the commentary was provided by those in the general field of higher education. In the summer of the preceding year, one of the first conferences on the impact of information science upon library school curricula was held at Case Western Reserve University under the direction of Alvin J. Goldwyn and Alan Rees,[100] and in September 1965, the American Documentation Institute held at Warrenton, Virginia, a symposium on education for information science.[101] Also, at their annual conferences, the American Library Association, the Association of American Library Schools, and the American Society for Information Science have held programs dealing with the educational problem, but none of these has had the impact upon the profession of the earlier meetings.

The relative ineffectiveness of all of these conferences arose from the failure to recognize that a conference is peculiarly suited to the communication of ideas, not to their generation. Advances in library education will come, like advances in all education, out of the creative and fertile mind of an individual, not the collective mind of a conference; out of the quiet of the study, not the hurly-burly of the conference hall. The history of education is sprinkled with great names, not great conferences.[102]

---

[98] Lester Asheim. "Library Education and Manpower." *American Libraries*. vol. 1 (April 1970), pp. 341–44.

[99] Sarah R. Reed, ed. *Problems of Library School Administration*. Washington, D.C. U.S. Office of Education. 1965.

[100] Alvin J. Goldwyn and Alan M. Rees, eds. *The Education of Science Information Personnel*. Cleveland. Western Reserve University. Center for Documentation and Communication Research, School of Library Science. 1965.

[101] American Documentation Institute. *Proceedings of the Symposium on Education for Information Science*. Washington, D.C. Spartan Books. 1966.

[102] For a good example of what a conference can achieve when properly used, see: Sarah R. Reed, ed. *Problems of Library School Administration; Report of an Institute, April 14–15, 1965*. Washington, D.C. U.S. Office of Education. 1966.
"The primary purpose of the institute was to provide new deans and directors of graduate library schools an opportunity to exchange ideas and information for the improvement of library education with resource people from the field of higher education and with their own experienced counterparts." *Ibid.* p. iii.

## THE UNRESOLVED SEARCH

Though much of the criticism voiced by Williamson and his successors is still valid, the search for a format in library education during the past half-century has made progress. Interdisciplinary programs are on the increase, especially at the level of the doctorate. At such universities as Case Western Reserve and the University of Texas at Austin, the doctoral degrees are awarded by the graduate school rather than the library school. The old quadrivium of cataloging, book selection, reference, and administration has been greatly modified and is no longer an inflexible requirement. The earlier "core" curriculum, though it still exists in many schools, is, in some instances, as at Case Western Reserve, being reshaped as a "foundations" program, and is set forth in Chapter 11. Information science and related aspects of library automation are being introduced into the curriculum, and instruction in cataloging is being reshaped accordingly. Finally, increasing attention is being given to theory, especially as it relates to the role of the library in the social order.

# Nine

# Winds of Change

Librarians, in general, have been reluctant to accept mechanical equipment. As commonplace a piece of equipment as the typewriter has not always had the acceptance of librarians that it enjoys today. At the Librarians' Conference at Lake George in 1885, Melvil Dewey reported on experiments that he and others had conducted in the use of typewriters, results of which were not particularly satisfactory. Dewey's presentation led to a consideration of the best type of handwriting for use in library cataloging.[1] Seventeen years after Dewey's presentation, a cataloger at the University of Texas was urging the use of the typewriter for the typing of headings on catalog cards because, with the use of these new machines the entries "can be written on these cards so neatly and satisfactorily that, to the casual observer, the difference," between them and conventional print, "will hardly be apparent."[2] Quite obviously, proficiency in typing as part of the library school student's arsenal of skills was slow in its acceptance, and the old "library hand" as it was taught in the earliest library schools became archaic less, perhaps, because of the typewriter than because of the availability of Library of Congress printed cards.

---

[1] "Typewriters in Libraries." *Library Journal*. vol. 10 (September–October 1885), p. 320; Henry J. Dubester. "The Librarian and the Machine." *Information Retrieval Today*, ed. Wesley Simonton. Minneapolis. University of Minnesota. Center for Continuation Study. 1963. pp. 165–76.

[2] Caroline Wandell. "Typewriters for Card Catalogues." *Library Journal*. vol. 27 (May 1902), p. 268.

## MICROPHOTOGRAPHY

Advances in photographic technology, particularly in Germany and the United States, that followed the First World War, and especially the development of fine-grain emulsions for photographic film, gave rise to a variety of new methods for reproducing documents and other forms of text, new techniques which were surveyed in Robert Binkley's classic *Manual on Methods of Reproducing Research Materials*.[3] Among the early innovations in library technology, however, one of the most spectacular was the microfilm. So promising was this new invention that in the 1930s there appeared many prognostications of a future in which books would become a curiosity, supplanted by roll film, flat film, and eventually micro-opaques. In a relatively short time, libraries, especially the research libraries, had accepted these microforms almost as a commonplace. Their impact on library school curricula, however, was less dramatic. In the summer of 1939, the Graduate Library School at the University of Chicago and the School of Library Service at Columbia inaugurated courses in microphotography.[4] But these courses were short lived, and few other schools included such offerings in their curricula. The library problem *per se* was overshadowed by the technology; most of those working in the field tended to come from the sciences, and were photographic technicians rather than librarians. Attention to the subject in library education usually appeared in courses in the technical services, documentation, or curatorship. In the final analysis, miniturization, though its engineering was relatively sophisticated, presented no revolutionary bibliographic procedures. It widened the resources of the bibliographer without in any serious way making his conventional operations and point of view obsolete. Its major impact was upon physical rather than content accessibility.

## THE NEW WORLD OF SIGHT AND SOUND

With the rise of the new technology there came the "new media" of graphic representation, both visual and auditory. The modern audio-visual,

---

[3] Robert C. Binkley. *Manual on Methods of Reproducing Research Materials*. Ann Arbor, Mich. Edwards Brothers. 1936.

[4] See announcements of these courses in *Journal of Documentary Reproduction*. vol. 2 (March 1939), pp. 45–46; and (December 1939), pp. 265–66. Also: "Rockefeller Foundation Provides Training in Microphotography." *Ibid*. vol. 2 (March 1939), pp. 53–54.

or "materials," center had its origins in the explorations of Thomas Wedgwood and Sir Humphrey Davy into the effect of light upon nitrate of silver, the heliographs of Niepce, and the tinfoil cylinders of Thomas A. Edison. But many decades were to pass before the librarians' devotion to the book permitted them to accept the photograph, especially the motion picture, and the sound recording as integral parts of the library's store of graphic records. The picture collection has been the librarian's stock-in-trade for many years, especially to work with children and young people, and lantern slides were not uncommon in libraries even in the early years of the present century. In certain types of special libraries, particularly those serving museums, schools of music, advertising agencies, and motion picture producers, such materials have been—and still are—one of the most important parts of their total resources. But one may search in vain through the indexes of *Williamson, Reece,* and other standard early works on library education for any reference to anything other than books and, occasionally, manuscripts.

Enthusiasm for audio-visual resources appears to have infiltrated librarianship from education, especially public school education, though the way had been prepared for it by early association of libraries with museums. Slides, posters, models, and layouts had long been standard equipment in the elementary and secondary school classrooms, but the more recent popularity of films and filmstrips was intensified by the introduction of the 16mm sound film. Strauss and Kidd credit the advent of the documentary film, in the 1930s, with considerable influence in the promotion of audio-visual materials. The success of motion pictures in the Armed Services Training Programs contributed greatly to the widening of their acceptance as legitimate instructional devices by the general public.[5] Educational television further expanded the audio-visual horizon, and all of these developments touched, in one way or another, the services of both the public and academic libraries.

The early concept of audio-visual materials is implicit in the mandate given in 1924 to the A.L.A. Committee on Visual Methods, which in 1941 became the Audio-Visual Committee. The purpose of the original committee was "to study library activities as they relate to moving pictures, lantern slides, stereoptican reproduction, microscopic equipment, educational exhibits, and museum material."[6] If one may judge from the published literature of the 1930s, the librarians' original concern with these "visual aids"

---

[5] L. Harry Strauss and J. R. Kidd. *Look, Listen, and Learn.* New York. Association Press. 1948. pp. 3–13.

[6] American Library Association. Committee on Visual Methods. "Report." *A.L.A. Bulletin.* vol. 25 (May 1931), p. 276.

was largely confined to their organization, servicing, and display; and their introduction into the curricula of the library schools was limited, fragmentary, and largely fortuitous. At George Peabody College for Teachers, as early as the 1930s, all library school students were required to register for a course in audio-visual aids, and the Demonstration School and the library school worked closely together with M. Lanning Shane serving as a consultant to both.[7] It was at Peabody, too, that Louis Shores began the development of a program of library school instruction in the audio-visual field that, a few years later, was to achieve fuller development at Florida State University.

The audio-visual program at the University of Illinois Library School dates from 1942, when the materials and equipment collected by Gwladys Spencer were used as the core around which the subsequent program was developed. Some five years later, the reorganization of the Illinois curriculum brought into being a Demonstration Laboratory for materials and equipment, and with it the abolition of a special course in the subject, with a transfer of the course content to the established courses of instruction. Thus, the faculty sought to eliminate the presentation of audio-visual resources as something apart from librarianship and to achieve their fuller integration with the totality of library materials, operations, and services. In 1951, C. Walter Stone reported continuing growth and expansion of the program, not only within the library school, but also with reference to other departments of the University, since no other department offered such instruction on a regular basis. Throughout, the program was "designed to achieve complete lateral integration with the library school curriculum," an objective that has been supported by the establishment of the Library School as a departmental subdivision of the Communications Division of the University. Stone added, however, that "if in time it becomes clearly desirable to have a separate A-V course to lay the groundwork for intelligent appreciation, handling, and use of equipment and materials in subsequent work projects, the course will be recommended for introduction on the elementary (undergraduate) level and will be regarded as a part of the basic core of knowledge and skills required for admission to graduate study."[8] By 1954, however, Stone reported that though the philosophy of the Library School had not altered, "we believe that in the end . . . it will not be necessary to

---

[7] M. Lanning Shane. "Audio-Visual Aids and the Library." *College and Research Libraries.* vol. 1 (March 1940), p. 145.

[8] C. Walter Stone. "Demonstration A-V: A Report on the Audio-Visual Program at the University of Illinois Library School. *University of Illinois Library School Occasional Papers.* no. 19 (February 1951), pp. 8–9.

conduct audio-visual courses. However, at the present time, because we have a need to train people who will go out and fill what are known as audio-visual jobs in librarianship, we need an audio-visual course which allows for some degree of specialization."[9] Illinois had, therefore, added to their program as originally envisaged "a special course in audio-visual work, a demonstration, training, service and recruiting unit which allows for a great many special activities as well as full service. We also have what is known as an audio-visual field work program."[10]

In 1953 there appeared a *Demonstration Laboratory Manual*, prepared by two research assistants in the library school at Illinois, Ronald C. Tollafield and Constance C. Janssen, working under the direction of Walter Stone. This manual, which was to be used in conjunction with demonstration and practice sessions conducted by the audio-visual demonstration laboratory at Illinois, was designed to provide the library school student with a guide to the techniques and maintenance of audio-visual equipment. In addition to an appended glossary of technical terms and a selected bibliography, the compilations included discussions of motion pictures, recordings and transcriptions, filmstrips and slides, flat pictures, charts and maps, and displays and exhibits. Illustrations were kept to a minimum to encourage use of the manual with demonstrations and practice work.[11]

Complete revision of the audio-visual curriculum took place at Illinois in 1955 and was based on the assumption that: an emerging cross-media approach to knowledge, information, and instruction, will require that every librarian have some familiarity with the selection and servicing of nonbook materials; increasingly school librarians may be expected to operate libraries with "materials centers," since a growing number of public and academic libraries will incorporate audio-visual services in their programs; and audio-visual material will assume an ever greater importance in the totality of

---

[9] American Library Association. Audio-Visual Board et al. *A Pre-Conference Workshop on Audio-Visual Materials, Feb. 1, 1954. Proceedings.* Berkeley. University of California. School of Librarianship. 1954. p. 22.

[10] *Ibid.* p. 19.

[11] Ronald C. Tollafield, Constance C. Janssen, and C. Walter Stone. *Demonstration Laboratory Manual; Using Audio-Visual Materials and Equipment.* Urbana, Ill. University of Illinois Library School. 1953.

Though designed for quite a different purpose, the *Manual* invites a measure of comparison with *The Audio-Visual Way*, prepared a few years earlier to provide school teachers and school librarians with an introductory guide to the resources for audio-visual materials and the techniques of their evaluation and use. See: Florida State Department of Education. *The Audio-Visual Way.* (Bulletin No. 22B) School of Library Service and Training, Florida State University. Tallahassee. 1948.

educational and informational services offered by libraries to their communities.

The program at Illinois came to a focus in the work of the Demonstration Laboratory, and in addition, special activities were carried out with the cooperation of the Urbana Public Library. The total program emphasized the "how" of the audio-visual field as well as the "why."[12] Early courses and programs in audio-visual materials were also offered at the University of Indiana,[13] William and Mary College,[14] and Florida State University.[15]

By 1954, Louis Shores found that, in general, the teaching of audio-visual subjects in library schools might be categorized into three types: (1) the campus-coordinated program in which the library school is dependent upon a central audio-visual unit serving the entire university; (2) a limited program in which the library school maintains its own independent resources, small though they may be; and (3) an extended program, like that at Florida, in which the library school maintains a "wholly-owned audio-visual subsidiary" that serves the entire parent institution.[16] However, at about this same time, Irving Lieberman reported that though "some library schools have recognized a responsibility to do something about audio-visual materials in the library school curriculum, such instruction has varied from school to school, from casual mention of the existence of other kinds of materials than books, to the organization of formal separate courses in audio-visual materials. . . . In general," he concluded, "library schools have done very little, simply because they have not known what should or could be done."[17]

In 1952, the Carnegie Corporation of New York awarded a grant of $28,000 to the School of Librarianship of the University of California for a two-year "experimental project on Audio-Visual Instruction in Library Education," the objectives of which were:

1.  To isolate, identify, and develop that which should be taught to

---

[12] C. Walter Stone. "A-V Training at Illinois." *Association of American Library Schools Newsletter.* vol. 8 (January 1956), pp. 7–10.

[13] Margaret I. Rufsvold. *Audio-Visual School Library Service: A Handbook for Librarians.* Chicago. American Library Association. 1949. p. iii.

[14] Mae Graham. "Training for School Librarians in Audio-Visual Materials and Their Use." *A.L.A. Bulletin.* vol. 40 (June 1946), pp. 199–200.

[15] Hazel A. Pulling. "Training for Audio-Visual Service." *Wilson Library Bulletin.* vol. 25 (December 1950), pp. 310–11.

[16] Louis Shores. "A-V Patterns in Library School Programs." *Association of American Library Schools Newsletter.* vol. 6 (July 1954), pp. 16–20.

[17] Irving Lieberman. *Audio-Visual Instruction in Library Education.* New York. Columbia University. School of Library Science. 1955. p. vi.

the first-year library school student that will enable him to promote, organize, and administer a collection of those materials that differ from books in format or administrative requirements.

2.   To demonstrate the ways in which such course content can be integrated with the curriculum at one library school, e.g., the University of California.

3.   To develop instructional materials to support the program of instruction in this field.

4.   To publish a sufficiently detailed report of the project to make the results of the inquiry useful to other library schools.[18]

The inquiry revealed, among other things, that though all but two of the sixty-one library schools investigated included instruction in audio-visual materials in some part of their programs, sixty-nine percent were doing "a less than fair job," and only three schools "could be rated as giving a good performance."[19] Though eighty-six percent of the respondents indicated that a basic course in audio-visual materials was available to their students, in more than half of these the course was established in the department of education. Only eleven percent offered courses in the library school, and fifteen percent indicated courses in both schools. With respect to the integration of audio-visual material with other segments of the library school curriculum, the results of the study revealed that the greatest amount, seventy-seven percent, was in the materials courses, sixty-seven percent in technical processes, fifty-nine percent in administration, and thirty-seven percent in bibliography and reference.[20] Of the schools responding, thirty-seven percent were using, and fourteen percent would consider using, a required laboratory course for which credit was, or would be, given; but nineteen percent were using, and four percent would consider using, such a laboratory but without credit. An extracurricular laboratory was in use in three percent of the schools. However, "several" schools questioned whether a laboratory in such manual skills had any place in a graduate professional program, a point that seems very well taken indeed.[21] The data of the study also revealed that good equipment, though it was conspicuous in a limited number of schools having well-developed programs, was relatively scarce, many of the schools having to depend upon loans from other parts of the

---

[18] Summarized from *Ibid.* pp. vi–vii.

[19] *Ibid.* pp. 84–85.

[20] *Ibid.* p. 85. The report does not explain the bases for the calculation of these percentages.

[21] *Ibid.* p. 87.

parent university. This may account for the fact that library schools generally have made relatively little use of such materials as teaching aids in their own courses. Library school faculties seem to have been more enthusiastic about such aids for others than for themselves.

An important segment of the California study· was the development of a test instructional program in the School of Librarianship at Berkeley. This two-year pilot operation involved:

1.   Thorough instruction of the school faculty in audio-visual materials and equipment to enable them to incorporate audio-visual techniques and methods in their courses.

2.   Regularly scheduled previews of films relating to the several parts of the School's curriculum.

3.   An extensive interrogation of the recent graduates of the School respecting their previous training in audio-visual materials and the importance of such material in their current professional needs and their past professional experience.

4.   The design of a first-year curriculum at Berkeley that would place audio-visual materials in their proper perspective with respect to the other subjects taught.

5.   Evaluation of the audio-visual program by the students in the first-year curriculum.

6.   The promotion of audio-visual workshops for in-service librarians in California.

7.   Representation and participation of the School of Librarianship in university-wide audio-visual activities.

8.   Exploration of the importance of audio-visual instruction to the school librarian and its implication for curriculum planning in the library school.

9.   The planning of programs of activities for professional associations.

10.   Exploration of the relation of the School to the development of noncommercial television programs.[22]

The Lieberman study resulted in twelve recommendations and conclusions relative to anticipated future development of audio-visual instruction in library schools:

---

[22] *Ibid.* pp. 97–120.

1.  The integration of all materials of communication should be taught in library schools, both by precept and by example.

2.  Such instruction should be diffused throughout the entire library school curriculum.

3.  Audio-visual instruction should be considered from a pre-service as well as an in-service viewpoint.

4.  Library school students should acquire skills in manipulating audio-visual equipment.

5.  Integrated instruction should lead to special elective courses in the audio-visual field for those students wishing such intensive training.

6.  A knowledge of standards for selection and evaluation of audio-visual materials is as essential as such knowledge respecting books.

7.  A comprehensive bibliographic service for audio-visual materials should replace the present scattered and uncoordinated bibliographic guides.

8.  The utilization of audio-visual materials with both individuals and groups should be improved.

9.  Courses in the technical processes and library administration should devote an increasing attention to the organization of materials respecting audio-visual resources.

10.  Audio-visual resources and skills should be related more closely than has been done in the past to such special activities as work with groups, discussion leadership, and community-wide planning.

11.  There should be an improvement in the means for exchanging locally produced, as well as commercially produced, audio-visual material.

12.  The entire library school faculty needs improved familiarity with audio-visual resources, and the ways in which such resources can contribute to the enrichment of all course offerings in the library school.[23]

As early as 1953, Raynard C. Swank argued convincingly for the importance of the audio-visual field to librarianship,[24] while Margaret Rufsvold emphasized the growing significance of these newer media for library education as techniques in teaching, as a segment of the curriculum, as a subject for research, and as an area of public and professional service.[25] The School Library Standards for 1960 devoted much attention to audio-

23 *Ibid.* pp. 121–30.
24 Raynard C. Swank. "Sight and Sound in the World of Books." *Library Journal.* vol. 78 (September 15, 1953), pp. 1459–64.
25 Margaret I. Rufsvold. "Library Education and the Newer Media." *A.L.A. Bulletin.* vol. 55 (February 1961), pp. 140–42.

visual resources, and pointed out that "the annual budget for the acquisition of audio-visual materials, exclusive of equipment, should not be less than one percent of the total per pupil instructional cost."[26] Moreover, the school librarian should "have an extensive knowledge. . .of audio-visual materials suitable for use by students and teachers."[27] This belief was based on acceptance by the authors of the *Standards*, the statement adopted by the American Association of School Librarians in 1956 that "the school library . . .should serve the school as a center for instructional materials. . .books —the literature of children, young people, and adults—other printed materials, films, recordings, and newer media developed to aid learning."[28] Yet despite this ferment among the librarians, the literature clearly reveals that leadership in these new media has been firmly in the hands of the educationists, and that efforts to expedite research into the values of the new techniques for all forms of education, have had slight impact upon the library schools. Even Miss Rufsvold, who believes that "ultimately the public schools. . .will be able to buy commercially prepared programs much as they now purchase films and textbooks," and who envisages "a trend toward a national curriculum due to nationwide television teaching," admitted that "library educators, on the other hand, will have to develop their own programs until our professional publishers find it feasible to produce them."[29]

Abram W. Vander Meer of Pennsylvania State University, in an address before the University of Chicago summer conference of 1959 on "New Definitions of School Library Service," convincingly indicted the new educational media on several counts. He charged that the field was "preoccupied with almost anything rather than content," that there was a serious lack of availability to individuals of the means of communication, that the concept of education upon which the field was based was dominantly *passive* rather than active with respect to participation by the learner, that there was an excessive concern with embellishments, "eye appeal," and other characteristics peripheral to the substantive content, and that the field was torn by conflict and factionalism deriving mainly from "a lack of knowledge of the total communication process."[30]

However, he saw these charges ameliorated somewhat by an increasing

---

[26] American Association of School Librarians. *Standards for School Library Programs*. Chicago. American Library Association. 1960. p. 84.

[27] *Ibid.* pp. 60–61.

[28] *Ibid.* p. 11.

[29] Rufsvold. "Library Education and Newer Media." p. 140.

[30] Abram W. Vander Meer. "A Critical View of Educational Media." *Library Quarterly*. vol. 30 (January 1960), pp. 48–51.

improvement in the quality of material available to the individual, a growing rapprochement between audio-visualists and librarians, a broadening of the scholarship respecting the new educational media and a consequent decline in fetishism, and, finally, "a dramatic upsurge in research," brought about largely through the work of the Educational Media Branch of the U.S. Office of Education, and given increased potential through the basic investigations of B. F. Skinner and his associates.

The present writer finds it difficult to share in Vander Meer's optimism, despite a compulsion to do so. Perhaps the nadir of the audio-visual movement was reached at a conference, sponsored jointly by the library school of the University of Illinois and the U.S. Office of Education, which was held in Chicago in the spring of 1963,[31] of which this writer has written in rather intemperate terms.[32] Pessimism also seems to be substantiated by the experiences of Florida Atlantic University and other massive installations of media. Old pedagogues do not easily learn new tricks. Though many of the excesses of the audio-visual enthusiasts seem to be passing the "scholarship" of the movement is still neither very broad nor very penetrating. Even Vander Meer admits that much of the research which he applauds is "more general than analytical, more applied than basic."

"I think the biggest revolution in education will come from better use of books," Francis S. Chase of the University of Chicago is reported to have said, "not from television and teaching machines. We've never really taken advantage of the printing press."[33] Not until educators place more emphasis on learning than on teaching, and give the student the major responsibility for his own education, will Carlyle's definition of a university as a collection of books be fulfilled. Whatever one's personal opinion may be with respect to the new media and the zeal with which they have been promoted by their most ardent advocates, the fact remains that these new techniques and methods will have an important, and probably a lasting, impact upon the operations of the library. Thus, Figure 9-1 shows the position these new developments might occupy in the library school.

The 1968 *Standards for School Media Programs* recommend a unified program for the acquisition, servicing, and administration of all

---

[31] Harold Goldstein, ed. *Proceedings of the National Conference on the Implications of the New Media for the Teaching of Library Science, Chicago, Illinois, May 27–29, 1963*. Champaign, Ill. University of Illinois Book Store. 1963.

[32] Jesse H. Shera. "O! Medium, O! Media" *Library Journal*. vol. 88 (November 1, 1963), pp. 4149–51. Also: idem. "The Cult of the Audio-Visual." *Wilson Library Bulletin*. vol. 36 (November 1961), p. 251.

[33] Charles E. Silberman. "The Remaking of American Education." *Fortune*. vol. 63 (April 1961), p. 201.

**The Educational Media Program in the Library School**

| Services | Research | Instruction |
| --- | --- | --- |
| Consultant Services | Faculty | Master's Degree Candidates |
| Materials selection | Advanced Students | Basic instruction in core |
| Organization | Consultants and Other Specialists | Advanced work preparatory to specialization |
| Direction of use | | |
| Plant and facilities planning | | Sixth-year Program |
| Staffing | | Advanced Specialization |
| Budgeting | | Supervisors for district and regional media centers |
| Establishment, development, and evaluation | | |
| Demonstration and Laboratory Resources | | Doctoral Program |
| Professional Information Services | | Research |
| Collection and dissemination of recorded information relating to educational media | | Utilization of Educational Media in the Educational Program of the School |
| Programs equipment, research results legislation | | Classroom presentation |
| | | Self-instruction |

**Figure 9-1.**

learning materials for all schools, and urges that schools having separate school-library and audio-visual departments combine them into a single operating and administrative unit.[34] As John Rowell has pointed out, in these *Standards*, "For the first time every school, large and small, has a measure by which to evaluate the adequacy of its media center. For the first time every school has an authoritative basis for asking for additional personnel and materials. For the first time every school can lay out long-range goals with evidence to substantiate them."[35] If the librarians of the future are to deal intelligently with these innovations, library schools dare not ignore them in their own educational programs. But the library school student must know *what* he is threading into his projector, not merely *how* it is done.

We have devoted considerable space to these new media because, despite all the excessive claims made for them, we believe that hospitable relationships with traditional teaching methods will be found. The work of Skinner and his successors may very well make possible the programming of a variety of instructional materials related to patterns of individual need as indicated by learner response and behavior. The contribution that programmed instruction can make to education may prove to be the program rather than the machine with which it is manipulated. It is the organization and presentation of content that lies at the heart of the educational process, and these new media should compel the educator to think through what it is that he is attempting to do in a way that has never been forced upon him before—just as computer applications are forcing the librarian to think of his processes and objectives in new analytical terms. But certainly much work remains to be done before the printing press will be displaced as the most important single instrument in the technological arsenal of education.

## SPECIAL LIBRARIANSHIP

The Special Libraries Association was formed in 1909 by John Cotton Dana and a group of fellow dissidents because of their belief that the American Library Association was not fully aware of the bibliographic

---

[34] *Standards for School Media Programs.* Chicago. American Library Association. 1969. Prepared by a special joint committee of the American Association of School Librarians and the Department of Audiovisual Instruction of the National Education Association. See also: John Rowell and Frances Henne. "AASL and DAVI Issue New Standards for Media Programs." *The Instructor.* vol. 78 (November 1968), pp. 81–84.

[35] Rowell and Henne. p. 81.

needs of the specialist. In an announcement of the 1911 SLA conference there appeared the statement:

> It might be desirable to place in charge of a special library, one who has no library training but who has extensive training in the problems and the scientific literature of the special library or business served and who has an aptitude for the reorganization of information, and who therefore may be relied upon to learn and apply the necessary library methods.[36]

A. G. S. Josephson of the John Crerar Library observed (in a letter to the president of the Association) that "to place in charge of a library a person who is not a librarian is to invite failure";[37] but he qualified his remark by saying that by a "librarian" he did not necessarily mean one who has attended a library school. Thus, the battle was joined.

In 1913, in the Department of Chemistry at the University of Illinois, Marian Sparks offered the first course in chemical literature, and thus was begun an educational genre of which the model has been Professor M. G. Mellen's course at Purdue. However, Josephine A. Rathbone voiced what was probably the attitude of most library school faculties in 1917 when she told the SLA convention, "Each special library is a special problem involving special knowledge of a special subject"; and though she admitted, as did many of her colleagues in library education, that the demand for special librarians was increasing, the market was still too small to justify an extensive program in special librarianship.[38] Those few schools which were offering a second year of study for advanced students might well consider, she thought, offering courses in special librarianship, but the one-year schools should concentrate on the conventional curriculum with perhaps some supplementary lectures on the requirements of the special library. The basic program, she believed, was essential for any kind of library practice, and the needs of the special librarian were no exception.

The four-week course in "The Business Library" offered in 1919 by the Library Service School at Riverside, California, may be regarded as the first formal instruction in special librarianship,[39] though, traditionally, the course offered at Columbia University in 1926–27 by Linda Morley has

---

[36] *Special Libraries.* vol. 2 (September 1911), p. 66.

[37] *Ibid.* (October), p. 86.

[38] J. A. Rathbone. "Library School Courses as Training for Business Librarianship." *Special Libraries.* vol. 8 (November 1917), pp. 133–35.

[39] W. A. Southern, "Education for Special Librarianship." *Special Libraries.* vol. 39 (November 1948), p. 317.

been held to be the prototype of present-day education for special librarianship in library schools.

Slowly and sporadically the schools began to schedule lectures by prominent special librarians in their vicinities, and to permit library school students to enroll for practice work in special libraries. Charles C. Williamson, in his 1923 survey, identified one school which invited lecturers to speak to its students on "industrial, commercial, and financial and other special libraries," and provided opportunities for students to gain "experience in such libraries."[40] Moreover, he argued that at least one library school should make provision for an advanced "special business library course."[41] He also found that of the eleven schools he surveyed, six devoted some classroom time to indexing, though the amount of attention given was not great.[42]

The general disregard of special librarianship that Williamson found among the library schools brought from him a rather serious indictment: "To bring about a reasonable degree of efficiency in library service, adequate provision must be made for specialized training. . . . While library service has been growing more and more highly specialized, and doubtless will continue to do so, the training afforded by the library schools has for the most part remained general."[43] Despite the fact that specialized library training was feasible, the library schools had "taken no steps to meet" these new responsibilities and challenging opportunities. "The schools," he wrote, "explain their failure to provide specialized training partly on the ground that there is insufficient demand for it, while librarians reply that there is a potential demand which would become actual if the schools were equipped to turn out well-trained specialists."[44] He quoted an unidentified university librarian as saying:

> The best reference people I have met in my own experience are not library school graduates but university-trained people who have somehow gotten into library work. I recognize, however, the extraordinary value of the addition to their other equipment of the training afforded by library schools, and I am always seeking persons who have had that training for our staff,. . .however, I have given other considerations foremost place and have made a known scholarly attainment the basis

---

[40] C. C. Williamson. *Training for Library Service: A Report Prepared for the Carnegie Corporation of New York*. New York. 1923. p. 21.

[41] *Ibid*. p. 100.

[42] *Ibid*. p. 22.

[43] *Ibid*. p. 91.

[44] *Ibid*.

of selection. I would rather have such people with an imperfect knowledge of library techniques, than the best trained technician who lacks university training and some graduate study.

This anonymous librarian suggested as the ideal "some such sort of scholastic library work as was given for so many years at Göttingen by Dziatzko. Such work could be done at Harvard, Yale, Princeton, Michigan, Chicago, perhaps at Minnesota and Cornell."[45] Williamson did not argue against the importance of the traditional library school program, but "when all professional schools are put on a graduate basis and the work of the first year is organized as a thoroughly well-rounded and complete general course, graduates from all the schools should naturally expect to take a second year of special training wherever accredited courses are offered in the special fields they desire to enter."[46] Such specialization during the second year of graduate study was, he said, "the only satisfactory solution."[47] But it is to be noted that he was talking about a specialization within librarianship, not specialization in a subject field. With the establishment of the master's as the first professional degree in library science, there was some discussion of awarding certificates for an additional year of study in a special area, and indeed in a number of schools such sixth-year programs are now under way.

In the spring of 1926, Williamson was appointed to the deanship of the library school at Columbia University, and in plans for the curriculum, serious consideration was given to the educational needs of the special librarian. The new program sought to present the student with a maximum degree of flexibility in his electives without losing the values of the foundation, or core, courses. As Ernest Reece said, the aim was "not specialization, but moderate emphasis of individual interests."[48] Though the program did not penetrate very deeply into the details of special library work, it did represent a break with tradition and a measure of improvement over the old inflexible curriculum, and probably went as far as conditions then justified in the preparation of first-year library school students for possible careers in special librarianship.

Indifference on the part of most library schools to the needs of special librarians was not due to any absence of pressure from the special librarians themselves. In 1926, an SLA Committee on Training was formed under

[45] *Ibid.* p. 95.
[46] *Ibid.* p. 100.
[47] *Ibid.* p. 97.
[48] E. J. Reece. "Preparation for Special Library Work at the School of Library Service, Columbia University." *Special Libraries.* vol. 25 (September 1934), p. 180.

the chairmanship of Rebecca B. Rankin, and the association membership voted that a summary of the Committee's conclusions be presented to Dean Williamson "as a suggestion to him in the establishment of future courses." The Committee's report to *Special Libraries* suggested no less than eighteen "specific courses of instruction" which, in addition to such standard library topics as subject bibliography, cataloging, and classification, included business economics, applied psychology, business appliances, typewriting, editorial work, indexing, filing, subject terminology, special library administration, and publicity. It was assumed that the student "would be granted time and required to take other courses in Columbia University at the same time, preparing himself in a special field—for instance, courses in chemistry, engineering, banking and finance or whatever kind of specialization he elects, for which he has aptitude or earlier training or experience." Realistically assessing the likelihood of such a program being put into operation, the Committee reluctantly accepted the outline for Linda Morley's special library course "as a less satisfactory alternative" expressing the hope "that it may be a step in the direction of a better course as outlined in the first part of this Report."[49]

During the next few years, while still compromising on Miss Morley's course, the Committee continued to press for an extensive program in special librarianship, and promulgated so-called minimum standards leading to "a certificate from the graduate library schools or a degree from the undergraduate schools for the satisfactory completion of the professional curriculum." It was in touch with the Board of Education of the ALA, it urged the SLA chapters to conduct local workshops, and at the request of Dean Williamson, it considered the matter of Home Study Courses, rejecting them on the grounds that they "do not appeal to us as being particularly adapted to special library courses."[50]

With the introduction in 1927 of the master's degree at the Columbia University library school, plans were made for a sequence of courses dealing directly with the problems of special librarianship which would enable the student to pursue appropriate studies both in the School of Library Service and elsewhere in the university. Even a doctoral program was envisaged. However, in 1934 Reece reported that no student had evinced any interest in pursuing a master's degree in special librarianship, and he concluded the plans at Columbia were in advance of the field.

---

[49] R. B. Rankin. "Training for the Special Librarian." *Special Libraries*. vol. 17 (November 1926), p. 330.

[50] R. B. Rankin, "Training for Special Librarians." *Special Libraries*. vol. 18 (September 1927), pp. 226–28; and vol. 19 (July–August 1928), pp. 200–2.

Harriet E. Howe of the University of Denver was one of the first, if not the first, library school director to consider seriously the failure of the library schools to prepare students for library service in highly specialized subject fields. Her conclusions, she said, were "formed from (a) personal experience among special librarians both in the East and in the West, (b) visits to many library schools, (c) study of the library school curriculum, and (d) experience in trying to put a theory into practice."[51] Though her argument was strongly colored, as one might expect, by the fact that she was writing at a time when economic distress was of such magnitude that library school graduates, regardless of their subject preparation and interests, were happy to accept any position that offered a wage above starvation, she advanced some very important points. She began with the effective argument that library schools could not afford to establish extensive special programs for a small number of students, nor could the students justify an excessive expenditure of time in preparing for a career which economic conditions might never permit them to enter. She urged that undergraduates, beginning if possible with the freshman year, prepare themselves with a subject specialization that would fit them for a special library service in the field of their choice, and she even urged advanced graduate study in that field. On the other hand, she defended the relevance of the general library school program for special librarians:

> The library school student preparing for a special subject library can work toward his objective in a class in which different types of library service are discussed. The advantage is that while he focusses his attention upon one phase of work, he hears other phases discussed and has an understanding of all kinds of library service, a distinct asset for the special librarian.[52]

She was arguing, of course, for the importance of the student's grasp of the essential unity of librarianship, whatever special applications there might be. The most important single statement that Miss Howe made, however, was her frank assertion that "experience has shown that it is more commonly the lack of sufficient subject knowledge rather than of sufficient library techniques that hampers the library school graduate in a special subject library. His special knowledge may not be adequate to the demands made upon him by experts."[53]

---

[51] H. E. Howe. "The Library School and the Special Librarian." *Special Libraries.* vol. 24 (June 1933), p. 107. See also: M. L. Alexander. "President's Page." *Ibid.* p. 112.

[52] Howe. "Special Librarian." p. 111.

[53] *Ibid.* p. 109.

Ernest J. Reece in his study of library school curricula, assumed a somewhat more conservative attitude than that of Miss Howe toward the education of the special librarian. He assigned considerable weight to the economic impracticability of employing highly specialized faculty to teach a very limited number of students, and raised the question of whether the demand for such specialized training might not be easily exaggerated. Employers, he observed, "often speak confidently about the need for special forms of service without having created the necessary positions and put into their budgets the requisite salaries."[54] He further observed that the problems involved in the introduction of specialized curricula

> exhibit their separate character most unmistakably when the factors concerned in setting them up are considered. They are unlimited in inclusiveness and length. All conceivable forms of service are contemplated; and it is assumed that students will be able to give a functional interpretation to the teaching, however it is organized, and to use their acquirements in unanticipated ways. The programs lack solidarity, implying the same study, ordinarily, for no two persons. Coordination is distinctly the individual's problem, and balance may be the last thing to be desired. Only in a qualified sense can what derives from them be regarded as a curriculum at all, since each scheme of study remains hypothetical until a candidate for it appears, and since in view of their range the possible components by no stretch could be assembled in a compact discipline.[55]

Seven years later Reece's concern over the possible fragmentation of the curriculum into clusters of specializations was even more intense. Courses that meet the demands for specialization, he believed, "need embody no matter that is basically new. Particular classes of libraries require the same kind of equipment for their conduct that is necessary for libraries generally—a fact often overlooked by those who advocate special instruction."[56] Elsewhere he wrote, "In spite of its many varieties there remain elements of homogeneity, if not of unity, in library work, since its differences are largely in application. Even a cursory view reveals a common core of aim, function, setting, scope, and process."[57]

---

[54] E. J. Reece. *The Curriculum in Library Schools.* New York. Columbia University Press. 1936. p. 111.

[55] *Ibid.* p. 109.

[56] E. J. Reece. *Programs for Library Schools.* New York. Columbia University Press. 1943. pp. 60–61. See also: idem. "A Look Ahead for Library Schools." *Bulletin of the American Library Association.* vol. 32 (January 1938), p. 45.

[57] Reece. *Curriculum.* p. 11. It should be noted that Reece recognized the importance of *subject* specialization to supplement the library school program: "It is reasonable

There were then still too few positions and too few prospective candidates, and librarianship was not sufficiently differentiated to admit of, or justify, intensive specialization. "Probably the preparation never ought to be partitioned to such a degree. If the librarian is to be roundly equipped, it would seem that the important things are not the adaptations and the other specifics, but the central and universal acquirements which he might hope to use wherever he is. To take any other view would result in narrowness. The general subjects, therefore, should remain dominant, other elements being merely a fringe. The fact that librarians still like to migrate and that there are few certification bars or other restrictions to keep them from doing so are all the more reasons for seeing to it that specialization does not begin too early."[58]

But despite Reece's concern, specialization (at least in certain quarters) was very much on the march. Dissatisfaction with traditional library school curricula was increasing within the ranks of special librarians, and the lines of conflict were becoming more sharply drawn. It is not possible to trace even superficially the arguments that have surged in the literature from the 1930's to the present over the need for and the character of the professional education of special librarians. The writing is tremendously repetitive and lacking in constructive suggestions based on reliable data. In general, the position taken by each writer reflects his own educational experience. SLA continued its vigorous insistence upon specialized education for the special librarian, many local chapters of the Association presented workshops and short courses for special librarians from time to time, and slowly the accredited library schools introduced limited instruction in this area, usually restricted to a single, rather isolated, course. Linda Morley published a study of all this activity in 1947,[59] but a more detailed and extensive survey was made by George S. Bonn for the International Conference on Scientific Information (ICSI) held in Washington in 1958.[60]

---

to suppose that adequate service can be rendered by persons not versed in the subjects concerned and in the methods of searching applicable to them, however adept they may be in manipulating manuals, handbooks, encyclopedias, and indexes. If in these circumstances a librarian is to be more than a caretaker and a purveyor, he must assemble material which he cannot know, uncover data he cannot recognize, and organize facts he cannot interpret, except he is himself something of an expert in the field. Unless they bring under their command the bodies of knowledge which their books and other materials represent, librarians must increasingly affect functions for which they are unequipped." *Ibid.* p. 22.

[58] Reece. *Programs.* p. 62.

[59] L. H. Morley. "Special Library Education in the United States and Canada." *Journal of Documentation.* vol. 3 (June 1947), pp. 24–42.

[60] G. S. Bonn. "Training for Activity in Scientific Documentation Work." *Proceedings of the International Conference on Scientific Information, Washington, D.C., No-*

A conference that was particularly significant for the development of specialized education for librarianship was the CNLA Princeton Conference of 1948. The conservatives, who believed that the library schools were already doing as much as they should with special subject offerings, were well represented and were very vocal. Nevertheless, the areas of agreement were perhaps larger than might have been expected: specialized subject bibliography was being neglected; the number of specialized courses demanded by special librarians was unrealistic; and workshops, short courses, and similar activities could have value, but were limited in their effectiveness and should be carefully planned with only highly restricted objectives.[61]

In reporting on this conference to the Special Libraries Association, Beatrice V. Simon made four points with respect to the discussion: (1) special librarians as a group are less concerned about academic or status symbols than are other groups in the library profession, particularly the academic librarians and the public librarians who are caught in civil service classification requirements; (2) no mention was made of the fact that the great majority of special libraries are one-man operations, a situation which greatly intensifies the need for general library training, whereas the specialized training so strongly emphasized presupposes a staff with highly specialized division of function; (3) there was no recognition of the fact that the great bulk of library work is nonacademic in character; and (4) there was excessive emphasis on quantity, to the neglect of standards of quality.[62] Miss Simon remarked that the survey of library school offerings in special librarianship initiated a year earlier by Hazel Pulling showed that scarcely more than one-third of the accredited library schools were actively engaged in providing even a minimum program for professional preparation in that area.

Perhaps the most important result of the Princeton meeting, however, was the general recognition that the group was deliberating without any real factual data on which to base its arguments, conclusions, and points of view. They therefore recommended

that if and when a joint committee on education for librarianship is

*vember 16–21, 1956.* National Academy of Sciences—National Research Council. vol. 2. 1959. pp. 1441–88.

[61] H. Lancour, ed. *Issues in Library Education: A Report of the Conference on Library Education, Princeton University, December 11–12, 1948,* New York. Council of National Library Associations. 1949. p. 53.

[62] B. V. Simon. "Subcommittee on Library Education." *Special Libraries.* vol. 40 (October 1949), pp. 336–37.

appointed, a thorough survey be made by the committee to determine the most desirable educational preparation for special librarians, to serve as a guide to library schools in developing programs of training.[63]

The Joint Committee on Library Education, of which five of the twelve members were special librarians, was brought into being by the CNLA, and with it a subcommittee on special library education.[64] This subcommittee assigned six areas for special study to seven of its members, who were chosen because of their knowledge' and experience in the areas they represented. The result was the publication, in the *Library Quarterly* for January 1954, of recommendations for special programs—for financial librarianship by Eleanor S. Cavanaugh; law librarianship by Julius J. Marke; science and technology librarianship by Melvin J. Voigt; medical librarianship by Mary Louise Marshall; law librarianship by Leon Carnovsky; theater librarianship by George Freedley; and journalism librarianship by Chester M. Lewis and Harold M. Roth.[65]

At the outset, the subcommittee formulated certain assumptions upon which these special sequences were to be based: (1) that preparation in a subject field is essential to special librarianship; (2) that except for law, where a professional law degree is necessary, subject specialization could be limited to undergraduate preparation in the special field; (3) that preparation for special librarianship should be centered in the library schools; (4) that though little deviation from the traditional library school program would be necessary, most library school curricula included courses of little or no value to the special librarian; (5) that the value of the special courses to be added to the library school curriculum "lies primarily in the practical information regarding the materials and in an awareness of the fundamental problems relating to their organization and use";[66] (6) that cooperation between the library school and the appropriate subject departments of the university is desirable; and (7) that the offering of subject specializations by the library schools be closely related to demand, since the demand for science librarians, for example, far exceeds that for librarians specializing in music or the other fine arts. One must admit that the seven special programs outlined added little to what had already been said, though the subcommittee performed an important service by bringing together expert opinion on the subject of special library training. The members agreed

---

[63] *Ibid.* p. 54.

[64] See: *Special Libraries.* vol. 41 (March 1950), p. 106.

[65] "Education for Special Librarianship." *Library Quarterly.* vol. 24 (January 1954), pp. 1–20.

[66] *Ibid.* p. 2.

that a solid general education, to which should be added an equally substantial appropriate undergraduate major and a good working knowledge of foreign languages, was desirable. There was general agreement, too, that certain basic courses in the traditional library school curriculum—specifically cataloging and classification, reference, bibliography, and administration—could not be eliminated. However, differences of opinion arose concerning the amount and kinds of special library courses to be required, admirably exemplifying Wyer's dictum that the librarian of each variety of special library "thinks that training for his type of work should be different from the training of every other type."[67]

Subsequently four additional program outlines were prepared under the auspices of the subcommittee: map librarianship by Bill M. Woods, librarianship in art and architecture by Eleanor F. Norfolk, theological librarianship (Protestant) by Robert F. Beach, and theological librarianship (Catholic) by Rev. James J. Kortendick. Though they were published only in mimeographed form for the benefit of the subcommittee, they showed a marked improvement over the earlier statements in their grasp of the problems to be considered, their awareness of the expanding functions of the special librarian, and their obvious consciousness of the need for integration between library education and subject knowledge.

Attempts by the Joint Committee to carry forward the work that the subcommittee had so bravely begun failed because the CNLA could find no financial support. Proposals for funds to undertake an extended inquiry into the character and nature of the special librarian's functions and the kind of formal education appropriate to the effective execution of those functions were unsympathetically received, and the work of the group has, therefore, of necessity, languished. Nevertheless, such a committee could still be effectively used to advance the study of special library education if it were provided with adequate recognition and support; had it been given such backing in the past, much of the waste and uncoordinated effort that have characterized exploration of this field could have been avoided.

## DOCUMENTATION

In library education, documentation courses have tended to develop parallel with, but only coincidentally related to, special librarianship. The Special Libraries Association sponsored in 1965 the first of a series of

---

[67] James I. Wyer. "The Training of the Special Librarian." *Special Libraries.* vol. 23 (September 1932), p. 342.

annual postconvention forums on the training of special librarians. The inauguration of this series may be viewed as a manifestation of professional solidarity in the face of threatening competition from documentalists and information scientists, or as evidence of the willingness of special librarians to entertain these interlopers, and to learn from them, in the hope of containing them. As Goldwyn and Rees have written, "The nebulous no-man's land between librarianship, documentation, information retrieval, and information science cannot be instantly clarified."[68] The history of disputation over documentation is almost as long as that over special librarianship, and with the emergence of other specially denominated breeds of librarians, the confusion has become compounded.

On February 13, 1918, Ernest A. Savage, Chief of the Coventry Public Library, addressed the British Institute of Automobile Engineers on "The Utilization of Accumulated Data Relating to the Automobile Industry." A summary of the paper and a report of the discussion that followed were published in the *Library Association Record* citing "the sympathetic attitude of technical experts with respect to the proposed Technical Libraries."[69] Mr. Savage urged the creation of a central information bureau to provide engineering data and other essential technical and managerial information to the entire automotive industry, but his audience, and the unidentified reporter, were not slow to see the implications for expanding the plan to include similar services to science and technology in general. "The scheme which Mr. Savage laid before his audience," observed the writer in the *Record*, "is one that has exercised France, Germany, America, and Belgium for years past. . . . Great Britain has given relatively little attention to it."[70] He continued:

> The French call it *documentation*: an excellent word and so English in form that we see no reason why it should not be adopted. It is certainly better than information—and bureaux of information—which Mr. Savage employed as the English equivalent. *Documentation* explains itself. It means getting in touch will all documents bearing on a subject. Documents, of course, must be understood in its wide, original sense of everything that contains information or proof.[71]

---

[68] A. J. Goldwyn and A. M. Rees, eds. *The Education of Science Information Personnel—1964.* Cleveland. Center for Documentation and Communication Research, School of Library Science. Western Reserve University. 1965. p. i.

[69] This report is without indication of authorship. *Library Association Record.* vol. 20 (March 15, 1918), pp. 77–82.

[70] *Ibid.* p. 81.

[71] *Ibid.*

Savage apparently said little about the kind of professional training needed by the staff of his proposed information bureau, but he did observe that "it should be in the hands of a man librarian with engineering knowledge."[72]

In the June-August issue of the *Record* for the same year, J. G. Pearce, of the research department of the British Westinghouse Company at Manchester, wrote optimistically of the expanding future of documentation and observed that the field should be given serious attention by the government Department of Scientific Research. The program of coordinated information services which Pearce envisaged was to be under the general supervision of a director of research; "the detailed work of administration, however, and the task of collecting, abstracting, indexing, and translating information and of distributing it, must be placed in the hands of those who have been adequately trained in library science."[73] England was becoming aware of the need for specialized library service to science and technology, and at this stage no distinction was drawn between the educational preparation of the professional librarian and that of the information specialist or documentalist—the latter was regarded as no more than a specialty within the former. The lines of demarcation that in later years were to be so harshly drawn were not present in these early stages of development.

On this side of the Atlantic, however, documentation made little impact upon librarianship until the 1930s, and even then the word was largely interpreted in terms of photographic, especially microphotographic, processes and techniques. It was the Second World War and the need for rapid and precise access to masses of intelligence data that focused attention upon unconventional methods of bibliographic organization and information analysis. In 1950 the official journal of the American Documentation Institute began publication, and that same year Helen Focke inaugurated, at the School of Library Science at Western Reserve University, the first library school course in documentation. This course included, in addition to the indexing and abstracting methods she had taught the year before, the use of punched cards and some consideration of other methods of bibliographic organization. Other unconventional techniques of subject analysis were added to the course as they developed.[74] Slowly, other library schools began to include similar courses in their curricula, and today most, if not

---

72 *Ibid.* p. 78.

73 J. G. Pearce. "The Future of Documentation." *Library Association Record.* vol. 20 (June–August 1918), p. 165. See also: W. Kenneth Lowry. "The Use of Computers in Information Science." *Science.* vol. 175 (February 25, 1972) pp. 841–46.

74 H. M. Focke. "Education and Documentation at Western Reserve University— Yesterday, Today (and Tomorrow?)." *Library Science.* Tokyo. no. 3 (1965).

all, of the accredited library schools offer at least some elementary instruction in documentation.

In 1955 the Center for Documentation and Communication Research was established in the School of Library Science at Western Reserve, for the development of a program of teaching and research in the emerging field of information retrieval. For a number of years its program was substantially concerned with the use of computers and computer-like devices, for the organization, storage, and retrieval of information in libraries and other bibliographic centers. Subsequently it was expanded to include the theory of information science, the mathematical foundations of information retrieval, and the application of automation to the noninformational aspects of librarianship. Case Western Reserve has consistently held to the conviction that documentation and information science are an integral part of the totality of librarianship, and all students pursuing the documentation program are required to have first prepared themselves in the fundamentals of librarianship.

When the importance of prompt and accurate information to the national security was highlighted because of Sputnik I, the National Science Foundation became concerned about the need for improving the undergraduate, graduate, and professional training of science information personnel. In the spring of 1960, the NSF Office of Science Information Service sponsored a small conference in New York City, to which were invited a selected group of educators and practicing information specialists in the hope that they could identify the tasks performed by documentalists and information specialists with a view to describing the kinds of education required to equip such workers for efficient service in this rapidly expanding field. As one result of this conference, Leonard Cohan and Kenneth Craven surveyed some two hundred individuals engaged in information work for the Federal Government, industry, and research organizations, asking them to check off on a list the tasks at which they spent their time. The tasks most often checked correspond to the subjects customarily taught in conventional library schools—bibliography, reference work, cataloging, and administration—while checks for such activities as mechanization, research in information science, and the interpreting of information were few.[75]

Though some librarians saw in these findings evidence that nothing more than conventional librarianship need be taught or learned, it must be remembered that Cohan and Craven's respondents were naturally conditioned by their own educational experiences; one can scarcely use in his

---

[75] L. Cohan and K. Craven. *Science Information Personnel*. New York. Modern Language Association of America. 1961. pp. 5–6.

work that which he has not learned. In the long run, Cohan and Craven unfortunately intensified the cleft between the conventional and the non-conventional by recommending the establishment of new schools to provide a kind of specialized education not offered by the library schools.

It is evident from the above that by the early 1960s the terms *librarian, documentalist,* and *information specialist,* and their variants, were becoming badly confused. Therefore, the invitational conference on the Training of Science Information Specialists, held at the Georgia Institute of Technology in April 1962, attempted to reach agreement on the precise meaning of some of the terms, and the following definitions were presented to the group for consideration:[76]

1.  *Librarian*—A person having formal training in library science and possessing a degree from an accredited library school. It is used here in preference to the term professional librarian.

2.  *Special Librarian*—A librarian, who by virtue of special interests and talents chooses to operate in a special discipline, and for that purpose requires a broadened and intensified knowledge of his selected field—to which he must adapt the library techniques basic to all library practice.

3.  *Science Librarian*—A librarian with a broad, though not necessarily deep, acquaintance with science, and a comprehensive knowledge of the literature of science. He differs from the literature analyst in two respects. (1) He is a librarian, and therefore is qualified to deal with the usual problems associated with the operation of a library. (2) While he can and does perform science literature searches, he cannot, in general, critically evaluate the scientific content of literature. The technical literature analyst interacts with information in the books; the librarian interacts with the books.

4.  *Technical Literature Analyst*—One who is trained in a substantive technical field, who has, in addition to the depth thus provided, some breadth of technical knowledge, and a thorough knowledge of the technical literature. He can analyze the literature for the researchers who are investigating problems in the areas of the analyst's technical competence. Analysis implies a search, an organization, and an evaluation of the literature in question. In his ability to deal with the technical literature the analyst

---

[76] Mimeographed statement presented to the conference. Two conferences were held at Georgia Tech, the first on October 12–13, 1961, and the second on April 12–13, 1962. Both were supported by the National Science Foundation and were limited to some thirty-five to forty invited participants from science, librarianship, and library education.

differs from the conventional science librarian in that he is sufficiently deep in science to enable him to make value judgments of its literature. At the higher levels this person generally performs not only analysis but synthesis of the literature as well.

5. *Information Scientist*—One who studies and develops the science of information storage and retrieval, who devises new approaches to the information problem, who is interested in information in and of itself.

Though there was considerable disagreement over the first four definitions because of their restrictiveness and deviation from reality, there was general acceptance of the definition of an *information scientist* as one who engages in research into the theory and practice of information handling.

## INFORMATION SCIENCE

One result of the Atlanta conferences was to stimulate in schools of engineering an interest in the training of information scientists. The Georgia Institute of Technology, with the assistance of a grant from the National Science Foundation, inaugurated a curriculum for the training of science information analysts and information scientists with a minimum of deference to librarianship. Lehigh University followed with a somewhat comparable instructional pattern. The extent to which these new programs differ from their library school predecessors is evident from a selection of the offerings at the Georgia Institute of Technology: Introduction to Probability; Electronic Computations; Comparative Programming; and Operations Research. At Lehigh students are offered seminars in Syntactic Concepts; Design of Experiments; Industrial Information Systems; Engineering Psychology; and Mathematical Models of Learning. A few of the library schools (Drexel Institute of Technology, the University of California at Los Angeles, the University of Chicago, the University of Minnesota, the University of North Carolina) initiated programs of varying degrees of intensity relating to information science. At the School of Library and Information Science of the University of Maryland, all beginning students are required to take a course in computer technology and its application to library operations. Professional education in all of these information-related fields, like the terms themselves, has been confused in pattern and uncertain as to objectives.[77] Early in 1965 the Massachusetts Institute of Technology announced a mas-

---

[77] See: J. C. Donohue. "Librarianship and the Science of Information." *FID Proceedings.* Washington, D.C. Congress. 1965.

sive program (INTREX, an acronym for Information Transfer Experiments) directed toward defining the "library of the twenty-first century," and a conference to identify needed research was held at Woods Hole, Massachusetts, in August of that year.[78]

To bring together in a kind of synthesis the diverse and disparate experiments in the professional education of science information personnel currently being conducted by library schools, engineering schools, institutes, and universities through interdisciplinary programs, to foster a common understanding of the educational problems, and to achieve some agreement among those concerned respecting academic standards, were the expressed purposes of a conference on the Education of Science Information Personnel—1964, held at Western Reserve University in July of 1964.[79] The problems of communication among the invited guests were, because of great divergencies in background and points of view, extremely difficult, but some measure of understanding was attained, and the published proceedings do provide a useful summary of the educational situation as it then existed.[80]

In a sense, the symposium on Education for Information Science held under the auspices of the American Documentation Institute at Airlie House, Warrenton, Virginia, in September of 1965, may be regarded as a continuation of the Western Reserve meeting. However, the invitees at Airlie devoted themselves almost exclusively to a dialogue, that was frequently turgid and pretentious, over the credentials of information science and the kind of discipline it may be; the attempts to formulate a theory of information science; and the pedagogic aspects of this projected discipline.[81] The results of the symposium would seem to bear out John Berry's belief that whatever credentials as a respectable academic discipline information science can present, "it is grudgingly accepted by librarianship, and is accepted for exploitation by science."[82] Perhaps most important of all, the symposium

---

[78] C. F. J. Overhage and R. J. Harman, eds. *INTREX: Report of a Planning Conference on Information Transfer Experiments, September 3, 1965*, Cambridge, Mass. M.I.T. Press. 1965. Also: Jesse H. Shera. "Librarians' Pugwash or INTREX on the Cape." *Documentation and the Organization of Knowledge*. London. Crosby Lockwood. 1966. pp. 115–24.

[79] Goldwyn and Rees. *Science Information Personnel.*

[80] See: R. Swanson. "Report on a Conference on the Education of Science Information Personnel." *American Documentation*. vol. 16 (January 1965), pp. 34–35; or Ralph Parker's review of the published proceedings in *Library Journal*. vol. 90, no. 19 (November 1, 1965), pp. 4746–48.

[81] B. Heilprin, E. Markuson, and F. L. Goodman, eds. *Proceedings of the Symposium on Education for Information Science, Warrenton, Virginia, Spetember 7–10, 1965*. Washington, D.C. Spartan Books. 1965.

[82] J. Berry. "It's a Wise Child . . ." *Library Journal*. vol. 90 (November 1, 1965), p. 4724.

dramatically underscored the fact that there were tides running that could drastically alter the entire philosophy of librarianship and education for librarianship should take them seriously into account.

"In the modern world. . .all citizens must have at least some empirical knowledge of Semiotics, Information Science and Technologies, or Informatics," Robert A. Fairthorne wrote for the 34th FID Conference in Moscow. "Many people have to specialize in various aspects of these activities. Whatever label may be preferred it denotes interests in aspects of production, manipulation, and application of signs and symbols. . . . I emphasize the essentially social nature of what I will now call, for temporary convenience only 'Information Sciences, Technologies, and Activities,' abbreviated as ISTA. I do this to curb a dangerous tendency to bring in every and any science or technique or phenomenon under the 'Information' heading. Certainly hitherto distinct activities and interests should be unified, if indeed they have common principles. However, one does not create common principles by giving different things the same name. The test of unification is whether it reduces the amount of disjunct among empirical matters that must be learned, and skills that must be acquired, by replacing them with the need to master some general principles and to acquire skill in developing and applying them."[83]

Fairthorne goes on to say that up to the present time the only unity within Information Science, other than its common origin in the uses of language, "has come through overlapping techniques and technologies. It has not come from the application of common principles." The one fundamental topic of Information Sciences is that of language, "its physical, social, referential, and intensional aspects." Thus, he concludes that Information Science "centers on the knowledge and services needed for effective discourse by other people," and at the present time the field is "more a federation of technologies than a set of special activities developed from common principles."

Harold Borko sees in information science a true discipline "that investigates the properties and behavior of information, the forces governing the flow of information, and the means for processing information for optimal accessibility and usability. It is concerned with that body of knowledge relating to the origination, collection, organization, storage, retrieval, interpretation, transmission, transformation, and utilization of information. This includes the investigation of information representations in both natural and artificial systems, the use of codes for efficient message transmission,

---

[83] Robert A. Fairthorne. "The Scope and Aims of the Information Sciences and Technologies." MS paper presented to the 34th FID Conference. Moscow. (September 1968). passim.

and the study of information processing devices and techniques, such as computers and their programming systems."[84]

Glynn Harmon believes that information science evolved not only as an expansion, or metamorphosis, of documentation and information retrieval, but also directly or indirectly incorporated or paralleled "several prevailing objectives and concepts of the communication and behavioral sciences and other contributory disciplines." He also hypothesizes that "in the early 1970s, information science will possibly achieve completeness as a disciplinary system. By 1990, it should achieve a relative state of maturity; specialization within its ranks could become intense. But new fusions and fissions with attendant name changes could occur within the next two decades."[85]

From this brief account of the faltering steps toward a definition of *information science* and the attempts to identify an education program

---

[84] Harold Borko. "Information Science: What Is It?" *American Documentation*. vol. 19 (January 1968), pp. 3–5. Hoshovsky and Massey reply to Borko in a paper emphasizing the "output" of information science. Alexander G. Hoshovsky and Robert J. Massey. "Information Science: Its Ends, Means, and Opportunities." American Society for Information Science. *Proceedings. 1968 Conference*. New York. Greenwood. 1969. pp. 47–55.

The Russians, it should be noted, have made information science subordinate to social science. Thus, they wrote for a UNESCO sponsored conference in September 1970, "Information science is a discipline belonging to social science, which studies the structure and general characteristics of scientific information, and also general laws governing all scientific communication processes." Committee for Mutual Economic Assistance. *Information on the Activities of the Bodies of the Council for Mutual Economic Assistance in the Field of Scientific and Technical Information During the First Part of 1970*. Fifth Session of the Central Committee to Study the Feasibility of a World Scientific Information System, UNESCO-ICSU, September 30–October 1, 1970. Moscow. (September 1970), p. 7.

At Fukuoka, Japan, research in information science has been made a branch of statistics. T. Kitagawa. *Information Science and Its Connection with Statistics*. Fukuoka, Japan. Research Institute of Fundamental Information Science, Kyushu University. 1968.

At Ohio State University, information science is combined with the Computer Research Center. See: Ohio State University. Computer and Information Science Research Center. *Report to the Office of Science Information Service, National Science Foundation, June 1969–1970*. (Grant no. ON 934-A) Columbus, Ohio. 1970.

[85] Glynn Harmon. "On the Evolution of Information Science." *Journal of the American Society for Information Science*. vol. 22 (July–August 1971), pp. 235–41. See also: Jesse H. Shera. "The Sociological Foundations of Information Science." *Journal of the American Society for Information Science*. vol. 22 (March–April, 1971), pp. 76–80; Louis Vagianos. "Information Science: A House Built on Sand." *Library Journal*. vol. 97 (January 15, 1972), pp. 153–57.

that will prepare students for its practice, certain conclusions can be drawn. Librarianship is the generic term and information science is an area of research which draws its substance, methods, and techniques from a variety of disciplines to achieve an understanding of the properties, behavior, and flow of information. Information science is not souped-up librarianship or information retrieval, nor is it antithetical to either. Rather information science contributes to the theoretical and intellectual base for the librarian's operations. Clearly a new pattern of relationships among the older disciplines is beginning to emerge as information science, the strands of which first seem to have been woven at the Georgia Tech. conferences of 1962 and 1963, which were following the leadership of Robert Hayes.[86] With respect to the professional education of the information scientist, Saracevic and Rees have found that there are three main types of programs: (1) those which are library school-based and are derived mainly from interest in information retrieval; (2) those which are engineering school-based and which have strong ties with departments of electrical engineering, computer science, and applied mathematics; and (3) those which are dispersed among several subject departments of a university, such as philosophy, psychology, or linguistics. Analysis of the various curricula reveals striking similarities. "All emphasize the existence of basic tools and methodologies from other disciplines such as mathematics and logic. All demand an insight into the phenomena, processes, and systems involved in communication. All endeavor to illustrate the application of such scientific methodologies to the investigation of communication phenomena. Differences do, of course, exist with respect to emphasis. A reasonably clear differentiation between information *science* and information *technology* can be found in the various educational programs."[87]

Though most of the research and development in information processing and handling has taken place outside the library schools and represents nonlibrary-oriented effort, Rees and Riccio have found that the schools are responding to change and have revised their curricula accordingly. Their survey of course offerings in this field, by the ALA accredited library schools, indicates that, at the time of their study in 1967, seventeen schools gave courses in data processing and library automation; nineteen in documentation and information storage, retrieval, and dissemination; and six in re-

---

[86] See: Jesse H. Shera. "Of Librarianship, Documentation, and Information Science." *UNESCO Bulletin for Libraries.* vol. 22 (March–April 1968), pp. 58–65; and Borko. "Information Science." pp. 3–5.

[87] Tefko Saracevic and Alan Rees. "The Impact of Information Science on Library Practice." *Library Journal.* vol. 93 (November 1, 1968), pp. 4097–98.

search and methodology. Thus they conclude that, "the crucial issue at the present time is not whether library schools need to teach information science and engineering but rather how should it be taught and by whom. By this we mean whether as an interdisciplinary venture in conjunction with other university departments or perhaps by a truly interdisciplinary school of librarianship, which is an approach already being explored by several library schools."[88]

The Rees and Riccio findings seem to be supported by those of Lester Asheim's study of accredited library school curricula for the year 1966–67. From his work with the ALA Committee on Accreditation, he found that twenty-two of the forty-one accredited schools had added eighty-five new courses, of which sixteen were in information science, and, in addition, two schools had added entirely new programs in this field. Moreover, eleven schools "are definitely planning the addition of courses or programs in information science."[89] Asheim is careful to add, however, that his statistics were drawn exclusively from the tabulation of questionnaires submitted to the Committee on Accreditation and that there was no attempt on his part to evaluate the work being done.

Since a profession must educate for the future of a world in change, the problems of education can never really be "solved." Programs (both in library schools and outside) have been predicated on local experience, highly personal assumptions of what is, and hypothesizing about what should be, rather than on any precise knowledge of what the information worker does and needs to know in order to do it. Experimentation and exploration are needed, but there must be careful planning, solidly based on precise knowledge, and judiciously interpreted if the training of a substantial, not to say disastrous, number of professional unemployables is to be avoided. Information is the librarian's business and he is the one person who, by virtue of his historic role and social responsibilities, is best qualified to become a specialist in the emerging information-related studies.

Some hint of the future role of the computer and related forms of automation in the library world may be evinced by the success with which they have been used in many libraries for circulation control, book ordering, and record keeping. The computer with on-line terminals dispersed over

---

[88] Alan Rees and Dorothy Riccio. "Information Science in Library School Curricula." *International Conference on Education for Scientific Information, Queen Elizabeth College, London, 3rd to 7th April, 1967.* International Federation for Documentation. The Hague. Federation Internationale de Documentation. 1967. pp. 29–37.

[89] Lester Asheim. "The State of the Accredited Library Schools, 1966–1967." *Library Quarterly.* vol. 38 (October 1968), pp. 323–37.

an extensive geographic area for centralized cataloging already promises substantial reductions in cataloging costs and may eventually revolutionize the teaching of conventional cataloging in library schools.[90]

## THE TREND TO SOCIAL ACTION

The demand for "relevance" by the Social Responsibilities Round Table, and related movements in the ALA, can be traced back to the nineteenth-century faith in the public library as a social force that would, through the promotion of reading, save mankind from poverty, crime, vice, alcoholism, and almost every other evil to which flesh is heir. But a more striking parallel to the present day unrest is to be found in the pleas of the young librarians for social action during the 1930s, for ferment was also taking place in the profession during that decade. The storms of crisis that battered the American economy during the last years of the Hoover Administration and the first of Roosevelt's promoted an awareness that the library had sociological roots, and that the librarian should have a vigorous and vocal social consciousness. This conviction was especially strong among a relatively small group of young librarians who were demanding an end to conservatism and complacency with development in their stead of a dynamic social role for the library.[91] During these years, the librarian had ample time to read, and the youth, if they were not actually reading Marx, were at least steeped in the writings of Thurman Arnold, on Recent Social Trends. These were the days when Stanley Kunitz was editing a *Wilson Bulletin* that voted for Franklin Roosevelt on every page, and was surrounded by a little coterie of kinspirits who were deeply troubled by racial segregation at the Richmond, Virginia, ALA conference of 1936, the economic crisis, the rights of librarians to preserve the integrity of their book collections, the Spanish Civil War, and the rising tide of totalitarianism

---

[90] LaVahn Overmyer of the School of Library Science, Case Western Reserve University, has surveyed the use of automation and other forms of mechanization in libraries as of 1970, under a grant from the U.S. Office of Education. This study, as yet unpublished, also devotes some attention to the implications of automation for library education. Report issued in mimeographed form from Case Western Reserve University, Cleveland, Ohio, 1970.

For an amusing report of one librarian's experiences with mechanization see Margaret Francine Morris. "Experiences with a Library Network." *RQ* vol. 9 (Fall 1969), pp. 39–44.

[91] Jesse H. Shera. "Plus ça Change." *Library Journal*. vol. 95 (March 15, 1970), pp. 979–86.

in Italy and Germany. "The only test that we can apply to the content of the public library," wrote Harold Laski, "is the test of significance." But, he continued, "it is not enough, in my judgment, to stop there. The library's business is not the collection of books, but their circulation. . . . Every home in this country into which there is not a constant flow of books represents a failure of the public library system. There are many such homes. There are prejudices we have not broken down, avenues we have not explored."[92] William F. Ogburn, who was not only a distinguished sociologist but also a participant in many investigations into the impact of social change upon the utilization of human resources, told the first summer institute of the Graduate Library School, that because the library was a creature of society, shaped by the social forces and trends in the world beyond its walls, it had an important stake in what was happening in society, and the librarian, therefore, must concern himself with society, he must teach himself to develop "attitudes of foresight."[93] Ogburn's words fell upon sympathetic and responsive ears, and they carried the weight of authority. But it was Lowell Martin who wrote the real *credo* for the youth of his generation. The core of the library's being, he wrote, "is the transmission of group culture and knowledge as recorded in printed materials."[94] Thus he derived the social functions of the public library as an agency of social control which conserves and transmits the social heritage, and inculcates the experiences and values of the past to its contemporary society, to the end of promoting social solidarity and unity. But the public library, he declared, also has an individualizing function, for it enables the individual to appreciate present trends and future values, enhance the quality and richness of his personal life, and even provide a means for increasing social mobility—"for climbing the social ladder." The position of the public library, therefore, makes it "an integral factor in both the anabolic and catabolic processes which comprise the metabolism of social life."[95] In these pages, indeed, echoed the voices of William Graham Sumner, Karl Mannheim, and Lester F. Ward.

"If it is true," Wilhelm Munthe inquired, "that the library is—as

---

92 Harold J. Laski. "The Uses of the Public Library." *Wilson Bulletin.* vol. 10 (November 1935), pp. 175–76.

93 William F. Ogburn. "Recent Social Trends—Their Implications for Libraries." *Library Trends.* University of Chicago, Graduate Library School. Chicago. University of Chicago Press. 1937. pp. 1 and 12.

94 Lowell A. Martin. "The American Public Library as a Social Institution." *Library Quarterly.* vol. 7 (October 1937), p. 549.

95 *Ibid.* Also: Margaret E. Egan. "The Library and Social Structure." *Library Quarterly.* vol. 25 (January 1955), pp. 15–22.

Theodore Roosevelt once put it—next after the school 'the most effective influence for good in America,' or, as Franklin D. Roosevelt said in 1936, 'the world's largest educational system,' how can it escape the same social evaluation and scientific examination to which all the other institutions of society are subjected?"[96]

Mary U. Rothrock, who, through her experience with the Tennessee Valley Authority, had had a better opportunity than most librarians to see what librarianship could accomplish in economically and culturally deprived areas, rejected, in her presidential address before the ALA in 1947, the library "as a passive conservator of man's cultural heritage," which she said "was little more than a vestigial trace from a vanished past," and in its place she espoused "a more positive responsibility in getting the insides of books into the minds of men."[97]

But, in the main, the profession at large was apathetic to the new sociology of librarianship. Joseph Wheeler expressed what was probably the view of an overwhelming majority of librarians when he stated that the profession was suffering from "a well-meant over-dose of social viewpoint."[98] Officially, the ALA turned a deaf ear to pleas for collective action in all matters that related to the involvement of the library in social action, but whether the ferment that was beginning to take place might have eventuated in professional schism can never be known; Stanley Kunitz's League for Liberal Librarians never got off the pages of the *Wilson Bulletin*. The coming of the Second World War directed the thoughts of librarians into new channels of concern. Not until after the midpoint of the century was there again any real attention given to the library's social role, and even then it was expressed mainly in terms of intellectual freedom and the struggle against censorship.

By the late 1960s, the public library discovered that it was being propelled into a new world in which social action could not be avoided whatever might be the dictates of conservatism. The crisis has been brought about by the flight to suburbia and new patterns of urban living, especially those in the inner-city. The conventional neighborhood library has discovered that it has neighbors who no longer want a quiet retreat, but are seeking information, demanding books that will help in passing literacy

---

[96] Wilhelm Munthe. *American Librarianship from a European Angle*. Chicago. American Library Association. 1939. p. 145.

[97] Mary U. Rothrock. "On Some Library Questions of Our Time." *Bulletin of the American Library Association*. vol. 41 (August 1947), p. 243.

[98] Joseph L. Wheeler. *Progress and Problems in Education for Librarianship*. New York. Carnegie Corporation of New York. 1946. p. 9.

tests, provide an understanding of Negro history, and make available texts in Spanish. Inner-city librarians in such metropolitan centers as Baltimore, Boston, Chicago, Cleveland, Detroit, Los Angeles, and New York are finding that their libraries are no longer places of quiet middle class respectability, but that they must reach out to the city's poor and the ghetto-bound. Programs tailored to the Black community share library resources with those directed to the interests of the teen-agers among the poor. Programs on premarital pregnancy share time with those on drug addiction. Even rock-and-roll concerts have been used to lure the youth to library doors. Librarians are beginning to learn to work with social agencies in the deprived areas of the city. In some libraries the age-old tradition of the library fine for delinquency in returning books is being abolished in an effort to prevent antagonism toward the library and its services. Librarians are reexamining their conventional roles in the community, and as a result are redirecting services, broadening programs, and in a variety of ways radically altering conventional methods. These activities of the library are still too recent for anyone to judge of their impact on the curricula of the library schools, but the time may not be far distant when specialized training for work with the disadvantaged of the inner-city or Appalachia may be an accepted specialty, and appropriate educational programs may begin to appear in library school catalogs.

The basic role of the library is not changing, it is the dynamics of that role, its expression in implementation, that is undergoing alteration. Lowell Martin has identified some ten changes in the environment of the library and in the library itself which he believes will have significant impact upon the practice of librarianship in the twenty-first century. Our society is changing, he says,

> from a people seeking productivity alone to a people also seeking value and fulfillment,
>
> from an educational system concerned with numbers to one seeking to develop quality,
>
> from a society of workers to a society of specialists,
>
> from a readership limited to the elite to a readership extended to the underprivileged,
>
> from the first step of building strong collections to the further step of outreach of resources through the whole society,
>
> from the traditional book to communication in new and ingenious forms,

from routines that sap our time and energy to machines that free us, from your own separate library to a unit within an area-wide resource, most important, from an assumption that what we do is automatically socially significant to a professional recommitment to library purposes.[99]

Unfortunately, the library profession has not developed a social philosophy or a body of research findings to support it. Philip Ennis, after reviewing the confused and disparate pattern of library users, concluded that librarians must "consciously put a priority marking on library objectives and press forward in concentrated bursts. . .picking up support and doing an effective, albeit a limited, job." The alternative is "to drift with the accidental pressures of demands and to move rudderless with the tide of fluctuating and residual public interests."[100] To yield to the latter, he believes, will lead eventually to the demise of the public library and the assumption of its true responsibilities by other agencies.

A philosophy of librarianship is an essential ingredient in the librarian's store of professional competencies without which he will find himself rejected by the lay world. "Not only is the base of power shifting from property and political criteria to knowledge," William Heston told a workshop for library trustees in 1968, "but, as Daniel Bell again tells us, 'what is so crucial is not merely the change to knowledge but to the character of that knowledge itself.' He contends that what has 'become decisive for society is the new centrality of theoretical knowledge, the primacy of theory over empiricism, and the codification of knowledge into abstract systems of symbols that can be translated into many different and varied circumstances.' Thus, we can easily see that the continued growth and evolution of our society will be by innovation, and we all know that theoretical knowledge is now the key to innovation."[101] Heston goes on to point out that the day of the tinker-inventor is rapidly passing, that it is no accident that industries are increasingly tending to cluster around great centers of research, especially university complexes, and that there is a real relationship between economic growth and education. He points to the development

---

[99] Lowell A. Martin. "The Changes Ahead." *Library Journal.* vol. 93 (February 15, 1968), p. 716.

[100] Philip H. Ennis. "The Library Consumer: Patterns and Trends." *Library Quarterly* vol. 34 (April 1964), p. 178.

[101] William M. Heston. "Today's Information Needs and Community Problems." Address before the Case Western Reserve University Trustees' Workshop. September 7, 1968. *Bulletin of the Ohio Library Association.*

of polymer chemistry, from which were created man-made fibers, as being the first "modern" example of an industry based principally upon theoretical knowledge.

But theoretical knowledge is as important to the behavioral as to the physical and biological sciences, and the same can be said of librarianship as one branch of the behavioral disciplines. At long last the universities are beginning to recognize that the proper study of mankind is man as a social being in all his manifestations. "The metamorphosis of the modern urban university," A. J. Goldwyn told the same trustees' workshop, when introducing Mr. Heston, "during the past few years has been so rapid and so dramatic that even those of us who have lived in—and through—the change can scarcely believe it. Not long ago the university protected—or hid—its scholarly community behind a high wall which served at the same time to shut out the 'real world' outside. Times have changed, the wall has tumbled. Now the university—and particularly the graduate professional schools— has experienced a profound reorientation."

Most of the elements of change that have been cataloged briefly in the preceding pages of this chapter—mechanization, the new media, specialization, documentation, information science, and social action—have come from without the profession of librarianship, and library education has, in the main, reacted to, rather than initiated change.

Clearly, the center of gravity of librarianship is steadily and irresistibly moving away from the humanities and toward the science of society. The importance of *belles lettres* in the library is not to be devaluated; the humanities will always be important to the librarian for their traditional role as stimulants to the imagination and the other intangible contributions that they make to the richness and growth of the human spirit; but these properties, too, have a sociopsychological base. One should not forget the impact of an *Uncle Tom's Cabin*, or the Wagnerian hero, on the structure of a society. Even those librarians and documentalists who are serving the needs of science dare not overlook the sociological foundations of communication. Surely no profession is more involved than that of the librarian in all the social processes. A science librarian who does not understand the forces that are at work within his social *milieu*, will have his effectiveness diminished however thoroughly he knows the *Gmelin Handbuch* or the *International Critical Tables*.

# Ten

# The Academic Setting

The most striking facts about education for librarianship are the confusion by which it is beset and the general lack of enthusiasm for it, and in this it is not significantly different from all other formal education from the elementary school to the highest levels of the university. The high school cannot make up its mind whether it is preparing its students for life or for college and, in consequence, does neither well. The junior college is little more than an extension of the high school with, as in the case of the community college, an overlay of vocationalism. The liberal arts college, when it does not resemble a teacher-training institution, is part high school and part university. The university is distinguished from the college by the fact that it is a composite of graduate curricula and professional schools. The graduate school exists primarily to confer the doctoral degree, which has become the official insignia of the academician. The reasons why a professional school should be attached to a university and, indeed, what a professional school should be like, have not been satisfactorily explained. In fact, the professions themselves have not been precisely identified. Such are the charges with which Robert Maynard Hutchins opened his classic essay on *The Higher Learning in America*. Therefore, before one can consider the meaning of education for librarianship, he must first consider the meaning of education itself, and before he can consider the meaning of education, he must ask what education is.

## WHAT IS EDUCATION?

"Education," said Alfred North Whitehead, "is the acquisition of the art of the utilization of knowledge."[1] But one must understand his use of the term *utilization*, for Whitehead is not confusing immediate and final ends. Material prosperity and adjustment to the environment have certain undeniable values, but they are not good in themselves, and there are values beyond them. "By utilizing an idea," he says, "I mean relating it to that stream, compounded of sense perceptions, feelings, hopes, desires, and of mental activities, adjusting thoughts to thoughts, which forms our life."[2]

Education is the process by which the intellect is trained; it is the cultivation of the intellectual powers.[3] As Carroll Newsom has said, "All education is really self-education. . . . Learning cannot be passive, one who would develop the powers of his mind must seek deliberately to 'match his wits' with problems provided by his natural and man-made environments. He must accept the wisdom inherent in the statement 'One learns to think by thinking.' "[4]

The ancients distinguished five intellectual virtues, or habits. They recognized three speculative habits: intuitive knowledge (the habit of induction), scientific knowledge (the habit of demonstration), and philosophical wisdom (a combination of intuitive reason and scientific knowledge directed toward first principles and first causes). To these three were added the two virtues of the practical intellect: art (the capacity to make decisions according to a true course of reasoning), and prudence (the application of right reason with respect to action).

The end which education seeks, then, is the creation of an intellect—an intellect, as Hutchins says, that will be properly disciplined, properly

---

[1] Alfred North Whitehead. *The Aims of Education*. London. Williams and Norgate. 1947. p. 6.

[2] *Ibid*. p. 4.

[3] "Education could be described as the mnner by which. . .social bodies perpetuate themselves from generation to generation. Hence education becomes transformed when there are social revolutions. Moreover, attempts at social innovation turn to pedagogical questions first." Karl Jaspers. *The Idea of the University*. London. Peter Owen. 1960. p. 61.

[4] Carroll V. Newsom. *A University President Speaks Out*. New York. Harper. 1961. pp. 1–2.

"Facts, observations, discoveries, as items, are but the nutrients on which the tree of knowledge feeds, and not until they have been thoroughly absorbed and assimilated, have they truly enlarged the body of knowledge." Paul Weiss. "Knowledge: A Growth Process." *Science*. vol. 81 (June 10, 1960), p. 1716.

habituated, "an intellect able to operate well in all fields. An education that consists of the cultivation of the intellectual virtues, therefore, is the most useful education, whether the student is destined for a life of contemplation or a life of action."[5] If the aim of education is the discipline of the intellect, it must operate not alone through the imparting of information, but by the cultivation of understanding to the end of achieving wisdom, and those studies which do not bring the student closer to wisdom have no place in the program of higher education. It is against this norm of the training of the intellect that educators must determine what education they shall offer, and it is through the attainment of wisdom that their students must lay the foundations of their moral, intellectual, and spiritual lives, for only through wisdom can they recover a rational view of the universe and their role in it.

This philosophy of education is rooted in the classical tradition and required by the intricacies of the contemporary culture. It is rooted in tradition because it is fundamentally Platonic and Aristotelian. It was transmitted through the medieval world in which the intellectual and spiritual life was largely the monopoly of a monastic elite. It was given increased strength during the Age of Enlightenment, and it suffused the spirit of the German university of the nineteenth century. From Cardinal Newman came what is perhaps the most vigorous nineteenth-century English statement of it:

> I say a University, taken in its bare idea . . . . educates the intellect to reason well in all matters, to reach out toward truth, and to grasp it.[6]

There is no denying the validity of the classical concept of education, but to a young nation in which freedom and democracy were on the march, a country which in its emotional complexion and its cultural pattern was remote from the ancient Graeco-Roman civilization, the rigidly prescribed curriculum of the classical tradition appeared excessively authoritarian. President Eliot of Harvard probably performed a useful service in breaking up the classical tradition to the extent of opening the whole field of study to the student's choice. But it was with the advent of the philosophy of John Dewey that Jacksonianism in education achieved its

---

[5] Robert Maynard Hutchins. *The Higher Learning in America.* New Haven. Yale University Press. 1936. p. 63. Cf. Sidney Hook. *Education for Modern Man.* New York. Knopf. 1963. Chapter 2. "The Ends of Education."

[6] John Henry, Cardinal Newman. *The Idea of a University.* New York. Longmans, Green. 1935. pp. 125–26.

fullest expression, and though his leadership was most conspicuous in elementary and secondary education, he exerted considerable influence over the course of higher education as well. Dewey's emphasis on education as experience in problem-solving, thus preparing the individual to meet new and changing life situations with increasing success, forced him to defend a program of study that stretched flexibility to the limit. Dewey's curriculum had to include every subject and every method, no matter how novel, that might help in or contribute to the solution of those life-problems that the college, and the society which supported it, might regard as socially important. Thus he and his disciples grouped and regrouped subjects, courses, and departments into ever-changing patterns of problem-solving activities.

But the elective system did not fulfill its promise, and it encountered a steadily mounting criticism. A. Lawrence Lowell rejected much of Eliot's elective system and, in his inaugural address, declared emphatically that the function of the college is to train the mind. The college graduate, he insisted, "ought to be trained in hard and accurate thought, and this will not come merely by surveying the elementary principles of many subjects."[7] He quoted in support of his view President Hadley's aphorism, "The ideal college education seems to me to be the one where a student learns things he is not going to use in after life, by methods that he is going to use. The former element gives the breadth, the latter element gives the training."[8] More than three decades later, the Harvard Committee on the Objectives of a General Education recognized publicly that the elective system not only gives a freedom to the student who is not qualified to exercise it intelligently, but also that it is a "divisive force" in that it "divides the student's work into compartments . . . many of which are simply islands of experience."[9] This disjointedness prevents the student's program of instruction from becoming a unified whole, and makes of it a cluster of scattered and often unrelated parts. Small wonder, then, that James Rowland Angell should have complained, "Coming out of an obscure past, universities have always eluded precise definition, and never more so than today."[10] But four years later, President Day of Cornell University gave the answer in his inaugural address:

[7] A. Lawrence Lowell. "Inaugural Address." *At War with Academic Traditions in America.* Cambridge, Mass. Harvard University Press. 1934. p. 36.

[8] *Ibid.* pp. 36–37.

[9] Harvard University. Committee on the Objectives of a General Education. *General Education in a Free Society.* Cambridge, Mass. Harvard University Press. 1945. pp. 13–14.

[10] James Rowland Angell. "The University Today; Its Aims and Province." *The Ob-*

A great university should be a place in which there are relatively undisturbed opportunities to live with ideas. . . . Men and women on a campus like this should learn how knowledge is gained and wisdom won. They should through practice improve their command of the difficult art of critical thinking. . . . They should strive for intelligence. They should learn what it means to abide with reason. They should through sustained effort achieve accessions of intellectual power. They should, in brief, . . . come to know what is really meant by the intellectual life.[11]

Frank Aydelotte recognized, as must indeed every serious student of the nature of the educational process, that it is far more than a process of absorption:

The amount of knowledge which a student can accumulate in his college years is limited in any case, and to us at Swarthmore it seems clear that the most useful thing the college can do for him is to train his mind and develop his power of thought.[12]

The small denominational colleges have, quite naturally, applauded Christian education as the supreme value of the higher learning. These colleges, which have slowly, and often inconspicuously, slipped quietly away from denominational inspiration and support and have come to regard themselves as being "independently endowed," have been careful not to forsake the faith of the founding fathers. The growth of state universities greatly intensified concern of the service of higher education to the commonwealth, though Jefferson had stressed this role of education many decades earlier.[13]

But "mental discipline" has been regarded as the primary purpose of education from the time when John Harvard made his historic bequest to the struggling colonial college at New Town on the banks of the Charles and the assembled pastors laid their books on the table in Samuel Russell's parsonage "for the founding of a college in this colony." "It is a hard

*ligation of the Universities to the Social Order*, ed. H. P. Fairchild. New York. New York University Press. 1933. p. 7.

[11] Edmund E. Day. "Inaugural Address." *Proceedings and Addresses at the Inauguration of Edmund Ezra Day, Fifth President of Cornell University*. Ithaca, N.Y. Cornell University Press. 1937. pp. 29–30.

[12] "Report of the President of Swarthmore College." American Association of University Professors. *Bulletin*. vol. 23 (March 1937), p. 251.

[13] Thomas Jefferson. *Notes on the State of Virginia*. Chapel Hill. University of North Carolina Press. 1955. pp. 146–51.

saying," wrote Samuel Eliot Morison in his history of Harvard, "but Mr. Eliot, more than any other man, is responsible for the greatest educational crime of the century against American youth—depriving him of his classical heritage."[14]

The philosophies of Eliot and Dewey have, after a fashion, been reborn in the student activism of the late 1960s, and the impact of this burgeoning student power upon educational theory is still to be evaluated. That education has many shortcomings no one can rightly deny, but neither is there evidence that the students have valid solutions to their educational problems. Education by its very nature is *not* democratic, any more than is the practice of medicine. The student should have a voice in his educational experience, but that experience should not be under his control. Education implies discipline, not a ruthless authoritarian discipline of some man-made academic hierarchy, but a discipline of the intellectual powers, and such discipline does not grow out of chaos.

The aim of education, then, is not so much to impart learning, as to develop the capacity to learn. All too often, John W. Gardner charges, we are "stuffing" the heads of our students "with the products of earlier innovation rather than teaching them how to innovate. We think of the mind as a storehouse to be filled rather than as an instrument to be used."[15]

"The university cannot remake a world," said Daniel Bell. "It cannot even remake man. But it can liberate young people by making them aware of the forces that impel them from within and constrict them from without. It is in this sense, the creation of self-consciousness in relation to tradition, that the task of education is metaphysics, metasociology, metapsychology, and, in exploring the nature of its own communications, metaphilosophy and metalanguage."[16] In much the same sense Gardner speaks of the first purpose of education as the fostering of "individual fulfillment . . . to nurture the free, rational, responsible men and women without whom our kind of society cannot endure."[17]

Paul Weiss, Sterling Professor of Philosophy at Yale, has written of the task of education in terms peculiarly relevant to the professional school. The task, he said, "is to teach the student to try to realize ideals more

---

[14] Samuel Eliot Morison. *Three Centuries of Harvard.* Cambridge, Mass. Harvard University Press. 1936. p. 389.

[15] John W. Gardner. *No Easy Victories.* New York. Harper and Row. 1968. p. 68.

[16] Daniel Bell. *The Reforming of General Education.* New York. Columbia University Press. 1966. p. 152.

[17] Gardner. *No Easy Victories.* p. 69. See also: idem. *Excellence.* New York. Harper. 1961.

comprehensive and fundamental than those which are usually socially cherished." Education, he goes on to say, "is society's way of making society better, by directing students to truths and values not now enjoyed, cherished, or perhaps known. It should not be viewed, as Dewey does, as an agency for preserving the values of the society. At the very best, school is a means by which these values are focussed on in order to be transmitted and *transformed*."[18]

In a somewhat more pragmatic vein than that of Weiss, Henry Steele Commager told the students and faculty of the University of Kentucky: "The next generation is going to need proportionately far more doctors, engineers, librarians, architects, biologists, psychologists, poets, musicians, and statesmen than the past, for the elementary reason that the tasks that have to be done require more and more experience. Therefore, perhaps the most urgent task facing the educational establishment in this or any country is the manufacture of intelligence."[19]

## THE NATURE OF A UNIVERSITY

The design of an educational system, and a university as one form of educational system, is a resultant, of five variables, or forces: (a) a set of educational goals, either implied or specifically stated; (b) the characteristics of the students; (c) a given educational pattern or configuration; (d) a body, or bodies, of knowledge relevant to the needs of the culture; and (e) the environment. No system, however carefully designed, can maximize all of these variables at any one time. Bentham's doctrine of "the greatest good for the greatest number" is a goal that, as von Neumann and Morgenstern have shown in the *Theory of Games and Economic Behavior*,[20] is mathematically impossible. Thus, at the outset, it must be recognized that anyone who seeks a more nearly perfect educational world must inevitably be faced with irreconcilable choices. Education, as much as politics, is the art of compromise.

---

[18] Paul Weiss. *The Making of Men.* Carbondale, Ill. Southern Illinois University Press. 1967. p. 34. (Italics are his.)

[19] Henry Steele Commager. "The University and the Community of Learning." *The Commonwealth of Learning*, by Henry Steele Commager. New York. Harper & Row. 1968. p. 199. See also: Brand Blanshard. "Value: The Polestar of Education." *The Goals of Higher Education*, ed. William D. Weatherford, Jr. Cambridge, Mass. Harvard University Press. 1960. pp. 76–98.

[20] John von Neumann and Oskar Morgenstern. *The Theory of Games and Economic Behavior.* 3rd ed. New York. Wiley. 1964.

Jacques Barzun states at the very beginning of his study of the modern American university, that it is like no other anywhere in the world, and that it is set apart by its structure, management, sources of support, relation to Church and State, and its responsibility to the public. "As for the one element that universities share all over the world—teachers and students—it is, despite appearances, less homogeneous in interest and purpose than it used to be, hence cannot be relied upon to give a uniform character and destiny to culturally diverse institutions."[21] Richard Hofstadter espoused much the same point of view when he told the assembly at the 1968 Columbia University commencement that a university is "a community of a very special kind—a community devoted to inquiry. It exists so that its members may inquire into truths of all sorts. Its presence marks our commitment to the idea that somewhere in society there must be an organization in which anything can be studied or questioned—not merely safe and established things but difficult and inflammatory things. . . . It is governed by the ideal of academic freedom applicable to faculty and students."[22]

The university developed, as it emerged from medieval Europe, three basic and clearly defined purposes: to prepare young men for the professions of law, medicine, the clergy, and, perhaps, teaching; to preserve the heritage of the past and to pass it on intact to future generations; and to expand the boundaries of knowledge through research, the last being the great contribution of Göttingen and her sister universities in Germany during the eighteenth and nineteenth centuries. To this triadic function the two great universities of England added a fourth, which was to train an elite class for the responsibilities and tasks of government.

Because the American colonies were unable to establish universities they created something quite different, the independent American college, which remains to this day a uniquely American development, occupying an intermediate zone between the high or preparatory school and the university. Throughout the Colonial period and even into the early decades of the Republic, American students were quite young; boys entered Harvard or Yale at the age of twelve or thirteen, while a John Trumbull or a Cotton Mather could enroll at an even earlier age. Not only were these students young, but also, for the most part, they came from simple middle class households without learning and sophistication. Hence they had to be taught elementary subjects in a sharply defined and prescribed cur-

---

[21] Jacques Barzun. *The American University*. New York. Harper & Row. 1968. p. 1.
[22] Richard Hofstadter. "The 214th Columbia University Commencement Address." *The American Scholar*. vol. 37 (Autumn 1968), p. 584.

riculum. Thus evolved the long tradition that students must be taught only in formal courses, and that they are intellectually, physically, and morally in *statu pupiliari*, characteristics which are still extremely strong in higher education.

In the latter half of the nineteenth century when the first American universities came into being, they were not substitutes for the college, but rather extensions of it, and their standards were, in the main, collegiate rather than those of a true university. Perhaps because the antecedents of the college were Cambridge and Edinburgh and those of the university Göttingen, Berlin, and Leipsig, an academic schizophrenia resulted. Moreover, education in a democratically oriented society is certain to differ from that in an authoritarian state. Because the new nation did not have the agencies to carry on the work of research and other cultural activities as did the Old World, such functions and responsibilities were given to the universities, and as a consequence there developed schools of agriculture, engineering, social work, hotel administration, and even librarianship. There emerged, therefore, at such campuses as Cornell and the great state universities, institutions that were not limited to the four conventional "faculties," nor to the traditional functions of training and research, and there developed a miscellaneous agglomeration of heterogeneous activities, academic and otherwise. As Henry Steele Commager has said, "By the twentieth century the special character of higher education in the U.S. was pretty well set. It was an education that was to be open to all, that was dominated by the collegiate idea, that inevitably took on the habits of *in loco parentis*. It was required to teach everything that society wanted taught or that special interest groups in society were strong enough to get taught; and it was expected to acquiesce in the democratic notion that all subjects were equal; it was expected to respond to all the demands of government or society, to serve these masters in every way that it could serve."[23]

A university, then, is not just a big college, nor is it made by grafting onto the undergraduate curriculum some advanced courses in selected academic or professional subjects. Though, historically, the university was related to the college, the essential difference between them derived from

[23] Henry Steele Commager. "Are Today's Universities Relevant?" Syndicated article in the *Cleveland Plain Dealer*. (Sunday, June 22, 1969), p. 1-AA. Also: Jacques Barzun. "Tomorrow's University—Back to the Middle Ages?" *Saturday Review*. vol. 52. (November 15 1969), pp. 23–25 and 60–61; John W. Aldridge. "In the Country of the Young." *Harper's Magazine*. vol. 239 (October–November 1969) pp. 56–64; 93–107; Robert F. Goheen. *The Human Nature of a University*. Princeton. Princeton University Press. 1969.

the former's "enlarged conception of the social role of higher education," and its unique "contribution can be summed up in a word: research. Both the college and the university existed to teach, to treasure, and to transmit knowledge, but for the university the task of *adding* to knowledge was primary."[24] "The idea of the university," wrote Karl Jaspers, "derives its educational force from the primary human will to know."[25] The emergence of the modern American university coincided with the rise of industrialism, the growth of corporate business enterprise, increasing urbanization of the population, a changing and increasingly complex social structure, and the advancement and heightening prestige of science. The university, and the professional schools which proliferated within it, were molded by all of these changes. "The intensified division of intellectual labor reflected an enlarged functional complexity of society outside the academic walls. The most urgent demand of this society was for specialized skills, and the definition of skills fell increasingly under the influence of the natural sciences. . . . The attempt to be 'scientific' therefore spread from the sciences themselves into every sphere of intellectual life."[26] With all of these forces beating upon the university and each demanding its share of attention, small wonder that John S. Millis declared that in a university the forces of unity are less strong than those of diversity, or Harry Gideonse, when he spoke of the university's lack of organic cohesion, characterized it as "atomism packed tight."[27]

Teaching, research, and public service are the three missions of the modern university, wrote James A. Perkins in expressing a widely held view, therefore the university's integrity demands that the coherence of its several roles be maintained—"the harmony with which it is able to pursue its aims—whatever their special nature."[28] But "the university is no longer a self-sufficient world: it has a central role in the drama of higher education in the world at large. The university must achieve not only an internal harmony, but a harmony that is in a state of constant adaptation to the outside world."[29]

[24] Richard Hofstadter and C. DeWitt Hardy. *The Development and Scope of Higher Education in the United States*. New York. Columbia University Press. 1952. p. 57.
[25] Karl Jaspers. *The Idea of the University*. London. Peter Owen. 1959. p. 66.
[26] Hofstadter and Hardy. *Higher Education*. p. 57.
[27] Harry Gideonse. "The Values of Youth and Accelerated Social Dislocation." *Modern Educational Development; Another Look*. Report of the 30th Educational Conference of the Educational Records Bureau. New York. 1966. p. 3.
[28] James A. Perkins. *The University in Transition*. Princeton. Princeton University Press. 1966. p. 33.
[29] *Ibid*. p. 59

Clark Kerr sees the university of the future as a "multiversity." Its justification is to be found in its historical emergence and its consistency with the social *milieu*. "It has few peers in the preservation, and dissemination, and examination of the eternal truths; no living peers in the search for new knowledge. Inconsistent internally as an institution, it is consistently productive. Torn by change, it has the stability of freedom."[30]

John R. Platt has represented the modern university as a "five-legged animal," of which four legs are: "the knowledge of everything that a man has done, or written, or thought, . . . the transmission of this knowledge to the next generation, . . . the generation of discovery of new insights or new knowledge in literature and the arts and the sciences, . . . the application of all this knowledge in writing and consulting and inventing, for its value to industry and government and the public. . . . The fifth leg of the complete animal is innovation—the trunk of this wise elephant, let us say, reaching forward to grasp the future. By innovation I mean a different kind of public service, . . . the kind that enlarges the achievements of man and transforms societies, . . . input-output matrices and Keynesian economics, that show us how to avoid economic dislocations and depressions, or theories of information and feedback and competitive decision-making and operations analysis, that change our whole approach to problems of communication and conflict and organizational structure. . . . The universities are coming to be not only repositories of knowledge and trainers for the future but places where the most important contribution may be the search for new understanding and the combining of ideas into new patterns."[31]

Robert Paul Wolff has rejected the declared purposes of the universities as a basis for his analysis of academic norms, and has turned instead to four basic models which would appear to encompass the range of contemporary suppositions about the university's function: the university as "a sanctuary for scholarship," as a "training camp for the professions," as a "social service station," and as an "assembly line for establishment men." The last he regards as an "anti-model," that is, what the university appears to be to the student radical.[32] Wolff's treatment of the

[30] Clark Kerr. *The Uses of the University.* Cambridge, Mass. Harvard University Press. 1963. pp. 6 and 45.

[31] John R. Platt. "The University as a Five-Legged Animal." *Science.* vol. 165 (August 15, 1969), p. 649. Cf. José Ortega y Gasset. *The Mission of the University.* New York. Norton. 1944. Chapter 2. "The Fundamental Question."

[32] Robert Paul Wolff. *The Ideal of the University.* Boston. Beacon Press. 1969. Hutchins complains that the modern university is not "being thought of as an autonomous community of masters and scholars pursuing the truth," but rather as "the

university as "training camp for the professions" is particularly relevant to the present study, for it is this practice that has probably done more than any other to dilute and adulterate education for librarianship. The demand for professional training, in all areas, has tended to make large segments of the undergraduate curricula resemble trial runs for the professions. Such downgraded professional training tends to encourage excessive specialization. Even more serious in its effects, is the strong tendency to present substantive materials in terms only of the profession attached to it.

The central role of the university has changed little over the centuries —through the art of teaching and the explorations of research to refine, organize, and transmit knowledge to successive generations of students. To this traditional statement of double purpose, there has been added the responsibility to give or provide services, a response mainly to the needs of certain professional schools, such as medicine, nursing, education, and social work, where it is desirable and even essential that the student be given supervised experience with those aspects of his work which can best be learned in an operating situation. Universities have tended to move slowly and with caution in the direction of providing services, because of the belief that a university is not a service agency and large-scale commitments to service will jeopardize teaching and research by diverting energies and resources to which they have the prior claim. But the assumption of service responsibilities has been justified on the basis that in many professions initiates cannot be adequately prepared without "clinical" practice and that some research can be done only in a service situation. Thus, service has been regarded as a means to an end, not an end in itself, and if in the process some people are cured of a disease, have the discomforts of hospitalization eased, their teeth repaired, or their family problems straightened out, so much the better. Thus, as John S. Millis has pointed out, service is not really a purpose of the university.[33] Rather one should say that service provides a pedagogical and research environment in which students can learn more effectively and inquiry can be conducted more reliably than is possible in the conventional classroom or laboratory. The real duty of higher ed-

---

nerve center of the knowledge industry, dedicated to national power, prosperity, and prestige." Robert M. Hutchins. *The Learning Society.* New York. Praeger. 1968. p. 105.

[33] John S. Millis. "A University President's Perspective." *Medical Ventures and the University: New Values and New Validities.* Evanston, Ill. Association of American Medical Colleges. 1967. Chapter 9. pp. 157–63.

ucation is to educate leaders, not to be a doctor for the nation's social ills. When a university conducts services as ends in themselves it has lost its way and is prostituting its social mission.

The university of today would seem to be confronted by two major problems that are central to its success. The first is the need to redefine the purpose, functions, and role of the university in the setting of contemporary social circumstances, and the second is the imperative to renovate the university's anachronistic organization and administration.[34] Four forces are pressing against the university of today that impel a modification of its statement of purpose. The first, and perhaps the most important so far as this study is concerned, is the tremendous growth of human knowledge, and the impact of that growth upon the changing balance between science and art, between knowledge and skill. Historically art has preceded science in the sense that skills have been developed based upon experience rather than theory. The historical development of library practice is an excellent illustration of this chronology, as are many of the sciences and the professions.

The second force acting upon the university is the very sharp decline in the time interval between the discovery of knowledge and its application or introduction in practice—from test tube to box car as the chemist is wont to say. For most of man's history, knowledge has accumulated slowly, and only recently has its rate of growth become exponential. Today, however, science has caught up with art and in some fields has surpassed it; as a consequence knowledge and skill are much more closely related and interdependent than they have ever been, while the lines of demarcation between science and art are becoming less and less distinct. One might rightly say that knowing and doing are now one world, not two, as they were, for example, in the golden age of Athens.

The third force is the insistent demand by society that knowledge be put to immediate and practical use. Because the university has consistently produced knowledge from which new skills were derived, there is the ever increasing expectation that this transformation will increase in velocity in the future, and when it does not happen society is disturbed and impatient. In short, the public demands that box cars come from test tubes with ever-increasing rapidity and volume. This expectation holds true for the social as well as the physical sciences, but it tends to mitigate against theoretical research by distracting the attention of the university always toward immediate and practical ends.

---

[34] *Ibid.* p. 157. Much of this and following paragraphs are drawn from the Millis essay.

This demand for immediate results has led to the fourth force that reacts upon the university: that the professor descend from his alleged ivory tower and be a doer as well as a knower. This recurrent demand that the modern professor be a man of affairs has, without question, contributed greatly to bringing the university into the mainstream of the life that flows about its ivy-covered walls, and it is all to the good so long as it does not draw the academic community away from its true purpose. But the benefits of community participation have sometimes been abused to the point at which the professor has been more concerned with what goes on outside his classroom and laboratory than what goes on within them. To maintain a balance is no simple or easy task. Moreover, this force does create inequalities and imbalance among the faculties of a university. Society calls upon the physicist and mathematician to help in winning the race in outer space, the urban sociologist in preventing juvenile delinquency, the political scientist in solving the complex problems of government, the educational psychologist in aiding the slow learner. Today's professor is a new kind of "wandering scholar."[35] But, in the areas of the humanities the gulf between knowing and doing seems almost as wide as it ever was. The art historian and aesthetician are members of the faculty, but painters and sculptors practice their art outside the university. The musicologist and the historian of the drama are in the university, but the composer and the actor are in show business. The university today is both ivory tower and marketplace which may well necessitate a reassessment of the purpose of the university.

This reassessment will not be easily achieved, it will be won at a heavy cost in shattered ideals. These historic disputes of learned men prove that "controversy is essential to a healthy condition in the citadel of learning."[36] The real purpose to which the university must be dedicated is the never-ending search "to find what fancies of the human brain are warranted and what are not . . . to find standards for . . . adapting new ideas as part of the cultural heritage."[37] There can be no doubt that the growth of knowledge and achievement in action are the products of "both conflict and cooperation, both a struggle among beliefs and a sharing of beliefs. These are the terms on which those within the citadel of learn-

---

[35] Barzun. *American University*. Chapter 2. "Scholars in Orbit."

[36] James B. Conant. *The Citadel for Learning*. New Haven. Yale University Press. 1956. p. 9. See also: Robert Brustein. "The Crisis at the University." *Revolution as Theatre*, by Robert Brustein. New York. Liveright. 1971. pp. 85–170 and Nathan Glazer. *Remembering the Answers*. New York. Basic Books. 1970.

[37] Conant. *Citadel for Learning*. p. 10.

ing have lived and worked effectively in the past; these are the only terms which will ensure the safety and vitality of the citadel in the future."[38]

## THE SEARCH FOR COHERENCE

The planning of the undergraduate curriculum is a search for unity. The classical tradition in education possessed a unity peculiarly its own, a unity that derived from the Seven Liberal Arts enriched by the philosophy of the ancient world. But the so-called free-elective system introduced by President Eliot opened to the American student a flood of specialized knowledge then streaming from the great European universities. Over the intervening decades this flood has swelled until it threatens the coherence, the intellectual discipline, of the undergraduate program. To this problem the "area of concentration" or "major" was only a partial solution. Such areas of concentration became increasingly vocational and threatened further the unity of the college, and there emerged an enormous variety of aims and methods among colleges, and on a smaller scale, within any one college. Thus was liberal education robbed of structural design or even of any clear coherent meaning. The reversion to the classical tradition as exemplified in liberal, or general, education was a reaction against Eliot's introduction of electives, John Dewey's emphasis on the *process* of learning and the *continuity* of experience, and a growing institutionalization of the college and the university in which the department was the locus and object of power rather than a larger entity that would have cut across conventional interdisciplinary lines. Thus emerged at such institutions as the University of Chicago, Harvard, Columbia, and Yale a curriculum that was largely prescribed and unvarying, and based on a conception of "eternal verities"—a hierarchy of knowledge, as the specification of a major tradition of thought—or of a body of great or fundamental ideas or great books as the organizing concept of the course.[39]

---

[38] *Ibid.* p. 21. Cf. Weiss's statement that a university is "a combination of colleges, professional schools, and graduate schools in equipoise." English universities, he holds, have tended to neglect the graduate schools and concentrated on the college. Continental universities have tended to emphasize graduate study. If the American university is to draw from both the English and Continental models it must bring them into balance. Weiss. *Making of Men.* pp. 106–7.

[39] Bell. *Reforming of General Education.* p. 24 ff. Also: Russell Thomas. *The Search*

The restoration of unity was sought along a number of quite divergent paths. There were those (exemplified by the experiments at St. John's College at Annapolis) who sought this unity in a course of study which emphasized the great writings of the European and American past, and certainly there is much that is commendable in this view. But in certain areas, particularly the sciences, innovation rather than tradition was the fundamental characteristic of the scholarship, and students soon discovered that so thorough a foundation in the "great books" of science left them unprepared for the revolutionary changes that science was experiencing. Thus the pragmatists turned to science itself, and the scientific method, for this saving unity; but they were immediately confronted by the vexing question of whether the so-called scientific attitude could be applied with validity to the entire horizon of life. Subsequently, there were those who recognized the spirit of change in contemporary life, and reacted against an educational philosophy that had emphasized the traditions of Western civilization; they, therefore, cast off the traditional and formalized divisions of knowledge and attempted to organize the student's educational program around contemporary problems and questions which young people might be expected to meet in mature life. Overt manifestations of this philosophy were more apparent in the high school than in the college, but higher education was by no means immune to it. It relentlessly severed the student's association with his past and left him without roots; it ignored the obvious fact that the present is the product of the past and can be comprehended only in terms of historic origins. It fell a victim to its own timeliness by failing to consider that because conditions within contemporary society change with great rapidity, there is no assurance that the problems which students study today will have any resemblance to those which they will face tomorrow. Relevance to the present, then, cannot be made a unifying principle for the simple reason that it is a point of view, an attitude of mind, on the part of the instructor rather than a basic theory of education.

Adler and Mayer have sought unity in the harmonizing of nature and art, which they believe to be the peculiar characteristic of the educational process. Learning is natural to man, they assert, because "he learns by experience and discovery from both the human and non-human events in his environment." But man also learns by instruction "of an intentional and methodical character known as teaching," and this is an art. Man readily accepts both types of learning, and the product of this pro-

---

*for a Common Learning.* New York. McGraw-Hill. 1962. Part 1. "The Historical Background of General Education."

cess of education, "the altered condition of the learner, who moves from ignorance or error to knowledge, is a natural product. But it is also a product of art."[40]

Thus for Adler and Mayer the unity of education is externally derived, it is a unity of process inherent in the fact that "the essence of education is human association, of adults with children and of adults with adults. It is, therefore, in any well-developed society, one of the greatest of all social enterprises, . . . society's practical effort to maintain and improve the peculiar combination of the practical and artistic processes of education."[41]

The educational philosophy of Adler and Mayer make an interesting comparison with that of Jacques Maritain who may well have been influential in the forming of their own thought. Maritain holds that higher education should restrict itself to "universal knowledge," universal in the sense that all the parts of human knowledge would be represented in its "architecture of teaching." This architecture would be planned according to the "qualitative and internal hierarchy of human knowledge," and "from the bottom to the top," the arts and sciences would be grouped and organized according to their growing value in "spiritual universality."[42] Thus he sees four orders of subjects: the first would be concerned with the realm of useful arts and applied sciences; the second with the realm of "those practical sciences—practical either because they belong to the domain of art or because they belong to the domain of ethics"; the third would be the realm of the speculative sciences and fine arts, that is "with the liberal arts proper and with that disinterested knowledge of nature and man and of the achievements of culture which liberates the mind by truth and beauty"; and the fourth with philosophy in all its manifestations.[43] In the university, these four orders would be represented by a "Teaching City" comprised of a cluster of "Institutes" that would be related to each other in a variety of ways rather than established as separate Faculties. The first Teaching City would be concerned with the "technical means of human life . . . the practical domination and utilization of matter"; the second with the means for the maintenance of human life itself; the third with the intellectual ends of human life; and the fourth with "the Trans-sensible realm of Being, Spirit, and Divine Reality, and

---

[40] Mortimer J. Adler and Milton Mayer. *The Revolution in Education*. Chicago. University of Chicago Press. 1958. pp. 37–38.

[41] *Ibid*. pp. 38–39.

[42] Jacques Maritain. *Education at the Crossroads*. New Haven. Yale University Press. 1943. pp. 76–77.

[43] *Ibid*. pp. 77–78.

the ethical realm of the aims, conditions, and rational ordering of human freedom and conduct."[44] The medieval ancestry of such an educational program is unmistakable.

Philip H. Phenix, who is professor of philosophy and education in Columbia University's Teachers' College, has based a projected curriculum upon six possible types or "realms" of human meaning: *Symbolics* (language, mathematics, nondiscursive symbolic forms); *Empirics* (physical science, biology, psychology, social science); *Esthetics* (music, visual arts, arts of movement, literature); *Synnoetics* (personal knowledge); *Ethics* (moral knowledge); and *Synoptics* (history, religion, philosophy). From these realms of meaning Phenix elaborates a philosophical theory for the curriculum of general education based on the idea of logical patterns in disciplined understanding. His central thesis is that knowledge in the disciplines has patterns or structures and that an understanding of these typical forms is essential to guidance in teaching and learning.[45] The program he envisages has much relevance to the undergraduate preparation of the librarian, and in many respects would seem to be very close to an ideal.

So the search continues, as it inevitably must, for a unifying philosophy of higher education that will provide a durable frame of reference within which the college and the high school can perform their appointed tasks. This educational philosophy must seek a harmony between the traditions of Western civilization and those of other cultures to meet the demands of the contemporary scene. It must provide the youth with substantial roots in the past, with competence for the present, and with adaptability to the future. Its logic must have sufficient depth for the acceptance of the total richness and variation of modern life, and strength enough to give goals and direction to the educational system. It must be sought in the peculiar character of the American civilization, a civilization which is not entirely New World since it derived from the old; one not wholly given to innovation since it acknowledges certain fixed values. It must embody, as the authors of the Harvard study of general education have said,

. . . certain tangibles of the American spirit, in particular, perhaps, the ideal of cooperation on the level of action irrespective of agree-

---

[44] *Ibid.* pp. 78–79.

[45] Philip H. Phenix. *Realms of Meaning; A Philosophy of the Curriculum for General Education.* New York. McGraw-Hill. 1964.

Reference should also be made to: G. W. Ford and Lawrence Pugno, eds. *The Structure of Knowledge and the Curriculum.* Chicago. Rand McNally. 1964.

ment on ultimates—which is to say, belief in the worth and meaning of the human spirit, however one may understand it. Such a belief rests on that hard but very great thing, tolerance not from absence of standards but through possession of them.[46]

The unity of education, then, is to be found in an understanding of the social phylogeny of the culture, the environment from which it evolved, the influences by which it is shaped, the possible directions of its future development. For as the aim of education is the training of the intellect, so education must concern itself with man as primarily an intellectual being. But, inasmuch as the intellect cannot properly be divorced from its biological and social environment, these aspects of the human experience cannot be neglected. For as the ontogeny is said to recapitulate the phylogeny, so must the education of the individual recapitulate the intellectual experience of the culture, and the student can prepare himself adequately for the life that stretches out before him only by reliving in a limited but intense way the intellectual life of his cultural antecedents.

## THE SECONDARY SCHOOL

One should emphasize that the attribute of unity is not restricted to the higher learning, but should pervade the entire educational system. The American college cannot be held completely responsible for all the ills by which it is beset. Certainly much of the inability of the college to define objectives and achieve a satisfactory unity arises from the failure of secondary education to provide it with an adequate scholastic base. Perhaps the high school is more to be pitied than censured; the Harvard Committee on General Education defended the secondary school at least to the point of observing that it has "the incomparably difficult task of meeting, in ways which it will severally respect and respond to, masses of students of every conceivable shade of intelligence, background, means, interest, and experience. Unlike the old high school in which no one was compelled to stay if he could not or did not wish to do the work, the modern high school must find a place for every kind of student whatever his hopes and talents. . . . The tendency is always to strike a somewhat colorless mean, too fast for the slow, too slow for the fast."[47]

But however one may excuse or explain its shortcomings, one cannot

---

[46] Harvard University. *Education in Free Society.* p. 41.
[47] *Ibid.* p. 9.

escape the obvious fact that the modern high school, with its proliferation of courses and its ever-lengthening calendar of extracurricular activities, suffers from a confusion of goals, misdirected emphases, inadequate instruction, increasing public apathy, and lack of support. Its basic anti-intellectualism all but crushes the spirit of the superior student, while rewarding mediocrity. Only when the college is freed from the necessity to correct the inadequacies of the high school can it achieve any substantial progress in developing its own rational program and meeting its own responsibilities. The downgrading, the lowering of standards, that permeates the entire educational system stretching to the doctoral examination, can be arrested only by bold and constructive action at the level of secondary education.

James B. Conant has placed the responsibility for educational reform at all levels, even the elementary, squarely on the shoulders of the graduate and professional schools:

> The place to begin to set standards in American Education is at the last rung of the educational ladder—the graduate level. Requirements for admission to law and medical schools and to graduate schools of arts and sciences should include evidence by examination of a wide and solid academic education. The requirements might be as follows: the ability to write a competent essay; a good reading, writing, and speaking knowledge of at least one modern foreign language; a knowledge of mathematics through the calculus; a knowledge of physics, chemistry, and biology at the freshman level of our most rigorous colleges; at the same level of competence, knowledge of American history and political institutions and English and American literature.[48]

Conant would have the secondary curriculum emphasize five basic areas: (a) history and related social sciences; (b) English composition and literature; (c) mathematics; (d) the physical sciences; and (e) foreign language.

It is interesting that the head of the department of physics at the University of Illinois, in writing about the education of scientists and engineers, who argues vigorously for increased specialization in the high school program, should emphasize history and literature so strongly. Of history he says:

---

[48] James B. Conant. *Slums and Suburbs*. New York. McGraw-Hill. 1961. p. 145.

To the extent possible we must cultivate a general awareness of the principles first appreciated by Polybius, that the successes and failures of societies do not just happen but have a variety of sources which are deeply rooted in the societies. More explicitly, American wealth and strength is not a birthright of our population, but can be retained in the future only by doing the proper things. Our secondary schools must place more emphasis on world history, and not merely on domestic and regional history. The history of Mesopotamia, Greece, Rome, or Europe is basically as important to the average American as the facts surrounding our own Revolution or Civil War. In fact, the importance of our national history becomes completely comprehensible only when viewed in the light of the former.[49]

To the fundamental study of history this physicist would add the related studies in the sciences of society, especially economics and government. Of English composition and literature, he wrote,

The ability to formulate one's ideas in clear concise English and to comprehend the ideas of others is still the most critical aspect of education for science and engineering as for most other fields.

The logical discipline of mathematics underlies all knowledge, not merely the physical sciences, and its neglect has brought great deficiencies to the education of youth. Some understanding of the physical world is not only essential to man's adaptation to his environment, but it supplies avenues to knowledge which may reveal hidden talents for later specialization. Finally, a knowledge of foreign language, training in which should have begun in the elementary school, will help to overcome a provincialism which in a world of international tensions we can no longer afford, and will eliminate the embarrassment which every American feels when he encounters a situation in which reliance upon at least one language other than his own is required. The ineptness of the average American scholar in any language other than English has long been a national disgrace that is increasingly serious.[50]

---

[49] Frederick Seitz. "Factors Concerning Education for Science and Engineering." *Physics Today*. vol. 11, no. 7 (July 1958), p. 15.

[50] See: James D. Koerner, ed. *The Case for Basic Education; A Program of Aims for Public Schools*. Boston. Little, Brown. 1959.

## THE UNDERGRADUATE PROGRAM AND GENERAL EDUCATION

Rooted in the educational system of Classical Greece and shaped by the curriculum of the Seven Liberal Arts of Medieval Scholasticism, the concept of general, or liberal, education emerged as a response to the need for unity in the college program, as a reaction against the chaos that was resulting from the free elective system, and as a rejection of progressive education. Perhaps, most of all, general education was a protest against rising vocationalism in the college. Doubtless such statements are a simplification of the complex origins of general education, but certainly these forces played a major part in stimulating its popularity.

General education is, as Jencks and Riesman have said, not easily defined. They would consider it more "a mood" than a movement, especially if the term "movement" implies a specific organization, program, or a common sense of identity.[51]

Behind the concept of general, or liberal education is an image, an image of "the whole man," a kind of modern version of the Renaissance man, a man who is articulate, with a feeling for clarity of expression, and a competence in some language other than his own; he must be at home in the world of quantity, numbers, and measurement; he must be able to think rationally, logically, and objectively; he knows much about the world of nature and the society of which he is a part; he is sensitive to aesthetic values; he is aware of his cultural heritage; he knows his responsibilities as a citizen; he acts with maturity and a perspective that is born of wisdom, conviction, and tolerance; he has an understanding of method without being a "methodist"; he possesses a sense of values both social and personal; in him the "two cultures" are united; he is a humanist in the broadest sense. The liberally educated man has not been poured into a mold, he is not a type, but always a unique person in which his attributes as a citizen and a social being are balanced with individuality.

George Stoddard has defined liberal education in terms of four standards: (a) the content must be enduring, not ephemeral, trivial, or merely descriptive—abstract principles, not techniques, must be constantly emphasized; (b) subjects must be approached as a whole, not as fragmented parts; (c) the student should approach the course without reference to

[51] Christopher Jencks and David Riesman. *The Academic Revolution*. Garden City, N.Y. Doubleday. 1968. p. 492.

immediate, practical, or technical applications; and (d) "liberal education is a common language . . . while based upon the most advanced thinking, and creating it is a form of intellectual currency that can be acquired in some degree by every student."[52] One may say that there is general agreement that a liberal, or general, education should include an exploration of meanings, and the relationships among them, with particular attention to problems of values; it should involve an exploration of the empirical, rational, and mystical approaches to knowledge; it should involve familiarity with both inductive and deductive reasoning; and it should encourage the student to ask questions, even those for which there are no firm answers.[53]

General education can be structured in a variety of patterns. It may be organized about the conventional academic disciplines, or it may be developed in large interdisciplinary segments that cut across traditional course boundaries. In some institutions which have received wide public attention it has been oriented around "the Great Books," or "great ideas." Though curriculum structure is not to be deprecated it is less important than the attitudes of the students and teachers and the spirit of inquiry which animates the academic atmosphere.

Two lectures delivered in 1963 shook the foundations of liberal education, which up to that time had seemed so firm, and revealed the ferment that was even then beginning to change the psychology of the academic world. The first was Clark Kerr's discourse on the "multiversity" mentioned above; in the second, Jacques Barzun charged that "both teachers and students are responding to the spirit of the times. They are impatient with everything that is not directed at the development of talent into competence. . . . The meaning of this is plain: the liberal arts tradition is dead or dying. . . . The trend seems to me so clear that to object would be like trying to sweep back the ocean. It would be foolish to repine or try to prolong a tradition that has run its course."[54] Though both Kerr and Barzun described the academic situation as they saw it, they immediately became the whipping boys of change as though they had created the forces each had described.

Barzun's warning is substantiated by Jencks and Reisman,[55] while

---

[52] George D. Stoddard. "A New Design for the College of Liberal Arts and Sciences." *School and Society.* vol. 90 (May 1, 1965), pp. 321–23.

[53] Paul Woodring. *The Higher Learning in America.* New York. McGraw-Hill. 1968. pp. 202–3.

[54] Quoted by Fred M. Hechinger. "The Problem of Change." *New York Times Book Review.* July 17, 1966. p. 3.

[55] Jencks and Reisman. *Academic Revolution.* pp. 492–504.

Nicholas von Hoffman sees the rise of the "multiversity" as one of the major causes for the rejection of the liberal curriculum.[56] The history of education, says Woodring, records a continuing battle between those who would educate for immediate and practical ends, and those who "take a longer view";[57] the latter believe that the goal of education is preparation for an expanded life rather than a vocation. The curriculum of most undergraduate colleges represents an uneasy compromise of these two views. There are very strong forces on the side of vocationalism and liberal education will need all the support it can muster. The Land Grant College Act of 1862, the Smith-Hughes Act of 1917, and most recently, the Defense Education Act, all suggest that legislators are prone to look upon education in terms of what the student can do with his education—right now. Yet, the fact remains that the old agricultural college, fostered by the Morrill Act, the polytechnic institutes and schools of mines, are either defunct or have completely changed their characters. Increasingly the schools of engineering are recognizing that at least some liberal education is essential to the engineer if he is to be something other than an alleged "slide-rule boy." One must not forget that there is a fundamental error in Barzun's characterization of the liberal tradition in education as being "dead." The history of American higher education is cyclical: the elective system liberated the college from a cohesive but rigid and obsolete curriculum, while in its beginning general education sought to save the undergraduate program from excessive and dangerous fragmentation. At the present time "single-minded probing in depth," exerts an extremely powerful influence in education, but fragmentation will again eventually have to be arrested, as Daniel Bell well knows and von Hoffman suggests. Perhaps Bell is on the right track when he proposes that there should be a series of courses for seniors in which the liberal arts are brought to bear upon the student's specialty and tested against relevant problems of contemporary society. As every reader of *The Saber-Tooth Curriculum* is aware, it is foolish to prolong a pedagogic convention long after it has lost its utility. But the teaching of today's facts and technologies is more akin to J. Abner Peddiwell's "clubbing little woolly horses"[58] than to the study of the great writings of the world.

[56] Nicholas von Hoffman. *The Multiversity*. New York. Holt, Rinehart, and Winston. 1966.

[57] Woodring. *Higher Learning*. pp. 199–214.

[58] Harold Benjamin. *The Saber-Tooth Curriculum*. New York. McGraw-Hill. 1939. Experiences at the University of California at Santa Cruz point up many of the problems of attempting to reform undergraduate education. See: Luther J. Carter.

Liberal education, to the present generation, may seem remarkably old-fashioned—a prescription from those who are "over thirty" and hence not to be trusted. But the great achievements to the credit of the classical tradition in education cannot be denied, while today's education has often all too willingly followed a popular rejection of intellectual goals. Whether overtly expressed or not, the basic idea underlying all educational practice is a sense of heritage, but heritage is not to be interpreted as meaning mere historical retrospection. Education, at whatever level, seeks to indoctrinate the young into the culture, to make them "good citizens," to bring them into a harmonious relationship with the social and physical environment within which they will lead their lives. Thus, there is always present the impulse to mold the student into a pattern sanctioned by his society, to generate within him an understanding and acceptance of the goals which the culture has created. If this were not so, the society would become discontinuous. Education can, of course, play its part in shaping the culture, but if education departs too drastically from cultural sanctions, either it or the culture must give way; the two cannot long exist in disharmony. Higher education must inevitably be a process of revealing to the student the intellectual forces that have shaped the human mind. Only thus can the student come to understand himself as a part of an organic process in which contemporary standards of judgment, ways of life, and forms of government bear the marks of man's cultural evolution. Only through such understanding can the student become a "good citizen," where being a "good citizen" means not only understanding the mores of his society, but also an ability to contribute in some constructive way to the growth and improvement of that civilization in which he finds himself.

The importance to education of this necessity for citizens capable of growth is difficult to overemphasize. It is impossible to escape the fact that contemporary American society, like any society, rests on the acceptance of a substantial body of common beliefs, and that a major responsibility of education is to perpetuate them. But this imperative is not antithetical to the belief in the need for independent insights leading to change. The emphasis of James and Dewey on pragmatism, science, and the scientific attitude—the knowledge of the scientist that the full truth can never be known and that man must forever be led by facts to revise his approximations of it—is itself a philosophy of education founded on obedience to facts and hospitable to change that is an essential element in the evolution of contemporary thought. The need to promote change, then, does not conflict with a program of education based on the cultural heritage, but

"University of California at Santa Cruz: New Deal for Undergraduates?" *Science.* vol. 171 (January 15, 1971), pp. 153–57.

rather is a fundamental ingredient in it. Therefore man must look back upon antiquity, not because of antiquarian curiosity, but because ancient thought has meaning for contemporary life. The Hellenic concept of an ordered universe, of political freedom flourishing under rational law, and the role of reason in shaping man's inner life, none of these was achieved without painful skepticism, even the sacrifices of martyrdom, and though less dramatic, but no less essential, the tedious observation of the scientist and the hard testing of experience. To comprehend the spirit of Socrates is itself the negation of traditionalism. The great writings of the past are great intellectual monuments not because they *are* old, but because they *were* new. Arnold Toynbee sees in a rapidly changing society general education's most potent argument. "The price of specialization," he has written, "is a myopic and distorted view of the Universe. An effective specialist makes, all too often, a defective citizen and an inadequate human being. . . . Specialization is an answer to the increase in the quantity and complexity of knowledge, but this at a price."[59]

The unity of a general education, then, is to be found, as Clarence Faust has expressed it, in the need "to provide all students with the means for acquiring, and demanding of all students evidence of having acquired, the understanding of society and social institutions, the knowledge of the physical world in which they live and the grasp of the methods employed in the natural sciences, the competence to understand and appreciate literature and the arts, and the ability to express themselves clearly and effectively."[60]

Perhaps no one has enunciated a more eloquent defense of the importance of general education to the professional man, than did John Stewart Mill in his inaugural address at St. Andrews University in 1867:

> Men are men before they are lawyers, or physicians, or merchants, or manufacturers; and if you make them capable and sensible men, they will make themselves capable and sensible lawyers or physicians. What professional men should carry away with them from a University is not professional knowledge, but that which should direct the use of professional knowledge, and bring the light of general culture to illuminate the technicalities of a special pursuit. Men may be competent lawyers without general education, but it depends on general education to make them philosophic lawyers.[61]

---

[59] Arnold J. Toynbee. *Higher Education in a Time of Accelerated Change.* New York. Academy for Educational Development. 1968. pp. 7 and 9.

[60] University of Chicago College. *The Idea and Practice of General Education.* Chicago. University of Chicago Press. 1950. p. 11.

[61] Quoted by Thomas. *Search for Common Learning.* p. vii. Hofstadter discusses the

There could scarcely be a better credo than Mill's statement for the undergraduate preparation of the librarian. If any profession, or neo-profession stands in need of a solid general, or liberal, education, certainly it is librarianship.[62]

Today there are unmistakable indications that all higher education is moving away from a vertical toward a horizontal dimension that transcends traditional disciplinary boundaries to seek a universal function common to all curricula, whether preprofessional or not, quite independent of the administrative divisions which have conventionally separated undergraduate students according to their particular vocational objectives. For the librarian, this trend toward the horizontal is particularly significant because no discipline is more innately interdisciplinary than that which concerns itself with the management and utilization of graphic records, and no knowledge can rightly be regarded as irrelevant to its practice. Librarianship is a service created to benefit all ages of the population and all degrees of intellectual capacity, including those who are intellectually as well as economically disadvantaged. It cannot be self-sufficient and the structure of its preprofessional education cannot be vertical. Librarianship must draw from and be sustained by the three great branches of human knowledge—the humanities, the social sciences, and the sciences—that comprise the several faculties of a university.

The unity of the undergraduate curriculum must be derived from two obvious and simple truths: (1) that the processes of thought for the achievement of truth in one discipline often differs from the processes of

---

anti-intellectual influence which vocational education has exerted on higher education. Richard Hofstadter. *Anti-Intellectualism in American Life.* New York. Random House. 1962. pp. 262–64.

[62] The importance to the librarian of a good general education with some undergraduate specialization was recognized more than a half century ago by Western Reserve University. The Library School *Bulletin* for 1908–1909 recommends that all undergraduates preparing themselves for library careers should study French and German, all the history, literature, and English available to them, with heavy emphasis on psychology, sociology, and economics; and in the sciences, geology, physiography, biology, and "nature study." The concept of a general undergraduate education as a prerequisite for professional study in librarianship was indigenous in the plan proposed by William H. Brett of the Cleveland Public Library and Charles F. Thwing, president of Western Reserve University, to Andrew Carnegie for the establishment of a library school at Western Reserve. Though the Library School opened its doors in 1904, it was not until 1920 that graduates of accredited colleges were admitted without being required to pass a qualifying examination in general education which included the areas of literature, history, science, art, and a reading knowledge of two foreign languages. Western Reserve University. School of Library Science. *Bulletin.* 1908–1909. p. 12.

thought required to attain truth in another; and (2) that the subject matter, methods, and objectives of disciplines which historically have become separate academic departments may be categorized into major groupings with fundamental and essential traits in common, and that these common traits make possible a treatment broader than that of the separate academic departments. These unities are not to be bought at the price of precision and rigor; general education is not to be equated with generality.

The substantive ingredients and their proportion in the student's program will vary according to his interest and the area of librarianship that he chooses to practice, but all, in greater or less degree, must be represented. Thus an inescapable conclusion would seem to be that a sound liberal education during the secondary school and undergraduate years is a prerequisite for every librarian.[63] As Ralph Beals wrote a quarter of a century ago, "A tragic irony of our times is the spectacle of library school faculties, whose natural allegiance lies on the side of the angels, sitting on the sidelines—mute, inglorious, and impotent—while general education, the only defensible preparation for their students, is destroyed by the academic departments and the other professional schools which lay down detailed and conflicting requirements for admission to the advanced instruction offered under their auspices."[64]

## THE BASIC AREAS

The three basic areas of the humanities, the social sciences, and the physical and biological sciences, should not be taught as composites or surveys of selected conclusions from their constituent departmental fields, nor should they be presented as superficial formulations of widely general problems. On the contrary, they should be considered exact, penetrating treatments of the basic principles and methods of each area studied in the most precise and rigorous manner possible within the intellectual comprehension of the student. Through an understanding of the historical development, the present state, the methodology, and the critical appraisal

---

[63] Jesse H. Shera. "Toward a New Dimension for Library Education." *Bulletin of the American Library Association.* vol. 57 (April 1963), pp. 213–17. Also: idem. *Libraries and the Organization of Knowledge.* London. Crosby Lockwood. 1965. pp. 161–67.

[64] Ralph A. Beals. "Education for Librarianship." *Library Quarterly.* vol. 17 (October 1947), p. 299.

of each of these areas, the student will acquire the wisdom—the intellectual capacity—requisite to the formation of sound judgments. The objective is the development of the capacity to formulate clearly the differences among conflicting lines of argument and to discover that critical point nearest to which truth may be believed to lie.

Thus, the task of the humanities program is to promote in the student the intellectual power to formulate judgments which are concerned with the appreciation of the arts of mankind—the training of students in the exercise of those disciplines which contribute to an intelligent appreciation of the creative spirit in whatever form it may manifest itself. The social science sequence should be directed toward an understanding of man's development as a social being, with particular emphasis on a comprehension of the democratic tradition in the resolution of political conflicts, and the expression of human personality in varying social and cultural *milieus*. The objectives of the science program should be to impart an understanding of the conclusions of science, to foster an application of the methods and processes of reasoning through which those conclusions have been reached, and to inculcate in the student attitudes of thought and judgment by which he may follow the application of a scientific discipline in a particular instance to acquire an understanding of the conclusions reached thereby. It is especially important that the student get an understanding of conclusions as resulting from the interpretation of valid evidence and as instruments for the prediction and control of determinable aspects of nature or of natural phenomena.[65]

In these three interdisciplinary sequences and, indeed, throughout the entire program of study, historical perspective must not be sacrificed to an excessive emphasis upon the problem-unit method. Admittedly, the student can learn much from a selective situational analysis, particularly in the social sciences, but even in the physical sciences there is much to be gained from a recapitulation of the experience of mankind as knowledge has grown from generation to generation by each climbing upon the shoulders of its predecessors. At the completion of his course of study, the student should possess a real sense of chronology, of historical continuity, without which he cannot achieve either an understanding of the present or a sense of the future. What is past *is* prologue; there is a unity which binds together the past, the present, and the future, just as there is a unity of knowledge itself. The human adventure is both a temporal and a substantive continuum. The philosophical speculations of Democratus concerning the nature of physical matter have meaning for the "nuclear

---

[65] Thomas. *Search for Common Learning.* Chapter 5.

age" just as the discoveries of the modern scientist ramify throughout man's behavior as a social being, as a creator of the beautiful, or as an inquirer into the meaning of life.

Supporting the basic interdisciplinary sequences are a cluster of auxiliary studies which are essential to the completion of a general education. A liberal education is one that liberates the student's mind, and it accomplishes this by providing him with the intellectual disciplines which will free the mind from slovenly habits of thought. He must learn to analyze and interpret that which he reads and hears, to seek out the premises and conclusions of arguments, to recognize valid evidence, and to discover the presuppositions which have led to the particular choice of the premises employed. Such competence implies not only becoming acquainted with a part of the vast store of human knowledge, but also the means by which knowledge of different kinds is gained, the methods by which hypotheses are formulated, the manner in which premises may lead to conclusions, and the conclusions validated. These intellectual skills necessitate the study of a cluster of related disciplines to which mathematics is central; mathematics not in the narrow sense of manipulating numerical data as a means of reckoning, but in the deeper sense of a discipline that is pertinent to almost every intellectual activity of which man is capable. Mathematics, then, should be supplemented by the study of logic, both classical logic and Boolean algebra, the principles of reasoning and scientific method, and philosophy—studies which will encourage clarity and precision of definition, validity of assumption, and rigorousness of reasoning. To the librarian, particularly, these disciplines are basic because they underlie all classification theory and all attempts to organize knowledge usefully.

Communication is so essential to the culture that proficiency in both its oral and written forms need hardly be emphasized, yet the illiteracy of the average college graduate, not to mention those who have achieved advanced professional degrees, is appalling. In some degree this unhappy situation arises from an erroneous, though perhaps well-intentioned, attempt to make formal courses in English composition into a device for directing the preparation of term papers and other written exercises for adjacent courses in science, social science, and literature. But oral and written English composition are independent courses in their own right for which the foundation should be laid in the elementary and secondary school, and nothing should be admitted to them which does not serve the end of improving oral and written expression. There are two ways in which the context of the undergraduate program can assist instruction in composition: (1) by providing a body of information that may be used as a substantive basis for the development of skills in the communication of ideas; and (2) by providing an awareness, or consciousness, of method that will support instruction in the logical and proper ordering and organizing of material so that its presentation will achieve a maximum of effectiveness. Therefore, courses in writing and public address should draw substance from the subject courses but should never be subservient to them, for composition is creative, not editorial.

A reasonable proficiency in the ability to read at least one foreign language possesses not only practical utility, but also provides a better insight into and an understanding of alien cultures. The inability of the average American student to communicate in any language other than English is almost incomprehensible to the scholar reared in the European tradition. Geographic isolation is probably the major cause of this linguistic deficiency, but the inadequacy of contemporary methods, or the lack of method, in foreign language instruction must bear its share of the blame. To such a low estate have college language requirements fallen that even the average doctoral candidate is terrified by a page of German. Encouragement to European travel during the junior or senior year, practiced in some colleges, may prove to be a partial corrective to a disturbing tendency to renounce the foreign language requirement, but it would seem that the work in foreign languages can, and should, be related closely to the substantive context of other parts of the undergraduate program.

The programs of study in English and foreign language should be brought to a focus through a course in linguistic problems, the object of which is to give the student some understanding of the nature and functions of language as an instrument of communication. Here the student would consider such topics as phonetics, the history and relationships of languages, the principles of comparative grammar, and semantics. Thus the student comes to regard language from four distinct points of view: (1) a system of vocal sounds, (2) a changing historical phenomenon, (3) a structured system of symbolic representations subject to varying forms of analysis, and (4) an instrument of communication through symbolic expression.

The objective of a general education is to equip the student with the knowledge and the intellectual discipline necessary for a meaningful integration of the several fields of knowledge, of the nature of knowledge itself, and of the place and value of the great disciplines in relation to each other. There is a need, therefore, that the program of general education culminate in a course which will instill in the student an understanding of the culture—its scholarship, its social organization, its physical equipment. He must come to view his inherited culture not as a fragmentation of its constituent elements, however significant they may be, but as a complex of interrelated parts, each with its fundamental role, and each contributing to the totality which is our contemporary civilization. Moreover, the individual disciplines are themselves unified systems of interrelated subordinated fields, and each branch of knowledge has its philosophy, its science, its history, and its technology.[66] There is, therefore, a need for a course that will give the student an opportunity to synthesize his general education in such a way as to enable him to develop for himself an intelligible and unified theory of human knowledge in relation to the culture of contemporary American life. Such a course should be more than synthesis, though it is based on synthesis; its real purpose is to stimulate the student to test, perhaps for the first time, his own intellectual powers, and give full rein to his "long, long thoughts." In such a course Adler and Mayer's "essence of education" as "human association" should attain its most complete expression; it should provide the student's first real opportunity to harmonize nature and art, which is the "fundamental peculiarity" of education. Here natural process and artistic undertaking blend in a unity in which the student, stimulated by the artistry of the teacher and the excitement of natural discovery, begins the formulation of his own philosophy upon which adjustment to the environment depends. Here he should discover the extent to which he has been successful in, to use Hutchins' phrase, "the cultivation of the intellectual virtues," here the student will discover the real meaning of learning as distinct from "being taught."

## SUBJECT SPECIALIZATION

Beyond the program of general education lies subject specialization. General education, if it has been successful, has educated the student for intelligent action. By developing correctness of thinking, it has started him on the road toward practical wisdom. The student has completed his general education by achieving a solid knowledge of the foundations of the several intellectual disciplines, he knows something of the various subject fields, he should be able to use language and reason effectively, and he should possess some understanding of man both as an individual and as a social being. He has laid the foundations of good citizenship by equipping himself with the basic intellectual skills that are essential for

---

[66] See: Henry E. Bliss. *A System of Bibliographic Classification.* New York. H. W. Wilson Company. 1936. pp. 75–77.

intelligent action regardless of the transformations in society to which, later, he may be called upon to adjust.

Concurrent with his general education the student who is preparing himself for one of the professions will need an undergraduate specialization, or major. The question, therefore, becomes not should there be specialization, but what kind of specialization should it be? Specifically, for the librarian, the question is, what kind of specialization should it be for what kind of librarian?

Traditionally, subject specialization at the undergraduate level has been viewed as a bridge from general education to a graduate or professional degree. Basically, it is vocational in its aim and is predicated on the assumption that the student will pursue the discipline he has elected to the point at which he becomes one of its practitioners. Thus, the growth in the number and variety of vocations has been reflected in a great expansion of the college curriculum. Hutchins speaks bitterly of the chaos that is the "higher learning."[67] Though he concedes the probable necessity in some fields for a practical training which is essential to the young man or woman embarking on the independent practice of a profession, he is alarmed by the pride which the academic community exhibits in this bewildering disorder of course offerings and with the resistance that meets any attempt at its reduction.[68]

Toynbee has warned that the great danger in today's emphasis upon subject specialization in any field and for any profession derives from the false assumption that the problem of the rapid proliferation of knowledge can be solved by merely increasing the length of time to be spent in mastering it, and by using that additional time in carrying specialization to ever greater extremes. Such a policy, he says, "is based on two fallacies: (a) that the amount of potential knowledge has merely increased in content, whereas this potential knowledge is now also changing in content all the time, and this faster and faster; (b) that specialization is the best preparation for life in the present-day world."[69] These are fallacies, he says, because the assumption that lies behind them is that the world is static, "and that specialization is the key to finding one's feet in modern life. . . . Specialization puts the specialist out of harmony with life as a

---

[67] Hutchins. *Higher Learning.* pp. 89–119.

[68] "If I were scoring a university for its performance, I'd count as negatives the number of required courses, the number of lecture courses. . . . I'd count as positives the number of students actively engaged in imaginative research with faculty, the hours of open debate, the courses of open discussion." C. West Churchman. "Scoring the University." *Science.* vol. 163 (February 16, 1969), p. 665.

[69] Toynbee. *Higher Education.* p. 8.

whole, and life, under all conditions, is a unity." Thus he holds that even graduate education "should be a counterpoise to specialization, not an accentuation of it; it should mainly be devoted to a general preparation for life."[70] His is, admittedly, an extreme view but there is enough truth in it that it should not be ignored.

This proliferation of course offerings in subjects and fractions of subjects presents a particular problem to the library recruit. The terrifying multiplicity of courses makes possible the almost indiscriminate accumulation of credits which will eventually lead to a higher degree, but leaves the student totally unprepared for a satisfying career in librarianship. Until the higher learning is redefined and unified, until it can bring order out of its tangled departmentalization, until it is rationally ordered as the medieval university was ordered about theology, or Greek thought was unified by the study of first principles, the library recruit has no choice but to affiliate himself with one or more of the traditional, or classical, subject disciplines—chemistry, biology, history, literature, language, political science. Only thus can he achieve any measure of proficiency in a subject field; only thus can he be reasonably certain of discriminating between the important and the trivial.

Any reform plan for higher education must provide for a liberal education, academic specialization, and an appropriate bridge to graduate or professional study. To avoid curricular confusion and the proliferation of degrees, Woodring proposes that the A.B. degree "be made to signify liberal education and nothing else, and that no other baccalaureate degree be offered. The master's is a more appropriate degree for engineers, architects, public school teachers, social workers and other professionals.[71] Such a program, he believes, would, by assigning all preprofessional study to the postbaccalaureate years, enable the student to reduce his undergraduate program by one-fourth. Thus he represents something of a compromise between Hutchins' University of Chicago College and the conventional four-year undergraduate curriculum.

Daniel Bell, like others before him, sees each department regarding its major solely in terms of preparation for graduate study in its subject. "Yet an analysis of career plans indicate that, except for physics and chemistry, a sizable number of students do not intend to remain permanently in their field of major study but plan either to cross over into other disciplines or, more often, to enter one of the professions."[72] Thus he

---

[70] *Ibid.* p. 9.
[71] Woodring. *Higher Learning.* p. 220.
[72] Bell. *Reforming of General Education.* p. 292.

proposes a "double track," the one being preparation for graduate study and the other providing a broad background in a cluster of related disciplines. He also decries the failure of the separate departments to consult each other and work out rather precisely defined combined sequences of appropriate related courses for each of the subject majors. Certainly both of Bell's proposals would hold much of value for the undergraduate preparation of the librarian.

The precise configuration of the undergraduate program can, of course, be substantially varied in accordance with the strengths of any particular college or university, but the major elements that contribute to an appropriate course of study are suggested in the diagram in Figure 10-1. The important consideration is that librarianship is not a self-sufficient discipline, it is essentially integrative, and the greater the strength the student brings to his professional preparation the better prepared he will be for a successful career. The success of many of the "old-line" librarians of an earlier day derived, in spite of a program of professional training that was lamentably weak, from the very fact that they brought with them a rich college preparation in the classical tradition which gave them, perhaps quite unconsciously, an inherited scheme of values and a sense of what librarianship is all about; without a thought of analyzing what they were doing or why they were doing it, they possessed a kind of instinctive sense of its rightness.

## UNDERGRADUATE COURSES IN LIBRARIANSHIP

In a position paper prepared by Lester Asheim in his role as the first director of the ALA's Office of Library Education, a kind of civil service categorization of library personnel is developed in five levels of which only that of "Library Assistant" is relevant to the immediate discussion.[73] Asheim envisages this grade, which he places immediately below the two professional classes of "Professional Specialist" and "Librarian," as re-

---

[73] Also: idem. Lester E. Asheim. "Education and Manpower for Librarianship." *Bulletin*. American Library Association. vol. 62 (October 1968), pp. 1096–1106. "Library Education and Manpower." *American Libraries*. vol. 1 (April 1970), pp. 341–44. Reference should be made to the treatment of middle level supportive staff defined in the report developed by the Interdivisional Ad Hoc Committee of the Library Education Division and the Library Administration Division of the ALA: "The Subprofessional and Technical Assistant; A Statement of Definition." *Bulletin*. American Library Association. vol. 62 (April 1968), pp. 387–97. (Popularly known as the "Deininger Report.")

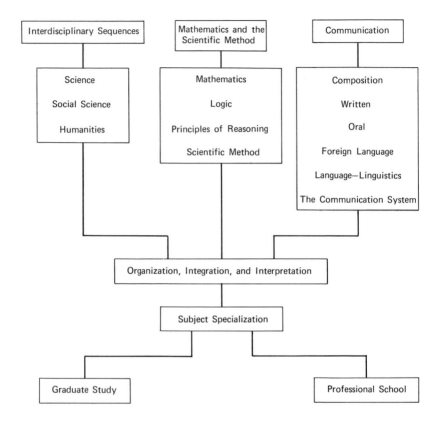

**Figure 10-1.**

quiring for adequate education, "a bachelor's degree from a good liberal arts college with the emphasis on general education." He believes that instruction in the fundamentals of library practice may be obtained "in a variety of ways: through on-the-job training and guided experience, through course work following the bachelor's degree offered by graduate schools as a prerequisite to the master's program (but preferably not for graduate credit), or for courses offered at the undergraduate level within the B.A. program. Courses in library subjects offered at the undergraduate level should be, insofar as possible, a contribution to the liberal education of the student rather than professional or technical in the narrow sense."[74]

---

[74] Asheim. "Manpower for Librarianship." p. 1101.

Asheim maintains that such library courses should constitute "a preprofessional minor" as "recommended by the graduate library schools," and should be articulated with the graduate program. He warns that "a major in library science represents too great an inroad into the student's general education"[75] and should be discouraged.

Asheim is insufficiently vigorous in his opposition to the dilution of the student's undergraduate studies with superficial courses in elementary library techniques; his theoretical structure would be meaningless in practice unless it were supported by the authority of a certification system that as yet librarians have been generally unwilling to accept. Library administrators have always been careless about the lines of authority and responsibility that demarcate their tables of organization, and job descriptions have a way of fading in actual practice. Asheim's boundaries are especially fragile, and the record of library school accreditation that the ALA has written certainly is not one to inspire confidence in its ability to enforce standards for the rational organization of personnel.

The library recruit should be particularly on guard against these undergraduate courses in "librarianship." The collegiate years are much too valuable to be frittered away on superficial expositions of library techniques—unblushingly vocational, they seriously encroach upon subject knowledge and discredit the graduate professional program by giving it a false and unprofessional orientation. The intellectual sterility and the substitution of technique for substance that these courses represent can, and indeed in many instances do, lead librarianship into the error of the professional educator of mistaking the technician for the teacher, of confusing that which is to be taught with the manner of its teaching. Librarianship can be a respectable discipline in its own right, with its unique body of theoretical knowledge and its own principles, but these are not to be comprehended through drill in routines or parroting of lists of titles.

Nor is the argument for the alternative proposal that subject specialization should be reserved for the graduate program rational, for without adequate undergraduate preparation, the door to graduate study in any of the major disciplines is firmly closed. The undergraduate with a library major or even minor will likely find that he is an unwelcome applicant for graduate courses in almost any subject field. Librarianship is an auxiliary discipline in the sense that it may be related to a variety of disciplines and areas of knowledge, and its introduction into the undergraduate program lowers the intellectual standards of librarianship itself, and breaks the continuity of general education with the beginnings of subject concentra-

---

[75] *Ibid.*

tion. By every test these paraprofessional courses are interlopers in the college program.

Rejection of traditional undergraduate courses in librarianship does not mean that the library as a social agency should be disregarded in the college program. The point to be emphasized here is that the focus of the undergraduate treatment of librarianship should be directed toward comprehension of the library system as an integral part of the communication process, and not upon a diluted survey of library skills. The study of social communication, then, is the bridge which the profession has been lacking in the past, the proper bridge over which the library recruit progresses from college to library school. Only by insisting on such a route can the prevalent misconceptions of what librarianship is be effectively dispelled. Not until the undergraduate program is purged of superficial courses in library work can the profession expect to attract to its ranks young people with the abilities and motivations it needs.

## TRANSITION

The four-year undergraduate program must not be terminal for the librarian and thus narrowly preprofessional. It must provide the foundation for further academic study and future intellectual growth. It must acquaint the student with the fundamentals of the intellectual disciplines thus enabling him to think about and deal with substantive intellectual problems, particularly as they relate to society. It must train him to use language skillfully and reason judiciously. It must awaken in the student an understanding of man and the relationships that connect man with man, and it must foster that which will eventually flower as wisdom.

"We need to distrust a system of thought," wrote Lewis Mumford, "that has cut itself off deliberately from the culture and the cultivation of the whole organism. . . . Don't think I don't admire my superiors when I see them at work, the great mathematicians, the great physical scientists, . . . I recognize that the really great ones—the Faradays, the Einsteins, the Clerk Maxwells—bring to their science their whole personality and this is what saves them, and perhaps also adds to their greatness."[76]

Admittedly, the ever-present danger in the crossing of disciplinary lines of the existing academic setting is a potential loss of quality control

---

[76] Lewis Mumford. "Closing Statement." *Future Environments of North America*, ed. F. Frazer Darling and John P. Milton. Garden City, N.Y. Natural History Press. 1966. p. 728.

and an acceptance of superficiality in the guise of breadth. Nevertheless, undergraduate course offerings should be sufficiently great to permit considerable latitude for choice, especially across departmental boundaries, and maximum flexibility consistent with undergraduate subject mastery should be encouraged particularly in the junior and senior years.

There should be no sharp dichotomy between undergraduate liberal education and graduate professional study separated by the granting of the baccalaureate degree. The character of professional education is not determined by its position in the academic sequence, but by its purpose, its relation to the entire context of learning, and by the methods employed by the teacher in teaching and the student in learning. Vocational utility no more determines the educational value of professional training than bracketing it with the graduate school engenders maturity. If properly educated, the student should be prepared to enter the fifth and subsequent years of study qualified to pursue a substantial amount of independent work and capable, on his own initiative, of utilizing his past educational experience in perceiving relationships, making value judgments, and exercising his imagination. In short, he should be able to use effectively the liberal education with which he has presumably been equipped. Higher education, then, may be seen as a progression in which the granting of the baccalaureate degree is little more than a signal to the student that he is on the right road.[77]

---

[77] Jesse H. Shera. "Toward a New Dimension." p. 167.

# Eleven

# The Professional Program

When C. C. Williamson urged the abandonment of the library training class and proposed that the university become the chief port of entry to the profession of librarianship he was recognizing a growing trend toward professional education on the part of universities, and expressing the belief that librarianship would gain in professional identity by such affiliation. The rise of professional education during the latter half of the nineteenth century, and particularly during the early decades of the twentieth, grew out of an enlarged conception of the social role of higher education.[1] Since the emergence of the university in the United States coincided with a period of tremendous scientific, industrial, and urban growth, the intensified division of intellectual labor reflected an enlarged functional complexity of society outside academic walls. To such changes the university was almost certain to respond. The most urgent need of this new society was for specialized skills, particularly in the sciences, and

---

[1] The term professional education, like the term profession itself, is variously defined and subject to considerable controversy. As used in the present chapter in relation to library education it encompasses those courses dealing directly with the theory and practice of librarianship. Basic, or foundation, courses are those required of all students in the professional program regardless of the student's specific area of interest. Courses required for effective practice in a particular area of librarianship will be designated as specialized courses, and professionalized courses are those the content of which has been drawn from other disciplines but are oriented toward librarianship, e.g., children's literature, storytelling, and many of the courses in the information science program.

Adopted with modifications from James Bryant Conant. *The Education of American Teachers.* New York. McGraw-Hill. 1963. pp. 21n. and 45n.

the new professional schools that were proliferating were at least molded by these demands, when they were not actually *created* by them. Traditionally the function of the college had been, and still is to a very large extent, to teach, to treasure, and to transmit knowledge, while that of the university is to add to knowledge. The new professional schools were more like the college, and a very restricted kind of college at that, hence their advent was not always welcomed in a research environment.[2] Robert M. Hutchins, for example, who has always been averse to the presence of such schools in the university because, among other reasons, their programs and objectives are not oriented toward research, believes that such subjects could be learned better "on the job or in training schools set up for these purposes. These training schools might be located in the vicinity of the university. The teachers and students might avail themselves of its resources. But, since their object would be different from that of the university, they could not be regarded as members of it and could have no part in its management. An intellectual community cannot be built out of people who are not pursuing intellectual interests."[3] One can have much sympathy for Hutchins's point of view, at least so long as such training is not intellectual, but it seems unfair to condemn those engaged in such activities to eternal anti-intellectualism if they are honestly striving to give intellectual substance to their pedagogic goals. A community of scholars should not be a closed society, at least not closed to those who can present proper credentials for admission.

## THE PROFESSIONAL SCHOOL IN THE UNIVERSITY

In view of Hutchins's enthusiasm for the unified curriculum of the medieval university, there is an inconsistency in his attitude toward professional education. In the medieval university the schools of theology, law, and medicine were all built upon the foundation of the trivium and the quadrivium. Basically, it was the professional schools that distinguished the university from the college and gave the former its chief reason for existence and its reputation for greatness.[4] There is no reason why a pro-

---

[2] Richard Hofstadter and C. DeWitt Hardy. *The Development and Scope of Higher Education in the United States.* New York. Columbia University Press. 1952. Chapter 3. "Graduate and Professional Education."

[3] Robert Maynard Hutchins. *The Learning Society.* New York. Praeger. 1968. p. 112.

[4] John S. Diekhoff. "The Professional School in the University." *Journal of Education for Librarianship.* vol. 6 (Fall 1965), pp. 103–10.

fessional school must represent a degradation of the educational ideal, nor must it be oriented toward the training of technicians. A professional school can teach its students to think as well as any other constituent element in the university.

Ernest C. Colwell, when he was president of the University of Chicago, expressed the belief that "the university is a faculty engaged in study. All else on the university campus is auxiliary and subordinate." Thus, it is the concentration upon research, and the teaching of research, that distinguishes the university from the college on one hand and the professional school on the other. Therefore, he says that one of the initial consequences of moving a professional school to a university is to arouse a sense of inferiority in the faculty of the professional school, and hence push it in the direction of research. This inferiority complex *is not* essential to the integration of a professional school faculty into the university, but the impetus toward research as a habit of mind *is*.[5]

The philosopher of higher education, as well as the university administrator, dare not forget that the university is provided by society with legal sanctions and material support so that it can carry out its responsibilities for the benefit of all who have the capacity to profit from higher education. The university came into being to provide those studying for the professions both intellectual stimulus and practical training. Thus, the university must continuously serve the needs of society which implies changing as society and the professions change. During the Middle Ages it was mandatory for the university to train the clergy, and subsequently the doctors, lawyers, and public officials. Until the seventeenth century, the knowledge of God, theology and philosophy, were the all-important foci of the university. Since that time the growth of science and the technologies that developed from it, have steadily increased the demand for specialized training.[6]

Carroll Newsom holds that "it becomes one of education's essential objectives to perfect a person's potential talents so that his specific contribution to society will be superior in its significance and contribution. The implications of such a principle, in spite of our great advances in the various areas of professional education, is still on the frontier of educational understanding and will continue indefinitely to provide a major challenge to our society."[7]

[5] Ernest C. Colwell. "The Role of the Professional School in the University." *Education for Librarianship*, ed. Bernard R. Berelson. Chicago. American Library Association. 1949. pp. 15–16.

[6] Karl Jaspers. *The Idea of the University*. London. Peter Owen. 1960. p. 133.

[7] Carroll V. Newsom. *A University President Speaks Out*. New York. Harper. 1962. p. 51.

Clark Kerr has pointed out that the new and evolving professions look to acceptance by the university as an index of their professional identity and status. This attitude "creates," he has said, "new roles for education but it is also part of the process of freezing the structure of the occupational pyramid and assuring that the well-behaved do advance, even if the geniuses do not. The university is used as an egg-candling device; and it is, perhaps, a better one than any other that can be devised, but the process . . . does for some professions what the closed shop has done for some unions."[8]

If the great advantage to the professional school from affiliation with the university is, as Colwell believes, that the former is stimulated to pursue research and self-criticism; the great asset of the professional school to the university is that the school's faculty "is insurance for the university against triviality," and the besetting sin of a faculty devoted to study is always triviality. The research worker runs a constant risk of devoting himself to "piddling, insignificant work. The professional school, however, cannot avoid a concern with matters of great importance to contemporary society."[9]

John W. Gardner sees an ever increasing role for the university in service to society; such, he says, was the view of Thomas Jefferson and Benjamin Rush, though the movement did not come fully into its own until the establishment of the land-grant colleges. So he sees the seeming antagonistic traditions of separatism and involvement existing side by side in the great universities.[10] His point of view can mean only an ever growing role for the professional school in the academic world. This view is largely shared by Henry Steele Commager, who is of the opinion that "the new interests are probably more important than the new knowledge," and that the spectacular growth of professional studies "is impressive." "What we now teach in most of our colleges," he told the faculty and students of the University of Kentucky in 1965, "has long been relegated to the *lycee* or the *gymnasium* or the technical school, and what we now teach in our professional schools has been accepted as the proper business of the university."[11] Thus he sees the need for the American university to move closer to the European pattern though "the mounting requirements— and expense—of advanced and professional education will call for a more

[8] Clark Kerr. *The Uses of the University.* Cambridge, Mass. Harvard University Press. 1963. p. 111.

[9] Colwell. "Role of the Professional School." pp. 20–21.

[10] John W. Gardner. *No Easy Victories.* New York. Harper and Row. 1968. pp. 86–87.

[11] Henry Steele Commager. *The Commonwealth of Learning.* New York. Harper & Row. 1968. p. 201.

effective collaboration among universities and between universities and other institutions and agencies than now obtains. There will have to be a clearer division of labor."[12] Richard McKeon, whose roots are thrust much too deeply in the Chicago tradition to permit him to minimize the value of general education in today's complex society, nevertheless acknowledges that universities are being transformed by social change arising from the growth of technology and man's aspirations to satisfy basic needs. Thus, "the professional schools, and even the non-professional departments of universities have taken over the training of experts and technologists needed in industry and government."[13]

René Dubos of Rockefeller University believes that the university must assume a more active role in society than it has done in the past if our culture is to avoid catastrophe. In his opinion, the quantitative expansion of the economy—the continuous production of more and more of everything for larger and larger numbers of people—will soon come to an end in a state of equilibrium and be self-regenerating in both energy and materials. The ecology of highly industrialized nations in the Western World has been in a state of disequilibrium for a considerable period of time, and this instability is increasing at an alarming rate. Thus, if man is to survive he must, with the aid of science and technology, develop a "steady state." Dubos's "steady state" is not to be equated with stagnation; rather it will mean a drastic change in our value system. This steady state might in the end generate a scientific renaissance, and surely it will challenge our powers of response and adjustments to a totally different economy. But such a renaissance "will not happen without a conscious, and probably difficult, effort on the part of the scientific establishment. So far, universities and research institutes have, in general, remained aloof from the problems that the world will face in an acute form before the century is over. But the pressure of public opinion will soon force scientists out of this aloofness. . . . Many discoveries have been a function of the conditioning scientists receive as members of society. The constraints inherent in the world of the immediate future make ideas concerned with design, rather than accumulations of facts related to growth, the dominant needs in the advancement of science and technology."[14] What Dubos has said of science is equally true for all other forms of intellectual endeavor, and especially those relating to the structuring of professional services.

---

12 *Ibid.* p. 202.

13 Richard McKeon. "Universities in the Modern World." *Issues in University Education*, ed. Charles Frankel. New York. Harper. 1959. p. 13.

14 René Dubos. "A Social Design for Science." *Science.* vol. 166. (November 14, 1969), p. 823.

Jencks and Riesman, after sampling "six major species" of professional schools[15] have identified certain patterns or tendencies by which they may be characterized. The first of these patterns is the one in which professionalization is accompanied by a tightening of the ties between the professional school and the profession itself. Such professional groups represent a subculture that, because its members share certain values and attitudes as well as specialized knowledge, feels itself separate from and superior to the laity. In such situations, professional schooling is crucial to the development of these subcultural attitudes—perhaps even more crucial than the transmission of knowledge. The importance of the professional school varies from one profession to another, though schooling is becoming increasingly important for all professions whatever their character.

A second phenomenon has been a growing tendency for professional schools either to affiliate with a multipurpose university or to expand into one. One consequence of this trend has been the tendency for the school to diminish its initial occupational commitments. Also, this characteristic seems to have encouraged those charged with the education of future professionals to take a more academic and less practical view of what their students need to know than was true before university affiliation. Moreover, the tendency of professional schools to "herd" under the protection of the university has made them more aware of each other, and encouraged a broader view of their responsibilities than was characteristic of the isolated training school not situated on a campus.

A third generalization that might be made is that the ways in which professional schools sift and screen potential applicants may be more important to the shaping of the profession than the substance the schools actually try to teach. It is easier to change a profession by recruiting new kinds of apprentices than by changing the rules of apprenticeship. Standards for admission can be manipulated in three ways: by age restrictions, by setting intellectual qualifications, and by offering special rewards for a selected minority of students.[16]

Jencks and Riesman conclude their discussion of professional education with a rather fancy, though quite illuminating, figure that has some relevance to the education of the librarian. They see a profession not as a pyramid up which the neophyte scrambles along an ever narrowing slope to possess an exclusive pinnacle of talent and power, but rather as a factory surrounded by a wall, the gates of which are guarded by educators

---

[15] Seminaries, medical schools, military academies, engineering schools, teachers' colleges, and graduate academic departments.

[16] Christopher Jencks and David Riesman. *The Academic Revolution.* Garden City, N.Y. 1968. pp. 199–256, but especially pp. 251–56.

who admit only those whom the educators regard as having the proper qualifications. These gatekeepers make their own rules and confer occasionally with one another, but never with the management of the factory inside the walls. They reject some petitioners whom the management would admit, and accept others who have neither been invited nor wanted.

The dangers in the situation are mitigated somewhat by the fact that there are many gates in the wall, and since the gatekeepers' standards vary, failure at one portal does not preclude success at another. Also, there are secluded spots where the determined can climb over the wall without confronting any gatekeeper, and once inside, the intruder's right to be there will rarely be challenged. "Such arrangements obviously leave a lot to be desired," say the authors. "It is therefore tempting to make the educators involved scapegoats whenever there are serious problems within. But this is almost certainly unfair. If the educators listened more carefully to the management and admitted only those who were wanted and needed, the situation might well be worse, not better."[17]

Contemporary attitudes toward the professional school in the university community have tended to polarize around those who hold that the catholicity and adaptability of the university reflect the pragmatic genius of the American people and the refusal of the academic world to resist change and rest content with past accomplishments, and, at the other extreme, those who hold that academia is experiencing a deplorable excursion into vocationalism which can bring only disintegration to the university as an integrated scholarly enterprise.[18]

The protracted debate over whether the professional school with its stigma of vocationalism is an interloper in the academic community has generated more emotion than substance, and in the final analysis is specious. The professional programs of study that first arose in the universities of the Middle Ages were unblushingly vocational. The American colonial college prepared young men for the ministry, or teaching, or public service, and felt no need to apologize for its aims. Every advanced study in the academic curriculum is directed toward the preparation of the student for a career of some kind, and hence is vocational. Higher education would certainly be of questionable value if it were aimed solely at a disembodied culture and divorced itself from the realities and problems of its world. American higher education, ever since the days of Eliot and Gilman, has sought the development of true professions.

---

[17] *Ibid.* p. 256.

[18] John S. Brubacher and Willis Rudy. *Higher Education in Transition.* New York. Harper. 1958. p. 378.

There is no question that the professional school belongs in the university; if it is a true professional school it does not belong anywhere else. The requirement is to make certain that the educational program *is* professional, not the apprentice training of a trial-and-error craft.[19] "It is our contention that the need for reform of professional education on a national scale has become urgent," wrote the authors of the study of professional engineering education at the University of California at Los Angeles. "Demands upon the professional school are unprecedented. Professional higher education, now more than ever, faces critical problems calling for immediate solutions: how to turn out men who can anticipate and solve the pressing problems of modern society; how to marshal the limited educational research resources of a school to develop effective programs; how to develop a professional course of study that will avoid the early obsolescence of its graduates in a rapidly changing society; how to maintain the cutting edge of an educational program at a price that a university faculty is willing or can afford to pay."[20]

The professional school must possess a program of study that has intellectual content, that presents a definite theoretical structure from which emerges a corpus of scholarship, and is organized in a systematic way. All too often, regrettably, library education, from the days of Dewey, has not exhibited these characteristics, often not even held them out as objectives, and the consequences for librarianship have been little short of disastrous. Williamson saw this clearly enough when he wrote his famous report for the Carnegie Corporation, but even he was far from successful in his efforts at Columbia. Wilson at Chicago was more successful than anyone, either before or since, in giving the library school a true professional status, but, for a variety of reasons, his achievements faded with the passing of time. The record is indeed a sorry one.

---

[19] "It is just because the fundamental liberalizing influence is so often ineffective that, in America for example, efforts are being made to broaden specialist studies by 'a twenty per cent admixture of the humanities.' And it is just because the young are so obstinately utilitarian and preoccupied with getting a job that any attempt to depart from what is strictly relevant to qualification is resented as a waste of time, and even of 'their' money." Roy Lewis and Angus Maude. *Professional People in England*. Cambridge, Mass. Harvard University Press. 1953. p. 221.

[20] University of California at Los Angeles. Educational Development Program. *A Study of a Profession and Professional Education*. Los Angeles. Reports Group. School of Engineering and Applied Science. University of California at Los Angeles. 1969. p. xi.

## THE NEGLECTED SEARCH FOR A PHILOSOPHY

It is a truism that the main outlines of the educational program for any profession must be set by the characteristics which distinguish a profession from all other human activities, refined by those properties which differentiate the particular profession from all other professions, making it the kind of profession it is. In a not very discriminating way, Melvil Dewey acknowledged this when he based the curriculum of his school upon a listing of tasks performed in the typical library of his day, and this "job analysis" approach has not been entirely abandoned.[21] "In the numerous decisions and procedures incident to adapting the curriculum," Ernest Reece wrote in 1936 in a study of trends in library school curricula, "the conditions of library work necessarily are the main guide, and largely may predetermine the path."[22] Seven years later he wrote that "there has been relatively little change in the substance of their basic programs in the fifty-odd years of their history."[23] Robert D. Leigh echoed the same point of view when he wrote for the Public Library Inquiry, though he saw the years immediately following the Second World War as a turning point in library education and the beginning of a new era.[24] So one could go on and on with all the "landmark" contributions and discussions of library education, all of them repeating the same tired old criticisms that have fallen largely upon deaf, or at least unresponsive ears.[25]

But blame for a failure to develop an adequate theory of library education cannot be laid entirely at the doors of the library schools. Despite insistence, in large measure justified, that it is the responsibility of

---

[21] Columbia University. Library and School of Library Economy. *Circular of Information*. 1884.

[22] Ernest J. Reece. *The Curriculum in Library Schools*. New York. Columbia University Press. 1936. p. 92.

[23] Ernest J. Reece. *Programs for Library Schools*. New York. Columbia University Press. 1943. Preface.

[24] Robert D. Leigh. "The Education of Librarians." *The Public Librarian*, ed. Alice I. Bryan. New York. Columbia University Press. 1952. p. 324.

[25] Wilhelm Munthe. *American Librarianship from a European Angle*. Chicago. American Library Association. 1939; Keyes D. Metcalf, John Dale Russell, and Andrew D. Osborn. *The Program of Instruction in Library Schools*. Urbana, Ill. University of Illinois Press. 1943; J. Periam Danton. *Education for Librarianship; Criticisms, Dilemmas, and Proposals*. New York. Columbia University. School of Library Service. 1946; Joseph L. Wheeler. *Progress and Programs in Education for Librarianship*. New York. Carnegie Corporation of New York. 1946; Chicago. *Librarianship*; J. Periam Danton. *Education for Librarianship*. Paris. UNESCO. 1949.

the educational system to lead the profession, such leadership is difficult when the profession itself does not know its destination. As John Wakeman wrote in his valedictory as editor of the *Wilson Library Bulletin* that the librarian of today serves "a society in flux poised between annihilation and Utopia, torn by the technological revolution, swept by great social movements and great political changes, confused by a babble of conflicting traditions. Such a society 'desperately needs both stimulus and a sense of continuity. It needs documentation of the truths which in simpler times it held self-evident. It needs the raw materials of reflection and discussion, the makings of a consensus, the intellectual heat that will finally melt the contents of the melting pot.' In short, society needs, as never before, effective access to recorded knowledge, and effective access to recorded knowledge is the librarian's business. Therefore, if this recorded knowledge 'is needed in greater quantity now, and more quickly, packaged differently, and distributed in new ways, then that is how we librarians must supply it.' "[26]

The significance of the communication system to the ability of the individual to make the best possible decisions in every aspect of his daily life defines the context of librarianship and the environment in which it must operate. But librarianship today is overburdened with the pressures of daily routine, and even though larger issues are recognized, they are obscured by the demands of detail and a preoccupation with means which engender neglect of ends. To develop the student's capacity to relate means to ends is the responsibility of education. But means and ends are not static entities, they change with circumstance and they interact upon each other. In the contemporary world of rapid and drastic shift in which no man lives all of his life in the world into which he was born, or even works all of his life in the world of his early maturity, education must do more than reflect existing means and ends. It must, as best it can, anticipate the future. The "fifth leg" of John R. Pratt's educational animal is an important part of the entire university program but it is an especially vital organ in education for those professions in which change is most drastic. It is just such a transformation in the role of the librarian, redefined by the increasing dependence of society upon its graphic records, that the professional library school must be prepared to meet. It must differentiate means from ends within the context of the present but in anticipation of the future.[27]

---

[26] John Wakeman. "The Context of Librarianship." *Wilson Library Bulletin.* vol. 37 (December 1962), p. 348.

[27] Jesse H. Shera. "Theory and Technique in Library Education." *Library Journal.* vol. 85 (May 1, 1960), pp. 1736–39.

The first responsibility of a profession is to know itself, which means, first, knowing what a profession is; second, knowing what kind of a profession it is; and third, knowing what differentiates it from all other professions. There is in every profession a quintessential element that distinguishes it from other human activities and which may derive from the intellectual content of its discipline, the technology of its practice, the responsibilities which society has placed upon it. It may be defined in terms of all or any combination of these. But librarianship, unfortunately, has been little given to professional introspection. For generations, librarians have accepted the social responsibility for custody of mankind's graphic records, hammered out empirical procedures for the organization and servicing of those records, and argued indifferently the right of their technology to qualify as a science.

But librarianship is not a science, if science is understood in the popular, narrow, even misleading, sense of an aggregate of facts, observations, laws, theories, and techniques accumulated in a linear series of discrete discoveries that terminates in an increment of information concerning the nature of phenomena. If science is only normative or positivistic, then librarianship is not a science at all. Rather, it shrinks to a body of technical procedures and skills that expedites man's access to the written word.

If science is understood to mean a deposit or accretion of empirical discoveries crystallized or economized at appropriate intervals into theories, principles, or laws that enable a highly articulated professional group, or school of thought, to comprehend the totality of the phenomena with which the group is concerned, then librarianship is a science. Science is not to be defined merely in terms of the materials upon which it works, the procedures it employs, or even the laws or principles that it evolves. Science, as a generic concept, also embraces the psychology and sociology of the scientific community, the universe in which it operates, and the influences that encourage acceptance or rejection of innovation. Thomas S. Kuhn, in *The Structure of Scientific Revolutions*, speaks of the *paradigms* of science, by which he means the structure of schema which, at any one moment, gives coherence to modes or schools of thought within the scientific complex.[28] If librarianship is concerned with the act of mediation between man, either individually or collectively, and his graphic records, then the paradigm of librarianship as a science is to be sought in the total communication process in society and in its epistemological, sociological, psychological, and institutional ramifications. An inquiry into the nature

---

[28] Thomas S. Kuhn. *The Structure of Scientific Revolutions.* Chicago. University of Chicago Press. 1962. pp. 43–51.

of librarianship is therefore prerequisite to the planning of a program of professional graduate study and the first responsibility of a school of library science within a university complex.

In large measure librarianship has based its claims to professionalism and the right to be described as a science upon the technology that, over the years, its practitioners have developed and which its initiates must master. The conventional response of librarianship, already burdened with the stigma of technological vocationalism, to the growing importance of graphic records to society has been to introduce new technologies and skills derived from the applied sciences. This has been especially true for that aspect of librarianship known as documentation. Thus, librarians hoped to increase their efficiency by making possible a more rapid and accurate performance of those duties for which they were traditionally charged.

There is nothing wrong with this search for increased efficiency in the engineering aspects of librarianship. That librarians are, with the aid of the engineer, developing a highly efficient technology, and that the proliferation of recorded knowledge necessitates a revolution in that technology are scarcely debatable. But a technology is a means, not an end. Lacking theory to give it direction and purpose, it drifts aimlessly. If it reaches its goal it does so only by fortuitous circumstance. Excessive attention to technology is especially dangerous to the librarian. The doctor who learns about the human body in health and in disease can bring his technical skill to bear upon the problems presented by any individual who seeks his aid. But the librarian, seeking to relieve the congestion in the information resources of his "patient," is much less fortunate. One human body is very like another, but the varieties in the information needs and their susceptibility to correction are infinite. To the doctor a heart is a heart, and its responses and behavior can be predicted with a high degree of accuracy; but to the librarian a book is no such stable entity to which the response of the human mind can accurately be foretold.

A sophisticated technology should be an important part of every librarian's professional equipment, and its neglect in his education would prove disastrous, but a technology, even when it is mathematically derived and electronically implemented, is not all or even the essential part of librarianship, and it must not dictate the credentials with which the librarian gains entry into the sacrosanct halls of science. To condemn library techniques as little more than clerical routines does not diminish the importance of such routines to the practicing librarian, or deny that their mastery by the competent librarian should not be taken for granted. Routines are simply not indices of the librarian's professional position. Similarly, the librarian who has equipped himself with the technology of the engineer has not thereby proved his professionalism.

Whatever the substance of the curriculum that must be taught, the redirection of an educational system is difficult enough when it has the support of the professional, but when it must constantly confront a tide of resistance from the practitioners, the charting of a new course can be accomplished against only the heaviest of odds.[29]

The task of redirection is further complicated by the necessity to absorb into a well-structured and truly professional program, established in a university, methods and techniques inherited from apprentice training, which are still valid and appropriate even though they possess the very characteristics which have aroused the ire of critics. A feeling of inferiority and a sensitivity to the charge of vocationalism has led to an excessive emphasis and reliance upon symbols or policies that promise to confer prestige—academic degrees, certification, accreditation—rather than to the formulation of an educational philosophy. Loose talk about making the library school curriculum "more interdisciplinary" or "more scholarly" have all too often sputtered out with the introduction of such courses as descriptive bibliography, the history of papermaking, the study of fine bindings, or, if the school desires to be particularly advanced, progressive, and ahead of time, classes in statistics or documentation, sometimes masquerading as "information science."

A somewhat more rational approach than the above to the search for an adequate theory of library education may be seen in the attempt to identify a discipline, or branch of knowledge, to which librarianship is clearly and meaningfully related and to translate its theory and findings into such terms as will illuminate librarianship. "The lack of any adequate connection with a theoretical discipline," wrote Metcalf and his associates, "to serve as its foundation is perhaps the greatest weakness in the library school program."[30]

Glynn Harmon holds that librarianship is an integrative discipline that

---

[29] Using data collected from librarians in thirteen large public libraries and faculty in twelve library schools, Anna C. Hall found that librarians placed a high "priority on complex skills and abilities," believed that most factual knowledge needed in librarianship was adequately taught, whereas the higher intellectual skills and abilities were relatively neglected in those courses required of all students in the master's program, and that in many schools important subject matter needed by librarians, but not unique to librarianship, was omitted. Anna C. Hall. *An Analysis of Certain Professional Library Occupations in Relation to Formal Educational Objectives.* Pittsburgh. Carnegie Library of Pittsburgh. 1968.

[30] Metcalf, Russell, and Osborn. *Program of Instruction.* p. 19.

is a part of a larger suprasystem known as the behavioral sciences. Integration of the behavioral sciences into a patterned mosaic of an interrelated and interdependent system has, however, been frustrated by the lack of communication among its dependent systems. Harmon suggests the unity of science movement as a possible means for ameliorating this fragmented condition.[31]

Bernard Berelson, in an article on the behavioral sciences for the *International Encyclopedia of the Social Sciences,* traces the development of the term, "which can be distinguished from the social sciences as designating a good deal less but, at the same time, somewhat more." The social sciences traditionally include the fields of anthropology, sociology, economics, political science, and much of psychology, along with history and statistics. Behavioral science, however, which became current in the United States in the 1950s, includes, "sociology, anthropology (minus archaeology, technical linguistics, and most of physical anthropology), psychology (minus physiological psychology), and the behavioral aspects of biology, economics, geography, law, psychology, and political science." Berelson is right when he says, "The edges of any such broad concept tend to be fuzzy—as are the edges of the social sciences themselves. . . . Given time the term will probably settle down to one or two generally accepted meanings, if it has not already done so."[32]

Berelson and Harmon may not agree on what subdisciplines constitute the behavioral sciences, but such a lack of agreement emphasizes Harmon's contention that there has been a lack of integration in this new field. Harmon's thesis suggests the reason for the failure of the Graduate Library School at the University of Chicago to achieve an adequate integration between the Library School and the Social Science Division of the university. With the most laudable intentions, the Library School directed students to the Social Sciences Division for adjunct courses which, at best, resulted in no more than fragmentary patchings. The school never accomplished a satisfactory integration either in the planning of its program of study or its execution. Such integration as there was came from the instructor in the adjunct course and usually was ignored or neglected. Yet what was done at Chicago was, in its limited way, the beginnings of a trend

---

[31] Glynn Harmon. *Human Memory as a Factor in the Formation of Disciplinary Systems* (unpublished doctoral dissertation). School of Library Science. Case Western Reserve University.

[32] Bernard Berelson. "The Behavioral Sciences." *International Encyclopedia of the Social Sciences.* New York. Crowell, Collier, and Macmillan. 1968. vol. 2, pp. 41–42.

that other library schools have emulated. At Case Western Reserve University, students, particularly at the doctoral level, are encouraged to enroll, wherever relevant to their interest, in other departments.

Other attempts to achieve unification are under consideration, but at least there would seem to be general agreement that the constituent elements in the behavioral sciences should no longer be treated as isolated.[33] But before one can *properly* relate librarianship to the behavioral sciences, a reasonable degree of consensus as to what the behavioral sciences are must be achieved. Abraham Kaplan holds that it is the subject matter, rather than any body of techniques, that makes this newly developed field distinctive.[34] But this search for a theoretical foundation for librarianship in other fields has resulted only in narrowing the concept of the library's function in order to make it fit the confines of a related discipline, and every such attempt has proved inadequate because of the scope and variety of the library's role.

"Even a village library embraces interests of surprising breadth," wrote Ralph Beals in discussing the professional education of the public librarian, "and readers may call upon the librarian for assistance at any point. . . . It is obvious that the general librarian can never expect to rival the economist, the chemist, or the musician in his knowledge of economics, chemistry, or music; but unless he knows more about chemistry and music than the typical economist, he is likely to fail as a librarian. . . . What the general librarian knows about economics or chemistry or music we still expect him to acquire as if he were to become an economist, a chemist, or a musician. As a result, we are not offering an adequate subject foundation for general librarianship. The creation of such a foundation, a body of knowledge about knowledge for the general librarian, is one of the obvious needs of the future."[35] Beals might well have added that the same criticism holds for the professional education of librarians serving the specialized needs of economists, chemists, and musicians. In short, we have not evolved a body of knowledge about the knowledge that any librarian should have in order to perform his responsibilities as society, if it is willing to underwrite adequate support, has the right to expect.

---

[33] See, for example: Walter J. Ong. "Crisis and Understanding in the Humanities." *Daedalus*. vol. 110 (Summer 1969), pp. 617–40; Talcot Parsons. "Unity and Diversity in the Modern Intellectual Disciplines." *Daedalus*. vol. 96 (Winter 1965), pp. 40–43; and Floyd W. Matson. *The Broken Image*. Garden City, N.Y. Doubleday. 1969. pp. 3–29.

[34] Abraham Kaplan. *The Conduct of Inquiry*. San Francisco. Chandler. 1964. p. 32.

[35] Ralph A. Beals. "Education for Librarianship." *Library Quarterly*. vol. 17 (October 1947), p. 297.

Traditionally, higher education in general—and professional education in particular—has progressed serially along more or less rigid disciplinary channels in which the student moved from an introductory or primary course to courses of increasing degrees of specialization in the subject of his choice. Undergraduate instruction has been predicated on the assumption that the student is preparing himself for a graduate or professional school, and graduate courses were pointed toward the doctoral or a professional degree as the ultimate achievement. In some disciplines the postdoctoral rung has been added to the academic ladder. Always this pedagogic sequence has been the vertical communication of the tried and true to the immature and inexperienced student by the mature and experienced teacher in the conventional atmosphere of the classroom or laboratory. Vertical education is not learning but being taught. To this pedagogic continuum library training, like many other forms of professional education, was grafted, either during the third or fourth year of college or following the granting of the baccalaureate degree. In the past it had been assumed to flourish best when it was an offshoot of the humanities branch of the academic tree. But, regardless of the stem to which it was affixed, it drew little nourishment therefrom and did not become an integral part of the living organism. This vertical pattern of education, by encouraging increasing degrees of specialization along a sequential continuum, has sacrificed liberal, or general, education to professional, semiprofessional, and vocational instruction to the point at which undergraduate education has become hardly less preoccupied with the cultivation of occupational skills than have the professional schools themselves.

The renovation of professional education is not to be accomplished by merely doing more intensively and extensively that which has been done in the past; it must be achieved by restructuring the educational system. In contrast to the conventional vertical transmission of information, horizontal education is a sharing of knowledge, through inquiry, exploration, and research, by the informed with the uninformed, and its primary prerequisite is not a receptivity to instruction but the desire to know.

In a narrow sense, education can be described as the instrument by which societies, or groups within a society, perpetuate themselves; certainly the organization and content of a curriculum reflects the social structure and the values a society seeks, as well as its accumulated knowledge and experience. Even when narrowly interpreted, education is seen to be altered when there are drastic shifts within a society or when attempts at social innovation promote educational reform. Because both education and librarianship are constituent elements in the communication system, librarianship—and the professional education that is propaedeutic to its practice—must reflect this change from a vertical to a horizontal structure.

Research alone, despite the power of its prestige in society and especially on university campuses, will not lift education for librarianship from its Slough of Despond. We do not mean to imply that the value of research is to be minimized. Research is important to all professional education, but it is not a theory of librarianship, or even a matrix for the shaping of library educational goals. The synthesized and crystalized experiences of the field and the derivation of general principles from practice are the real source to which education for librarianship must look for its rationale. These experiential fragments must be integrated into a reasonably well structured body of knowledge before the goals of the educational system can be defined.[36]

Carl M. White recognized that an adequate integrating theory of librarianship must be developed analytically rather than parasitically when, in 1948, he told the annual conference of the Graduate Library School of the University of Chicago:

> The approach I am suggesting is that instead of planning our [library] specialist's education in terms of the *form* of work he is to be paid for doing, we plan it in terms of the *content* of understandings he will require, and then we see whether that content cannot be brought into relation with similar content required in other forms of library work. In this way we shall avoid the excessive proliferation of separate courses for separate forms of work, and thus not be beguiled into pulverizing the concept of a profession into a miscellany of educationally discrete activities.[37]

Thus, some way must be found to *generalize* the program of study. The mere straining out of all materials which are not suitable for formal education, which are extraneous to the real needs of the profession, or which, though a necessary part of the librarian's technical equipment, may best be learned elsewhere, does not go far enough. The critical scrutiny of existing programs of study for relevance and significance is, of course, essential to any reexamination of library education, but the philosophy of education for librarianship is not to be discovered through a process of

[36] Margaret E. Egan, Helen M. Focke, Jesse H. Shera, and Maurice F. Tauber. "Education for Librarianship—Its Present Status." *Documentation in Action*, ed. Jesse H. Shera, Allen Kent, and James W. Perry. New York. Reinhold. 1956. pp. 54–56.

[37] Carl M. White. "Discussion." Chicago. *Librarianship*. p. 229.

elimination, however rigorous it may be. Education for librarianship is not a residuum—it is not that which remains after all irrelevancies have been stripped away.

In an address before the 1964 conference of the University of Chicago, Abraham Kaplan, of the Department of Philosophy of the University of Michigan, identified three major areas as comprising the basis of the intellectual foundations of library education. The first area, he said, was "humanistic," though he sharply rejected the interpretation of humanism as exemplified in the dualism of C. P. Snow's "two cultures." By the humanistic foundation of librarianship he meant, "knowledge of the uses, and therefore, of the users of information . . . nothing other than knowledge of people and of the various things that people do and of the various ways in which in the course of these doings they generate and transmit and interpret ideas or information."[38] Consequently, he assumes that the student, during his educational experience, "whether as an undergraduate or in a graduate library school itself, will have been exposed to something of the sociology of knowledge, to something of the history of ideas, and to something of the structure of inquiry, not merely in some area that might happen to be of special interest to him but in broad historical and cultural terms."[39] But this knowledge must be buttressed by "an appropriate set of values . . . an inculcation of the love of learning, of the love of ideas, or the love of truth."[40] Specifically, Kaplan was thinking about "a certain kind of social responsibility that is involved in resisting the pressures of various interest groups and institutions or social conditions in which you operate, which interfere with the proper discharge of your functions." The professional education, therefore, ought to make it possible to "recognize and discharge that kind of responsibility."[41]

The second group of basic elements that Kaplan identified were the "specifically vocational," which he says involves learning "how" as distinct from merely learning "that." Thus, he acknowledges his debt to Kant in distinguishing between the faculty of judgment, "which is the faculty of relating general principles to particular cases," and the faculties of understanding and reason, "which operate to produce and combine these general principles." Despite the fact that rules can be provided for the

---

[38] Abraham Kaplan. "The Age of the Symbol—A Philosophy of Library Education." *Library Quarterly.* vol. 34 (October 1964), p. 300.

[39] *Ibid.*

[40] *Ibid.* Regrettably, Kaplan weakens this admirable list by adding "and even of the love of books."

[41] *Ibid.* p. 301.

application of a principle to a specific case, judgment will always be required in the application of those rules to the cases they govern. Moreover, the specific content of the skills will change as the instrumentation with which they operate changes.[42]

Finally, the third area recognized by Kaplan is described by "the whole set of disciplines which I lump together under 'metasciences,' " which are sciences not about subject matters provided by man and nature "but about subject matters provided fundamentally by our ideas *about* man and nature, or by our language, or by our way of transmitting and processing the information that we have derived. . . . I mean disciplines like mathematics, logic, linguistics, semantics, and, in the narrower sense, theory of information, and maybe cybernetics."[43]

The only alternative to these three areas as the basis for professional studies "would be a narrow specialism or a really quite impossible encyclopedism."[44] These studies, Kaplan said, are central to the education of the librarian, not because they underlie the new computer technology and other technologies related to automation, but because there is central to these metasciences, the concept of structure, order, form, "which seems to me to be precisely the central concern also of library science."[45]

## THE OBJECTIVES OF THE LIBRARY SCHOOL

From this philosophy of library education, fragmentary and ill-defined though it may be at the present time, must be derived the objectives of the library school. These objectives, growing out of a soundly developed theory of librarianship, must provide a basis for the integration of dissident interests within the profession. The traditional definition of a library, as a collection of books organized for use, by implication defines the librarian as one who is little more than a keeper of the collection, or at best a cataloger, and merely describes what is done in libraries by librarians with only the vaguest reference to specific social goals toward which the operations of the librarian are directed. The only generally accepted definition which attempts to specify the role of the librarian is actually no more than an enumeration of purposes for which books are used: education, information, recreation, aesthetic appreciation, and research.

---

[42] *Ibid.*
[43] *Ibid.*
[44] *Ibid.* p. 302.
[45] *Ibid.*

But important as these functions are, they define the use of *books* wherever they may be found; no one of them establishes any ineluctable tie with librarianship, and there is no one of them for which the library has sole responsibility.

The first criterion for the evaluation of the librarian's program of professional study must be expressed in terms of the social function of the library as a unique and important channel of the communication network and the degree to which the program comprehends the *entire* library system, both as an inherent unity and as a sum of its constituent parts. Early in the present study, the theory was developed that the social function, or role of the library, is to maximize the effective social utilization of the graphic records of civilization. The value of such a definition to education for librarianship is its essential objectivity; the point of view which it establishes for the librarian is that of an impartial observer of the social process, and substitutes for his own subjective value-system an objective study of what society itself expects to get from graphic records at any stage in its development or in any part of its structure. From the relating of the role of the library to its social *milieu*, to an understanding of the social utilization of graphic records, it becomes possible to describe those activities which are peculiar to the library, shared only at the margins with other groups or agencies, and always intimately intertwined with the changing needs of the supporting culture.

The second criterion for evaluating professional education is the degree to which it extracts from the totality of the librarian's knowledge and skills those which are appropriate to the objectives and processes of graduate study. Expressed in terms of education for librarianship, this means the emphasizing of those professional activities relating to the collection, organization, and utilization of graphic records. Stated in terms of their social objectives, these professional responsibilities are of two kinds:

1. Advancement of the general cultural level through the provision of library materials which enrich the experience of the individual.

2. Advancement of the "scholarship" of the society; i.e., its scientific knowledge and managerial effectiveness, through provision of the specific information needed in the research, investigation, and decision-making processes.[46]

These two responsibilities stand almost in direct opposition. The first is focused upon the user—his tastes, his education, his interests, and his

---

[46] Margaret E. Egan. "Education for Librarianship of the Future." Shera et al. *Documentation in Action.* p. 206.

experience. It implies an intimate and highly personal relationship between reader and book. The second, by contrast, is environment-oriented in that it relates to such variables in the situation as the subject field, the type of problem to be solved, the method or methods of investigation being used, or the kind of decision to be reached. Here the characteristics of the user, other than his capacity to understand what is set before him, are relatively unimportant. The lines of demarcation between these two responsibilities are not always clear and distinct, and though one may, in general, say that the first is the domain of the public, the school, and the college library, and the second is the concern of the special library or information center, there is a constant recrossing of lines of responsibility. This interrelationship is proper; the public library should serve the informational needs of the specialist, and the special librarian may appropriately administer to the cultural tastes of his clientele. But it is the failure to keep these two responsibilities properly identified in the librarian's professional thinking that has led to much error in the delineation of the librarian's social role, and a consequent confusion respecting the kind of professional education he will need.

It is this confusion that compels the abandonment of the earlier concept of the "general" librarian as the basis for all professional education in librarianship, and dictates the third objective—the need of the professional curriculum to provide the intellectual discipline, the specific knowledge, and the technical skills required for any one aspect or segment of the library's function. Librarianship is, in the final analysis, a cluster of specializations united by certain bonds of knowledge that are common to all bibliothecal activity. But these specializations are no less specialized for being, in some instances, broadly based or even "general."

Ralph A. Beals, addressing the Library Association of the District of Columbia, charged the profession with failure to achieve its promise to adjust services to the needs of the clientele, or even to know or understand what those needs might be:

> In the late nineties there was some talk of standard libraries, particularly standard branches of public libraries; that is, identical in every particular, down to the latest novel, which could be established anywhere without reference to the community to be served. This talk was never taken very seriously; but I sometimes wonder whether our ability to verbalize our intentions of suiting libraries to readers may not have outrun our ability to translate our intentions into realities; whether we do not sometimes underestimate the difficulties of

such a task; and whether, in this connection, the means to the end are not sometimes exalted into ends in themselves.[47]

He compared the librarian to the anthologist, both of whom are artists, for the library, like the anthology, must be an artistic creation and not a neatly packaged and standardized product:

> Without detracting from the claims of librarianship to be a science or discounting the contributions already made to the science of librarianship, which I myself think very great, I should like to suggest that the librarian, like the anthologist, is also an artist. . . .
>
> In the larger, scholarly libraries, the librarian, like the editors of the *Patrologia,* or the *Monuments Germanise Historica,* sets himself the high task of representing the many subjects that crowd the limits of his spacious canvas, and his particular delight is in the minuteness and accuracy of his rendering. The special librarian customarily works a narrower field; like Bishop Stubbs, he seeks to collect every *important* document bearing on the causes, growth, and consequences of his subject, forging all together as "the links of a perfect chain." The public librarian, presiding over an institution created by society for this purpose, cannot, if he would, evade the responsibility of portraying the full range of our civilization in all its pulsing human aspects—cosmic and intimately personal, grave and gay, sublime and humdrum. But scholarly, special, or public librarian, each in his own way is an artist, working under the age old limitations of the artist, to communicate the good, the true, and the beautiful in whatever terms may prove perceptible to those with eyes to see or ears to hear.[48]

Finally, the professional program of study must be intellectual. The whole purpose of any curriculum in higher education, wrote Joseph Schwab is to "provide an intellectual challenge to students and the fullest possible opportunity to develop the arts of recovery, enquiry, and criticism appropriate to each discipline."[49] The objective of education is the training of the mind, and the professional degree must not stand as a denial of this objective. Only to the degree to which it is intellectual is it pro-

---

[47] Ralph A. Beals. "The Librarian as Anthologist." *D. C. Libraries.* vol. 12, no. 2 (January 1941), p. 20.

[48] *Ibid.* pp. 20–21.

[49] Joseph J. Schwab. *College Curriculum and Student Protest.* Chicago. University of Chicago Press. 1969. p. 183.

fessional and properly a part of the university community. Thus one may summarize the four objectives by which the professional program of study is to be judged: (1) it must represent a well-developed theory of the social function of the library; (2) it must extract from the totality of the librarian's knowledge and skills those which are professional; (3) it must present librarianship as a unified cluster of specializations as opposed to the earlier concept of a "universal" librarian; and (4) it must be directed toward the training of the intellect. Only to the degree to which the professional program of study can meet these criteria can it maintain its position as a graduate program in an academic setting or be anything other than vocational training in manipulative skills.

## CRITERIA OF THE PROGRAM

Reduced to their elementary and most basic terms the tasks of the library school are two-fold: to provide the best possible professional education to highly qualified and motivated students who seek to excel in that branch of librarianship in which their interests reside, and to advance the practice of librarianship through a program of research and related investigatory and developmental activities. This duality is not internally inconsistent or antagonistic; the two parts of the whole are natural allies. If the program of the school is to achieve its highest potential of excellence the two parts must be brought into a reasonable balance, for both teaching and research suffer if either is neglected.

It is the thesis of this study that the first professional degree should be based upon an undergraduate program that has provided the student with a sound general, or liberal, education which has equipped him to take his place in society as a citizen, and an undergraduate specialization, or cluster of specializations, which have reflected his special subject interests, utilized his special competencies, and introduced him to some understanding of one segment of human knowledge and experience. Thus equipped, the student should be prepared to undertake graduate professional study directed toward his acquiring:

1.   A fundamental understanding of the role of the library in the communication process of society together with the historical development of the library and of library materials as social instrumentalities shaped by and responding to their coeval culture.

2.   A comprehension of the basic theory and the appropriate systems for the organization and interpretation of library materials, and

especially the intellectual content of those materials, together with the necessary skill to deal practically with the techniques and routines relating to library organization and use.

3. A knowledge of the principles and methods of research as applied to the investigation of library problems, together with the ability to evaluate research results, especially research in librarianship, in terms of the appropriateness and reliability of the methods used and the validity of the results obtained.

4. An understanding of the basic principles of administration and their application to libraries as organizations of people working together to achieve specific goals, with special emphasis upon the administration of libraries serving the field of the student's special interests.

5. A mastery of the basic elements of a library specialty, or cluster of specialties (e.g., children's work, school libraries, and educational media).

6. Exposure to practical library experience, when the student has not previously had such experience, as exemplified by a well-supervised work-study program or internship which makes possible controlled experience, this experience to be coordinated with classroom instruction through formal review of a particular library problem developed from the working situation in which the student has been placed.

7. Contact with the professional field of librarianship through lectures, discussions, and other special events which will bring the student into contact with a variety of librarians outside the academic setting.

8. Encouragement of contacts, either formal or informal, of the student with other departments and schools of the university to ensure that he does not lead his academic life in a sterile library vacuum.

If these criteria are to be fully and successfully met there must be a continuous review of the curriculum both with respect to keeping it up-to-date with current developments and trends in librarianship and related areas of knowledge, and to utilize new methods of instruction. There must be a constant interaction between student and faculty in an atmosphere in which both are learning, both are sharing an educational experience. The research program of the school must relate in fundamental ways to the understanding of librarianship and be relevant to the aims and objectives of the school, rather than be tailored to the whims of a fund-granting agency. Freedom of inquiry for both faculty and students must be encouraged. The participation of both faculty and students in appropriate extracurricular, as well as curricular, professional activities that will both enrich their arsenal of professional skills and extend their knowledge and understanding of the problems of the field, should be encouraged so long as such activities are kept in proper perspective and do not interfere with the performance of direct educational responsibilities. Continuing contact with alumni is important not only to aid them in their professional development and advancement, but also to enlist their assistance in the evaluation of the school's program. Cooperation with the faculties of other departments and schools of the university is vital if the library school is to take full advantage of its position in the academic community, though it is important to remember that the initiative for such cooperation will, in the vast majority of cases, have to come from the library school.[50] This activity is probably the most difficult to achieve of all, yet at the same time it is one of the most important to the viability of the school. Finally, there must be an active awareness on the part of the faculty of the field of librarianship itself, both in the practice of librarianship and in library education, if the school is to assume its proper share of professional responsibility at local, state, national, and even international levels.

## THE BASIC PLAN

Viewed in the light of these criteria, the main outlines of the professional course of study begin to emerge. The search for a unified theory of librarianship implies a professional philosophy which is expressed in the curriculum as a basic course structure required of all students. This basic philosophy bifurcates into two groupings: communication as a social process, together with the theory and historical development of the library, and the body of professional knowledge of librarianship as a human activity. The study of communication must emphasize the importance of social organization and social development as conditioning factors in the communication process. The theory and history of librarianship should not only trace the development of the library as a social agency from the earliest times to the present, but also relate the library to its coeval culture, specifically to such instruments of communication as language, speech, writing, the alphabet, pictorial representation, books, periodicals, and the newer media such as films, sound recordings, and the computer-related

---

[50] Wilfred L. Saunders. "The Library School in the University Setting." *Library Education: An International Survey*, ed. Larry E. Bone. Champaign, Ill. Graduate School of Library Science. 1968. pp. 73–107.

techniques for the transcription of information. In short, it should view the library against the background of the social organization, the physical equipment, and the scholarship of the culture of which it is a part.

In addition to a comprehension of a unified theory of librarianship, the librarian must possess the technical skills necessary for the effective organization and exploitation of large accumulations of recorded, or graphic, materials, and he must be able to use fully the resources that lie outside his own library. The librarian of the future cannot place his faith in the skillful use of one standardized and inflexible system, such as a standard classification or list of subject headings, a basic list of reference sources, or a universal body of operating techniques. He must be trained to analyze the needs of a particular library clientele and to adapt familiar procedures or devise new ones on the basis of well-established principles which will ensure that he will not emerge with a hopeless maze of unrelated and even contradictory practices. The librarian, therefore, must acquire competence in the means by which librarians perform their functions, and he must be thoroughly familiar with the technical aspects of professional practice—the selection and acquisition of material, the organization and interpretation of collections, the library as an administrative and operational organization, the changing concepts of services to be rendered, and the means for the evaluating of results. He must learn all this in relation to underlying general principles so that he may attain a genuine mastery of his professional practice, not mere skill in its application. Only thus can he be brought to an understanding of his profession, its organization and responsibilities.

Finally, the librarian must have some understanding of the processes by which knowledge is advanced—of the research process. This is essential for three fundamental reasons: (1) he may himself, in the course of his professional career, wish to engage in some investigations of his own, even though they may be no more than a simple evaluation of the effectiveness of a single operation; (2) certainly he will be called upon to evaluate the research of others, and he must, therefore, be able to winnow the wheat from the chaff; and (3) unless he has some appreciation of the meaning of research and the means by which research is conducted, he cannot appreciate the needs of an important segment of his clientele.

"It is all very well . . ." Ralph Beals said in the address quoted above, "to reflect on the ends of librarianship, the characteristics of the profession, the characteristics that distinguish librarianship among the professions, and the place of professional schools in universities, but what has all this to do with education for librarianship? What would a curriculum look like if designed with these considerations in mind?

Even if the factors thus far mentioned exhausted the possibilities—and they do not; and even if all critics were to agree that all the factors mentioned were relevant—and they will not; the number of different programs that could be evolved logically from the foregoing considerations is very great."[51]

Beals's suggestion, as he is careful to point out, "is no more than an attempt to sketch one program as illustrative of the possibilities." He assumes that a good general education, that had been defined in some detail, would be required of all students admitted to the graduate program, and that this undergraduate preparation "would be attested by examination, not by certification." Moreover, he would have the achievement of the student tested, at the end of his graduate program, also by examination. "Ideally this examination should be designed and administered by persons other than those offering the instruction." Here, of course, he was reflecting his experiences with the independent and centralized examining office at the University of Chicago.[52] "Until graduates of library schools are subjected to a comprehensive test, the degree in librarianship will have no readily understood meaning." This examination, and the courses preparatory to it, might well, according to Beals, exhibit the following generalized pattern:

1.  Subject field—thirty percent.

2.  The theory of communication, the ends and means of librarianship, and the nature and administration of social institutions—twenty percent.

3.  The formation and use of book collections—twenty percent.

4.  Seminar and thesis—twenty percent.

5.  Directed practice—ten percent.

Beals's plan, though it displays certain characteristics of the time in which it was formulated (e.g., the thesis requirement which, in 1947, was almost universally required of master's candidates in the library schools), still has a remarkable relevance even after more than two decades in which

---

[51] Beals. "Librarian as Anthologist." p. 300.

[52] After Beals's departure from Chicago, some experimental work was done in enlisting the expertise of the University Examining Office in the design of comprehensive examinations in the master's program in the Graduate Library School. Regrettably, and for reasons that are not clear to those who participated in the experiment, which included the present writer, the results were far from satisfactory. However, there is considerable doubt about the validity of these unhappy results. The principles which Beals was espousing still seem to be valid.

librarianship has undergone rather drastic changes. Unhappily for library education, Beals did not live to see the rise of information science, and only in his last years, as director of the New York Public Library, was he much concerned with the emergence of documentation.

## THE FOUNDATION PROGRAM

From the time when the American Library Association began to concern itself seriously with the problems of library education there has been a continuing search for the principles of unity that would bind the educational program into a cohesive whole, and, following the Second World War and at about the time that the first-year master's degree began to replace the fifth-year bachelor's, the concept of a "core" of education for librarianship became popular. In general, this "core" was composed of introductory courses in cataloging and classification, materials selection, library administration, and information sources, courses believed to be so fundamental to the practice of librarianship that they should be required of all students regardless of the library specialization which they might pursue.

The goal, however admirably motivated, proved nevertheless to be elusive, and even as early as 1953, when the Graduate Library School of the University of Chicago held its widely publicized workshop on "The Core of Education for Librarianship," it was becoming clear that the concept was not viable.[53] The difficulty lay in the apparent fact that the "core" was not really a core at all. It was biased throughout in favor of the public library, and much that the program contained had only marginal relevance to the practice of academic and special librarianship, and almost no relevance to documentation and information science. Indeed, for such specialties as school librarianship and library service to children, the core emphasized much that was of dubious value.[54]

But the weaknesses that were inherent in the concept of a "core curriculum" did not negate the need for, or invalidate attempts to create, an instructional program that would lay the basis for an integrated struc-

---

[53] Lester Asheim, ed. *The Core of Education for Librarianship.* Chicago. American Library Association. 1954.

[54] Jesse H. Shera. "Review of Asheim. *Core of Education.*" *College and Research Libraries.* vol. 15 (July 1954), pp. 348–52. See also the observations on the "core" concept by Harold Goldstein. "How Articulate is our Articulation?" *Journal of Education for Librarianship.* vol. 4 (Spring 1964), pp. 218–30.

turing of librarianship, to be required of all students before they embarked upon a relatively intensive exploration of the specialized aspects of librarianship.

The objectives of such a foundations course should be: (a) to provide the student with a generalized overview of librarianship in a way that will make clear the interrelationships and interdependencies of the variant forms and specializations of the field; (b) to present a theoretical structure of librarianship that will make clear these relationships; (c) to give something of the historical development of librarianship in relation to the communication processes of society and the emergence of the library as a social instrumentality; (d) to make reasonably certain that all students have a common background of understanding of the field prior to their entry upon their library speciality; (e) to relieve the subsequent courses of much of the technical detail, terminology, and standard procedures that must be mastered by the recruit before he can progress very far in his quest for competence; and (f) to provide those students who have not at the time of matriculation in the library school, decided upon a specific area of activity, some bases for making a rational choice in terms of their competencies and interests.

But the students are not alone the benefactors of such a course of study. Because a substantial proportion of the faculty participates in the undertaking, the course tends to break down artificial and psychological barriers among the members, encourage appreciation of the work being done in other programs in the school, and stimulate revision of advanced courses in ways that will increase their graduate quality. Thus, the faculty comes to know and understand itself.

One cannot present here a precise blueprint for such a course. Each school must work out the details for itself in terms of its own resources and needs.[55] Nevertheless, it is possible to identify the major areas that should be included in such an undertaking, and thus provide a theoretical framework within which specific presentations can be developed.

The schedule, which here can be no more than suggestive, might well be subsumed under five major groupings: People; Materials; Methods; Services (including research); and Institutions and Structure.[56]

---

[55] Helen M. Focke, together with Margaret Kaltenbach, were the architects of the Foundations Program at Case Western Reserve University.

[56] Adopted, with certain modifications, from Helen M. Focke. "Foundations of Library Science." *Journal of Education for Librarianship.* vol. 8 (Spring 1968), pp. 241–50.

I. *Introduction*
   a. Objectives of the course
   b. The plan of the course
   c. The character of professional education, with particular reference to the professional education of the librarian—theory and practice
   d. Orientation to the resources and facilities of the school and other housekeeping matters

II. *People and Communication*
   a. Communication
   b. Communication and the individual
   c. Communication in society
   d. Knowledge and the growth of knowledge
   e. Censorship and intellectual freedom
   f. Evolution of libraries
   g. The social role of the library
   h. The library in the future

III. *Materials: History, Types, Distribution*
   a. Origin and development of graphic records to the invention of printing
   b. Graphic records from the invention of printing to the present (emphasis on technology)
   c. Recorded information today: the book, its publishing and distribution
   d. Recorded information today: periodicals, documents, reports, patterns of research publication
   e. Recorded information today: non-book materials; other forms of the graphic record: films, sound recordings, miniaturization
   f. Selection of library materials: general principles and problems
   g. Building the library collection: quality control

IV. *Tools for Access to Materials: Bibliographic Organization*
   a. Descriptive and enumerative bibliography
   b. Trade and national bibliographies
   c. Subject bibliography
   d. Reviewing and evaluating media
   e. Media for access and evaluation of non-book materials
   f. Development of the library catalog and its functions
   g. Forms of the modern library catalog

       h. Basic descriptive cataloging
       i. Introduction to classification
       j. Subject analysis; the subject catalog
       k. The computer in information storage and retrieval

V. *Tools for Access to Materials: Information Sources*
       a. Reference sources: types and evaluation
          Retrospective bibliography
          Dictionaries
          Encyclopedias
          Annuals
          Compilations of data
       b. The structure of the literature
       c. The reference process; search strategy

VI. *The Institutionalization of the Library*
       (Related to the historical development of libraries)
       a. Major types of modern libraries
       b. The library's external relations and support (government; parent institution)
       c. The library's internal relations, organization, administration
       d. Personnel management
       e. Basic principles of scientific management
       f. Library standards
       g. Physical plant: equipment and housing
       h. Professional organizations: international, national, state, local
       i. The library and the federal government

VII. *Services*
       a. General services and those services peculiar to special types of libraries
       b. Services to particular types of users
       c. Services to readers individually
       d. Services to groups
       e. Information services at various levels
       f. New services: interlibrary cooperation, information centers, data banks
       g. Evaluation of services
       h. Rise of information science

VIII. *Research in Librarianship*
       (Generalized presentation)

IX.  *Summary*
  a.  Integration, overview, and recapitulation
  b.  The future of the library

Because the sequence is presented largely as a series of lectures, it is important that provision be made for small and intimate discussion groups in which students can consider the substance of the lectures and the readings, clarify problems, and interact with the faculty in ways that the lectures do not permit. Also, one of the major responsibilities of the coordinator of the program is to make certain that all participating faculty cover the areas for which they are responsible in such ways as will contribute to a unified whole.

An example of the degree to which such a course may compel the review and appropriate revision of the entire master's program is to be seen in the possibility that such a course as general library administration may be dropped completely in favor of courses in the administrative problems of various types of libraries, e.g., public, academic, school. With such a sophisticated introduction, the course in cataloging can be greatly strengthened, and that in book selection made, what it has always really been, a treatment of book selection in public, or generalized, libraries.

If the library school program is to derive, as we believe it must, from an understanding of what knowledge is common and unique to practice of librarianship *qua* librarianship, whatever the area of library specialization, and what knowledge is common to all librarians in a given field—but different from that required in all other library specialization—then the foundation for such understandings must be laid in a generalized orientation program such as that outlined above. The proliferation of courses envisaged by many who have written of the curricular needs for effective training in library specializations, for example the mass of documentation generated by the Committee on Education for Special Librarianship of the Council of National Library Associations, shows quite clearly that unless there is this common denominator which, when found, will reduce the number of specialized groups to a realistic optimum, programs will fragment to the point at which chaos becomes a real threat, or it will become impossible to serve adequately any specialized group except, perhaps, those few for which there is the most active and articulate demand.

## THE INTELLECTUAL BOUNDARIES OF THE FIRST GRADUATE YEAR

One of the first tasks in programming the first year of professional study is to establish the content of the foundations program and to define the relationship of subject knowledge to competence in librarianship in the several special fields of library practice. The elements common to the derivative forms of librarianship, such as information science, and the parent discipline must be fully exposed if curriculum content and degree structure are to meet the demands of the present and the anticipated needs of the future. If educational facilities are to be properly aligned with professional requirements, knowledge of what professional librarians do and how they do it, modified by an understanding of what they *should* be doing and how it *should* be done, is a *sine qua non* for those who are to make the decisions that will determine the pattern for library education. Such decisions cannot be made for all time; they must be flexible and responsive to the changing environment within which the librarian operates. Intellectual and procedural ossification is the occupational disease of all educators from kindergarten through the postdoctoral years.[57]

The first year of graduate professional study should bring to a synthesis the undergraduate liberal program, basic instruction in librarianship, and the subject matter of the student's major; the student must learn to relate the fundamental theory and basic techniques of librarianship, in a meaningful way, to the substantive content of his undergraduate education. An understanding of librarianship requires not only mastery of basic knowledge but also development of the capacity for rigorous analysis— the cultivation of a toughness of mind—that will promote the student's intellectual growth and prepare him to contribute to the growth of his profession. During this first year, the student should begin as soon as possible his initiation into that particular branch of librarianship in which he expects to practice. But the treatment of these specializations during the first graduate year can, at best, because of the limitations of time, be no more than introductory; it is the basic essence of librarianship that must be transmitted at the master's level, together with an introduction to one of the specialties in the profession toward which the graduate may direct his future interest and attention.

The master's degree, now generally awarded after the successful completion of approximately one calendar year of graduate professional study, is terminal for far too many students. Though it is generally acknowledged that one year, even when it excludes the requirements of a thesis or paper, as it now generally does, is an inadequate amount of time for mastering the fundamentals of the profession and achieving some compe-

---

[57] Much of what follows has been taken, in modified form, from the present writer's "Toward a New Dimension for Library Education." *Libraries and the Organization of Knowledge* by Jesse H. Shera. London. Crosby Lockwood. 1965. pp. 162–65.

tence in a specialty, the placing of the short-sleeved gown and abbreviated hood over the shoulders of the candidate itself implies a certain finality. Yet the profession is becoming more and more insistent that the library schools (or any other schools for that matter) graduate specialists in the various areas included in their educational offerings. Thus, the students and the schools are both caught in the toils of a growing, changing professional situation.

There are three possible ways of escape from this predicament: (1) revise the content of the master's curriculum so that it includes a minimum of "foundation" material and a maximum of specialty-oriented material; (2) let the specialists be trained in other schools, with the essentials of librarianship added to their programs in capsule form by the library staff or by librarians added to the faculty for this purpose; (3) define the master's program as comprising the fundamentals of librarianship, and institute a new degree (between the M.S. and the Ph.D.) designed to qualify graduates in the various specialties.

Most library schools have felt the pressure to accept the first of these possibilities, and many have yielded to it. Attrition of the core has been a fairly persistent phenomenon in library education. This pressure is particularly difficult to resist when a fund-granting agency is prepared to finance the development and implementation of a brand spanking new curriculum for the training of specialists in certain kinds of librarianship, but will make no money available for the development of a sound core program on which the many library specialties must build. Moreover, this approach to the problem may not be entirely irrational. The core as it is now understood may well be overburdened with elementary material, excessive detail, and unnecessary routine, and much of it may be obsolete or irrelevant to the needs of the specialist. One finds it difficult to believe that the core today should be identical with the core of ten years ago, much less that the core ten years hence should have a common boundary with the core as it exists at the present time. But to say that the core is changing in content is not to say that the period of time for its mastery should necessarily be reduced. Documentalists, for example, may not need today's basic course in cataloging, but it is entirely possible that the character of the course itself may change so that it will encompass a broader scope of basic knowledge essential to the professional preparation of all students, including documentalists. Again Don R. Swanson of the Graduate Library School of the University of Chicago has told the alumni that, in his opinion, "the future librarian must be well grounded in techniques of operations research and systems analysis, [and that] advanced research should be carried out by those with a mature scientific perspective that can best be achieved by a solid grounding in mathematics."[58] To one who sees these techniques as belonging to a specialization, the conclusion would seem to be that the line of demarcation between core and specialization may not be as sharp as has been assumed, and that its definition is becoming increasingly blurred.

Programs for the training of students by subject specialists, with only nominal participation (if any) by the librarians, the second of the three possibilities, have been inaugurated in institutions such as Lehigh and Georgia Institute of Technology. This development, too, has largely been encouraged by certain of the fund-granting agencies, especially the National Science Foundation, in which there exists considerable skepticism about the merits of conventional library education and its appropriateness for information specialists and others serving the complex information needs of research workers in the sciences. Such programs are predicated on the assumption that the science information specialist is first of all a scientist and that librarianship is to be equated with cataloging, classification, and other traditional forms of bibliographic organization. Adherents to this philosophy do not see the librarian as a literature specialist, hence the programs which they have developed emphasize such areas as: Syntactic Concepts; Logico-Mathematical Theories; Computer Programming; Data Processing; and Languages for Science. As specialized additions to a basic library curriculum, these courses can readily be justified, but hanging in midair, as it were, they are completely divorced from the realities of professional practice.

The third alternative, a middle-level program designed to encourage advanced study rather than research will be dealt with in a subsequent section. Before consideration of the master's program is dismissed it is necessary to consider the problem of library specialization during the first professional year.

## THE PROGRAM OF LIBRARY SPECIALIZATION

Over the years library education has achieved an approximation of agreement among the several library schools concerning the basic techniques and concepts which must be taught. But it is at the level of library specialization that diversity becomes most evident, for specializations in library school curricula have developed in a haphazard manner in response

[58] Don R. Swanson. "GLS Curriculum—The Shape of Things to Come." University of Chicago. *Graduate Library School News Bulletin.* no. 28 (January 1964), p. 4.

to local needs, or assumed needs, the availability of instructional talent, the quest for institutional prestige, the dictates of transitory enthusiasms or fads, interinstitutional competition and rivalry, and, most recently, the demands of student activism. Certainly no one could rightfully charge that the library schools have been unique among agencies of education in this disregard of thoughtful judgment in curriculum planning, but it is true that they have been among the most serious offenders. Careful and intelligent planning is as essential to the specialized program as it is to the basic curriculum, and it must represent the coincidence of a favorable employment market and adequate instructional resources. Specialization is not something that is superimposed upon the basic curriculum, a superficial tinkering with tradition; it penetrates to the very heart of the program of study; it has its own body of theory from which practice is derived; it stands solidly on its own two feet; it is integrated with the basic program, not dangled from it.

Despite the need for restraint in the introduction of specializations, one scarcely needs elaborate statistical procedures to prove that the irresponsible growth of specialization has been all too characteristic of library education since the 1940s.[59] The urge to offer a variety of specializations, in a kind of shotgun approach, has been very strong, especially among the less well established and newer institutions which have sought to compensate for impoverished general programs by creating "unique" specializations, e.g., comparative librarianship, Latin American studies, Black studies, service to the disadvantaged and the aged, and the like. Many such programs are no more than a single superficial course which treats the subject at a level far below that expected of a graduate school. This trend toward excessive specialization, fostered as it all too often is by the fund-granting agencies and their emphasis on "innovation," is probably characteristic of a profession in flux at a time of social mutation. The library school administrator, like educational administrators generally,

---

[59] Statistics gathered by Lester Asheim have shown that for the academic year 1966–67, twenty-two of the accredited library schools added eighty-five new courses of which sixteen were in information science. Two schools added entirely new programs in that field and eleven other schools were "definitely planning the addition of courses or programs in information science." Lester Asheim. "The State of the Accredited Library Schools, 1966–67." *Library Quarterly*. vol. 38 (October 1968), pp. 323–37. His findings are in agreement with those for the same period assembled by Alan Rees and Dorothy Riccio. "Information Science in Library School Curricula." *International Conference on Education for Scientific Information Work. London, April 3–7, 1967.* The Hague. Federation Internationale de Documentation. 1967. pp. 29–37.

feels himself pushed into unrestrained and often irrational "specialization," simply to secure additional financial resources and to avoid the stigma of conservatism and opposition to change. Specialization of function is, of course, the product of growth of a field of human endeavor, but too often educators tend to labor under the illusion that the introduction of specialization will signify growth, thus confusing consequence and cause.

No one would properly argue that the information needs of today's culture, with its many highly specialized subcultures, are substantially the same as the book needs of a half-century ago, and that library school curricula, even at the level of the first graduate year, should not respond to such shifts. Nevertheless, one finds it difficult to understand why the critical demands of the present for new types of library and bibliographic services must inevitably presuppose the need for a wholly new profession with independent curricula provided by a special department or school. Even a study as early as that made by Cohen and Craven for the Modern Language Association showed clearly that librarians, trained in conventional library programs, are doing the largest part of the information work demanded by specialists, and that the work they are doing is encompassed in the definition of conventional librarianship. Thus, the authors wrote, "literature searching—bibliography, reference work, and subject analysis (including classifying subject headings and indexing) were by far the most frequently cited essential elements in science information work."[60] That such work is done in places which may or may not be called libraries and that for those who do it education for librarianship ranks second in importance only to subject knowledge of the field of activity does not alter the fact that an information specialist is basically a librarian.[61] Many so-called specializations are scarcely more than restatements, in a different

---

[60] Leonard Cohen and Kenneth Craven. *Science Information Personnel.* New York. Modern Language Association of America. 1961. pp. 23–26.

But the authors did not follow their own data, but rather proceeded to recommend a wholly new curriculum designed, as they believed, to meet the needs of the information scientists.

[61] See: Raynard C. Swank. "Documentation and Information Science in the Core Library School Curriculum." *Special Libraries.* vol. 58 (January 1967), pp. 40–44. Also: Robert S. Taylor. *Curriculum for the Information Sciences.* Bethlehem, Pa. Lehigh University. Center for the Information Sciences. (Report no. 12). 1967.

See: Alan M. Rees. "Modifications in Curriculum for Biomedical Libraries in Library Schools." Paper presented at the Third International Congress on Medical Librarianship. Amsterdam, the Netherlands. May 6, 1969; and Alan M. Rees and staff. *Report on Education for Medical and Hospital Librarians.* 3 vols. Cleveland. Center for Documentation and Communication Research. Case Western Reserve University. 1968.

vocabulary and a new jargon, of wholly conventional understandings. The importance of specialization to the librarian is not to be minimized, but distinctions should not be made where there is no difference, and the program of study should not be so highly fragmented that the professional mobility of the graduate is placed in jeopardy.

Robert G. Cheshier, looking at specialization in the one-year library school curriculum from the perspective of his experience in developing the program for the education of medical librarians at Case Western Reserve University, has seen five distinct advantages: such programs tend to draw a relatively small number of students and this reduces the student-faculty ratio and permits a type of concentration that is not practicable with large numbers of students; they provide for the involvement of practicing librarians in a creative teaching role which buttresses and strengthens their operational activities; they encourage the "use of library facilities as laboratories," and "because the subject literature is small, such usage can become . . . pragmatic . . . in the sense that a student can be quickly oriented and knowledgeable"; the smallness of the universe makes possible its consideration from many points of view; and, finally, such specialization expedites the drafting of "resources not generally available," including "facilities and personnel whose activities can be served at the same time that education takes place."[62]

But, as director of the Cleveland Health Sciences Libraries, he also saw certain dangers in specialization. Students in the program tend to become an "elite, both in their eyes and in the view of their fellow students." Specialization can be limiting in that it tends to discourage the student from generalizing about the specifics to which he is exposed. Both of these factors, said Cheshier, "are sociological, but their impact is real and disturbing." The ready availability of financial support for many specialized programs "can create real problems within the library *milieu*." Specialization tends toward ever increasing narrowness, and "when this occurs both the faculty and students can too easily view any offerings not slanted to the specialization as lacking in importance or pertinence." The low student-faculty ratio and the elite atmosphere of specialized programs often encourage undue participation in the "social and organizational dynamics of a specialized program." Such activity can be a serious distraction from the student's real educational purpose, when it is permitted to become excessive.

---

[62] Robert G. Cheshier. "Specialization in Library Education." Unpublished statement presented to a doctoral seminar on library education. Case Western Reserve University. Autumn 1969. pp. 1–2.

Cheshier has pointed out that "specialization requires unusually able faculty," and that in the development of such a program, sociological factors play a very important role.

Yet, he concludes that, despite the problems and dangers, such programs can be justified: they upgrade the educational atmosphere of the school, promote desirable student-practitioner interaction, and the students develop a highly desirable professional attitude, as he expressed it, a "possessive attitude" toward the program, and "in our experience this has been a very valuable asset."

"Any form of library education," wrote Horst Kunze for a *festschrift* honoring the present writer, "must be aimed at a specific kind of librarianship, which, in turn, is determined by nation-wide library developments." But he admits that "it is unrealistic to expect the library curricula to produce, today or tomorrow, competent specialists for *all* branches of library service. It follows then, that the best preparation for the multi-faceted demands of library practice is obtainable through serious study of the fundamentals of librarianship, paralleled by a *practicum* or several separate excursions into the service, in application of what has been studied. . . . The graduate library schools can offer to their students merely the prerequisites for professional competence. It is the practice of librarianship that produces a librarian who is useful to society. But this may be accomplished within a shorter period of time with the aid of an educational armamentarium sufficient for continued study and learning after graduation."[63]

In an attempt to provide a basic first-year curriculum that would overcome the weaknesses in specialized fragmentation, but at the same time "qualify any beginning student for any beginning position in any kind of library," Barbara Denison has proposed the generalized program outlined in the following table. Miss Denison's program, which allows for no library specialization during the initial year, is predicated on the assumption that the student would return to school after a period (perhaps two or three years) of professional practice, and pursue a specialization of his choosing during the sixth year, after which he could qualify for candidacy in the doctoral program or consider his professional education as terminating with the completion of the sixth year.[64]

---

[63] Horst Kunze. "On the Professional Image and the Education of the Librarian." Paper presented for publication in a *festschrift* edited by Conrad H. Rawski, honoring Jesse H. Shera.

[64] From unpublished memorandum presented to the curriculum committee of the faculty of the School of Library Science, Case Western Reserve University. April 1969.

**Curriculum Plan**

*M.S. in L.S.*

Unit I: *History and Theory of Librarianship* — 4 weeks — Summer
  (How we got where we are, current thinking, projections)
  Changing social role, kinds of libraries for different purposes, communication
  Librarianship as a discipline
  Research: concepts, impact, relevance

Unit II: *The Library as a System* — 2 weeks — Summer
  (Including libraries with branches)
  Administration as an art/science
  Budgeting and funding
  Planning and administering a program
  Library surveys

Unit III: *Libraries in Systems or Networks* — 2 weeks — Autumn
  State agencies

Unit IV: *Libraries within Other Organizations* — 4 weeks — Autumn
  Sociology of fields or groups served

Unit V: *Librarianship as a Profession* — 1 week — Autumn
  Structure of the profession
  Nonlibrarians in libraries, at all levels
  Range of specialties within librarianship
  Salary expectations
  Professional literature
  Professional organizations, staff associations, unions

## Curriculum Plan (Continued)

| | | |
|---|---|---|
| Unit VI: *Structure (Sociology) of Knowledge* <br> Nature, history, and bibliographic organization of literatures | 4 weeks | Autumn |
| Unit VII: *Access (To All Knowledge)* <br> (Including resource libraries, interlibrary loan, abstracting and indexing services) | 2 weeks | Autumn |
| Unit VIII: *Selection and Maintenance of a Collection* <br> (Criteria for choosing from all knowledge, and for discarding) <br> Library purposes and policies <br> Community study, including organizations and individuals <br> Censorship | 2 weeks | Autumn |
| INTERSESSION | | |
| Unit IX: *Mediation* | 4 weeks | January |
| (Utilizing own collection and outside resources) <br> Role of library and librarians <br> Also nonlibrarians and paraprofessionals <br> Reference service <br> Other kinds of service (including those outside of the library) <br> Special services for special groups | 6 weeks | Spring |
| Unit X: *Organization of Collections* <br> A. Definitions (cataloging and classification terms) <br> Form of catalog card <br> Structure and nature of catalogs and indexes <br> Special materials requiring special handling | 4 weeks | Spring |

B. History and theory of universal schemes for the organization of knowledge, including nonlibrary (systems in historical settings)

    Logic of informational organization

    Necessity for special schemes

C. Tools and resources (history, updating)

    Experimentation

    Research—theoretical and applied

Unit XI: *Summation*      1 week    Spring

Unit XII: *Short Subjects* (On demand)      4 weeks    Spring

Students to arrange with faculty members for any kind of "program" they wish on whatever subject they desire, for example, some kind of session or sessions on book arts and rare books, library architecture

Presumably there would be a minimum number of students required before the sessions would be scheduled

Miss Denison's plan represents a carefully developed compromise between what is and what might be, and many of the areas which it includes are very important. But it is useful to hypothesize the ideal, unhampered by restrictions on resources—economic, material, or personnel. If the present writer could have the school of his dream, he would begin with the students, admitting only those who could demonstrate the possession of a solid undergraduate general education supplemented by a major in a respectable academic discipline, or cluster of related disciplines. This undergraduate program would be followed by graduate study through the master's degree, and preferably beyond, again in a substantive field. Some near-professional experience in a library situation would greatly strengthen the student's library school study, indeed the quasi-apprenticeship is now being required at many of the English schools of librarianship, especially at the University of London.

Thus equipped, the student would be ready for library school and a program, genuinely graduate in character, that would be heavily weighted in subject bibliography, bibliographic organization, and the structure of the literature in his appropriate discipline. Specialization, or emphasis, would by no means be confined to the conventional academic studies, or the old tri-partite library divisions of "public, academic, and special." Provision would be made for those students concerned with such social problems as race relations, aid to the disadvantaged, vocational rehabilitation and re-training.

Admittedly such a program would be expensive for both the student and the university, but good education is not to be sought at the bargain counter, and "expensive" is only a relative term. Bibliography and bibliographic organization are central to the practice of librarianship and their centrality must be recognized in the professional education of the librarian. Librarians who are true bibliographic specialists in the broadest sense will amply justify the social investment they represent, and so educated could once again become, as they were in centuries past, the proud and worthy masters of the recorded word.

Such a proposal as this immediately raises the question of the appropriate education of the librarian in the small and even medium-sized community library, but the answer would remain essentially the same. Perhaps less attention would be given, for them, to subject specialization and more to generality, but generalization itself is a form of specialty (the general practitioner in a small community does not need to know less about medicine than does his counterpart in the city). The great weakness of the librarian in the small system is that he has had too limited a view of the profession, and he needs to know, much more than he has in the past, about librarianship as practiced elsewhere—like the bantam rooster who introduced his hens to an ostrich egg, not to criticize their efforts, but to let them know "what is being done in other communities." Moreover, it is not unreasonable to hypothesize that, as systems and networks grow, the librarian of the small town will be increasingly drawn toward the metropolitan library, and if he cannot exploit the resources of his area or region he cannot serve his community well.

If one accepts the statement that the major aspects of librarianship expressed in terms of its social goals are the promotion of the general cultural level through the provision of materials and services that will contribute to the enrichment of the individual, and the extension of knowledge and social effectiveness through the provision of specific and often highly specialized information required by the research and decision-making process, one may conclude that it is from the confusion of these two objectives that much of the muddled thinking about library specialization has emerged. It has been the resolute attempt to force upon the education of the library specialist the now largely obsolete concept of the "general librarian" or librarian as generalist that has been the source of much of the dissatisfaction of the librarian specialist with the library schools. There can be no doubt that from the days of the training class even to the present, library education has been strongly influenced, not to say dominated by the needs of the public librarians, or perhaps more precisely, their needs as the public librarians perceived them. Therefore, criteria of specialization in the library school must make possible a differentiation, not between general and special, but between the two major areas of specialization—the "cultural" and the "scientific."[65] Each of these areas is a cluster of specializations in its own right; the former is not more general than the latter, or the latter more specialized than its counterpart.

## CULTURE AND SCIENCE IN LIBRARY SPECIALIZATION

Culture, as one of the social goals toward which the library, especially the public library, strives, is probably best described by Matthew

---

[65] The terminology is most unsatisfactory. "Culture" is here used in the popular sense, not in the anthropological sense in which it was properly used in the opening chapters of this study. "Scientific" is used to designate anything that is not "cultural." The English language has no terms to express adequately these ideas, even though the areas of human activity for which each stands are generally well understood. Cf. Matthew Arnold's use of "sweetness" and "light," or "Hebraism and Hellenism" in *Culture and Anarchy*, or again C. P. Snow's *The Two Cultures*.

Arnold. He distinguished culture from mere curiosity; though the sheer desire to see things as they are, a passion that is natural and proper in an intelligent human being, is its foundation.

> But there is in culture another view . . . a view in which all the love of our neighbour, the impulses towards active, help, and beneficence, the desire for removing human error, clearing human confusion, and diminishing human misery, the noble aspiration to leave the world better and happier than we found it—motives eminently such as are called social—come in as part of the grounds of culture, and the main and pre-eminent part. Culture is then properly described not as having its origin in curiosity, but as having its origin in the love of perfection.[66]

Later he says that the aim of culture is not only stated in the words of Montesquieu, "To render an intelligent being more intelligent," but also, in the words of Bishop Wilson, "To make reason and the will of God prevail."[67]

The goal of the public library, then, stated in cultural terms, is the perfection of the individual and, through the individual, the perfection of society. It is rooted in the nineteenth-century social philosophies of Carlyle and Ruskin, and on this side of the Atlantic, in the faith in the perfectibility of man and the optimism of an expanding frontier. Today the philosophy of general education is the modern prototype, and its conditioning factors are both psychological and sociological—an understanding of man as both an intellectual and a social being—and it is in this sense that it is a form of specialization. Thus, the librarian who would devote himself to the cultural services of the library must discipline himself in those branches of knowledge that are directed toward the better understanding of man individually and collectively. Therefore, the librarian's understanding of graphic records, their acquisition and selection, must be related to their cultural significance, the extent to which they promote the intellectual, ethical, and moral values of human beings. The same criteria must be applied to the organization and interpretation of library materials; for schemes of classification and techniques of subject analysis which pretend to be scientific, which take as their models schemes for the taxonomic classification of knowledge and the precise terminology of the scientist, are not, in many situations, appropriate to the library servicing the cultural needs of the

---

[66] Matthew Arnold. *Culture and Anarchy*. London. Macmillan. 1903. p. 7.
[67] *Ibid.* p. 8.

child, the adult in the middle years of life, or the aged. The public library is in a period of transition, not to say crisis, and in these changing concepts of the services it is to render lies the key to the character of the professional education required by its staff. What these changing concepts will bring may not now be clearly visible in detail, but at least it is becoming apparent that the public library must develop a closer integration with related agencies and organizations, which are also concerned with the improvement of the individual and the society of which he is a part, than has been true in the past. The public library may well be called upon to reshape its practices and procedures to emphasize enticement rather than retrieval. The public library cannot afford to follow blindly the whims of popular demand and rationalize its lack of standards on the easy assumption that it is a tax supported institution and therefore should respond to the requests of the entire community. Historically the library was brought into being by and for the intellectual elite, and if it is to work constructively with the disadvantaged in the community the librarians must understand the needs of this new clientele. A missionary zeal to do good may, in the end, bring disaster and alienation. The public library is neither the people's "university," nor a social service agency, but it possesses some elements of both and it must educate its practitioners to the bibliographic needs of those segments of the population which have been denied the intellectual wealth of their more fortunate neighbors.[68]

Since Berelson wrote of the library's public for *The Public Library Inquiry*, two major changes, both actual and potential, may be identified in the public library's clientele. First, the characteristics of the population itself have altered dramatically. The "baby boom" of the post-World War II period, just beginning when Berelson wrote, has altered the age distribution. Following a period of relatively low birthrate during the Depression and the Second World War, the "baby boom" has rolled forward like a mammoth tidal wave, creating demands for more schools, more teachers, more children's library services. As this rising tide has progressed from preschool, to grade school, to high school and college, it has altered conceptions and emphases in the education of youth. Combined with educational changes embodying the use of multiple resources, this demographic change has inevitably affected public library service. Even where school libraries have approached adequacy, the demand has been heavy; where

---

[68] See: Kathleen Molz. "The Public Library: The People's University?" *American Scholar.* vol. 34 (Winter 1964–65), pp. 95–102. Also: idem. "Education for Sensibility in the House of Facts." *American Libraries.* vol. 1 (January 1970), pp. 29–32.

school libraries are weak or nonexistent, the public library has had to struggle to maintain itself as a service to the total community against the rising flood of "school-assignment questions." In the 1970s, the wave will create an increasing number of adults who must be served by public libraries, many of whose staffs have had little or no experience in serving adults. Public libraries, and library education, must recognize that these new adults differ in many ways from those of an earlier period for whom the traditional adult services were designed.

The second major change relates not to a difference in population, but rather to a difference in social concern. Whether the charge that the public library has, on the whole, served only white middle-class America, is true or not, attention has shifted to the needs of minorities and the handicapped. It is here that many of the innovations and experiments in new modes of public library service are being tried. The Black community is now the most visible, though it is by no means the only group receiving special attention. Puerto Ricans, Chicanos, Indians, the blind, the homebound, the physically handicapped—all these segments of the population are now the targets of a variety of outreach programs. Encouragement and stimulation have come not only from a general social concern but also from the federal programs under the *Library Services and Construction Act* and, to some degree, under the *Economic Opportunity Act*. The future of these programs is uncertain in view of possible economic problems. Such specialized services are expensive and they will call for careful scrutiny when in direct competition with other needs; some, however, will surely survive, and the movement as a whole has released creative thinking about alternative methods of service which may well have a long range effect on traditional librarianship.[69] The task of educating the public librarian is perhaps the most complex and difficult of all, certainly it is that segment of librarianship about which our knowledge is the least precise and reliable.

The specialized communicational services, by contrast, emphasize retrieval and serve the two great divisions of man's scholarship, i.e., the sociohumanistic disciplines and the natural sciences. The sociohumanistic comprises the humanities and the social sciences, and the librarian's professional specialization here must emphasize the history and theory of scholarship, the structure and characteristics of the literature and bibliographic apparatus, and the special problems the field presents with respect

---

[69] The author is indebted to Dorothy Sinclair of the faculty of the library school at Case Western Reserve University for information respecting the changes in the clientele of the public library since Berelson made his study.

to organization and service.[70] For the natural sciences the pattern is much the same. Here the history and methods of science are particularly relevant, as are also the structure and characteristics of the literature of science and the historical changes through which it has passed. The monograph, the journal, the transactions and proceedings of societies, the research report, the literature of patents; all are important aspects of the structure of scientific literature which the professional librarian must master.

Because in the sciences there is a need for the retrieval of exact information, information which is often fragmented into minute units and widely scattered,[71] particular attention must be given not only to the major bibliographic instruments, but also to the latest developments in mechanized literature searching. This is the area of librarianship in which technological development is most rapid and the procedures least standardized. Moreover, it is subject to the most exaggerated claims. Therefore it is particularly important that the student be equipped with a body of theoretical knowledge that will enable him to define the parameters of the problems to be solved, analyze as objectively as possible the validity of each "solution," and develop the intellectual skills necessary to winnow the genuine from the spurious. This implies an understanding of the special problems of organization and presentation that must be solved if the sciences are to be adequately served, and how and under what conditions the contributions and limitations of such bibliographic aids as the index, the classification scheme, the abstract, and the literature survey may be most effectively used in the totality of the scientific process.[72]

A rational division of responsibility among the several library schools for library specialization would be not only desirable for the future, but almost inevitable. In many instances carefully planned internships, workshops, institutes, and other forms of the short course can prevent hasty and ill-considered plunging into specializations for which a school has few,

---

[70] Conrad H. Rawski. "Subject Literatures and Librarianship." *Library School Teaching Methods; Courses in the Selection of Adult Materials,* ed. Larry E. Bone. Urbana, Ill. Graduate School of Library Science. University of Illinois. 1969. pp. 92–113. See also: Dewey E. Carroll. "Toward a Systems Oriented Approach to Subject Literatures and Problems of Selection in Libraries." *Ibid.* pp. 73–91.

[71] See discussion of the "Law of Scattering" by S. C. Bradford. "The Documentation Chaos." *Documentation* by S. C. Bradford. 2nd ed. London. Crosby Lockwood. 1953. pp. 144–59.

[72] Jesse H. Shera. "How Engineers Can Keep Abreast of Professional and Technical Developments." *Papers Presented at the 1962 Design Engineering Conference.* New York. American Society of Mechanical Engineers. 1962. pp. 49–53. Also: idem. "On Keeping Up With Keeping Up." *Documentation and the Organization of Knowledge* by Jesse H. Shera. London. Crosby Lockwood. 1966. pp. 72–83.

if any, of the minimum essentials. One course does not a program make, and unrealistic hopes are not the stuff with which achievement is won. Library education is experiencing an inflation that can be disastrous. The profession is rapidly approaching a point where there are too many schools and too many specializations. The literature of the "educationists" has many sins for which it must accept responsibility, nevertheless, those who are charged with the establishment of new schools or evaluating and restructuring the curricula of established ones would be well advised to consider thoughtfully certain of the "neoclassics" such as the writings of Tyler, Taba, Bloom, and a few others.[73] Such works as these will go far toward clarifying educational objectives and procedures in professional education. These and similar inquiries must be read, of course, in the light of the problems of library education, and they will yield up to the reader only the applications which he brings to them, but there is real substance in those pages and all too few library educators have an awareness, much less an understanding, of the insights such studies can bring to the tasks and problems of the library educator.

The diagram in Figure 11-1 can be no more than suggestive, and the interrelationships cannot all be shown in a two-dimensional figure. Such a pictorial representation cannot be a blueprint; rather it is a hypothetical configuration which should provide some awareness of the intellectual topography of the first professional graduate year; and it may provide some indication of the interrelationships of those areas of study which comprise the discipline of librarianship.

## THE SIXTH, OR POST-MASTER'S YEAR

That a single calendar year provides insufficient time for the initiate to acquire the professional education he needs has long been recognized by both students and faculty of library schools. Moreover, the steady deterioration of the master's degree, not only in library education, but also in all fields of graduate study, has been a distressing phenomenon. During

---

[73] Ralph W. Tyler. *Basic Principles of Curriculum and Instruction.* Chicago. University of Chicago Press. 1950; Hilda Taba. *Curriculum Development, Theory and Practice.* New York. Harcourt, Brace and World. 1962; Benjamin S. Bloom et al. *Taxonomy of Educational Objectives. Handbook I. Cognitive Domain. Handbook II. Affective Domain.* New York. David McKay. 1956 and 1964; James B. Macdonald et al., eds. *Strategies of Curriculum Development.* Columbus, Ohio. Merrill. 1965.

| Stage I—All Students | Stage II—Major Groupings | Stage III—Specialized Groupings |
|---|---|---|

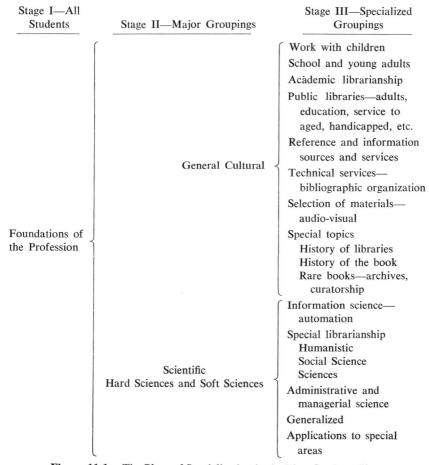

**Figure 11-1.**   The Place of Specialization in the First Graduate Year

the first three decades of the present century, the Graduate School of Yale University made a valiant attempt to revive the deteriorating status of the degree by requiring two years of graduate study, Latin and one modern foreign language, and a master's thesis. But competition and the economic hardships brought on by the Depression compelled the abandonment of this noble plan because it was handicapping Yale in the competition for students. The residential and thesis requirements of the Graduate Library School of the University of Chicago still, in the eyes of many, penalizes the student by requiring him to surmount academic barriers that block the way to a degree that is little, if any, more prestigious than that of other library schools. Nevertheless, one can at least admire the determination in the school beside the Midway to remain true to its original principles in the face of the most severe competition. The "academic Gresham's law," that cheap education tends to drive out excellence, has brought only harm to graduate and undergraduate study. Courage is required to go against the current, but even more necessary is money, for without financial support excellence cannot survive. In education, the myth of "the better mousetrap" is little more than wishful thinking.

The ALA Board of Education for Librarianship was, in the opinion of Louis Round Wilson, guilty of a serious error when, in 1926, it accepted the ruling of the Association of American Universities that a certificate, or a second bachelor's degree be awarded for the first year of professional study in librarianship. This acquiescence, Wilson believed, "has been responsible for much of the confusion concerning the proper content of the pre-professional, professional and graduate-professional curricula and for salary discrimination against holders of second Bachelor's degrees, since it was not clear what the degree stood for."[74] Nevertheless, one finds it difficult to criticize the position taken by the Association of American Universities, for the Williamson Report, published only three years earlier, was scarcely one to inspire confidence in library education on the part of the academic community.

In contrast to Wilson's position, and, in a curious way, something of a substantiation of his point of view, Ralph Munn wrote in 1936, of the professional education needed by the staff of the Carnegie Library of Pittsburgh, that "except for the director and about six department heads and specialists, I believe the Pittsburgh staff does not need more bibliographical or technical training than is now given in one-year library schools."[75] Obviously Munn did not see the accelerated rate of change that even at the time he wrote, was beginning to be manifest, nor did he envisage the role that the librarian of a large and important metropolitan public library might play in the communication system in society. Yet Munn must be acknowledged as one of the leaders of the library world during the period of his greatest professional activity. The obvious fact remains that, except for a very few people such as Wilson, the need for anything beyond the first professional degree was not widely recognized until very recent years, and even today this need has been poorly articulated.

In 1965 Raynard Swank envisaged the sixth-year program, leading

---

[74] Louis Round Wilson. "Historical Development of Education for Librarianship in the United States." Chicago. *Librarianship*. pp. 50–51.

[75] Ralph Munn. *Conditions and Trends in Education for Librarianship*. New York. Carnegie Corporation of New York. 1936. p. 15.

to some form of academic recognition exemplified by a certificate or other formal device, as one of four approaches to advanced specialization.[76] Two years later Swank was still seeing the sixth year as presenting a great opportunity for specialized education. He was convinced that, confronted as we are "with all the new content and roles of librarianship that confound us in these times, we need to pay more attention than ever to the nature, scope, and purpose of the general curriculum, wherein lies the unity of the profession. At the same time, we must intensify our specialized curricula, wherein lies the diversity of the profession. . . . We cannot succeed at both within the fifth year."[77] Moreover, Swank believed that if a sharp distinction were drawn, during the fifth year, between library education for service and library education for research, the sixth year could be used to carry both forward to advanced levels. He did not hold that the sixth year could be accepted as adequate for the education of faculty in graduate library schools nor did he regard the M.Ph., the D. Arts, or the Certificate of Candidacy as substitutes for the Ph.D. But the sixth-year program, properly designed, "could become a staging period both for practitioners who later want to enter teaching and research and for researchers from other disciplines who do not want to enter library practice."[78]

Rev. James J. Kortendick and Elizabeth Stone of the Catholic University of America, after conducting an intensive interrogation of 365 "middle and upper-level" practicing librarians in the federal government service, drawn from a total population of 1,347 such individuals, concluded that: there exists a need for a post-master's program that would upgrade professional librarians, that the program should be interdisciplinary, should relate to "on-the-job" needs, be based in a library school, a "systems format" should be used in planning and implementing the program, a multimedia approach to instruction seemed desirable, and financial considerations would seem to necessitate a "part-time" basis if students in appreciable numbers are to be attracted. The subjects which seemed to be most in demand were library administration and management, library automation, and such specialized courses as building and evaluating collections, current practices in acquisitions, special library administration, search logic and tactics, and systems analysis for library and information

---

[76] Raynard C. Swank. "The Graduate Library School Curriculum." *Problems of Library School Administration*, ed. Sarah R. Reed. Washington, D.C. U.S. Office of Education. 1965. pp. 20–28.

[77] Raynard C. Swank. "Sixth-Year Curricula and the Education of Library School Faculty." *Journal of Education for Librarianship*. vol. 8 (Summer 1967), p. 15.

[78] *Ibid.* p. 19.

center operations.[79] Prior to the Kortendick-Stone study, Mrs. Stone had conducted a comparable inquiry, using librarians from a diverse sample of all types of libraries—public, special, school, and academic.[80] Her findings also indicated a feeling that practicing librarians needed continuing education, and that such programs should be a joint responsibility shared by library schools, the U.S. Office of Education, library administrations, and even publishers. Certainly no one can deny the value of sound continuing education programs to the practicing librarian, but one wonders whether the questionnaire approach to the problem has any real validity in predicting support for such programs when "the chips are down."

In a study carried out at the University of Chicago in 1967–68 of eleven of the twelve accredited library schools then offering post-master's programs, Floyd N. Fryden found that in general the objectives of the programs were divided among three distinct categories: (1) to prepare teachers for faculty positions in library schools at either the undergraduate or graduate levels, or both; (2) to provide means for practicing librarians to improve their upward mobility; and (3) to enable practicing librarians to improve performance.[81] Obviously the programs were planned to be complementary to the students' first professional year, though in some schools courses have been offered which are open to master's candidates as well as to those seeking added knowledge. Most of the programs were no more than two years old at the time the study was made, only three of the programs were formally inaugurated before the fall of 1966, and two had received no support from the provisions of Title IIb of the Higher Education Act of 1965. One of the two programs, however, was the recipient of state aid. In eight of the schools there was a remarkable coincidence of availability of federal support and the inauguration of the programs. Thus, one cannot but wonder whether it was the schools' response to a professional need, or the prospect of easy federal money that was respon-

---

[79] James J. Kortendick and Elizabeth W. Stone. *Post-Master's Education for Middle and Upper-Level Personnel in Libraries and Information Centers.* Washington, D.C. Catholic University of America. 1970.

[80] Elizabeth W. Stone. *Factors Relating to the Professional Development of Librarians.* Metuchen, N.J. Scarecrow Press. 1969. Also: Elizabeth W. Stone. "Continuing Education in Librarianship; Ideas for Action." *American Libraries.* vol. 1 (June 1970), pp. 543–51.

[81] Floyd N. Fryden. "Post-Master's Degree Programs in the U.S. Accredited Library Schools." *Library Quarterly.* vol. 39 (July 1969), pp. 233–44. The schools surveyed were: University of California at Los Angeles, Columbia, Emory, Florida State, Illinois, Louisiana, Maryland, Minnesota, Pittsburgh, Western Michigan, and Wisconsin. After the study had been completed, the author discovered that the University of Texas also had such a program.

sible for the sixth-year development. One can guess that these programs, because they lack adequate structure and objectives, are extremely "soft" and very exposed to the vicissitudes of governmental largess. The picture of these programs which Fryden presented is not one to inspire confidence, and it raises many more questions about the direction in which library education is moving than it answers.

In 1968, J. Periam Danton inaugurated a study of sixth-year programs, under a contract with the Committee on Accreditation of the ALA, to supplement Fryden's inquiry.[82] Nine schools were added to the Fryden list, though it is to be noted that, of the total of twenty, Drexel, Louisiana, and Maryland had abandoned their programs, at least temporarily, after a year or two of trial. Danton's inquiry included not only an intensive review of the schools, their programs, and objectives, but also the graduates and their employers. All of the schools conceived of their programs as providing some kind of library specialization, one-third of them emphasized preparation for teaching in library schools, and more than one-third emphasize information science and automation. This is not surprising as, in the early days of evaluating applications for grants under Title IIb of the Higher Education Act, priorities were placed on "innovation" in library education. Whether or not "form follows function," at least it follows financing. Nine of the twenty schools also offered doctoral programs, but in general such schools regarded the sixth-year specialist program as being a separate and largely independent activity. Curricula varied to the point at which generalization was virtually impossible. Nine schools required no single course or seminar of all students in the sixth-year program, though seven made mandatory a course in research, or research methods. Thus, one can conclude with reasonable accuracy that the programs are highly flexible and individually tailored to the student's needs. Stated positively, such a characterization would seem, at least at first blush, to signify virtue, but it can, and in many cases probably does, imply only a hodge-podge of courses thrown together with little plan or forethought, with no Divinity to shape their rough-hewn ends. Perhaps Danton's most

---

[82] J. Periam Danton. *Between M.L.S. and Ph.D. A Study of Sixth-year Specialist Programs in Library Schools Accredited by the American Library Association.* Berkeley, California. September 1969. Draft copy.

The schools, with dates of establishment of the programs were: Atlanta, 1967; Chicago, 1969; Columbia, 1961; Drexel, 1966; Emory, 1966; Florida State, 1967; Illinois, 1964; Kent State, 1968; Louisiana State, 1967; Maryland, 1967; Minnesota, 1966; Peabody, 1954; Pittsburgh, 1963; Rutgers, 1966; Texas, 1967; Toronto, 1950; UCLA, 1967; Wayne State, 1967; Western Michigan, 1966; and Wisconsin, 1966.

distressing finding is that few schools *required* students to enroll in courses in other disciplines, all did no more than *encourage* such interdisciplinary study. Also a limit, usually no more than half of the credit units, was placed on the amount of such study. It is impossible to escape the conclusion that, despite Williamson's admonition of a half-century ago, library schools are still far more isolated than they should be from the academic environment which university affiliation was supposed to provide.

Evaluations by the students of the programs is not convincing. Only 153 responded to the inquiry, of which one-half indicated satisfaction but one-fourth reported positive dissatisfaction. The remainder of the sample was "content," whatever that may mean. Danton admits that these results are "disturbing." Employers of "graduates" of the sixth-year programs seemed generally satisfied with the benefits received from this educational experience of their staff members, though the sample was necessarily small and of dubious statistical validity.

Danton's faculty findings, however, are truly disturbing. Sixty percent of the full-time faculty in the library schools surveyed hold no degree higher than the BLS/MLS, and many of these are teaching in sixth-year programs. Such a situation would not be tolerated in a graduate subject department of any reputable university. The present writer does not hold to the doctrine of the educationists that a degree is necessarily the mark of instructional competence, but the situation depicted by Danton would seem to be carrying "liberalization" too far. Danton's final evaluation of the sixth-year programs appears to be somewhat more optimistic than his data substantiate. He concluded that, in general, the sixth-year programs are basically sound in conception, viable, functioning well, and, in some instances excellently, though all could be improved. Because these programs are very recent in origin and their life expectancy may be brief, it is probably unfair to be overly critical of them; nevertheless, from the studies of both Fryden and Danton it is difficult to view such programs as doing anything more than perpetuating the ills and problems that beset the conventional master's program in librarianship. There can be no doubt that a program between the M.L.S. and the doctorate is needed, and it could provide a welcome opportunity to enrich the first professional year of study in many ways, but before library educators plunge headlong into such undertakings they would be well advised to put the first year of study in order. Until both the fifth- and sixth-year programs can be developed soundly, students should devote the time in the sixth year to graduate study in an appropriate subject discipline. Two weak programs will not make one strong one, and library educators cannot compensate for the inadequacies of the fifth year by piling a sixth on top.

The answer to the problem posed by the sixth year will depend on the future admission policies of the library schools. If the schools should insist on the possession of at least a subject master's degree and a measure of quasi-professional experience prior to admission to the basic library school program, the sixth year could then be devoted to intensive exploration of subject bibliography and bibliographic organization. By contrast, however, if students are admitted directly to library school from college with an undergraduate subject major, the sixth year should be devoted largely to graduate study in the appropriate subject areas. These alternatives are, of course, not mutually exclusive, a school can pursue both. The basic consideration is that in the future the library schools graduate only those who combine technical competence in librarianship with a mastery of the recorded knowledge of a discipline.

## CRISIS AND CHANGE

That education for librarianship is rapidly approaching a real crisis seems to be beyond dispute. Increasingly it is coming under attack; some of the criticism is invalid and arises from misapprehension of the nature of the educational process in general and of professional education in particular.

Perhaps the most distressing feature of library education today is the seemingly inexplicable enthusiasm of college and university administrators for the establishment of new library schools. The rapid proliferation of these undergraduate and weak graduate programs, inadequately financed, poorly staffed, and neglectful of the problems of curriculum construction, cannot but bring great harm to the profession by flooding it with mediocrity. Unhappily this trend has had the full support of library administrators who have cried out for more "professionals" to augment their staffs.

The first step, then, must be to arrest this onrush into library education by greatly strengthening and stiffening accreditation requirements, both through the adoption of precise and rigorous standards applied with much more discrimination, even severity, than has been the policy in the past. Above all, the competence of the faculty must be a primary consideration of the accrediting agency; to say merely that "the faculty shall be adequate," is very far from being enough as a standard of excellence.

If there are to be attracted to library schools faculties with the competence and dedication that library education desperately needs, salaries must be commensurate with responsibility. So long as faculty are required to make financial sacrifices in order to teach, the educational system will suffer, but more will be said about the faculty problem in Chapter 13.

The curriculum of the first professional year, especially, stands in serious need of a thorough overhauling. The old "core" must be streamlined to emphasize those elements that are fundamental to the practice of all librarianship whatever the specialization. There must be a reconciliation between what might be called conventional librarianship and the emerging study of information science. Mechanisms must be evolved to enhance the dialogue between faculty and students in the library school and faculty and students in other departments, disciplines, and professions in the university. Students, alumni, and practicing librarians should be brought into the intellectual operations and decision making processes of the schools. The Library Education Division of the ALA and the Association of American Library Schools should exert more leadership in library education and give more support to the schools than they have exhibited in the past. To say merely that library education should be "relevant to today's needs," a slogan mouthed *ad nauseam* by today's young dissidents, can be misleading. The relevance of today may well be the irrelevance of tomorrow, and the library school must educate for the future while not neglecting the demands that will be placed upon its graduates when they embark upon their first professional jobs. Yet the spirit that lies behind this slogan is unmistakably clear and in large measure justified. An educational program that is fragmented in approach and limited in concept can result in the training of facile technicians in an atmosphere of intellectual sterility or chaos.

One can say of education for librarianship much the same as Kathleen Molz has said of the practice of librarianship, that it is "implacable of purpose."

> The requirements of society dictate something more to us than a resistance to change; if institutions resist modernization, then leaders will come who will modernize them. Personally, I am not sure what the decision of the profession is really going to be; to serve as the granite, the rock diverting the course of the stream; or to move into the swift flowing water which finally shapes the course of history. Like rock and flood, the contrarieties are there; resistance to change or commitment to revolution. I suspect that most libraries and colleges and schools will try to straddle the fence, find some middle ground between the two extremes. What I feel uncertain about is whether that middle course will be possible.[83]

---

[83] Kathleen Molz. "Education for Sensibility."

The chairman of an Irish corporation, so an old story goes, on hearing the financial report of the business for the year, observed, "This is all right in practice, but how will it work out in theory?" His query is as appropriate for education as it is for industry. Robert M. Hutchins, in a symposium on higher education in America, cites Henry Steele Commager as saying that the American university is the greatest success in the history of the world without advancing any theory of its function other than that it should continue to perform any task society assigns to it. Hutchins adds that "perhaps any theory of the American university is impossible." But Hutchins remains unshaken in his belief that the university "needs a brain," and concludes, in words that have a special relevance for library education, "The brain, if it can be found, might then decipher the idea of the enterprise."[84] Library education certainly needs a brain. The present writer would not pretend that he has discovered it, but he does express the hope that he may have suggested some places where a search might profitably be conducted.

---

[84] Center for the Study of Democratic Institutions. *The University in America.* A symposium by Clark Kerr, Rosemary Park, Jacques Barzun, and others. Santa Barbara, California. Center for the Study of Democratic Institutions. 1967. p. 8. (Occasional Paper on the Role of Education in a Free Society.)

# Twelve

# The Doctoral Program and Research

As early as 1891, Melvil Dewey, then director of the New York State Library School at Albany, established the degree of Doctor of Library Science, but it was his intention that the degree should be awarded *honoris causa* for conspicuous professional achievement rather than for research. There is no record that the degree was ever granted.[1] The doctorate at Columbia was not awarded to a library school student until 1953, and thus was preceded by the universities of Chicago, Illinois, and Michigan.

The establishment of the Graduate Library School at the University of Chicago in 1926, included immediate provision for the awarding of the earned degree of Doctor of Philosophy, and ignited a heated discussion of what constituted appropriate research in librarianship that would qualify the candidate for the doctor's hood. Until the appointment of Louis Round Wilson as dean of the new school in 1932, the program was quite unstructured, there were few if any formal classes, and individual work under the direct supervision of the appropriate instructors was emphasized. Wilson introduced a substantial measure of formalization, initiated the concept of the social sciences as providing the appropriate intellectual foundation for advanced study in librarianship, and insisted that students supplement their study with appropriate courses in other divisions and schools of the University. Because many of the Chicago graduates, espe-

---

[1] Ray Trautman. *A History of the School of Library Service, Columbia University.* New York. Columbia University Press. 1954. pp. 29 and 65.

cially those during the Wilson era, themselves entered the field of library education, subsequent doctoral programs have been heavily influenced by these early developments on the Midway.

## THE STRUGGLE FOR SURVIVAL

From the day of its inception, and even before when the idea was but a dream, the program at Chicago waged an uphill battle. Only the lure of a Carnegie endowment persuaded the administration of the University to adopt this unwanted child, and once reluctantly taken into the academic community, it was treated at best with a tolerant indifference, and at worst was threatened with dissolution. It was damned by critics as prime evidence of the deterioration of the doctorate when entrusted to the vocationalists. Within the library profession itself the criticism was, if anything, even more devastating than that from the outside. Public librarians such as Wheeler and Munn could see no need for it whatever; the conventional library school program, which taught students the "how" rather than the "why," was held to be quite adequate to the profession's needs. That these critics were worrying about "a cloud no bigger than a man's hand," would seem to be apparent from the early records. As late as 1949, Bernard Berelson wrote: "All of the Doctorates have come from one school. . . . In an average year—and in this case, there is still such consistency that almost every year (of the past ten) is average—about four Doctor's degrees are awarded."[2] Yet there was a curious ambiguity in the attitude of the profession toward the Ph.D. for, despite the widespread criticism of it and the denial of its value in librarianship, Berelson was able to point out that the first consequence for the students in the doctoral program "is just what it should be: they learn something. . . . The second consequence for the students is that they get good jobs in librarianship." This last point he supported with statistics: "The Ph.D.'s in librarianship now make an average salary of nearly three hundred percent of their salary at admission. When the fifty or so currently active Ph.D.'s came to the Graduate Library School, ten were head librarians and now twenty-eight are; thirteen held minor positions and now none of them do."[3]

---

[2] Bernard R. Berelson. "Advanced Study and Research in Librarianship." *Education for Librarianship*. University of Chicago, Graduate Library School. Chicago. American Library Association. 1949. p. 214.

[3] *Ibid.* pp. 19–20.

For the schools the major advantage in a doctoral program was also twofold: first, "when properly administered," the program has "the effect of vitalizing the school, of keeping it plastic, curious, alert, alive"; and second, such programs increase "potentially, and in some cases actually," its influence upon the profession. "Such influences come partly through the impact of the research that is generated and published and partly from the work of the graduates and their improved effectiveness."[4] As to the impact upon the profession, Berelson again found a twofold result: "The first is the increment to the profession of trained personnel with broad educational orientation. . . . The important point here is not so much the contribution of such people; they are persons of ability and most of them would have made their marks sooner or later. My point is that with the aid of advanced training, they made it sooner. . . . In other words, advanced training has brought such Doctoral graduates into full service some ten to fifteen years *before* they would have reached such positions otherwise."[5] But doctoral programs have brought to the profession not only an increment of personnel, but also an increment of knowledge. "Whether that increment is impressive or disappointing depends, of course, upon the standards by which it is evaluated."[6] Berelson thought it was some of both. Some of the accomplishments of graduate study merit considerable praise, but are "disappointing when viewed against the possibilities and the need."[7]

In the decade that followed Berelson's observations, six library schools inaugurated doctoral programs—Illinois, Michigan, Columbia, Western Reserve, California, and Rutgers.[8] Also, there appeared from time to time, doctoral dissertations in the field of librarianship in graduate departments other than library science—Louis Shores's *The American College Library*, Sidney Ditzion's *Arsenals of a Democratic Culture*, Howard McGaw's *Marginal Punched Cards; Their Use in College Libraries*, Eugene Wilson's *Pre-Professional Backgrounds of Students in the Library School*, and Thomas S. Harding's *The Literary Society in the Development of the Early American College Library*, to name a few. Quite obviously, librarianship was beginning to achieve a measure of recognition as an appropriate subject for doctoral research. Yet, Berelson's ambivalent reaction to the products of library research would seem to be supported by the available

---

[4] *Ibid.* p. 220.

[5] *Ibid.* p. 221.

[6] *Ibid.* p. 223.

[7] *Ibid.* p. 224.

[8] J. Periam Danton. "Doctoral Study in Librarianship in the United States." *College and Research Libraries*. vol. 20 (November 1959), pp. 437–53. Lists the doctoral dissertations in librarianship 1930–1959.

evidence. During the first thirty years of the existence of such programs 129 dissertations were produced of which 80 came from the University of Chicago.[9] Of the 129 dissertations appearing between 1930–59, 45 dealt with the history of books, printing, publishing and the history of libraries, whereas other categories were far less frequently represented: library government and administration, 13; studies of the technical services, 11; studies of reading and reading interests, 9; content analysis, 8; and bibliographic organization (which might be regarded as the antecedent of documentation and information science), 9. Even such scattered and fragmentary statistics as these show clearly the humanistic origins of library research and the persistence of the humanistic tradition despite the efforts of Wilson and Waples to channel students into the behavioral sciences.

Two decades after Berelson confessed to a degree of skepticism about the state of doctoral study in librarianship, J. Clement Harrison wrote a sterner verdict than that of the former Chicago dean: "The doctoral programs in library science . . . have not been insignificant. On the other hand, in terms of both quantity and quality, they have been disappointing. I think the average annual output has been something like six. . . . Of the quality of the doctoral dissertations in library science it might be said that, with certain notable exceptions, most of the candidates have obeyed the injunction that if something is not worth doing at all it is not worth doing well!"[10] By and large, the objective observer must admit that, since Harrison wrote, the situation has improved little and that doctoral writing has much for which it should be ashamed even though it may not be worse than that in some other areas of the "soft sciences."

## ANTITHESIS OF FORM AND FUNCTION

But librarians are not alone in raising some fundamental doubts about the doctorate. The malaise that infects advanced graduate study in librarianship has its counterpart in, if it is not a direct reflection of, the doc-

---

[9] The first doctoral dissertation in library science was Eleanor S. Upton's *A Guide to Sources of Seventeenth-Century English History in Selected Reports of the Royal Commission on Historical Manuscripts.* (Chicago 1930). The first non-Chicago dissertation was Rolland E. Stevens' *The Use of Library Materials in Doctoral Research.* (Illinois 1951).

[10] J. Clement Harrison. "Advanced Study; A Mid-Atlantic Point of View." *Library Education, an International Survey,* ed. Larry E. Bone. Urbana, Ill. Graduate School of Library Science, University of Illinois. 1968. p. 330.

torate generally. "For graduate schools to continue to follow their outmoded tradition has critical consequences almost beyond belief," wrote Carroll Newsom.[11] Much the same uncertainty that besets the undergraduate curriculum can be applied to doctoral study. "The graduate schools are not beyond criticism"; wrote John Diekhoff, "they probably do not do their job any better than undergraduate schools."[12] And he quotes with approval the statement by Charles W. Jones to the effect that the direct object of the Ph.D. program is to develop "love of learning, not to produce research scholars."[13] This statement is debatable; "love of learning" should be a prerequisite for doctoral study, not its end product.

The absence of unity and coherence that characterizes the graduate school of today derives quite logically from the *Lernfreiheit* and the *Lehrfreiheit*—the freedom of the student to choose his courses and that of the professor to offer his wares—of the early nineteenth century German universities. Yale awarded the first American doctoral degree in 1861, but the real breakthrough in graduate study came with the appointment, in 1876, of Daniel Coit Gilman as the first president of Johns Hopkins University, which began as a graduate school with an emphasis on research. Charles W. Eliot at Harvard followed the Gilman example by emphasizing graduate and professional education together with research, and others followed in rapid succession—Andrew Dickson White at Cornell, James B. Angell at Michigan, Frederick Barnard at Columbia, William W. Folwell at Minnesota, David Starr Jordan at Stanford, William Rainey Harper at Chicago, and Charles K. Adams at Wisconsin. With the Hopkins influence came the doctrine of the preeminence of the department in educational decision-making, the idea of the "academic ladder," and the great proliferation of courses. "The elective system, however," observed Clark Kerr, "came more to serve the professors than the students for whom it was first intended, for it meant that the curriculum was no longer controlled by educational policy. . . . Each professor had his own interests, each professor wanted the status of having his own special course, each professor got his own course—and university catalogs came to include 3,000 or more of them."[14] Along with the Teutonic influence came one

---

[11] Carroll V. Newsom. *A University President Speaks Out.* New York. Harper. 1961. p. 104.

[12] John S. Diekhoff. *Tomorrow's Professors.* New York. Fund for the Advancement of Education. n.d. p. 59.

[13] Charles W. Jones. *"The Truman Report and the Graduate School." Journal of Higher Education.* vol. 20 (October 1949), pp. 357–58.

[14] Clark Kerr. *The Uses of the University.* Cambridge, Mass. Harvard University Press. 1963. p. 14. See also: Richard J. Storr. *The Beginnings of Graduate Education in America.* Chicago. University of Chicago Press. 1953.

that was typically American, not to say Jeffersonian, the establishment of the land-grant colleges. Surprisingly, the two blended well, perhaps almost too well, for together they further destroyed any real structural design for the graduate program. Moreover, in this blending may be seen again the two halves of science, the pure and the applied, or to say it another way, the shotgun marriage of theory and technique.

Though the doctorate has long been regarded as an essential prerequisite to teaching in the college and university, there is a growing belief that research and training for research is absorbing increasing amounts of the students' attention, and that such preparation has little to do with the success of the teacher. At the same time, there has been a stiffening reluctance to introduce a "teaching degree." Opposition to a new degree may be, as William Clyde DeVane has hypothesized, due to a fear of "the damage to scholarship resulting from a training and a degree that might be regarded as second-class," or a loss of caste through any departure from an orthodox position.[15] The only really important changes that have taken place in the doctoral programs have been a tendency to shorten the dissertation with less emphasis on originality, a belief that the dissertation should primarily represent the intellectual competence and skill of the candidate without regard to its uniqueness, a broadening of the program of study through ill planned interdisciplinary programs, and a lowering of the foreign language requirement. All of these changes would seem to be "downward," in that they tend to increase the ease with which the degree may be obtained. There is a danger that eventually the degree may not be useful to either the skilled research worker or the teacher, and, in preparing a student for truly competent research, postdoctoral programs will have to be developed.

This deterioration of the doctorate can well be attributed, at least in part, to the onward rush of normal schools and colleges to become "universities." "Universities by the dozen now offer the Ph.D.," complained Jacques Barzun, "some genuine, some travesties, because the college market wants the label on its faculty members, even the junior colleges. . . . As long as college catalogs are printed with degrees following names, and people believe that all Ph.D.'s are created equal, those letters will exercise on American higher education the baneful influence that Lawrence Lowell so often denounced, blaming Daniel Coit Gilman of Johns Hopkins for needless invention."[16] Daniel Bell, the uncompromising supporter of

---

[15] William Clyde DeVane. *Higher Education in Twentieth Century America.* Cambridge, Mass. Harvard University Press. 1965. p. 154.

[16] Jacques Barzun. *The American University.* New York. Harper and Row. 1968. pp. 92–93.

general education, has complained that the graduate school has become central to the university and is threatening the college in general and liberal education in particular.[17] Hofstadter and Hardy have seen excessive specialization as the great danger in the doctoral program; "even in science this is jeopardizing the range of intelligence necessary to the elaboration of theory."[18]

Complaints against the doctorate are, of course, not new. William James spoke of "the Ph.D. octopus," and A. Lawrence Lowell attempted to create an aristocratic alternative to the degree by endowing, at Harvard, the Society of Fellows. The subjects, or at least the titles, of doctoral dissertations have long been the butt of popular American humor, and every experienced university administrator is all too painfully aware of the difficulties in raising financial support for pure research, or research that does not have an apparent immediate application to contemporary problems and needs. "Caught in this cross-fire between the intellectual elitists and the know-nothings," wrote Jencks and Riesman, "the graduate schools have inevitably been somewhat defensive, but they have made no concessions. Instead their faculty mostly concluded that the laity was beyond redemption, that stronger efforts were needed to prevent the subversion of the academy by pragmatism and indolence, that the primary problem was to . . . keep the citadel fortified against possible Luddite incursions."[19]

Bernard Berelson, after completing for the Carnegie Corporation a major statistical analysis of graduate education, concluded that almost from the beginning graduate education has been caught between growing numbers of students and an extremely rapid expansion of knowledge; as a result it has been compelled to diversify in fields, institutions, students, and objectives. The central characteristics of graduate programs, especially those relating to the doctorate, were established early in the development of an institution's history. Over the years there has been a substantial amount of self-criticism and evaluation concerning graduate study. From generation to generation the debate has been substantially the same, and

---

[17] Daniel Bell. *The Restoring of General Education*. New York. Columbia University Press. 1966. p. 275.

[18] Richard Hofstadter and C. DeWitt Hardy. *The Development and Scope of Higher Education in the United States*. New York. Columbia University Press. 1952. p. 193.

[19] Christopher Jencks and David Riesman. *The Academic Revolution*. Garden City, N.Y. Doubleday. 1968. p. 514. See also: Philip Handler. "The Federal Government and the Scientific Community." *Science*. vol. 171 (January 15, 1971), pp. 148–49. He holds that interdisciplinary programs should be based on a solid training in the conventional disciplines.

the debaters have more often been the humanists and social scientists rather than those engaged in the physical or hard, sciences. There has been an inherent clash between service and standards, teaching and research, the university and the college, academic and professional objectives, among different classes and types of institutions, and among different fields. Paper standards have deteriorated through elimination of the publication requirement for the doctoral dissertation, a shifting of the comprehensive examination to an earlier and less "culminating" position than that which it had previously held and the virtual elimination of the "minor" field.[20]

Hans Rosenhaupt finds in Berelson's statistics evidence that graduate school faculties generally are so preoccupied with their own work that they are quite content with the situation as it is. But perhaps the most serious charge that he brings against graduate study is that of pedantry. "So many authors read, so many dates remembered, so many quotes identified." If unchecked, these tendencies will stifle "joy of discovery, curiosity, the creation of new insights, the courage to say what has not been said before."[21]

With regard to the doctoral program, Berelson recommends: that the norm of a four-year doctorate should be enforced by the university; there should be a general "tightening," by increasing the clarity, compactness, and specificity of the course of study with close supervision and direction of the student by the faculty; the dissertation should be shorter than it has been in the past; postdoctoral study should be regularized; foreign language requirements should be left to the departments; and the final oral examination as a defense of the thesis should be eliminated.[22]

Through the findings of Oliver Carmichael's study of graduate education, and analysis of the criticisms of it, Carmichael evolves an integrated program for the talented fifteen to twenty percent who might anticipate pursuit of the Ph.D. The course of study would be of seven years duration, beginning with the first two years of college, and would progress through predoctoral education, not unlike the premedical and prelaw courses which have long been a feature of professional education.[23] His proposal is, in

---

[20] Bernard Berelson. *Graduate Education in the United States.* New York. McGraw-Hill. 1960. pp. 216–19.

[21] Hans Rosenhaupt. "Graduate Education." *American Education Today*, ed. Paul Woodring and John Scanlon. New York. McGraw-Hill. 1960. p. 185. The author is clearly speaking primarily of the humanistic disciplines.

[22] Berelson. *Graduate Education.* pp. 234–42.

[23] Oliver C. Carmichael. *Graduate Education, A Critique and a Program.* New York.

some respects, comparable to the program at the University of Chicago during Hutchins's administration, and that set forth by Paul Woodring.[24] All of these ventures have been an attempt, consciously or unconsciously, to give reality to a concept of the university enunciated, among others, by Paul Weiss, that "a university is a combination of colleges, professional schools, and graduate schools in equipoise, where men are encouraged to sustain and contribute to the next major turns of knowledge. . . . It makes possible a leisurely and expert contact with the basic and pivotal attainments of mankind."[25]

## THE DOCTORATE IN LIBRARIANSHIP

The doubts, uncertainty, and pangs of growth that beset the faltering steps toward the doctorate in librarianship are only a reflection of the schizoid conflict between teaching and research that has harassed graduate study generally almost from its beginnings. The inauguration of doctoral study at the University of Chicago opened a Pandora's box of vexing questions about the need for and the utility of such a degree in a service-oriented occupation, and engendered an argument concerning the intellectual content of the program and the objectives it would serve.[26] Reread today, these debates seem more concerned with rationale and polemics to convince the skeptical than with real substance. We will not here concern ourselves with what Rawski has called "the rosy-cheeked" debates over theory versus practice, library school "methods," grading systems, language requirements, credit hours, the structure and execution of examinations, and all the other logistics of the degree. These matters are largely determined by local university policy. Accrediting bodies can play with them to their heart's content—it gives them something to do and, hence, justifies their existence. We are here concerned with the philosophical rationale, assuming that rationalization is possible.[27]

---

Harper. 1961. Part 2. "Program." See also Chapter 10 for his appraisal of the graduate program.

24 Paul Woodring. *The Higher Learning in America, A Reassessment.* New York. McGraw-Hill. 1968. pp. 216–28.

25 Paul Weiss. *The Making of Men.* Carbondale, Ill. Southern Illinois University Press. 1967. p. 107.

26 See, for example: Charles C. Williamson. "The Place of Research in Library Service." *Library Quarterly.* vol. 1 (January 1931), pp. 1–17.

27 Conrad H. Rawski. "Doctoral Programs, Case Western Reserve University." *Journal of Education for Librarianship.* vol. 8 (Spring 1968), pp. 259–64.

One must begin any discussion of the doctorate, the present writer is convinced, with the assumption that the Ph.D. is a research degree and that it is awarded for evidence that the student is qualified to pursue reflective inquiry. The prize, then, is not for those who would improve or extend their technical proficiency or otherwise seek assistance to climb an occupational ladder. Certainly the doctorate of philosophy is not a professional degree, or some form of certification that testifies to mere professional expertise. But the task of defining basic research for an activity or profession that, over the centuries, has been service, rather than research oriented, is not easy.

The first problem, then, is to identify that in librarianship which is "researchable," for at this level librarianship must not be construed as a kind of handmaiden of other disciplines. Library research, as Rawski has written, must embrace "emphatically the locus problem librarianship has been so slow to recognize."[28] This locus is the underlying theory of librarianship itself. Rawski calls it a *froehliche Wissenschaft*, perhaps to distinguish it from a "dismal science," as economics has on occasion been characterized, but he warns that it has serious implications and is not to be taken lightly. "Rigorous exercise," he goes on to say, "in disciplined examination articulates a basic intellectual armamentarium regardless of specialization or realm of interest. The 'strong inference' created here is, perhaps, less important than the challenge of random applicability, the horizontal thrust of inquiry once the relevant facts of a problem area have been established. Student initiative and effort operate in terms of problems and the situations and contexts attendant upon these problems, and not in terms of a 'program,'" and he has rightly concluded that this is the distinction between "learning" and "being taught."

One can scarcely emphasize too strongly the underlying principle that at the level of the doctorate, and preferably at any intermediate grade, the course of study must be interdisciplinary. The basis for such an assumption does not derive from any sense of academic insecurity giving rise to a fear that without it there can be no program, nor is it necessary for the maintenance of status in a generally suspicious academic community. The interdisciplinary imperative arises from the very fundamental fact that librarianship is an integrative system and hence an object of reflective inquiry, to use Rawski's phrase. To say that research in librarianship cannot

---

In the preparation of this, and the succeeding section, I have received very substantial assistance from my colleague, Professor Conrad H. Rawski, who has been the chief architect of the doctoral program at Case Western Reserve University.
[28] *Ibid.* p. 262.

stand alone, that it is not self-sufficient, that it cannot look exclusively within itself for the solution to its many vexing problems is not to disparage it or its place in the academic world. Interdisciplinarity is of the greatest importance to research and education in all academic disciplines, as Harold Cassidy has shown.[29] But if this integration is to enrich, organize, and deepen the librarian's understanding of his profession, its nature and scope, its responsibilities and requirements, there must be a permanent, implicative, two-way relationship. Such a relationship will not emerge from the loose codisciplinarity of studies in discrete areas connected, as is the case in so many so-called programs in library schools, by nothing more than an educational mystique. Wilson and his associates at the University of Chicago in the 1930s were struggling toward an integrative discipline of librarianship, but despite their innovative efforts they never achieved a true synthesis. Had Waples and Butler been able to reach a common ground of understanding, and had what is now understood as information science been perceived a generation earlier, the contribution of Chicago to education for librarianship, and to research in librarianship, might well have been greater than it was. The foundations were laid on the Midway, but the superstructure has, indeed, been slow in building. Again to quote Rawski:

> We have a great deal to learn. Our limited efforts will not necessarily provide revelatory insights. And there will be misdirection and error. But, uneven as these efforts may turn out to be, they all contribute to the "knowledge within"—that edifice of subject matter concepts, descriptions, and theories, critical evaluation, and eventually, more inclusive epistemological insights, which, if it is ever built, will constitute the discipline of librarianship.[30]

## THE CURRICULAR MATRIX

Without disregarding the Rawski warning that we do not as yet have all the answers to the problem of curricular planning, it is still possible

---

[29] Harold Gomes Cassidy. *The Sciences and the Arts; A New Alliance.* New York. Harper. 1962. p. 24. Cassidy presents the university diagrammatically in terms of the surface of a sphere with philosophy as the north pole, the technologies as the south, and the disciplines which are used to define the arts and sciences arranged as a continuum about the equator.

[30] Rawski. "Doctoral Programs." pp. 263–64.

to suggest a matrix for the doctoral program that is based on a view of librarianship encompassing all that is required, both materially and intellectually, for effective access to recorded knowledge.[31] Such a view implies the inclusion of the relevant areas of information science and information and communication theory, together with the necessary fundamental and substantive subjects.

A program which purports to produce graduates who have the competencies required for professional research and teaching in librarianship, must concentrate on formal study of the theoretical bases and their areas of application. It must provide advanced study in subjects and fields pertinent to librarianship and its problems and be focussed on theory and knowledge (*Wissen*) rather than the acquisition of skills (*Koennen*). The diagram in Figure 12-1 may help to clarify these relationships.

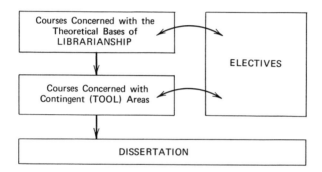

**Figure 12-1.**

Courses concerned with the theoretical bases of librarianship would have to address themselves to,

1. Fundamentals—the goals and principal concerns of librarianship, the "*bibliothecal*" activities (i.e., the acquisition, preservation, organization and housing, and making available of materials), the basic properties of these materials, and the internal and external controls they require. Next come the *service* activities involving human communication, social, and even clinical contexts, and a variety of *supportive* activities and attendant competencies, "ranging from top level administration, management

---

[31] Phyllis A. Richmond. "The Ph.D. in Library Science." *College and Research Libraries.* vol. 31 (September 1970), pp. 313–17.

and planning to maintenance and receiving and shipping . . . including the professional hierarchies and organizational systems and patterns." These areas to be treated in terms of all forms and situations of library service.[32]

2.    The profession of librarianship—its characteristics, history, theory, organizational structure, and sociology.

3.    Education for librarianship—its rationale as professional education, its history, its relationship to higher education generally, and its major areas of concern.

The "tool" courses deal with subjects directly related and/or requisite to competent inquiry in the areas set forth above. The foremost of the fields involved might be grouped as follows:

1.    *Method*: mathematics, statistics, philosophy (especially logic), philosophy of science, systems analysis, computer technology, and the history of science and technology.

2.    *Science and Social Science*: the physical and biological sciences, anthropology, psychology, sociology, economics, education.

3.    *Communication and Organization*: linguistics, management (including organization, administration, and operations research).

These listings are, of course, intended to be no more than suggestive. Curricula should be planned individually in the light of the student's interests, competencies, education, and professional experience. Most entering students will probably need, during their first year, some basic and applied mathematics or statistics, logic, philosophy of science, history of science and technology, though there should be no hard and fast rules. Doubtless, too, many students may want to "fill in" advanced courses in the conventional library school program, and, if they are preparing to teach in library schools, a period of carefully supervised teaching should be provided. At the advanced level, i.e., for second and third-year students, course selection should be directly related to individual research interests or the problems to be investigated in the dissertation. It is important to note that in this phase of the program it is problem analysis which determines the course of study (and not the *fiat* of sundry curriculum committees).

---

[32] Cf. C. H. Rawski. "The Interdisciplinarity of Librarianship." *Toward a Theory of Librarianship; Papers in Honor of Jesse Hauk Shera.* ed. Conrad H. Rawski. In press.

## RESEARCH

Because the doctorate of philosophy is a research degree, and should remain such, and because the concept of research in librarianship is still largely foreign to a profession oriented toward service rather than analysis of bibliothecal phenomena or introspection of its own activity, special attention should here be paid to the research process itself.[33]

"When on board the H.M.S. *Beagle*," wrote Charles Darwin in the Introduction to *The Origin of Species*, ". . . I was much struck with certain facts in the distribution of the organic beings inhabiting South America, and in the geological relations of the present to the past inhabitants of that continent." Darwin surmised that these facts might throw some light on "that mystery of mysteries," the origin of species. Therefore, upon his return home, he began his inquiry "by patiently accumulating and reflecting on all sorts of facts which could possibly have any bearing on it."[34] First he turned to that which was immediate—the plants and animals of the farm and barnyard—and comparing them with their kind "in a state of nature";[35] he reflected that the lesser variability to be observed in the wild might be "due to our domestic productions having been raised under conditions of life not so uniform as, and somewhat different from, those to which the parent species had been exposed under nature."[36] "*The Origin of Species*," Kuhn has written, "recognized no goal set either by God or nature. Instead, natural selection, operating in the given environment and with the actual organisms presently at hand, was responsible for the gradual but steady emergence of more elaborate, further articulated, and vastly more specialized organisms."[37]

Here we cannot, of course, trace out in its entirety the thread of Darwin's argument, though it would be most instructive so to do, for in it is to be seen the almost perfect representation of the research process. Darwin was probably not aware that he had embarked on "research"—

---

[33] The section that follows has been largely taken from the author's essay, "Darwin, Bacon, and Research in Librarianship," which appeared originally in *Library Trends* (vol. 13 (July 1964), pp. 141–49), and reprinted in the author's collection of essays, *Libraries and the Organization of Knowledge* (London. Crosby Lockwood. 1965. pp. 208–16), and is here reproduced with the kind permission of the publishers.

[34] Charles Darwin. *The Origin of Species*. New York. Modern Library. n.d. p. 11.

[35] *Ibid*. p. 13.

[36] *Ibid*. p. 15.

[37] Thomas S. Kuhn. *The Structure of Scientific Revolutions*. Chicago. University of Chicago Press. 1962. p. 171.

though in his *Autobiography* he speaks of his mind as "a kind of machine for grinding general laws out of large collections of facts"[38]—or that he was engaged in any recondite enterprise. He was simply following the admonition of Francis Bacon, from whose *Advancement of Learning* he quotes on one of the fly-leaves of the *Origin*:

> To conclude, therefore, let no man out of a weak conceit of sobriety, or an ill-applied moderation, think or maintain, that man can search too far or be too well studied in the book of God's word, or in the book of God's works; divinity or philosophy; but rather let men endeavour an endless progress or proficience in both.

He also quotes from Whewell's *Bridgewater Treatise*:

> But with regard to the material world, we can at least go so far as this—we can perceive that events are brought about not by insulated interpositions of Divine power, exerted in each particular case, but by the establishment of general laws.

Shorn of its mysticism and its methodology, research since (at least) the time of Bacon has been an answering of questions by the accumulation and assimilation of facts which lead to the formulation of generalizations or universals that extend, correct, or verify knowledge.

One cannot talk about the philosophy of modern research without going back to Bacon, for every serious investigator of natural and social phenomena since the seventeenth century is deeply indebted, consciously or unconsciously, to Baron Verulam, Viscount St. Albans. But Bacon's insistence upon strict application of the experimental method for discovering the facts of nature has now been so fully absorbed into modern scientific practice, and has become so commonplace with the passage of time, that one is apt to forget that Bacon was really protesting the *haphazard* accumulation of observation. He knew, of course, that experimentation had been practiced long before his time; but, as he wrote, "the manner of making experiments which men now use is blind and stupid . . . wandering and straying as they do with no settled course, and taking counsel only from things as they fall out, they fetch a wide circuit and meet with many matters, but make little progress. . . . [They] make their trials carelessly, and as it were in play."[39] The true research worker does

---

[38] Charles Darwin. *Autobiography. Life and Letters.* London. Murray. 1887. vol. 1. p. 101.

[39] Francis Bacon. *Novum Organum. The Works of Francis Bacon.* Popular Edition, Based Upon the Complete Edition of Spedding, Ellis, and Heath. Boston. Houghton, Mifflin and Company. n.d. p. 100.

not embark on a fishing expedition. Chemists do not make random mixtures to see what will happen, nor do biologists thrust under their microscopes the first living organism that comes to hand. Experimentation comes after hypothesis, not before it. Indeed, one can agree with Pierce Butler that "there is no such thing as scientific research until a theoretical hypothesis has been formulated."[40] To be sure, Darwin's curiosity was aroused by his observations of variety in species, but he did not begin his systematic study of its manifestations in domestic animals and plants until he had hypothesized the outcome of his inquiry.

But it was Bacon who established the pattern. "For hitherto," he wrote, "the proceeding has been to fly at once from the sense and particulars up to the most general propositions. . . . My plan is to proceed regularly and gradually from one axiom to another, so that the most general are not reached till the last."[41] Again, he wrote in one of his most famous passages, "The men of experiment are like the ant; they only collect and use: the reasoners resemble spiders, who make cobwebs out of their own substance. But the bee takes a middle course; it gathers its material from the flowers of the garden and of the field, but transforms and digests it by a power of its own."[42] Clearly, to be an effective research investigator one must resemble the bee—purposeful, industrious, and imaginatively selective in the assembling of evidence.

Moreover, for an inquiry to qualify as research, its results must be generalizable. Darwin's work had implications, applications, and consequences far beyond the boundaries of biology, and Bacon well knew that "axioms rightly discovered . . . [will] draw after them trains and troops of works."[43]

This criterion that the results of investigation must be generalizable raises again the age-old problem of pure as opposed to applied research. The fallacy of the dichotomy rests in the assumption that these terms are absolutes, that they are discrete. Research is no less "pure" for leading to useful results, though it most certainly does not have to possess immediate applicability to qualify as research. Bacon, the practical politician and public figure, was suspicious of the tendency of human beings to engage in the artificial kind of speculation that leads nowhere; he wanted all scientific activity to be well established on the bedrock of concrete prob-

[40] Pierce Butler. *An Introduction to Library Science.* Chicago. The University of Chicago Press. 1933. p. 108.
[41] Bacon. *Novum Organum.* p. 42.
[42] *Ibid.* p. 131.
[43] *Ibid.* p. 101.

lems: "On account of the pernicious and inveterate habit of dwelling on abstractions, it is safer to begin and raise the sciences from those foundations which have relation to practice."[44] Yet Bacon was not unmindful of the value of those inquiries which have no immediate applicability, but represent the pursuit of knowledge for its own sake: Science should be willing to carry out "a variety of experiments, which are of no use in themselves, but simply serve to discover causes and axioms: which I call *Experimenta lucifera*, experiments of light, to distinguish them from those which I call *fructifera*, experiments of fruit."[45] Such experiments possess the great advantage that "they never miss or fail. For since they are applied, not for the purpose of producing any particular effect, but only of discovering the natural cause of some effect, they answer the end equally well whichever way they turn out; for they settle the question."[46] Man can maintain his compatibility with nature only by understanding the secrets of nature without regard to immediate and practical ends. "Truth, therefore, and utility are here the very same things: and works themselves are of greater value as pledges of truth than as contributing to the comforts of life."[47]

From both Darwin and Bacon we learn that research in its generic sense is much more than a method or system of methods, a technology, or a body of practice. Though it may involve any one or all of these, it is not defined by them alone. Nor is it to be equated with invention, with which it is so frequently confused by the layman. It is an intellectual act that begins with the asking of a question (emerging from an awareness of one's ignorance) and progresses through the critical examination of evidence that is both relevant and reliable, to the revelation of truth that is generalizable and universal. Its goal is the perfectibility of human knowledge through the pursuit of truth, a goal that can never be attained, but which must always be assumed to be attainable. The more deeply we penetrate into the nature of the atom, Enrico Fermi once observed, the more we are aware that Nature always keeps two jumps ahead of us. He was saying, albeit graphically, no more than that the search for knowledge is interminable, that it has no end, that there is always some place else to go. This is not the counsel of despair, but a challenge to initiative.

Described in terms of its sequential acts, research is an intellectual process whereby a problem is perceived, divided into its constituent ele-

---

[44] *Ibid.* p. 169.
[45] *Ibid.* p. 135.
[46] *Ibid.* p. 135.
[47] *Ibid.* p. 157.

ments, and analyzed in the light of certain basic assumptions; valid and relevant data are collected; hypotheses (if any), are, through objective testing, rejected, amended, or proved. The generalizable results of this process qualify as principles, laws, or truths that contribute to man's understanding of himself, his works, or his environment. Stated another way, research is the systematic attempt to discover new facts or sets of facts, or new relationships among facts, through the formulation of a preliminary explanation or hypothesis which is subjected to an appropriate investigation for validation or disproof.

Hans Selye has identified three properties which he believes should be present in every research result. "It is characteristic of great basic discoveries that they possess, to a high degree and simultaneously, three qualities: they are not only true but very true and in a very special sense; they are generalizable, and they are surprising in the light of what was known at the time of the discovery."[48] But he warns that "in science, things are not true or false; they can be true only within certain statistically determinable limits which tell us the likelihood of the same observation repeating itself in the future if we try to repeat it again." Moreover, the fact that a finding is generalizable is no measure of its significance or importance, e.g., the statistical accuracy with which the color of hormone C was predicted from the first ten that could be prepared in pure form. Therefore, the results must also be surprising, that is, the unexpectedness of the discovery at the time when it was made.[49] Again, Marion Levy has written, "In scientific work it is more important to be fruitful for further work than to be right."[50] Research is the stern disciplinarian that it is, not because it is recondite or esoteric, but because it minimizes the subjective. Yet it is pursued by human beings who are themselves inescapable complexes of both reason and emotion, and in research the latter must be suppressed if the former is to prevail. Reasoning or observation that is diluted with emotion becomes sophistry or dogma. We submit that these are particular threats to research in librarianship, for librarianship is dominantly a service, and a service is always in jeopardy from emotion.

It was Ralph A. Beals who categorized library literature into the tripartite classification of Glad Tidings, Testimony, and Research, finding

---

[48] Hans Selye. *From Dream to Discovery*. New York. McGraw-Hill. 1964. p. 102.

[49] *Ibid*. pp. 102–5. See also: Jesse H. Shera. "The Trickster in Library Research." *Wilson Library Bulletin*. vol. 41 (January 1967), pp. 521 and 533.

[50] Marion J. Levy, Jr. *Modernization and the Structure of Society*. Princeton. Princeton University Press. 1966. p. 7.

precious little of the last.[51] This poverty of research in librarianship was explained by C. C. Williamson, in an address delivered at Western Reserve University in 1930 and subsequently published as the opening essay of the first issue of the *Library Quarterly*, as a consequence of the fact that librarians are basically empiricists, untrained in research and the scientific method. There exists, he charged, "a deep-rooted prejudice among library workers against subjecting their activities to scientific scrutiny."[52] This was undoubtedly the attitude of the typical librarian in 1930, and there is still much of it today. Research is emotionally disquieting, it does question old beliefs and sweeps aside tradition, often leaving in its wake disbelief, uncertainty, and shattered ideals.

Yet, despite the librarian's conventional antipathy for research, at the University of Chicago in the decade of the 1930s some progress was made in laying a solid foundation for the application of research to the library as a social invention. Pierce Butler attempted to formulate the principles of a science of librarianship; Carleton Joeckel encouraged studies in the application of the techniques of scientific management and administration to the operation of libraries; William Randall focused the attention of his students upon the application of theories of the organization of knowledge to principles of library classification and bibliographic organization generally; Douglas Waples went beyond librarianship to the fundamental problem of the social effects of reading. And Dean Louis Round Wilson set forth, in *The Geography of Reading*, the social, cultural, economic, and other environmental influences related to the geographical distribution of libraries and library resources.

The advent of the Second World War exerted two powerful influences upon research in librarianship. First, it abruptly terminated the developments at Chicago by dispersing the faculty, and from this interruption the program initiated by Wilson and his colleagues never recovered. Second, the war raised research in general to such a high level of prestige, and rewarded its practitioners with such rich endowments, that librarianship was forced into a form of activity which had been largely alien to the profession and for which librarians generally were unprepared. To this pressure for research, librarians responded in a variety of ways, most of them hastily devised and ill-considered. The library schools began to talk glibly of research and to establish courses and seminars in library research

---

[51] Ralph A. Beals. "Implications of Communications Research for the Public Library." *Print, Radio, and Film in a Democracy*, ed. Douglas Waples. Chicago. University of Chicago Press. 1942. pp. 165–67.

[52] Williamson. "Place of Research in Library." p. 10.

and research methods. They substituted for the fifth-year bachelor's degree the degree of Master of Science in Library Science, and they rushed all unawares into doctoral programs. Wanting desperately to "do research," they looked to such fund-granting agencies as the federal government and the foundations, and the response to their applications was surprisingly generous. Dollar diplomacy came to librarianship, with research as the key by which the coffers of wealth were to be unlocked. One can scarcely blame the librarians—even a starving man will founder if his normal diet is not restored by degrees, and librarians had been hungry for a very long time.

Because research had for so long been foreign to librarianship, when librarians did take the plunge they became overenthusiastic converts to method. Librarians, as John Livingston Lowes once wrote of the humanists, tended "to become enamored of the methods, and at times to forget the end; to allow, in a word, the fascination of the means to distract [them] from the very object for which they are employed."[53] Because librarianship used as a model the methods of social science research, it relied so heavily upon statistics that, for a time, research in librarianship came to mean, almost inevitably, statistical investigation; and the value and significance of a research project came to depend upon the demonstrated degree of skill in statistical manipulation.

Because the methods and techniques of librarianship itself had been empirically derived, it is not surprising that research in librarianship was also empirical at first. As a result, much library research has been little more than what Beals called "testimony," the implications of which are almost always personal and hence likely to be idiosyncratic. The evidence offered in support of testimony is experience, usually undifferentiated experience consisting of impressions and appraisals of complex phenomena by those whose predispositions tend to favor *ex parte* conclusions.

While in some situations valid experience rightly interpreted can contribute to the research process, of much library research one cannot but wonder whether the process of winnowing the data has been carried far enough to yield wholly trustworthy results; whether the size and character of the sample are such that the results can be reliable; whether the reporters of the data were skilled analysts and observers; whether conditioning factors had been isolated and appraised with accuracy; whether central tendencies had been slighted in favor of the picturesque, the un-

---

[53] John Livingston Lowes. "The Modern Language Association and Humane Scholarship." *Publications of the Modern Language Association.* vol. 48, p. 1403. Supplement 1933.

usual, or the fortuitous; and finally, whether the conclusions reached would be respected by qualified authorities. To be sure, for the solution of many stubborn library problems, undifferentiated experience is the only source of information available to the investigator, but it requires careful scrutiny and judicious appraisal if it is not to be misleading.

Because of the empirical character of library research, and its excessive dependence upon local observations and limited data, more frequently than not it is provincial and parochial rather than general in its applicability. Such investigations tend to be "service studies" rather than true research. Yet librarians cannot be entirely condemned for the quantification of localized experience—into that trap the social sciences fell before them, and even the physical sciences were by no means immune to the lure of counting masquerading as objectivity. In 1906, the University of Chicago catalog observed, "it seems probable that most of the grand underlying principles [of physics] have been firmly established, and that future advances are to be sought chiefly in the rigorous application of these principles to all the phenomena which come under our notice. It is here that the science of measurement shows its importance."[54] An eminent physicist has remarked that the future truths of physical science are to be looked for in the sixth place of decimals. In short, all scientific inquiry, at one stage or another in its journey toward a valid scientific method, has been guilty of that error to which Bacon pointed: the fallacy of investigating "the nature of anything in the thing itself."[55]

"To restore to intellectual life," writes Arthur Bestor in the *Restoration of Learning*, "the unity that the forces of modern life are threatening to destroy constitutes one of the most significant tasks to which thoughtful men and women are addressing themselves today."[56] In the modern world of research the cooperation of scholars and scientists from a variety of disciplines, in a team attack upon problems of great complexity, is one of the most distinctive and important features. Though as Hertz and Rubenstein have pointed out in their pioneering study of team research,[57] the research process itself is as old as the history of man, and though the incessant striving for *system* in the solution of problems has evolved the *scientific method* as it is understood today, the recent intro-

---

[54] The University of Chicago. *Annual Register July, 1905–July, 1906*. Chicago. The University of Chicago Press. n.d. p. 245.

[55] Bacon. *Novum Organum*. p. 123.

[56] Arthur Bestor. *The Restoration of Learning*. New York. Alfred A. Knopf. 1955. p. 58.

[57] David B. Hertz and Albert H. Rubenstein. *Team Research*. New York. Columbia University Department of Industrial Engineering. 1953.

duction of team research represents *organization* for the purpose of reducing the uncertainty of outcome and minimizing the possibility of failure. Team research, then, born of man's continually growing awareness of the complex interrelationships within the world of knowledge and the interdependence of phenomena, stands as tacit admission of the essential unity of the research process. However, the fact that the team approach is to be encouraged in some areas, does not mean that the solitary scholar is obsolete. There is a place, and a very important place, for the individual working alone in pursuit of his research. Because librarianship itself is concerned with all human knowledge, the use of interdisciplinary team research for attack upon library problems is especially important and promising. One can identify offhand a number of areas in which library research could profitably seek assistance from other branches of intellectual activity:

1. *Library administration*—political science, government, management theory, operations research, systems analysis, personnel management, budgeting.

2. *Knowledge and society*—epistemology, cultural anthropology, social psychology, communication research, social organization, philosophy, library criticism.

3. *Education and communication*—the structure and operation of the brain, psychology, the assimilation and utilization of information, linguistics, the new media, educational theory, communication theory.

4. *Man-machine relationships*—automation, cybernetics, information science and systems, logic, theory of classification, scientific method, structural linguistics.

The areas here designated are intended to be no more than suggestive; certainly they are not definitive. They may, however, serve to indicate the opportunity for enrichment of research in librarianship through synthesis with other disciplines, some of which are themselves quite new and as yet not fully formalized. One should also point out that in certain areas (e.g., neurophysiology), the librarian can do little but evaluate the findings of others in terms of their relevance to his professional responsibilities.

## TOWARD A THEORY OF LIBRARIANSHIP

If education for librarianship *per se* has suffered from the absence of a theoretical base and the fundamentals such a theoretical base provides, the research that library education, and the library profession generally, has spawned has suffered even more. Claude Bissell has declared that the first characteristic of a great university is that it must be "a stronghold of scholarship in the pure theoretical subjects that lie at the basis of any expansion of knowledge." He does not suggest that the professional faculties are always, or necessarily, derivative or secondary, "for the application of theoretical knowledge . . . demands a knowledge of traditional practice, a sensitivity to the human situation, a nice ordering of idea to special situation that together create separate and autonomous disciplines." But, "a university cannot be described as great unless it can, within itself, generate knowledge in the pure, theoretical disciplines."[58] Research in librarianship, therefore, must turn to those pure studies from which it can derive its intellectual foundations.

Kuhn has argued that "normal science" presupposes a conceptual and instrumental framework that is accepted without question, and even perhaps unconsciously, by an entire community of scholars—a consensus. Innovation thus occurs only through a breakdown of previously accepted rules. Such breakdowns of the accepted "paradigm" generate "crises" which cannot be resolved within the accepted framework, and the discipline can return to normal only after a new conceptual framework has been accepted. Such breakdowns, and the consequent transition to a new paradigm, a new basis of professional practice, is the historical narrative of revolutions in scholarship.[59]

The paradigms of the "normal" science of librarianship, have never been fully articulated, but they are present none the less, and they have been accepted by the library community—conservation, education, recreation, information, inspiration, and aesthetic appreciation; these in themselves may be said to constitute a kind of paradigm, and explicitly expressed or not they underlay the whole of the *Public Library Inquiry*. But such values are not acceptable as a structure for library research. One must search more deeply than the identification of such values for the theory of what librarianship is in cognitive rather than normative terms.

Nor do quantitative measures of circulation, book collection, staff, or staff salaries have any significant meaning except in the making of certain administrative decisions. Such statistical analyses contribute only to service studies of particular localized situations or for comparisons between or among libraries; they are not without value, but they offer no

[58] Claud T. Bissell. *The Strength of the University*. Toronto. University of Toronto Press. 1968. pp. 153–54.

[59] Thomas S. Kuhn. *The Structure of Scientific Revolutions*. Chicago. University of Chicago Press. 1962.

credentials as research. Thus, the search for a structured theory of librarianship that will allow us to relate it meaningfully to other disciplines must be pursued as a valid prerequisite to a research program.

As Rawski points out: "Professional knowledge is sought as a means to attain *and to continue to attain* what we desire [to be] true. Hence, professional knowledge must strive for more than after-the-fact assurance. It must seek explanatory relevance and predictive power. Both explanation and prediction depend on conceptual reconstruction of the objective patterns of events (i.e., facts subsumed under general principles), and thus link the quest for action knowledge to scientific inquiry. Stated narrowly, the knowledge situation here involves a schema which leads from data described in observables to grounds for expectation in terms of observables via interpretive connectives and theoretical statements permitting argument, and requires concepts, propositions, and theorems which the diagnostic vocabulary of records of past experience alone cannot provide. To avoid Shera's fallacy *the librarian means to do good, and by dint of self-sacrifice and hard work he does what he means to do, and therefore that which he does is good*, we need theory."[60] Such a theory will allow us to grasp and understand our problems in terms of librarianship, its goals, concerns, activities, properties, and relationships, and to proceed systematically and critically in the pursuit, not of knowledge, but of what Rawski calls "the right kind of knowledge."[61] It is only this kind of knowledge and its generalizable concepts and propositions which will enable us to equip adequately the coming generations of librarians to cope with change, to anticipate, to initiate knowingly, and thus creatively to address the future.

A profession that would know itself—that would anticipate or, to use Dennis Gabor's phrase, "invent the future"[62]—must support and engage in productive research. But research, important as it is, is not the be-all and end-all of life, or even of professional life; and every librarian does not have to be a "researcher" in order to prove the vitality of the profession. Research is too important to be left to dilettantes and amateurs, and its pursuit should be reserved for those who are qualified for it by aptitude, education, and motivation.

---

[60] Editor's introduction in *Toward a Theory of Librarianship; Papers in Honor of Jesse Hauk Shera*. ed. Conrad H. Rawski. In press.

[61] *Ibid.*

[62] Dennis Gabor. *Inventing the Future.* New York. Alfred A. Knopf. 1964.

# Thirteen

# The Faculty

The teacher stands at that crucial point where students and the educational experience meet. The student, of course, has much to do with the excellence of an educational system; he is implicated through his motivation, attitude, preparation, and degree of participation. Perhaps it is not too much to say that true learning, as distinct from being taught, exists only when students have the will, the "incentive of self-impulse" as Nathan Pusey calls it, to achieve a state of understanding. In this formalized process of acquiring education the teacher is a catalyst, and where there is no good teacher the student suffers. Reduced, then, to its most elemental terms the school is a duality of student and teacher—Mark Hopkins on one end of a bench and the learner on the other.

## WHAT MAKES THE GOOD TEACHER GOOD?

The competent teacher, like every other accomplished artist, is born, not made. Such a generalization does not imply that proficient teachers emerge fully robed from some process of spontaneous biological generation. The artist is not born a master of his instrument or his materials. The teacher, too, must grow, and stretch, and learn his art. But without native ability, no amount of pedagogical experience or training will lift the neophyte from mediocrity.[1] "Most professors become good pro-

---

[1] John S. Diekhoff. *Tomorrow's Professors; A Report of the College Faculty Internship Program.* New York. Fund for the Advancement of Education. n.d. Chapter 1.

fessors only if it comes easily and naturally," was the conclusion of Jencks and Riesman. "Those who do not have much natural flair seldom know how to begin remedying their failings even if they have the impulse. They certainly get little help from their colleagues. The reasons for this are not hard to discover. . . . A professor's book can be evaluated in 'objective' terms, whereas his course syllabi, lectures, and examination questions can be valued only 'subjectively.' The adjectives re-enforce the prejudices of the profession."[2]

No one has as yet been able to define the essential characteristics that make a great teacher great in any but the most general of terms, much less establish valid tests for prognostication of success in teaching.[3] President Robert Goheen of Princeton has said that those who would reduce teaching "to a formula are doomed to failure. There will always be teachers who will break all our rules and yet be profoundly successful. In other words, it is the good teacher, not teaching in the abstract, that counts."[4]

If one is to attempt, even in a limited way, to judge success in teaching, he must begin with an understanding of the role of the teacher in the educational process. The teacher at various times and in differing situations plays many roles—counselor, student, leader, magistrate, even minister. "Teachers are people who are constantly provoked into telling other people—younger and dependent people—what they ought to do," Robert Redfield once told the graduates of the University of Chicago Laboratory School. "They feel like delivering sermons, but they find themselves awkwardly in places where sermons are inappropriate. A sermon belongs in church, not in school. . . . That teacher or college professor who has the nervous habit of straightening his tie as he lectures, is really [responding to] his impulse to turn his collar around the other way."[5] But most of all

---

"Teachers, Born or Made?" See also: John D. Millett. *The Academic Community.* New York. McGraw-Hill. 1962. Chapter 3. "Faculty."

[2] Christopher Jencks and David Riesman. *The Academic Revolution.* Garden City, N.Y. Doubleday. 1968. p. 531.

[3] Logan Wilson reported that he was unable to find any "infallible means for developing or detecting good teaching." Logan Wilson. *The Academic Man.* New York. Oxford University Press. 1942. p. 22. See also: James B. Conant. *The Education of American Teachers.* New York. McGraw-Hill. 1963. p. 113.

[4] Robert F. Goheen. *The Human Nature of the University.* Princeton. Princeton University Press. 1969. p. 80.

[5] Robert Redfield. *The Social Uses of Social Science.* Papers of Robert Redfield. vol. 2. Chicago. University of Chicago Press. 1963. p. 262.

Henry M. Wriston has defined the good teacher negatively and by the process of elimination: "The ideal faculty man. . .ought properly to find administration dis-

the teacher is a communicator and what he communicates is an enthusiasm for learning and the knowledge which is the stuff of learning. Enthusiasm is, of course psychological, and the ability to communicate it is personal and individualistic, and the extent to which it is, or can be, a product of the teacher's professional education is open to question. But there can be no doubt that the communication of knowledge rests squarely and firmly upon the mastery of the knowledge to be communicated. To cite the old story of the mountaineer who was conspicuously successful in the training of hunting dogs, the teacher must, first of all, "know more than the dog."[6] There are many ways, of course, by which the teacher's knowledge may be acquired—through formal study, through directed but independent reading, from his own research, from associates, colleagues, and other professional contacts, and through experience in the act of teaching itself. "One learns much from books," an ancient Chinese proverb is alleged to assert, "more from his teachers, and most from his pupils."[7] The unfortunate fact remains, however, that, according to Bruner, because of the pedagogical philosophies of professional educators, a relatively high rate of turnover in teaching or an interest in either continuing study or research, a proportionately large number of teachers do not have the opportunity, or do not make the opportunity, to master the subjects they are supposed to be teaching.[8] But the possession of substantive knowledge does not, in itself, guarantee successful communication. Probably everyone, at one time or another, has known teachers who have had much of importance to say but were unable to transmit it effectively to others. Certainly no one would

---

tasteful. A man who positively enjoys sitting on committees, arguing about university affairs, or haggling about the wording of regulations, is unlikely to be passionately interested in teaching, scholarship, or research. This I believed in 1925, when I began to administer; I believed it even more deeply when I retired in 1955." Henry M. Wriston. *Academic Procession*. New York. Columbia University Press. 1959. pp. 119–20.

[6] I. A. Richards has resorted to a rather fancy figure of speech to exemplify the intellectual imbalance between teacher and pupil. "There is, as it were," he has written, "a piece of elastic between you and your audience. You must not snap the elastic or you have lost them. On the other hand, you must have the biggest possible tension on the elastic and this must be pulling on them most of the time. This is the whole point of teaching. Otherwise, why do it?" Ivor A. Richards. "The Teaching Process." *A Handbook for College Teachers*, ed. Bernice Brown Cronkhite. Cambridge, Mass. Harvard University Press. 1951. p. 12.

[7] Earl Johnson of the University of Chicago calls it the "teacher-learning situation." Earl S. Johnson. "The Art of Teaching." Association of American Library Schools. *Report on Meeting, January 28, 1957*. p. 34. (Mimeographed)

[8] Jerome S. Bruner. *The Process of Education*. Cambridge, Mass. Harvard University Press. 1961. p. 88 ff.

deny that scholarship, especially as it is exemplified in productive research, can, and indeed has, enriched the vitality of teaching; the Germanic tradition in American higher education has been largely responsible for the widely held conviction that the productive scholar cloistered in his book-lined study, or busily engaged with retort and test tube in his laboratory, is the stereotype of the ideal professor. Of all the influence exerted by the German universities upon comparable institutions in the United States, the urge to engage in research, especially pure research, was by far the most important and most persistent. Even today it is generally believed in many segments of the academic community that teaching and research are, in the university, almost inseparable.[9] Professor Daniel Bell, of Columbia, for example, has argued strongly for the close alliance of teaching and research. He acknowledges that research has become such an overpowering source of prestige on the university campus that teaching as such has often been subordinated to publication with the result that superior teachers have been denied proper rewards. Nevertheless, he raises the question whether, "in the light of rapid advances going on in every field, the distinction between research and teaching is tenable in a university context . . . and can one have superior instruction except by those who are themselves involved in the research process—*and who are capable of translating*, not necessarily their findings, which may be quite limited, but their modes of procedure into an adventure for the student?" Again he has asked, "If, in the broadest sense, a university is a community of scholars, can one truly separate research (or scholarly investigation or critical or reflective inquiry as represented in publication) from teaching?"[10] Certainly the tradition of scholarly research has greatly strengthened graduate and professional education in America, but the central point of argument in Professor Bell's questions is the phrase, "who are capable of translating," for one must certainly acknowledge that the best research investigators do not always make the best "translators." One could even argue, from the basis of unfortunate experience, that there can be a real antithesis between the ability to conduct research and the capacity for its effective communication. To draw a sharp dichotomy, or create a false antithesis between teaching and research is to misunderstand the nature of the educational process, both at the undergraduate and graduate levels. President Pusey of Harvard, has clearly stated the need of the good teacher also to be a productive scholar:

[9] See Karl Jaspers. *The Idea of the University*. London. Peter Owen. 1960. Chapter 4. "Research, Education, and Instruction."

[10] Daniel Bell. *The Reforming of General Education*. New York. Columbia University Press. 1966. pp. 66–67. (Italics mine.)

The faculty have in the first place to be convincing examples of the life of learning. It is not necessary that each member of a faculty be one of the world's great scholars . . . but it is necessary that he be a scholar, that his scholarship shall have brought him to secure knowledge of his subject, that his knowledge be his own—and that he have some ability, some method or artistry, to communicate both his learning and his enthusiasm for the field of his inquiry and his sense of its importance, to younger minds finding their way into that world illuminated by intellect where his own chief pleasure is found.[11]

This ability to communicate, to translate, is not a constant but a variable; success in the act of communicating changes from individual to individual and even in the same individual; teaching, which at first seems to be a dismal failure may eventually be revealed as providing an exciting intellectual experience. Good teaching can at least seem to violate all the basic tenets of good communication. Thus Irwin Edman has written of John Dewey:

> He had none of the usual tricks or gifts of the effective lecturer. He sat at his desk, fumbling with a few crumpled yellow sheets and looking abstractedly out of the window. He spoke very slowly in a Vermont drawl. He looked both very kindly and very abstracted. He hardly seemed aware of the presence of a class. He took little pains to underline a phrase, or emphasize a point, or, so at first it seemed to me, to make one. Occasionally he would apparently realize that people in the back of the room might not hear his quiet voice; he would then accent the next word, as likely as not a preposition or a conjunction. He seemed to be saying whatever came into his head next . . . what came next did not always have or seem to have a very clear connection with what had just gone before.

But Edman confesses that he soon discovered that

> what had seemed so casual, so rambling, so unexciting, was of an extraordinary coherence, texture, and brilliance. . . . I had been listening to a man actually thinking in the presence of a class. . . . It was this last aspect of his teaching that was most impressive—and educative. To attend a lecture of John Dewey's was to participate in the actual business of thought. Those pauses were delays in creative thinking, when the next step was really being considered, and for the

---

[11] Nathan M. Pusey. *The Age of the Scholar.* Cambridge, Mass. Harvard University Press. 1963. p. 148.

glib dramatics of the teacher-actor was substituted the enterprise, careful and candid, of the genuine thinker. One had to be scrupulously attentive and one learned to be so.[12]

Quite obviously, apart from the content of that which is to be communicated, the ability to communicate—to teach—is essentially a personality trait and is psychologically based or derived.[13] Moreover, any attempt to deal in a generalized way with the characteristics of the "best" teacher or the "best" methods to use in teaching is essentially profitless. "Before you decide whether a teacher is good," Warren Weaver of the Sloan Foundation has advised, "ask, good for what? . . . Is the criterion of goodness the mechanical success with which information is transmitted, the sympathy and warmth with which a young mind is led to unfold— or the influence a great character can have on the whole life of a student?"[14] Warren Weaver "profoundly disbelieves" the results of evaluation of teachers by their students, and he adds, "It will not even work to ask alumni— presumably wiser, surely older, and hopefully more eclectic—which teachers they remember with greatest admiration." It is his opinion that "the only useful judgment concerning university teachers comes from their immediate working colleagues. . . . Fellow teachers, through their skillful and intimately informed judgments, will come nearest to recognizing good teaching. The immediate colleagues of a teacher will know what the students really think, for they will have obtained this information in effective informal ways, will have available the evidence of student records, will be aware of the general community opinion, and will have put all this information through the sieve of their own competence."[15]

Evelyn Kossoff of the University of Kentucky has reviewed the conventional techniques for measuring teaching efficiency and finds them artificial, synthetic, and quantitative. In her opinion it is possible to devise a system of evaluations based on *concrete* teachers rather than on abstract teaching traits. Instead of focusing on similarities and generalities, the focus should be on the concentration and analysis of *unique* qualities of teaching

---

[12] Irwin Edman. "Columbia Galaxy." *Great Teachers*, ed. Houston Peterson. New Brunswick, N.J. Rutgers University Press. 1946. pp. 196–97.

[13] See: William James. *Talks to Teachers*. New York. Holt. 1929. Chapter 1.

Arthur Bestor has based his judgment of the good teacher upon the possession of three characteristics: (1) thorough knowledge of the subject; (2) ability to translate that knowledge into practical purposes; and (3) character. Arthur Bestor. *The Restoration of Learning*. New York. Knopf. 1956. p. 270.

[14] Warren Weaver. "Good Teaching." *Science*. vol. 151 (March 18, 1966), Editorial, p. 1335.

[15] *Ibid.*

traits exhibited by individual teachers. A teacher's effectiveness should be evaluated in terms of the particular set of circumstances in which he operates—the students with whom he is attempting to communicate, the subject matter with which he is dealing, and without recourse to any formalized artificial standard against which *all* teachers are to be measured. She recognizes and accepts the obvious fact that only human subjective opinion can provide effective evaluations, but rejects questionnaires, "evaluation instruments," and computers. "I have no objection to evaluation of teachers by human observers," she concludes, "Criticism of humans by humans I consider fair play. I object only to the evaluation of humans by 'instruments' and 'mechanisms' to which are attributed superhuman powers of perception, precision, and perspicacity. I ask only that we recognize the limitations of all forms of human judgment, and that we leave the final evaluations to the Almighty Evaluator, Who alone knows all the facts and understands all the motives relevant and requisite to the pronouncement of final judgment on all human beings."[16]

Teaching as an act of structured intellectual communication can take many forms,[17] and it is probably most effective when it approaches the discourse of equals. But in that flow of communication that characterizes the act of teaching, the teacher, like the artist, sets his own rules in his own way and lets the results speak for themselves—such is the essence of academic freedom. Probably no other profession is so highly personal as teaching in the sense that the teacher reveals himself to his students; nor is any so subjective. The teacher plans his own work, tests the results of his teaching with his own examinations and passes his own judgment upon the success of his accomplishments. This self-appraisal seldom receives any outside review other than the dubious, and often internally inconsistent, verdict of his students. If his courses are popular he assumes that his teaching is effective. If his classes are small he rationalizes the response to the severity of his demands for performance and his unwillingness to tolerate mediocrity. The good teacher, then, is a scholar and an artist with something important to say and the freedom to say it under conditions of his own creation. Thus David Riesman has written:

---

[16] Evelyn Kossoff. "Evaluating College Professors by 'Scientific' Methods." *American Scholar.* vol. 41. (Winter 1971–1972) p. 93.

[17] Gilbert Highet discusses some of these in the opening chapter of his *The Art of Teaching.* New York. Knopf. 1950.

The Johns Hopkins chapter of the American Association of University Professors has collectively agreed that there is no such thing as "good" teaching in the abstract. American Association of University Professors. *Bulletin.* vol. 18 (October 1932), pp. 454–55.

No one should underestimate the miseries of having to set one's own goals. It is much easier, in my observation, to meet a payroll . . . than to do research or to try to help students learn something. For creative intellectual work is never done, and it is certainly never done to one's satisfaction. To be sure, professors and creative people, like other people, try to find outside judgments in order to avoid having to set their own goals.[18]

The function of the teacher is to evoke wisdom through the stimulation of imagination and motivation by the communication of information, knowledge, and, above all, insights. But only when the teacher is truly the master of his subject will he widen and deepen the sensitivity of his students to the end that they will learn to deal wisely with the problems of a difficult and changing subject in a complex and changing world.

The young learner is, by nature, "a little copy-cat," to use Barzun's phrase, and the good teacher must turn him into an independent and self-motivated thinker who not only learns but also studies.[19] Learning, even at the higher levels, must begin with a measure, at least, of imitation, but its ultimate aim is to further the growth of certain independent habits of intellectual activity rather than to provide for the passive acceptance and absorption of information to be retained. To be educated is to possess the power to propound alternatives and to choose wisely from among them. Thus the teacher must make possible the growth of those intellectual capabilities that are essential to rational choice. Teaching, therefore, must create an environment that provides for and encourages the act of learning; it must systematize and direct the process of the student's coming to know.

Because the student is by nature a "little copy-cat," for a variety of reasons—eagerness for new facts or knowledge, the desire to get good grades, honest admiration for the professor, or even the dedication of a "willing vestal"—the great occupational hazard of the teacher is self-replication, the desire to make the student in the teacher's image. Yet, the greatest joy a teacher can have is to see a student pick up the ball where he himself has dropped it and advance it a few more yards. In the achievements of the student lies the justification of the teacher, and it is by the performance of his students that the teacher shall be judged. As Paul Weiss has written: "The teacher himself is also ignorant; he too is a learner. The

---

[18] David Riesman. "The College Professor." *Education in the Age of Science*, ed. Brand Blanchard. New York. Basic Books. 1959. pp. 277–78.
[19] Jacques Barzun. *The Teacher in America*. Boston. Little, Brown. 1945. p. 21.

student in turn is his teacher's teacher; he reveals what the impact of knowledge is on innocence, what effect honesty and competence, friendliness intertwined with dignity, have on the outlook of the young. By guiding the student toward fulfillment the teacher incidentally learns something of the nature of freshness, creativity and growth."[20] But one hopes that the teacher gains much more than the values Weiss has set forth.

## THE TEACHER'S CHANGING ROLE

Concern has frequently been expressed that the era of the great teachers has passed. The virtues and influence of the great teacher are, perhaps, most evident when viewed in retrospect and with historical perspective. But those who pass such judgments on the present are often looking backward through the Indian Summer haze of "the old grad."[21] Whether or not one rates the present state of teaching as being low, it is certainly true

---

[20] Paul Weiss. *The Making of Men.* Carbondale, Ill. Southern Illinois University Press. 1967. p. 36.

In *Prologue to Teaching* (New York. Oxford University Press. 1959), Marjorie B. Smiley and John S. Diekhoff have brought together a rich anthology, with accompanying commentary of readings on education and the profession of teaching.

See also: Joseph Adelson. "The Teacher as a Model." *The American College*, ed. Nevitt Sanford. New York. Wiley. 1962. pp. 396–417.

Vannevar Bush's chapter on "Of Teachers and Teaching" in his *Pieces of the Action* (New York. William Morrow. 1970. pp. 236–70) is discursive and even, at times, rambling, yet it contains many touches of insight and wisdom that make it worthwhile as well as pleasant and enjoyable reading.

[21] Barzun says that teaching "is not a lost art, but the regard for it is a lost tradition." Barzun. *Teacher in America.* p. 12. Carroll Newsom holds that "synthesis is becoming a forgotten art within academic circles." Carroll V. Newsom. *A University President Speaks Out.* New York. Harper. 1961. p. 93.

Veysey, after looking at the historical record, has suggested that the "good old days" at Alma Mater may not have been quite so happy as the old grad sometimes thinks, and that "bright college years" were not always "with pleasure rife." Laurence R. Veysey. "The Gulf Between Students and Faculty." *The Emergence of the American University*, by Veysey. Chicago. University of Chicago Press. 1965. pp. 294–302.

Goheen holds that it is the responsibility of the entire academic community to preserve a proper balance between teaching and research "and preserve the dignity of the teaching-scholar as teacher, not solely as scholar." Goheen. *Human Nature of University.* p. 86. See also: Henry Steele Commager. "The American Scholar Revisited." *The Commonwealth of Learning*, by Commager. New York. Harper & Row. 1966. pp. 113–29; and Joseph J. Schwab. "The Professor's Professor." *College Curriculum and Student Power*, by Schwab. Chicago. University of Chicago Press. 1969. pp. 251–55.

that the role of the professor, especially in graduate and professional education, is undergoing important changes. The rank and recognition of the individual in his profession is becoming more important as a source of prestige than the particular institution with which he may be affiliated, and the rewards of scholarship are increasingly related to one's standing in his discipline instead of years of devoted service to his school. The reputation of the teacher comes not so much from what he does in the classroom as his activities outside its walls. There is change, too, in the multiplication of tasks and the differentiation of functions within the professorial role. The professor who, in an earlier day, taught his classes, personally directed the studies of a few doctoral students, and wrote a book or two and some articles, now serves as teacher, research worker, project director, administrator, and, at times, even fund raiser. He serves on a variety of committees, both within his own university and for his professional associations. He will be a member of a number of editorial boards of professional journals, asked to participate as a referee for project proposals to fund-granting agencies, invited to serve on national, state, and local commissions, and he will attend innumerable professional meetings, both national and international. In addition to all this he must conduct conferences, edit symposia, prepare reports, and "publish or perish."[22] In recent years, also, the expansion of the market for the professor's services has greatly increased his mobility.[23] This mobility is very largely the result of the growth and

---

[22] "Teaching can become extremely shoddy as the whole competitive pressure focuses on quantitative measure of research productivity and ignores ability to hand on old research traditions and inspire new ones. I think of this when I hear graduate professors denounce 'methods courses' in normal schools and teachers' colleges, for the denouncers could often themselves profit from courses in educational psychology, and are overprotected by their reputations and academic disciplines from the feedback of student trauma and justified complaint." David Riesman. *Constraint and Variety in American Education.* Garden City, N.Y. Doubleday. 1958. p. 141n. See also: Jacques Barzun. *The American University.* New York. Harper & Row. 1968. Chapter 2. "Scholars in Orbit."

[23] See: Howard D. Marshall. *The Mobility of College Faculties.* New York. Pageant Press. 1964. Particularly p. 56 ff.

"The material base, even the physical location of the professor was changing. He drew his sustenance now from outside the university and could take it with him wherever he thought he would feel more comfortable elsewhere. In many fields he could develop into an executive presiding over a large staff who carried on his work while he travelled from meeting to meeting, consulting and negotiating. For him the university could be a place to hang his hat, one to which he owed no obligation and in which he felt no interest. The professor might belong to an intellectual community, but it was not one having a local habitation and a name; it was not a university community as that term had been understood since the Middle Ages."

proliferation of institutions of higher learning and the resulting intensifi-
cation of demand for faculty of recognized ability. At a time when the
responsibilities and obligations of the teacher are experiencing such drastic
change, it is not surprising that teaching, as teaching, tends to suffer, and
that if teaching is being neglected all the blame cannot be attributed to the
intrusion of research.[24] One may quite logically suggest that the changing
role of the teacher, and the dissipation of his time and energies that divert
him from teaching have played more than a minor part in the growing wave
of student dissatisfaction with the educational experience. It is also possible that a sharp decline in governmental and other support for research
and other nonteaching activities may possibly return the teacher to his old
place in the classroom. If there are no generally accepted criteria for the
identification of those qualities which make for success in teaching, and
if the role of the teacher is undergoing constant change, perhaps at an
accelerated rate, without any real sense of direction and lacking purposeful
evolution, it is largely so because of what Jerome Bruner calls "the absence of an integrated theory of instruction as a guide to pedagogy." Lacking such a theory, there is in its place only "a body of maxims."[25] At

---

Robert M. Hutchins. *The Learning Society.* New York. Praeger. 1968. pp. 107–8.
Clark Kerr speaks of the "un-faculty" in *The Uses of the University.* Cambridge,
Mass. Harvard University Press. 1963. pp. 65–67.

[24] Bell. *Reforming of General Education.* pp. 99–101. See also: Paul Woodring. *The
Higher Learning in America.* New York. McGraw-Hill. 1968. "The Academic
Life." pp. 117–53.

[25] Bruner. *Process of Education.* p. 31.

The absence of any generalized theory of instruction as a guide to evaluating
success in teaching is clearly evident in the editorial by Warren Weaver. "Good
Teaching." p. 1335.

William R. Hutchison argues that the two factors in academic life that most
seriously conflict with teaching are the traditional lecture-course methods which he
regards as an abuse imposed upon both teacher and student, and the fragmented
program which atomized the student's time and attention by dividing it not only
among a number of courses and their requirements, but also between "long-range
and short-range obligations," and between curricular and extra curricular demands.
In short, he is of the opinion that there are as many activities to divert the student
away from the business of learning as there are to draw the faculty from teaching
and research. William R. Hutchison. "Yes, John, There Are Teachers on the Faculty." *The American Scholar.* vol. 35 (Summer 1966), pp. 430–41.

One should scarcely be surprised, therefore, when Carroll Newsom states that
"the actual place of the teacher in the educational picture is far from clear" and
again, that "there is actually grave doubt about the effectiveness of the activities
that are maintained in a large number of classrooms in facilitating the learning

the present time, therefore, it would seem that the best that can be done is to identify four "maxims" which define an equivalent number of generalized characteristics of the successful teacher: (1) competence in the appropriate subject, (2) effectiveness of verbal communication, (3) a sincere concern with, perhaps even dedication to, teaching, and (4) a genuine liking for students coupled with an understanding of their problems and points of view. The first two are largely acquired and can be learned, though native ability is, of course, not to be ruled out; the last are psychologically derived and the product of rigorous self-discipline.

Former President Hadley of Yale has, perhaps, put his finger on the central problem in defining the attributes of the successful teacher in individual terms when, in reality, teaching is essentially a social phenomenon. "Teaching is more than a theory," he wrote in the *Atlantic Monthly*, more than half a century ago, "it is an act. It is not a subjective or individual affair, but a course of conduct which creates important social relations and social obligations."[26] What the distinguished former president of Yale University was saying is that there is for the professor a role that transcends all others, and that is to exercise to the full the responsibility of the intellectual to his society. It is the responsibility of the professor to pursue the truth wherever he finds it, that is an axiom that cannot be denied, but it is also his duty to expose error, to analyze actions according to their motives, causes, and hidden intentions. It is the professor's task to pursue truth through the jungle of distortion, misrepresentation, ideology, and special interest, and to flush out the lies hidden in polemics and special pleading. The scholarly expert is, in large measure, replacing the free-floating intellectual of the early decades of the present century, who believed that the wrong social values were being honored, and hence rejected society. If the new "postindustrial" society is to grow by building and strengthening democratic institutions rather than by totalitarian means the responsibility must largely lie with the academic intellectuals. Both as teacher and seeker-after-truth the new academic scholar-expert dare not retreat to an ivory tower.[27]

---

process." Newsom. *University President*. p. 3. See also: James B. Conant. *The Citadel of Learning*. New Haven. Yale University Press. 1956.

[26] A. T. Hadley. "Academic Freedom in Theory and Practice." *Atlantic Monthly*. vol. 91 (February 1903), p. 157.

[27] Noam Chomsky. "The Responsibility of Intellectuals." *The Dissenting Academy*, ed. Theodore Roszak. New York. Pantheon. 1967. pp. 254–98; Daniel Bell. *The End of Ideology*. New York. Free Press. 1960; Robert Boguslaw. *The New Utopians*. Englewood, N.J. Prentice-Hall. 1965.

## THE LIBRARY SCHOOL FACULTY

Despite general agreement that the quality of the library school faculty, like the quality of the faculty in any other educational institution, is a major determinant of excellence in the program of study, definition of the credentials that are essential to qualify a candidate for professorial status usually evaporates in not very meaningful pronouncements respecting personality, leadership, breadth of education, teaching ability, professional competence, interest in students, practical experience, and demonstrated ability to add to the sum of professional knowledge. In short, the qualities that make them successful in any field are valid for library education, and the directors of library schools are as confused about the characteristics of the good teacher as are most educators.[28] Doubtless no one would quarrel with any of these attributes as being important to the profile of the good teacher, and any library school dean or department chairman would be happy to add to his faculty any person possessing all of them. Yet they are not of equal value, and the relative importance of each varies from discipline to discipline and specialization to specialization. However, except for a recurrent insistence upon the importance of practical professional experience, which is somehow always equated with subject knowledge and teaching ability, library educators generally have not attempted to assign values or weights to any of them. The vagueness of librarians' thinking about the characteristics of a good library school faculty is graphically illustrated by the standards for library school accreditation approved in 1951 by the American Library Association. Of the faculty these standards say only that

> the faculty shall be adequate in number, have authority and competence to determine and to carry out a program designed to achieve

---

[28] See, for example: Joseph L. Wheeler. *Programs and Problems in Education for Librarianship.* New York. Carnegie Corporation of New York. 1946. p. 46; and J. Periam Danton. *Education for Librarianship.* Paris. UNESCO. 1949. pp. 32–34.

Andrew Osborn makes the point that library school faculties "tend to be followers rather than leaders and originators. . . . It is rare for the library school instructor to be ahead of the practicing librarian in theory or practice, and this is one of the most perplexing difficulties the library schools have to resolve in developing their faculties and in improving their instructional programs." Andrew D. Osborn. "Education for Librarianship." *Personnel Administration in Libraries,* ed. Lowell A. Martin. Chicago. University of Chicago Press. 1946. p. 126.

the objectives stated in these standards and other objectives of the library school.

The instructional program must be the responsibility of a corps of full-time faculty sufficient in number to provide stability and continuity of instruction, to carry the major portion of the teaching load and to represent a variety of competencies.[29]

If these standards present only the most inconsequential of generalizations about the characteristics desired in a library school faculty, they say nothing about the professional preparation a teacher should have; one can only surmise that they were written and approved by people who knew very little about educational needs and placed a low premium on the importance of professional education to the future of librarianship. One should say in defense of the librarians, however, that whereas the graduate school is the generally acknowledged agency for the preparation of teachers in the academic disciplines, entree to professorial status in a professional school is usually achieved through the practice of the profession itself with little regard for evidence of concern with research. Law school faculties tend to be recruited from the ranks of practicing lawyers; the faculties of medical schools are staffed both by practicing physicians and surgeons and those dedicated to scientific inquiry. Only for instruction at the elementary and secondary school levels are there rigidly prescribed curricula for the preparation of the teacher. The influence of the training class is still strong in library education, and the teaching staff for that level of instruction was drawn from the department heads and other supervisory personnel of the library in which the program was presented. Courses in cataloging were taught by the head of the catalog department, reference tools by the head of the reference department, and library administration by the chief librarian himself. When the training classes were moved from libraries to university campuses, the belief in the importance of practice to the professor changed but little, and many schools enlisted a disproportionate number

---

[29] American Library Association. Committee on Accreditation. *Standards for Accreditation, Adopted by the Council of the American Library Association, July 13, 1951.* Chicago. American Library Association. 1951. p. 2.

The statement of interpretation of the Standards, though more detailed than the Standards themselves, are also vague and filled with generalizations that basically are meaningless. American Library Association. Committee on Accreditation. *Statement of Interpretation to Accompany Standards for Accreditation Adopted by the ALA Council July 13, 1951.* Chicago. American Library Association. 1960. pp. 7–11. (Mimeographed)

of faculty who divided their time between teaching and desk work. If there is any consensus at all among librarians respecting the preparation of library school faculties, it is to be found in a general insistence that the teacher, at some time in his career, "has met a payroll."[30]

The value of practical experience to the teacher's reservoir of competence cannot be denied, and excessive separation of the classroom from reality is an ever-present danger. But, ironically, librarians whose lives are supposedly dedicated to the book, have a fear of "the Ivory Tower" and a distrust of book learning. Experience can be the source of error as well as of wisdom, and practice in a narrow field, however rich it may have been and however long its duration, can make a narrow teacher. Moreover, practice can tie one too closely to the present, and the professional school must train for the future. The faculty of the Graduate School of the University of Chicago during the 1930s was subjected to almost constant vilification from the profession because some of its members were not and had never been practicing librarians. Yet, much of the strength of that faculty derived from the very fact that it was unimpeded by conventional patterns of thought about library problems, and for that reason it was free to explore areas of inquiry which in the past had been surrounded, quite unintentionally no doubt, by tradition and opinions based on experiences and practices no longer relevant to changing needs. There are, to be sure, certain areas of librarianship for which practical experience is a prerequisite to successful teaching, and for which no faculty member should be considered who has not served an adequate apprenticeship. Library administration, for example, would be quite sterile and remote from reality if taught by one who had never been confronted by the day to day problems of operating a library. Moreover, there is danger in remaining away from administrative practice too long, and some provision might well be made for teachers of administration to be granted leaves of absence from time to time to permit them to return to practice. But there is danger, too, in excessive attention to practice, for the kind of library in which a teacher has had experience will almost inevitably color his classroom presentations. The teacher's experience should enrich, not dominate, his teaching; yet those who can successfully subordinate their own experience to

---

[30] The Western Reserve Institute of 1962 on the future education for librarianship, was unable to reach agreement on whether "faculty members should have practical working experience in the field of their specialties," and whether field experience for faculty is essential or only highly desirable. Frank L. Schick and Ruth Warncke, eds. "The Future of Library Education; Proceedings of an Institute Co-sponsored by the U.S. Office of Education and Western Reserve University, Cleveland, Ohio, April 25–28, 1962." *Journal of Library Education*. vol. 3 (Summer 1962), p. 54.

the larger requirements of instruction are rare. The anecdote and the personal reminiscence are at one and the same time the enemy and the enrichment of teaching, and to master their effective use raises the presentations of the pedagog from histrionics to elucidation. Yet rich as his knowledge may be in the theory and practice of library administration, his performance will be weak if he is not widely read in the literature of administration itself—public administration for the public librarian, and the administration of higher education for the academic librarian.

## WHAT KIND OF FACULTY?

When librarianship was conceived in only technological terms and library training was little more than the transfer of that technological skill to the recruits to library practice, there was good reason for insisting that instruction be held firmly in the hands of those who had themselves been practitioners of the art. Today, however, a broadening of the concept of librarianship and a growing awareness of the role of the librarian in society has placed entirely new demands upon the library school faculty. The interdisciplinary relationships of librarianship necessitate educational programs that are interdisciplinary and courses should be taught by faculty qualified in the subject disciplines concerned. If the library is to be presented as an important element in the communication process, then, obviously sociology, anthropology, communication, and linguistics must be represented in the student's educational experience. The inclusion of these disciplines may be accomplished in several ways: by bringing to the faculty of the library school those adequately prepared for graduate instruction in the nonlibrary subjects on either full-time or part-time appointment, instructors who are specialists in their disciplines without regard to any competence in librarianship *per se*;[31] and by sending students to the appropriate subject courses in the graduate or other professional schools of the parent university. Of this last alternative more has been said in the

---

[31] The Western Reserve Institute of 1962 agreed that "faculties should be required with competencies and specialties to meet new demands in such fields as research (including statistics), the several subject areas, administration, documentation and information retrieval, information science, the effects of reading upon behavior (all ages and levels), and programmed learning and other teaching methods." The Institute also agreed that "the faculty should be selected representatives not only of generalists but also of specialists in various disciplines, including, when this is desirable, specialists who are not librarians." Schick and Warncke. "Future of Library Education." p. 54.

section on curriculum. There is no one best procedure. The policy to be followed will vary from school to school and from subject to subject within the individual school, depending upon the school's program, the qualifications of its faculty, and the strengths of the several departments in the graduate school. It is the responsibility of the dean, in consultation with his faculty, to choose that which is best for his particular students from among the resources available to him. Each procedure has its advantages and dangers, but the one basic consideration that must always be kept in mind is that the student must be made aware of the relation of these disciplines to the profession and practice of librarianship. Failure in the past to understand the importance of this fundamental principle has narrowed professional vision, sent into library practice graduates with inadequate intellectual breadth, and thus threatened librarianship with the loss of social responsibilities naturally its own. Such attrition is, perhaps, best seen in the rise of information science which threatens to go its own way with a resulting serious loss both to information science and to librarianship.

One very important means for strengthening the student's educational experience, without increment to the resident faculty, is a form of interinstitutional cooperation that would make possible a student's studying under a particular specialist in another university or library school. If libraries can cooperate in the use of their books, surely library schools could transfer such practices to instructional programs. Admittedly, there are a number of prickly logistic problems: schedules, compensation for the cooperating university, living costs for the student while absent from his campus base, and the like. But such problems are very far from being insoluble if the effort to attack them is sincere. Already, students are beginning to demand attention to such a procedure, and they have the continuing growth and complexity of knowledge very much on their side. The time is past when the school calendar is drawn up for the convenience of the faculty alone.

The problem of enlisting the faculty instructors with special competencies inevitably raises the question of the roles of resident (full-time) and nonresident (part-time) appointees. Since the days of the training school, library education has relied heavily upon part-time instruction, a situation which, at least in part, was the result of the schools trying to "make do" on a minimum of financial support.[32] Over the years there has been a trend away from the use of nonresident faculty as a theoretical ideal, but such philosophizing has not been reflected in practice. Though most

---

[32] Danton. *Education for Librarianship*. pp. 36–39; C. C. Williamson. *Education for Librarianship*. New York. Carnegie Corporation. 1923. pp. 42–44.

library school deans would doubtless agree that reliance upon a substantial proportion of such faculty is not only undesirable, but deleterious to library education, the growing student enrollment in library schools has compelled an increasing use of part-time instructors, including doctoral candidates.[33] That such use represents a rather desperate attempt to meet the exigencies of a serious shortage in available faculty does not lessen the potential danger to the quality of professional graduate study.

Dependence upon nonresident faculty can be justified as a permanent policy only on the basis that it introduces into the curriculum special competencies which, though they are essential to the school's program, do not require the services of a full-time instructor, and the policy can, perhaps, best be defended in respect to joint appointments with other departments and schools of the university with which the library school is affiliated.[34] The wiser practice would seem to be to send the students to the teacher and his courses rather than to bring the teacher to the students. The importance of other disciplines to graduate library education can scarcely be overemphasized, but such study is best obtained within the environment of the discipline, and not in diluted courses in the discipline designed for librarians.

No one really knows what the optimum size of a library school is, or what an appropriate student-faculty ratio should be. Sarah Reed considers ten faculty members to be "desirable for multi-purpose accredited graduate library school programs with fully developed curricula in the areas of school, public, academic, and special librarianship."[35] President Dearing of the State University of New York at Binghamton, told the 1965 Washington institute on problems of library school administration:

> As to adequacy of numbers, it might be emphasized that in addition to providing coverage for each of the essential specialties, there are some subtle but significant effects of the way in which faculty members complement, reinforce, and stimulate one another. I have heard it argued by a chairman of a physics department, in the language of

---

[33] Sarah R. Reed. "Students, Faculty, Funds—1966 vs. 1964." *Journal of Education for Librarianship.* vol. 7 (Fall 1966), pp. 97–104.

[34] The classic statement of the advantages and disadvantages of the part-time instructor, and it still has much relevance though it is too long to quote here. Williamson. *Education for Librarianship.* pp. 42–44.

[35] Sarah R. Reed. " 'The Faculty Shall Be Adequate in Number, Authority, and Competence.' " *Journal of Education for Librarianship.* vol. 5. (Spring 1965), p. 263.
    See also: Reed. "Students, Faculty, Funds." p. 12.

his discipline, that a minimum of 12 faculty members is required to constitute a "critical mass." By this I believe he meant that a group smaller than this, while it might provide basic coverage in a sufficient number of the sub-fields of physics, could not provide the degree of interaction and stimulation which is prerequisite to research productivity and the vitality and excitement and validity in teaching which is thought to be inextricably related. . . . I would suppose that 12 is not a magic number, and that research does not play precisely the same role in a library school as in a science department. Moreover, I wonder what is conventionally done, or could be, in the matter of intimate professional association with members of related disciplines.[36]

The president's warning of the need for an adequate full-time faculty was well taken, for Florrinell Morton, whose paper he was criticizing, had espoused the discouraging assumption that "the library schools must continue to use part-time faculty perhaps in increasing numbers," though she recognized that such faculty must be brought "into more effective dialog with full-time faculty . . . if they are to contribute to a unified program rather than teach courses in isolation."[37]

The proper student-faculty ratio is also a matter of considerable debate. According to Miss Reed's statistics, "On the basis of full-time equivalent enrollment, there were 20 students per full-time faculty member in 1966 compared with 16 in 1964."[38] Full-time equivalency is scarcely a valid measure of student load, since the part-time student requires as much, and often more, time for advising and personal guidance as does the full-time student. Moreover, in all professional schools individual work with students is probably a more important part of the faculty's responsibilities than in undergraduate colleges and graduate schools. Personal guidance is especially important in such service professions as librarianship, in which the student, once he has entered the field, will himself be expected to devote a major proportion of his effort to the advising of clientele. Class lectures and assignments are but one segment of the student's educational experience, and direct contact between student and teacher, so long as it

---

[36] G. Bruce Dearing. "Criticism of Working Paper No. 1." *Problems of Library School Administration; Report of an Institute, April 14–15, 1965, Washington, D.C.,* ed. Sarah R. Reed. Washington, D.C. U.S. Office of Education. 1965. p. 10.

[37] Florrinell F. Morton. "Faculty Adequacy. Working Paper No. 1." *Library School Administration,* ed. Reed. p. 8.

[38] Reed. "Students, Faculty, Funds." p. 12. Miss Reed's statistics need updating, but the use of part-time instructors in library schools has certainly not diminished since she wrote.

does not degenerate into a paternalistic, or perhaps, maternalistic, relation, can scarcely be overemphasized.

The proper student-faculty ratio, then, is a function of many variables: the nature of the classes and subjects to be taught, the level of instruction, the amount of required student advising, and the research or professional activities expected of the teacher. Quite obviously, a school that supports a large research program or the curriculum of which is designed for study at the doctoral, or postdoctoral, level, will require a higher ratio of faculty to students than one engaged only in elementary and generalized instruction. There can be no established pattern that is applicable to all schools. The introduction of new teaching methods, especially the use of audiovisual materials and programmed instruction, may in the future substantially reduce the time required for classroom instruction and correspondingly increase the number of students that can be given adequate attention at any one time. The ten principles set forth in 1929, by a special committee of the American Association of American Library Schools on the service load of library school faculties still have considerable validity.[39] About all that one can say is that in most, and probably in all, library schools the "mass" of the faculty is too small to be very "critical."

But the problem of building a faculty is, of course, not alone a matter of numbers. Central to the responsibilities of the dean is the building of an adequate faculty. Such a statement is very easy to make and very difficult to implement. A good school can be wrecked if its senior faculty all retire within a short space of time, yet one could argue conversely that such a situation could, if properly administered, provide an excellent opportunity for the infusion of new blood in key positions, thus making possible extensive innovation and experimentation that otherwise would be denied by the conservatism, of an "old guard." Young faculty with promise can be discouraged if the path to promotion is "locked" by arbitrary budgetary restrictions on the number of available high faculty positions. Yet, no faculty can be "all chiefs," and the dean must reconcile himself to a certain amount of loss, from time to time of those promising youngsters he would gladly retain were his faculty infinitely expansible.

A faculty should have balance both in professorial rank and subject competence, and balance is not normally the result of chance. There must, therefore, be a plan, but as Wriston warns, "it must never become a rigid mold. . . . Every time a formula is substituted for responsible judgment there is official defeasement. Rules make decision easy but rob it of wis-

---

[39] Ernest J. Reece. "The Service Loads of Library School Faculties." *Library Quarterly.* vol. 1 (January 1931), pp. 37–38.

dom. . . . A plan is a guide for normal situations; when something unusual supervenes, seize the opportunity and let the plan stay on ice for a while."[40]

The job analysis approach to the planning and staffing of faculty positions is not as applicable to university situations as it is to elementary and secondary education, to say nothing of business and industry. The faculty itself usually has, and certainly should have, a great deal of influence in the appointment of new colleagues.[41] In large measure the faculty member makes his own job, he does not admit of being fitted into a neat compartment as civil service planners would like to think of employees. Ability is the only criterion for faculty appointment and promotion. If the dean stays in his job long enough the faculty will almost inevitably reflect his philosophy, though they will not necessarily always be in agreement with him, indeed it would be unfortunate if they were.

The faculty not only makes a school great or mediocre, it *is* the school, and there is no more important responsibility of the dean, nor one for which there are fewer guides, than that of building the faculty. But one should also add that a superior faculty is the dean's greatest achievement and his highest reward.

## THE DOCTOR DILEMMA

President Dearing called it "the Ph.D. syndrome," and more than a half century ago William James wrote of "the Ph.D. octopus,"[42] but by whatever name it is known, for better or worse, certainly the library schools have fallen a victim to its popularity with whatever virtues and vices it may be accompanied. Increasingly the library schools are demanding the doctorate of their faculties and faculty candidates, and, hence, its importance has grown to the point that its validity as a prerequisite to teaching merits special consideration. One can sympathize with the burning desire of the nineteenth-century American educators to raise the academic stan-

---

[40] Wriston. *Academic Procession*. pp. 111–12.

[41] John Walton. *Administration and Policy-Making in Education*. Baltimore. Johns Hopkins University Press. 1959. p. 89.

[42] William James. "The Ph.D. Octopus." *Harvard Monthly*. vol. 36 (March 1903), pp. 1–9. Reprinted in his *Memories and Studies*. New York. Longmans, Green. 1911. pp. 329–47. What James called the Ph.D. octopus was the organization of scholarship into professional disciplines, which was, he believed, hostile to learning and incapable of meeting the human needs of the student. He was pleading essentially for the claims of feeling and individual experience as against the deadening weight of institutions and institutionalization.

dards of their institutions to the levels of Göttingen, Oxford, or the Sorbonne, but it is difficult to forgive subsequent generations of schoolmen who have forgotten that, in England and on the Continent the doctorate is not necessarily a passport to the teaching profession, and who have made James's phrase appropriate even today.

The higher degrees were instituted for the laudable purpose of promoting scholarship, especially in the form of original research,[43] an objective which is entirely commensurate with the role of the university and its professional schools in modern society. It is well for a nation to have research in abundance, and, though ideally the pursuit of scholarship should bring its own rewards, no one should complain if a diploma and an academic hood certifying mastery of a field of knowledge and the achievement of proficiency in scholarly inquiry act as a challenge, a spur, and a reward for the intellectually ambitious.

The doctoral degree in librarianship is still enough of a rarity that it imparts a vague sense of professional recognition and honor, conferring at least the outward manifestations of great learning. It is therefore not surprising that a young profession, often unable to attract professors of eminence to the faculties of its schools, seeks to compensate for the obscurity of the names on its instructional staff and atone for its sense of academic inferiority by an abundance of decorative titles which follow the names in the pages of school catalogues. What James could say of the Ph.D. in general as early as 1903, can be said today, with even greater force, of education for librarianship. The degree, he wrote, "is in point of fact already looked upon as a mere advertising resource, a manner of throwing dust in the Public's eyes."[44] When, to the pressure to maintain academic respectability, is added the mandate of the accrediting bodies, the tentacles of the octopus tighten to the point of strangulation.

The American student can scarcely be blamed if, during the past half century or more, he has become the most degree-conscious person in the world. Colleges and universities have increasingly taken the position that the doors to success in teaching, and the professions are forever closed against those who do not have the appropriate alphabetic series following their names.[45] When, to these economic drives, are added the social necessity of a bachelor's degree for entry into the local university club, the forces of the entire cultural complex are united with the academic pres-

---

[43] See: Veysey. *Emergence of American University.* pp. 175–76.

[44] James. "Ph.D. Octopus." pp. 329–47.

[45] See: Robert Maynard Hutchins. *No Friendly Voice.* Chicago. University of Chicago Press. 1936. p. 176.

sures to exalt the degree at the expense of education, teaching, and research.

This degree syndrome has been characterized by the proliferation of new institutions and instrumentalities of higher education. Colleges, even normal schools, have been converted into "universities" with reckless abandon, and entirely without regard to the curricular, instructional, library, and other resources that are essential to adequate educational programs. "Doctoral degrees" have been awarded by departments and schools which are inadequate even for graduate study at any level.[46] This uncontrolled growth has, in large measure, been stimulated by the availability of federal money, in unprecedented amounts, for aid to higher education. A growing demand was thus created for teachers and other types of educational manpower, including even librarians. One can applaud the objectives that prompted such action, but their implementation may well prove to be a disservice to the youth of the nation. Not only has this federal generosity been shockingly wasteful, and often stimulated that which would best have been left unencouraged, but also, when the horn of plenty is either empty or flows with only a petty trickle, serious academic maladjustments are almost certain to result.

There is, of course, nothing in the doctoral degree that guarantees, or even prognosticates, the capacity of its possessor to teach, nor anything in the generally prescribed course of study that is likely to prepare him for a successful teaching career. In fact, Jacques Barzun is hard pressed to determine what the degree really does evince.[47] The difficulty, of course, lies in the fact that the doctoral degree as it now exists represents a confusion of two divergent objectives. Originally created as a formal recognition that the advanced student has achieved a prescribed level of accomplishment in preparing himself for the life of a scholar, it has been prostituted to the need for licensing or certifying teachers. No one can deny the importance of preserving standards, but it is wrong to conceal the need for licensing through a pretense of promoting scholarship. If scholarship had been consistently looked upon as a special form of creativity, and teaching as an art, this confusion in the objectives of the Ph.D. degree would not have resulted.

James offered three possible solutions to the problem of the doctorate,

---

[46] In 1966, the governor of the state of Ohio announced a plan to have a college or university within thirty miles of every resident of the state. One is reminded of the statement attributed to Henry A. Beers, that "A man who hasn't money enough to found a college goes West and founds a 'university.' "

[47] Barzun. *Teacher in America.* p. 196.

of which the first was prophetic. Let the universities, he said, give the degree "as a matter of course . . . for a due amount of time spent in patient labor in a special department of learning. . . . Native distinction needs no official stamp. . . . On the other hand, faithful labor, however commonplace, and years devoted to a subject, always deserve to be acknowledged and requited."[48] This is exactly what has happened. Now that the Ph.D. has become the official seal of academic respectability, educators are afraid to let it go, however empty its symbolism. As a second alternative James proposed that academic institutions abandon their "unspeakably silly ambition to bespangle their lists of officers with these doctoral titles. Let them look more to substance and less to vanity and sham." James proposed as his third course, that every student "of native power" be encouraged by his faculty advisors to rebel against the system when its empty formalism interferes with "the free following out of his more immediate intellectual aims," and that he should not be made to suffer for his independence. James offered as a substitute, private letters of recommendation from instructors, "which in any event are ultimately needful," and which should "completely offset the lack of the bread-winning degree."[49] But this, too, has its dangers. "Individuality" can too often be used as a shield to hide mediocrity, dilettantism, and laziness. Letters of recommendation can be devoid of meaning as the formal statements of credit for which they are a substitute. The degree, with all its faults, still testifies to a measure of competence and a substantial quantity of plodding perseverance; it is at least evidence that the student has subjected himself to a modicum of self-discipline.

Thus it becomes possible to establish certain generalizations respecting this highest of earned academic degrees and its relation to professional education:

1.  The doctoral degree, as a badge of academic scholarship, has seriously declined in value since James launched his attack upon it.

2.  Despite this deterioration, it still retains substantial values as an indicator of the scholarly attainments of a faculty, and the concern of that faculty with the promotion of research. Regardless of its faults, it is very far from being discredited as a symbol of a faculty's true worth.

3.  The presence or absence of the degree in the credentials of a prospective faculty member must be evaluated with reference to many

---

[48] James. "Ph.D. Octopus." pp. 344–45.
[49] *Ibid.* p. 345.

other qualifications; e.g., a demonstrated capacity to teach, research productivity, and mastery of the materials of the subject field.

4.   The lack of the degree by a substantial proportion of the faculty places a heavy responsibility upon the dean of the school, which he must be prepared to meet in dealing with the profession at large, the academic community of which his school is a part, and the accrediting agencies.

5.   The doctorate is not a protective device, an academic shield, behind which the dean can escape from the obligations his office places upon him to select the best faculty obtainable. The burden of proof must always rest with the dean to defend his appointments and the promotions he recommends.

The growing tendency among educational institutions to insist upon the doctorate as a prerequisite to faculty appointment is infecting library schools, and many deans are finding themselves severely handicapped in attracting candidates to their faculties because of such a generally restrictive policy. Sarah Reed, in discussing the critical shortages in library school faculty, pointed to the fact that in the twelve years between 1952 and 1964 only 131 doctorates in librarianship were awarded, the maximum number for any one year being only 19.[50] Obviously she is assuming that the doctorate is, at least, the proper, if not the necessary, source for academic manpower. This growing insistence upon the doctorate is, in part, a wholly admirable attempt to improve the level of graduate library instruction, but it also represents a confession of academic inferiority, an attempt to keep up with the chemists, and the physicists, and all the others in the academic pack. Such playing of the sedulous ape to the other departments of the university is definitely not wholesome, and it does not reflect favorably upon the ability of library schools to be discriminating in the development of their faculties. President Dearing made a very important point when he told the Washington Institute on Library School Administration:

> In my opinion the possession of a doctorate is only the most convenient and unchallenged qualification for a faculty position. Any capable student preparing to enter the profession can be wisely counseled to acquire his degree as expeditiously as possible. However, there are many areas in higher education to which the degree has little relevance, and there are many kinds of training and experience which could legitimately be considered as appropriate qualifications

50 Reed. "Faculty Shall Be Adequate." p. 263.

in lieu of the doctorate for participating in the program of graduate instruction. . . . .I see no reason why there should be any difficulty about a faculty member without a doctorate offering a part, though obviously not a whole, of the instruction which leads to a doctorate.[51]

The provision of Title IIb of the Higher Education Act of 1965, the guidelines of which assigned priority in the giving of financial aid to those preparing to teach in library schools, is wholly admirable if it does not encourage the creation of library school courses in "how to teach library science," or promote a synthetic doctoral degree.

The professional preparation of the individual faculty member will depend upon, and vary according to, his role in the instructional and research program of the school. He should be competent, i.e., be formally trained and professionally experienced, in those areas in which he will be guiding the intellectual development of his students. In addition, he should be knowledgeable in the field of higher education, and should have at least read widely in the substantial literature of academic administration. The writings, even the reminiscences, of distinguished educators is a particularly fertile field for the assimilation of wisdom; some of these writings have been cited above, but there is a rich literature that begins with Plato and terminates with the observations of today's educational leaders which every teacher can explore with profit. It has been our observation that the literature of higher education is superior to that relating to the elementary and secondary school, perhaps because it is less addicted to the jargon of pedagogy, less intensively structured, and hence more liberal in its point of view.[52]

Bernard Berelson, whom no one would accuse of being prejudiced in favor of courses in pedagogy, has written in his study of graduate education prepared at the request of the Carnegie Corporation, "But the general question remains of training in teaching as a part of the graduate program and it faces all the old hurdles: *whether* there is anything to teach, *what* it is, *when* should it come, . . . *how* should it be done, and *who* will do it. At the least, it may be fair to say that training in *what* to teach may not be sufficient for a college or university teacher but it is necessary, whereas training in *how* to teach is neither. Here I must confess to my own prejudice since it is in opposition to the general run of opinion of those concerned: until some hard evidence is in, I remain skeptical that

---

[51] Dearing. "Criticism of Working Paper." p. 11.
[52] Jesse H. Shera. "Twelve Apostles and a Few Heretics." *Journal of Library Education.* vol. 10 (Summer 1969), pp. 3–10.

formal training in teaching is a more effective way to get a good under-graduate teacher than simply selecting those doctoral students who are seriously interested in that kind of work. But the college presidents say it matters, and so do the recent recipients, and I defer to them—though not without some reservation."[53] In this passage Berelson was, of course, speaking of undergraduate teaching, but without doubt his insistence upon a subject doctorate as a prerequisite for the teacher of advanced graduate and professional courses would be even more emphatic than he has indicated above.

There may be more things in teaching than are dreamed of by the Doctor of Philosophy, but their evaluation is difficult. The tendency of professional schools, particularly those in librarianship, to enter lightly into programs of training at the level of the doctorate without a substantial proportion of the faculty having been subjected to the rigors of advanced graduate study and the discipline of the dissertation, is disturbing.

## THE RESEARCH FUNCTION OF THE FACULTY

The place of research in education for librarianship was dealt with in the previous chapter; here it is necessary to deal with the problem from the point of view of faculty administration. As John Diekhoff has written in his now classic work on the *Domain of the Faculty*: "Perhaps no product of the graduate school is more likely to be an effective . . . teacher than the productive scholar, not because 'productive scholarship' is a condition of good teaching but because love of learning is a condition of both scholarship and teaching. The real enthusiast for knowledge will pursue it and will communicate it, in books and articles or in the classroom, or by both means."[54] But to say that teaching and research are inseparable and not a dichotomy, does not imply that every member of a faculty must be engaged in research or that those primarily engaged in research must always have classroom responsibilities. There is, of course, a natural affinity between teaching and research, for the teacher should be learning along with his students, particularly at the levels beyond the first professional degree, but an excellent teacher should not be rejected simply because he is not enthusiastic about the pursuit of new knowledge, and a "research

[53] Bernard Berelson. *Graduate Education in the United States.* New York. McGraw-Hill. 1960. p. 225.
[54] John Diekhoff. *The Domain of the Faculty in Our Expanding Colleges.* New York. Harper. 1956. p. 53.

man" can be a welcome addition to a faculty even though he may have little stomach for the classroom.

The faculty of a true university is a community of scholars, therefore the faculty of a graduate library school, if it is to share in and contribute to the academic community of which it is a part must, on the whole, be chosen not alone for its instructional talent but also for its ability to advance the frontiers of truth. Hutchins has insisted that "a university may be a university without doing any teaching. It cannot be one without doing any research."[55] This is probably an exaggeration, but at least it underscores the importance of research ability as an attribute of the faculty. Of course there are scholars who do not publish, and they may be wholly admirable teachers, but, again to quote Diekhoff, "failure to publish is not what makes them good teachers, and it does not follow that a faculty member is a good teacher because he does not publish. He is not likely to be a good teacher unless he shares the enthusiasm for knowledge of the productive scholar."[56] The teacher who "explains" his failure to engage in productive scholarship with the excuse that he does not have the time, or is too preoccupied with his students to engage in research, is not really a frustrated productive scholar, and would not be if he were given a sabbatical every year. The dedicated research man will pursue research in spite of almost every impediment that can be placed before him. When it comes to a choice between the classroom and the study or the laboratory, one can be sure that it is the classroom that will be neglected. It is virtually impossible to prevent a productive scholar from being productive. Thus has written Dean Melvin E. Haggerty: "Students are better served in an institution peopled with scholars, though half the classes do not meet, than in one in which the schedule is perfectly kept by a faculty from whom has passed the power to think about new problems and the will to solve them and whose members have ceased to yearn for the company of other scholars."[57] The teacher who does not know all the answers, who "stands helpless before his problems, part of the time; . . . is much closer to the student than the man who just teaches, because the man who merely teaches knows all the answers."[58]

The neglect of research and the proliferation of data gathering mas-

---

[55] Hutchins. *No Friendly Voice*. p. 175.

[56] Diekhoff. *Domain*. p. 53.

[57] Melvin E. Haggerty. *The Faculty. The Evaluation of Higher Institutions*. vol. 2. Chicago. University of Chicago Press. 1937. p. 96.

[58] J. Robert Oppenheimer. "Research in the University." *Freedom and the University*, ed. Edgar N. Johnson et al. Ithaca, N.Y. Cornell University Press. 1950. p. 101.

querading as research, is largely responsible for much of the disapproba-
tion that has been heaped upon library schools by colleagues in other parts
of the university, even though some of the most critical may themselves
be residents of glass houses. As Barzun says, "It ought not have to be
said that no specialized skill implies the possession of any other, that the
ability to discover new knowledge is extremely rare, and the power to
put it into writing rarer still. Compared with this the ability to teach is
relatively widespread."[59] If scholarship were regarded as a special form
of creation and teaching were recognized as an art, much confusion would
be eliminated.

In a sense teaching and research are a dichotomy. Education is synthetic and generalized, and is becoming increasingly so. Research is analytic and detailed and is becoming increasingly specialized. The teacher
aims at comprehensiveness, but the goal of much research is the discovery
of facts. Many of these discoveries are as yet but partially comprehensible
to their sponsors, and hence cannot be absorbed into an intelligible scheme
capable of synthesis in the classroom. A school that decides to engage in
both teaching and investigation must face squarely the responsibilities that
such a decision of necessity imposes. First, it must accept the responsibility of doing a good teaching job for its students. It must understand
what the educational needs and the consequent educational developments
of librarianship are, and what they are going to be in the immediate future.
A professional school that does not train its students with an eye to the
future is not only a stagnant school, it is contributing to the decay of its
profession. Many library schools seem to have remained largely oblivious
to what is taking place in librarianship beyond their own immediate confines, particularly the most striking phenomenon of the contemporary library world—the unprecedented growth and increasing complexity of the
scholarship of our culture and the new social forces that are swirling about
their doors. Every library school must, therefore, ask itself whether, in
view of the revolution in librarianship today, it does not have responsibilities beyond the training of its students.

The apparent conflict between education (or teaching) and research
can be resolved only when they are administratively recognized as separate, but interdependent, halves of a unified whole. Since its inception at
the end of the nineteenth century, education for librarianship has been
primarily concerned with teaching, and much of this teaching has been
at the vocational level of technical instruction. Except in a few centers,
such as the University of California at Berkeley and at Los Angeles, the

---

[59] Barzun. *Teacher in America.* p. 207.

University of Chicago, Case Western Reserve University, the University of Illinois, and Rutgers University, over the years the library schools have shown little concern for, or interest in, research, despite the fact that there has been much talk about it along with a generally unhealthy proliferation of doctoral programs. Yet the revolutionary changes that are taking place in the production and use of recorded communication are intensifying the need for basic and fundamental research in all aspects of librarianship. Thus, if the library school is to meet its educational responsibilities, it must recognize the importance of research and take active steps to build a faculty qualified for its prosecution.

For the library schools the decision to engage in research is particularly difficult to implement, partly because the profession itself has never been truly convinced of the importance of research to its professional advancement, and in part because library school faculties themselves have not, in the main, been subject to the discipline of research and hence are inexperienced in it. But the issue of research must now be faced, and the time is right to begin gradually and experimentally to establish in the professional schools, or perhaps among them as jointly sponsored undertakings, research centers or institutes. The staffs of these centers would be members of the faculty only if they were engaged in fundamental research and participating in the instructional program of the university. The teaching faculty, on the other hand, would contribute to the work of these centers in proportion to the time they wished to devote to research. Only those students seriously interested in research and evincing promise of becoming research workers would be admitted to study in such centers. Once admitted, they would serve as senior research assistants and, at the same time, secure practical experience as research fellows. The centers would not themselves be degree-granting agencies, but would recommend students for degree candidacy in the school of which the center is a part.[60]

In addition to their devotion to pure and applied research, these centers might engage in operational activities insofar as possible without

---

[60] Clark Kerr has called these research scholars who do not engage in teaching the "unfaculty": "Now some scholars are added to the faculty in exclusively research capacities—and increasingly with titles suggesting professorial status. They have no teaching responsibilities and are not as yet fully accepted members of the academic community." He adds, however, that "there has been an almost frantic remaking of the rules—new titles created, new relationships established, new classes of citizenship formulated and only partially assimilated. . . . If there can still be said to be a 'faculty' at all it is most certainly a different composite than before." Clark Kerr, *The Uses of the University.* Cambridge, Mass. Harvard University Press. 1963. pp. 66–67.

jeopardizing their primary responsibility for investigation. Such operational activities could serve the dual purpose of providing a laboratory for the testing of the research being conducted at the centers, and making available facilities whereby students could become familiar with professional activities and technical routines. Finally, the operational aspects of the centers would provide a certain amount of bibliographic service to an appropriate clientele, though at no time should such services be permitted to dominate the true research function. In short, the centers would serve the library school much as a hospital or dental clinic serves medical and dental education.

More than thirty years ago Robert Hutchins proposed the formation of research institutes in universities when he considered the state of the higher learning in America.

> I should insist that a university is concerned with thought and that the collection of information, historical or current, had no place in it except as such data may illustrate or confirm principles or assist in their development. It is perfectly clear, however, that the mere collection of information is of great importance and it must be carried on somewhere. It is useful and economical, perhaps even essential, to have it carried on in part under the auspices and protection of universities and in connection with them. . . . So information on subjects important to the public should be gathered, analyzed and published. . . . They are at what may be called the research level. . . . I suggest, therefore, that research institutes be established at universities, in which all the current and historical facts now collected by professors, and more, can be assembled. . . . It may be desirable in certain cases also to attach to the university on the same terms technical institutes in which the students may become familiar with . . . routines, of course some care should be exercised to see to it that the routines are worthy and susceptible of communication.[61]

Robert Ulrich has presented the scholar as both communicator and explorer. Universities he holds to be "living incorporations and symbols of man's insatiable thirst for truth," and though fallible human reason can never hope to achieve ultimate truth it must remain always the "vision of a goal." To pursue this goal the scholar-teacher must have the courage

---

[61] Robert Maynard Hutchins. *The Higher Learning in America.* New Haven. Yale University Press. 1936. pp. 109–11.

to "envisage new methods of inquiry and new ways of organizing research."[62]

## THE FACULTY AND EXTRAMURAL ACTIVITIES

"Publication and professional society contacts are the evidences that the individual is still alive, that he still reaches out for intellectual stimulation and the comradeship of alert minds. Because this is true, the college teacher who . . . has commerce with his colleagues of similar interests throughout the land contributes to the spiritual life of an institution in far greater measure than he who is merely busy with his institutional and personal duties."[63] Thus wrote Dean Haggerty, and though one may be pardoned some skepticism regarding the "spiritual" contribution of the professionally active teacher's contribution to his school, there certainly can be no doubt about its intellectual value.

The professions generally accept as a self-evident truth the obligation of the individual to contribute in a variety of ways to the associations and organizations which represent his professional interests. Indeed, in some professions (among which medicine is a conspicuous example) such affiliation is almost indistinguishable from certification, licensing, and the right to practice. Such patterns of conduct probably derive from the medieval guilds, but may be traced to the priesthoods of the pre-Christian era, the banding together of the elite among primitive tribes, and ultimately to the human need for forms of social organization beyond the family or the clan.

The contemporary professional society, however, can probably be traced more directly to such historical antecedents as the scientific societies that originated in England and on the Continent during the latter part of the seventeenth century.[64] In the United States, these voluntary associations of scholars had their counterpart in such organizations as the American Philosophical Society founded in 1743 by Benjamin Franklin and the American Academy of Arts and Sciences founded in Boston in 1780. Both of these associations provided forums for the presentation of

---

[62] Robert Ulrich. "The American University and Changing Philosophies of Education." *Issues in University Education*, ed. Charles Frankel. New York. Harper. 1959. pp. 40–41.

[63] Haggerty. *Faculty*. p. 95.

[64] Martha Ornstein. *The Role of Scientific Societies of the Seventeenth Century*. Chicago. University of Chicago Press. 1938.

discoveries resulting from observation and experimentation, and both provided platforms for the debate of theories, philosophies, and points of view. The growth in scientific and technical knowledge that characterized the nineteenth century was an important stimulus to the proliferation of such voluntary associations, associations which represented a great diversity of professional interests. The earlier societies, though their interest in what was taught and how it was taught was extensive, evinced no overt or formalized responsibility for education. During the same century, however, through the leadership of such educators as Henry Barnard and Horace Mann, professional groups concerned with the improvement of education became extremely active and influential, especially with respect to the improvement of the common schools. By 1853, even the librarians launched an attempt, which proved to be abortive, to form a professional association,[65] but success was not achieved until the centennial celebration in Philadelphia in 1876.

The modern professional association represents a convergence of two streams of influence. First, the heritage from the early scientific societies brought enthusiasm for the cultivation of knowledge both for its own sake and for the improvement of mankind. Thus the founders of the American Academy stated their objective:

> The experience of ages shows that the improvements of a public nature are best carried on by societies of liberal and ingenious men, writing their labors without regard to nation, sect, or party, in one grand pursuit.[66]

The second stream was the urge for the advancement, in power and prestige, of the profession itself. In its extreme manifestations the professional association exemplifies the contemporary organizational revolution.[67]

Certainly man has a legitimate right to organize himself in ways that will serve his best interests as he sees them, and indeed he would be very stupid to do otherwise. Furthermore, such organizations are not necessarily inimical to the best interests of society; they can, and often do, benefit others than their own members. They are a very potent form of social control whereby a society maintains standards of behavior, exacts

---

[65] George B. Utley. *The Librarians' Conference of 1853*. Chicago. American Library Association. 1951.

[66] Quoted by A. Baird Hastings. "The College Teacher and Professional Societies." *Handbook*, ed. Cronkhite. pp. 173–74.

[67] See: Kenneth E. Boulding. *The Organizational Revolution*. New York. Harper. 1953. p. 202.

penalties for improper conduct, and promotes and rewards excellence of performance. But they can also become empty shells from which life and function have long since departed. At its worst, a professional association gone haywire can become a first-rate public threat and it can even cause professional education to worry about its future.

Today librarianship is threatened as never before with the danger of excessive organization. Associations, international, national, regional, state, and local, in a wide variety of areas of librarianship: public, academic, school, special, documentation, information science, *ad infinitum*, even *ad nauseam*, are proliferating like the dragon's teeth of Greek mythology. To these activities have been added a multiplicity of special conferences, institutes, "seminars," and workshops, all of which have been encouraged by the easy availability of support from the Federal and state governments, as well as from a number of private fund-granting agencies. There have been library schools that sponsored an institute or workshop almost fortnightly. The school that does not, at least occasionally, engage in such activity becomes suspect. Judicious participation in all of these activities can be justified on the grounds that it promotes the intellectual development of the faculty and brings prestige to the school. But programs are plagued with repetition, the platitudinous, and the promotional, and they are fast becoming a burden that can threaten instructional and research programs.

Further inroads on faculty time are also being made by the demand for consultant assistance, and other forms of advisory service, many of which can make substantial contributions to the teacher's income, while improving his contact with library problems outside the "ivory tower." In general, these activities are probably more fruitful to the teacher and the school than conference and workshop participation, but even they can become a burden that robs the teacher of time and energy that should be devoted to obligations more closely associated with his professional responsibilities. There are no set rules, guidelines, or formulas that will facilitate decisions in any of these extramural activities; they must be carefully reviewed as they appear, always with regard to the individual faculty member's particular situation. The faculty should be allowed as much freedom as possible so long as the needs of the students are held to be paramount.

But all demands upon faculty time do not come from outside academic walls. Every school has its own mechanism, often quite highly developed, for stealing the teacher's precious hours. The faculties of library schools are now growing to the point where a reasonable measure of organizational structure is probably inevitable, but it is also dangerous. A faculty should, of course, be run democratically in so far as democracy is possible. But true democracy is not to be mistaken for its mechanical facade. A faculty committee, properly controlled, can be an important aid to the administration, but, run berserk, it can also be a great waster of time. No one ever did an honest piece of research or wrote a good book while sitting in a committee meeting. Committee service can create the delusion of academic achievement when it is often no more than procrastination. An unnecessary or an inactive committee can be a drag upon the progress of the school, and a committee that gets the notion that it is a substitute for the dean can be a real danger. But such a danger is not very great. Few faculty committees have ever confronted their "King Johns" with a "Magna Carta." More relevant to the prevailing situation is the wish of a regrettably unknown professor who said that when he died he wanted it to be in a faculty meeting because, "there the transition from life to death would be imperceptible."

# Fourteen

# Administration

Organization, says Kenneth Boulding is "anything that is not chaos,"[1] and it permeates the entirety of the universe, all phenomena, physical, biological, and social, though it is largely with the last that we have been concerned in this volume. Chester Barnard has defined organization as "a system of consciously coordinated activities or forces of two or more persons. In any concrete situation in which there is cooperation several different systems will be components. Some of these will be physical, some biological, some psychological, etc., but the common element which binds all these other systems into the total concrete cooperative situation is that of organization."[2] Organization, then, consists of structures, and it is inherent in the concept of culture. A culture is a structure of subcultures which, in turn, have their own structures by which roles are defined and implemented. Without organization, without the assignment of roles, rational productive effort, work, could not be accomplished. Boulding suggests that even in the "teaching" process there may be "something akin to the growth of organization. Knowledge, indeed, can be regarded as a form of organization. In its verbal expression it consists of a structure of related contexts, in each of which any 'word' or symbol can play the appropriate role, provided that the code is understood."[3] We are, however, not here concerned with the

---

[1] Kenneth E. Boulding. *The Image*. Ann Arbor. University of Michigan Press. 1956. p. 19.

[2] Chester I. Barnard. *The Functions of the Executive*. Cambridge, Mass. Harvard University Press. 1947. pp. 73–74.

[3] Kenneth E. Boulding. *Beyond Economics*. Ann Arbor. University of Michigan Press. 1968. p. 134.

semantic or philosophical problem of whether the teaching process exemplifies the concept of organization. The present concern is with the structure of the academic community as a subculture and the roles which are assigned to, or have been accepted by its constituent elements, and the problems that the harmonizing of these constituent units raise. In other words, we must here look at the university generally, and the library school in particular, as an operating organization more or less apart from its social role of promoting intellectual growth, though the two are, of course, interdependent, and one should not be viewed in isolation from the other. "The irony of our present situation," wrote John Gardner, "is that the academics, despite themselves, have discovered the joys of organization. The scholar may say that he despises organization, but he quite complacently accepts—even demands—the benefits which it brings."[4]

Gardner's "academics" are entirely right; the university exists only to the extent that it is organized. The idea becomes concrete in the organization. To quote Jaspers: "The polarity of persons and institutions begets opposite errors. On the one hand, there is the cult of personality, the emphasis on originality and even eccentricity. On the other hand there is an emphasis on oppressive and empty organization. Both extremes lead to unreasonableness."[5] To escape the horns of this dilemma is not easy. Eccentricity, when supported by sound scholarship, must be tolerated, and new personalities must be welcomed. Ideas are generated and ideals realized only through the individual effort of people. There must always be a sense of rank and merit, and a recognition of seniority. Again to quote Jaspers: "The ultimate problem posed by the institutional structure of the university is the place of human beings in it. For its vitality the university depends on persons, not institutions, which are no more than a physical prerequisite. The university is judged by its ability to attract the best people and provide them with the most favorable conditions for research, communication, and teaching."[6]

Allen Wallis has seen as the great task of modern university administration the reconciliation of the traditional decentralization of the academic community with the need for increased centralization imposed by the assumption of new socially important functions which are burgeoning and which could not have been provided satisfactorily had not the university assumed responsibility for them. He concluded that universities should "retain such responsibilities, or accept new ones, only if they are compatible

---

[4] John W. Gardner. *No Easy Victories*. New York. Harper and Row. 1968. p. 97.

[5] Karl Jaspers. *The Idea of the University*. London. Peter Owen. 1960. p. 83.

[6] *Ibid.* pp. 89–90.

with the decentralized decision-making that is essential to the basic purposes of universities, or if they contribute substantially to activities that are essential to these basic purposes."[7]

## THE DEAN

"The task of the administrator," said Robert Maynard Hutchins, "is to order means to ends,"[8] (Barzun uses the phrase, "to distribute resources to the best advantage")[9] and a dean is basically an administrator. But the dean, like the university president, is a very special kind of administrator; he is not like a business executive, who has a degree of authority that is denied to the dean. The dean may be, as Hutchins suggested, more like the political leader than a business executive, but the political leader owes his allegiance to his party, and his first obligation is to keep it in power, and his main instrument for the maintenance of power is patronage. But the dean's overriding concern is not that of keeping himself in power, and he has no patronage to dispense. The dean presides over but one room in the house of intellect, and he should conduct his office with a maximum of democracy by generally allowing each member of the faculty to pursue his own course in his own way. In short, he must maintain at all times an active appreciation and respect for the demands of educational excellence and academic freedom. Democracy does not imply the privilege of the dean to abrogate his responsibilities. If his task is to align means with ends he must know thoroughly, and constantly be aware of, both. But he should not get the notion that he can "boss" the faculty; he is indeed fortunate if he is able to lead it. Rather, he can, and should, stimulate it, and he must insist upon making those decisions that are rightfully his by virtue of his office and the responsibilities and obligations that the university administration has placed

---

[7] W. Allen Wallis. "Centripetal and Centrifugal Forces in University Organization." *Daedalus.* vol. 93 (Fall 1964), p. 1081.

See also: Barnard. *Functions of the Executive.* Chapter 17. "The Nature of Executive Responsibility"; Herbert A. Simon. "The Proverbs of Administration." *Public Administration Review.* vol. 6 (Winter 1946), pp. 53–67; and Simon. *Administrative Behavior.* New York. Macmillan. 1947. Chapter 7. "The Role of Authority."

[8] Robert Maynard Hutchins. "The Administrator." *The Works of the Mind,* ed. Robert B. Heywood. Chicago. The University of Chicago Press. 1947. p. 136. Reprinted under the title of "The University Administrator," and with the addition of "The Administrator Reconsidered: University and Foundation," in Hutchins's *Freedom, Education, and the Fund.* New York. Meridan Books. 1956. pp. 167–96.

[9] Jacques Barzun. *The American University.* New York. Harper and Row. 1968. p. 95.

upon and expects of him. Such insistence is not likely to make him the benign and well-beloved shepherd of his flock, though there may be times when he must leave the ninety-and-nine to go in search of the one lamb that has strayed from the fold. But the objective of the university is the progress of learning, not the popularity of the dean. The dean, as is true of other university administrators, for whom, as Hutchins said, the peculiarities of academic administration "have a morbid fascination," will derive little help from the literature of scientific management. He can find his best source of professional knowledge from studying the behavior of successful university administrators and reading thoughtfully their autobiographical writings and collected essays that are the fruition of a lifetime of administrative experience. Beyond that he is on his own with little more than his good sense to guide him.[10]

What makes prediction of success in university administration particularly difficult is that it must constantly travel a perilous knife-edge between bureaucracy, which as an organization of human beings the university cannot escape, and the minimization of that bureaucracy which is essential if the university is to be a free community of scholars. Administration is not an end in itself; the university has a brain as well as a body; and the purpose of that brain is to give meaning, coherence, and unity to the organism and its activities. If the purpose of the university is maieutic, if it is aiming at the ancient Hellenic ideal of the training of the mind, then success in university administration rests first upon the maintenance of harmonious human contacts and relationships which is the most difficult of tasks.[11]

At the outset it must be observed that the dean of a professional school is like no other dean, or perhaps there is no such thing as the *genus* dean. Because he presides over a relatively autonomous unit, or school, within the university complex, he has more freedom of action than does the dean of the college or the graduate school.[12] In some respects he is

---

[10] John Walton. *Administration and Policy Making in Education.* Baltimore. Johns Hopkins University Press. 1959.

[11] Robert Maynard Hutchins. *The Learning Society.* New York. Praeger. 1968. pp. 117–21. Also: Harold R. W. Benjamin. *Higher Education in the American Republic.* New York. McGraw-Hill. 1965.

[12] Dean Roy Nichols has pointed out that the dean of a graduate school is not a dean at all, in terms of the usual connotation of the title: "He has a faculty to be sure, but he does not recruit it, pay it or promote it. He cannot effectively either reward or admonish it. He cannot deal effectively with departmental heads in any direct face-to-face relationship in any realistic atmosphere of academic negotiation. The department heads know, and he knows, that they must look to other deans for new appointments, promotions, increases in salary; they must negotiate elsewhere than

comparable to the president of a liberal arts college, in others more like an academic vice president or provost. His responsibilities and privileges vary from situation to situation and university to university. If he presides over a very strong professional school, such as a medical or law school, he can be very powerful. If his school is weak, or is given a low priority in the administrative councils, he will be handicapped in his operations despite his theoretical autonomy. Also, there are those schools, a frequent phenomenon in library education, which have no dean but only a director or chairman, the latter if the school is ranked only as a department. The academic totem pole, or more precisely, the pecking order, is often very subtle, understood if at all only by those who have had long experience with its vagaries and its politics. But it cannot be denied that the responsibility for the recognition of the school as an integral and respected part of the academic community rests squarely upon the shoulders of the dean. If the dean is not himself a scholar who can command respect from his peers, and if he cannot build a faculty that is accorded equal respect by other faculties in the university, his school can scarcely rise above mediocrity. Regrettably, library education has, over the years, suffered seriously from just such incompetent, or at best inconsequential, leadership.

## THE DEAN OF THE LIBRARY SCHOOL

The office of the dean of a library school, like that of any other professional school, stands at the point of junction where educational and research ambitions—the *program*—collide with administrative decision and economic necessity—the *realities of organization.* Thus the dean must somehow seek a resolution, or reconciliation, of these competitive forces within the limbo of practitioner demands and student protest and the urge for "relevant" reform. The spokesmen for each of these interests has the right to be heard for each has something vitally important to say. The first requirement of a dean, therefore, is that he be a statesman. The school will inevitably become the lengthening shadow of its dean as a journal is the lengthening shadow of its editor or a university of its president. His is the responsibility to mediate conflicting and divergent forces and weld them into an effective instrument for the advancement of learning. Obviously he must be a statesman, but also he must be a scholar and a resolute admin-

---

in his office." Roy F. Nichols. "The Ambiguous Position of the Graduate School Dean." *Journal of Higher Education.* vol. 30 (March 1959), pp. 124–25. See also: Oliver C. Carmichael. *Graduate Education.* New York. Harper. 1961. p. 188 ff.

istrator. He will have to go a great many places where he does not wish to go and listen to a great many voices that he does not wish to hear, and often he will have nothing to guide him but his own instinctive intuition. To say that the dean must have the skin of a rhinoceros is to mouth a popular fallacy—nothing could be further from the truth. The dean must be sensitive to every wind that blows. The winds will often be chill and the exposure painful but that is the price he pays for his office. The very minimum function of the dean is to decide, and since he has to make more decisions than most men he has the opportunity to be either a very good or a very poor administrator. Moreover, he will soon discover that all too often he is forced to work from a negative position, and that in the majority of cases he will be deciding *against* something rather than *for* it. As Hutchins once told an audience in Rockefeller Chapel at the University of Chicago, "Almost every decision an [academic] administrator makes is a decision against somebody. This is true even of decisions that look as thought they were for somebody, like a decision to raise a man's salary. The administrator quickly learns that such a decision is really a decision not to raise the salaries of other men in the same department."[13]

It has been said that the way to become a good administrator is to administer, but it also is the way to become a bad administrator. Habits are formed by action and the behavior of the administrator is probably more the result of habit than of any kind of formalized training. The besetting fault of the dean is likely to be not so much that he is a "bad" man, but a weak man, that is, he can decline to make decisions. To say that a successful dean cannot avoid the making of decisions does not imply that he must say either "yes" or "no" to every proposition or problem that is placed before him, there are other ways than these of making his decision known—that is where his statesmanship applies.

If the dean is to perform his highest function, which is to discover, define, and clarify the aims of his school, he must possess, as Hutchins has indicated, four characteristics: courage, fortitude, justice, and prudence or practical wisdom. Prudence, or practical wisdom "is the habit of selecting the right means to the right end." But prudence cannot be exercised without courage "which is the habit of taking responsibility." Fortitude is "the habit of bearing the consequences," and justice "is the habit of giving equal treatment to equals."[14] Justice, Justinian is supposed to have said, is "the steady and abiding will to give to each man that which of right belongs to him." Thus stated positively, the injunction is relatively easy to put into

---

13 Hutchins. "Administrator." p. 141.
14 *Ibid*. pp. 137–38. See also: Hutchins. "Administrator Reconsidered." pp. 185–96.

practice, but the real rub comes when one attempts to deny to each man that which does not belong to him.

President Eliot of Harvard, we are told, came to look upon patience as the chief requirement of an administrator, but Hutchins rejects it because he considered it a snare and a delusion which administrators usually have too much of rather than too little. He also excludes temperance "which, in the case of the administrator, would be the habit of refraining from making decisions that should be made by his subordinates." Such matters he said, "are between administrators and should not be discussed before the uninitiated." Finally, Hutchins has deliberately excluded the three theological virtues of faith, hope, and charity, "though the administrator needs them more than most men." But they "come through divine grace, and I am talking about what the administrator can accomplish by his own efforts. Since it is not within his power to obtain the theological virtues, I must leave him to work that he may deserve them and pray that he may receive them."[15]

There is one attribute of the administrator as dean, however, that Hutchins has either intentionally or unintentionally omitted from his list, though it was certainly not absent from his own personality. Perhaps he regards it, like the theological virtues, as of divine origin. What Wriston has said of the university president is equally applicable and appropriate to Hutchins's administrator and to the library school dean.

> Finally, in administering the faculty the president must not lose his sense of humor. There will always be rebels who will fight whatever he does. There will always be "liberals" in politics who prove to be hard-shell conservatives in matters academic. There will be dogmatists who will resent his failure to worship their particular golden calf. There will be those who needle him as a matter of principle, because there should be no such thing as an "administration" in a society of scholars. These slings and arrows are not outrageous fortune, they are the common hazards of his office. Once the lesson is learned a president can bear them not so much with fortitude as with laughter. He can smile at the rebels and the rock-ribbed liberals. . . . He can shrug off the dogmatists and needlers. Furthermore, he should save some of his laughter for himself, because no man is deft enough to do all a president is obliged to attempt without being ludicrous from time to time.[16]

---

[15] Hutchins. "Administrator." pp. 137–38.
[16] Henry M. Wriston. *Academic Procession*. New York. Columbia University Press. 1959. p. 128.

If the goal of the dean is to order means to ends, his first responsibility is to build, within the limits of the resources available to him, the strongest possible faculty that can be recruited and then endow those scholars with the freedom to pursue its educational and research programs in ways that seem most appropriate to them. "I think I can understand brother Waples," Dean Louis Round Wilson once told the present writer, "when he talks about the third and even the fourth dimension in research, but when he gets to the fifth I fall off the sled. Nevertheless, I think what he is doing is important and he should be given every opportunity to follow his own course." Here speaks the academic administrator at his very best. Having fulfilled this responsibility to his faculty, the dean must, Janus-like, look to the university administration and interpret to his superior officers the program and needs of the school, and at the same time interpret the reasoning and problems of the administration to his faculty and students. There are, as we shall see, many lesser duties than those dealt with above, but all are subordinate, though related, to the scholarship of the school and the faculty that is its embodiment. "I have known father to hire men," one of the sons of president Henry Churchill King of Oberlin observed, "whom he knew would be sources of trouble to the administration and create dissension on the faculty, but he hired them because he believed that they had something important to contribute to the intellectual life of the college."

The dean who would be a good dean and not merely an office-holder will soon discover that the strain upon his character is greater than that upon his intellect. The dean who is afraid of anybody or anything, who cannot stand criticism, especially unjust criticism, who cannot give equal treatment to equals, who is unwilling or unable to appeal for support from those he may have alienated, is lost. All of these responsibilities are inherent in building and maintaining a good faculty.

Beyond his duties as an administrator, the dean should be a scholar, preferably a productive scholar, but certainly one who understands and appreciates the scholarship of others. The scholarship of the dean does not necessarily have to be in the field of librarianship; there are examples of successful deans who have not been practicing librarians nor have they had formal library training. The dean should, the present writer believes, possess the doctoral degree. Ideally he should have library training and library experience in a senior administrative position, the latter preferably in an academic library since he will be part of an academic community. Such a background of education and experience can give him a distinct advantage in dealing with the profession and with the alumni of his school. Also he would be better equipped to work with the faculty in the planning and development of curricula and research programs. But every situation must be weighed in the light of the individuals involved—there can be no fixed policy, no absolutes.

It would be well if, from time to time, the dean could engage in some teaching, for if he is remote from the classroom he will lose touch with the real purpose of his school. His teaching is likely to be subject to rather frequent and irregular interruptions, but it will be very good for him, and it will help to break down that artificial barrier which his office inevitably creates. The dean, then, is administrator–scholar–teacher; certainly he cannot fulfill these three roles all the time; and administration he cannot escape, but he should, at one time or another throughout his deanship, engage in the other two.

The policy of limiting the service of the dean to a specified period of time or rotating the office among members of the faculty at regular intervals is not to be recommended for a professional school, and it is doubtful if it is a wise practice anywhere in the university. The dean, if he fulfills his responsibilities properly, needs time to think and to build. Rotation of the office stifles initiative and reduces the dean to an office-holder and an academic errand boy. Obviously the dean should not hold his office indefinitely; the well of innovation eventually runs dry and strain and tension take their toll, but if there is an optimum length of service it has not yet been discovered; its calculation would depend on many variables not all of which can be expressed mathematically. The building of a faculty, the dean's first responsibility, takes time, and change cannot be accomplished overnight, especially where an excessive amount of tenure is involved. An inadequate dean will probably reveal his weaknesses rather quickly, but a strong dean requires time to bring his program to fruition. Nevertheless, the dean should not have academic tenure as dean. He serves at the pleasure of the university administration, and if the president is legally saddled with a dean in whom he has little or no confidence, the president is denied *his* ability to build the kind of university he envisages. There is no substitute for mutual confidence between dean and president, for each, by the nature of his office, is heavily dependent upon the other. Administrative theory is deceptively simple, but, perhaps because it is founded on human relationships, one finds its basic tenets violated again and again.

Thirty years or more ago the appointment of a single individual to serve both as dean of the library school and director of the university library was not uncommon, but in the 1950s, the policy was beginning to be seriously questioned, and it was put to rest by Robert D. Leigh's now classic study.[17] Admittedly there should be the closest possible cooperation

---

[17] Robert D. Leigh. "Single or Combined Directorships for the Library and the Library School?" *Library Quarterly*. vol. 27 (July 1957), pp. 161–72.

and coordination between library and library school; the former can well serve on occasion as the laboratory or training ground for the latter, so long as such practices do not interfere with the services the library is expected to perform, and the library staff is properly compensated for its share of the effort. It was quite natural, then, that the assumption would be made that the best way to achieve such coordination would be to have a single head for both organizations. No point would be served here in describing in detail the investigatory procedures by which Leigh exploded this early assumption; suffice it to quote briefly from his conclusion: "Administrative logic indicates that the library school and the library perform essentially different functions, serving a different clientele, calling for the entire energies of persons of distinguishable as well as distinguished executive talents, each profiting by a position of high academic and administrative status inside and outside the university or college. Administrative logic also indicates that daily operations and the professional interests and growth of both the library and the library school personnel call for friendly cooperation."[18]

The value of Leigh's study is not to be minimized, for it brought the problem to a focus and provided a demonstrated base for the right answers, but the separation of library and library school would probably have proceeded as it has in any event. The growth in libraries and the increasing complexity and expansion of educational and research programs in library schools have made a combined directorship virtually unworkable. One may charge that we have knocked over a straw man, or broken down an open door, but the point is worth emphasizing because, unfortunately, there are still some university administrators who see this combined position as a move toward efficiency without perceiving the inefficiencies that lie hidden in such a policy.

The dean has many ways to fail and few ways to succeed, but with all its pitfalls and false pathways, his can be one of the most rewarding of occupations. To see a program grow and develop, to see it given reality and vitality is certainly one of the most satisfying of academic experiences. Not even the medical profession can offer such rewards as does education, for the doctor only saves lifes while the educator builds them, and the doctor knows that eventually he must fail, while the educator knows that his chances for success, even distinguished success, are very great.

---

[18] *Ibid.* p. 172.

## THE STUDENTS

In many ways one can sympathize strongly with the student activist movement. Contrary to opinion on both sides of "the generation gap," the university does exist for the students, though educators themselves have not infrequently forgotten this axiom. There is no doubt that repeatedly library school students have been shortchanged; they have not been exposed to the kind of educational experience they had every right to expect. One may regard it as a promising sign, therefore, that students are being increasingly encouraged to participate in the decision-making process of the school, through representation on important policy committees. It is regrettable that the voice of the student seemed inaudible until it was amplified by the decibels of riot, but for this the educational system has itself to blame.[19] One may also find a little disquieting the fact that, in general, library schools have been only slightly touched by the waves of dissent that have swept across the campus.

The great danger in student activism is not that it is irrational or unjustified, but that it will emphasize the wrong elements in the educational system, that it will lead to more, rather than less, vocationalism, and that it will make education far too pragmatic and practical, and hence subject to obsolescence with even minor shifts in the cultural *milieu*. Student activism, like other revolutions, carries within itself the danger that, despite the rationality of its origins, excess will triumph, at least for a time, and in that victory much harm will result.

During the decade of the '60s, the student body in colleges and universities, including the library schools, were undergoing marked changes, of which a dramatic increase in numbers, though most conspicuous was, perhaps, not the most important. The life style of the students was being drastically altered. There was a weakening of family ties, generally explained in terms of "the generation gap." There has always been a generation gap; whether it is becoming wider than ever before is open to question.

The paradox that today's students present to higher education was emphasized by Eric Severeid when he told the CBS television audience on September 14, 1970:

---

[19] See: Robert Maynard Hutchins. *The Learning Society*. Chapter 1. "The Circumstances." and Harold Taylor. *Students without Teachers*. New York. McGraw-Hill. 1969. Part 1. "The University and its Students"; and Edward H. Levi. *Point of View*. Chicago. University of Chicago Press. 1970.

At the top level these students may well be the best ever, excepting perhaps the returned GIs after World War II, the best informed and most mature. At the bottom level, which includes unprecedented numbers driven in by parental and social pressures and fear of the draft, they are pretty surely the worst ever, the most self-indulgent, the most illiterate and lazy-minded. So the pressure is intense, not to drive them up to the old standards of performance but to drive the standards down to their level. Some, however unprepared, will rise and make it by their own hard efforts. A great many will end up with degrees and no education worth the name.

In general the students of recent years have been more adequately prepared for college, more independent, more concerned about involvement in social problems, more impatient with the restraints of old moral values and codes, and more serious-minded than ever before in the history of American higher education. Ideals, too, were changing. The grey-flannel suit, the key to the executive washroom, and the lure of the laboratory are no longer the great symbols of success. These students, born into an era of inflation, are almost indifferent to economic rewards. Plagued by the evils and maladjustments in society that these young people have seen all about them, service to the community and the nation became the great watchword.[20] Though the library schools have not felt the impact of these new currents as strongly as some other parts of the university, paradoxically, the library profession is feeling, especially within the ALA itself, the full force of demand for reform. The point of view may be poorly articulated, the movement diverse and lacking in leadership, and confused by internal inconsistency, but youth must and will be heard.[21]

The real problem in responding to the demands of today's youth and realizing a fruitful dialogue with them is the ability to identify that which

---

[20] Christopher Jencks and David Riesman. *The Academic Revolution.* Garden City, N.Y. Doubleday. 1968. pp. 28–60.

[21] Jacques Barzun. *American University.* Chapter 3. "Students or Victims?" Also: Barzun "Tomorrow's University—Back to the Middle Ages?" *Saturday Review.* vol. 52 (November 15, 1969), pp. 23–25 and 60–61; and John W. Aldridge. "In the Country of the Young." *Harpers.* vol. 239 (October 1969), pp. 49–64 and (November 1969), pp. 93–107.

John S. Millis speaks of the "upside-down university," referring to the traditional organization chart which places the board of trustees at the top and a block representing the students at the bottom. The true situation he believes would be represented by the students at the top, since it is for them that the university is supposed to be working, and the trustees at the bottom, where they should be as the foundation, especially the financial foundation of the institution.

is truly "relevant," for much of today's relevance may be tomorrow's irrelevance. "I find myself deeply divided on the issue of relevance," wrote Robert Paul Wolff, "My own education was a perfect example of all that the radicals reject. . . . The portions of my education which proved most useful to me in my attempts at social criticism have been precisely those which originally seemed least relevant to politics or society. . . . When I turn to the social critics whose work I admire, I find the same grounding in a technical mastery of some academic discipline. . . . The original and important intellectual work always proceeds at a considerable distance from immediate problems, and for that reason frequently seems 'irrelevant' or 'abstract.'

"Still the question remains: how can you get the bright, concerned student to sit still for the technical study which alone will prepare him for genuinely relevant work later on? . . . Must they postpone their critical analysis of society until all passion has died in them and they have reconciled themselves to the tedium of the academy? I don't know the answer save to say that honest, brilliant, dedicated teachers will always evoke interest and application from their students no matter how abstract the subject matter of the courses."[22]

The identification of talent in the student is as hazardous as is the prognostication of teaching in the faculty. The most prevalent means for evaluating the student's intellectual potential is the standardized test, and in many situations it has proved to have a high degree of predictive ability. But its use in the hands of those unskilled in psychological measurement can result in serious injustices. Many people fail to perform at their best under test conditions, and such measures do promote fear of social manipulation and the reduction of the individual to a statistic. As John Gardner has pointed out, such tests will always meet with public resistance and disapproval because they are designed to do an unpopular job.[23] But Gardner has admitted that there is no really workable alternative to the tests, and "whatever their faults, the tests have proven fairer and more reliable than any other method when used cautiously within the limits for which they were designed."[24]

A major complication in the identification of talent derives from the fact that career success places a heavy emphasis on those attributes which

---

[22] Robert Paul Wolff. *The Ideal of the University*. Boston. Beacon Press. 1969. pp. 77–79.

[23] John W. Gardner. *Excellence*. New York. Harper. 1961. Gardner has given an excellent discussion of the values and weaknesses of standardized tests in Chapter 5.

[24] *Ibid*. p. 49.

are not necessarily related to scholarly achievement. Judgment of the student, therefore, should not be based upon his intellectual gifts. There are mysteries in the development of the individual which we are very far from understanding. The personal interview has long been a favorite as a basis for judgment, especially in library schools, and indeed it has the advantage of personal contact with the individual as a human being. But all too often the interview is biased in favor of conformity to middle-class standards of manner, dress, cleanliness, and other behavior patterns more often, perhaps, learned in Sunday school than anywhere else. Interviews can be very prejudicial to some types of individuals.

Undergraduate grades are also an unreliable source for evaluation of a student's potential. Any course grade can be, and often is, as every teacher knows, an "elastic slide rule." Records of academic performance are strongly colored by the prestige of the college, the intellectual content of the courses taken, the personal situation of the student as an undergraduate including economic dependence, family security, and general health. The elapsed time interval between the granting of the baccalaureate degree and the application for graduate study is also a factor that must be given serious weight. It is not an uncommon practice for a school to refuse admission to all applicants who have a grade average lower than a certain cut-off point, but such a policy rigorously applied can result in injustices to a student and a loss to the profession.

But of all the "evidence" of academic and career potential, probably the letter of recommendation should be given the lowest priority. At the best it will come from someone whom the applicant knows will write a favorable response, and at its worst it can be pure hypocrisy and deceit. The present writer will not soon forget a particularly distressing case in which a student was not only admitted but given a handsome fellowship on the basis of a particularly strong letter of recommendation. Too late to avoid serious disillusionment and pain was it discovered that the letter had been written by the applicant's employer only because he wanted to sever relations in the easiest possible, and most cowardly way.

In the selection of students, then, there is no easy course. When all the evidence is in, a composite profile derived from all of the above sources would seem to promise the greatest degree of success, but even then some worthy student will be barred who might have been a "mute inglorious Milton."

> Some heart once pregnant with celestial fire;
> Hands, that the rod of empire might have sway'd,
> Or waked to ecstacy the living lyre.

Conversely, despite all safeguards, there will be those who will slip through who should not have been admitted; a greater danger since there are more of them in the world than of the "inglorious" Miltons.

The placement of graduates is a responsibility traditionally assumed by the school, rather than being delegated to a central university placement service. In 1960, Martha Simpson found that eighty-five percent of the schools included in her survey of accredited institutions conducted their own service.[25] The situation appears to have changed little since Miss Simpson wrote.

Arguments for retention by the schools of this service have been impressive and vigorously advanced. The position customarily taken has been that the faculty knows better than anyone else the qualifications of the student and the demands of the field; the school maintains the records necessary to support the service, and these cannot be transferred to another office, perhaps quite remote from the quarters of the school; contact with visiting recruiters keeps the faculty current with developments in the profession and in addition is good public relations; a centralized office with diverse responsibilities, that include all or most parts of the university, would tend to neglect library school students; the practice provides the school with one additional means for keeping in contact with the alumni, and to check on the progress of previous graduates already employed in the recruiter's library.

All of these arguments seem valid, but they are not inherent in the schools' retention of the service. All of them can be overcome by close coordination between placement office and library school. A placement service can often provide facilities, e.g., interview rooms, organized data, well scheduled programs, and similar conveniences that are beyond the means of the library school. The maintenance of an appropriate placement service that both student and interviewer have a right to expect, constitutes a very heavy burden that few if any library schools are prepared to meet. The principle of centralized placement conforms to sound administrative theory by consolidating like operations in a single unit, rather than dissipating them throughout the organization. If the centralized placement service is operated efficiently, with a high degree of coordination between central office and library school, and if the central office assigns a competent person, who either knows or is willing to become thoroughly familiar with the library school, its students, and its graduates, there can be no doubt in the mind of

---

[25] Martha Simpson. *A Study of Placement Systems in Library Schools Accredited by the American Library Association.* Unpublished Master's Thesis. Division of Librarianship. Emory University. June 1960.

the present writer that the centralized service is superior to the conventional pattern, and in the writer's experience it has been very successful. As is usual in most administrative situations, the real key is the people involved.

It is customary for library school graduates to complain that their school loses interest in them after they have secured their first position. The charge probably exaggerates the real situation somewhat, but it is true that few schools follow the careers of their graduates closely or that the graduates keep the school properly informed of their progress and professional situation. Neglect of the graduate is injurious to both the school and the alumnus. The success of the graduates is the true measure of the school's success, and the latter has a vital stake in the former's future. A body of distinguished alumni is the supreme achievement of any school; yet how casually, even indifferently, alumni and school customarily work together for mutual advancement.

## FINANCE

"No nation," wrote John Ruskin in *The Crown of Wild Olive*, "ever made its bread either by its great arts, or its great wisdom. . .but its noble scholarship, its noble philosophy and its noble art are always to be bought as a treasure, not sold for a livelihood." Yet money motivates education, even as it does the mare, and the university administrator cannot escape the dismal science of economics, free himself from finances, or be rid of the burden of the budget. A university is not an economic enterprise; it is forced to exist in a world in which men live by taking in each other's washing, and the university has no tangible laundry.

Every institution in society is economic—it must have some means for acquiring an income if it is to survive in our system of specialized production. In contemporary society there are but three principal methods through which income is achieved. The first is through the sale of a product or a service. This is the method of the marketplace, in which goods or services compete with each other for their share of the total gross market. This method is the foundation of capitalism, and a derivative of it is the use of money, through investment (or lending) to earn more money. The second method, which is the prerogative of government, is through the taxation of the earnings of the marketplace, whether those earnings are the rewards of enterprise or income from investment. The third is through gifts or loans which themselves are the result of either enterprise in the marketplace or the taxing power of government. (The actual fabrication of money, either legally or illegally, does not come within the scope of the present discussion.) All three of these methods of achieving economic survival, then, depend upon the seller's capacity to satisfy a human want or need. In the Garden of Eden, presumably, there was no economy, for in it there was no want nor any need until man first tasted the forbidden fruit of the Tree of Knowledge and became aware of his boredom.

But the groves of academe are no Garden of Eden, rather they are a nursery for trees of forbidden fruit. To the extent that higher education sells a product or a service, it partakes of the nature of an economic enterprise operating in the marketplace. To the extent that higher education receives, either directly or indirectly, income derived from tax support, it is an agency of government and essentially a socialistic institution; and to the extent that it receives gifts for its support, it is an object of charity. Though a university is not an economic enterprise, to the degree that higher education contributes to the intellectual advancement of society, it is an essential part of the economic system. Theodore W. Schultz argues that education is an investment in human capital just as a factory is an investment in physical plant capital, and the one is no less a real contribution to the health of the marketplace than is the other.[26] Similarly, the studies of Machlup, Harbison, and others have shown a direct correlation between a society's or region's expenditures for higher education and economic well-being.[27] Thus, though higher education is a part of, and cannot be understood without reference to, the national economy and the system it represents, higher education is a very special kind of enterprise, an undertaking established not to earn or save money, but to *spend* or "invest" it intelligently and efficiently for the production of an intangible good.

## DIRECT INCOME FROM STUDENTS

Conventionally, the economics of the marketplace are based on direct charges for products sold or services rendered, and the markup provides the margin of profit—the rewards. In an earlier day this system even pre-

[26] Theodore W. Schultz. "Education and Economic Growth." *Social Forces Influencing American Education.* National Society for the Study of Education. Chicago. University of Chicago Press. 1961. p. 46.

[27] Fritz Machlup. *The Production and Distribution of Knowledge in the United States.* Princeton University Press. 1962. Chapter 4. "Education."

Frederick Harbison and Charles A. Myers. *Education, Manpower, and Economic Growth.* New York. McGraw-Hill. 1964.

Seymour E. Harris, ed. *Higher Education in the United States: The Economic Problems.* Cambridge, Mass. Harvard University Press. 1960. Section 6. "Economics and Educational Values."

vailed in education. At the great medieval universities, and perhaps even earlier in the peripatetic schools of Greece, the student in effect dropped his coins in the turnstile at the door of the classroom, and the professor pocketed the "take." This system of direct reward to the teacher was eminently profitable to an Abelard or a Duns Scotus, who could "empty Paris" whenever he chose to go elsewhere, taking his students with him. But we can only speculate about the economic status of the average academician, who could recruit no such devoted band of disciples. With the increased bureaucratization of the university, the federation of autonomous units that characterized its medieval ancestry was eventually lost to the highly structured academic commonwealth of the present day. As the costs of education rose (to almost astronomical heights in the present century) the share that could be charged directly against the student declined proportionately.

Professor Seymour E. Harris has pointed out that in 1958, charges to students accounted for about twenty-five percent of the total educational revenue, and that by 1970 this figure would likely rise to some forty percent.[28] John D. Millett, who has probably studied the financing of higher education more deeply than any other single individual, observed that in 1960, the total operating expenses of higher education were 5.6 to 6 billion dollars, and added, "It seems likely that nearly 40 per cent of this total amount was derived from student charges, since almost all auxiliary service income results from charges to students."[29] The figures cited by both men pertain to all higher education. The student in the private or independent[30] college or university bears a significantly larger proportion of his educational costs than does his counterpart in a publicly supported institution, but in no situation does the student begin to approach paying for the full cost of his education.

Professor Harris insisted that an increasing proportion of the costs of higher education must be borne by the student; Schultz believes that all three of the major sources of income must advance in a more or less constant ratio; and Sidney Tickton of the Fund for the Advancement of Education is of the opinion that the student's share of costs will continue to increase, but that it can and will be met "with the aid of scholarship money, . . .if the education provided is distinctive, has a high degree of excellence,

---

[28] Seymour E. Harris. "Financing Higher Education: Broad Issues." *Financing Higher Education, 1960–1970,* ed. Dexter M. Keezer. New York. McGraw-Hill. 1959. p. 36.

[29] John D. Millett. *The Academic Community: An Essay on Organization.* New York. McGraw-Hill. 1962. p. 48.

[30] "Independent" is here used to mean those institutions which have no church or other affiliation; e.g., Harvard, Yale, the University of Chicago.

and is sufficiently differentiated from that provided by other types of higher educational institutions to be worth the higher price."[31] Such optimism may be justified, especially if personal income keeps pace with educational costs. But Tickton has "cheated" somewhat by introducing scholarships and other forms of financial aid into his argument, for he is only saying, in effect, that students could pay the entire cost of their education if someone else picked up the bill. One finds it difficult, however, to suppress the haunting concern that higher education, particularly private and independent higher education, may be approaching dangerously near to a point at which it must price itself out of the market; indeed there are disturbing indications that such is already happening.[32] Despite all the impressive statistics that have been marshalled to prove that education is a richly rewarding investment for the individual, and that college and university degrees return their costs to the graduate manyfold in increased earning power, the fact still remains that the majority of the population will not sacrifice the present or mortgage even a small piece of the future to buy a share of higher learning. The present writer once heard a distinguished scientist assert, not entirely facetiously, that he was "not impressed" when he was repeatedly told that the United States spends more money annually for tobacco, movies, and liquor than it does for education: "I like to smoke, drink, and go to the movies, and that has nothing to do with my concern for education." But in a capitalistic society, money is the index of value and the measure of priorities, and if society is unwilling to pay the price of education, then there is something wrong with society or with education, or possibly with both. Wherever the fault lies, the economic crisis that education faces is critical, and it is not likely to be solved by the direct methods of the marketplace.

---

[31] Sidney G. Tickton. *Letter to a College President*. New York. Fund for the Advancement of Education. 1963. p. 27.

[32] Sylvia Porter has painted an alarming picture of the soaring costs of college education resulting from the impact of inflation upon the economy. In a syndicated column appearing in the *Cleveland Plain Dealer* for June 17, 1970 (p. 3–B), she estimates the annual cost of a college education, at one of the Ivy League colleges, approximates $5,000 to $6,000 per student. "Smaller private college costs may easily run $3,000 to $3,500. Costs of public colleges are not far behind." High as these expenses are they represent only one-third of the total instructional costs at private and only one-fourth in public colleges. Miss Porter sees no relief in sight. Educational costs are sky-rocketing, private donations, though on the increase are not keeping pace with costs, support from federal sources is actually declining. Thus, she reaches the disturbing conclusion: "You, the parents, and you, the college students, must for now at least shoulder the giant share of these educational expenses."

## GOVERNMENT SUPPORT

"For the institution of higher education as a whole in the United States," Millett has written, "about 50 per cent of educational income and about 35 per cent of all operating income are being provided by government. In terms of social purpose, our national security, and financial support, higher education has begun to assume more and more the appearance of an agency of government."[33]

Governmental concern for higher education dates back to the late Middle Ages and the beginnings of the Renaissance. As the universities began to challenge the cathedral schools and divest themselves of their monastic associations, royal charters for new universities were granted, and many founded under church auspices enjoyed patronage from the nobility and even from the crown. On this side of the Atlantic, state and federal concern for higher education began long before the passage of the Morrill Land Grant Act of 1862. Following the Northwest Ordinance of 1785, which provided lands for the support of public elementary and secondary schools, an act of 1787 provided lands for the support of public higher education. Jefferson's proposals for the University of Virginia are a landmark in the movement for state support.[34] Today every state of the Union has at least one state-supported university and many have a complex network of state colleges and universities. With the passage of the Morrill Act and subsequent legislation, federal aid to higher education became massive, and at the present time virtually no college or university, public, private, or independent, is lacking some form of federal investment. Such subsidization is a natural outgrowth of the conviction, which dates back to Colonial times, that the education of youth is a public concern, and that the opportunity for universal education is essential to a democratic society and to the social mobility and economic well-being of its citizens.

There is no need to dwell at length upon the financial situation of state-

---

[33] Millett. *Academic Community* p. 53.

[34] Freeman Butts and Lawrence A. Cremin. *A History of Education in American Culture*. New York. Holt. 1953. p. 198 ff.

Clark Kerr. *The Uses of the University*. Cambridge, Mass. Harvard University Press. 1963. pp. 51–52.

Marjorie B. Smiley and John S. Diekhoff. *Prologue to Teaching*. New York. Oxford University Press. 1959. Part 2. "Schools for All."

Richard Hofstadter and Wilson Smith. *American Higher Education: A Documentary History*. Chicago. University of Chicago Press. 1961. vol. 1, Part 3. "The Nation, the States, and the Sects."

supported higher education or those universities, colleges, and junior colleges that have been established by municipalities, except to point out that they must compete with similar agencies and other services in their respective governmental units for their share of the revenues. Though they can be, and have been, embarrassed by legal restrictions, local accounting procedures, and the intellectual limitations of those who directly or indirectly control their purse-strings, in general they are more responsive to the upward thrusts in the economic cycle and perhaps somewhat slower to feel the pinch of deflation than are their privately supported counterparts. The public till is an economic buffer even when legislative bodies are most dollar-conscious. In many ways the financial position of these public universities and colleges is to be envied, even when they think their lot is hard.

Federal and local government has also assisted private and independent higher education by providing exemption from taxation, principally from real property and gift taxes. Especially since the close of the Second World War, the federal government has provided loans or gifts, often on a matching basis, for plant construction, the purchase of equipment, and the stocking of libraries. Also, the so-called G.I. Bill provided scholarship aid to students pursuing the baccalaureate or advanced degrees, and in recent years a number of federal assistance programs have been inaugurated, particularly in science and medicine. Perhaps, however, the most spectacular government funding has come in the form of grants or contracts for research, of which the Manhattan Project was a dramatic example. Daily the faculties and administrators of colleges and universities beat upon the doors of such fund-granting agencies of the federal government as the National Science Foundation, the National Institutes of Health, the U.S. Office of Education, the Atomic Energy Commission, and other offices. Many universities employ specialists whose major, if not sole, responsibility is to seek out support for research and to assist in the preparation of proposals geared to the psychological orientation of any one of a number of government agencies. With the passage of the National Defense Education Act of 1958, and its legislative descendants, particularly the Higher Education Act of 1965, a whole new array of academic activities have received financial assistance from the federal government in a variety of ways. This is not the place to debate the question of the relevance of research to the objectives of higher education, but in most cases, contract research—underwritten by committed funds—generally contribute only peripheral support to teaching programs.

Such largess has developed mainly because of the importance of higher education, and especially the research responsibilities of higher education, to the national security. Though there will be fluctuations in governmental aid as a long-term trend, these contributions seem unlikely to disappear. "On the contrary," wrote Millett, "governmental financial assistance to colleges and universities to educate needed talents and to perform vital research will unquestionably grow."[35] Bruner has written, an "almost inevitable consequence of the national security crisis is that there will be a quickened flow of federal funds in support of education. . . . The National Defense Education Act is only a beginning."[36] Indeed, one might say with considerable accuracy that federal funds are beginning to take the place of private philanthropy in support of private and independent higher education.

That support of colleges and universities is a proper function of government has not only been accepted, but also welcomed, by the great American public. But government funding is not without its dangers. This warning does not imply fear that the bureaucracy will interfere with academic freedom or impose its political ideology, either Republican or Democratic, upon the teacher. But the availability of government money has, up to the present time, led to an overemphasis upon government interests, especially science, both in teaching and research, and it has tended to channel research to the extent that, all too often, proposals are shaped to please the bureaucrats instead of the investigators. Moreover, until very recently, investigation of serious social problems has suffered from lack of federal funding. Governmental regulations and accounting procedures can tie up administrative offices and personnel until, like Gulliver enmeshed in the Lilliputian web, the educational giant is immobilized. All too few administrators have the courage to refuse a handsome subvention even when it threatens to distort or reshape their educational or research objectives. John S. Millis, when president of Western Reserve University, acknowledged the existence of the dangers to the university which lie, often concealed, in excessive dependence upon government grants, particularly grants for sponsored research. "I wish to devote a portion of this report," he wrote to the Trustees of the University in 1963, "to a discussion of questions which are being actively debated both inside and outside of the universities. The questions are: What effect is the rapidly growing emphasis upon research having upon the university? Is the university being diverted from its historic purpose? Is it becoming unbalanced? Is it in danger of losing its freedom because of increasing dependence upon outside sources

[35] Millett. *Academic Community.* p. 52.
[36] Jerome S. Bruner. *The Process of Education.* Cambridge, Mass. Harvard University Press. 1961. p. 76.

of support, particularly upon government support?"[37] Millis did not answer any of these questions. He concluded only by insisting that they must be dealt with seriously and soon, for they are "coming upon us with great rapidity," and they are "becoming more insistent each year."[38]

Not only are the universities threatened with the unresolved problem of the extent to which government funding should be permitted to dictate the profile of higher education, but also there is the obvious fact that federal money, unlike endowment, is "soft" money. It is not, in itself, income-producing or self-perpetuating. It must be sought annually or biennially. Such support comes, often, at the whim of a capricious bureaucracy, and there is no guarantee that it will not evaporate whenever there is a change in the policies or programs of the sponsor, when Congress becomes frightened of its own prodigality, or when, for any reason, anti-intellectualism, which is always latent in the popular mind, breaks out.[39] Nevertheless, the stern fact remains that someone is going to have to bear the escalating costs of education if its intellectual standards are to be preserved, and all the costs cannot be forced down upon student tuition and faculty income. In a democracy, the education of the citizenry, at all levels, is a proper—even inevitable—concern of government, and it is the responsibility of the citizenry to make as certain as possible that its elected officials exercise their powers in the nation's best interest.[40]

## ENDOWMENT

Patronage of the scholar by men of wealth dates at least as far back as the Golden Age of Greece, and a generous endowment still remains the nearest we know to the ideal method for the support of independent education. Endowment wisely invested provides stability to the budget; it is "hard" money that acts as a buffer against violent swings in the economic cycle. A properly balanced portfolio of investments will respond relatively

---

[37] John S. Millis. *Research . . . How Much? Report of the President, 1961–1962.* Cleveland. Western Reserve University. 1963. p. 1.

[38] *Ibid.* p. 4.

[39] Campus disturbances, and other excesses in student conduct in recent years illustrate this point admirably.

[40] Jesse H. Shera. "Financial Support for and Income and Expenditures of Library Education Programs." *North American Library Education—Directory and Statistics, 1966–1968*, ed. Frank L. Schick. Chicago. American Library Association. 1968. pp. 1–4.

quickly to inflationary pressures and retard the effects of deflation. Because education is always something of a gamble, because there are no accurate means for predicting success either in teaching or in research, the quality of an educational system does not become apparent until long after the student has left the halls of ivy. "Patient money" is higher education's great need, and "patient money" is exactly what unrestricted endowment can provide. It frees the academic community from dependence upon the "buyer," from the hand-to-mouth existence of government grants and contracts, and from the matrix of bureaucratic domination whether wisely or unwisely imposed. To the independent or private colleges and universities, it stands as does tax support to public colleges and universities. It is their lifeblood.

Excessive hunger for endowment can, of course, make higher education subservient to the donor. "Education," wrote Millett, "is a dangerous business," for "it is committed to change. It expects first of all to change individuals by augmenting their store of knowledge and by developing their ability to reason. Beyond this, the educated person may become an instrument of social change. . . . Creative change is the province of a higher education which is a part of society rather than an escape from it. Higher education by its activity appears to threaten the positions of leadership in the established institutions of society. Higher education may question the ways and means by which men produce goods and services, the ways and means by which men live together, the ways and means by which men govern themselves and others, the ways and means by which men express their ultimate concern for the Ultimate. Higher education may declare that what is thought to be knowledge is no more than folklore and convention."[41] Such ideas may be repugnant to the potential donor, or the trustee, both of whom are likely to have a strong vested interest in the maintenance of the *status quo*. One need not be an octogenarian to recall the too-often repeated aphorism that America has replaced "the little red schoolhouse with the big red university," or Robert Maynard Hutchins's rejoinder to the industrialist who wanted to know whether communism was being taught at the University of Chicago College, "Yes, we teach communism in the College and cancer in the Medical School." But university fac-

---

[41] Millett. *Academic Community*. p. 55.

    See also: Robert M. Hutchins. "The Professor is Sometimes Right." *No Friendly Voice*. Chicago. University of Chicago Press. 1936. pp. 155–61.

    Hutchins is supposed to have replied to a visitor who had expressed surprise that the university had accepted gifts from an organization known to represent strong "right-wing" predispositions, "The University of Chicago purifies the source of all its income."

ulties are not nearly as radical as some people seem to think, and the tradition of academic freedom, which is well entrenched in the mores of American culture, has been a strong deterrent to interference with the right of the teacher to his own convictions. In actual practice, the pressures against academic freedom have been exercised more by state and local governing bodies than by the wealthy patrons of education.[42]

But the day of large personal philanthropy is waning, if indeed it is not over. Modern tax laws have taken their toll of such huge private fortunes as those of the Rockefellers, the Dukes, and the Stanfords. The private foundation has largely displaced the individual as the dispenser of spectacular largess, and corporate and committee decisions have replaced those of the individual. Increasingly benefaction is becoming institutionalized. One finds it difficult to say whether this change is good, bad, or only different. Certainly it has introduced more "machinery" into the process of benefaction. It has freed philanthropy from individual whim, but has substituted the idiosyncracies of the corporate mind, and apprehension over the possible loss of tax exemption status. Value judgments as to which entails the lesser annoyance (humiliation?) to the applicant probably rest on one's personal experiences.

## FINANCE AND ACADEMIC ORGANIZATION

In higher education, absolute authority is as abhorrent to the American as is absolute power in business, government, or even the church. Though the modern university has the loosely structured associated federation of its medieval forerunners, nevertheless a pluralism of substantially autonomous units has always been regarded as a safeguard against excessive control from the top. As a consequence of its inherent distrust of authority, higher education has built up a community, rather than a hierarchy, of colleges and schools within each university.

The tenuousness of administrative controls over the university components has brought much criticism from without the academic world and a demand that higher education be put "on a more business-like basis."[43]

---

[42] See: Robert M. MacIver. *Academic Freedom in Our Time.* New York. Columbia University Press. 1955.

Richard Hofstadter and Walter P. Metzger. *The Development of Academic Freedom in the United States.* New York. Columbia University Press. 1955.

[43] See: Beardsley Ruml and Donald H. Morrison. *Memo to a College Trustee.* New York. McGraw-Hill. 1959. This is a good example of the business executive's reaction to the financial and administrative management of colleges and universities.

This relatively loose administrative control is reflected in academic budgetary procedures. As Henry Wriston has said, "The relationship of the president to the budget is a strange mixture of delegation of authority and personal control. It would be beyond human power for him to 'make' the budget all by himself. . . . Decentralization is the first necessity; only by such methods can the vast mass of requisite data be gathered and put in reviewable order. Delegation is the second essential; the business office must collect, organize, calculate, and predict. Advice is the third step; without help no president can know enough to make the enormous range of decisions required to arrive at wise conclusions. This assistance must come from department chairmen, from deans who are responsible for the first review of sections appropriate to their realms of action, from officers dealing with the maintenance and operation of the plant. How orderly and rational that sounds!"[44]

But the position of the university president, as we have shown above, is not like that of his counterpart at the head of a business or industrial corporation, and he is not entirely to be blamed if his budgetary procedures are not as tidy as managerial theory holds that they should be. In a corporation, those to whom budgetary responsibility is delegated have, in general, the same objectives and point of view as the president, and may differ from him only in degree of boldness. But the great danger to the president of a university lies in the delegation of excessive authority to those whose business it is to "run" the financial operations, people who are not educators in the strict sense of the word and who see the university only in terms of assets and expenditures. He who pays the fiddler calls the tune, and it is the comptroller who issues the salary checks. The figure, as well as the letter, killeth; to both the spirit giveth life.

President Wriston could have made an even stronger case for the uniqueness of the position of the college or university administrator. As John Fischer has written, "Professors grumble constantly, as we all know, about academic administration—but in fact most universities have less administration per square yard than any other institutions in American life. Typically the president is a sort of Merovingian king, presiding nervously over the savage and powerful barons who run their separate schools, departments, laboratories, and institutes like so many feudal fiefs. He has only very partial command over the university's budget; because of the tenure rule he cannot fire an incompetent or lazy professor; and his control over

---

[44] Wriston. *Academic Procession*, pp. 167–68. It is odd that Wriston gives the deans no authority to initiate "sections appropriate to their realms of action."

what happens in the classroom is only marginal."[45] No one would deny the faculty their right to security and academic freedom, but it is purchased at a price. The A.A.U.P. and the accrediting agencies are powerful organizations, and no president runs afoul of them without peril to the public relations, and even the academic standing of his university. Moreover, even if the president had a great deal more authority than he does, he probably could not expedite reforms however necessary he thought them to be. Though higher learning is dedicated to change, and the faculty hospitable to innovation in the resolution of political and social issues, when it comes to the world of education the professor is almost always conservative. "The reasons which make it almost inevitable that the professor should be right," Hutchins has written, "about the world, the country, or other people's business, have no application to his own. The professor is not always right about education, because there he has vested interests, personal ambitions, and ancient habits, all of which he wishes consciously or otherwise to protect. Every great change in American education have been secured over the dead bodies of countless professors. In education the professor is a practical man," and Hutchins defines a "practical man" as one who "practices the errors of his forefathers."[46]

But of all the handicaps under which the academic administration labors in safeguarding the efficient use of its funds, perhaps the most vexing is the inability to assess with any degree of accuracy the excellence of its product. Business and industrial management can establish quality controls, balance sales against inventory, and measure with a high degree of precision the contribution that each segment of the organization makes to the efficiency of the whole. Not so the university administration. No one has yet devised an objective impersonal method for quantitatively assessing the monetary value of a student's knowledge. There are not even any valid tests for the prognostication of success in education. Good teachers are distinguished from poor ones mainly on the grounds of such rather dubious evidence as hearsay, student gossip, and a kind of campus osmosis. There is no solid, safe yardstick by which a dean or department head can justify his budgetary recommendations. In the end the administrator must rely on

---

[45] John Fischer. "Is There a Teacher on the Faculty?" *Harper's Magazine.* vol. 230 (February 1965), p. 18.

[46] Hutchins. "Professor." pp. 157 and 156. Hutchins has said that the only way to fire a university professor is to catch him in the act of fornication, in broad daylight, and with twelve witnesses. Yet one must not forget that of all the distinguished university administrators of the present era, Hutchins was probably the most vigorous and uncompromising in defense of academic freedom.

his own personal judgment; but if he depends too heavily upon himself, or overrrules the considered opinions of his advisors too often, he is in danger of being charged with favoritism, recrimination, or incompetence.

Because there are so many ways for the administrator to lose and so few to win, he almost inevitably shores up his decisions with things that can be measured quantitatively: research productivity, consultant jobs undertaken, research contracts awarded, prizes won, pages published in learned journals, books authored. Yet the validity of such counting is always open to question for, though the administrator is not expected to judge the actual value of such activities, he equates them all as being quantitatively equal—and thus subconsciously denies their validity as tests of educational achievement.[47]

In the topsy-turvy economics of the academic world, it is probably pointless to belabor the administrator for not finding "a better 'ole"—if he knew of one, he would doubtless run to it. "On many occasions," wrote Millis, "we have had to make a quantitative decision based on moral judgments." Qualitative answers, Millis pointed out, must be given to such quantitative questions as: How many students should the university undertake to educate, and in how many, and in what, fields of knowledge? What quantitative limit, if any, should be imposed on the research program? In making such quantitative determinations, the university administration must make "judgments of the moral responsibility of the university to its society." All such decisions must be based on "the consideration of quantitative data of financial and physical resources, an assessment of human potentialities, but always measured against the moral responsibility of the university to assume its full share of the task of furnishing our society with educated men and women."[48] "Moral judgment" is a fine euphemism for informed opinion or educated hunch, but it does not engender objectivity in the assessment and decision-making process.

## THE FINANCIAL PROBLEMS OF THE LIBRARY SCHOOL

The preceding pages have dealt with the problems of academic economics as a whole for the simple and obvious reason that a graduate (pro-

---

[47] In actual practice these conventional quantitative measures probably have more validity than the unproductive faculty member would like to admit. Criticism of them provides an excellent rationale to excuse intellectual inertia. We have heard too many members declare themselves to be "perfectionists," for whom publishing for the sake of publishing, or to receive a promotion is "abhorrent." We have yet to find a faculty member who rejected a promotion because of his fine sense of perfection.

[48] Millis. *Research*. p. 4.

fessional) library school is a part of a larger community, and it is in the light of its academic setting that the financial problems of the library school must be viewed. Moreover, these problems of the library school may be considered as a microcosm of the whole university budget. If the substance of librarianship is interdisciplinary, so also are its finances. The administrator of a library school must argue for his share of the university's resources, but he cannot argue effectively if he does not understand how those resources originate, are allocated, and expended. If library school deans have failed to get what they believed to be their fair share of the university's funds, if their schools have seemed to be academic poor relations, it could well be, at least in part, because their schools have not been in the main current of the academic community. If university administrators have not thought of library schools as integral parts of the university, it may be because the deans have not thought of themselves or their schools in that way either. The first task of the library school administrator, as a responsible budget officer, is to understand the position of his school in the fiscal as well as the intellectual program of the parent organization.

But, though the administrator of a library school must be concerned with financial matters, he is much more than a budget programmer. As a university is first and foremost an educational instrument, so the library school administrator is first and foremost an educator. Higher education does not exist for the purpose of maintaining a neat set of financial records nicely balanced between income and expenditure. A budget is not an end in itself; it is created to improve, whenever possible, the efficiency and effectiveness of the organization it is created to serve. The task of the administrator is to align means with ends, and for the academic administrator this means knowing what the objectives of his school are, the means by which they may be achieved, and the resources, both human and fiscal, needed to achieve this educational goal. The great weakness in most library school fiscal operations is their absence of plan. The administrator works from year to year, from budget to budget, arguing each year as best he can for his share of the university's income, but without any real sense of direction, purpose, or ultimate end. He is like the chess player who thinks only of capturing the nearest pawn, without concern for any strategy that will lead him to a checkmate of his opponent's king. The preparation of the budget, then, should be a form of strategy, not a series of maneuvers to outwit the university administration—a well-ordered, long-term campaign to align resources and goals, viewed always in the context of what library education should be.

A clear sense of priorities measured in the light of ultimate objectives, then, is the basic budgetary responsibility of the dean. If he and his faculty are alert to their educational needs and opportunities, it is unlikely that any university, however wealthy, will have enough money to meet their legitimate demands. As Wriston has said, "Any time a president boasts that, 'our resources are adequate for our program,' you can be certain that the program is impoverished. With all that needs to be accomplished . . . money will always be short."[49] Budget preparation may be almost as much a process of elimination as of innovation. Again to quote Wriston: the president (and one might add, by extension, the dean) "must spot the program that is 'living on its legend,' and balance its continuance against new proposals which may offer greater promise of educational advance. If he does not do this the educational program will rapidly ossify, and all the work of a curriculum committee, all the insights of some alert professor cannot stop the process. If every new idea must wait upon increased resources so that it may be piled atop all the old procedures, the situation soon becomes hopeless."[50] Admittedly, library schools are usually spread so thin, and they are so likely to be lacking in program depth, that there is little opportunity to eliminate one educational endeavor, even when it is "living on its legend," to make room in the budget for another; and it is often next to impossible to add any new activity without some sort of compensatory adjustment. It is the responsibility of the dean to make certain that his budget is as nearly educationally watertight as he can make it, and that every item in it can be defended with complete honesty.

If it is the obligation of the dean to interpret and defend his budget to the university administration, so it also is his responsibility to make certain that his faculty comprehends the educational program of the parent organization and the financial circumstances within which it must be carried out. A faculty is a sensitive organism, both intellectually and emotionally; if it is not a little taut, intense, edgy, it is probably not taking its work very seriously. But if it is made up of intelligent and reasonable men and women, as indeed it should be, it will either accept a rational explanation of financial stringency, or seek appointment elsewhere. Acting as the channel of communication is not always easy; no one likes to be a bearer of ill tidings, and not infrequently the beliefs, procedures, and objectives of the dean confict with those of the administration. But somehow he must come to terms with both the administration and his faculty or he faces very unhappy, and even disastrous, consequences.

The dean would be well advised to communicate to the students, at appropriate intervals, interpretations of university policy and the school's financial position. Much of the student unrest has arisen, the present writer

---

[49] Wriston. *Academic Procession.* p. 168.
[50] *Ibid.* p. 169.

believes, not from youthful irresponsibility, but from the failure of academic administrators to communicate to the students information that they should have. Such communication, however, should be not merely a strategy to avoid crisis, it should be a useful part of the students' educational experience.

In the final analysis, when the dean deals with the financial problems of his school, as with all administrative matters, there is no substitute for Hutchins's administrative virtues—courage, fortitude, justice, and prudence or practical wisdom. We would not attempt to assign a position of pre-eminence to any one of these, but it is, perhaps, notable that Hutchins has placed courage and fortitude first. Certainly, courage and the fortitude to "carry through" are essential in dealing with the budget. An administrator who administers is bound to cause trouble for the budget officer. "If a university has a deficit of a million dollars," we once heard Hutchins remark, "as every well-run university has, then it makes little difference whether. . ."; the key phrase here is "well-run university." The Rockefeller Brothers Fund report of 1958 stated prophetically, and more elaborately:

> It will not be enough to meet the problem grudgingly or with a little money. The nation's need for good education is immediate; and good education is expensive. That is a fact which the American people have never been quite prepared to face. At stake is nothing less than our national greatness and our aspirations for the dignity of the individual. If the public is not prepared for this, then responsible educators, business leaders, political leaders, unions, and civic organizations must join in a national campaign to prepare them.
>
> But first our national leaders will themselves have to grasp the full scope of the problem. Perhaps the greatest problem facing American education is the widely held view that all we require are a few more teachers, a few more buildings, a little more money. Such an approach will be disastrous. We are moving into the most demanding era of our history. An educational system grudgingly and tardily patched to meet the needs of the moment will be perpetually out of date. We must build for the future in education as daringly and aggressively as we have built other aspects of our national life in the past.[51]

Alfred E. Smith, when he was still "the Happy Warrior" and governor of New York, said that "the trouble with 'pay as you go' is that you don't

---

[51] Rockefeller Brothers Fund, Inc. *The Pursuit of Excellence: Education and the Future of America.* New York. Garden City, N.Y. Doubleday. 1958. p. 33.

pay and you don't go." There was never a better aphorism for education to heed—in librarianship, or out.

But if the financial plight of higher education is serious, that of professional library education is, generally, far worse. The fiscal needs of library schools have very low visibility, indeed, on the ledgers of the university. University administrators, legislators, and trustees have been submitted to a vast outpouring of demands for increased support for medicine, science, social work, nursing, and on *ad infinitum,* but as Professor Doi observed, in commenting on an earlier paper dealing with finance by the present writer, "If the professors of library sciences are sounding their trumpets within the confines of the university, only those blessed with the keenest of ears can hear them."[52] There can be no doubt respecting the validity and pertinence of the professor's charge, but it is not so much that library schools have not made enough "noise" about their accomplishments, they have not made the right kind of "noise"; they have not been convincing in stating and fully documenting their needs. One cannot blink the fact that fiscally, as well as intellectually, library education stands very low on the academic totem pole, and that it lives apart from the rest of the university. The situation is a sorry one and needs the highest form of administrative and professorial skill to effect reform. The present writer finds it difficult to be optimistic about the outcome. As Doi warns, "Library education seems to me to have a narrow basis of support. When the school of library education begins to falter and fall, do not count on others within the university to rush to its aid."[53] The professor of education from the University of Michigan's Center for the Study of Higher Education, unquestionably knows whereof he speaks, and he concludes his observations on a note which, if not pessimistic, is at least an admonition that there are dangers ahead for library education. "I believe I am correct in saying that university administrators are generally less well-informed on the problems of library education than on the problems of most other disciplines and professions. This holds true, I believe, even in the universities that have graduate schools of library education. Your administrative colleagues need to be better informed of your problems. Some will want to be, others will be resistive. But the initiative for their education will have to come from you."[54] Despite the esteem with which poverty is held in the Christian ethic, in this world at

---

[52] James I. Doi. "Critique of Working Paper No. 4." *Problems of Library School Administration,* ed. Sarah R. Reed. Washington, D.C. U. S. Office of Education. 1965. p. 46.

[53] *Ibid.* p. 48

[54] *Ibid.*

least, money is still the measure of value. Both libraries and library education have long argued from poverty, and this is not the way to salvation.

## ACCREDITATION

Licensing, certification, or accreditation are the means by which a society, or segment thereof, maintains a measure of control over standards of accomplishment. Indeed, such certification is an essential element in most definitions of a profession. But accreditation of educational systems, particularly by voluntary associations, is virtually unique to the United States; in most other countries it is a function of either the church or the state. American higher education developed in such a chaotic fashion that, by the end of the nineteenth century, standards became mandatory. Thus modern accreditation in higher education dates from the period 1890–1915.[55] Almost from the beginning, the influence of the regional associations was paramount—the New England Association of Colleges and Secondary Schools (1885); the Middle States Association (1889); and the very influential North Central Association and the Southern Association (1895). Until approximately 1930, emphasis was upon "minimum standards" applied quantitatively. In the early 1930s, however, the North Central Association initiated a massive redefinition of function by reducing the policing aspect and broadening the bases of evaluation to encourage initiative and experimentation.

But accreditation activities were not limited to the general associations; specialized groups, beginning with medical schools and followed by law and many others, spread rapidly until some thirty organizations are recognized by the National Commission on Accrediting.

Concern with the accreditation of library schools dates from Williamson's justly famous report of 1923 to the Carnegie Corporation. Williamson proposed the formation of a National Certification Board which would include among its functions some supervision of library schools. On June 30, 1924, the ALA created the Board of Education for Librarianship, and its first official recommendation was the proposal of "minimum standards" for four types of schools: (1) a junior undergraduate school that could be associated with either a library or an institution of higher education, but requiring only one college year for admission; (2) a senior undergraduate school which must be associated with a degree granting institution, and for

[55] William K. Selden. *Accreditation; A Struggle for Standards in Higher Education.* New York. Harper. 1960.

which three years of college would be sufficient for admission; (3) a "graduate" library school for which the baccalaureate degree would be necessary for admission; and (4) an advanced graduate library school which could confer the master's degree and even the doctorate. The report also set forth specifications for curriculum, quality of instruction, degree requirements, and evidence that the school equipped "students with technical knowledge and social understanding to meet the requirements of the profession."[56]

By 1933 the ALA Board recognized only three types of schools, based on admission policies: (1) those requiring the baccalaureate degree for admission and giving only graduate work; (2) those requiring the baccalaureate degree but offering only one year of advanced study; and (3) those giving a full year of library training but not requiring four full years of college for admission. By 1948 these standards had become obsolete and were suspended; also the distinction of schools by type was abolished, and the master's degree was becoming generally accepted as appropriate to completion of the first full year of graduate study. The old fifth-year degree of Bachelor of Library Science was definitely on the way out. Concurrently there was a growing rejection of undergraduate vocational or professional programs in favor of general, or liberal education. In 1951, the Council of the ALA adopted the new standards, and a review of the accredited library schools was inaugurated.[57] Some 1951 standards were relatively specific, while others were quite general and hence required interpretation. A substantial degree of latitude was left to the accrediting team in exercising judgment.[58] These standards were, of course, developed over a period of

---

[56] "First Annual Report of the Board of Education for Librarianship." *American Library Association Bulletin.* vol. 19 (July 1925), pp. 235–48.

[57] A good historical account of the history of library school accreditation is to be found in the following: Leon Carnovsky. "The Evaluation and Accreditation of Library Schools." *Library Quarterly.* vol. 37 (October 1967), pp. 333–47; Louis Round Wilson. "Historical Development of Education for Librarianship in the Unitetd States." *Education for Librarianship*, ed. Bernard Berelson. Chicago. American Library Association. 1949. pp. 44–59; Robert D. Leigh. "The Education of Librarians" *The Public Librarian*, ed. Alice I. Bryan. New York. Columbia University Press. 1952. pp. 299–425.

[58] American Library Association. Committee on Accreditation. "Standards for Accreditation." *American Library Association Bulletin.* vol. 46 (February 1952), pp. 48–49.

American Library Association. Committee on Accreditation. *Statement of Interpretation to Accompany Standards for Accreditation Adopted by the ALA Council July 13, 1951.* Chicago. American Library Association. 1955.

Robert L. Gitler. "Accreditation: Agencies, Practices, and Procedures." *Journal of Education for Librarianship.* vol. 1 (Fall 1960), pp. 61–74.

time by practicing librarians and those engaged in library education, submitted to the faculties of library schools for critical review, and eventually approved by the ALA Council. But even at the time of these presentations there was much dissatisfaction with the vagueness of the statement. In 1971, the profession has again addressed itself to a review of accreditation standards, but the preliminary draft presented for discussion shows very little improvement over the earlier document.[59]

It was the plan of the Committee on Accreditation to review each accredited school every ten years, but the interval, which in most instances was not rigidly maintained, came to be regarded as too long in view of the rapidity with which change was taking place in many of the schools. Thus, in 1968, accredited schools were required to submit annually, data that would make possible a reasonable check on the status of each school. Every effort is being made to simplify the questionnaire form, but at best this annual responsibility does place something of a burden on the schools. Nevertheless, if the data thus gathered are properly used and rigorously applied, the system could aid materially in raising the standards of professional education in librarianship. One should also add that the Committee is empowered to authorize a full-dress review whenever it seems warranted.

Though there has been much discussion concerning the accreditation of undergraduate library programs, the Committee on Accreditation has not yet seen fit to enter upon such an undertaking, despite some pressure from the field. The Office of Library Education at ALA headquarters has been devoting considerable attention to the problem. Such undergraduate programs can be a real menace to the profession, and, though they may be worthy of serious consideration, professional sanction of them must not be taken lightly. The dangers to a sound liberal education and undergraduate subject specialization are very great indeed, and the present writer has as yet seen no proposals for these programs which would not seriously lower the standards and performance of the profession. Once again the educational system is threatened by the "academic Gresham's law"; and cheap and mediocre education could easily drive out standards of excellence. If colleges could divest themselves of much that properly belongs in the high school, then there might be room in the undergraduate years for sound preprofessional programs that would not damage the student's experience. In short the entire educational system needs a thorough overhauling, but there is little evidence that such a revolution is in the making. On the contrary,

---

[59] American Library Association. Committee on Accreditation. "Tentative Draft of Revised *Standards for Accreditation*." Chicago. American Library Association. 1971. (Mimeographed.)

pressures for the lowering of standards, to extend educational opportunities to the disadvantaged, admirable though they be, would seem to indicate that the trend is quite the reverse. Thus these undergraduate programs can do serious injury to the effectiveness of library service, and the academic prejudice against professional library education will grow.

The Committee on Accreditation has grave responsibilities for the welfare of the profession, and the profession, recognizing that fact, has endowed it with commensurate authority. Yet, the committee has not come to grips with fundamental issues regarding the standards and their application. It has lacked courageous and truly professional leadership. It has tended to accredit "from the bottom," rather than "from the top," thus focusing attention on the minimum rather than the optimum. It has yielded to pressures both from the schools and from the profession. Over the years it has worked "hard" but seldom taken its responsibilities seriously. It appears not to know what education, especially professional education, is all about. Librarianship has always been wary of self-criticism, and nowhere has this been more strongly manifest than in library education. The profession has failed to be tough-minded about the right things. During those periods when the demand for librarians is declining, "natural selection" may help to solve some of the problems that librarianship has been neglecting, but this is indeed a painful, not to say brutal, way to solve the problem of educational standards. Library education needs a watchdog; there can be no doubt about that, but over the years the bark has been far worse than the bite, and often the bark is little more than a distressed kind of whimper, or at best no more than a low growl. Library school accreditation doesn't scare anybody, except, of course, those who see what it may be doing to the profession.

# Epilogue

# The Hungry Sheep Look Up

All Western philosophy, according to Alfred North Whitehead, is footnotes to Plato, and much the same, with equal validity, can be said of educational theory. Every major philosopher since Plato has written, at one time or another, on education and all have been influenced by his insight. *The Republic* remains today the classic statement of educational theory, and its most penetrating analysis. In order to talk about the good life, Plato's argument ran, one must first talk about the good society, and if one is to talk about the good society one must begin with a consideration of the educational system that will bring that society into being and sustain it. Hence there is no vision of the good life that does not imply a set of educational policies and goals, and conversely, educational policy has implicit within it a conception of the good life.

The relationships between education and the good life that Plato so clearly perceived, hold with equal validity for the interdependence of professional education and the good professional life. Unfortunately, however, education for librarianship has missed the deeper meaning of this Platonic concept by confusing the good professional life with the skilled craftmanship of the practitioner. The big question that library education has implicitly been asking is not "why it should be done," but "how it should be done 'right.' " As a result there has been much prognostication about the coming of the "push-button" library of the twenty-first century. During the past several decades an increasing amount of material has been published which purports to delineate the *library* of the future; we have written some of it ourselves, but almost nothing exists in print concerning the *librarian* of tomorrow. Yet human resources (manpower) are obviously the most

**493**

important of all library resources. When one attempts to define the librarian of the future one is immediately caught up in a vicious circle—for the kind, or kinds, of librarians the profession is going to need will obviously depend upon the kinds of libraries in which they will be employed; and the kinds of libraries in which they will work will, of course, be shaped by the kind of librarians who will design, administer, and operate them. Then hen theory of eggs is as valid as the egg theory of hens.

Any consideration of library education that implies redefinition must begin with certain fundamental assumptions: (1) that man's dependence upon and demand for graphic records will increase as society becomes more and more complex; (2) that the library is becoming too important to the expansion of knowledge to be left to the librarians alone, a somewhat facetious statement in which there is both menace and promise for a profession confronted by staggering problems growing from technological and social changes; (3) that, for the foreseeable future at least, the book is here to stay; and (4) that computers in the library have come to stay, too. From these assumptions one can variously envisage the library of tomorrow as being: (1) full of computers and magnetic tape, (2) full of systems analysts, (3) full of cost accountants, or (4) full of bibliophiles. Doubtless all of these varieties of people and things will have a part to play in the library of tomorrow, but we are still old-fashioned enough to want to see the library full of books and competent librarians—the best books and librarians who are expert in the organization and servicing of bibliographic materials, well educated, thoroughly competent in the subject areas with which they are dealing, highly motivated, and alert to the potentialities and opportunities for change.

The library schools as they exist today must be charged with two serious weaknesses: (1) they have not attracted to their doors in suffcient numbers those exceptionally qualified students who give promise of enriching the profession with imagination, flexibility of mind, and outstanding subject competence in their undergraduate records. "In comparison with university schools of medicine, engineering, and law," Ralph A. Beals told a meeting of New England academic librarians twenty-five years ago, "university schools of librarianship have been conspicuously unsuccessful in defining their requirements for the admission of students; in drawing upon relevant resources elsewhere in the university; and in contributing to or even influencing the scholarly enterprise at large or in related fields."[1]

---

[1] Ralph A. Beals. "Education for Librarianship." *Library Quarterly*. vol. 17 (October 1947), pp. 299–300.

But for a quarter of a century his warning has gone largely unheeded except for sporadic introduction of the Miller Analogy Test or the Graduate Record Examination. (2) Again, as Beals has pointed out, the schools have failed to strengthen their curricula by drawing upon the resources of the universities of which they are a part. They have remained as islands in the stream of academic life, and the waters have flowed about them without in any serious way irrigating an all-too-barren curriculum. The same charge was made by Williamson a quarter of a century before Beals wrote.

*Lycidas*, you will remember, is an elegiac poem written by Milton in memory of Edward King, who had been drowned while crossing the Irish Channel. Into this elegy, Milton has introduced a denunciation of the English clergy under the tyranny of Archbishop Laud. In keeping with the pastoral setting of the poem the clergy were likened to shepherds, not shepherds with crooks but shepherds and crooks, who presided over their emaciated flocks with more concern for personal self-interest than for Christian principles or doctrine, leaving them "to scramble at the shearer's feast." Thus Milton says of the deprived worshipers, "The hungry sheep look up and are not fed." This line, in language not too metaphorical and to be taken with a certain degree of literalness, represents the plight of the library school student today—students who are starved for real intellectual substance and challenge, but who get "at the shearer's table," large servings of a conventional library technology served in the most unimaginative and uninspiring of ways.

In a savage and rather bitter attack upon the state of scholarship in the humanities, Kenneth Eble has made, nevertheless, some criticisms that the library educator would do well to translate into the terms of his own discipline. "The cant words of the Student Left—relevance, involvement, participation, confrontation, innovation, turning on—have antonyms that as rigidly define the attitudes of a large part of the academic community. . . . Humanistic scholarship must have the support and respect of its young and vigorous practitioners, if it is to make any difference to the world at all. . . . The waste of conventioneering puts me off. The vanity of scholars and scholars' projects lowers my respect for scholarly work. The stepping up of production of M.A.'s and Ph.D.'s to set them to doing tasks they don't really enjoy toward ends they don't much believe in troubles me even as I am engaged in doing it. . . . The shame of humanistic study in the face of so much that needs to be done is the vast amount of learning that means little to the person doing it, little to the scholar supervising it, and nothing whatever to the society that supports it. Part of the scholar's task must be that of removing some of the undergrowth that scholarship has encouraged to grow up around formal study in the humanities. Another part is to make humanistic scholarship generous enough to attract more of the intelligence, imagination and energy of the young scholars." In concluding, Eble spoke of "the estrangement that graduate students in the humanities characteristically feel toward their disciplines," and he added, "I experienced that estrangement as a graduate student; I am living through it now as a scholar solidly established in middle age; I hope I can avoid carrying it on into my dotage."[2]

Wherein lies the source of mediocrity in library education? At least part of the answer has come from the poverty of its leadership. Far too much of the pressure for change, experimentation, expansion, and innovation has come from outside, not only of the library schools but also from without the profession itself. One need scarcely be surprised that the restless youth of the profession, looking at its leadership and seeing mostly mediocrity, is in revolt. One must recognize, painful though it may be, that such progress as has been made in librarianship has come largely from governmental subvention and much of that is the product of circumstances which librarians have been most reluctant to recognize, the importunate demands of war.

The library school should be the main source of professional change —of new ideas. But its leadership has not been able to weld an effective bond between that which is traditional and that which is solidly substantial in the new. Innovation and experimentation have been allowed to slip into non-library hands, a transfer which has meant a serious loss to the profession and much repetitive waste by those unfamiliar with the library problem and its ramifications. Endlessly talking about education and research, librarianship has rarely understood either. Thus library education is today paying the price of its failure to be concerned with the theoretical foundations of the profession. It has not sought for, much less developed, a viable theory of librarianship out of which education and research could have emerged. As a result ends have often been confused with means, and means with ends.

Dr. Sheldon Schiff, who is director of the Woodlawn Mental Health Center in Chicago, has charged professional education generally with socializing their students to an invariable standard of values, and to "accepted" and "preferred" theories and practices. In addition, professional education encourages the development of a rationale which limits the pro-

---

2 Kenneth Eble. "The Scholarly Life." *American Scholar.* vol. 39. (Winter 1969–70), pp. 119–22.

fessional capacity of the practitioner for growth. This socialization process provides the base upon which the highly specialized knowledge and the techniques and practices of the profession are taught. There have been developed no effective measures of the student's ability to perform as a professional after he has received his degree. Educators have assumed that a student's performance in his course work is significantly related to his future success as a practitioner.[3]

But if the hungry sheep look up and are not fed, the blame is not entirely to be laid at the door of the library schools. The practicing librarians are not being as helpful as they could be, and their operating programs are not coordinated with professional education as they should be. Indeed, the library administrator, perhaps because of the inadequacy of his own professional education, has been a serious drag upon the educational preparation of the librarian by failing to understand the true meaning of professional education, and by overburdening promising young recruits with dull routines and repetitive tasks that are not professional, not challenging, and not conducive to the encouragement of initiative. One can scarcely condemn the library schools for a failure to develop a philosophy of professional library education, when the profession itself has been unable to define its own goals while jumping from one "band wagon" to another in the hope of attracting community attention and support. Admittedly library education should lead the profession, but if the intellectual gap between the classroom and the librarian's office becomes so great that one is beyond the horizon of the other, the trail will be difficult to follow. The profession has seldom been able to communicate to the schools what it wants taught, and when communication has taken place it has usually emphasized the lowest technological level. Thus, the library schools must not only educate the professional leaders and pursue an active program of research, but also they must take the initiative in reforming the library system to provide their graduates with an environment hospitable to innovation. If practicing librarians disapprove of this role for library education, then they themselves must exercise leadership in promoting change.

Despite all the pleading that has appeared in print during the past several decades, librarians have still failed to differentiate between those activities that are truly professional and those that are not. Small wonder that the college student, looking at what goes on in libraries, wants no

[3] Sheldon K. Schiff. "Training the Professional." *University of Chicago Magazine.* vol. 62 (January–February 1970), pp. 12–13.

part of it, or that the ambitious young library school graduate suffers a period of acute disillusionment, before he, too, loses his youthful dreams and his initiative and becomes submerged in a morass of routine.

The library profession is, in the opinion of the present writer, faced with a very serious crisis the magnitude of which most librarians are scarcely aware. The profession cannot go on as it has in the past; it must either remold itself into a true profession or it must surrender its age-old responsibilities to others. Librarians worry about technological unemployment as a result of increased automation, yet insist upon promoting undergraduate and technical library courses which train enrollees in those very routines which the computer is most adept in performing. In other words, to ameliorate today's crisis there are those who would increase that proportion of the staff most vulnerable to technological unemployment. Librarianship, if it is to survive as a profession, must rise above the computer, above the engineer, and above the systems analyst; yet the profession has not yet developed an educational program nor a working environment which gives evidence of providing such a transformation. If it be true that one-half of the work that is done in libraries is not professional, and this writer believes that this proportion is not too far from being correct, then professional education is not needed for one-half of the library's operations; but the remaining half of what goes on in libraries should be truly professional in its demands, and we should develop schools that are qualified to prepare candidates for such responsibilities rather than giving "Mickey Mouse" courses in the guise of professional education. If the above figures are even approximately accurate, librarianship needs not more library schools, but very much better library schools that will challenge the highly qualified student, and libraries that will offer him positions of professional responsibility in a context of intellectual challenge in which he can grow, exercise his imagination, and push the profession into a position of real social utility. The problem of staff adequacy will not be solved by proliferating mediocrity. If librarians attempt to compete with the computer on its own terms they are sure to lose, for the computer is a slave and he who would compete with slaves must accept the conditions of slavery.

Abraham Kaplan has spoken of "the law of the instrument," by which he meant that machines have a way of dictating their own ends, that we adapt solutions to problems, not in terms of the problem, but in terms of the capabilities of the machine. Simply stated, "the law of the instrument" says that, given a hammer, a small boy will soon discover that everything needs hammering, or, expressed in the librarians' frame of reference, given a Xerox machine the librarian will soon develop a need to reproduce everything in multiple copies.[4]

Here and there have appeared sporadic attempts to apply computer technology to library education, such as the so-called LEEP project at the University of Syracuse (Library Education Experimental Program), which has been subsidized by the U.S. Office of Education. The Syracuse undertaking, for example, is an effort to discover ways in which the MARC II tapes from the Library of Congress might be used for the generation of bibliographic information needed in library school courses. Quite obviously, considered in Kaplan's terms, this is indeed getting the technological cart before the pedagogic horse. What should be investigated first are the educational needs, and from them the proper and appropriate mechanisms and technologies could then be derived.

But with all its weaknesses the Syracuse undertaking does accentuate the need of library education for bold and imaginative experimentation, and the importance of diversity in educational programs. "Let's give up striving for complete coverage of some body of knowledge." Stefan Machlup wrote in the *A.A.U.P. Bulletin* in 1967, "Let's instead provide the students with an enormous choice of educational materials. . . . All of these can be tightly or loosely 'programmed,' linear or branched. And let's make sure there's a constant and lively dialogue, with the faculty doing its share of the listening."[5]

Again, F. Champion Ward has pointed out that any proposal for a rigid standardization of an educational system poses two contrary "dangers." The first is agreement upon a national curriculum, whereas "educational uniformity is believed by most Americans to be incompatible with political democracy." The contrary danger is that diversity "will simply be a euphemism for uneven quality in the actual performance of different educational institutions purporting to be engaged in the same task." Thus, he concluded, "an attempt should be made to keep general, higher education at a good standard, while respecting pluralism. I believe that the answer lies in a limited pluralism. . . . There should be deliberate exploration of superior minds and settings for the purpose of developing new forms of general education."[6]

---

[4] Abraham Kaplan. "The Age of the Symbol." *Library Quarterly*. vol. 34. (October 1964), pp. 303–4.

[5] Stefan Machlup. "In Defense of Diversity." *Bulletin of the American Association of University Professors*. vol. 53 (Autumn 1967), pp. 337–38.

[6] F. Champion Ward. "Principles and Particulars in Liberal Education." *Humanistic Education and Western Civilization*, ed. Arthur A. Cohen. New York. Holt, Rine-

Two areas of knowledge are central and fundamental to the librarian's professional competence: an understanding of society and the communication system that operates within it, and a substantive knowledge of the intellectual content of graphic records and their bibliographic organization for effective access to them.

Bibliography, like communications, is central to librarianship, and has been ever since the first collection of clay tablets was brought together by the Sumerians, or whoever it may have been. Yet today many librarians do not appreciate the importance of substantive bibliographic knowledge, and they are paying dearly for this neglect. To maximize the social utility of graphic records—that is still the goal of librarianship.

The librarian operates in an environment of ideas, ideas expressed in bibliographic form, but, as Theodore H. White has said, "technically this environment changes from decade to decade. Whoever shapes the ideas, whoever creates the applause or the denunciation, or whoever seizes the moral heights in the world of ideas controls the politics, not of today but of ten years hence."[7] The goals of librarianship and of library education do not change, though the means by which they are achieved may be in rather constant flux, and what the library school student learns today can shape the profession of tomorrow. Every library school educator pays lip service to the reality of change, but few succeed in reshaping their programs to make them relevant. One must admit, however, that part of this unresponsiveness to change is due not so much to a lack of hospitality to innovation as to the severe financial restrictions under which library schools operate. An outstanding school costs money, and a superior faculty has the right to command salaries commensurate with its qualifications. Money alone will not make a school great, but a school cannot be great without it.

Higher education is experiencing drastic change, both in intellectual content and manner of presentation. New methods of instruction are being developed, methods which will place an increasing degree of responsibility upon the student for his own educational progress. In this trend, the use of the library will become more and more important, and will demand a new kind of library, one that has not only books and other printed materials, but also a wide variety of educational media, so that it is the acknowledged learning center of the educational program. Students are entering the colleges and universities in greater numbers than ever be-

hart, and Winston. 1964. p. 136. See also: Jesse H. Shera. "In Defense of Diversity." *Journal of Library Education.* vol. 4 (Winter 1964), pp. 137–42.

[7] "Notable and Quotable." *Wall Street Journal.* May 13, 1970. p. 18.

fore; many of them are better educated, more mature, more highly motivated, and insistent upon a greater voice in their educational experience than has been true in the past.

All of these changes prognosticate a new role for the librarian, a role for which the conventional library school curriculum is no longer adequate. If librarianship and library education do not respond to these new needs, the responsibility for library service will pass to other hands, and the librarian, as we know him or her, will face a new competition from without the profession far sharper and more devastating than any engendered by the machine.

Librarians cannot solve their problems alone; they must seek the active assistance of specialists in many disciplines, especially those in the social and behavioral sciences. The profession must cease the senseless outcry for more library school programs of any kind that will turn out ever greater numbers of so-called professionals. As this study draws to a a close there is a shift in the market for librarians, and one can see disturbing warnings of a declining demand that are a little too reminiscent of the Great Depression of the 1930s, with the added specter of inflation. Yet, despite these signs and portents, conventional library schools are proliferating at an uncontrolled rate, and accreditation is being granted with little thought for the intellectual content of their programs. The situation is serious and can very easily become critical. The picture that education for librarianship presents today is not one to inspire confidence in the future of the profession. One has but to attend a typical meeting of the Association of American Library Schools or the Library Education Division of the ALA to become aware of how little substance lies behind the rhetoric spoken, and how casually librarians take their responsibilities for professional education. For too long library education has been intoxicated with the heady wine of governmental support and the process of withdrawal may be very painful, but it is to be hoped that a period of agonizing reappraisal may give the profession the intellectual maturity that it has seldom displayed.

We who are charged with the responsibility of educating professional librarians must not forget that the library school is part of the university and that it owes an allegiance to higher education as well as to librarianship. In the days of crisis that have confronted the house of intellect during the last years of the 1960s and the early years of the '70s, it is easy to yield to the pressures of "relevance" or to align ourselves with reaction. We must not forget what a university is. President Kingman Brewester of Yale, in 1969, opened his Phi Beta Kappa–Sigma Xi address before the American Association for the Advancement of Science, by pointing out that the very existence of the university "presupposes that some people have something special to contribute to the thinking of others. . . . The university by its nature cannot avoid making judgments. It must decide, or someone must decide in its name, who shall be allowed to enter. It must decide who deserves the opportunity of intial junior appointment, who deserves the lifetime security of senior appointment. It must decide who is the most deserving of the honors, certification, the credentials of accomplishment."[8]

The president of Yale went on to say, in words especially relevant to library education, "I do think we should be more forthcoming in our admission of the weaknesses and contradictions in our university inheritance." Relevance, he believes, is not a valid test when it is interpreted to mean concern with topical problems, for today's relevance may well be tomorrow's irrelevance. Thus, he concludes, "a university must glory in the privilege of doubt. Intellectual progress is made by finding fault with the last best thought you had. Argument is for the purpose of learning, not for the therapy of dogmatic assertion. Serenity is sought in the exhaustion of reason, rather than by turning off the hearing aid."[9] In all too many library schools, and libraries, students and staff members alike, not to mention teachers and administrators, have sought serenity by turning off their hearing aids, or narrowed their world by looking down a tunnel.

The library has often been called the memory of civilization, and so it was and is, but the Queen, in *Through the Looking-Glass*, told Alice that it was a great advantage to have a memory that worked both ways. Alice replied that she feared that her memory didn't work in that fashion. She couldn't remember things before they happened, to which the Queen replied, "It must be a very poor memory that works only backward."

For many centuries librarianship was one of the most honored of the professions, it was the province of the true scholar. Why, in the past century, it has fallen so sadly into disrepute is for the social historian to delineate. Librarians and library schools must be concerned both with the onset of the malaise, and with its amelioration and cure. Let us view automation as a symbol of the change that the future may hold for the profession. If we insist upon training sorcerers' apprentices instead of *professional* librarians, we will indeed be crying out, *"Die ich rief die Geister werd ich nun nicht los."* Or, to go back to Milton—the hungry sheep look up, and must be fed.

---

8 Kingman Brewester, Jr. "If Not Reason, What?" *American Scholar.* vol. 39 (Spring 1970), p. 243.
9 *Ibid.* pp. 249–51.

This index has been coordinated with the analytic table of contents, and topics which are brought together in one section under a specific identifying heading in that table of contents are not included here; nor are names of authors not cited in the body of the text but only referred to in bibliographic footnotes.